New German Cinema

Thomas Elsaesser

New German Cinema
A History

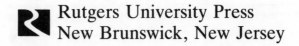

Rutgers University Press
New Brunswick, New Jersey

First published in cloth and paperback in the United States
by Rutgers University Press, 1989

First published in cloth and paperback in the British
Commonwealth by Macmillan Education, Ltd., 1989

Manufactured in Hong Kong

Library of Congress Cataloging-in-Publication Data
Elsaesser, Thomas.
New German cinema.
Bibliography: p.
Includes index.
1. Motion pictures – Germany (West) – History.
I. Title.
PN1993.5.G3E57   1989   791.43′0943   88–42997
ISBN 0–8135–1391–X
ISBN 0–8135–1392–8 (pbk.)

Contents

List of Illustrations

x

Acknowledgements

The idea for a book on the New German Cinema goes back to 1975, when Tony Rayns asked me to contribute a general introduction to his collection of essays on Rainer Werner Fassbinder. With a talent as singular and powerful as Fassbinder's radiating at the centre, it seemed necessary to examine in more detail the field of force that West Germany's political resolve to finance a national film culture had generated for the country's film-makers. Since then, the New German Cinema has become common currency – not least because of a number of excellent studies which now exist on the films, their directors and the conditions that gave rise to them.

While I have benefited greatly from this literature, my thanks are in the first instance due to the institutions and individuals that over the years have given me the opportunity to present, discuss and argue views which without their prompting I would never have tried to formulate. After Tony Rayns' and the British Film Institute's commission, it was Dudley Andrew who invited me to teach at the University of Iowa in 1977. Similarly, between 1980 and 1986, colleagues at the University of California Los Angeles, Santa Barbara and Irvine have been kind and generous hosts. Among them, Janet Bergstrom, Edward Branigan, Natasa Durovicova, Anne Friedberg, Naomi Greene, Lea Jacobs, Lynne Kirby, Patrice Petro, Eric Rentschler, Garrett Stewart and Charles Wolfe were particularly encouraging. Beverle Houston at the University of Southern California, Peter Kopec at the State University of Oregon, Pat Mellencamp and Roswitha Mueller at the University of Wisconsin, Milwaukee, David Bordwell at the University of Wisconsin, Madison, Bernd Moeller at the University of Texas, Austin, Kaja Silverman at Simon Frazer University, Vancouver, Mary Ann Doane at Brown University, Providence, Phil Rosen at Clark University, Worcester and Ingrid Scheib-Rothbart at the Goethe Institute in New York all allowed me to speak to knowledgeable and appreciative audiences. Tim Corrigan, Ramona Curry, Miriam Hansen, Tony Kaes, Judith Mayne, B. Ruby Rich and Marc Silberman contributed with their enthusiasm and energy to the high standard of the conferences I was privileged to attend, and their work continues to keep the New German Cinema a lively and exciting topic.

Helga Rulf at the Goethe Institute in London has been a friend and support ever since she helped me organise a season of New German films at the Gardner Arts Centre, University of Sussex in 1971. In West Berlin during various stages of my research I have been greatly aided by Jutta Brückner, Clara Burckner, Harun Farocki, Erika and Ulrich Gregor, Rene Gundelach, Ingrid Oppermann, Ulrike Ottinger, Karsten Witte, Hans Helmut Prinzler and the staff of the Library at the Deutsche Kinemathek. Noll Brinckmann, Werner and Martje Herzog,

Gertrud Koch, Ulrich Kurowski, Claudia Lenssen, Enno Patalas and Jack Zipes were important sources of insight, information and friendship.

Thanks go to my editors at the British Film Institute, Ed Buscombe and Geoffrey Nowell-Smith, to Roma Gibson and Lisa Hardy; to John Rignall, Ginette Vincendeau and Richard Combs for having taken the trouble to read parts of the manuscript at various stages, to Wolfgang Borgfeld for a crucial piece of typing, to Eric Rentschler for his attentiveness and acumen, and especially to Helen Boorman, who knows the book better than I do.

Incorporated in the argument are parts of articles which first appeared elsewhere. I would like to thank the editors of *Fassbinder*, of the *New Statesman*, *October*, *On Film*, *Cinetracts* and the *Monthly Film Bulletin* for their permission to use this material, details of which can be found in the bibliography. All translations from the German are my own except where indicated otherwise. In general, films are referred to in the text under their accepted English title. Reference to the index will provide the German title; conversely, films are listed by their German title in the filmography, with the English title in brackets.

Film stills were provided by Clara Burckner at Basis-Film, by the Stills Collection of the National Film Archive, by Recorded Releasing and Mainline Pictures. My thanks to them, and to Dina Lom.

Finally, I have to admit that the subject of this book is of more than scholarly interest to me. Although the films of Fassbinder, Herzog and Wenders were in the 1970s as vital and formative a film experience as Godard, Sirk and Minnelli had been during the 1960s, they were also a shock. They returned me to the country I had left the year the Oberhausen Manifesto was published, but they opened wounds, memories and regrets that reached beyond cinema, and brought a dissatisfaction and a restlessness which I soon recognised as the depressive disposition of a whole generation. The book is dedicated to those who know the intellectual rewards and emotional ravages of such a disposition, and who believe in the cinema, nonetheless.

Thomas Elsaesser
London

Introduction

'The Germans are Coming'?[1]

This book does not provide a complete survey of West German film production from the early 1960s to the present. Rather, it outlines a framework for understanding in a historical perspective what has come to be known as the 'New German Cinema'. The perspective is a double one. It situates the New German Cinema as a national cinema within the economic development of the West German and European film industries, which have always been rivalling with Hollywood – usually without success – for dominance in Europe's domestic markets. But the study focuses also on the cultural issues raised by the revival of independent film-making in Germany, which happened partly on a competitive basis and partly in collaboration with national broadcast television. The lead taken by television set an example increasingly followed in other countries such as Italy, France and Great Britain. In Germany, the TV/film alliance brought a gradual change in independent feature films as 'cinema', away from the idea of mass entertainment (still vigorously and successfully pursued by Hollywood), but also distinct from television's notion of family entertainment.

I could have made my task – and the reader's – much easier if I had opted for one of the two models currently available when writing about 'national' cinemas or 'new' film movements: concentrating on individual directors or on specific themes and genres. For instance, I might have proceeded in the way John Sandford and Jim Franklin did when writing their respective books on the *New German Cinema*.[2] Sandford, for instance, gives a brief general survey of the landmarks and turning points, introduces the directors who have come to prominence and discusses their work in chronological sequence with chapters on Alexander Kluge, Jean-Marie Straub, Volker Schlöndorff, Werner Herzog, Rainer Werner Fassbinder, Wim Wenders and Hans Jürgen Syberberg. He concludes with a summary of other film-makers or individual films that deserve special mention. Klaus Phillips, as editor of a volume on *New German Filmmakers*,[3] follows a similar model: his Introduction charts the success story, particularly in the United States, of New German films and film-makers since the Oberhausen Manifesto, and thereby leads up to seventeen specially commissioned articles on twenty different directors from Achternbusch to Wenders.

A more themes-and-issues approach is taken by Eric Rentschler and Tim Corrigan. Rentschler in *West German Cinema in the Course of Time*[4] strongly objects to what he sees as the far too starry-eyed picture usually presented by American commentators in their efforts to 'hype' the films and make cult figures of the directors. He isolates some of the themes and stylistic traits that critics have discovered in the films, and discusses in depth generic trends such as the *Heimatfilm* or literary adaptations. However, his main purpose is to shift attention back to Germany itself and point out the struggles and difficulties which the film-makers have had to endure. He gives more scope than his American colleagues to the generally negative pronouncements of German critics and the equally pessimistic self-advertisements of German film-makers about the situation of their cinema. Corrigan's *The Displaced Image*[5] is textually oriented: it takes half a dozen individual films which are treated as key examples not so much of the New German Cinema but of contemporary art cinema, and its often intimate relation with contemporary film theory. A thematic–generic account of 'The New German Film', finally, can be found in Hans Günther Pflaum/Hans Helmut Prinzler's *Cinema in the Federal Republic of Germany*,[6] written as an information handbook for the Goethe Institutes.

In the chapters that follow many reasons, I hope, will be given for why I have chosen a different route, confusing as it may be since most readers' interest in the New German Cinema will in all likelihood have been sparked off by watching particular films, by one of the well-known directors, or at least on a subject that presented an intriguing picture of West Germany, its past or its people. I have tried to bear these legitimate demands in mind, and hope readers will see their own questions addressed in one form or other. They will probably find certain points discussed at greater length than they had ever cared to consider them.

This is partly, I suspect, because the book argues against at least two tacit assumptions that have, in a way, become received wisdom. One is that the origins of the New German Cinema date back to the Oberhausen manifesto of 1962, or rather, that a continuity exists between the films following Oberhausen, and those of Fassbinder, Wenders and Herzog which gave the New German Cinema a recognisable identity. For the sake of greater historical accuracy and so as to identify a common set of moral stances (which translate into stylistic choices), I have stressed some of the discontinuities, suggesting that Oberhausen belongs at least as much to the 1950s as it does to the 1970s.

To understand the renewal of film-making in Germany and the conditions for its brief international success, it seems to me that a distinction needs to be made between the Young German Film and the New German Cinema in terms of the politics of film-making, as well as in terms of style and subject matter. What does, superficially at least, unite the Young and the New German Cinema is a militant platform around the concept of the *Autorenfilm* (cinema of authors), but here again I see this as a complex, often contradictory term, undergoing many a sea-change in the course of its twenty-year history.

The second accepted view is that the New German Cinema was an avant-garde in the traditional mould, battling against the films and film-makers that had gone before, overturning the old order and creating the new; that its leading figures shaped their uniquely personal vision, spontaneously and untutored, out of an irrepressible urge towards self-expression. The paradigm of the 'new' is applied to this cinema, even though directors such as Fassbinder, Wenders, Syberberg and Schlöndorff have a demonstrably complex approach to their filmic forebears, to Hollywood, the German commercial cinema and the European art cinema, which cannot be accounted for by any simple antagonism or revolutionary break.

In fact, the concept of the *Autorenfilm* had primarily a strategic function, and the book tries to contextualise the often heroic self-representation of the film-makers, by showing how the star directors were part of a broadly-based movement inside Germany to win new audiences as well as representing a unique marketing

2

asset internationally. Such a view does not mean the heroes have to be toppled from their pedestals – although the image of a solitary and persecuted, or even a collective and triumphant struggle has to be seen for what it is: a discourse, a stance, a necessary fiction to enable and motivate productivity. More importantly, it requires one to see direct and indirect government subsidy – the chief economic reason for the flourishing film production in West Germany during the 1970s – in a wider context than that of the State supporting artists of genius. Instead, subsidy has become part of the politics of culture, where independent cinema is a protected enclave, indicative of a will to create and preserve a national film and media *ecology* amidst an ever-expanding international film, media and information *economy*.

Authors' Cinema or Spectators' Cinema?

The chapters proceed by first outlining a number of historical factors determining the German funding system, mainly from the perspective of the film-makers trying to gain access to production funds. My argument is that the apparently incompatible objectives of a national cinema – to be economically viable but culturally motivated – can be seen to have produced in West Germany different sets of debates or ideological fields, in which the contradictions were negotiated, contained and even temporarily resolved. These aim to legitimate film and film-making, once they are no longer justified by the automatic logic of financial profit, or the less self-evident logic of a public service like state television. Even as an economic activity it is difficult to decide whether film-making results in goods or services. As an ideological activity, the question remains – whom or what does it represent? Independent cinema funded in this way requires a context or a definition which German directors were called upon to elaborate and verbalise. The films, their makers, film criticism and theory have in this field of culture become closely related to each other.

In Chapter 1 I outline the history and economic structure of a 'mixed film economy'. From this follows a conception of the cinema as a social space and of film as a commodity – but of a special kind. Within West Germany, which since its foundation in 1949 has had a modern capitalist 'social market economy', culture occupies a compensatory function rather than standing in opposition to industry. The delegation of the state's interventionist role to television and to the Film Subsidy Board ensured that film-making became part of official culture and entered into a primarily ideological arena, as opposed to staying in a strictly economic field. West German films, being produced outside box-office returns, had to define both their mode of production and their use-value differently.

The second chapter is thus concerned with the modes and models of production prevailing in West Germany. A 'cultural' mode of production distinguishes itself from economic modes of film production in so far as its logic is not determined by the profit motive (at least not directly). Even the traditional rationale of show business (namely that it provides pleasure and entertainment for the largest possible audience at the lowest possible price) does not have the same force with products situated at the very margins of the mass market.

The question of what determines cultural products is usually answered unprob-lematically, by assuming the author's intentionality or desire for self-expression as *raison d'être* and origin. Yet in the case of the New German Cinema the mode of production is such that neither authorial self-expression nor audience expectations

3

are inscribed unambiguously in the films. Rather, one might say that as aesthetic objects, they are shaped by processes of self-representation and self-legitimation. For while the conditions of film-making have had a much more directly determining effect on the films than in a purely commercial system, they are at the same time less representative of anything other than themselves, since their efficacy as objects of pleasure remains largely untested at the German box office. Their use–value, to authors as well as audiences, therefore depends on the status that cultural production, but also cultural consumption has in a given social and political context: what it means, in other words, to make films and go to the cinema.

In France and Italy, for instance, the cinema enjoys a very high cultural prestige, in Britain less so, and in Germany – prior to the emergence of the New German Cinema – even less. On the other hand, once film-making becomes totally absorbed into television, its cultural currency falls, being regarded as no different from ordinary television programming and on tap like other domestic utilities. German film-makers fiercely resisted such an absorption, which explains why the discourses of legitimation and justification took up so much space.

The main idea that the third chapter, devoted to the *Autorenfilm*, wants to put across is that the film-maker as *Autor* and originator of a given film occupies a double function within a double circuit: s/he is an 'artist' in the conventional bourgeois sense, and a producer in a pre-capitalist sense, engaged in a cottage industry. As artisans with a craft mentality, the film-makers faced an economic situation that gave them the status of a self-employed entrepreneur, but with the State playing the leading role in a system of patronage. Since the State also acts, via delegates such as television, as direct employer, the film-maker is servant of several masters, while having to maintain an image of autonomy and independence. Many of the political controversies arose out of the contradiction between 'self-directedness' and 'other-directedness'.[7]

The signs of these splits are that West German film-making comprises both more and more varied films than those recognised as 'art cinema' and generally identified with the New German Cinema, mainly because subsidised films are aimed at several distinct groups of spectators. Chapters 4, 5 and 6 try to retrace the strategies adopted in pursuit of audiences. Given that the commercial cinema, too, had to cope with an increasingly fragmented public, the many hesitations of West German cinema since the war between family entertainment and soft-core pornography, between *nouvelle vague*-ish post-Oberhausen films and the international art house productions of the New German Cinema can best be understood in the light of a more-or-less conscious process of reorientation towards a new public, different from the one that used to go or still goes 'to the movies'. This is borne out when one looks at the debates around art films versus genre films; the demands for government measures to subsidise distribution and exhibition alongside production; the polemics of film-makers with the hostile press of the old commercial film industry; the superstar status of certain directors and, finally, the reliance on festivals and the international press for prestige in West Germany itself. In other words, the search for a public manifests itself across a whole area of debate, conflict and strategy which begins to assume cogency only when viewed as belonging to the larger historical problem of the cinema's place in the changing context of entertainment, leisure, information and education.

The central argument of the book, then, is that far from the New German Cinema constituting only acts of self-expression by a small number of highly gifted and personal directors, the logic of its production, the history of its failures

4

and successes, and the aesthetic-formal strategies that give it a degree of stylistic coherence, derive from the various ways the films attempt to address spectators. Crucial for the New German Cinema, as for the more overtly spectator-oriented commercial cinema, was the issue of identification, in the general sense of providing the audience with a coherent or meaningful place in the fiction. The commercial cinema does this with a narrative of conflict, complication and resolution which proceeds from cause to effect via the central characters, but also through the processes of narration, how the story is told, how knowledge is distributed and revealed across the film's progress. The central characters, apart from functioning as agents for this narration may also act as role models. The films of the New German cinema differ to a greater or lesser extent from this norm, mainly by employing unconventional narratives, a feature typical of European art films.

Quite untypical for this art cinema is the New German Cinema's search for positive heroes and exemplary stories, often reflected in the choice of titles. At the same time, the notion of a 'place in the fiction' is considerably extended to include what would normally be regarded as 'documentary modes', while German film politics and film practices conceive of the cinema as a particular social space. 'Going to the cinema' briefly became an activity and an experience comprising but not confined to entertainment.

Equally typical are more complex modes of narration and an often unusual deployment of the specifically filmic forms of identification. These are not dependent on clearly motivated characters, but have to do with camera-placing, editing, and what in German is called *Einstellung*: a useful term because it means both 'scene, take' in the cinematographic sense, and stance, point of view in the moral sense.

The search for more indirect modes of spectator-involvement may also explain why many German film-makers tended to work with narrative forms closer to the documentary and the film essay. I have chosen the term 'cinema of experience' to describe this major tendency within New German film-making. This helps to distinguish it from the perhaps more habitual form of involvement via genres ('experience of cinema') and allows me to discuss the social, political and aesthetic consequences: they range from the revival of melodramatic modes designed to enlist the spectator on behalf of victims, outsiders and outcasts, to films whose strategies of identification are deliberately ambiguous and contradictory, as in the work of many avant-garde and feminist directors. There, questions of gender and sexual identity imply a more theoretical reflection about the nature of cinematic identification itself and also highlight the role of minority audiences and subcultures. Specific target spectators – women or a working-class audience, for instance – implied the redefinition of the cinema as a means of militant self-awareness and self confirmation. This conception contrasted with the cinema as a refuge from self-consciousness and self-awareness, the search for a kind of post-ideological space, attracting spectators to an experience of 'pure being as pure seeing': a desire perhaps best met by the films of Wim Wenders and Werner Herzog.

A National Cinema: Self-projection or Self-parody?

In so far as the New German Cinema – as has sometimes been said – is an invention of the critics and the result of shrewd marketing strategies, it is useful to look at the terms in which the films have been viewed outside West Germany.

But here, too, the question has to be put in a wider context, for this must include the directors' response and defence. For instance, some reacted to the commodity status of their products by an excess of personality, and often parody, in order to escape the mandate as ambassadors of Germany asked to legitimate German culture: reactions which can be studied in the films themselves. This inevitably implies an analysis of what sort of mythical construct emerges of the 'nation' and of 'Germany'. If for the domestic spectator it is more a matter of identifying with this or that character or stance and recognising certain experiences, in the international context, a national cinema will be perceived as presenting or projecting an identity, a narrative image of an entire country.

Chapters 7, 8 and 9 explore these aspects more fully. Films by Fassbinder, Herzog, Wenders, Syberberg, Kluge, Reitz, Schlöndorff, von Trotta and Helma Sanders-Brahms are discussed in so far as they have a bearing on the construction of a specific myth of Germany, its history and culture. The common extra-filmic referents, such as Nazism, urban terrorism or the post-war family which many of their films share are only the most obvious signs of this self-analysis as self-stylisation. For the internationally-oriented directors, the concept of authorship, media star status and self-consciously German subjects did at various points become essential ingredients of prestige and success. One can, however, discern in their work other strategies designed to compensate and substitute for what they lack in terms of box-office appeal: elements in the films which generate recognition and repetition similar to that offered by the commercial cinema through genres and stars. Among these are the frequently literary source material and the trilogies or series associated with a specific director or actor, or both.

The book thus looks at the concept of independence when applied to film-making today, as situated between the commercial cinema on the one side, and television on the other. The question is not only whether under these circumstances the traditional opposition of commerce/culture is still valid, but also whether there can be an independent cinema at all. If independent of market forces, as the New German Cinema was for a time, can it be independent of the conditions of production as well? The New German Cinema presents an exemplary case of an independent cinema shaped by very special circumstances, and the book suggests that these affect the films themselves and not just how they are made.

If much of what follows is concerned with the 1970s, it is because they were a decade of transformations for the visual media outside Germany too. The New German Cinema coincided with major changes in the economic structures of the film and television industries. New technologies were beginning to be introduced which necessarily affected the social use and significance of media products. For instance, given the way that every national broadcast television system recycles old cinema films and given the wide availability of home video, a form of film culture is developing in most advanced countries, with often quite noticeable effects on new national production as well. Thus, Chapter 10, beyond the specific case of West Germany, looks in conclusion at the general conditions and possibilities of film-making in the two decades that witnessed the resurgence of Hollywood, the transformation of the traditional European art cinema, as well as the victory of television, which effectively now determines in most Western countries the economic survival of other media including the cinema.

The United States in many ways still holds the key to future developments. By the sheer quantity and proliferation of their products in this domain they are in the position to define the norms, set the expectations as well as the pace of change. Other countries try to maintain themselves on a terrain staked out by

6

the competition. West Germany is one example, but the implications affect all developed countries whose sense of cultural identity is based on a need to maintain markers – and markets – of difference *vis-à-vis* the products of the international entertainment businesses. Their standards or economic priorities control in most industrial and industrialising countries network television and commercial film-making. For reasons which will form the substance of this book, West Germany's film-makers seem to have been remarkably successful in doing battle on two fronts for at least a limited period.

1:

Film Industry – Film Subsidy

Creating a Commodity

Four factors have shaped the New German Cinema: a system of public funding for feature film production; a legal framework for television co-production; an international reputation for four or five individual directors and, finally, the politicised and media-conscious student movement of the late 1960s and 1970s.

These factors are distinct but inter-related. They are distinct from each other, in so far as they relate to different parts of the film industry as traditionally conceived. One might even say that public funding, television participation and the star director cult each in its way corresponds to an alternative strategy for the three divisions of the commercial cinema: production, distribution and exhibition. Subsidy bypasses the need to generate capital on the open market; television centralises distribution and exhibition; new demands from audiences create new venues and uses for films; the star director, finally, can substitute for generic recognition, attracting an international art cinema audience, and publicise cultural values.

To consider finance and production without a look at the audiences and their expectations would be misleading, because in some crucial respects government funding worked in West Germany only to the extent that it was able to combine aid for film production with the creation of a film culture: this meant subsidising the exhibition infrastructure as well. The overall result of state aid for the cinema was to establish, for a commodity as dependent on export as film, both an internal market and a more diffusely defined international reputation. A 'culture industry', in other words, for the world market; and for domestic consumption a parallel/alternative structure to television, which would function as a kind of 'cultural ecology', in the sense of mitigating the worst excesses of a commercial system that basically operated quite outside the state's control. Film began receiving support partly in analogy with technological research grants for pilot schemes and prototypes, and partly comparable to funds available for public parks, museums and national monuments. This was true above all for the 1970s. With a change of government in 1983, official film policy began reverting to more directly 'economic' criteria. Independent production was left in the hands of television, or to producers who had in the meantime become experts in playing the subsidy-television-tax shelter game. 'Cultural' aid became once more concentrated on first-time film-makers, and only the most commercially profitable productions now are rewarded with bonuses. Today the German Cinema has acquired if not a film industry, then a Film Establishment.

In retrospect, public funding, the *Autorenfilm*, the student movement and television co-production none the less do represent inter-related moments of the

8

New German Cinema, since they follow each other chronologically even more than they imply each other logically. State prizes and regional first-film subsidy began to make an appreciable impact from 1966 onwards; the authors' cinema had its ideologically most active phase between 1968 and 1974, which coincided with the period of highest politicisation in the age group most likely to go to the cinema; and by the time the triumvirate of star directors (Fassbinder, Herzog and Wenders) emerged as an identifiable group at international festivals, the television framework agreement had begun to take effect. Domestic production of independent features (and more modestly of documentary films) experienced a boom. Finally, beginning in 1974, the art cinema circuits the world over discovered the existence of the New German Cinema.

The impression of successive waves, amplifying and building on each other, is almost inescapable. Hence the tendency for critics to construct a classic rise-and-decline story: after the groundswell of the 1960s, the crest of the wave carried the individual geniuses of the star directors to the top in the 1970s.[1] The death in 1982 of the most prolific and gifted among them, Fassbinder, soon followed by the end of the political era of Helmut Schmidt, symbolically broke the wave, dispersing the creative energies and scattering the remaining talents.

This account, attractive though it may be as a narrative, is too metaphorical by far. It seriously misrepresents the structural features and different historical forces at work. One may agree that by the mid-1980s the New German Cinema was no longer new, and possibly no longer either German or cinema (happening mostly on television), but to know what exactly determined these shifts requires a look at underlying factors and a knowledge of its pre-history.

Hollywood Divides and Rules

The economics of the West German cinema have to be seen in the wider context of the United States' film industry. This is true of every Western European country since 1945, and it could be argued that the Hollywood hegemony dates back not to the end of the Second but to the First World War.[2] However, only in Germany after the collapse of the Nazi régime did American interests penetrate distribution and exhibition virtually without obstacle. The reason was that economic objectives complemented political goals. They reinforced each other (especially during the formative first decade between 1945 and 1955) rather more than in other countries, because the newly created two German states rivalled with each other politically and ideologically. In a famous speech Spyros Skouras, Head of 20th Century-Fox, argued:

> it is a solemn responsibility of our industry to increase motion picture outlets throughout the free world because it has been shown that no medium can play a greater part than the motion picture industry in indoctrinating people into the free way of life and instil in them a compelling desire for freedom and hope for a brighter future. Therefore, we as an industry can play an infinitely important part in the world-wide ideological struggle for the minds of men, and confound the Communist propagandists.[3]

Thomas Guback, in his book *The International Film Industry*, has detailed how despite these fine and patriotic sentiments, the Hollywood film industry held the Military Government to ransom over the use of American films for re-education and propaganda purposes. Only when the Motion Picture Export Association was satisfied its earnings on the German market could be converted into dollar

From film noir to neo-realism: location shot from one of the first post-war German films (Wolfgang Staudte's The Murderers Are Among Us, *1946)*

holdings and that there were no restrictions on the free movement of capital, did Hollywood follow its words with deeds. This happened when the United States Senate passed the Information Media Guarantee Program in 1948, which effectively gave the go-ahead for the commercial exploitation of the German market:

> The reluctance of American companies to send films to West Germany . . . was a result of concerns with revenue. Even the Military Government's objective, to reeducate Germany, was not sufficient incentive for the companies. The event which turned the trickle of American films into a torrent was, clearly, the initiation of guarantees by the American government. That the IMG program was lucrative to Hollywood was apparent when . . . Congressman H. R. Gross attacked film industry lobbying in Washington and the IMG, declaring that . . . the 'Motion Picture Export Association has been given a pretty good ride on the Informational Media gravy train . . .'.[4]

By 1951 over 200 American films were released annually in the three Western-occupied zones. For the German cinema, trying to re-establish indigenous film production out of the ruins of what had, from the 1920s onwards, been one of the most prosperous and technically advanced film industries, this saturation of the market proved a permanent handicap. To appreciate both the intentions of the Americans and the consequences of their policies, one has to remember that, throughout the 1930s and early 1940s, the German film industry had been progressively centralised and put under state control. The UFI holding company created by Goebbels comprised the old UFA, with its extensive, vertically integrated production, exhibition and international distribution branches, but also included technical laboratories, patent rights and subsidiary interests such as publishing, sheet music and recording.

Such a media empire with massive monopoly potential was clearly perceived as a rival to the MPEA, and in line with American policy towards other key German industries, the Allied Occupation Forces insisted that UFI should be dismantled. Actual implementation of the directives ran into difficulty, and some of the production activities of UFA, as well as parts of its exhibition circuit, functioned throughout the 1950s with a semblance of continuity. The reasons for the delays in breaking up the UFI giant were manifold, but also reflected the West German government's growing realisation of just how disadvantageous the piecemeal dismantling and disposal of UFI holdings would be to the survival of the German cinema.[5]

The Military Government was none the less able to keep a very close watch over film production. As a strategic pro-Western stronghold, built up by the United States to counter Soviet influence east of the Elbe river, the artificial political entity called West Germany was subject to very strict controls regarding press, radio and film. Charged with vetting and granting licences in virtually every field of economic and information activity, the Allied Control Commission ensured that no vertical integration or cartel formation could develop in the German film industry. As Guback points out:

> In contrast to East Germany where only one large company was authorized, the Americans, British, and French agreed to place the new West German film industry on a thoroughly competitive basis . . . The Western Powers believed that the new German industry should be composed of small independent units. The three levels of the film business – production, distribution and exhibition – were to be separated, and within each level there was to be competition among companies.[6]

Two priorities determined United States thinking on the German film industry: to let production resume along lines that implemented the pro-capitalist, anti-communist 'hearts and minds' re-education programme of free enterprise, and to stop it from becoming a monopoly. Practically, it meant stopping this free enterprise freeing itself from Hollywood, and from achieving economic dominance either within Germany itself or by expanding into European markets. 'Information control will provide the Germans with information which will influence them to understand and accept the US program of occupation',[7] read one of the first directives relating to the mass media in April 1947. Secretary of State Byrnes was equally unequivocal when he announced: 'What we have to do now is not to make the world safe for democracy, but to make it safe for the United States.'[8] As far as the film industry was concerned, it was a policy aimed at imposing the Hollywood mode of production, but without the Hollywood means of production.

By licensing a host of small independent production companies, the Control Commission bequeathed to the post-war film industry its most persistent problems, namely chronic liquidity crises, under-capitalisation, and a narrow-based home market orientation. Throughout the 1950s, too many one-off production units were forever chasing the little investment capital available for film financing. Of the 102 production companies registered in 1954, for instance, according to Erhard Kranz about 70 per cent had 'a basic working capital of less than DM 20.000'.[9] Small wonder that most of them ended up in the bankruptcy courts.

Selective licensing was only one of the control mechanisms available to the

On the set of Helmut Käutner's In Those Days *(1947)*

Military Government. Another affected exhibition, rather than production. From very early on, the MPEA persuaded the State Department to block any moves that might have limited the number of American films distributed in Germany after the IMG programme had been passed:

> [The MPEA's] policy became one of bringing into Germany as many films as it thought the market could absorb. Not only that, but the American industry thwarted the establishment of an import quota in Germany. Discussions in Washington between MPEA representatives and the State Department resulted in an order to the U.S. High Commissioner in Germany that the Department wanted no quota on the importation of American films. An official German quota never materialized.[10]

Quota restrictions were a safeguard applied after the war by every other European country, including Britain, in order to stem the tide of Hollywood pictures. Although it must be said that these measures rarely achieved their aim, they did point to the urgent need for government intervention in the film industry, even amongst political allies. The German authorities at first found it difficult to press this argument for ideological reasons, since it was deemed to be part of the civil population's democratic duty to watch Hollywood movies. For the Americans, sound business sense happily coincided with a moral mission, and a whole generation of Germans grew up with the schizophrenic experience of watching John Wayne ride through Monument Valley, or Humphrey Bogart wander down those mean streets, while their (German) voices never left the cavernous spaces of the dubbing studio.

A further aggravating factor was that among the Hollywood imports pouring into Germany around 1950, a large number dated from the pre-war and inter-war period. These films had long since recouped their production cost in the United

Hollywood, UFA or DEFA style? The Murderers Are Among Us *and (right) Harold Braun's* Between Yesterday and Tomorrow *(1947)*

States, and could now be sold on the German market at rates that decisively undercut new West German productions. Such dumping practices forced indigenous producers to keep their budgets as low as possible if they were to retain the chance of returning a profit. Without using explicitly political pressure, Hollywood was able to manipulate the market in the decisive early years, keeping any challenge to its dominant position permanently at bay. German distributors retaliated by re-releasing scores of Nazi entertainment films from the 1930s and 1940s, also at dumping prices, but this made the situation for new productions even more difficult.

1945: No New Beginnings

Politically, the proliferation of small production companies gave the impression of a new start. The famous 'Zero Hour' for West German society and industry also seemed to apply to film-making, fostering illusions of autonomy and independence. At the same time, since parts of the old UFA organisation survived both the nationalisation of the central production unit at Neubabelsberg (which became the East German State company DEFA), and the Allied Forces' deconcentration measures, there was an ominous impression of continuity with the infamous recent past of German cinema. The Americans had, for instance, in their zeal to license only reliable (that is anti-communist) Germans, encouraged the more right-wing and politically opportunist members of the profession to take over rebuilding the German film industry. One of the officers charged with 'denazifying' film industry personnel reported how in practice his task was impossible, 'since virtually all directors, writers, actors, cameramen and technicians (qualified to make films) had been more or less active members of the NDSAP [the Nazi Party]'.[11] According to Pleyer's calculations, as late as 1960, 40 per cent of the directors active in the West German film industry had either been working in the industry before the arrival of Hitler or had started their careers during the Nazi era.[12] Erich Pommer, the former production head of UFA in the 1920s,

13

returned in an American Army uniform to supervise reorganisation of production facilities from Hamburg. Although able to help colleagues such as Helmut Käutner to obtain production licences (Käutner founded his own short-lived unit, Camera Film GmbH) Pommer – like many émigrés – knew how great the hostility towards him was for not having stayed during the war. There were to be many directors (Fritz Lang, Douglas Sirk, Billy Wilder, William Dieterle, Robert Siodmak and Frank Wisbar) who found to their surprise that the West German film industry in the 1950s seemed to consist of nothing but white-washed former Nazis.

Those who had stayed developed a siege mentality, and the 'old boys' network became a closed shop, suspiciously warding off both outsiders and newcomers. And yet, looked at from purely commercial perspectives, Germany possessed a wealth of professional and technical talent. Many directors who had made films under the Nazis were capable of successful entertainment films, and also of tackling contemporary issues: the German cinema, ever since the coming of sound, had a number of genres with a strong realist, socially critical slant, which resurfaced after the war as the so-called 'problem film', associated with directors like Käutner, Kurt Hoffmann, Wolfgang Staudte, Gerhard Lamprecht and Rolf Thiele. In many ways, their films could, under different circumstances, have competed at least technically with the standard Hollywood production. The more ambitious directors even tried to emulate other national film styles, such as Italian neo-realism.

The problem lay elsewhere. As a result of Hollywood's 'divide and rule' policy, production was dispersed between Berlin, Munich and Hamburg and lacked the

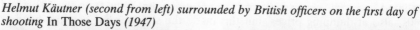

Helmut Käutner (second from left) surrounded by British officers on the first day of shooting In Those Days *(1947)*

investment to create a sound infrastructure. Consequently, distributors became the real force in the industry and gained the upper hand over both production and exhibition. Yet it was the American Major companies who controlled the German market both directly and indirectly. While some cinema chains, in the aftermath of the botched UFI decartelisation plans, had been quietly taken over by a handful of German entrepreneurs, distribution was heavily dominated by Hollywood firms and its subsidiaries. Even distribution companies not set up by the Majors were only able to weather the crises in the industry (notably in 1953 and 1961) where they had ties with US companies. These were increasingly able to dictate their own terms – block and blind booking contracts – to the entire exhibition network. By the early 1970s, not a single commercial distributor had survived in West Germany that was not American-controlled and, here too, Hollywood effectively ran the show without seeming to do so. Wenders, who himself once worked in a distributors' office, has given a graphic account:

> During that time I saw a lot of movies, because personnel were given free tickets. The films I saw were almost always a continuation of what I had witnessed in the office. And vice versa: the distribution system is only an extension of the films it handles. From production to distribution, the same brutality was at work: the carelessness with images, sound and language, the stupidity of German dubbing, the infamy of the block and blind booking system, the indifference of advertising, the unscrupulousness in exploiting the cinema-owners, the bloody-mindedness when making cuts in the films.[13]

West German producers as a rule had to go to an American company in order to get their own film into German cinemas, a situation that applied not only in the 1950s and 1960s. Many of Fassbinder's, Herzog's, Wenders' and Schlöndorff's films are in fact distributed in Germany by United Artists or the CIC chain.[14] Of course, this works both ways: it meant that from a certain point onward, the star directors did begin to have access to production guarantees and a world market.

Given the stranglehold over distribution, the limitation on growth imposed by the Allied Forces and widespread nepotism, the German film industry in the 1950s was ailing. It was not only confined to the home market, but distinctly provincial and incestuous in its outlook on world cinema, neglecting for instance the art cinema as an alternative to Hollywood, out of a misguided concentration on purely 'commercial' criteria. While the many independent companies set up in the late 1940s seemed a promising start for a new film culture, many of the films that might have sown the seeds of an art cinema were never adequately distributed. This was particularly true of some of the early DEFA productions, such as *The Blum Affair* (*Affäre Blum*, Erich Engel, 1948), *Rotation* (Wolfgang Staudte, 1948), but also of *The Lost One* (*Der Verlorene*, 1951) directed by and starring Peter Lorre.

Home market orientation, the central weakness of the post-war German film industry as an industry, has itself to be seen in another context. From the early 1920s onwards, German films (although spectacularly unsuccessful in breaking the Hollywood monopoly on the American market) were considerable export earners in Latin American countries, in South Africa and the Far East, in France and Italy, but particularly in Central and Eastern Europe. After 1933 the film industry continued to hold and aggressively increase its foreign markets. With the beginning of the war, as the régime began to integrate UFA and other production companies into the UFI holding group and administrative control became centralised under Goebbels' Ministry of Propaganda, Hitler's obsession

Peter Lorre in The Lost One *(1951)*

with economic autarchy also affected film production and exhibition. Severe import restrictions closed the market to Hollywood films, and German production was stepped up to meet the shortfall.

During the war the film industry boomed, having almost the whole of the annexed and occupied countries in Europe as a captive audience. For the two decades prior to 1945, therefore, the industry had operated under the assumption that the German market was economically profitable, albeit on the back of military and political expansion of territory. The end of the war brought the collapse of this hinterland, putting an end to the artificial production boom. The division of Germany, along with the redistribution of its Eastern provinces between the Soviet Union and Poland, meant that even the German home market had shrunk to approximately one third of its pre-1933 size. Export after the war was further cut down by the revulsion felt among most audiences for German-produced or German-speaking films.

Illusions of Autonomy

As a reflex, and in view of the obviously unsuccessful struggle against Hollywood supremacy, acquiescence in a retreat to a mere share of the home market seems understandable. But given the experience of other European countries, notably Britain, the economic outlook of a commercial film industry based on the box office receipts of its national market alone is not encouraging. The major recession in audience demand hit West Germany in the late 1950s: the introduction of television and the increasing availability of private cars changed leisure and

16

entertainment as drastically as elsewhere in Europe and America. Cinema admission dropped from an all-time high in 1956 of 817 million to an eventual 192 million in 1968.[15] This picture is further darkened when one considers that German productions were worst hit by the general audience decline, while the Americans were able to increase their share of the market, having more or less successfully exported their own crisis in audience attendance through domestic cutbacks, European-based production units and monopolistic distribution practices.

West Germany's poor showing in exporting its films is, however, surprising when one considers the rest of its economy, which has remained strong because of its leading position in world trade. For the film industry, the figures were depressing even during the relatively buoyant years of the mid-1950s: in 1955, a total of 15 million DM was earned in exports (including script rights, leasing of German actors and other incidental services) while 138 million DM worth of films was imported.[16] The tendency to remain something of a Bavarian cottage industry persisted well into the 1960s. Neo-imperialist 'Sissi' films, dreaming of Viennese pastry and Hapsburg glories, the Bavarian mountain musicals, beermug-and-lederhosen comedies made few friends and fewer admirers for the post-war German Cinema abroad, even though some films from the 1950s are due for a revaluation.

A consequence of catering exclusively for a home market was that the average feature lacked production values. Since German films as a whole had to break even on 15 to 20 per cent of the national box office receipts, each film had to be made in a very cost-conscious way and producers hardly ever pooled resources in order to undertake an expensive film, preferring low yields to high risks. As Volker Schlöndorff, one of the first of the new generation of directors to have experience in international co-production pointed out in an interview in 1972, when the disaster of his American/German/Czech film *Michael Kohlhaas – der Rebell* (*Michael Kohlhaas, the Rebel*, 1969) was well behind him:

> It simply makes good sense for a film industry to undertake three or four times a year projects which cost 5 to 8 million DM, because this way a large number of technicians and other professionals are employed and trained, it is a healthy shot in the arm for the industry itself. The Italians and the French are very clever to produce something like *Borsalino* once in a while, which not only raises the industry's infrastructure to the latest stage of technology, but can also be used to break into the World Market: in its wake, they can sell a Truffaut or a Chabrol, and the notion of the 'French film' gets international currency two or three times a year. If France produced only Truffaut or Chabrol films, it could not export films at all. This is one of the things wrong with the German film industry ever since the 1950s. One always started from the assumption that a film had to earn 80 to 90% of its money at home.[17]

As long as production values were low on films aimed at the commercial audience, a vicious circle set in. Not only could German films not compete on the international market, they also looked shoddy and drab in the home market compared with Hollywood glamour and spectacle. That the German film industry was operating at a loss, for instance, could be seen from the 1967 figures for the national box office. German films accounted for 40 per cent of the films on offer, but represented only 24 per cent of the market share in earnings.[18]

For a brief period in the 1950s, it became government policy to make the film industry less dependent on imports and to regain for German producers the majority of the home market. It was an unrealistic goal, and may well have been put forward mainly as an argument to silence growing criticism that the Adenauer government was putting up less resistance to US pressure than other European countries. The political will to make a decisive intervention was lacking. The dismemberment of the UFA empire was not carried through because there was said to be a shortage of capital among private buyers. On the other hand, large finance institutions with the necessary funds were reluctant to invest. As the initial report on the UFI negotiations put it in 1949, banks were 'unwilling to lend money to finance the purchase (of UFI properties) since very high rates of interest can be obtained in making industrial loans with less inherent risk than in the motion picture industry'.[19]

As a result, the Adenauer government, fiercely committed within the post-war boom economy to let market forces determine investment, refrained from anything more decisive than loans and tax incentives for the film industry, often with strings attached that amounted to political censorship. However, by the mid-1950s, it became clear that government action would have to be taken if there was to be a German cinema at all. The professional bodies of the industry, such as SPIO (*Spitzenorganisation der Deutschen Filmwirtschaft*), and its trade press, rapidly transformed themselves into a permanent parliamentary lobby. The record of these attempts to lobby for credits and subsidies, the unsuccessful role played by successive Christian Democrat governments trying to mediate between purely economic, directly ideological and broadly cultural objectives provides the underlying continuity between the old, the young and the new German cinemas.[20]

Government Intervention: Sponsorship or Censorship?

In line with its contradictory position of executing the wishes of the US Administration, while holding the interests of its own bourgeoisie as its mandate, the Christian Democrats decided as early as 1950 to make available to the industry so-called guaranteed credits (*Ausfallbürgschaften*). The government guaranteed the banks the credits they gave to distributors, who in turn advanced a distribution guarantee to the producers. The intention was to encourage small producers to raise money for films, but the actual effect was rather the reverse: the system of passing the buck was administratively heavy-handed, it tripled the producers' dependencies and, in the final instance, brought film-making under the direct control and censorship of the State. Scripts, contracts, shooting schedules and production estimates down to the last detail had to be approved by a board of state-appointed trustees, who also had the right to block funds for productions already underway if recommendations were not implemented. After only two years the system had to be modified, not only because of high financial losses. Even SPIO protested against the unacceptable level of interference:

> We note with growing concern that . . . the era of guaranteed credits . . . stands under the sign of governmental control, which makes film production into the executive organ of an apparatus directly dependent on the State.[21]

The 1952 modifications, however, had even more disastrous effects. They removed the last vestiges of support for a 'pluralistic' film production and reversed the anti-trust implications of the original credits: henceforth, only producers who promised a package deal (usually eight films in a row) could apply for guaranteed credits. This limited the use of credits to those who already had a dominant position in the market. For most producers a programme of eight films was beyond their capacities: they died either the slow death of financial asphyxiation

18

or a fast one by over-committing themselves and going bankrupt. None of the companies which had accepted credits under these terms survived into the 1960s. If 1955 shows one of the highest annual figures for production (120 films compared with 84 in 1954) it was because the government announced that it would stop credits altogether. The rush was on to get in at the last minute, for it had become more profitable to produce films than to sell them: a calculation that was to hold true for the next 20 years.[22]

By 1956 the industry had experienced another shift of power in the distributors' favour: many had formed their own companies to produce the required eight films. Guaranteed credits had actively encouraged a monopoly situation in the market, but in the process had destroyed the economic initiative and independence of the exhibition sector. The concentration of capital that took place meant that a handful of buccaneer producers held most of the key positions (Arthur Brauner of Central Cinema Company, Waldfried Barthel of Constantin, Ilse and Walter Kubaschewski of Gloria were the movie moguls of the 1950s). Their policies were shrewd but extremely conservative:

As a producer I know that there are projects where it is completely pointless to invest even a single mark more than is absolutely necessary. With *Heimatfilms* for instance it is pretty clear in advance how much they can return at the box office because one knows the audience, almost to the exact number of spectators likely to see such films. If I invest, say 1.2 Millions instead of 900,000 DM, I am throwing capital straight down the drain. The additional 300,000 won't lure a single extra viewer away from his cosy television set.[23]

In fact the government had already swung over to a pro-monopolist film policy by 1953. In a hurried undercover action it had finally disposed of UFA at way below its true value by asking the Deutsche Bank – history repeating itself ominously – to found three separate companies to develop the various assets of the former state monopoly. In 1956, the three firms were openly reunited as a consortium headed by the Deutsche Bank and the Dresdner Bank. The new production-cum-theatre-chain giant turned out to be a dinosaur. It came too late to combat American supremacy, and its organisational structure was already anachronistic at its inception. In 1961, the second major crisis year, UFA collapsed and most of its assets were acquired by Bertelsmann, a publishing group which used UFA's debts as tax write-offs. Once again, government interference had brought the kiss of death to any hopes for a national cinema. It simply aggravated the internal contradictions of the industry as a whole.[24]

After the guaranteed credits were scrapped, lobbying for subsidies via tax relief began. Mindful of the poor reputation and poor quality of the German cinema, however, the government administered tax relief indirectly. An institution that had hitherto existed only at individual state level was centralised in 1955, becoming the FBW ('Filmbewertungsstelle Wiesbaden'); its purpose was to award quality ratings to films of 'artistic merit' (*wertvoll* – valuable, or *besonders wertvoll* – especially valuable). A film with a quality rating was entitled to considerable relief from entertainment tax, which meant that it showed profit for the distributor on less real revenue. Given the low returns even on successful films, a quality rating often decided if a film was to be distributed at all. The so-called quality incentive worked as an additional means of censorship, economically penalising politically inopportune films. Jean Marie Straub's *Chronicle of Anna Magdalena Bach* (*Chronik der Anna Magdalena Bach*, 1968) had to fight a long and much-publicised battle to get a rating at all. Since ministerial or local civil servants

19

made up 40 per cent of the FBW membership, the state had a massive share of the vote determining filmic 'quality'. *De facto*, the incentive functioned as an actual disincentive to producers and directors to tackle 'difficult' subjects. Instead of quality and experiment, it encouraged mediocrity and conformism, and the official list of 'valuable' films for the 1950s reads more like a roll call of the world's worst movies than a guide to a nation's film culture.[25]

The ratings were of economic significance only for as long as the federal states continued to tax films. With a deteriorating market, entertainment tax was greatly reduced, and the FBW's function dwindled accordingly. The intervening period between 1962 and 1967 saw the decisive struggles for a new German cinema, which not only revealed the dilapidation of the established film industry, but gave prominence to another sort of subsidy altogether. It tended to displace the combat zone from the film industry to the shadowy domain of 'culture'.

One of the peculiarities of the German federal system is that affairs of culture and education are under the jurisdiction of the individual states rather than the federal government. Yet, at the time, it did not seem to make sense to encourage a 'regional' film industry. The federal government's interventions were thus limited to direct economic measures, like the guaranteed credits and the UFA handouts to the banks. Entertainment tax and quality ratings being matters for the individual states to administer, the only level at which federal initiative did not violate the cultural sovereignty of the states was an international one. Thus it was the Ministry of the Interior, with funds to subsidise arts festivals, operas and cultural activities in West Berlin, which emerged as a sponsor, via the international film festivals (Berlin, Oberhausen, Mannheim). Among the Minister's privileges is the award of annual prizes for the best German feature film, and of production grants for 'cultural' short films (*Kultur-und Dokumentarfilme*).

Until 1961, when no prize for the best feature film was given for lack of suitable entries, the political bias of the awards was unmistakable; the Minister regularly honoured films with a distinct anti-communist and pro-NATO slant, usually stories dealing with Germany's divided state from a Cold War perspective. When challenged on this, a Ministry spokesman once tartly replied: 'these prizes are gifts. It is our right to choose to whom we want to present them.'[26] However unlikely such a policy was to encourage better films or help the international standing of the German film industry, it was the Ministry of the Interior which became, especially during the Brandt government, one of the most important sources of finance for young film-makers. Given their close links with government sponsorship, it was perhaps not surprising that the first articulated protest and counter-organisation emerged from the ranks of the state-subsidised makers of 'cultural' shorts.

The Oberhausen Manifesto: Subsidy for Exporting Culture

Of the 26 film-makers, writers and artists who signed the Manifesto at the Oberhausen festival, most had acquired film experience through short films either subsidised by the Ministry or commissioned by oil companies and the chemical industry. Some, like Kluge, Reitz, Schamoni, Senft, Spieker and Houwer, had won prizes at international festivals. What stung them into action was a justifiable sense of being neglected at home:

> The collapse of the commercial German film industry finally removes the economic basis for a mode of film-making whose attitude and practice we reject. With it, the

Alexandra Kluge in Yesterday Girl *(1966)*

new film has a chance to come to life. The success of German shorts at international festivals demonstrates that the future of the German cinema lies with those who have shown that they speak the international language of the cinema. This new cinema needs new forms of freedom: from the conventions and habits of the established industry, from intervention by commercial partners, and finally freedom from the tutelage of other vested interests. We have specific plans for the artistic, formal and economic realisation of this new German cinema. We are collectively prepared to take the economic risks. The old cinema is dead. We believe in the new.[27]

Even if the intentions seem rather general, to publish them at this point was none the less a shrewd move. The advocates of the Young German Film did not attempt to storm the industry that had left them out in the cold, but rather assumed its demise as a proven fact – a premature assumption as it turned out. They put forward a programme which was a calculated mix of professional and 'ideological' demands, obviously addressed to the Minister of the Interior in his role as representative of the country's cultural interests abroad.

The truly innovative aspect of the Manifesto was that so many film-makers were able to unite on a common platform, despite the diversity of artistic and filmic interests. As a group, their influence on government circles was considerable. Thanks to spokesmen like Alexander Kluge, who became and remained the leading film politician of the independents, the Oberhausen group successfully lobbied members of the Bundestag, of special commissions and ministerial assistants. The most tangible result was the formation in 1967 of the Kuratorium Junger Deutscher Film, a key institution in the later development of the German cinema because it was explicitly charged with putting the proposals of the Oberhausen Manifesto into practice. With direct government funding, but a selection committee made up mostly of film journalists, the Kuratorium sponsored the first films of Kluge (*Yesterday Girl; Abschied von Gestern*, 1966), Hans Jürgen Pohland (*Cat and Mouse; Katz und Maus*, 1967), Peter Fleischmann (*Hunting Scenes from Lower Bavaria; Jagdszenen in Niederbayern*, 1968) and Werner Herzog (*Signs of Life; Lebenszeichen*, 1968), as well as sixteen other fully or more often partly financed films between 1965 and 1968.[28]

The starting capital of the Kuratorium amounted to 5 million DM over three years, with an average of 300,000 DM per film. The idea was that of a pump-priming operation, in the form of interest-free loans, to be paid back and reinvested in future production. In fact, very little of the money was ever returned. None the less, the measure was singularly successful. Twenty films, even over three years, represented a sizeable percentage of the output of a country whose film industry was in permanent crisis.

Not surprisingly, the work of the Kuratorium was felt to be a threat to the established film industry, whose representatives began to lobby parliament for a new form of tax concession to boost production almost as soon as the Kuratorium had been set up. After years of public debate and bitter feuds between the Kuratorium lobby and the commercial lobby, parliament passed the Film Subsidy Bill (FFG).[29] The Bill provided for a levy on every cinema ticket sold in West Germany (the so-called *Filmgroschen*, totalling about 15 million DM annually) to be passed on to the Film Subsidy Board (the *Filmförderungsanstalt*, or FFA) for allocation. Unlike the Kuratorium, the FFA was an official federal institution; as such it could only dispense economic aid and could not discriminate on criteria of quality.

Once the Bill was passed, the Ministry of the Interior ceased to fund the Kuratorium directly and merely recommended to the federal states that they support it with a total of 750,000 DM per annum, a drastic reduction in its operational scope compared with the original 5 million DM over three years. This was the more severe for the Young German Film, as the FFA was designed to help only those already established as producers. The Board automatically subsidised a producer whose film had grossed 500,000 DM or more during its first two years of release, up to an amount of 250,000 DM, or 50 per cent of production cost. This amount could only be used for financing another film. In other words, the subsidy was intended mainly as a commercial production bonus, with the only concession to quality being that a film with a FBW rating had to gross only 300,000 DM for its producer to be given a grant for his or her next project. This reinstated the economic and political significance of the Censorship Board (FBW), whose role had shrunk with the gradual abolition of entertainment tax on films. Since cinemas were closing at the rate of one a day, and audiences were staying away by the million (a loss of 700 million spectators between 1956 and 1976), independent productions had to aim for a quality rating and thus adjust themselves to the ideological criteria of the FBW if they hoped to qualify for subsidies from the FFA. In fact, of the hundred-odd films that had received production grants from the Board by 1972, no more than ten could be said to belong to the Young German Film.[30]

The reasons for this are simple. One had to have made a film (the so-called

Referenzfilm) before applying to the Board, since the Bill did not initially provide for subsidies on scripts or script outlines, as in the case of the Kuratorium. Once the reference film was made, it needed a distributor. Production was again at the mercy of the prevailing distribution system, a situation not synonymous with an objective assessment of popularity. When a distributor was found, financial success still depended on the amount of publicity he was prepared to invest. It was therefore less than fair to conclude that the Young German Film was a failure with the public simply on the grounds that its films did not return a profit. Alexander Kluge, for instance, maintains that caught between the monopoly position of the distributors and the 'automatic' (that is non-quality oriented) subsidy system operated by the FFA, the young cinema never actually had a chance to prove itself.[31]

Although presented as equitable to all parties, the Film Subsidy Bill evidently advantaged the established distributors' production arm. Even the first amendment of the Bill (1971), empowering a special committee to award a further subsidy of up to 150,000 DM to films classified as 'good entertainment' and to give grants to directors who had won a prize at an international festival, did little to redeem the Board's function in the eyes of its opponents: it was dubbed the soap opera cartel (*Schnulzenkartell*). As a counter-offensive against Oberhausen, the Bill was effective in driving independent directors to look for better opportunities in television, and it hastened the dissolution of the original Oberhausen group. Some of the original signatories were prepared to 'go commercial', as we shall see, by trying to produce within the system the kind of pot-boiler that would give them the production grant necessary for the realisation of more personal projects.

This was the case with Peter Schamoni, Hans-Jürgen Pohland and Rob Houwer, who were soon considered commercial directors and producers. Other directors occupied an in-between position: actively interested in production values, quality entertainment and the future of the 'industry', they tried to make films for an international public. Johannes Schaaf, for example, when asked what he thought was wrong with German films, replied:

> We always try to keep the entertainment value as low as possible, which is ridiculous; no other country in the world makes films that way. I believe German directors always disregard the public's need to be entertained. If you look at Brook's *A Midsummer Night's Dream* what strikes you is, on the one hand, the clear and exciting interpretation of the Shakespeare text, and, on the other all the show-values, so that the production could easily be put in an entertainment slot on TV and everyone would be delighted. I think it is important that a film can be consumed on different levels.[32]

Schaaf gives a description of how the Subsidy Bill might ideally have worked, but the actual Bill was not only detrimental to the Oberhausen activists, it was also disastrous to the industry itself. While the availability of easy money for commercial producers made production shoot up virtually overnight (1966 – 96 films; 1968 – 107 films; 1969 – 121 films), it encouraged a policy of throwing subsidy quickies on to the market. These recouped their investment in the shortest possible time by catering to a pornography clientele, largely recruited from Germany's two million immigrant workers (the *Gastarbeiter*), or by purveying infantile, low-brow schoolboy comedies to adolescents of all ages. The sex wave and the classroom comedies ruined the market for commercial producers, since each new series had a briefer span before it ran aground on the public's apathy. They permanently disaffected the more demanding cinema audiences, and led to

23

the closure of virtually all cinemas not located in the larger cities.

As with the guaranteed credits of the 1950s, a production boom was foisted on a shrinking market, with predictable results; for the sake of short-term profits, the industry was prepared to jeopardise its economic future by creating a volatile and occasional public, unpredictable in its demands and tastes. The situation was not helped by the fact (again paralleling the experience of the 1950s) that production was largely in the hands of the distributors, who via block booking were able to dictate programme policy to the cinemas. In extreme cases, cinema owners had to take German porn films in order to be able to show an international success like *Midnight Cowboy* or *Cabaret*, even if they knew that there was no demand among their regulars for sex films. The distributors' restrictive practices virtually starved second-run cinemas out of existence, a fact commemorated by Wim Wenders in *Kings of the Road* (*Im Lauf der Zeit*, 1976), where a woman would rather close her cinema altogether than be forced to show 'smut'.

By 1972, ten years after Oberhausen, the success and failure of the Young German Film could be seen in perspective. Government intervention in film production did not in itself distinguish the post-Oberhausen from the pre-Oberhausen period. As Kreimeier notes, the Oberhausen Manifesto was only the last in a long line of pamphlets and polemical pronouncements lamenting the situation of the German cinema.[33] Most of them vacillated between advocating economic measures to boost domestic production, and pouring scorn on the international reputation of a film industry that had become the standing joke of European film critics and journalists.[34]

What Oberhausen had contributed was, firstly, organised rather than individual protest – by film-makers instead of critics; and, secondly, an argument for cultural rather than fiscal government intervention. Out of the Manifesto had emerged a pressure group, taking its place alongside, but decidedly in opposition to the film industry's own parliamentary lobby. It had the backing of Social Democratic and Liberal members of the Bundestag, who were keen to develop a distinctive cultural and media policy in anticipation of soon forming a new government. The legislation that materialised as the Film Subsidy Bill was a compromise, reflecting the strength of the industry in the lobbies, but also the fact that the government of the day was a Christian Democrat one, destined to remain in power until 1969.

The Kuratorium, unquestionably the major achievement of the Oberhausen initiative in the area of cultural subsidy, instituted a parallel structure, a system of film-making that bypassed rather than challenged the industrial mode of production. It modelled itself on forms of patronage and commission as they had traditionally applied to writers, painters and the fine arts generally. For although the monies advanced by the Kuratorium were loans, they were in practice rarely demanded back. Thus the idea of establishing a revolving fund for first-time film-makers was not in fact how it worked in practice. As will be argued in more detail in the next chapter, the scheme implied a notion of film as an art work and an act of self-expression whose value lay in the fact that it existed at all, and only secondarily in its possibility of circulating as a commodity.

In this respect, the Young German Film was distinct from other comparable art cinemas, such as the *nouvelle vague* in France, whose films functioned as alternative products, but within a more or less traditional film industry, comprising commercial outlets as well as *cinémas d'art et essai*. They could address a socially stratified and self-selected, but none the less cinematically literate audience. By contrast, Young German films were made with a far less assured sense of an actual audience, and often bore little reference explicitly or implicitly to national

24

or international film culture. The early films of Syberberg or Herzog, for instance, were to a remarkable degree objects *sui generis*, outside any recognisable tradition of film-making either commercial or avant-garde. Kluge's essays on celluloid, and even Jean-Marie Straub's or Vlado Kristl's films seemed, in contrast to the French directors' love of the cinema, inspired by what one might almost call 'cinephobia', a revulsion against the commercial film industry and its standard product, the fictional narrative film.

'Trying to Build a Rolls-Royce with Money for a Bicycle'

It was in many respects a 'poor cinema' that had emerged out of the efforts of the Kuratorium. By having to rely on subsidies which were intended only as starting capital, film-makers were faced with the choice either of trying to measure themselves against expectations they could not live up to in terms of budgets and production values, or of defiantly proving that films could be made at a fraction of the cost usually invested in a feature film. The cinephobic reflex was a matter of necessity as much as the reflection of an aesthetic choice.

> If you only get subsidies, they are necessarily a temptation to either cheat or go bankrupt . . . For what are the criteria of a selection committee when it picks a particular script for subsidy? Doubtless the criteria which individual members of the committees have derived from the films, say of Fellini, Rosi or Truffaut. But their films are made on considerably higher budgets. This means that you have to submit a script that meets these criteria, but then it needs at least six to eight hundred thousand marks in order to get made. [. . .]. To get out of this dilemma [the director] starts his eight hundred thousand mark film on, say, three hundred thousand, which means a shorter shooting schedule, he cannot afford professionals but has to ask his friends, his actors are picked off the street. Of course he isn't naive, but tries to make a virtue out of necessity and it becomes a matter of style. Only his film was not planned this way. [. . .]. It is like trying to build a Rolls-Royce with money that is just enough to put together a bicycle.[35]

While the industry-oriented measures of the levy-and-rebate principle led to the speculative exploitation of an already depleted market, the quality-oriented subsidy forced film-makers into competition with each other at the script and project stage. The Kuratorium subsidy was 'too little to live on and too much to die from',[36] and while the assumption of producing a hand-crafted object in the editing room gives the film-maker a sense of total control, the illusion of artistic autonomy is immediately dispelled in the subsequent phase, when the film appears before a public bringing to it a more or less precise set of expectations. Schaaf's explanation of the failure of the Oberhausen films is convincing, but it contrasts interestingly with the criticisms made on directly stylistic grounds, which will be discussed in a subsequent chapter.

The major problem, therefore, with the films sponsored by the Kuratorium in the years between 1964 and 1971 was the absence of a distribution strategy into which the films might have fitted. Given that they were made outside the commercial system, and given the exhibition situation in Germany for non-Hollywood distributed products, the Young German Film existed in a vacuum within the home market, having to rely on the few outlets for European art cinema, and on one or two distributors exploiting the novelty value of the label while it lasted. Launching the films of Schlöndorff, Reitz, Schamoni or Schaaf commercially – to mention only some of the directors whose films might have met conventional expectations – would have required a sizeable publicity effort, which the film-makers were not able and the distributors not willing to undertake. Prestige, rather than financial gain, motivated the film-makers. The target audience had to be critics, journalists, festival visitors, through whom directors could campaign not only against the distribution system as it had been monopolised by the Majors, but on a much broader front for a reorganisation of the cinema's infrastructure altogether. However, the case on behalf of the Young German Film even after ten years was not self-evident.

First there was the fact that, by 1971, over 30 full-length feature films produced with public money had failed to find any form of exhibition other than occasional screenings at festivals or in the presence of the director. The industry's trade press predictably used the figures to argue that the Young German Film was bankrupt, and that the Kuratorium, the Ministry of the Interior and the Project Commission of the Film Subsidy Board were misguided in their criteria, ignoring the 'real' needs of the market and the public's true interests.

Second, opponents could point to a number of opinion polls such as the Dichter Study commissioned by the Film Subsidy Board.[37] Its finding showed that audiences who had seen films by Young German directors were unable to name common characteristics or identify what the label stood for. But not only was there no brand recognition, many spectators felt 'irritated' or 'annoyed' by the films' flippancy and lack of seriousness. The elliptical story-telling made them feel 'intellectually inferior'. Some even expressed 'anxiety', because of the 'disconnectedness' or 'lack of story', and of images evoking 'disagreeable associations'.

Alexander Kluge, who along with many other critics took stock at the start of the 1970s, also judged the Young German Film to be wanting in several respects:

> The problem was to create films that could play on the home market, but which became economically viable only if they reached interested audiences abroad. The first step was to win the confidence of international festivals on behalf of German films, and to counteract the prejudices dating from the Nazi films. The first products of the Young German Film seized this chance. It would have been necessary to [. . .] follow this up and produce exportable films that could count on international coverage. However, this second step did not happen. The Film Subsidy Bill, by the nature of its incentives, once more oriented German film production towards the home market, in the case of commercial films by stipulating audience ratings that could only be achieved via extensive exploitation of provincial markets. Similarly, the exclusion of independent producers from this market made these dependent on the equally provincial criteria of German selection committees for prizes, German journalists or the requirements of German television channels.[38]

Kluge, writing in 1973, could acknowledge the exceptionally poor performance of the Young German Film, while turning the tables on its critics. The economic crisis, he argued, must be met with a double strategy which oriented production unequivocally towards the international art cinema. The home market, on the other hand, needed a general renewal of film culture from the bottom up, an alternative distribution system, a more internationally literate critical establishment, different exhibition venues, and the development of new use-values for the film medium. With this, he read quite accurately the signs of the times since *Filmwirtschaft in der BRD und Europa*, from which this quotation is taken, was written not only as a 'white paper' for the 1974 revision of the Film Subsidy Bill, but was published on the eve of the German Cinema's major international successes and its transformation into the New German Cinema.

As far as the development of a specifically German film culture was concerned, several factors indicated that such a renewal was indeed underway. From 1969 onwards, the Kuratorium, recognising distribution as the most pressing problem of independent film-makers, had set aside a fund specifically for film promotion. The *Filmverlag der Autoren* was founded by a group of directors who had decided to pool their resources for distribution and enter the market directly. Its history is itself a very instructive chapter in the struggle for a brand name identity, and the efforts to move from an art cinema production model into a national–international distribution system.[39]

One consequence of the Oberhausen initiative was to draw attention to the problem of training and education. In 1962 Kluge, Reitz and Detten Schleier-macher set up West Germany's first film school, the Institut für Filmgestaltung Ulm, for which they had hoped to recruit Fritz Lang.[40] The Deutsche Film und Fernsehakademie Berlin followed in 1966, and the Hochschule für Film und Fernsehen opened in Munich in 1967. Even though among the internationally known directors only Wim Wenders graduated from a film school (Fassbinder was turned down when he applied to Berlin), each institution developed a quite distinct aesthetic. Both the 'Berlin School' and the 'Munich School' (as they came to be known) had its own approach to subject matter, style and politics which were to have a formative influence on the way television and the cinema evolved.

Parallel to the academies, a number of archives were also founded in the wake of Oberhausen: the Siftung Deutsche Kinemathek and the Freunde der Deutschen Kinemathek who run the Arsenal, a Berlin cinema functioning as a permanent and public cinémathèque. Shortly after the start of the Arsenal in Berlin, the Frankfurt Senator of Cultural Affairs, Hilmar Hoffmann, campaigned successfully for the concept of the so-called *Kommunale Kino*,[41] an art house or programme cinema funded by local authority grants. This policy, imitated or modified by many other West German cities, greatly increased the number of venues open to New German films as well as for revivals from the international repertoire, thus laying the basis for the kind of cinephile film culture which brought new audiences into contact with the cinema. Of special significance was the opening of the Munich Foto und Film Museum, which under the directorship of Enno Patalas (since 1973) became a cinémathèque and began collecting and restoring mainly German films from the beginnings to the present day. At the other end of the spectrum was the work of the Internationale Forum des Jungen Films (since 1971), initially a parallel event to but soon an integral part of the Berlin Film Festival. Headed by Ulrich and Erika Gregor and administered by the Friends of the German Kinemathek, the Forum also functions as an information and distribution centre for independent, avant-garde and Third Cinema.

The legacy of Oberhausen was thus to set in motion the development of a film culture, whose diverse manifestations and activities only incidentally required a particular kind of product as its material support. Almost as important as the films, the film schools and cinémathèques and the contracts with an international and avant-garde cinema were the new writing about the cinema, the publishing ventures and other local or regional media initiatives – all of which revalued the experience of going to the cinema. At the same time, more directly political issues had created a militant public which looked to film-makers for new forms of communication and agitation. These audiences contributed their own exhibition spaces.

Cinema as *Kultur*

Wherever the self-regulatory mechanisms of the economy cannot assure the participation of all citizens, the democratic state has to help and intervene. Since the participation of the masses in the communicative processes of the cinema cannot be assured without the arbitrating intervention of governmental institutions, a film policy is necessary.[42]

West Germany was the first major capitalist country where the State, directly via its Ministry of the Interior, indirectly via grant-awarding bodies, assumed for film-making the role of patron traditionally associated more with education and the performing arts than with the cinema.

The objective [of film subsidy] is motivated, above all, with the argument that film, along with literature, theatre, music and the fine arts, constitutes an autonomous art form, and furthermore represents a particularly suitable medium for education. Films with cultural, socio-political and paedagogic relevance therefore deserve similar subsidy on the part of the state as is enjoyed by other forms of education and expressive art forms.[43]

The intricate network of grants, stipends, prizes, bonuses, seed-money and financial risk-sharing that followed from this decision[44] amounted to the expression of a political will to see film acquire the status of 'Kultur'.[45] One of the historical conditions that had made the practice of subsidy possible was already described by Horkheimer and Adorno in their *Dialectic of Enlightenment*:

In Germany the failure of democratic control to permeate life had led to a paradoxical situation. Many things were exempt from the market mechanisms which had invaded the Western countries. The German educational system, universities, theatres with artistic standards, great orchestras, and museums enjoyed protection. The political powers, state and municipalities, which had inherited such institutions from absolutism, had left them with a measure of freedom from the forces and exigencies that dominated the market, just as princes and feudal lords had done up to the nineteenth century. This strengthened art in this late phase against the verdict of supply and demand, and increased its resistance far beyond the actual degree of protection.[46]

Horkheimer and Adorno are thinking of the early part of the century. They could not have anticipated that cinema, the mass medium and product of the 'culture industry' par excellence, would one day be protected from the forces of the market rather like the string quartet.[47]

Even though the money involved still made film quite marginal in comparison with the annual budgets of municipal theatres or state opera houses,[48] the German cinema during the 1970s became a new cultural force: not by bringing a paying public back to the box-office, and perhaps not even by the number of films it produced, but because of the debates it engendered at home, and the publicity it attracted abroad. This at any rate, is how some of the directors themselves saw it, for instance Reinhard Hauff: 'On the arts pages we are strong, in the film industry we are marginal figures.'[49]

As far as the industry was concerned, the cultural brief was perceived as a major threat, since it shifted the very ground-rules of film-making. Yet trade representatives were not prepared to take issue with the principle of subsidy itself, nor the need for government intervention. Instead, they attacked the subsidy system as 'undemocratic'. During the public debates leading up to the 1977 revision of the Film Subsidy Bill, the president of SPIO declared:

We need to make a basic decision. Either we want the selective subsidy system which I personally consider elitist and dirigist, because today in Germany an elite decides what films are to be made and which aren't. If we carry on like this, the market share will soon be below 1 per cent. Or we want a more market-oriented subsidy, which to my mind is the only democratic one, because it takes into consideration the audience at the box office.[50]

Thus, while one part of the film industry sought to attract from the US Majors the capital they could not raise in Germany,[51] another part was just as vigorously elbowing towards public funds as the independents, to whom the space they had conquered on the arts pages gave the feeling of participating in a national film culture. The German government in the meantime had found a 'crucial artistic medium for the manifestation of national identity'.[52]

Culture as Commerce

If the spirit of Oberhausen can be credited with having injected into the body-politic a new idea of film-culture – an achievement which, as we shall see, probably outweighs its contribution to film form and film language – the legislation it promoted in the area of film production at first seemed to founder on the impossible task of reconciling economic and cultural priorities. Indeed, no sooner was the 1967 Film Subsidy Bill before Parliament than its shortcomings were apparent even to the legislators:

> Renewal and improvement of the German cinema on a purely commercial basis would remain incomplete without a simultaneous raising of quality standards, and a vigorous support for research, development and education in the area of film-culture. We also need continuing subsidy for new film-makers and the strengthening of existing impulses for reform. The Film Subsidy Bill [. . .] should therefore, as soon as possible, be supplemented by an increased cultural subsidy.[53]

Since the Bill was heavily slanted in favour of the commercial film industry, the levy which made up the bulk of the funds available accrued only to producers capable of delivering enough exhibition outlets to clock up the stipulated 300,000 DM from paid admissions – a figure which was by itself rather arbitrary.[54] Even though film prizes, the project commissions of the Film Subsidy Board and the Ministry of the Interior tried to redress the balance on the side of cultural aid, the two types of financing resulted in totally different types of product.[55]

The first amendment to the Bill in 1971 therefore attempted to mesh the commercial and the cultural system, by disqualifying pornographic and low-quality films from receiving automatic subsidy, and at the other end by changing the system to a threshold of minimum attendance and lowering this for films that had received a quality rating or a festival prize. The number of film prizes was also increased, and their cash value raised. The Film Subsidy Board as well as the Kuratorium were empowered to spend funds on promotion and distribution. Cinemas were given prizes for the best programming schedules and interest-free loans for acquiring 16mm projection equipment. The Goethe Institute and German Embassies set aside money to pay for rights, buy extra prints or title them for showings abroad.[56] More money became available for the Berlin Film Festival and the Forum. The range and direction of these changes owed much to the lobby organised by Alexander Kluge, whose 'white paper', as we saw, advocated a more staggered, heterogeneous, quality and export-oriented package of funding measures:

Production cannot be understood as simply the manufacture of individual products, but needs to envisage the production of infrastructures and new types of audiences, which is to say, the transformation of the markets.[57]

The first amendment thus showed the new Social Democratic government firmly committed to an alternative film culture, with state intervention present at virtually all levels from production to distribution, publicity, exhibition, export, education and preservation.

Apart from the increased participation of the federal authorities in the funding system, regional production or project grants also began to open up for film-makers. The result was that the various grant-aid bodies overlapped in their activities, especially in the area of production subsidy. Instead of opting for one type of grant-aid, a German film-maker would apply to the Ministry of the Interior, the Film Subsidy Board, the Regional Development Fund or the Special Film Fund of the Free State of Bavaria – all for the same project. The city-states of Berlin, Hamburg and the Land Northrhine-Westphalia started similar regional schemes. This multiple-entry point system proved to have distinct advantages. Because the funds came out of so many different pockets – federal, regional, local – and from quite distinct spending authorities – industrial investment, regional development, education and science, national and international trade – the sums were a relatively small item in each budget.

Diversification spread the risks more evenly, for the sponsor as well as the producer. The combination, accumulation and circulation of different types of subsidy (prizes, loans, levy-money), which could make up 80 per cent of the overall production budget, encouraged the kind of initiative on the part of the film-maker that required forward planning and stimulated productivity on other than a one-off basis, which is the traditional bane of independent film-making. Even if only moderately successful a film could already provide, via a prize or access to automatic subsidy, the financial basis for the next one.[58]

In other words, the multiplication and decentralisation of grant-aid energised production quantitatively, rather than stifled it. Competition between the different regional authorities further stimulated production, and some of the schemes were organised according to cooperative principles: the Hamburg funds, and the Northrhine-Westphalia subsidy system being administered by the film-makers themselves. Berlin, on the other hand, offered particularly generous conditions for film-makers who could provide the so-called *Berlin-Effekt* and prove that they created jobs and employed laboratories or service industries in a city existing on the strength of a wholly subsidised economy.[59]

This seems to suggest that West Germany spent fabulous sums on funding its film production. But according to figures on film subsidy in other countries of the European Community, throughout most of the 1970s Germany was well behind Italy and only slightly ahead of France and Britain. It was the mixing of different forms of subsidy, the financing by fund-raising, and the mesh of federal and regional grant-aid within the overall strategy of the Film Subsidy Bill that distinguished Germany from the rest.[60]

The Idea of 'Quality' in Subsidy

Because the Film Subsidy Bill attempted to yoke together a double objective – that of *Wirtschaftlichkeit* (economic viability) and that of *Qualität* (quality) – the selection criteria for funding became one of the most fiercely debated and contested areas of the subsidy system. The full arguments will be aired in a later chapter, but the ambiguity surrounding the key terms – *wirtschaftlich* meaning 'commercially oriented' as well as 'profitable' and *Qualität* being taken either to mean 'good entertainment' or implying a certain cultural status and ambition – proved highly instructive. Once profit-taking at the box office is only one index or motive for production, factors which are usually considered stable, such as the relation of audience-figures to success or the calculation of long-term or short-term investment to returns become variables, while highly variable and unstable criteria such as quality have to become measurable and calculable.

The traditional film industry would at best understand the two key notions as naming different constituencies or markets; film journalism would see them as diametrically opposed ('commerce versus art'), but the legislators in West Germany intended them as 'complementary criteria, two priorities when examining a project in view of its eligibility for subsidy'.[61]

Ideally, the two criteria are compatible and complementary. Kluge thought that a term like *Brauchbarkeit* ('usefulness' – for the industry, for the nation, for the general good, for the preservation of the cinema as a public space and a particular kind of communal experience) would yield sufficient gradients and differentiations to test and assess a project's suitability, without polarising the subsidy system between 'culture' and 'commerce'. But such a correlation of long-term and short-term objectives, of material and immaterial benefits, and other basically non-equivalent entities can only be implemented if indeed the state is patron.

In practice, the allocation of quality subsidy rarely worked according to such 'socialist' principles, but rather oscillated between deciding either on a project's chances of success at the box office or on its potential prestige value abroad as well as on the 'arts pages'. That such yardsticks ultimately cannot measure either 'quality' or 'width', as it were, and yet have a certain logic which deeply affected the actual production of films under this system is the paradox of the German cinema in the 1970s.

The victims were the film-makers, both collectively and as individuals. It is doubtful, for instance, whether the selection process could ever have helped to bring into being a profession as opposed to single films. Even in West Germany, out of the relatively large number of first-time directors, few make it past their second or third film:

> For fifteen years German film has continued to produce new directors and film-makers. A complete list would contain almost three hundred names. Every year new names are added to the list and every year heralds the dawn of three, four or five promising talents. But every year also signifies the leave-taking, hardly noticed for it is silent, from almost as many hopes. The waste of imagination and innovation is tremendous.[62]

German film-makers enjoyed the privilege of being virtually exempt from calculating the direct financial returns of their films. But finding themselves thus sealed off did not mean they had escaped another, perhaps even crueller form of competition. Werner Herzog put it succinctly in 1972: 'I owe a lot to film subsidy. Without the Federal Film Prize and the script award I could hardly have worked at all. If you like, I'm on artificial respiration.'[63] The implication is presumably that some had their oxygen supply cut off, while others made it to where the air was less thin. Since very few directors imposed themselves at the box office, and only a few more were able to impress the subsidy committees on a regular basis, film-makers in Germany are often part-timers. They have second jobs – not, of course, in the film industry, but as teachers, academics, writers and even lawyers.

While new German directors turn their creative ability into pictures and sounds, their productions are sold off at cut prices. Only a few of the films produced in Germany reach cinema audiences; only a fraction bring in enough to cover the cost of production. Though the Federal Republic may be the richest film country, it is also the poorest cinema country.[64]

The Role of Television

A rich film country and a poor cinema country: this paradox can only be explained if one takes into account the one factor most would agree was not only crucial in transforming the ailing Young German Film into the more robust New German Cinema, but also in reconciling (by eliminating) the contradiction between commerce and culture – television. Given the continuing weakness of the distribution sector, the shrinking of audiences and the disappearance of cinemas especially in rural areas, even the most sophisticated government and regional funding policy and most buoyant urban film culture could not have created the resonance that the term New German Cinema began to acquire in the public mind by the mid-1970s. By then, the films had found audiences quite different from those that had rejected the Young German Film. Apart from spectators who began frequenting the *Kommunale Kinos*, the New German Cinema reached an art cinema audience abroad and a television audience at home: developments which in turn helped the film-makers to find distinctively German subjects, and so give a meaning to the term New German Cinema over and above its marketable brand name.

That television should enter the picture is itself the result of specifically German conditions, combining with general tendencies among the formerly competing mass media. What is specific is the internal structure of German television. West German television is organised along lines quite different from those of the British or American systems. Being a monopoly of the State, regionally divided and separately administered, the various channels commission much of their broadcast material from outside the institution, either by purchasing finished product or by sub-contracting and co-production.[65] There is no commercial broadcasting as such, each network being a public corporation answerable to the regional government of the day. Television could thus be brought within the kind of legislation represented by the Film Subsidy Bill. Thanks to the particular regional structure of German television, with altogether eight television companies supplying the two national channels and the more regional (in the afternoon) and highbrow (in the evening) third channel, a film-maker can either sell his or her finished film to television as a substitute for cinema distribution (and sell it several times to different TV companies), or s/he can offer the film at the project stage as a co-production, in order to close the gap between a government grant or prize and the required budget.

In this sense, television acts in much the same way as a commercial distributor's advance or a distribution guarantee. What is distinct from the overall policy of the government in respect of film, however, is that German television did not engage in film production in order to create a parallel structure, or merely to boost national prestige. Rather it anticipated and implemented on a large scale what other European networks, both commercial and government-controlled,

have increasingly practised: exploiting the cinema's residual glamour and attract-
iveness, for the purposes of advertising television's own appeal to a mass audience.
Television everywhere has co-opted the cinema and its history in order to create
a more special viewing experience for its own captive audience. A cinema film
still has the power to generate special expectations and a sense of occasion, even
when it passes on to the small screen. With it, the traditional distinctions between
production, distribution and exhibition become either blurred, or at least reshape
themselves in different forms.

German television channels produce fewer programmes themselves than either
British Independent Television (ITV) or the British Broadcasting Corporation.
Because they subcontract, with commercial companies or freelance independents,
film-makers can join the queue for commissions. The mechanisms for co-
production with an independent producer-director having been well-established,
the Film Subsidy Bill could bring television within its own terms of reference.
Such relatively smooth synchronisation of film production and television would
have seemed difficult to imagine in the British context, for instance, before the
arrival of Channel Four, which adopted a policy of commissioning feature films
based largely on that of German TV.[66]

If the terrain had not been prepared in this way, the second revision of the
Film Subsidy Bill might not have taken the decisive turn that it did. Compared
with the 1971 amendment, whose main effect had been to discriminate positively
in favour of various quality thresholds, the 1974 revision laid the groundwork not
only for the situation on the home market, but also for the standing of the New
German Cinema abroad. In order to grasp the complex and ever more powerful
role that television played in the history of the New German Cinema, both in
terms of production and in audience building strategies, the nature of West
German television in its socio-political functions has to be considered. This will
be done later, when looking at one of the most remarkable experiments in public
broadcasting – the *Arbeiterfilme* – produced by the prestigious Westdeutsche
Rundfunk (WDR) between 1968–1976.[67]

Two further contributing factors seemed to have played a part. One was that
the entire film and television sector in West Germany was, by British standards,
patchily unionised, giving producers few restrictions in respect of crewing or of
employing independent, non-union personnel. Secondly, Westdeutsche Rundfunk
(WDR) and Zweites Deutsches Fernsehen (ZDF) had, during the period in
question, Heads of Drama and Film who came to their posts via film-making and
film criticism. They were convinced supporters of the New German Cinema and
of independent film-making. The history of the commissioning policy of these
two channels is itself a vital part of the New German Cinema, since without some
of its special programming slots such as ZDF's *Das kleine Fernsehspiel* or WDR's
backing of television series like Fassbinder's *Berlin Alexanderplatz* (1979–80) or
Edgar Reitz' *Heimat* (1984), many of the most successful projects of the New
German Cinema would never have been realised.[68]

However, until 1974 the role of television was a haphazard one, with *ad hoc*
arrangements for co-production between film-makers and commissioning editors
being the rule. The Television Framework Agreement between the TV companies
and the Film Subsidy Board specified the amount each channel was to allocate to
feature film production, although not specifically to films by German directors.
For the first period of the agreement, the years from 1974 to 1978, 34 million
DM were invested in feature film projects which would have regular film
distribution and television airing. The time lag between first cinema release and

33

a television broadcast could be anything between six months and five years. The Framework Agreement also provided funds which the Film Subsidy Board could allocate to the development of promising projects, regardless of whether television would eventually act as the co-producer.

This, and various other amendments to the Film Subsidy Bill, helped to redefine television's role in relation to independent cinema. Rather than intervening directly in film production, as it had done at the time of the Kuratorium and the early phases of the Film Subsidy Bill, the Federal Government gradually delegated its role to intermediary institutions such as the Film Subsidy Board (which is a federal agency operating on the basis of committee decisions) and to the television companies (which, though public institutions, are autonomous in relation to the federal authorities). In contrast to the ideological and social vacuum in which the Young German Film had found itself, television's role as a public service and its sensitivity to questions of accountability involved film-makers in public debates. It led to an increasing politicisation, if not necessarily of the films themselves, then of the independent cinema's role within the overall structure of the media, within Germany's democratic institutions and the information industries.

By the mid-1970s, then, a clearer picture emerged of the different modes of production characteristic of the New German Cinema. Bringing television into film-making had diversified considerably both the products and the markets, the audiences and the forms of reception. Alongside films with an international art cinema appeal, which retained a prestige currency for German films abroad and fed back into the home market as successful international releases, films began to appear which were clearly more directly aimed at various sections of the national television audience. Political questions, social issues, current affairs and historical topics began to be treated in fiction films and documentaries in a manner unknown before in the Federal Republic.

At the same time, women film-makers found it easier to enter production than at any time previously, partly through *Das kleine Fernsehspiel* commissioning a majority of women, and partly through a more highly developed awareness of collective struggles and the formation of professional associations. Avant-garde and experimental work, which had fared particularly badly during the subsidy system because of the committees' preference for full-length feature films, began to appear again. Without the funding provided by television networks, these projects would have found it impossible to persuade a commission to back them, for lack of any distribution prospects. On the other hand, it might be argued that with television providing both the central funding authority and the main form of exhibition, many of the productions of the German cinema should no longer be considered cinema. A history of the New German Cinema might find its natural conclusion at the point where television modifies the way we now perceive a national cinema. Increasingly, we are obliged to view each country's films not primarily in relation to its erstwhile competitor and antagonist, namely Hollywood, but in relation to the dominant audio-visual institution – television – and its creation of a national culture as a complex form of social consensus and collective memory screen.[69] However, within the mode of production represented by television, some of the old antagonism between film-makers as individuals with set intentions, and the institution with different constraints and priorities, was bound to resurface.

For whether a director regarded television simply as a short-cut in the arduous process of finding film finance, or fully accepted television's role as both exhibition outlet competing with the cinema, and its best promotional showcase, his or her

34

mode of production had to take into account a bureaucratic structure more or less outside any individual's control, determining the product as well as its form of circulation. The Hamburg independent film-makers' festival of 1979, itself a protest event in response to the City of Munich's attempt to co-opt the film community for a commercially oriented film festival, voiced many of the misgivings film-makers felt about finding themselves no longer confronting the State as their prime sponsor, but television. The so-called Hamburg Declaration thus has to be read not so much as a *volte face* with respect to the Oberhausen Manifesto, but as its logical extension into the changed historical situation. Whereas in 1962 aspiring film-makers knew they had to turn to the government for assistance, by 1979 the appeal was to television. Yet because television represented both patron and consumer, the appeal could be ambiguously understood as an address directly to the public:

> Imagination cannot be administered. Committee minds must not determine what productive cinema is to be about. German films of the eighties can no longer be other-directed by committees, institutions and vested interest groups . . . We have shown that we are professionals. Therefore, we cannot regard ourselves as a guild. We have learnt that our ally can only be the spectators: people who work, who desire, dream and have interests, that is those people who go to the cinema and those who do not, and those who can imagine an altogether different cinema.[70]

What strikes one in this manifesto (apart from it being obviously drafted by a committee) are the coy and indirect references to television. In a supplementary declaration it becomes more evident that the film-makers wanted to be better represented on the selection panels of the television boards, rather than demanding the abolition of existing structures or radical changes in the co-production agreements. Only the women were precise in their demands: 50 per cent of all the monies to women, 50 per cent women on all the committees. For the rest it was not altogether clear whether the intention was to preserve the independent and freelance status of the film-maker-as-television-author, or whether the demands went in the direction of greater job security within the television institutions.

At the other end of the scale, but by no means in opposition to the film-makers in television, were those international directors who by the end of the decade had become bankable within the art cinema, and whose films were generally released via US-controlled Major companies. Fassbinder in particular had, throughout the 1970s, been able both to work in television and to raise finance for projects which did, in effect, satisfy Schlöndorff's requirement for a national film industry. Namely, that periodically it undertakes work of sufficient scope to bring the infrastructure up to the latest stage of technology. *Despair* (*Eine Reise ins Licht*, 1978), *Lili Marleen* (1980), or *Querelle* (1982) were films very much relying on well-equipped studios. Likewise, Wolfgang Petersen, first with *Das Boot* (*The Boat*, 1981) and then with *The Neverending Story* (*Die Unendliche Geschichte*, 1984), fully utilised new special effects equipment to bring German film-making to an international commercial standard. This seemed a far cry from Kluge's *Yesterday Girl* (1966) or Fassbinder's own *Katzelmacher* (1969). By the end of the 1970s the point had been reached where the ceiling of the subsidy system touched the floor of the international film industry.

2:

The Old, the Young and the New: Commerce, Art Cinema and *Autorenfilm*?

'Film Subsidy is no Pension Fund'

In one respect, the victory of the New over the Young German Cinema remained problematic: despite all its successes, it seemed to achieve little towards improving, as the Film Subsidy Bill had stipulated, 'the structure of the German film industry' – if this was predicated either on financial profit or long-term capital investment. By 1978 German films' share of the home market had sunk to 8 per cent;[1] West Germany was Hollywood's second-largest export market (after Canada and ahead of Great Britain), with no less than US$51.9m annual gross.[2] The lack of box-office revenue for German films highlighted the stark discrepancy between output and financial return, as well as the paradoxical relation between prestige and popularity.

During 1977/78, almost 60 German feature films were made, of which roughly half belonged to the New German Cinema: among them were Fassbinder's *Despair* (1977), Wenders' *The American Friend* (*Der amerikanische Freund*, 1977), Herzog's *Stroszek* (1977), Syberberg's *Our Hitler* (1977), Helke Sander's *Redupers* (1977), Herbert Achternbusch's *Beer Battle* (*Bierkampf*, 1977), Walter Bockmayer's *Flaming Hearts* (*Flammende Herzen*, 1978), Peter Handke's *The Left-Handed Woman* (*Die Linkshändige Frau*, 1978), Margarethe von Trotta's *The Second Awakening of Christa Klages* (*Das zweite Erwachen der Christa Klages*, 1977), Niklaus Schilling's *Rheingold* (1978), Wolfgang Petersen's *The Consequence* (*Die Konsequenz*, 1977), Hans W. Geissendörfer's *The Glass Cell* (*Die Gläserne Zelle*, 1978).

It was, in fact, the *annus mirabilis* of the New German Cinema. Yet the first German film to enter the year's list of box-office successes, at Number 38, was *Moritz lieber Moritz*, a children's film by Hark Bohm. It was seen by 400,000 spectators, compared with the 4.6m Germans who saw *Star Wars* that season.[3] Many of the films one now thinks of as the lasting achievements of the New German Cinema never made the Top 50 in their own country.

Until 1976, the low percentage could be correlated to the still declining trend in cinema attendances generally (1956: 817 million admissions per year; 1966: 257 million; 1976: 115 million), which went hand-in-hand with falling revenue (1956: 956 million DM; 1976: 591 million DM).[4] But by 1977 attendance figures had begun to increase again, and the press could hail a new cinema-going boom.[5] German films did not benefit from it: commercial exhibitors were among the strongest enemies of the New German cinema, fiercely opposed to any suggestion of a quota of state-subsidised films. Claiming that larger chains as well as small neighbourhood cinemas had to rely on American block-busters for profits, the industry lobby demanded the abolition of the quality clauses and discrimination by the Subsidy Board in favour of commercially oriented productions. A pro-industry critic for the right-wing *Deutsche Zeitung*, and himself a film director, wrote in late 1977:

> Film-makers like Kluge, Herzog, Geissendörfer and Fassbinder, all of whom have collected subsidies more than once, and who despite such public funding are incapable of directing a success, should in future be barred from receiving subsidies. Film subsidy is no pension fund for failed film-makers.[6]

Such venom was symptomatic of the divisiveness among West Germany's cineaste community.[7] Why was the New German Cinema so unloved in its own country and what were the reasons given by its critics? In 1968 the bad figures had been blamed on the self-indulgent films of the Obermünchhausner (a joke contraction of Oberhausen and München – where most of the rebel film-makers came from – and 'Baron Münchhausen' – a legendary braggard and liar). In the early 1970s it was the cultural subsidy and the cosseted *Autorenfilm* which caused films to be produced 'past the public'. By the mid-70s, the culprits were the *Gremien* (committees) and their preference for 'filmed literature'. In the late 1970s it was once more the *Autorenfilm*, now under fire from the cinephiles who wanted 'real movies'. Early in the 1980s, when some German films such as *Das Boot* (*The Boat*, 1981) were actually making money, the call was for power to producers with international experience. Attacked by distributors and producers, directors accused each other and feuded with critics, who in turn sided with industry interests in the name of the ordinary spectator. German film-makers acquired egos that were both arrogant and paranoid, unable to trust either the critics or the spectators.

'Germans just don't go to the Cinema'

For the film industry almost everywhere, the 1960s brought the demise of the traditional family audience. With spectators becoming younger and younger, and adult audiences more volatile in their tastes, the *Autorenfilm* and its cultural brief would have found it difficult to capture a national audience even in a country less divided and cut off from its sense of historical continuity. Again, figures indicate just how far the situation bordered on the hopeless:

> The average German spends three hours a day in front of his television set. The same statistically average German spends about three hours in the cinema per year. Of these he watches American films for about 90 minutes, then the rest, 30 minutes of porn films and German films for barely 20 minutes. Of the approximately 300 productions that could be counted as 'New German Cinema' about six were commercially successful in German cinemas and just about broke even: *Effi Briest* by Fassbinder, *Kaspar Hauser* by Herzog, *Katharina Blum* by Schlöndorff, *The Baker's Bread* by Erwin Keusch, *The Marriage of Maria Braun* by Fassbinder, *The Tin Drum* by Schlöndorff. What is striking is the large proportion of filmed literature among the commercial successes. Four of these six films are based on literary sources.[8]

The statistics in turn highlighted the fundamental dilemma of the independent cinema, whether state-subsidised or not. The instances of intervention in the German film industry had been mostly on the side of production, with little impact on the distortion of market forces due to the massive presence of American distributors who, in the 1960s, controlled up to 85 per cent of the national first-run film bookings. Arguments about the quality of German films or complaints about the power of the funding committees were therefore largely irrelevant. The stark fact was that a German film, however good, could not show a profit, nor reach a mass audience within the given exhibition system, unless it had an American distributor launching it in West Germany itself. If a production took more than 500,000 DM to make, it could not return its investment on the second-run or art cinema circuits. Yet, unless it cost more than 5 million, the Majors were rarely interested, since for an American distributor the economics of starting films in first-run cinemas are such that only above a certain budget (equated with certain production values) does it become viable to invest in sufficient prints, pre-publicity and local advertising to properly launch a new release.

The average German film, relying on public subsidies, television finance and the producer-director's own 15 to 20 per cent share was, from the beginning, caught in the trap between these two sets of figures. In order to be nationally popular, the German cinema had to become international. In order to be international, it had to have budgets, production values and access to markets comparable to those open to its main competitors. Elsewhere in Europe, the ties that French and Italian producers have with American Majors were incomparably

Filmed literature: Günter Grass, Heinz Bennent and Volker Schlöndorff on the set of The Tin Drum *(1979)*

better than those available to the authors' cinema. For New German films to prove themselves at the box office was like trying to sell home-made lemonade to the Coca Cola Company.

Werner Herzog's self-consciously titanic struggles might be said to have had just that in mind. When in 1972 he argued that 'one should get used to the fact that Germans just don't go to the cinema. Which is why it makes no sense to produce films for the German market alone',[9] he was only partly right. Blaming the unpopularity of German films on the audiences does acknowledge one dilemma of a cinema that is expected to be 'national' in what is essentially an international industry. But it ignores the structural problem of over-production or the feeling, not only voiced by the industry lobby, that less would be more, that the system produced too many first-time film-makers who were unable to develop a sustained oeuvre or even confirm their initial promise by an acceptable second film.[10] Crowding in the relatively small area of the secondary circuits, independent films tended to harm each other's business and were ghettoised even before they reached a public.

Their strength – diversity of form and appeal – was thus also an economic liability. Difficult to classify generically and therefore difficult to market by the criteria of the commercial cinema, the films that began to appear around 1968–70 set up expectations and echoes in so many directions that only a very well-defined film culture or a buoyant market could have absorbed them. A few examples at random illustrate the problem: *Chronicle of Anna Magdalena Bach*, 1968 (a European art film in the tradition of Dreyer and Bresson), *Zur Sache Schätzchen* (*Let's Get Down to Business, Darling*, 1967, a sex comedy borrowing from Swedish and Italian models), *Lebenszeichen* (*Signs of Life*, 1968, a literary, highly 'personal' film), *Kelek* (1969, an international avant-garde film), *Michael Kohlhaas, the Rebel* (1969, an international commercial co-production based on a literary classic), *Jet Generation* (1968, a 'swinging sixties' *nouvelle vague* imitation with thriller overtones), *Eika Katappa* (1969), a low-budget operatic camp extravaganza), *Jagdszenen in Niederbayern* (*Hunting Scenes from Lower Bavaria*, 1968, a realist social critique), *Liebe ist kälter als der Tod* (*Love is Colder Than Death*, 1969, a gangster melodrama).

Each of these films was in itself the programme for a New Cinema, defining a stance, and with it a potential audience. Some titles promised genre-based films – *Rote Sonne* (*Red Sun*, 1970), *48 Stunden bis Acapulco* (*48 Hours to Acapulco*, 1967) – or alluded with their English titles to mainstream Hollywood or rock music: *Deadlock* (1970), *Blue Velvet* (1970) and *Summer in the City* (1970). Others flaunted enigmatic names echoing the European 'art cinema' (*Malatesta*, 1970, *Neurasia*, 1969, *Cardillac*, 1969, *Fata Morgana*, 1971).

Finally, and most typically for the New German Cinema, a proliferation of programmatic, over-explicit or mock-didactic titles: *Film oder Macht* (*Film or Power*, 1970), *Auch Zwerge haben klein angefangen* (*Even Dwarfs Started Small*, 1970), *Geschichten vom Kübelkind* (*Stories of the Bucket Baby*, 1970), *Nicht der Homosexuelle ist pervers, sondern die Situation in der er sich befindet* (*Not the Homosexual is Perverse, but the Situation in which He Finds Himself*, 1970). If the production boom caused the exhibition bottleneck, it was largely because of the unfavourable odds in the market, and the titles themselves hint at the difficulty of envisaging audiences when there were virtually no cinemas to attract them.

A 'Cultural' Mode of Production

Even during the buoyant mid-1970s, then, when the New German Cinema undoubtedly peaked both in terms of the number of important films being made and in the growing self-assurance of its directors, the sense of crisis could not simply be put down to the film-makers' persecution complex and hypochondria.

Three basic anomalies typified the situation. The central ideology of the German cinema was that of the *Autor*, but the films themselves were massively determined by the production mode (state finance supporting artisanal values) and the exhibition context (either American distributor or television). Secondly, despite these common conditions and a united political front, no group style emerged, and the output remained amorphous and unfocused. Instead of authorship being conferred on a director's films retrospectively, to honour the perceived coherence of an achieved body of work, it was at the level of ambition and intention that someone became an author, while each individual work often seemed to remain economically and aesthetically a one-off effort.[11] *Autor* status became a euphemistic way of classifying the unclassifiable: no other national cinema was able to propagate so many directors as authors in such a short space of time. Finally, despite the diversity and individuality of the vast but not unlimited number of films, there is a persistence of similar thematic motifs and of certain configurations (the family, authority, the outsider), the recurrence of formal issues (identification and point of view), and above all, a remarkably consistent tone (often of melancholy, regret, nostalgia and loss).

Hence the need to try and account for the logic of this production and provide a rationale for the diversity but also the unity of the films. The most obvious answer is to treat the New German Cinema as a variant of the art cinema. European post-war cinema evolved closely in relation to two contradictory impulses: safeguarding the national film culture with government measures, while trying to develop a cinema formally distinct from that of Hollywood.[12] The film industry invariably wanted a national cinema that could compete commercially with Hollywood. Art cinema, however, is generally produced on the margins of that industry, neither in outright opposition to it nor a serious rival to Hollywood. In countries like Italy and France, it often succeeded in being nationally specific by capitalising on intellectual and literary traditions. It gained international recognition and hard currency where the films addressed themselves to an audience which most probably regarded cinema as a 'vulgar' form of mass entertainment, yet looked to film for a representation of modernist cultural themes. Existentialism, the absurd and alienation were never far from the critical discussions of, for example, the early films of Bergman, Antonioni, Resnais and even Losey: it meant that the art cinema auteur worked within a broad cultural consensus and for an identifiable public.

However, while some of this applies to the German situation, notably the origin and purpose of the funding system, interpretations of New German films in the European auteur tradition (with the possible exception of Herzog's) are almost as problematic as are the genre divisions sometimes put forward. Furthermore, the absence of either a film industry or an ideological consensus enforcing technical standards or representational norms makes analyses analogous to those attempted of Hollywood films inappropriate. Although the New German Cinema remained throughout, and despite interesting variants, a narrative cinema,[13] a reading of the films as narratives, and of the narratives as socially symbolic forms yields disappointing results – not least because of the almost total absence of romance plots. Also, it is precisely in the area of narrative that the output of the German cinema presents another major paradox, since the films are, by conventional standards, often artless in technique and badly constructed as drama, but visually intriguing. Moreover, they break many of the rules of classical narrative without, however, necessarily developing alternative paradigms such as can be found in, say, the films of Jean-Luc Godard or Jean-Marie Straub.

Thus, in economic terms (state-funded, anti-formula, promoted as national) the New German Cinema belongs to the art cinema, as opposed to genre cinema. But as an art cinema it is far less self-conscious about its film-historical place than the cinema of Bresson or Bergman, Rivette or Truffaut and, instead, much more aware of a (film-)political role and social issues (quite untypical for an art cinema).

The question arises whether the New German Cinema, because it generated a historically distinct 'mode of production'[14] also developed a distinct 'mode of representation'. Features which in the analysis of commercially produced films tend to be of minor importance, such as the different self-definitions of the directors, may take on a new prominence within the films themselves, while other factors, such as the 'mode of address' or the different patterns of recognition and identification, may be based on shared cultural experiences. On the other hand, evidence of specific formal features – the touchstone of identifying the classical narrative cinema as well as defining avant-garde modes of representation – are in the New German Cinema difficult to describe as anything more comprehensive and general than the styles of individual directors (for instance, the distinctive mises-en-scène of Fassbinder, Herzog, Schroeter or Wenders).

Yet the object here is to offer an account of the New German Cinema, rather than absorb the films into the stylistic idiosyncracies of art cinema or modernist auteurs (into which the German authors only fit with difficulty in any case). It is therefore the 'cultural' mode of production that must serve as the starting point not only for indicating what, if anything, the internationally recognised auteurs of this cinema have in common with their less well-known colleagues, but to highlight those aspects of the production logic that appeared to have had a determining effect on the films themselves.

The following tries to sketch three interdependent areas of structured significa-tion that can be found in the output of the New German Cinema and which will be taken up in greater detail during subsequent chapters. The first of these fields of meaning focuses on the ideological determinations: the concept of the Autorenfilm and its contradictory inscription of self-expression and state subsidy. The second concerns a number of institutional determinations, mainly to do with the status of a so-called independent cinema, existing between non-commercial exhibition venues (in this case, the Kommunale Kinos) and late-night television slots. The third field touches on the spectatorial determinations, the real, perceived or projected demands made by German audiences (but also critics and the State) on the cinema, and the directors' response to such expectations. The author-auteurs and their international productions mesh with these national determi-nations in complex but demonstrable ways, making the meaning most readily available to their art cinema audiences outside Germany often a mere abstraction of the specific historical inscriptions present in the films.

The polemics quoted earlier suggested that German film-makers were self-indulgent, and indifferent to their home audiences. I would want to advance the opposite hypothesis: that the films, their forms (ranging from realist narrative, documentary fiction to stylised fantasy), their subjects (dealing with matters of recognisable public debate) and titles (often quite 'uncinematic') imply a continuing anxiety about audiences, and can only be understood against the internalised and exterior pressures coming from a pervasive 'legitimation gap' affecting a cinema sponsored by the state and not supported by a mass public. In short, the vast majority of German independent films seem to me at some level always concerned with justifying film-making not so much as a creative individual act, but as a critical activity involving issues of public accountability. The German film-maker is 'other-directed' twice over: parallel to negotiating approval from the committees and state bureaucracies, he or she must also woo a public. The search for an audience constitutes the other, less commented-on aspect of the cultural mode of production.

Subsidy and Self-expression: The *Autorenfilm*

If for the first ten years or so the *Autor* proved the most decisive focus for both production and reception, it was also the most confusing concept in the New German Cinema. This was largely due to the way it combined a certain self-understanding of the film-maker as author in the legal sense, and his more directly ideological role as an artist and as the creator of personal works. The confusion was compounded by the existence of the term within the art cinema generally, where it often functions as a transcendent category of value. Not so in West Germany: *Autoren*, in order to be able to make films, as we saw, first had to create the conditions for making them. The authors' film is thus tied indissolubly to the authors' policy: the cultural-political demand for recognition and subsidy. Film aesthetics often became indistinguishable from film politics.

The cultural mode of production differs from the industrial mode (for which Hollywood is still the shorthand name), and from the avant-garde model of co-ops, workshops, galleries and aesthetic theory. Yet it shares elements of both these diametrically opposed conceptions of film and cinema, and is nevertheless neither a compromise between the two nor does it supersede them in practice. At one extreme, raising finance under the German system resembles, paradoxically, the Hollywood 'package deal', the norm in international film financing which succeeded the studio system. Commercial package deals are put together by a producer or an agency who sells to often quite unlikely clients or interest groups a package of stars, story and production values. In the 'cultural' mode of production, it is the individual film-maker who has to shop around, fill in the application forms, present proposals to committees, submit budgets and attend hearings, before knowing whether the project will ever become a film. What this has in common with the package deal is the add-on practice of separate financing sources combining to fund a single product. Where it differs is that the client is ultimately the State buying 'culture', and that the diversity is not in the ingredients of the product but in the number of decision-making bureaucracies involved in its genesis.

At the other extreme, what Pam Cook has defined as typical for the avant-garde does to a large extent also apply to the New German Cinema:

> Traditionally the relation of the avant-garde film-maker to her or his work has been artisanal, i.e. the film-maker, like a craft worker, is in control of all aspects of the process of production and distribution/exhibition, retaining rights of ownership over her or his film. The artisanal mode of production has several levels: it implies a particular mode of production which is small-scale and therefore, in a capitalist economy, lies outside the dominant system . . . Artisanal production stands in

42

opposition both to the capitalist economic organisation of the film industry and to the structure of labour within the industry (in terms of its hierarchy and organisation) . . . In general, because of its marginal position *vis-à-vis* the industry, artisanal film production has been supported by patronage of wealthy individuals, funding in the form of grants from State institutions and by the organisation of co-operative workshops.[15]

Most German directors manifested an extreme ambiguity towards the subsidy system and its effects on their work. Herzog, for instance, was already in a 1972 interview tired of passing round the begging bowl:

[What bothers me are] the quite apalling efforts involved in raising finance for film-making . . . Maybe three-quarters of my energies go into organisational matters. With more money, I could invest myself in a much more purposeful way.[16]

For Herzog, Wenders and Fassbinder, as their films began to earn automatic subsidy for investment in future production, the cultural model appeared to be of importance only as a secondary source of finance. They gradually phased themselves out of the subsidy maze, and once their reputations as directors were established, they possessed a 'value' which the international film industry understood, so that for them, a version of the Hollywood model re-emerged. Fassbinder once scornfully said that he could make an entire film in the time it took others to read the small print on the application forms of the grant-aid committees.[17]

Similarly, though surprisingly for someone widely considered to have been the mind behind the subsidy system, Kluge made no secret of his hostility to its practices. He once compared the committee hearings to a school board in session, and complained about the indignity of being treated with every new film like an examination candidate threatened with relegation.[18] Kluge also claimed that the German Cinema of the 1970s attained even its international reputation not *because of* the West German funding system, but *in spite of* it.[19] This may be a polemical exaggeration, but it points to the fact that estimations of the benefits of the subsidy system were by no means unanimous, and that the cultural mode stood in tension not only to the Hollywood ambitions of a Fassbinder or the fierce individualism of a Herzog, but also to the collectivist-egalitarian aspirations of a Kluge,[20] not to mention the political avant-garde positions of a Jean-Marie Straub. In fact, the secret of the subsidy system's 'success' may have been that it was in many ways self-contradictory.

For implicit in the Oberhausen rebellion was an ideological stance which has always been a main platform of the independent cinema: the right to self-expression, and the demand to use film as the medium for a personal vision. As a militant position from which to fight the film industry, the 'personal vision' argument lacks conviction. When the writer Alfred Andersch put forward the notion in the 1950s 'that the eye of the camera only starts seeing when a literary consciousness is behind it',[21] he echoed Alexandre Astruc's *caméra-stylo*, but Astruc had outlined an alternative and complementary practice rather than a competing one. The generation of Oberhausen on the other hand wanted to replace the film industry. Had they been avant-garde film-makers, they might have insisted on self-expression (though in actual fact, the German avant-garde directors were fiercely suspicious of this concept), arguing that they were concerned to protect their project from the contingent obstacles attending its realisation. But state-subsidised film-makers, in contrast to painters or writers, cannot escape their social obligations – after all, so the argument goes, they use tax-payers' money to fulfil a 'private' fantasy. Indeed, they are only too aware of the constraint which receiving public funds puts on self-expression. As Edgar Reitz explained:

> Practically, the situation today is this: you receive money from the Ministry of the Interior, and then you have to try incredibly hard to forget where the money comes from, and why it was given to you.[22]

However, what is valued by a government financing its film-makers is not a particular use-value or even propaganda function but, precisely, a relentless commitment to self-expression. Or at least a commitment to the idea of film as art, and of art as existing in the realm of aesthetic autonomy. This was part of the traditional compromise that subsidised art in whatever field had concluded with the powers that be, in order to escape the odium of being 'official' art, as most of the state-supported arts are in socialist countries. In Western democracies, the problem with patronage is that those who receive it must not appear to bite too fiercely the hand that feeds them, while displaying sufficient discontent to pass as independent. Much of the peculiarity of the New German Cinema can be traced along the fine line of this tension: between the role that the grant-awarding bodies projected onto the film-maker, and the image that film-makers had of themselves and of the cinema in general.

The task, thus, of mediating between mutually exclusive projections and expectations fell above all to the *Autorenfilm*,[23] a term serving as a sort of turnstile between ideology and practice, an ideal and a dogma so strong that for a time the renaissance of the cinema in Germany could be attributed to the fact that 'the author [was] a public institution'.[24]

> Autorenkino [was] in essence institutionalised directorial autonomy. It would also give rise to intense competition among individual Autoren . . . Likewise it would put the creators at the beck and call of the very institutions so much of their work aimed to call into question.[25]

While it disguised rather than eliminated the contradictions, the victory of the *Autorenfilm* gave state-funded film-making a certain identity.[26] But the author in the German cinema is neither a retrospective category of coherence applied to a film text, as is the case in Hollywood auteurism, nor was he, at least initially, the 'film director-as-superstar'.[27]

Instead, the *Autorenfilm* is more an example of an ideological concept and a discourse functioning as a form of coherence for the cultural mode of production itself. It determined the political and administrative machinery put in place to fund films practically and it furnished the criteria which validated film-making as 'art'. The ideology of self-expression, institutionalised, became a surrogate economic category: for by being accepted as an 'author' a film-maker found access to the subsidy system and could command a certain legal and financial power within it. Sheila Johnston even goes so far as to say that '*Autoren* were defined as such from the very outset, often before they had even made a film'.[28]

Crucial for the *Autorenfilm* were the statutes of the Kuratorium, which by and large set the pattern for the contractual relations between film-makers and film subsidy as cultural aid. By recognising as its legal partner, and answerable for the project, the person submitting a script and intending to realise it, they defined the author for all intents and purposes as the director:

> The film-maker should have autonomy in giving shape to his film idea without having to take legal or serious financial risks. He was to retain control over the direction and the entire production process.[29]

44

Was this a progressive move, intended to counter the employee status of the film director in German labour law, or did its regressive side predominate, confining German film production to glorified home movies?[30] By shaping the directors' self-definition and the films themselves, the ambiguities inherent in the concept of the *Autorenfilm* became themselves one of the most productive aspects of the German situation.

One feature, however, was only noted towards the end of the 1970s: assuming the main battle for control to be between the director and the producer, the ideologues of the *Autorenfilm* had left no separate or defined role for the script-writer. By its very nature, the subsidy system heavily favoured the director as his own script-writer, a bias which became a problem as soon as the German cinema needed to confront seriously the task of making films which were both narrative and aimed at the cinemas:

> A script-writer, e.g. Hark Bohm, wants to be and is immediately advanced to 'author' even if he happens to be a bad director. Conversely, no director – despite all the complaints about the difficulties of writing a good scenario – wants to entrust his idea to a professional writer, for fear the writer might turn into a film author himself.[31]

If one sees the *Autorenfilm* and the interpretations it received against a wider historical horizon – that of the legal or judicial status of film authorship prior to the War – it becomes apparent that not only did the writer feature prominently in the debate in the early years of German film history,[32] but authorship in the New German Cinema retained its literary associations very strongly at another level: in the notion (evident in a name like *Filmverlag der Autoren*) that distributors should regard a film director in much the same way as a publisher treats his author.

The legal contradictions emerging from authorship in the cinema were polemically probed – again from the writer's point of view – by Bert Brecht in his *Threepenny Opera Lawsuit*, written after the court case he and Kurt Weill had fought with Nero Film, the company making *The Threepenny Opera* in 1931. Brecht argued that in the film industry it is the producer (through the contracts he holds on the story, on the director, the script-writer, the cameraman, the technical crew, the actors) who appropriates the labour of others and makes himself the owner and thereby the author. The model of authorship in the cinema is thus that of industrial production, and not that of bourgeois notions of creative authorship. But as Brecht also pointed out, behind the producer stands that which he invests, namely capital, so that ultimately capital itself, in the human shape of the producer, appears as the author of a film. The various other authors – the writer for instance – are expendable or replaceable (as is evident in the Hollywood film industry, where even directors can be taken off a film). Brecht was thus not surprised that he lost his case:

> If in practice, the legal system is to enable production, how should it then be able to protect an ideology ('intellectual property is inviolable') which endangers production? . . . Capitalism is coherent in practice, because it must. But its coherence in practice obliges it to be incoherent in its ideology.[33]

Brecht's argument is that the bourgeois legal system has to step in and mediate between an artistic form of production and an industrial form of production, but finds itself ill-equipped to do so since both have become subsumed under the laws of capitalism and the market. The 'author' in the New German Cinema fulfilled a similar function: the ideological task was to hold together a bourgeois notion of art and a capitalist notion of production.

Norbert Kückelmann, a trained lawyer and co-founder of the Kuratorium, for example, argued that film had a special role in advanced industrial societies: 'Art is becoming more and more an instrument of . . . an individual's defence against pressure from economic and social power structures which are increasingly reducing art to a commodity. This is especially true of film art.'[34] Kückelmann seems to think that the commodity status of film constitutes a 'misuse', which the *Autorenfilm* could rectify by reinstating 'the extremely underprivileged director as true originator of the film work'.[35] Here, Kückelmann and the Kuratorium perform the role Brecht had diagnosed: creating a definition intended to arbitrate between positions that cannot be reconciled. .

Legitimacy and Legitimation

Only since the Romantic period has art or creativity been judged in terms of originality and valued for its personal, subjective form of expression. As a historical development it was not unconnected with the disappearance of private patronage and the need for artists to make a living on the open market.[36] The contradictions of the free market in matters of art re-emerge every time the state assumes patronage for an area of production where private property and personal authorship are regulated by the buying and selling of commodities and services, rather than by originality, artistic intention and subjective commitment. The authors' cinema inherited the dilemma, but could not resolve it other than practically with the director becoming the producer, acting as the author and hiring him/herself as writer and director.

In ideological terms, the nexus of autonomy and patronage as embodied in the *Autorenfilm* gave the quest for legitimation and legitimacy a momentum which in more ways than one predestined the New German Cinema to a restaging of the Romantic rebellion. The Oberhausen Manifesto, with its rhetoric of freedom ('the new film needs new kinds of freedom. Freedom from the conventions practiced in the industry. Freedom from the influence of commercial partners. Freedom from being under the tutelage of vested interests')[37] sounded a familiar note and served a particular strategy. Freedom having been the traditional battle-cry of the liberal bourgeoise and petit-bourgeoisie at least since the French Revolution, its invocation also served as a reminder of the bourgeoisie's own anti-feudal, 'revolutionary' ethos.

As a Bill of Rights, the Oberhausen Manifesto was plainly addressed to the West German State in its self-appointed role of representing not only Germany's liberal-democratic traditions, but defending the freedom of expression, of opinion, of movement and of trade against the rival claims of the other Germany: the anti-bourgeois socialist traditions represented by the German Democratic Republic. To take the constitution of a liberal democracy at its own word may often prove an effective way of bringing to the fore the discrepancies between ideology and practice. Yet it cannot by itself overcome the contradictions thus highlighted. This was to be true of the *Autorenfilm* as well:

One has to understand that neither as a paid director of a big company nor as a small producer-director is one in a position to control the market. National and international firms are in charge, and as an individual one cannot take them on, not even as an 'independent producer'. Which is why it is so important for

46

film-makers to recognize their situation, get organised, and stop deluding themselves about their 'freedom'.[38]

One of the reasons why the West German government ultimately welcomed the Oberhausen Manifesto and pursued such an apparently generous funding policy was its own 'legitimation gap'. In the political vacuum left by the collapse of the Weimar Republic and the Nazi State, and facing social and class divisions only exacerbated by the ideological and geographical splitting of Germany into two sovereign States, it was high culture which was meant to promote consensus and foster social cohesion.[39] Secondly, the notion of a national cinema, as opposed to a domestic film industry, corresponded quite closely to one of the major ideological tenets of the Federal Republic, namely to be the sole legitimate representative of German culture and German history. The cinema was a particularly effective way of arguing West Germany's case to be considered in this role, against the rival assertion of the German Democratic Republic. Already at the time of the UFA decartelisation plans in the early 1950s, one aim had been 'to export, as it were, culture, civilization, German prestige via German films – not only abroad, but also to help the German cinema at home to new esteem'.[40] The drive to legitimate West Germany in this way appears to have been largely successful, as the label 'New German Cinema' proves: who would insist on specifying New 'West' German Cinema?[41]

The State, addressed by the film-maker as patron, not surprisingly in turn addressed the film-maker, assigning him a specific role and public function. If the role was that of 'artist', the function was to represent 'national culture'. Werner Schroeter recognised the dilemma early on:

> With my mini-productions I am something of a marginal figure but I'm just as embroiled in 'Kultur' as is Fassbinder or Reitz. And I find this abominable. I think the worst danger for me and for others is that we become nationalised figures, common property.[42]

The promotion of film and the cinema as high art thus corresponded to both a domestic and a foreign policy aim: it supported artistic activity on a broad front, and provided an art form that could represent West Germany as the legitimate heir of German culture. This phrase was quite enthusiastically taken up by Werner Herzog when, on his first visit to the United States as a celebrity, he proclaimed that 'after Kleist, Büchner and Kafka, we are legitimate German culture'.[43]

The subsidy system protected film-makers from the 'market' which would never have allowed them to exist otherwise, by withdrawing them partially from the circulation of capital, and establishing a secondary circuit – that of cultural legitimation. They had to prove that the cinema was a serious art and that they were serious artists. But by obtaining the benefit of subsidy without actually having overcome the 'legitimation gap' which the cinema had always suffered in the eyes of the educated public when compared to the other arts, German films became involved in a much older dilemma: that of the artist and bourgeois society (for which he is enormously important as a symbolic figure). Kückelmann, in the above quotation, pointed out how the artist in some sense represents the last refuge of the sovereign subject, in the form of an individualism that has apparently escaped the negative consequences of modernity. His activity is not affected by the division of labour, and in a society of part-subjects, part-objects and commodities he holds up the image of the possibility of non-alienation. The ambiguity of such a position derives from the fact that it puts responsibility on society to keep the ideal alive for everyone as a practical human potential (which

47

is why the arts are funded), but the artist is also an alibi for a society far from working towards such a possibility. He is the guardian of a totality and wholeness, the loss of which the rest of society accepts as the price of technological progress and material well-being. In the satisfied post-war prosperity enjoyed by most West Germans by the mid-1960s, the self-tormented, but spiritually free artist was a highly-prized cultural asset.

Romanticism and *Kultur*

The co-option of film as an art that merited public subsidy brought the cinema from the margins to a position nearer the centre of German cultural politics. At this centre literature, but also the theatre and film, found themselves invariably confronted with the question of national identity and representative German culture. The critics' ambivalence, especially *vis-à-vis* directors such as Herzog and Syberberg who assumed this legacy of culture more overtly and stridently than others, was due to the fact that the very idea of *Kultur* is itself a profoundly embattled notion in German history. It not only polarised critics and film-makers, but film-makers among themselves. Already in 1972 Werner Schroeter insisted on dissociating himself from film as art and the director as artist:

> I have no intention whatsoever of playing a leading part [in the New German Cinema], and submit to the expectations of producing *Kulturscheisse*, even if it may be true that I carry around with me and into my films the past of this *Kulturscheisse*. I neither depend on it, nor do I admire it. The elements of this *Kultur* are the materials I play with.[44]

This antipathy of the labels 'art' and 'culture' must, however, be also judged as the sign of a new self-confidence. For instance, knowing his stature as the father of the Young German Film and theoretician of film-as-culture to be secure, Kluge could assume for the cinema a place alongside literature, philosophy and music while explicitly repudiating the name of artist:

> I don't know what an artist is. I'd say, my roots are in Hebrew theology; in the Critical Theory of Horkheimer, Adorno, Oskar Negt; in Walter Benjamin. On the other hand, Hölderlin, Kleist, James Joyce and Arno Schmidt are a source . . . not to mention music. The achievements of the classical arts – that is the tradition I understand myself in, as part of a profession which doesn't exist as a defined profession.[45]

Herzog and Syberberg would probably agree, but it is difficult to think of a non-German director, even a well-established auteur, placing himself in a similar line of descent. The pointed omission of any film-maker either past or present from Kluge's list of spiritual ancestors and influences underlines the different conception of film culture in Germany. It makes Fassbinder's or Wenders' cinephile attachment to father-figures such as Douglas Sirk or Nicholas Ray both comprehensible and provocative.

Despite denying an affiliation with art as it might have become ritualised in visits to the opera or the concert hall, Kluge and Schroeter, along with many other German directors, none the less place themselves in a recognisably German tradition – that of Romantic anti-capitalism – and their claims and counter-claims to cultural legitimacy and representation invariably also involved taking a stand in the fight for the right interpretation of the Romantic legacy in German history. The conflicts of art and politics, of absolute subjectivity within an absolutist

48

Prussian monarchy, for instance, was what made the person and work of Heinrich von Kleist play such a central role in German film culture during the 1970s.

Economically, the New German Cinema owed much to the political objectives of the Social Democrats who, since their entry into a Coalition government in 1966, had pressed for greater state intervention in the free market economy. Ideologically, however, the New German Cinema has to be seen against the background of the radical politicisation which started in the universities around 1963, and peaked in the late 1960s with the broadly-based movement known as the extra-parliamentary opposition. Although having its roots, as Kluge put it, in Horkheimer and Adorno's Critical Theory, which was itself an essentially romantic reading of classical Marxism, the extra-parliamentary opposition developed a rhetoric, if not a practice, that was extremely hostile to liberal notions of art, culture and subjectivity. As a response to the Vietnam war and Third World movements elsewhere, the outlook was internationalist rather than national.

Much of the New German Cinema did indeed appear to signal a return to Romantic, irrational and nationalist values and positions. To critics from this camp, unable or unwilling to see the peculiarity of a national film production within an international market place, such a return was interpreted as a counter-revolution. The fact that the neo-romantic tendency which came to be known as 'sensibilist' should be so prominent among film-makers (notably in Herzog, Wenders, Schroeter, Syberberg and Achternbusch) is in no small measure due to their self-conscious or militant exposure to the contradictions of their situation. For them, subsidy of cinema by the State revived, in the age of corporate capitalism and media conglomerates, a preoccupation with the processes of individual aesthetic production, with subjectivity and non-alienated labour. This was perhaps quite out of proportion with the importance of art as an instrument of critical reflection and cognition, but it exactly reflected the consequences of an art-practice under public funding. In this respect, it is arguable whether the political categories of left and right can be applied, for the 'Romanticism' which manifested itself in the New German cinema was itself a radical response to the crisis in critical thinking, regardless of whether it understood itself in the traditions of the Enlightenment, Romanticism or Modernism.

Yet the sense of Germany as a nation, with a culture specific to its history, has always been associated more with the phases of Romantic pietism and subjectivity than with Enlightenment rationalism or practical political engagement. Thus, although it might be true that literature and the arts flourish in Germany more often as a result of a failed revolution, this might well be in reaction to frustrated desires for change rather than a sign of resistance to change. No other European country, it seems, is as unsure of the meaning of its culture as Germany, or as obsessed with its national identity. The reasons are evident: the post-war division of Germany into two political entities, each with its own highly partisan version of national history fixated on the phenomenon of Fascism, has ruptured and set up barriers to any notion of cultural or historical continuity. Germany never became a nation state through a bourgeois revolution like France, or a civil war such as the United States experienced. Even more so than Italy, it was eventually united from above, developing geographical and social cohesion under a bureaucratic-imperialist monarchy, in the wake of the Franco-Prussian War of 1870.

Only the long-established reflex of regionalism and centuries of decentralisation can explain why so many Germans accepted what in effect were five fundamentally different political régimes in less than a century. Likewise, the division of Germany or the severance from its eastern provinces after the Second World War came to be accepted quite readily by a majority of the population, not so much because it was felt to be a just price to pay, but because German intellectuals had always tended to consider *Bildung* and *Kultur* fair compensation for political disenfranchisement and geographical division.

The ideological shifts that transformed large sections of West Germany's highly educated but traditionally a-political middle class into an ultra-left, radical intelligentsia between 1963 and 1973, strikingly confirms a recurrent cycle in German politics and culture: that of a brief, para-revolutionary surge followed by longer periods of conservative backlash and restoration. The pattern has repeated itself several times since the 1790s – when the poet Hölderlin, the young Hegel and Kleist became fervent admirers of the French Revolution only to turn, upon Napoleon's invasion of Germany and his alliance with a mercantile bourgeoisie, passionately conservative and to advocate political nationalism as well as cultural provincialism. Thus, periods of European and international 'rationalism' have in Germany been often succeeded by spells of pietist inwardness, safeguarded externally by politically reactionary régimes. German Romantic nationalism could appear militant, utopian and revolutionary, but in the context of Europe and world politics it just as often proved to be profoundly conservative.

The New German Cinema, in its international presence, shares many of the characteristics of such a Romantic, radical phase in German culture. In addition, it was polarised regionally, not so much between East and West as North and

Impulsive South: Harry Baer in Syberberg's Ludwig – Requiem for a Virgin King *(1972)*

South, and during the 1970s Munich predominated over Berlin or Hamburg. The polarisation has to do with the location of the traditional centres of film-making, but the fact that German film culture has a strong Bavarian flavour is reflected in the biographical data of many of the directors. Fassbinder, Herzog, Achternbusch, Geissendörfer and Adlon were all born in or near Munich. Kluge, Reitz, Hauff, Schlöndorff, von Trotta, Uwe Brandner, Schilling, Petersen and Lilienthal live in Munich. Wenders studied at the Munich Film Academy, wrote for a Munich daily paper and lived in Munich. Syberberg comes from Pommerania, but has lived in Munich since 1953. The stereotype, already exploited by Thomas Mann, of the sentimental, impulsive, romantic South and the cold, rationalist North transfers the historical tensions discussed above also on to the map, and the same configuration turns up in many of Syberberg's films (explicitly in *Ludwig – Requiem for a Virgin King* and *Ludwig's Cook*, but also in *Our Hitler*). It is furthermore a prominent motif in Fassbinder (*Effi Briest, Bolwieser, The Bitter Tears of Petra von Kant*) where it often conveniently symbolised a male/female polarity.

. . . *and frozen North: Irm Hermann in Fassbinder's* Effi Briest *(1974)*

'Author-oriented' versus 'Issue-oriented' Film-making

While this overview may seem to make the concept of the author a progressive one, the fact that many of the films produced under state sponsorship failed to reach the cinemas either in Germany or abroad indicated that the German Cinema had not found its identity as an art cinema. The designation of the author as the contractual partner and addressee of the funding system meant film-makers had to legitimate themselves as 'artists'. But the need to legitimate themselves with an actual audience, both for the sake of their professional self-image and in order to counter the accusations and hostility of the commercial film industry lobby, made directors seek active ways of adjusting themselves to what they perceived to be particular audience expectations.

In fact, the search for audiences provides the most obvious key to the apparent heterogeneity of the general output of the German cinema. The difficulties in classifying the films according to common stylistic or thematic traits begins to resolve itself when one relates them not only to the funding system but also to the other major determining factor – the conditions of reception. While initially after Oberhausen film-makers tried to find subjects and styles that would make their films resemble those, for instance, of the *nouvelle vague*, other directors very quickly turned to reworking genre formulas, accepting that the cinema lives from repetition and recognition as much as from originality and uniqueness. Neither kind of film is typical for the New German Cinema; and no theoretical and historical arguments are needed to realise that the bulk of the films made by German directors in the 1970s and early 1980s does not follow the logic of self-expression nor that of genre, but is intensely concerned with social and political questions. Some critics have therefore divided the New German Cinema into author-oriented films (where the emphasis is on self-expression, or the implied audience is the international, art house spectator) and issue-oriented films (dealing with social problems or controversial issues aimed at home audiences).[46]

On the face of it this makes good sense. Even at the time of the Young German Film, the tendency was to make films around issues: one of the few popular successes immediately following Oberhausen, Ulrich Schamoni's *Es* (1965), was about abortion; Kluge's *Yesterday Girl* (1966) was about vagrancy, petty crime and social work; Johannes Schaaf's *Tätowierung* (1967) was about youth criminality and foster homes. Fleischmann's *Hunting Scenes from Lower Bavaria* focused on social prejudice and sexual deviancy and Fassbinder's *Katzelmacher* (1969) on unemployment and racial prejudice towards foreign workers.

Equally remarkable is that over the past twenty years there has hardly been a single 'social issue' not dealt with by a major fiction film.[47] One explanation for the prevalence of 'issue films' must be the 'television-orientation' of many film-makers funded either directly or indirectly by the networks. By the mid-1970s it was clear that film production in West Germany would be decided by those film-makers who could either command an international following (and in turn feed a national narcissism) or at least address at home two kinds of audiences with the same films: those of television and those of the communal cinemas and non-commercial outlets, exploiting rather than ignoring the differences between the cinema and television.

This did not necessarily lead only to social documentaries or the dramatisation of current issues, although many films suggest that state-funded cinema is primarily

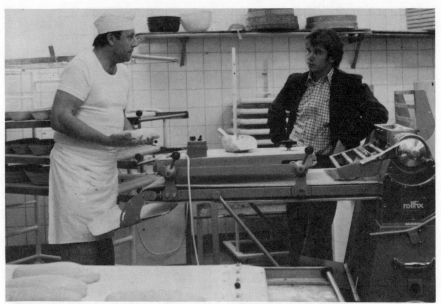

Gerhard Lamprecht and Bernd Tauber in Erwin Keusch's The Baker's Bread *(1976)*

a forum for social work. A popular book on women's films, for example, is divided into chapters called 'Young Girls, Mother–Daughter Relationships, Living Alone, Sexual Relations, Family, Pregnancy/Birth, Abortion, Women at Work, Women and Trade Unions, *Berufsverbot* [job discrimination], Women and Violence, What Makes Women Mentally Ill, Oppression and Resistance', and it ends with 'Growing Old, Handicapped Women, Foreign Women in West Germany, Women in the GDR, Women in the World, Film Classics, Experimental Feature Films'.[48]

A counter-example, where issue-orientation is used to find a way back to genres suitable for both film and television, is *Das Brot des Bäckers* (*The Baker's Bread*, Erwin Keusch, 1976). It is the story of a small-town bakery where the labour-intensive business of baking good bread comes into conflict with the demands of rationalisation, and the master baker finds himself isolated not only from his trade union but from his sons, who prefer to go to college. The film was a great success in the cinemas – the careful depiction of a milieu around a solidly constructed plot, reminiscent of 1930s German films (or Ealing comedies, in its sympathy for the family business), seen through the eyes of the outsider-hero and across the story of his apprenticeship. It did well on television too (not only in Germany), because of its appeal as a family sit-com with its crabby patriarch, a disgruntled assistant, the salesgirl attempting suicide and a mother energetically holding both family and business together. Yet its virtues for these markets were precisely what made *The Baker's Bread* unsuitable for the art cinemas or for launching its director as an international auteur.

That the independent cinema was exploring areas where television would do least damage to style and form could be seen in many films focusing on rural communities and confining themselves to family issues, such as *Ich dachte ich wäre tot* (*I Thought I Was Dead*, Wolf Gremm, 1974), *Paule Pauländer* (Reinhard Hauff, 1976) or *Albert Warum* (*Albert – Why?*, Josef Rödl, 1978). Similarly, a

Fritz Binner in Josef Rödl's Albert – Why?
(1978)

Maria Stadler in Doris Dörrie's Come
Rain or Shine *(1977)*

steady stream of films tried to capture the youth audience by blending the
American road movie with issues of truancy, juvenile delinquency and the
temptations of drugs: Rüdiger Nüchtern's *Schluchtenflitzer* (*Ravine Racer*, 1978),
billed as '*Easy Rider* in Lower Bavaria', Uwe Friesner's *Das Ende des Regenbogens*
(*The End of the Rainbow*, 1979), Adolf Winkelmann's *Die Abfahrer* (*On the
Move*, 1978), a German trucker film, for which Hark Bohm's *Nordsee ist Mordsee*
(*The North Sea is Murderous*, 1976) might have been the inspiration, where the
two central characters steal a sailboat rather than a car. In each case, the very
nature of the subject – the roads, the wide open spaces, the sensation of speed
or adventure – demands the big screen. All were shown on television but only
Winkelmann's film was a success in the cinema, and in Doris Dörrie's *Ob's stürmt
oder schneit* (*Come Rain or Shine*, 1977), a semi-fiction film about a rural cinema
owner, it is *Nordsee ist Mordsee* that prompts the heroine to say 'It breaks my
heart, sitting here in my ticket booth, with such beautiful films on the programme,
and nobody to come and see them'. By contrast, Wenders' *Kings of the Road*
(1976) worked in both media, not least because of the extraordinary care taken
over composition and pacing, and because it combined the temporality and
intimacy of television with the sense of space typical of the cinema.

Another index of both television-orientation and the inscription of exhibition
constraints is the seriousness and the didactic or pathos-filled stance of much of
New German Cinema during the 1970s. Even the films of Syberberg and Hauff,
Herzog and Fassbinder, Sanders-Brahms and von Trotta, whose target was an
international art house audience, were relentlessly earnest and often school-

Author-oriented or issue-oriented: 'Gastarbeiter' El Hedi Ben Salem (right) in Fassbinder's Fear Eats the Soul *(1974)*

masterly while manifesting a gesture of ambitiousness often patently at odds with the means at the film-makers' disposal. It was a 'poor cinema' not ashamed of thinking big. Assured of their television audience the films envisaged, but in a sense also despaired of, finding the audiences of that 'cinema of the future' which Kluge and Syberberg in their different ways never tired of evoking in their writing.[49]

A third reason for the issue-orientation may have been the desire to break out of the confines that the institutional pressures of public funding and broadcast television imposed on film-makers to style themselves as artists. One of the New German Cinema's most distinctive products of the early 1980s were films which combined an engagement with sexual politics and the women's movement with a highly idiosyncratic conception of film form, opening spaces for the self-representation of women, of homosexuals, and for social minority views treated from a partisan perspective.

This last point, however, also indicates the limits of thinking of such films as issue-oriented. For if television is partly responsible for the strong social and even sociological bias that the dual production and reception context makes apparent, it does not by itself explain the preference for 'issue films' and for several reasons. In the first place, many of the films that would fall under this heading were not financed by television. Secondly, virtually all would be claimed by their directors to be personal, authored works. Finally, among them are some of the major international successes of the New German Cinema. The distinction 'issue-oriented' versus 'author-oriented' which opened this section thus seems difficult to maintain, unless one can assume that the directors themselves divided their

55

Rüdiger Vogler and Hanns Zischler in   Walter Ladengast and Brigitte Mira in
Wenders' Kings of the Road *(1976)*   Herzog's The Enigma of Kaspar Hauser
                                          (1974)

own work along these lines, for which there is no evidence. One may have to
think of both 'issue-oriented' and 'author-oriented' as 'audience-oriented', and
to consider more closely not so much the institutional or sociological context of
reception but a more general condition of receptivity typical for the generation
and the decade in question.

'Contentist' versus 'Sensibilist'

If the decisive change which brought the national television networks into the
film-funding system as co-producers, commissioning editors and exhibitors of the
finished product thus eased the severely congested distribution situation, it also
contributed to the emergence of a new cinema-going public. Audiences only
began to return to the specialised art cinemas after television had developed a
new interest in film culture and a certain cinephilia, from which contemporary
film-making could also benefit. At the same time, a more broadly political film
culture gave a different value to going to the cinema, compared with the old
family audience, both as an aesthetic and as a social event (the pleasure derived
from a particular film and from 'going to the cinema' need not necessarily be the
same).

An intriguing account of this renewed interest in the cinema during the 1970s
in West Germany, which links it to social and political changes, is given in an
essay by Michael Rutschky entitled 'Dreaming the Real'.[50] Loosely inspired by
Siegfried Kracauer's pieces during the 1920s for the *Frankfurter Zeitung*, about
the cinema and the emergent *Angestelltenkultur* (culture of the white-collar class)[51]
Rutschky imagines (or describes) the case history of the student M., and his
movie-going habits.

> In the early Seventies, M. went to the cinema about three times a week, mostly in
> the evenings, but occasionally he would 'indulge himself' as he called it, and go to
> a film already in the afternoon . . . In the early Seventies, M. studied sociology.
> This was the subject he had switched to during the student protest movement.[52]

M.'s favourite films are *Last Tango in Paris*, *Taxi Driver*, *The Lacemaker* and, of
course, Wenders' *Kings of the Road*. According to Rutschky, this puts M. squarely
in one of the two factions that made up the cinema-public in the 1970s – the

56

Claus Eberth and Antje Hagen in Christian Ziewer's Walking Tall *(1976)*

Hanna Schygulla, Wolfgang Schenck and Ulli Lommel in Fassbinder's Effi Briest *(1974)*

sensibilist side, rather than the 'contentist' one. The sensibilist faction, disappointed by the 'failure' of the protest movement and their sociology and politics courses, had sought a refuge from dejection and melancholia in the cinema. In their opinion, words only served to aggravate the sense of being alienated from what is of value and from true feeling (hence the attraction of Herzog's films), or words were simply superfluous when compared to the self-evidence of images viewed through a camera (hence the reassurance emanating from Wenders' films).

To see *Kaspar Hauser* or *Kings of the Road* as manifestos of a revulsion against words (in the tradition of Novalis or Hugo von Hoffmansthal), and as a new partisanship for images, gives the romanticism implied in the films a concrete historical reference point in the distrust of verbalisation and of theory which followed the surge of political literature after 1968. The contentist faction, by contrast, more convinced than ever of the urgency of analytical categories and conceptual generalisations, expected a film to validate their views of social problems and of a political perspective:

> They would prefer Christian Ziewer's sociological realism, his films set among working-class people, to Wim Wenders' sensibilist films which seemed to them products of a decadent subjectivity. Or vice versa: *Kings of the Road* was a cult film for all those who had probably seen the film five times and who thought Ziewer's *Walking Tall* was nothing but an illustrated Open University lecture.[53]

Put like this, Rutschky's pair of opposites is very persuasive. It shifts the weight of the argument from auteurism-as-self-expression to the spectator and the conditions of reception. It also allows for the dual register outlined above. The success and fascination of a Fassbinder film might be precisely the way it knowingly accommodates both kinds of audiences, because the same 'texts', say *The Merchant of Four Seasons* (*Der Händler der vier Jahreszeiten*, 1971), *Fear Eats the Soul* or *Effi Briest* (1974), could confirm the 'contentist' (dramatised discussion of racial prejudice, economic and sexual exploitation, the repressiveness and sexism of Prussian moral codes). Few 'sensibilists', on the other hand, would mistake Fassbinder's camp revamping of Hollywood melodramas for 'an Open University lecture' (though *Effi Briest* might just qualify). Indeed, the 'contentist' versus 'sensibilist' opposition would roughly coincide with the division 'domestic audience' versus 'international audience'. In this case the international audience would include that section of the domestic audience whose film culture was sophisticated enough to view Scorsese, Wenders or Bertolucci as belonging to the same tradition: a cinema made doubly reflexive by alluding to the European art cinema and to Hollywood auteurism.

Rutschky's M. is meant to give an insight into what Kracauer would have called the 'psychic dispositions' of a symptomatic spectator of the New German Cinema. In this sense the cinema, as an experience, is almost more decisive than the film itself:

> It is not clear in advance on which evenings M. goes to the cinema; there comes a moment of decision. This moment is the experience of a vital lack, which can only be alleviated by a film. Reading, even reading a cheap paperback, would not help . . . When the decision is made, M. would call up his friends or an acquaintance, and there was usually at least one who had already half-decided to go to the cinema, too.[54]

'Going to the cinema' is in M.'s case obviously determined by a wider psychological context: the film is not experienced as a self-contained work, but as a sort of vehicle, transporting the spectator from solitude and boredom to sociability. It allows M. to unite a number of divergent motives: these are mainly negative in relation to his working life, typified by indecision, hesitancy, a half-wish. Such a spectator's choices of entertainment are narrowly related to his sociological status and affiliation: unmarried, middle-class, going to the cinema because the alternatives are less tempting; but even then, he is fussy and diffident. No mass medium can live on such a slender slice of the population, but it is the typical constellation for an art cinema audience, and films which share this knowledge with their audience can very accurately represent the experiences of a public as well-defined as this, and address themselves to its moods.

The picture Rutschky gives of the ideal type of a 1970s spectator corresponds very closely to the findings of the Dichter poll mentioned earlier. The reasons why cinema attendances had declined was that neither the cinemas themselves nor the films they showed did justice to the 'high expectations' associated with the cinema's educational or entertainment value. The cinema's enemy was not television ('a compromise solution for the disappointed film-goer') but the cinema itself. Among the leisure needs that made films potentially so attractive, according to the Dichter study, were a desire for culture and self-education, for social contacts, for permissible regression, as a catalyst for emotions, for making sense of the world and shaping experience.[55]

Such coherence as there was in the New German Cinema of the 1970s can, perhaps, be understood as part of the process of creating this sort of fit between at least some of the expectations surrounding the films, and the films themselves. It would explain, for example, why the concerted attempts at improving the cinema's cultural status were largely successful. The Dichter study had highlighted the low prestige value of the cinema as a public space, and of the image of the film spectator ('only rockers and dirty old men go to the cinema'): the New German Cinema became resolutely artistic and serious. Dichter had pointed out that spectators missed social relevance in the films, and that there was a lack of credible or interesting figures to identify with: the New German Cinema, as we shall see, tried to respond to both of these demands, even with a vengeance. According to the Dichter findings, cinemas provided less social contact than the theatre, which meant that a visit to the cinema did not satisfy as a complete evening's entertainment: cinemas accordingly turned their foyers into bars, some

Christian Ziewer's Dear Mother, I'm Fine *(1971)*

Werner Schroeter's Palermo or Wolfsburg *(1980)*

opened small galleries, or a bookshop. Finally, the poll predicted that the cinema of the future would have to be more flexible in its programming and diverse in its offerings: the *Programmkinos* did just that.

Equally telling, however, is the manner in which the films themselves 'managed' or transformed these partly contradictory social and psychological dispositions of the moment into recognisable attitudes and values (such as the ones described by Rutschky as typical for the sensibilists) or, on the other hand, appealed to more activist interests. The hesitancy, diffidence and indecision of the typical Wenders protagonist, the endless sitting around in bars drinking beer in Fassbinder films, or the resolute spunk of a character like Christa Klages in von Trotta's film by that title, are mirror-images of the spectator, foils for direct (though possibly masochistic) identification. By contrast, there are films which make identification itself the issue, both within the narrative (von Trotta's subsequent films come to mind) and in their narrational stance, as in so many Fassbinder films which use an 'inner frame' in the composition of shots to 'place' characters and events[56] or in Herzog's documentaries, where characters often stare aggressively into the camera. From Christian Ziewer's solid working-class types offered as role models in *Liebe Mutter mir geht es gut* (*Dear Mother, I'm Fine*, 1971), to Werner Schroeter's elf-like and angelic factory workers singing arias from Verdi in *Palermo or Wolfsburg* (1980), there is an extraordinarily broad spectrum of exemplary figures even within what might appear to be working-class subjects and settings. The directors outline these 'horizons of expectation' in the cultural discourses with which they arm themselves, by talking about 'making the spectator productive' or of 'the film only taking place in the spectator's head'; but most of them also try to establish such a horizon through the *mise en scène*, and the specifically filmic inscription of the spectator.

Towards a Coherent Spectator-position?

While Rutschky is able to give a convincing picture of the 'sensibilist' spectator, his categorisation of the 'contentist' faction is less satisfactory. The name itself, with its implied form/content distinction, seems cruder than the phenomenon it tries to describe. Not only is the category of 'contentist' too unwieldy when applied to specific films and film-makers, but also the opposition leaves out too much of the middle ground and, like all binarisms, is short on explanatory substance.

Given that, as both the Dichter study and Rutschky imply, a national audience can no longer be assumed to be sociologically uniform or representative, the implied spectator of German films is very rarely identical with the national, though in truth multinational, audience that makes the latest Hollywood film a block-buster. Rutschky's self-selected, self-conscious spectators could be called a domestic 'target audience', if the term did not suggest either too narrow a political orientation, in the form of preaching to the converted, or reflect too much the categories of market research, designed to deliver audiences ready bundled and labelled for the advertisers. None the less, some form of pre-construction of the viewers does seem to have informed film-making and film-funding policy.[57]

The problem with 'issue-oriented' thematic interpretations is that they invariably resort to speculations about how a film 'reflects' trends, or embodies the *Zeitgeist*, a critical option made more dubious by the fact that most films manifestly did not capture a mass audience. In the same way, sociological categories devised for television popularity ratings may tell us how many spectators a programme managed to reach, but they rarely analyse how it affected them: something which would require a study of long-term effects on attitudes. A more useful index might be the sort of critical reception reported by Rutschky:

> After a while, a lively discussion ensues, full of allusions which an outsider will not be able to follow. However, the film is not in the usual sense interpreted or criticised because the goal is not to locate some philosophical or political meaning. In fact, the conversation can come to an abrupt, unpleasant end if there is no spontaneous agreement in the group that the film was good. Even though a discussion may reach some sort of consensus, the evening is somehow spoiled, there is a coolness which destroys the mood.[58]

The difference between calling films 'spectator-oriented' rather than 'issue-oriented' or 'contentist' may at first seem trivial. However, it highlights the question of address: of who speaks in a film, on whose behalf and to whom. Are the workers' films, for instance, made by workers, or for workers, or simply about the working class? This is particularly important with regards to the women's films, or films about marginal groups, sub-culture lifestyles or minority interests: the very areas where film-making in Germany has been particularly innovative and coherent.

An approach focusing on spectator-positioning and narrational strategies ought to be able to encompass both sets of determining instances, author-oriented as well as audience-oriented. A good example would be the congruence between women's films and their implied audiences, which allowed women film-makers to let the authorial-autobiographical ambition towards self-expression coincide with and be reinforced by a female audience's desire for finding themselves represented and addressed in terms of their concrete life situation. Films like Helke Sander's *Redupers* (*Die Allseitig Reduzierte Persönlichkeit – Redupers*, 1977), *Der Subjektive Faktor* (*The Subjective Factor*,1980) and *Der Beginn aller Schrecken ist Liebe* (*Love is the Beginning of all Terrors*, 1986), where in two cases the director plays the lead, are shaped around personal-autobiographical themes, but the formal complexity is determined by a problem which is also a filmic one. It is how to give the female character in the fiction film a coherent identity, when the very thing that makes her a woman is the constant struggle and failure to cohere. The conflicting demands between private and professional life (*Redupers*), of who she is now/who she was then (*Der Subjektive Faktor*), feelings of jealousy as both proof and betrayal of love (*Der Beginn aller Schrecken ist Liebe*), are dramatised as questions of both identification and identity.

This dramatic-formal tension cannot be assumed to be the sort of spectator-screen interaction valid for all constituencies, and there are films which communicate with their audience via a quite different set of assumptions and strategies. It would thus make sense to see the various styles of film-making and the different film forms which emerged in the German cinema less as distinct genres (the women's film, the workers' films, the youth films, the gay-scene film, the coming-to-terms-with-the-Nazi-past film), and rather as so many modes of identification, distanciation, spectator-address and discursiveness. The New German Cinema would then be exemplary in its search for narrational stances appropriate for a national cinema functioning outside the commercial film industry but inside television, outside European auteurism but inside the art cinema, outside doctrinaire propaganda but inside a generally politicised media consciousness.

For despite the prevalence of social issues, the New German Cinema is actually

Angela Winkler in Schlöndorff/Trotta's
The Lost Honour of Katharina Blum
(*1975*)

Echoes of the Problem Film: Fassbinder's
Veronika Voss *(1982)*

rather poor in sociological detail; very few films give a convincing idea of West Germany's political reality or the workings of its social institutions. Even in the films of Schlöndorff, Hauff or Petersen (the most conventionally 'realistic' directors in the 1970s), one learns little about the political establishment. Schlöndorff's *The Lost Honour of Katharina Blum* is not an illuminating film about the German press, any more than Hauff's *Stammheim* (1986) conveys a convincing picture of German judges and the legal profession.

In 1978 Alf Brustellin and Bernard Sinkel tried, with their film *Berlinger – Ein deutsches Abenteuer* (*Berlinger, a German Fate*, 1975) to make a German *Citizen Kane*, but the film lacked a tight script and became too enamoured with its hero's grandiose death wish. A film dealing, for instance, with the division of Germany, such as Niklaus Schilling's *Der Westen Leuchtet* (*The Light Trap*, 1986, meant to allude to the Gunter Guillaume spy story), remained a helpless denunciation of luxury cars, villas and champagne breakfasts, while Hauff's *Der Mann auf der Mauer* (*The Man on the Wall*, 1983) used the other Germany as little more than a dramatic pretext for a love story. This reticence may well be due to the caution of television networks (all of which are headed by political appointees) to venture into politically sensitive areas. During a roundtable conference in Frankfurt in 1977, Kluge gave a lecture provocatively called 'Films that Were Never Made criticise the Films that Were Made', in which he named some of the stories that nobody would touch, although money was still forthcoming for the sixteenth film based on a novel by Heinrich Böll. Scriptwriter Gerhard Zwerenz added: 'German film-makers carry the censor's scissors in their heads.'[59] Six years later, taking Kluge's sentence as her motto, the critic Claudia Lenssen published a whole panorama of stories, types and situations 'forgotten during twenty years of old new German cinema'.[60]

On the other hand, it may be that the coolly analytical, left-wing stance typical of post-war European directors is simply not part of this cinema's repertoire of voices: it is difficult to imagine Rosi's *Salvatore Guiliano* or *Cadaveri eccellenti* made by a German. Similarly, even though, as we shall see, West German television and independent films have a very strong documentary tradition, one looks in vain for the kinds of essays Fred Wiseman has made about American institutions, such as *High School, Basic Training, Welfare* or *Law and Order.* In this respect some of the films from the despised 1950s, such as those by Staudte, Thiele and others, are more revealing than the products of the New German Cinema, as Fassbinder realised when, for his 'BRD Trilogy' (*Maria Braun, Lola, Veronika Voss*) he skilfully cited or reworked many of the dramatic and melodramatic clichés from the problem films of the Adenauer era.

The German cinema of the 1970s excelled in critical, melancholy, angry, desperately excessive and extreme attitudes and stances, which the audience was invited to recognise and share. It was the feel, the mood of West Germany (of its film-making, cinema-going generations and groups) that predominated over action narratives. The famous 'subjective factor' of the New German Cinema is an effect of the cinematic form and its modes of address and, to this extent, the 'contentist versus sensibilist' distinction is a misleading one. More accurately, one could speak of different sensibilisms being constructed through different filmic means. They are distinct from each other not by their degree of realism or fantasy, but chiefly by the degree of melancholy, fatalism, pathos, irony or loss and what these came to signify. Yet, although the images the German cinema gave of German sensibilities were by no means uniform, they did begin to codify themselves into story types, stereotypes, even something resembling genres – thus eventually taking specifically cinematic form.

The subsequent chapters are intended to argue this development in greater detail. Tracing the logic of production involves a close consideration not only of such apparently diametrically different forms as documentary and fiction film, which in the German cinema are part of a continuous spectrum and thus not opposed, but contiguous (due to the absence of commercial constraints on film production and the influence of television). It also necessitates a look at the kinds of self-representation of the author in the films, and a discussion of the idea of genre in the New German Cinema. I shall argue that, from the perspective of implying a specific spectator, film-makers redefined genres not so much internally, or for product differentiation, but in the light of their suitability as vehicles for particular forms of audience identification.

Finally, the argument for spectator-positioning requires the introduction of a non-cinematic concept – that of experience (*Erfahrung*), which in the German discussions around the shifts between aesthetic and political sensibilities has played a crucial role. Before embarking on these issues, it is important to recall the connection which the discussions around *Einstellung* (stance, position, but also frame and camera set-up) have with 'realism' as the central problem crystallising the failure of Oberhausen.

Making Fiction Films with Documentary Methods

The question of address first surfaced in Germany in the debates about realism (themselves very heavily influenced by the documentary strain in West German independent film-making) and in discussions about the political function of cinema. The latter can be traced back to the founding years of the Young German Film. Indeed, in the arguments about a 'critical' perspective on society, and the kind of cinema appropriate for such an objective, the confusion of address and point of view are a key to why the first films of the Oberhausen group failed to find audiences. In retrospect, the issues raised by the early critics of Oberhausen, notably Joe Hembus and Enno Patalas, set the terms for much of the theoretical debate inside West Germany, as well as for film-making itself. They were the theorists of sensibilism *avant la lettre*, and their targets were the documentarists.

The directors who came together at Oberhausen had gained much of their film-making experience via industry-sponsored 'cultural' shorts and, often enough, the funding left its traces on the product. Documentaries about Latin American countries or the Third World generally tended, if not to show the industrial activities of the sponsor directly, to extol the civilising influence of Western progress and technology. Not surprisingly, much of this film-making was in fact designed to help West Germany's industry present a favourable image of its business dealings with the Third World.[61]

Against the ideology of the Hollywood 'dream-factory' and that of the commercial German cinema 'remote from any relation with reality', the Oberhausen group could only base its aesthetic programme (as opposed to its economic and institutional one) on a conception of realism. Such realism, however, was not – as one might expect – neo-realist in inspiration, but satirical. This was precisely because as directors of commissioned work they had had to accommodate themselves to an ideology of photographic transparency and propagandist commentary, and they took revenge on this captivity by often brutally deconstructing the illusion of unmediated reality that the cinema can give. Their films played with the conventions of continuity editing and sound-image synchronisation by showing the object represented to be at the mercy of the act of representation. But they were not Brechtians: the result, when applied to feature films, was either involuntary or deliberate satire of the people portrayed. Jürgen Pohland's film about the jazz musician Tobby Fichelscher (*Tobby*, 1962) gave rise to the following remarks in *Filmkritik*:

> For a film of this kind, Pohland would have needed the stance of an ethnologue, that of Jean Rouch: the willingness to collect illuminating moments, and to fix this process of collecting on film, and thus show willingness to let the spectator participate in the gradual structuring of an idea and a theme . . . Tobby's own reaction to the film [was that] he felt himself unmasked and he left the premiere before the end.[62]

The charge, namely that the directors of the Young German Film did not respect the characters they portrayed, was to recur time and time again. Social satire, when intended, relies on a consensus and on generic rules: precisely what the German cinema did not have in the early 1960s and could not presume in its audience. The Oberhausen group had promised 'a new language of cinema', but in the eyes of their critics the early work of Reitz, Kotulla, Strobel and Tichawsky, as well as films like *Es* (*It*, Ulrich Schamoni, 1965), *Mädchen, Mädchen* (*Girls, Girls*, Roger Fritz, 1966), *Kopfstand Madam!* (*Stand on Your Head, Lady*, Christian Rischert, 1966), *Closed Season for Foxes* (*Schonzeit für Füchse*, Peter Schamoni, 1966) and *Der sanfte Lauf* (*The Gentle Course*, Haro Senft, 1967), seemed distinctly problematic.

> Racy and superficial, Ulrich Schamoni describes the sometimes gay and sometimes sad everyday life of a young couple in Berlin. Roger Fritz, less racy and even more

Sabine Sinjen and Bruno Dietrich in Ulrich Schamoni's It *(1965)*

superficial, describes the love between a rich, titled young man and a Bavarian girl from the people. Christian Rischert describes with dogged seriousness the inner problems of a young married couple in Kiel. Peter Schamoni describes with sluggish seriousness the tristesse of a couple in Düsseldorf. Haro Senft, most earnestly, describes the socially conditioned tensions between two young people in the Federal Republic.[63]

But the uncertainty of address also had another reason. On the occasion of Ula Stöckl's *The Cat Has Nine Lives* (*Neun Leben hat die Katze*, 1968), Peter M. Ladiges drew up a balance sheet of five years of independent film-making:

Something, I think, all the films of the Young German Cinema have in common, almost without exception: one can tell from them the tour de force, the effort it took to have made a film at all. For in fact, [the directors] do not just shoot a film, they are already advancing the argument for the next one. I think this is the most devastating consequence of the current film-political situation in the business. A psychological stress for all those who come before the public with their first film: the fear it might be their last.[64]

Ladiges emphasises the conditions of production, but he also draws attention to the special case of the woman film-maker:

One is often aware of overexplicitness – for fear of being misunderstood, which comes of course from insecurity of not having expressed it right. The uncertainties, however, also speak of something which the film as a whole addresses. In Ula Stöckl's own words: 'Never before have women had as much opportunity to

Uncertainty of address: Peter Schamoni's Closed Season for Foxes *(1966)*

organize their own lives as they would want to. But now they first have to learn that they can want'.[65]

The problem of Stöckl's film, according to Ladiges, has little to do with artistic self-expression: self-representation is first and foremost tied up with trying to make contact with spectators. The mode of address did not so much over-estimate the audience or under-estimate them, as it showed the difficulty of addressing them at all. The director behaved as if she already anticipated the audience's hostility or feared their impatience, and as if noise interfered in the communication. This noise was probably not imagined: it was, as Kluge would put it, 'the commercial system itself in the spectators' heads'.

Pornography and Art Cinema: Oberhausen Goes Commercial

My films will be ever more uncinematic, because the films one sees are becoming more and more cinematic. The commercial cinema is getting more cinematic, which is to say, more and more pornographic.[66]

Straub's remark can also be taken literally. While directors of the Young German Film foundered in their attempts at realism on the problem of how to address a non-existent spectator, the commercial film industry had resolved the question by aiming at the lowest common denominator among audiences: sexual voyeurism. It began to exploit the relaxation of censorship laws and became Europe's largest producer of soft-core pornographic films. An underground need had finally surfaced and, swelled by several millions of at first mainly male *Gastarbeiter* from Southern, Catholic countries, a volatile and furtive but none the less numerically quite sizeable clientèle began to oust, indeed eradicate, the last remnants of the family audience. In most suburban areas of West Germany, going to the cinema in the late 1960s became synonymous with indulging in licensed pornography.

Lack of success with their first films, and loopholes in the original Film Subsidy Bill, quickly turned a number of Oberhausen militants into producers of pornographic films. By 1966 Peter Schamoni and Rob Houwer headed production companies which, apart from investing cautiously in the films of their erstwhile comrades-in-arms, made sizeable profits out of sexploitation films like *Nights of Lovemaking in the Taiga, Quartet in Bed, Little Angel – The Virgin from Bamberg*. Since even films of a more ambitious nature had titles like *Playgirl, Let's Get Down to Business, Darling, Bengelchen Loves Back to Front* and *Let's Play Hide and Seek*, the impression arose that the Young German Cinema was aiming directly at the pornographic market under cover of the liberated and swinging 1960s. Straub's angry asceticism is all the more understandable when one learns that films with titles such as *The House of Pleasure* and *Don't Fumble, Darling* were awarded the quality rating which *Chronicle of Anna Magdalena Bach* only grudgingly received.

As Vlado Kristl was to find out when he made *The Dam* (*Der Damm*, 1964), the Oberhausen members' readiness 'jointly to take economic risks' was soon strained to breaking point when individuals faced the ruin of their careers and personal livelihood. Prudence dictated to some directors the compromises that for Kristl or Straub were merely a cover-up for cowardice, venality, and corruption. But, as Hans Günther Pflaum pointed out, even:

the circumstances surrounding Straub's [own film] illustrate the contradictory situation facing the cinema in the Federal Republic of Germany at the time of the emergence of the 'New German Film' . . . No less than eight names now appear in the production credits as sources of finance, indicating how laboriously money had to be accumulated for this project.[67]

Avant-garde Antics in Maran Gosov's
Little Angel – The Virgin from Bamberg
(1967)

Finances were raised either by securing a distribution guarantee, or by getting an established producer to back the project. The price was that a director had to provide the right mix of what the 'old' film industry regarded as commercial values: a salacious title, sex or show-business names. Straub, for instance, was offered complete finance on his Bach film by 'Atze' Brauner: all he had to do was to agree to Herbert von Karajan as J. S. Bach.[68]

The commercial film industry, more alert than the independent cinema, retooled its production in view of television by adapting one of the new medium's typical forms of reception and programming: that of the series. Crime stories and thrillers taken from Edgar Wallace's pulp novels set in Edwardian London; adventure series based on the Western novels of Karl May; pseudo-scientific sex education films; pornographic classroom scandals, such as the infamous *Schulmädchenreports* and *Lümmelfilme* formed the basis for a commercial revival of sorts. There were even signs that the film industry was prepared to risk larger financial investment in order to test these new markets and to imitate Hollywood's 'runaway productions'. The first Karl May Western, *The Treasure of Silver Lake* (*Der Schatz im Silbersee*, 1962), was greeted with enthusiasm by the public, perhaps because it had the production values of a prototype:

> This Rialto Production is like a virgin, falling in love for the first time: making up for inexperience by passionate intensity. For weeks the team toured Yugoslavia in search of the wildest landscapes. For a single scene entire pueblos and Western towns were built, without a thought for future use, each costume was hand-made, each prop lovingly crafted, and not a single take of any significance was left to the second unit. The whole enterprise was by American standards utterly wasteful. But the result had a certain authenticity which it would be hard to find in Hollywood westerns of this category.[69]

The calculations, however, had to be straightforward: the share of German films in the overall box office tended to be so low that only the economies achieved by

Pierre Brice and Lex Barker in Harald Reinl's The Treasure of Silver Lake *(1962)*

making series could return a profit on investment. Especially in the years between 1968 and 1971, when automatic subsidy was still being given even on pornographic films, series production led to a temporary boost in audiences which pushed the market share above the 8 per cent threshold.

Concentration on the domestic market had led German producers to stay with the tried and proven formulae of the 1940s and 1950s: melodramas, problem films, bio-pics, exotic travelogues, hit parade and *Heimat* films. But audiences who might have enjoyed variations on well-worn genres were also the ones increasingly watching only television: variety shows, pop music, quiz programmes, and the very popular crime series *Tatort*. The screening of films from the 1950s in large numbers on television was itself almost a revival of a national genre cinema. While one of the effects of television in the long run was to create the illusion, after the event so to speak, of a fundamental continuity in German films, this continuity only manifested itself at the level of production in the 1970s, when the old German cinema began to have an influence on the more commercially inclined directors of the New German Cinema, especially in their choice of actors. In the 1960s the disappearance from the cinemas of an audience for so-called 'good entertainment' was the most visible and outward cause for the much lamented decline of the German commercial cinema.

It seemed as if for the sake of a fistful of films the German film industry was prepared to damage its own infrastructure, oblivious to the fact that porn films neglected almost the entire non-male population as well as the majority of middle-class spectators, and thus the very groups which would become the New German Cinema's most important audiences. While this confirms that the spaces for an independent cinema had to be created elsewhere than on the remains of the traditional film outlets, from a commercial point of view the industry's strategy did have its own logic. If the series concept competed directly with television, the commercial producers also specialised in the area of demand where television was neither able nor willing to compete.

Finally, sex films were to some extent parasitic on mainstream cinema traditions in ways perhaps not altogether different from television's own attitude to the cinema: as a fully constituted, quotable body of familiar references, stereotypes and formulae. As we shall see, it was the Bavarian mountain musical, the *Heimat* film (popularised by Hollywood in *The Sound of Music*) that served as the genre to be 'deconstructed' by pornography. The New German Cinema's own sense of identity came at first from rejecting totally the associations that had formed around such genres. In a second move, it was the reconstruction of the concept of *Heimat* as both a synthetic myth and a reality with historical roots which gave film-makers, at least temporarily, the sense of belonging to a 'national' cinema.

The Oberhausen Style: Two Kinds of Spectatorship

Retrospectively, one can see that satire was the least satisfactory solution to the problem of address. Irritated by what they saw as the chief vice – contempt for the subject and contempt for the audiences – critics and spectators refused to identify with the films' implied mode of address:

> Two elements, which over and over again make the films of the Oberhausen group suspect: the tendency to despise people and the pseudo-esoteric penchant for formal excess. The two amount more or less to the same thing. Just as the Oberhausener seem to enjoy exposing people of a lower intelligence to the merciless ridicule of intellectuals, so they please themselves in the attitude of someone who can afford to ignore contact with the cinema stalls, and instead produce wild fantasies for an imaginary public of the day after tomorrow.[70]

Although this was written in 1964 and referred mainly to short films and documentaries (before any of the feature films had yet been made), on republishing his polemic twenty years later the author conceded that only Alexander Kluge's *Yesterday Girl* (1966) had been an exception. For the rest, his strictures seemed prophetic, since they were repeated, in slightly different form, many times during subsequent years. For Peter Schamoni's *Closed Season for Foxes* the unofficial tag-line was 'a film about philistines, for philistines, by philistines'.

> The conformism without commitment which Schamoni thinks he is (and seems so busy) attacking in his film, is in actual fact merely reduplicated by his film . . . *Closed Season for Foxes* is pretty well exactly the sort of film which his sullen hero full of self-pity might make if he were to succeed in switching from being a critic to directing.[71]

This may not do full justice to a film which in many ways is the first look at the provinces through the eyes of someone trying to break out, but it highlights the terms of the critical debate. Even more sharply, in an article entitled 'Young German Cinema – The Dead Eyes', Enno Patalas attacked Kluge, Kotulla and others for the lack of affection they had for their material, their condescending attitude towards the characters and the fact that nowhere did they let either the locations or the action develop a reality and a momentum of their own. Why, Patalas asked, can a trip to Italy not first of all be a trip to Italy, instead of serving as an occasion for sneering at German tourists and their consumerism (*Notabene Mezzogiorno*, Strobel and Tichawsky, 1962)? About Kluge's *Artistes at the Top of the Big Top: Disorientated* (1967) he wrote:

> The camera supplies particles of reality by the cart-load as if it was providing evidence for a trial. Images and objects are not there to be seen, felt, but to be interpreted and read. Instead of patiently observing one elephant, and let it work against the prejudices of the spectator, Kluge shows a whole herd of them, performing different activities, just as one can see them at least once a year in the newsreel. The same applies to his central metaphor – the circus. It is finally no more than a paradigm of 'art today' for him: any other might have done just as well, this one is particularly picturesque, it gives the story a bit of glamour and the magic of disorderliness.[72]

What was at issue was the morality implicit in a given mode of address. Many film-makers had come from documentary shorts, and when directors tried to apply the principles of documentary film-making to feature films it was deliberate policy and not accidental. Without reproducing the format of the social case history as an instance of general relevance, but also without personalising the issues as in the conventional fiction film, the ambition was to retain the authenticity of the documentary image, yet gain the metaphoric possibilities of fiction. Still, Patalas questioned the honesty of the documentarists' techniques. If Strobel and Tichawsky preceded their film *Eine Ehe* (*A Marriage*, 1968) with the assurance that 'documentary methods were logically extended to the fiction film', the logic did not even seem to extend to their treatment of sound:

Hannelore Hoger (left) in Alexander Kluge's Artistes at the Top of the Big Top: Disorientated *(1968)*

Conformism without Commitment?

Andrea Jonasson and Christian Doermer in Peter Schamoni's Closed Season for Foxes
(1966)

The few scenes (in *A Marriage*) where one hears sync-sound stick out clearly from the rest: for a brief moment one can hear people speak as they do in life – and as they do in the films of Wildenhahn, Straub, Erika Runge, Ula Stöckl – in a language that speaks itself and therefore carries, apart from the intended, always a host of unintended and often more important meanings. These brief moments aside, the directors do not allow their characters any physical identity . . . You don't even have to watch their lips to know that they do not say in the image what you hear on the sound-track: one constantly notices that gestures which belong to the movement of the spoken word have been sacrificed in the post-dubbing process.[73]

Such practices make it clear why a film-maker like Straub felt himself doubly in opposition – against the commercial cinema and against the directors of the Young German Film itself.

Two basic types of spectatorship solicited by the films of the Young German Film can be isolated. Both are important indicators of the differences between Young and New German directors. In one case, the mode of address belaboured the spectator by relentlessly selecting events and incidents as proof for a thesis, because the film assumed the spectators to be hostile, or their attitude to be one of indifference. In the other, the implied spectator shared the film's perspective and the mode of address presumed agreement, without actually creating it. Put more polemically, one aimed to indoctrinate and the other to ingratiate. In actual fact, the peculiar malaise experienced by spectators and critics alike over works by Spieker, Schaaf and Senft is due to the extent to which the films were a combination of both stances: posing their protagonists as case studies, while exposing them to ridicule or patronising sentiment.

Much of the subsequent work of Kluge and of Reitz, the uncompromising opposition of Straub, but also the beginnings of Fassbinder, Wenders and Herzog, can only be understood as a reaction to the dual impasse of Oberhausen. Film-makers of the first generation were trying to conjure up a consensus with spectators whom they already suspected of not existing, and doing so through a form of satire which understood itself to be critical, but was perceived as arrogant, derogatory and manipulative. Assessing thus the possible definition of the German cinema by the end of the 1960s, one is confronted with what is economically an art cinema (state-sponsored and anti-Hollywood). Yet within this art cinema one finds two strands: an authors' cinema growing confident of its audience only by a gradual process of self-definition and self-representation, and a cinema self-consciously social (almost in the terms of the contemporaneous Third World national cinemas), unsure of its stylistic traditions, but 'political' and prepared to be provincial.

3:

The Author in the Film:
Self-expression as Self-representation

The Author as Aesthetic Expert

For today's film production in Western Europe and the United States it is characteristic that films are produced as singular films, whether extravagant like Coppola's *Apocalypse Now* or modest like Rudolf Thome's *Berlin Chamissoplatz*. As pure 'author's films' they are responsible only to themselves. . . . These circumstances are very different from the earlier studio-based ones, though not necessarily to their advantage. For the cinema knows more than film-makers. 'Le cinéma a plus de talent que les cinéastes', Chris Marker wrote in 1953.[1]

The previous chapter wanted to locate some of the ideological divides associated with subsidising film as culture by discussing the *Autorenfilm* in the context of the European art cinema as well as in view of the legacy of German Romanticism. From this, the film-maker as artist emerged as a particularly contradictory figure. In practice he fully participates in a technological and capitalised world, while his ideological role involves a constant disavowal of this participation, almost as if a film could still be seen as a hand-crafted object. Yet cinema is also based on collective production and collective consumption, on generating series, genres and stereotypes. In so far as it is the art of this century, its power lies in the density of its myths and the transparency of its forms.

The *Autorenfilm* was constantly threatened by the opposite: the complexity of form and the paucity of mythic resonances. At the limit it came up against a basically unresolved contradiction between specialisation and intelligibility. The state-subsidised film-author is the equivalent of the researcher or the engineer, but as artist he is his inverse mirror-image. As specialist and expert, his competence is based on his ability to concentrate on the part while ignoring the whole. As artist, he is the negation of the specialist, in charge of preserving the unity of human endeavour and expressing it in his work. The subsidised artist, I have argued, has thrust upon him his role of representative: a middle ground where originality is compromised by speaking on behalf of others.[2] The label of author thus becomes a dubious value. Conferred by committees, in advance filled with social meaning, his status is, by an ironic twist, a subtle form of revenge society extracts for his privilege. Not surprisingly, therefore, the *Autorenfilm* gave rise to particular forms of self-stylisation. A quotation from Horkheimer and Adorno can illustrate the historical context. They had sarcastically added to their description quoted earlier:

What completely fettered the artist was the pressure [under a system of public patronage] always to fit into business life as the aesthetic expert.[3]

It is not difficult to see that directors, notably Fassbinder, Herzog, Syberberg, Wenders and Achternbusch, cultivated a public persona and a stylised self-image. They responded to the invitation to profile themselves as artists by an exaggerated, parodic or ironic cult of genius. Some became *enfants terribles*, others prophets or even pranksters. Usually, their individual psychology was blamed for the excesses in personality. But the madness has method: in the art cinema, the physical person and the projected persona of the director fulfil an essential role in both the sphere of production and that of circulation, for they provide a source of value and a context for meaning.

In Germany however, most film-makers tried to cope with or displace the role also in less flamboyant ways. Whether lawyers turned film-makers (Kluge, Kückelmann and Bohm), social scientists and economic historians (Schlöndorff, Jutta Brückner and Bernhard Sinkel) or literary historians and specialists in modern drama (Syberberg) they all went into print about the cinema and contemporary society, showing prodigious energy as cultural critics, publicists and theorists.[4] The fact that they expressed views and took positions publicly became an integral part of being film-makers. Both their prolixity as writers and their personality cult directly relate back to the problem of legitimation and the cultural mode of production, for not only did these directors have to become – *pace* Horkheimer and Adorno – business experts as well as aesthetic experts, the conditions of production and the part films played as cultural commodities demanded constant self-definition – of the artist but also of the product. The fact that the films were no longer cinema, and the cinema no longer entertainment but an exhibition (in every sense of the word) of individual works meant that, as with a painting or a piece of sculpture, the object and the person signing for it circulate together: each needs the other to support it and both need to attract the attention of a public.

After having argued that the New German Cinema, despite its allegiance to the *Autorenfilm*, did not function according to an ideology of self-expression, this chapter will try to show that it did: that self-expression as self-representation profoundly marked many of the films themselves, making them allegories of their own problematic existence, endlessly examining the question what is cinema, and what can films, produced in such a context, be 'about' except the conditions of their own impossibility? From Jean-Marie Straub's *Chronicle of Anna Magdalena Bach* to Werner Schroeter's *Dress Rehearsal*, from Kluge's *Artistes at the Top of the Big Top: Disorientated* to Herzog's *Fitzcarraldo* nothing is more consistent than the parables one finds of the subsidy system, the direct thematisations and indirect representations of its impact and paradoxes.

The pervasiveness as well as the diversity of the response to what it means to be a film-maker, for instance, can be gauged by the many portraits of artists, writers, musicians and philosophers in the New German Cinema. They may appear as heroic figures of resistance, as in Helma Sanders-Brahms' *Heinrich*, and Straub/Huillet's J.S. Bach or their Empedocles; they may be sensitive young men, in the tradition of the German *Bildungsroman*, as in Wenders' *Wrong Movement*, of the hard-boiled, hard-drinking kind (*Hammett*), or they can be pathetic victims of self-delusion (Fassbinder's Kranz in *Satan's Brew*). Directors may compare themselves to composers (as in Reitz' *Heimat* and Straub/Huillet's Schönberg adaptations, or Syberberg's fascination with Wagner). Their heroes

The director in double reflection: Armin Müller-Stahl in Kluge's The Blind Director *(1986)*
Frederick Forrest, hard-boiled, hard-drinking writer-hero in Wenders' Hammett *(1981)*

often feature in strongly independent professions, as artisans (Reitz' *Cardillac*), inventors (Reitz' *The Taylor from Ulm*), craftsmen (Wenders' *The American Friend*) or architects (Thome's *Berlin Chamissoplatz*), to name only a few. In Wenders' case they tend to be writer–photographers, writer–projectionists or writer–detectives (*Alice in the Cities, Kings of the Road, Hammett*), and sometimes they are even crash-landing aviators and entrepreneurs (Brustellin/Sinkel's *Berlinger – A German Fate*).

All of them have an idealist streak, coupled with a practical side. They have either visions, *idées fixes* or are diffident to the point of self-effacement about their artistic abilities. They feel ambivalent about power and social prestige, and are torn between introspection and narcissistic exhibitionism. The film-maker's contradictory craft, status and ambition is furthermore represented, parodied, analysed and mythologised in many guises. Syberberg's dictators (*Our Hitler*), mad kings (*Ludwig – Requiem for a Virgin King*) and pulp novelists (*Karl May*) are all extravagant *metteurs-en-scène*, mainly of other people's fantasies; and Herzog's Spanish conquistadors, adventurers and jungle aesthetes (*Aguirre, Fitzcarraldo*) revel in the physical exertion and danger attendant upon the realisation of impossible dreams. The last is typical in another respect: it is about a 'mixed' medium. Especially favoured is opera (in almost all the films of Schroeter) as having affinity with the cinema, because in Kluge's phrase both are 'power stations of feeling'.[5] But Kluge has also used the circus (*Artistes at the Top of the Big Top: Disorientated*) as an extended analogy.

Finally, the New German Cinema has its fair share of films about film-making: Fassbinder's *Beware of a Holy Whore*, Schilling's *The Expulsion from Paradise*, Wenders' *Lightning over Water* and *The State of Things*, Achternbusch's *Bye Bye Bavaria* and *Rita, Ritter* and Kluge's *The Blind Director*. There is a temptation to subsume these manifestations generally under the term 'self-reflexivity' or to discuss them as instances of meta-cinema. This they are, but I am more concerned to demonstrate how closely and at the same time obliquely they engage with the German funding system on the one hand, and the broader ideological or historical issues on the other.

Gustav Leonhardt in Jean-Marie Straub and Danièle Huillet's Chronicle of Anna Magdalena Bach *(1968)*

Sam Fuller and Patrick Bauchau in Wenders' The State of Things *(1982)*

The Author and the Avant-garde

Although many directors of experimental or avant-garde films in the 1960s were either not involved in the Oberhausen group at all, like Jean-Marie Straub and Danièle Huillet, or notorious dissidents, like Vlado Kristl, their work none the less tended to be drawn into the vortex of the debates that ensued. Rejection of Oberhausen and its consequences was as much based on a radically different conception of film, as it was motivated by political opposition to the idea of a state-funded national cinema.

> They could have made films with far less money, I mean the Oberhausen group, if they really had wanted to. They could have started much earlier, before the Bill existed. You can always tell when a film is made in order to make money.[6]

Straub, whose first two films *Machorka Muff* (1963) and *Not Reconciled* (*Nicht Versöhnt*, 1965) were produced without official subsidies, found that his script for a biography of J.S. Bach was turned down several times by the Kuratorium.

> It was of course idealist in the bad sense [to try and work within the subsidy system] because I didn't know the power relations yet that operated in film production and distribution. [We thought], if they try so hard to stop us making this film, then we just have to make it. I realized exactly what the score was when the Ministry of Culture in Düsseldorf rejected my application for subsidy three times in five years. They were desperate to prevent *Chronicle of Anna Magdalena Bach* from coming out in the cinemas . . . The only gap that is open [to avant-garde film-makers] is the Third Programme on television. It is obvious, a film made outside the system will never get inside. The system takes revenge.[7]

What characterises *Chronicle of Anna Magdalena Bach* above all is its careful avoidance of making the material – verbal, visual or musical – yield the meaning already established by the genre (biography of a great man) or by common historical hindsight. The stubborn difference between the documents and citations (the fact that they do not 'add up') is emphasised by the fiction of the diary of Bach's second wife. Because we expect her to unify the information given, if only by showing her emotions and reactions, the absence of any such perspective opens the view more strongly towards a historical inscription also of the present. In *Chronicle of Anna Magdalena Bach* Straub and Huillet confront the question of art in its relation to patronage: the dependencies it creates, and the discrepancy between, on the one side, the work's spiritual claims and, on the other, the material cares excluded from artistic form, which yet necessitate and justify its other-worldliness. The fact that patronage is self-evident for the Bachs makes it remarkable for us. 'Bach' is heard (rather than seen) struggling equally hard with poverty, child mortality, musical form, court intrigues, dull insensitivity, the blows of fate and bad medicine. He is seen with the only weapon at his disposal, which is his music. Deceptively coded as piety, J.S. Bach's response to adversity is one of the clearest articulations of the possible freedom that the artist can have in relation to social demands: the freedom to resist through the discipline imposed by form.

The materialism which the Straubs distil from the Bachs' historical situation becomes itself the most eloquent argument for the absolute asceticism of the work. Precisely because it is not an allegory of the subsidy system, but an act of resistance to it, *Chronicle of Anna Magdalena Bach*, even before it encountered its difficulties with the public and the press, was already a formulation and a critique of the *Autorenfilm* and its concept of the artist.

Vlado Kristl, who also began making films in 1963/64 (*Madeleine-Madeleine* and *The Dam*), was perhaps the most radical film-maker West Germany has ever

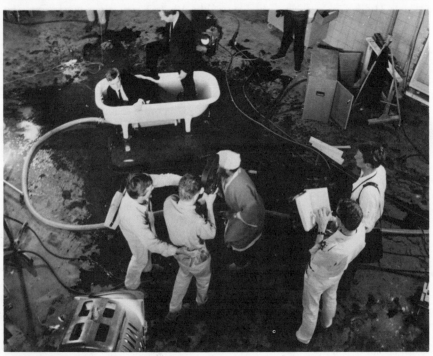

Vlado Kristl shooting The Letter *(1966)*

78

Movie-making: playing with the most expensive train set? Hellmuth Costard in The Little Godard *(1978)*

had. His raids on the commercial film industry were extended to desperado missions against the Young German Film itself, and he cultivated confrontation and personal antagonism as remorselessly as the destruction of narrative form and film syntax:

> My co-producer for *Der Damm*, Schleiermacher, was left with enormous debts over the film, and emigrated to Canada. The general shock was so great that, in fact, *Der Damm* precipitated the reactionary wave. Everyone became scared and rushed back to making commercial films. It was tough for Schleiermacher, who was Professor of Film at Ulm. He lost everything, Kluge had him kicked out of the Ulm Academy. Me he suspected of theft and called in the police. I only mention this, to indicate that those who seized power in the film business had recourse to very old methods. Even though they claimed to be socialists, Kluge and a few others were almost careless in the way they showed their true face . . . German films are by far the most accurate reflections of the Europe of our time. For film history they are more important as failures than where they were successful . . . The very early films of the Young German Film were much more necessary and deeper, but then they didn't ingratiate themselves with office workers and the petit bougeoisie, as Schlöndorff and company do today, who finger their way into people's dreams with 'beautifully' told phoney stories. The opposite, modern documentary films, get 'rewound' by television, and it dissolves whatever commitment they may have had.[8]

Kristl made these comments in 1972, after he had given up films for painting.

The Letter (*Der Brief*, 1966) was his own contribution to the polemic about the *Autorenfilm* and the artist's marginal and suicidal role in society. A man, asked to post a letter, decides to deliver it by hand. His itinerary takes him around the world, into the cross-fire of street battles and revolutions, to scenes of violence and love, but his inquiries for directions or his spontaneous assistance always meet with the same indifference. Finally arrived at his destination, he realises that the letter carried his own death sentence.

For Kristl such a scenario is already a betrayal of the cinema, since anyone can realise this film in his head. Thus *The Letter*, financed with money from the Kuratorium and a script prize, has as its subject the Kuratorium, and the form of film-making it seemed to predicate.

> All these scenes and sketches contain parables, comparable perhaps with Polanski's shorts . . . if only Kristl's scenes didn't constantly attack their own meaning, like the people in the film who all the time beat and insult each other . . . As one can see, Kristl cannot be counted among the institutional avant-garde. He lacks all interest for their group mentality and aesthetic fetishism.[9]

As far as the avant-garde was concerned the Kuratorium, rather than fulfilling the promise of Oberhausen, helped to betray whatever solidarity there was to share risks and responsibilities, by ultimately playing off one director against the other. Anyone committed to collaboration and the workshop ethic found himself necessarily frustrated by the subsidy system, which isolated the individual creator. In *Sekundenfilme*, a series of short sketches made in 1970 for Bavarian television, Kristl has a scene which he describes as follows:

> A sign says 'Young German Film'. Behind the house, in the field, some young men are shooting a film while talking about the Old Film. They accuse each other endlessly of making old films. When the money arrives, they start stabbing each other.
>
> Another sign says 'Old German Film'. Everyone is talking about the New German films they are about to direct or distribute. Producers exhort the directors to make the New film, and distributors speak of a new dawn, the New Cinema. When no money arrives, they start stabbing each other.[10]

Film oder Macht (*Film or Power*, 1970) is Kristl's filmed application form to the Project Commission. Taking the statutes and regulations by the letter he reduces *ad absurdum* the bureaucratic apparatus of submissions in triplicate of story outlines, scripts, treatments and budgets, of copyright and contracts. If a project can be described, itemised and put between the covers of a file, why bother to film it? 'The only and true description of the content is that I have made a film, which excluded any preparation whatsoever, of the kind that could result in material conventionally used as the basis for developing a film subject.'[11]

In the 1960s collective work was mainly associated with the Hamburg Film Co-op, and directors such as Helmut Herbst, Werner Nekes, Dore O, Klaus Wyborny and Hellmuth Costard.[12] From Costard in particular came further attacks on the 'cultural' conception of film and federal fundings. Costard made films taking issue with the commercial cinema (*Warum hast Du mich wach geküßt*, 1967, starts with a mock trailer for a bombastic spectacular), the quality rating (*Besonders Wertvoll* (*Quality Rating: Excellent*, 1968)) and the Kuratorium (*Der kleine Godard an das Kuratorium junger deutscher Film* (*The Little Godard*, 1978)). *Besonders Wertvoll* shows a penis in close-up mouthing the speech of a High Court judge defending the quality ratings, before spitting into the camera. Accepted for the Oberhausen

An image from Brecht's Kuhle Wampe *(1932) in Harun Farocki's* Between the Wars *(1978)*

Festival of 1968, *Besonders Wertvoll* was withdrawn for fear of police reprisals, which led to a walkout by most German film-makers, with the exception of Werner Herzog.[13] *Der kleine Godard* was Costard's attempt to document the technical, financial and political difficulties which he encountered with his project 'to shoot fiction films wholly without imagination' – itself an idea close to Kristl's deconstructions of the cinema before and behind the camera, as well as in the spectator's head.

> [Costard's] film shows what films usually do not give away, that the struggle for its production precedes the realized product. And maybe Costard can only show the general significance of his personal struggle, because he appears defeated, because only this intervention, this form of symbolic subversion remains open to him.[14]

Kristl himself was back at the 1984 Berlin Festival with a film entitled *Death to the Spectator* (*Tod dem Zuschauer*, 1983), funded by the City of Hamburg:

> Since this non-film addresses itself to non-spectators, it should be shown at non-festivals. With this the organizers have undertaken a difficult task, which resolves itself surprisingly easily when one considers that this 'Death to the Spectator' which happens to have found its way onto celluloid is as 'Death of the Spectator' a factual reality.[15]

Such pessimistic views regarding audiences of both television and the cinema can stand for an entire spectrum of avant-garde film-making in West Germany.

Its strict formalism is, like the Straubs', always derived from a political perspective. The German subsidy system, experienced directly by all film-makers, becomes for the avant-garde the occasion for a reflection about the cinema as an act of resistance. The films themselves are, as it were, merely the visible part, the aggression that conceals the promise of an as yet non-realisable, non-representable endeavour. The object is not to make cinema, nor even films, but to bear witness to the relentless 'packaging' of ideas, images, insights and information that characterises the media and their interdependence, of which the subsidy system is merely another example.

Harun Farocki, for instance, who began as an agitprop director making didactic shorts for teach-ins and political group work, is in his feature films concerned with the trade-offs between rivals and opponents. His first full-length film, *Between the Wars* (*Zwischen zwei Kriegen*, 1978), is ostensibly about the support German industrialists gave to Hitler by devising the so-called *Verbundsystem*, whereby the waste-products of the iron industry were used in the coal industry and vice versa. As a system of industrial rationalisation, it seems politically neutral, but Farocki is at pains to show the historical consequences of this different form of production.[16] A brief scene discussing the making and financing of his own film outside the subsidy system and without television seems merely a Godardian touch, until one comes across an article by Farocki on freelance work which draws the necessary analogy with the media's own *Verbundsystem* as it affects his status as producer at its margins.

Following the example of the steel industry . . . I try to create a *Verbund* with my work. The basic research for a project I finance with a radio broadcast, some of

The 'Verbundsystem' in Farocki's Between the Wars *(1978)*

82

. . . and in his Before Your Eyes: Vietnam *(1981)*

the books I use I review for the book-programmes, and many of the things I notice during this kind of work end up in my television features.[17]

Farocki is also the author of another formulation of the impossible options facing the avant-garde film-maker. *Before Your Eyes: Vietnam* (*Etwas wird sichtbar*, 1981) has at first sight little to do with the New German Cinema, because it deals with the impact of the images from Vietnam on the West German left and their conception of revolutionary action and agitprop. Again, passages which seem aphoristic in relation to the Vietnam War become graphically descriptive when seen in the light of independent film-making:

> It is not a question of doing either one or the other, but of joining the two. When you clear up your room by moving everything to one side, that's easy. Or when in your work-shop every time you use a tool you put it back where it belongs, that's easy, too. It's easy to produce something systematically, like a machine. And it is easy to produce something new, once only, like an artist.[18]

Farocki speaks from the vantage point of someone who wants to think the politics of film-making, the politics of warfare, and the representability of abstract relations such as they obtain under capitalism within a practice of cinema that is critical and at the same time formally accomplished. In Werner Schroeter's films, the definition of a specific filmic form also goes beyond a refusal to be co-opted. What the two directors have in common may be no more than the necessity of rethinking the cinema outside the parameters of state-funded independence. Whereas Farocki looks to the essay and the document for a form that can generalise

83

from the particular without becoming metaphoric, Schroeter circumvents narrative in favour of performance-inspired spectacle and drama. This mainly includes opera, but also dance theatre, stage melodrama, cabaret and even the rock concert.

Schroeter not only shows disregard for cultural legitimacy, but an almost serene indifference to the fact that his films have virtually no distribution and are only known to specialists. Indeed, one might say that he is above all a film-makers' film-maker. Fassbinder has said that he 'learnt massively' from Schroeter's films:

Werner Schroeter has been for more than a decade . . . the most important, most exciting, the most decisive and decided director of an alternative cinema, generally called 'underground', a name that limits, prettifies and finally suffocates it in a friendly and tender embrace. In truth, there is no such thing as an 'underground' film [and in Germany today], there are few among those who have had the chance to make films who did not copy what they could from Schroeter . . . Daniel Schmid is unthinkable without Schroeter, and so is Ulrike Ottinger; Walter Bockmayer was able to learn from Schroeter . . . And an especially smart Schroeter-imitator emerged, who just at the time when Schroeter was helplessly waiting [for funds], cleverly marketed what he had taken.[19]

Fassbinder's jibes against Syberberg (who was in fact the first to acknowledge his debt to Schroeter in *Ludwig – Requiem for a Virgin King*, 1971) are tendentious. How crucial Schroeter's *Eika Katappa* (1969) and *Bomber Pilot* (*Der Bomberpilot*, 1970) were for Syberberg, however, can be judged from comparing his films prior to *Ludwig* (for example, *San Domingo*, 1970) with almost all his films since. In the use of back-projection, operatic staging and acting, or the development of narratives around music and song collages, Schroeter was the initial inspiration.

Schroeter's early work can stand as a commentary on the subsidy system's pre-definition of film-making: what is exciting about his films is precisely what makes most of his projects unsuitable for the written treatment required by funding bodies. With less of Kristl's politico-anarchist black humour or despair, Schroeter's films challenge the most basic assumptions of narrative cinema and continuity editing by the sheer urgency of the states of mind he can communicate through the gestural language of images paired with song and music.

To an extent Schroeter's lack of interest in films that can get cinema distribution might reflect the fact that he is practically a hostage to television. He did in fact, with *Kingdom of Naples* (*Neopolitanische Geschwister*, 1978) and *Palermo or Wolfsburg*, make scripted, subsidised and commercially financed films, the latter winning the Golden Bear at Berlin in 1980. They are narrative films where the emotions of opera are starkly juxtaposed with, in one case, the history of a Neapolitan working-class family from 1944 to 1977, and in the other, the boundless need for love and capacity for devotion of an Italian guest-worker in Wolfsburg, home of the Volkswagen works. His spirituality contrasts with the superficial, callous behaviour displayed by the Germans he meets and which hides their own unhappiness.

Narrative or non-narrative form: Schroeter's boldness about strong emotions gives him a radically different attitude to the figure of the artist and to bourgeois (musical) art, compared to the more overtly political avant-garde:

It would be absurd to assert that the desire for beauty and truth is merely an illusion of our romantic-capitalist society. Undoubtedly, the desire for exalted, larger-than-life wish-fulfilment, as we find it in all traditional art, to which we can certainly add the modern 'trivial' media of cinema and television, corresponds to a very general human need. In my films I want to live out the very few basic human

'A few completely authentic feelings': Brigitte Tilg and Nicola Zarbo in Werner Schroeter's Palermo or Wolfsburg *(1980)*

moments of expressivity to the point of musical and gestural excess – those few completely authentic feelings: life, love, joy, hatred, jealousy and the fear of death, without psychologizing them.[20]

His most explicitly allegorical film about film-making between art and commerce is *The Death of Maria Malibran* (*Der Tod der Maria Malibran*, 1971). A young man (actually a woman dressed as a boy) with a proverbial feather in his cap wanders slowly through a snowy landscape. At a clearing he is accosted by a Caligari-figure (another woman, in cloak and top hat) who promises him a slice from his large loaf of bread, but only if the boy lets him gouge out his eyes. The boy agrees and becomes the older man's companion. Taking motifs from E.T.A. Hoffmann and the German silent cinema, Schroeter here anticipates much of the opening scenes of Herzog's *Kaspar Hauser*. The fable of *The Death of Maria Malibran* as a whole (of which the scene is only one episode) is as starkly pessimistic as the form is high camp parodic. Unlike Herzog, whose Romanticism in *Kaspar Hauser* almost takes itself seriously, Schroeter's film mixes Grand-Guignol, operatic excess, pop music schmaltz, transvestism and pastiche. The play with sexual ambiguity on the formal level contrasts with an unambiguous moral: an artist can only achieve perfection and truth by 'singing' about death. Schroeter's response to the social demands made on the 'artist' seems to be to sabotage any personality cult, by endlessly dissimulating sexual identity, without which neither narrative nor the star system functions in either the commercial or the art cinema.

Werner Schroeter (left) in his Dress Rehearsal *(1980)*

The Artist as Hero

I am convinced the economic conditions of production shape the content of a film
. . . Today I know that if I lived in a country with a flourishing film industry and a
flourishing film culture, my scripts would have interested a flourishing production
company. They would have budgeted my project and said, the film will cost two
million. And *Mealtimes* would have been a different film. With my second film,
Cardillac, I was already aware of the connexions, and they became the subject of
the film. I tried to give a portrait of the artist as an individual in all his absurdity
. . . but the result is: one can tell it's a film about a German film-maker and his
peculiar predicament.[21]

Edgar Reitz' comment indicates that German films often have as their subject
their own conditions of existence almost in spite of themselves: the work becomes
an act of self-analysis, as much out of frustration and resistance as self-
representation. *Cardillac* (1969) was one of the earliest of Young German films
about an artist, based on a story by E.T.A. Hoffmann – *Das Fräulein von
Scuderi*. It concerns a goldsmith during the French Revolution who, dependent
as he is on aristocratic patronage and commission, cannot bear to part with his
creations and by night robs and murders in order to repossess them. Since his
victims are members of the aristocracy, his deeds become confused with political
acts of revolutionary justice and he goes undetected. The parable nature of the
story is obvious: the artist-craftsman, torn between self-expression and patronage,

refuses to see his works become objects of the ruling class' need for luxury and self-display. He goes to the extreme of murder in a vain and pathetic effort to restore to the work its 'aura' and authentic value, while being mistaken for a political revolutionary.

Rather than opting for period adaptation, *Cardillac* is set in West Germany, with oblique but none the less explicit references. Cardillac's daughter – an exotic mulatto woman whom he treats like one of his crafted jewels – involves herself in a hippy commune and, as an example of the new moneyed aristocracy, Gunter Sachs plays Gunter Sachs, Germany's international playboy of the 1960s. Cardillac's crowning masterpiece turns out to be an electric chair with which he executes himself. The film never made it into the cinemas: critics found the style academic and the subject merely arty. *Cardillac* is almost an anthology of motifs clustering around the New German Cinema's fictionalised self-understanding: the split between artist and craftsman, the transposition of feudal patronage into West German show-business, the use of a literary work from the Romantic period, in a dramatic or allegorical context that allows for contemporary inferences.

1968 to 1971 saw the first spate of 'literary films'. The most obvious, but in truth rather complex, reaction to the demand for cultural legitimation (and the need to reject, or at least distance such a demand) was to take recourse in early nineteenth-century literature as intertext for current preoccupations. Critics quickly countered with charges of typically German *Schwärmerei*, of self-pity and pampered neuroses. Yet the need to locate in literature the point of departure for a tradition of radical art analogous to the film-maker's own situation, privileged those texts where an acutely experienced subjectivity clashes with an equally acute sense of duty, or comes to grief among bureaucracies and hierarchical power structures. For while sensibilism could be seen as simply a return to the Romantic motifs of the perennial, adolescent outsider, the (film-)political subtext renders the figure more symptomatic, and allows one to sense behind any naive reproduction of German inwardness a dual strategy. This was to locate film-making within the historical context of German *Kultur*, and to renew the links between theatre, literature and the cinema which had existed in the nearly 1920s – the last time German cinema had had an international reputation. The situation made one Romantic writer in particular an almost inevitable choice: Heinrich von Kleist.

In the general rediscovery of Germany's literary response to the French Revolution in the wake of 1968, Kleist became the patron saint of the New German Cinema at the same time as his plays were revived on every municipally subsidised stage from Hamburg to Munich. His work has been filmed many times over. Volker Schlöndorff made *Michael Kohlhaas – The Rebel* in 1969; Hans Jürgen Syberberg took another Kleist novella for his *San Domingo* (1970); in 1974 Helma Sanders-Brahms filmed *The Earthquake in Chile* (*Erdbeben in Chili*, 1974); Eric Rohmer came to Germany for his Kleist adaptation *The Marquise of O* (1975). Kleist's themes, especially in his novellas, were civil wars and revolution, which he attempted to understand in a double metaphoric perspective: as violent natural disasters become political by the promise of a new beginning. Yet the return to zero in stories such as *The Earthquake in Chile* is always betrayed by the everyday, the needs and desires of the moment re-establishing the *status quo ante*. As a conservative radical and political writer of subjectivity, Kleist's individualism of 'excess' has had a key role in 1970s German culture. Helma Sanders-Brahms makes the connection with the women's movement:

Ever since school I have felt an affinity for Kleist. He is so contradictory, awkward and extreme; qualities which somehow for me represent Germany. What fascinates me about Kleist is the huge gap between the demands he makes on himself and others, and the reality of his life. What annoys me about Goethe: in some fatal way it all comes right; life, the writing, love . . . he accommodates himself and calls it mastering one's life. Kleist does not accommodate himself, demands too much and comes to grief. There I recognize myself.[22]

Kleist's metaphysics of private revolt stand behind much of Herzog's early work, even where there is no directly acknowledged source. *Signs of Life* (1967), Herzog's first film, was based on an incident from the Napoleonic Wars that could have been written up by Kleist (it was used by Kleist's contemporary Achim von Arnim), just as another Kleist story could have been a source for *Kaspar Hauser: Der Eindling*, which had in fact already been filmed by George Moorse in 1967. What this indicates is not so much any direct literary influence, but the fact that a film-maker, however individualist and idiosyncratic she or he may be in her or his 'vision', shares in the processes whereby specifically German 'high-culture' reference points emerged for a cinema that, having distanced itself from both Hollywood and its own immediate commercial industry, was looking for self-definitions.

Kleist also signified the artist forced to write letters and petitions to patrons in order to make a living by his pen. What Bach had been to the Straubs, Kleist became to German directors in the 1970s: a figure across whose life and work a certain historical juncture could be represented. His life – and double suicide – became in turn the subject for fiction. Helma Sanders-Brahms returned to Kleist

Heinrich Giskes and Grischa Huber in Helma Sanders-Brahms' Heinrich *(1977)*

Hanna Schygulla and Rüdiger Vogler (in the background Natasha Kinski and Hans Christian Blech) in Wenders' Wrong Movement *(1974)*

in her *Heinrich* (1977), and theatre director Hans Neuenfels made *Heinrich Penthesilia von Kleist* (1982), where Kleist's play, rehearsal scenes and discussions around his politics and life were intercut to probe the writer's peculiar fascination for both men and women. The very title of a film like Jutta Brückner's *Kolossale Liebe* (*Mighty Love*, 1984, about the ageing Rachel Varnhagen, who headed a famous literary salon in Berlin of the 1820s) evokes Kleist, as does the characterisation of the manic depressive, highly lucid and radically egocentric heroine.

A comparable culture hero was Reinhold Lenz, an eighteenth-century poet and former friend of Goethe's who became insane. Indeed, preferences for either Kleist, Goethe or Lenz indicates interesting differences among the 'New Sensibility'. Lenz had mainly survived as the hero of a fictionalised autobiography written by Georg Büchner in the 1830s, who saw in Lenz' schizophrenia and spiritual turmoil a proto-revolutionary radicalism reacting not only to his social isolation but to a general estrangement of man from nature. Such 'cultural' schizophrenia made him in many ways a figure of the 1970s as well. In this guise, he figures in George Moorse's *Lenz* (1970), from where a line can be traced to one of the most influential books of the post-1968 generation – Peter Schneider's *Lenz*, a sort of manifesto of the 'New Sensibility'. But a film like Wenders' *Wrong Movement* (1974), perhaps the best-known version in the New German Cinema of the theme of the artist as a sensitive young man, would have been less assured in its tone and theme had it not been for these predecessors, which include Wenders' own *Alice in the Cities* (1973, itself loosely based on motifs from

89

Handke's *Short Letter, Long Farewell* in which the hero is reading *Anton Reiser*, another artist's novel from the time of Kleist and Büchner).

Of course *Wrong Movement*, written by Peter Handke, is an adaptation of Goethe's *Wilhelm Meister*, the classic in the tradition of the *Bildungsroman*. This may seem to make it an unlikely candidate for a parable of the German subsidy system, but Goethe's hero, hesitating between a bourgeois existence and his artistic vocation, takes up theatre management as an interim solution. Wenders' hero concludes his voyage through Germany by borrowing a super-8 camera to record from the Zugspitze, Germany's highest peak, the panoramic but also highly symbolic views before him. In this he is imitating not only one of Caspar David Friedrich's figures peering into the infinite, but Wenders' own camera which during a central discussion about life and art had followed the characters wending their way higher and higher up the slopes of the Rhine valley near one of Germany's best-known spots, the Lorelei. *Wrong Movement* is constructed so as to let the end of the fictional story symbolise the beginning of the film we have just been watching.

Wilhelm's dilemma is primarily presented as that of the writer trying to make his general anomie and estrangement from life productive, by learning to see himself less as a victim and instead as part of a story which he is merely called upon to record (a situation already to be found in Schlöndorff's *Young Törless*, 1966, after the novel by Robert Musil). But where Schlöndorff in the 1960s had worked into his film heavy allusions to authoritarianism and Fascism, Wenders' historical intertext is the Federal Republic itself. Among the many references to the cinema (Wilhelm in his home town dates an usherette) is included a screening on television of Jean-Marie Straub's *Chronicle of Anna Magdalena Bach*.

The Artist as Autodidact

The New German Cinema has, because of its mode of production, a particularly acute understanding of the avatars of culture in post-industrial societies, and many of the directors attempted to make productive the anomaly, the marginality of their work. Culture appears in their films not as an explicit discourse about the aesthetic point of view on life, but paradoxically, as almost its opposite. Their heroes valorise the non-signifying, the mute 'thereness' of things, contrasted with the aestheticising of the modern environment in commodity and consumer culture. It is easy to mistake this for naive Romanticism, as in Herzog's *Kaspar Hauser*, or see in it a sort of fetishism of the inarticulate, as in some of Wenders' films or early Fassbinder. But in *Kaspar Hauser* Herzog seems less concerned to juxtapose innocent nature and the inarticulate foundling with corrupt and fallen society (a possible but simplistic reading). Kaspar's non-natural as well as non-human condition challenges both society *and* nature. What is confronted in the film is the process of the making of an artist whose gift resides in being able to read society-as-nature and nature-as-social utopia who, in other words, has a radically artificial relation to both. Herzog's particular dialectic of marginal figures and over-reachers has to be seen, it seems to me, as part of a mythology of self-creation to do with the situation of the German cinema rather than as the sign of a regressive Romanticism.

Look at what's on TV. Look at Pan Am's posters of the Grand Canyon. Sometimes there is a gap between the advance of civilisation and its images. For such an advanced civilisation as ours to be without images that are adequate to it is as serious a defect as being without memory.[23]

The artist as hero is thus also present in a more oblique figuration: images of nature *after* man, or a view of the exotic as a surreal collision of incompatible value systems, such as one finds in other Herzog films (in *Fata Morgana*, 1971, or in his documentary about the deaf and blind, *Land of Silence and Darkness*, 1971, and in *La Soufrière*). Kaspar Hauser in this respect is the artist as autodidact, the self-created human being starting from zero who possesses a different form of apprehension, itself metaphorically represented by an emphasis on pure perception, unmediated vision and the beauty of the image. Herzog's self-image is in this respect highly instructive. He, like so many other German directors, appears to be a craven seeker of headlines to satisfy an inflated ego. But again one could argue that the context of intelligibility necessitated by the *Autorenfilm* has more to do with it than individual psychology. Consider how carefully constructed a persona it is:

I'd almost say, the news of my birth is nothing but a rumour. My grandfather, who was an archeologist, died mad, and I admired him very much. My mother is Yugoslav. I have a very complicated family. My father lives like a vagabond. He was married twice. I have many brothers and sisters, but some are half- or quarter-brothers. I wasn't brought up in the system. I am an autodidact and have never been to film school. While I was doing my studies I worked at night in a steel mill in Munich. For two years I was chained from 6 pm to 8 am. I made enough money to shoot my first short in 35mm. I hired a cameraman, and there was the Munich Institute for Film Research, a precursor of the Munich Film School today, and these bastards had three cameras locked in some kind of safe, and I went and 'borrowed' one of them. I think to this day they don't realize that one of their cameras is missing. Under these circumstances, I think it was right to appropriate the means of production.

What made me a film-maker? – I made myself a film-maker.[24]

Chained during the night to a welding machine in a steel mill, stealing a camera from a film school, and shooting his first film in 35mm instead of Super-8 or 16mm. An ancestry of madmen and vagabonds, self-taught and self-sufficient: it sounds more like a Herzog scenario than a biography. One can see the outlines of a very particular myth: that of the autodidact as Prometheus, defying the Gods and stealing fire for the benefit of mankind. Herzog's conversion to Catholicism, for instance, followed a similar pattern: he did it apparently to provoke a definitive break with his father. The personal and the public, the private and the mythological fuse in this idea, providing a further context for the films themselves. Prometheus joins Kaspar Hauser, as the two sides of the same attempt to conceptualise a radical fatherlessness and turn the state-subsidised artist into a rebellious martyr. The marginal becomes the exceptional and sensational, at which point it can insert itself as a commodity into the reigning order of production and circulation. Now, a Herzog film without a few tall tales would hardly be the authentic article.

The stance of the autodidact – as both orphaned foundling and all-powerful creator – is thus not only a successful stylisation of the two sides of the film-maker–artist as culture hero, it also refers back to one of the most favoured topics of post-war German cinema: that of the new start, whether literally as the 'zero hour' of 1945 or, more metaphorically, as the new generation's unwillingness to see their work in a continuity with the 1950s and the commercial cinema. 'We had no fathers, only grandfathers' was how Herzog put it, and in Wenders and Fassbinder, too, one comes across similar statements. Their value is as much symbolic as factual, since to believe in the start from scratch, or in the self-taught, self-created hero may be to assert a freedom the directors usually did not possess. It explains in part why Kleist's *The Earthquake in Chile* proved so influential: its theme is the possibility of a new start and the reasons why it fails. Reinhard Hauff's *Knife in the Head* (*Messer im Kopf*, 1978) uses the format of a political thriller about terrorist suspects for a story whose inner logic turns on a myth not unlike that of *Kaspar Hauser*. A man, shot by a policeman in a raid, loses his memory and has to start afresh: he can only do so by returning to the origin of his 'fall' and confronting the youthful policeman with his own terror.

The Author as Prophet

Herzog's stylisation of the cinema in terms of a heroic mythology and of film as a form of practical utopia finds its echo both in Syberberg and Kluge, however different the three directors are as film-makers and as personalities. Syberberg's own stylisation, as a public figure and writer of cultural criticism, tends more to that of a Cassandra, his country's prophet and national conscience haunting and haunted by the legacy of German history. Syberberg's practical notions of a cinema of the future, within the context of the growing mythologisation that the *Autorenfilm* underwent in the 1970s, indicate some of the contradictions with which such an oppositional concept of film-making, as a counter-practice to television, is fraught, when it endorses as fully as did Syberberg the role of the bourgeois artist. True to the logic of his convictions, Syberberg demanded not only public funds for film-making but also state-funded cinemas. However, unlike the schemes elaborated during the 1970s in support of community-based and municipally sponsored cinemas and exhibition spaces, Syberberg's suggestions aimed at creating an equivalent of state opera houses and theatres for the cinema, ideally modelled on Bayreuth and combining private patronage with state subsidy.

It has always been art which represented the better Germany, even Bayreuth has in every period been better than the government of the day. The New German Cinema, too, is Germany's best messenger abroad, so why not at home? We live in a democracy, and ought it to be said of it that it is incapable of presenting in attractive form what is new, if necessary from above, as was the case under princes and popes? We are awaiting the democratic politician who will recognize what needs to be done, like the feudal patrons. He will earn himself a place in the history of modern times in the way that Ludwig [of Bavaria] belongs to the history of Wagner's music.[25]

Such a vision of 'democracy from above' responds provocatively to the state's implicit demand for film authors to play their role as representatives, turning it into the demand that the state give the artist not only the means to create but also the institutions to exhibit, to be celebrated and given his due. Concretely, the idea reflects that distribution and exhibition were *de facto* the New German Cinema's Achilles' heel. This lack, combined with his admiration for the Paris cinemathèque, Syberberg stylises into the need for a Walhalla of the Seventh Art. However much it might have been said with tongue in cheek, it too provides a context for the films. So far it is mainly Syberberg's own work that seems designed to supply a Bayreuth of the cinema: *Ludwig – Requiem for a Virgin King*, *The Confessions of Winifred Wagner*, *Our Hitler*, *Parsifal* and *The Night* are conceived as a *Ring*, the high art version of an author's genre.

92

Ludwig in particular can be read as the transposition of problems of subsidy and patronage, along the lines suggested by the quotation above. The historical Ludwig of Bavaria was indeed Wagner's most lucrative and illustrious patron, staging *Tristan and Isolde* in the splendour and extravagance of his fantasy castles, often with himself as virtually the only spectator. Yet despite this aristocratic self-indulgence, Ludwig was an immensely popular monarch, who comes across in Syberberg's film as a sentimental, if cantankerous, typical Bavarian.[26]

Much of what Syberberg has written on this question, and not least his own self-presentation in the media as an artist in the bourgeois tradition, would indicate that the audience he envisaged for his films is a middle-class public, intellectually literate and considering itself in possession of *Kultur*, if not its embodiment. In other words, precisely that audience which is the main beneficiary of state-subsidised art, and goes to the theatre by subscription, attends concerts, loves the opera and occasionally visits an art exhibition. There is, furthermore, in Syberberg, a curious notion of aesthetic decorum which has to do with artistic forms considered serious (Syberberg's vocabulary in this respect is mostly musical: 'requiem', 'chorus', 'aria', 'melisma') and of subjects considered important if not portentous. Yet from everything one empirically knows about German audiences loyal to the cinema, the culturally active segment of the middle-class is rarely among them.

This paradox, of which Syberberg is himself aware, is the subject of *Karl May* (1974). What interests Syberberg in the creator of immensely popular adventure stories and boy's fiction from Wilhelmine Germany – apart from the story of the ageing writer pursued by intrigues, smear campaigns and money worries, which has obvious parallels with the film-maker (the role is furthermore played by the venerated 'old' German director Helmut Käutner) – is the contrast between Karl May's self-image as philosopher, prophet and serious artist, and the pulp qualities and appeal of his fiction. Karl May becomes the more instructive in the light of an article by Ernst Bloch, in which Bloch tried to argue that popular culture of low-brow or adolescent appeal, such as Karl May's novels, do contain a utopian political dimension. By pointing out that the Communist Party in the Weimar Republic had, in their rationalist zeal, left to the National Socialists and their propaganda the entire heritage of German romantic myths, popular fantasies and wish-fulfilling ideals, Bloch had accused socialist notions of art (as education and for raising class consciousness) of being counter-productive. For, as he put it:

A class-ideology always produces a surplus [of utopian thinking] over and above the historically given false consciousness, which is called culture, whose substratum is there to be inherited [by progressive thought].[27]

What Bloch wrote in 1932 became once more very topical in 1970, with the failure of the student left to formulate a progressive aesthetics that had popular support. Syberberg felt that the cinema, regarded from this aspect, is the heir to the fairground, the fairy tales, legends and popular myths of German Romanticism. They are the products, the 'surplus' of this false consciousness. Serving real needs, albeit in imaginary, escapist form, the cinema can still dream of liberation and, in this sense, it is heroic. Where petit bourgeois culture tries to bring everything into the cosy idyll of the home, truly popular art insists on otherness, on distinct times and places, on the need to escape and the need for change. A 'national cinema' ought to concentrate on showing in this impure, ideologically ambiguous medium the attraction of such forms of idealism and also their historical,

Kristina Söderbaum and Helmut Käutner in Syberberg's Karl May *(1974)*

'materialist' basis. It is therefore possible to recognise in the deliberately provoked clash between high culture and bad taste, *Kunst* and *Kitsch*, so typical of the films of Schroeter, Syberberg, but also Fassbinder (and other directors named by him as Schroeter disciples), the consequences of an art cinema trying to realise its claim to being popular and progressive.

Syberberg sees in Karl May both the popular artist, tossed between patronage and the market, and an occasion to think about the New German Cinema's failure to develop a genuine mass appeal. The irony lay in the fact that Karl May's books, made into 'German Westerns', had in the mid-1960s not only furnished 'Papa's Kino' with one of its most impressive strings of commercial hits: its producers were also the main beneficiaries of the first Subsidy Bill. Thanks to Karl May, Horst Wendlandt or Franz Seitz, for instance, demonstrated that one could, after all, make money with German films. The question was whether home-grown German entertainment was preferable to Hollywood super-schlock, and while Syberberg would never have talked to Seitz or Waldleitner, he did do business with Francis Ford Coppola, who distributed Syberberg's films on the art circuit in the United States while, along with his friends Lucas and Spielberg, cleaning up in Germany's commercial cinemas. Fassbinder, for his part, was prepared to go directly to the automatic subsidies Waldleitner had earned from sex comedies and Bavarian soft porn. The *Kunst–Kitsch* collages which made the New German Cinema so exciting to a New York avant-garde, who saw in the films evidence of a post-modernism prepared to deny any difference between high and mass culture in the age of the commodity, were in Germany itself more properly evidence that the ideological and practical opposition between the Old and the New Cinemas had by the mid-1970s begun to crumble, making way for bewildering forms of intertextuality.[28]

The Author at the Top of the Big Top

Syberberg needs the State to negate the status of commodity that his own product willy-nilly possesses. The government as patron is called in to disguise and shore up the contradictions that arise from the uneven development in different parts of domestic film production, between the national and the international entertainment and media industries. On the face of it, this interpretation of 'democracy from above' could not be further from the idea advocated by Alexander Kluge, who sees the renewal of the cinema, if anything, as a move towards a democracy from below. Both Syberberg and Kluge – even though their notions of culture are diametrically opposed – regard the irrational, the unconscious and fantasy as areas where the cinema reconstructs and re-forms a subjectivity that exists politically in social life and can appropriate a collective past. They have defined a new role for the cinema within the mass media: part but apart, which means for Syberberg to be the media's conscience and for Kluge to act as their meta-critique. This radically changes film and the cinema; for neither director is it a means of self-expression – hence Syberberg's own disagreements with the *Autorenfilm*.

Kluge has written more than any other film-maker about the place films ought to have in culture. This is partly the result of his immense and intense activity as a media politician, but corresponds also to his essentially pedagogic temperament. More clearly than most star directors, Kluge is against any attempt to up-grade the cinema by making it part of traditional art, just as he is against the notion of pure entertainment. Unlike Syberberg, whose fears of 'commercialisation' drive him towards an alliance with high art, Kluge sees the split itself as a false dichotomy. In so far as he rejects the 'recipe films'[29] of the commercial film industry, he is in accord with Herzog or Syberberg, and is resolutely anti-capitalist. In so far as it is a question of the cultural status of the cinema, however, Kluge understands film-making as a political practice, rather than as part of any official or legitimate culture. For him, cinema in the age of television and other media has a radically different function. Where its economic basis is government financed, its social task and responsibility is towards general emancipation. It is an instrument for people to realise needs and develop skills that the industrialised urban economies of the West (including the commercial cinema) have neglected or exploited one-sidedly. The cinema of the future, therefore, must be a counter-culture, an 'ecology', rather than an economy.

At the same time, the very concept of culture for Kluge is much too restrictive, if it does not allow the film-maker to come to grips with the mechanisms which transform culture into a commodity. In the tradition of the Frankfurt School and Critical Theory, Kluge sees culture as both an industry, and as a field of political struggle. In a study co-authored with Oskar Negt, which takes issue with Jürgen Habermas' concept of the 'public sphere', Kluge agrees with Habermas that the formation of cultural values is one of the chief areas of political intervention. Since the mass-media virtually hold a monopoly in producing, circulating and consolidating so-called public opinion, they create the consensus which for a majority defines reality. This public sphere, however, according to Kluge and Negt, is far less homogeneous than Habermas assumes, and therefore offers countless areas of resistance, non-accommodation and private rebellion, which Kluge calls 'life-energy produced through friction'.

Kluge's own films want to articulate these areas of resistance, to isolate those events in everyday life that are politically significant and even explosive in the family or outside, but which to the ordinary eye seem merely the private frustrations of living. Only the cinema can, according to Kluge, 'organize' these isolated moments because the principles of montage allow the dialectic operating here to become manifest visually and intellectually.[30] Not surprisingly, for Kluge, to be an independent film-maker does not coincide with having to assume the role of artist. He is not interested in creativity and artistic productivity *per se*, except as a special case of social productivity. Likewise, the idea of the artist as a sovereign subject needs to be superseded by more collective and interactive models of subjectivity.

All his films analyse processes of production: the family in particular, but even the opera, or an argument with a shop assistant is a 'power-station' or a 'building site'. No other director – or writer – is as obsessed as Kluge with production as a metaphor and a reality outside the shop floor and industrial statistics. This more than anything else seems to be the reason why women play the key role in his films. Not only do they bear the main burden of social and biological reproduction, they are also invariably involved in mediating and mitigating the conflicts on the production sites of human intercourse. For Kluge, women's form of productivity is superior to that of capitalism, just as it is also in a sense more archaic. Films like *Yesterday Girl* (1966), *Occasional Work of a Female Slave* (1973) or *The Patriot* (1979) can only be understood if their ostensible subjects (pregnancy, abortion, prostitution, the double exploitation of women at work and in the home, German history teaching, party political congresses) are also seen as parables of production. They show the way the mass media both incessantly represent forms of socially approved productivity, but inhibit, destroy or even criminalise the more 'natural' forms of productivity that human beings invest in their lives, and whose social value goes unacknowledged, even though it represents, according to Kluge, a huge untapped reservoir of energy, which can be mobilised. Unfortunately – such is the irony and dialectic of Kluge's world – this usually

96

Women, the production site of human intercourse: Alexandra Kluge (left) in Kluge's Occasional Work of a Female Slave *(1973)*

happens, on a collective scale, only during wartime: which is why Kluge's other major subject is war.

Over the years Kluge has transformed himself from a theorist of the *Autorenfilm* into a supporter of the *Zuschauerfilm*,[31] though not without taking his distance from either position inasmuch as they became slogans between embattled factions. His critique of the *Autorenfilm* and also his most directly allegorical film about his own film-making is *Artistes at the Top of the Big Top: Disorientated* (*Die Artisten in der Zirkuskuppel: Ratlos*, 1968). Kluge has said that the film was made 'in response to the frustrations I felt after the 1967 Berlin Film Festival, where we [Kluge, Reitz, Enno Patalas] were pelted with rotten eggs by the students.'[32]

The film is ostensibly about 'art' versus 'entertainment', and 'culture' versus 'business'. The debate, as in Syberberg's *Ludwig*, is framed by two limit-situations or qualitative reversals: the politicisation of art, and the aesthetisation of politics. Leni Peickert inherits a circus with which she intends to make socially relevant entertainment, her 'reform-circus'. Twice she goes bankrupt, until she is finally bought out by television. While the story and characters are barely credible, the film's argument proceeds dialogically, from an unstated premise: art today is best served by an impure medium, and it must be both political and popular.

Artistes at the Top of the Big Top: Disorientated caricatures and parodies many of the German New Left positions about target groups, strategies of confrontation and political entrism, about the use of agitprop and of campaigns with limited objectives. The main satirical thrust, and at the same time the self-critical context, is the Young German Film itself. Leni's various ideas for more realism as opposed to stunt numbers, her problems with finance, the endless squabbles with her backers and 'friends', the pompous debates and, finally, the sell-out to television are easily decodable as salient arguments for and against the *Autorenfilm*. The

97

antagonist seems less the commercial film industry (miraculously, Leni constantly inherits money – a reference to the Kuratorium?) than the political and formal avant-garde. Leni's basic problem, how to get a paying public to her show, is only half-heartedly tackled when someone suggests market research, and much more time is spent on crude attempts at making 'political' numbers, a circus equivalent of Godard's *La Chinoise*. Much of the post-Oberhausen euphoria and failure, of partial victories and unholy alliances comes through in the film via allusions to rope tricks and artistic suicides, trapeze numbers without a net, and mortgaging the caravans to pay for the elephants. The moral of the fable shows that in 1967 Kluge already saw quite clearly that the Young German Film would have to be state supported and finally be bailed out by television. Evidently his own experience as a lobbyist went into the film, perhaps too much for *Artistes* to stand on its own as a film. However, it makes clear Kluge's own 'reformist' position: the politics of the 'one step at a time' approach, even and especially in the cinema.

Where Kluge seems closer to the historical avant-garde is in his conception of cinematic forms diametrically opposed to Hollywood. He frequently invokes Brechtianisms like 'the realist method' and 'montage', and when asked about the film-makers that influenced him he mentions Eisenstein and Godard.[33] His idea of film form, however, is both theoretically very complex and in practice very eclectic, based more on sociological theories of communicative interaction than on filmic models. In literature he favours less the novelistic mode of classical narrative and more a combination of oral history, documentary journalism, and a whole variety of often nostalgically evoked folk idioms of narrative (ballads, nursery rhymes, fairy tales).

If one looks closely, his images often come from the pre-history of the cinema, the pictorialism of children's books and popular entertainment (magic lantern, cheap book illustrations and penny dreadfuls) or *Kitsch* reproductions of the classics as one used to find in parental bedrooms. Filmic references, where present at all, are most likely to be old newsreel. The chaos of his disparate visual sources and the often artlessly shot footage that makes up the narrative give the spoken or written word in his films almost invariably the dominant role. The result is that as a film-maker he is criticised by the 'Sensibilists' for depriving the visuals of any sensuous presence, by the political documentarists for manipulating his material, and by feminist film-makers because the sarcasm and irony of his commentary often makes his female protagonists twist and turn like helpless and manic puppets.

Feminist Authors?

When the battle-cry 'Daddy's cinema is Dead' raised hopes for an effective change in the landscape of film-making, it turned out after all to be the old conflict between sons and fathers. It is therefore symptomatic that among the 26 Oberhausen signatories not one was a woman.[34]

In the initial stages of the struggle over the *Autorenfilm*, women had very little part either in its theory or its practice. Or so it seems. Of the women directors active before 1970 (Ula Stöckl, May Spils, Dore O. and Erika Runge) only two made feature films. 'It went so far that for part of the time, I felt as if I was not present; not even misunderstood, just non-existent'.[35]

In the press Ula Stöckl was habitually associated with her male partner Edgar

Reitz, while May Spils, after making one of the most successful films of the Young German Film, *Zur Sache, Schätzchen* (*Let's Get Down to Business, Darling*, 1967), followed it up with commercially oriented productions and work mainly for television. The breakthrough for women into films therefore did not come from the vicinity of Oberhausen and the Kuratorium, although at Kluge and Reitz' Ulm Academy a large percentage of staff and students were women (Ula Stöckl, Oimel Mai, Beate Mainka-Jellinghaus, Claudia Alemann and Jeanine Meerapfel were all associated with Ulm between 1964–1980).

One significant aspect of feminism, however, directly overlapped with the underlying tenets of the *Autorenfilm*: the demand for self-expression and the right to a partial and subjective point of view. Here was both a contact point, and an area of friction, between the work of the women and the men. As Pam Cook argues in respect of feminism, self-expression 'is a concept which, with emphasis on the personal, the intimate and the domestic has always been important to the Women's Movement, and the personal diary form, for instance, has always been a means of self-expression for women to whom other avenues were closed'.[36] Helke Sander explains how this could become a source of friction:

> I always had work and found recognition, so long as I was an artist in the bourgeois sense. Things went downhill when I became a socialist, but real trouble only started after I began actively to work for the interests of women.[37]

When campaigning for their share of the subsidy system in subsequent years, women were particularly concerned to preserve the spirit of solidarity and group

May Spils (centre) filming Let's Get Down to Business, Darling *(1967)*

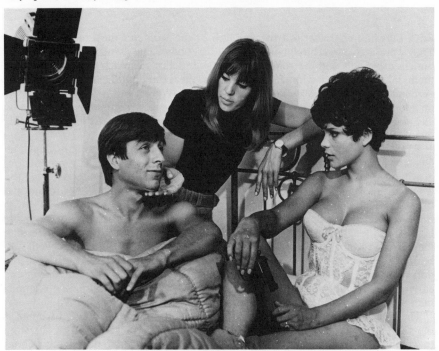

99

Helke Sander's Redupers *(1977)*

work that had characterised the strength of the women's movement generally. They were active in lobbying for professional bodies and associations, distrusting the *Autorenfilm*'s and the subsidy system's tendency to split film-makers and set them in competition with each other. At the Hamburg Festival in 1979 the *Verband der Filmarbeiterinnen* (Association of Women Film Workers) insisted on adding to the concluding Declaration their own, demanding representation on all commissions, committees and juries, as well as statutory parity in the awarding of subsidies.

From 1974 to 1979 feminists were working primarily towards establishing at all levels an alternative approach and a parallel system in the areas of film production, distribution, exhibition and publication, the latter two deriving support from the women's movement as the primary constituency. A leading figure on the organisational, critical and practical side was Helke Sander, who in 1974 set up the first German feminist film journal *frauen und film*. When she came to make her first full-length feature film in 1977 (*Redupers*), much of the history of German feminism, as well as the more specific problems of the artist as feminist, went into both the subject of the film and its theoretical conception. Unlike many of the documentaries and semi-documentaries made by women film-makers during the early 1970s, *Redupers* is explicitly personal, and represents a particular commitment on the part of the director, who also plays the lead.

The melancholy and euphoria of her endeavour as both artist and woman is the very subject of her film. *Redupers* is about the artist subsidised by the state (a woman photographer commissioned by the City of Berlin to do a project about

100

women in the divided city). It is a symptomatic film in that none of the issues are treated in anything other than the ambivalent light in which they present themselves to the naked eye even of an outside observer. As the guardian of wholeness and art, as well as of life in the form of a child (for Sander a double demand that is as intolerable as it is contradictory) her heroine is virtually paralysed by her growing awareness of how important a function in society the woman artist potentially has.

What is of interest in *Redupers* is the conflict between the ideological function of the commissioned artist, her marginalised position and the degree of specialisation and expertise needed beyond her actual art in terms of craft, organisational talent and skill in dealing with bureaucracies. Rather than being displaced, the conflict is starkly presented, without the narrative attempting to resolve the issues. Sander refrains from romanticising her heroine, and her film finds its dignity in a kind of stoic desperation. In many ways *Redupers* can be seen, on a different level of reflection, as a reply to Kluge's *Artistes at the Top of the Big Top* which was, like other of his films with female characters at he centre, quite severely criticised by feminists, not least for using a woman to represent a typically male perspective on state subsidy, independent cinema and the question of artistic creativity.[38]

The development of women directors has in some sense been dephased temporally in relation to that of the men, since they had to catch up almost a decade. Also, the self-representations and self-stylisations, as well as theoretical work on the cinema, often took a much more sophisticated form, both politically and aesthetically. If the biographical aspect seems to predominate in the films of Jutta Brückner, Claudia Alemann and Helma Sanders-Brahms, their feminist interests, as we shall see, are inextricably linked with investigating the social and historical forces that shape their heroine's lives.

But as in the case of Margarethe von Trotta, there is a tension between the more specifically feminist concerns, their recognition that as film directors they have to address a larger public, and that to do so means to look beyond addressing a mainly German audience. In particular, Helma Sanders-Brahms has been at pains to profile herself also as an international film-maker and auteur, since her success with *Germany Pale Mother* (*Deutschland bleiche Mutter*, 1979); just as von Trotta, after the world-wide interest in *The German Sisters* (*Die Bleierne Zeit*, 1981), sees herself as an international director.

The Artist as Artisan

If one of the effects of the mode of production is the attribution of 'quality', conferred on the film or the maker by the public discourses of *Kultur* and of artistic prestige, then for the director the cultural model necessitates training in all areas of film-making. This would especially include camera, lighting, editing and often hiring (or in Herzog's case, 'borrowing') the means of production, while operating a kind of workshop in his own home. 'I work out of my own apartment – in one room. I have no secretary. I do taxes, book-keeping, contracts, script writing, organizing, everything myself – as an article of faith.'[39]

One is not always aware how frequently directors also took on the jobs of editors (Franz Walsh was Fassbinder's pseudonym in the role) or cameramen (Fassbinder did the camerawork on his *The Third Generation* (*Die Dritte Generation*, 1979), and Kluge has called Reitz 'a cameraman of genius'). This is in spite of the fact that, apart from Schlöndorff and Wenders, no director of the first or second generation went to film school, and hardly anyone completed an apprenticeship as assistant director in the film industry – a fact that may explain why the myth of the autodidact and 'starting from zero' proved so pervasive and appealing.

When the Ulm Film School was founded in the wake of Oberhausen, and discussions began for Film Academies in Berlin and Munich, the goals were defined in terms of education and craft, rather than specialisation or vocational training. In Ulm the inspiration was the ideas of the Bauhaus, in Berlin a socialist hope for the all-round developed personality. But in practice, as most of those involved realised, the *Autorenfilmer* were shopkeepers:

> Wildenhahn calls [them] retailers, Alexander Kluge ascribes to them the status of small businesses, coming from the artisan section of the middle-class. Indeed, sociologically film-makers are traders; subsidy is their trading licence. Economically, the German cinema as a whole has the endearing role of the good old corner shop.[40]

The Oberhausen ideal, out of an anti-capitalist, anti-industry impulse, as Sheila Johnston rightly remarks, was almost stridently petit bourgeois. In many of the early statements by German film-makers one finds the image of the artisan even more than that of the artist: a pride in workmanship, in the physical aspects of film-making, the sensuousness of handling film equipment and the strip of celluloid in the editing room:

> The contact with things is the root of my view of work today, of my interest in details. My view of quality and morality, of beauty is shaped by the early encounter with the craft of my father . . . I have always had an artisan's approach to my own films. I think they are better in the details than overall. As finished works they hardly ever fulfilled the purpose for which they were intended. They were neither successful in the marketplace as goods, nor can one say that they corresponded to the critical trends of their day. My main pleasure was with the experience of quality in their making.[41]

Edgar Reitz, writing in 1981, neatly conveys the tension in which this conviction of artisanal pleasure found itself: as a defensive reaction to the demands, on the one hand, of being artists in the culture industry, and on the other of being wholesalers, or at least retailers in the marketplace. Herzog ironically remarked, when asked how it felt to be an independent producer: 'I'm like any market stallholder: registered as self-employed.'[42] In an almost literal sense, throughout the 1960s and 1970s, each film was a manufacture, which in so far as it came to the market at all, had to compete with the high-tech and expertly packaged articles of the international entertainment industry. When critics were able to point out how cheaply the Germans produced their films, or when Syberberg prided himself on the fact that his *Our Hitler* (1977) was shot in 20 days and cost no more than $500,000,[43] there was a danger of believing that artistic integrity, will-power, pluck and ingenuity were all that was needed for independent cinema to pull itself up by its bootstraps to international success. But it was just as much an indication that, for a certain period, West German film-making was no more than a cottage industry kept alive like a quaint local craft through the 'artificial respiration' of the subsidy system. The pride in quality and workmanship was necessary, not least to justify to the directors themselves the long hours and appalling odds involved in film-making.

Yet what from one perspective may appear as backwardness (and a consequence of the uneven development noticeable whenever Hollywood confronts different national or independent cinemas), can also be an advantage when it becomes a product differentiation and an exhibition value in its own right. Herzog expressed this paradox most completely, because he was able to transform the reality of his 'backward' situation as an artisan into a special brand image, to the point where the image almost became a parody. In 1972, it was still a modest ambition: 'Some people acquire houses, I own films. My films are my wealth and I feel that I possess all the attributes of a well-to-do person: I can work on something I enjoy, and I am independent.'[44] The very same image is used by Fassbinder: 'I want to build a house with my films. Some are the cellar, some the walls, and again, others are the windows. But I hope that in the end, it will be a house.'[45]

In Herzog's case, however, the presentation of himself soon oscillated between that of a Bavarian woodcarver, as in the artist-as-ski-jumper (self)portrait *The Great Ecstasy of the Woodcarver Steiner* (1973/4), and of a medieval stonemason:

> Some people have written that I'm a figure out of the nineteenth century, but they are wrong. The appropriate time for me would be the late middle ages. I feel close to the music and painting of that time. It would also fit the concept of my work. I don't feel like an artist, I feel like a craftsman. All the sculptors and painters of the period didn't regard themselves as artists, but rather as craftsmen. That is exactly how I feel about my work as a film-maker – as if I were anonymous, I couldn't even care.[46]

How deeply the craft mentality pervades the self-understanding of film-makers can be seen from an episode in Edgar Reitz' diary, when he was preparing a scene in *Heimat* (1984) at a watch-maker's shop: 'The camera was set up, in the close-ups it was my hands that took apart the watch, and I could have gone on forever [until the cameraman] said: "we're not here to make an educational documentary about watchmakers, we still have some action scenes to shoot".'[47]

The most accomplished and also ironic self-stylisation of the film-maker as artisan is Wim Wenders' *The American Friend* (*Der amerikanische Freund*, 1977). In the story of Jonathan Zimmermann, the frame-maker from Hamburg who gets embroiled first in the sale of fake paintings by a supposedly dead artist, and then in the mafia's international pornography business, Wenders made a double parable. It is not only the story of the German film-maker *vis-à-vis* Hollywood and its aftermath, of the relationship between art and commerce and between Germany and the United States: it is also about the value that is now attached to the New German Cinema abroad, as a cinema made up of craftsmen, sticklers for detail, but who get caught up in things bigger than they can handle. Even before his involvement with Coppola, *The American Friend* anticipated Wenders' troubles in Hollywood. The independent film-maker as artisan came up, inevitably, against the international film industry and the power of the producer mafia.

The Author as Producer

The programming of the artist-director into the subsidy system may account for the proliferation of self-images noticeable in German films. Practically, however, the main concern of the *Autor* was to attract as many forms of subsidy or prize money to his person and to keep control of them. Since both automatic subsidy and the film prizes of the Ministry of the Interior were awarded to the film's producer (reflecting the fact that this form of aid came from an economic as opposed to cultural source), the writer-director often enough also became his

The Ethics of a Craftsman: Bruno Ganz in Wenders' The American Friend *(1977)*

own producer. This took to its logical conclusion the ideology of the *Autorenfilm* with the director obtaining complete creative and executive authority, which he did primarily out of an economic motive, itself imposed on him by the subsidy system and its 'mixed economy'. Johannes Schaaf never forgave his producer for using the automatic subsidy earned by *Tätowierung* (1967), Schaaf's first film, in order to make a pornographic comedy.[48] Self-expression and creative control must thus also be seen under the aspect of economic-political necessity.

Most of those who set up their own production companies (Kluge, Wenders, Reitz, Herzog, Fassbinder, Syberberg and Schlöndorff among others), did so for other practical reasons as well. A frequent complaint among young film-makers was the absence of qualified or honest producers with whom they could have gone into partnership. Herzog spoke of 'gangsters'[49] and accounts of how Artur Brauner, West Germany's most powerful post-war commercial producer, had treated Fritz Lang while he was making *The Indian Tomb* and *The 1000 Eyes of Dr Mabuse* circulated as moral tales.[50]

However, along with the creative control which writer-director-producer status gave a film-maker, came also a permanent state of pressure. Some of the more eccentric behaviour of German directors on their way to recognition must have a partial explanation in the at once isolated and exalted position which their all-round responsibilities gave them. If the intention of the Kuratorium was that they should not suffer the 'legal or serious financial risks' attendant on a commercial film production they none the less, as the fate of Fassbinder and others was to show, exposed themselves not only to financial, but also to physical risk.

After eight years, two film-makers finally made their second film. In reply to my petit-bourgeois question, what in heaven's name had they been living off during all these years, they gave the laconic reply: debts. – How much did they owe? 300,000 DM. There was even a faint smirk. Another film school graduate: 'never again my own producer'. That was the mistake she made with her first film. For two years, the receiver came once a week. 'In the end, the man was really sorry for me and brought me cake baked by his mother.'[51]

Directors, though heading their own production company, in fact went into partnership with other directors (the famour *Filmverlag der Autoren* was started by Wenders, Brandner, Fassbinder, Herzog and others; Schlöndorff's company *Bioskop* comprises also film-makers Hauff and von Trotta). Alternatively they joined with one of the new producers spawned by the subsidy jungle (Wenders' company *Road Movies* was a joint venture by himself, the writer and film-director Peter Handke, and two producers with degrees in business law and economics). The most important production and distribution company for Berlin film-makers, 'Basis Film', came about when director Christian Ziewer decided that his film *Dear Mother, I'm Fine* (1971) needed as much attention in the distribution as in the production stage and he hired Clara Burckner.[52] Others, such as Herzog, employ the same executive producer, Walter Saxer, from film to film, who effectively takes on most of the roles of the traditional producer, with the exception – an important one – of raising finance.

If commercially-minded producers could deprive a director of the benefits of automatic subsidy, the reverse was perhaps more often the case: a producer–director helping another director to a start by putting at his disposal money from automatic subsidy and going into co-production. Wim Wenders, who while tied up with *Hammett* was receiving more automatic subsidy from previous films than he was himself able to invest in new projects, co-financed via his production company films like Chris Petit's *Radio On*, and wholly financed the film of his editor, Peter Przygodda, *Als Diesel Geboren* (*Born for Diesel*, 1979). The same is true of Schlöndorff, von Trotta and Hauff, who had automatic subsidy invested in a film by Herbert Achternbusch for which he was unable to get television co-production.[53]

The Author and the Committees

Politically, the *Autorenfilm* often demanded self-governing structures for film financing (as they were introduced at the regional level in Hamburg and Düsseldorf during the late 1970s). Various professional bodies, notably the *Arbeitsgemeinschaft Neuer Deutscher Spielfilmproduzenten*, set up as a counter-weight to the SPIO, were represented on virtually all the subsidy committees. Yet, by the middle of the 1970s, the very success of the funding system in penetrating and reorganising most aspects of the German cinema led to a widespread conviction of a takeover of film and film production by state bureaucracies. In the absence of market forces regulating supply and demand, film-makers confronted in the first instance neither Hollywood nor the domestic public, but the committees. The result was, as Volker Schlöndorff somewhat cynically remarked: 'In Germany we now make films for an audience of eleven, eight of whom sit on the Project Commission of the Film Subsidy Board.'[54]

The question of legitimation in the general sense gave way to a more specific problem. Had the *Autorenfilm*, even though the director took on the role of producer, perhaps simply moved the old producer/director hierarchy one step further along, with the committees acting as faceless super-producers? The dilemma was the unresolved split between material dependence on the vote and approval of committees, and the film-makers' moral superiority in questioning the committees' right to judgement. In practice one could detect a persistent but radical ambiguity. On the one hand there existed, for most of the decade, a latent process of self-censorship among film-makers who, understandably, had learnt to internalise the criteria of the subsidy boards, in order to get their projects vetted positively. On the other hand, the very subservience to an authority only partially accepted as legitimate made directors complain about a 'ghetto of culture'. The more successful the director, one might almost say, the more s/he became an enemy of the subsidy system: it deprived her or him of any realistic calculation of executive power.

The most vociferous criticism of the *Gremienkino* (cinema by committee) came not from film-makers, but from the critics. The absence of any precise reference points for a national film culture made expectations both pressing and diffuse, and the criticisms raised were correspondingly disparate and confusing. Because the films rarely found the kind of distribution that would put them in touch with a mass audience, critics and journalists had to stand in for a non-existing public, for an audience who otherwise might have been in at least some sort of dialogue with the film-makers.

What complicated the issue was the fact that no clear distinction could be made between the pressures from the grant-awarding institutions and those from the press, since many of the committees were in fact staffed with film journalists working for daily or weekly papers. This must account for the more than troubled and acrimonious atmosphere which existed between film-makers and their critics, since these critics not only took an active part in the formation of public taste, but also made decisions about the approval or rejection of specific projects. There have been, over the years, a number of highly publicised leaks from former members of the selection committees, whose revelations further helped to poison the climate. 'Critics went into the committees, practically became co-producers, in order then to write deferential court reports about the films they had themselves voted subsidies. I call this a scandal of the first order.'[55]

But the charge was less that of corruption for personal gain or even of hidden political censorship as much as for encouraging timid, dull films.

> After a brief period of relatively open possibilities for coalition, changing majorities, party-political trade-offs and even bold individual decisions, the consolidation of the funding institutions and their committees has, predictably, led to bureaucratic structures imposing themselves as cultural policy . . . The result: faceless films, averaged-out products of a consensus derived from disoriented mediocrity.[56]

While government funding for the arts generally is always fraught with precisely such problems of balancing expertise with impartiality, film-making in Germany for the first decade experienced a gap between the relatively generous funding provisions and the heavily bureaucratic structures created to administer them. With projects being scrutinised at so many stages by officials, the film-maker was part of state culture, but at a low level of organisation. He was faced with the basic contradiction of being treated as a free artist at one end of the system and as an accountable employee at another end.

Criticism of the *Gremienkino* indicated dissatisfaction not only with the way cultural subsidy was administered, but more generally became a covert attack on

106

the principle of the *Autorenfilm* itself, as it had become established over the previous ten years. The *Autor* was being blamed for having made the German cinema intellectual and elitist. By the late 1970s one could read virtually the same attacks, now from the left, that were voiced in the mid-1960s by the trade press on the right:

> Because they do not know their craft, because the physical qualities of cinema are unknown to them, the author-film-makers tried to compensate for their deficiencies with thoughtlessness (which they called a higher form of abstraction) and the invention of arbitrary rules (e.g. theories of montage), while letting themselves be celebrated as 'artists' . . . It almost seems as if [the low share of the domestic market] suited our film-makers very well, since they would rather work for small specialised audiences anyway . . . One has the impression that West German authors' cinema is the final desperate attempt at making expensive home movies and passing them off as a mass medium.[57]

The Author and the Literary Classics

The clearest sign of growing dissatisfaction with the concept of the *Autorenfilm* and the *Gremien* came in 1977, when a number of state prizes were awarded to films taken from well-known novels or treating literary figures. Helma Sanders-Brahms' *Heinrich* (1977), and Heidi Genée's *Grete Minde* (1976), after a novella by Theodor Storm, were mercilessly pilloried. Suddenly, all the problems of the German cinema were blamed on its uncinematic reliance on literature.

> Where are German movie authors like Paul Schrader or Robert Towne? Instead, we have committees calculating adaptations, a marketing of remaindered novels, culture from the book-cases of bourgeois homes, dusted-off classics of the German tongue. The tell-it-again cinema is booming.[58]

The predominance of literary classics as source material for the New German Cinema was itself an expression of the cultural legitimation gap. It was thus a symptom rather than a cause of the troubled relationship between film-makers and their clients, the critics. Seen as a reaction to a stiffening political climate, the literary adaptation films came to be regarded as a direct consequence of film-makers playing it safe for the subsidy committees, and thus as a collusion between directors out to please their judges and committee members nervous about backing politically sensitive subjects. Filmed literature sells German culture twice over, as film and as literature, while also going down well on television and even abroad in literature classes of Modern Language Departments. Is it not in the very nature of an official body to favour culturally prestigious material of proven artistic value? Quite apart from the fact that committees feel more comfortable reading scripts with literary pretensions than trying to imagine how the outline of a visual idea might work as cinema.

This cynical view seems as much part of the problem as it is its explanation. The attack on filmed novels, plays and costume dramas as uncinematic is itself not new, and is as common as its reverse, the dismissal of adaptation as a betrayal of the literary text. One of the mainstays of virtually every commercial film industry is the appropriation of the classics for the screen and for television. It could be argued, therefore, that the appearance of films based on Fontane, Kleist, Döblin, on Thomas and Heinrich Mann, Günter Grass or Heinrich Böll simply indicated that the New German Cinema had by the mid-1970s assumed the function of a film industry, at least in the special sense of having become the representative and dominant form of film-making in West Germany. Throughout the 1960s and 1970s 'commercial' German producers had carried on their habits from the 1930s, 1940s and 1950s: making films of Sudermann, Ganghofer or Johanna Spyri novels. The difference might be that the New German Cinema was renewing the tradition of an art cinema as it existed in the 1920s by choosing Kleist rather than Ganghofer and Böll rather than Simmel. But in each case it was a question of bringing into the cinemas an audience favourably disposed towards story material or drama already possessing a certain recognition value or seal of approval.

Secondly, it would be quite wrong to speak of literary adaptation as a genre. To shuffle together the nth version of Ludwig Ganghofer's *The Hunter of the Falls* (*Der Jäger vom Fall*, 1974) with Jean-Marie Straub's *Not Reconciled* (1965), Fassbinder's *Effi Briest* (1974) or Eric Rohmer's *The Marquise of O* (1976) is plainly absurd. The predilection for certain writers such as Kleist, Fontane, Storm and Büchner hints, as mentioned earlier, at particular affinities or parallels with the contemporary situation. The collaboration of post-war German writers with film-makers (Heinrich Böll and Günter Grass with Volker Schlöndorff, Peter Handke with Wim Wenders), or the cases of literary authors becoming film authors (Peter Handke, Herbert Achternbusch, Uwe Brandner and Thomas Brasch) need to be seen in the context of the changing function of literature itself, as well as the inherently literary bias of the authors' cinema.

Finally, if among the increasing number of feature films produced during the 1970s – an average of about 80 a year – a sizeable proportion were not based on literary material either classic or contemporary, the situation would require even more comment than it received. Although the selection process and the participation of television massively favoured narrative over non-narrative films, and feature length projects over experimental or documentary shorts, one of the major problems mentioned already in the late 1960s by directors such as Schlöndorff or Lilienthal was the dearth of professional scriptwriters in Germany.[59]

The very successes of the German cinema thus not only brought film-making closer to the basic story material of the commercial film industry, but attracted modern writers to the medium and fostered dual talents. In fact, the situation in West Germany only repeated with a time lag what had characterised most post-war European film-making – a symbiotic relationship between contemporary literature and national art cinemas.[60]

The reasons why the literary adaptations became such a polemical issue have also to do with the fact that originality and personal vision, crucial to the ideology of the *Autorenfilm*, were themselves profoundly literary criteria, and ultimately unsuitable by themselves for an evaluation of the cinema as either an artistic or a popular medium. While critics complained about impersonality, academicism, lack of innovation and a shying away from topical subjects, film-makers countered by accusing the project commissions of being responsible for the high number of filmed novels and plays. A veritable daisy chain of mutual recriminations demonstrated the ghetto mentality and parochialism of film culture, but also the ideological nature of the debate.

The Author in Television

If the committees became for the author-producer the good-bad objects that

Arthur Brauner, Horst Wendlandt or Luggi Waldleitner had been for Fritz Lang and commercial maverick directors like Rolf Thiele or Will Tremper in the 1950s, the television networks were much more formidable super-producers. It was not only that without their co-production blessing very few films could get made at all – nine out of ten have TV money written into the budget – but because of the 'domino effect', the committees (on which television is well represented) were reluctant to make awards if WDR or ZDF had already given the project the thumbs down.

Television has been very supportive of the German *Autorenfilm*, in practice and also ideologically. Heads of Drama and Film, such as Heinz Ungureit and Günter Rohrbach, became the godfathers of the New German Cinema. They became so not least by writing about it, entering into public debate and coining slogans and catchphrases (such as Rohrbach making his plea for the 'amphibious film', when the results of the framework agreement were attacked for having spawned uncinematic films). The phrase may not have been more than a euphemism for films that were neither fish nor fowl, a compromise between the film-maker's ambition to make 'real cinema', and the commissioning editor's concern that the home viewer should get enough close ups, shot-countershots, and a storyline that would survive a quick trip to the toilet or the fridge. But it led even in non-specialised journals like *Die Zeit* to public discussion about the specificity of the two media, and thus contributed, indirectly, to creating a new audience for the cinema.[61]

Günter Rohrbach or Eckhardt Stein from ZDF's *Das kleine Fernsehspiel* (which gave women directors as well as many foreign independent directors vital chances of directing first feature films) were not acting on a philanthropic impulse. Since German television sub-contracts much of its programming, the *Autor* perfectly fitted into its production system as a freelance worker, and television benefited from his or her existence in at least two respects.

Firstly in economic respects: from an 'author' the networks could expect work of high quality, done with total commitment at cost price, while the product itself could be advertised as art.

> Which employee would today work himself to the very edge of self sacrifice, as do these small entrepreneurs? There are those who know how to value such dedication. Television people know full well that during the long march on their desk-tops from left to right not much first-class material emerges. [After all, they] are mainly paid to chop bulky, awkward and oversized creativity into handy parcels.[62]

Secondly, there were ideological benefits. As Sheila Johnston concluded, after looking at different statements by German television executives:

> The reasons [for television companies favouring *Autorenfilme*] were also connected with their status as public corporations charged with mirroring 'the principle of a representative democracy'. As such, according to Friedrich Wilhelm von Sell (Intendant of the WDR) they had to follow the principle of 'mediating a plurality of opinions'. Von Sell argued that one way of ensuring that 'a variety of opinions on all important subjects' could be conveyed was by purchasing material from freelance sources . . . But as well as being representative, the television companies also had to be 'balanced' . . . The concept of the *Autor* fitted neatly into this pattern. By attaching a programme to a 'name' director, the television stations could both avoid the charge of 'excessive timidity' and at the same time acquire as an added bonus the prestige of a patron of the arts.[63]

However, with television reversing the balance of power in the subsidy system, gradually becoming both the majority fund-raiser and the chief exhibitor, the author as a necessary fiction diminished in importance. This came at about the same time as freelance television workers generally began to organise themselves in order to secure permanent posts within the institution, in preference to being celebrated as artists:

> At the ZDF, for years working as a reliable simpleton, who almost always brought back for the department rave reviews from abroad, which raised the self-esteem of these midwives to creation but did not stop them turning a blind eye to the fact that just about every film made by Werner Schroeter cost him more than he was paid.[64]

Harun Farocki once distinguished three types of freelance workers in television. There are those who simply fill the production slots with material. Regardless whether they report on an exhibition in a cultural programme or write a TV play, they completely blend with the institution. Then there are those with a name (known to the network, if not to the public) who convincingly convey the impression of speaking on their own behalf while miraculously confirming the consensus. Finally, those ('remains and reconstructions of the autonomous bourgeois artist-personality') whose livelihood does not depend on the medium, but whose appearance in its constitutes itself an event because they already belong to the so-called real world 'covered' by television.[65]

Independent film-makers generally entered television as the second category. Occasionally, as with R.W. Fassbinder, they advanced to the third. The question of direct or indirect political censorship (as opposed to simply no longer being commissioned) poses itself at the first and second level. A good example were the so-called *Arbeiterfilme* made by film-makers like Christian Ziewer, Erika

Hanna Schygulla in Fassbinder's The Third Generation *(1979)*

110

Runge, Helma Sanders-Brahms and Fassbinder in the early 1970s. These were *Autorenfilme* but, because they dealt very specifically with social and political issues, they brought to crisis point two sets of television practices: the enforcement of a clear demarcation line between news, current affairs and documentary on the one hand, and drama (that is, fiction) on the other. Secondly, they violated the unwritten rule that 'balance' and 'objectivity' must be seen to be present on topical and political issues, which in German television means framing the programme with a studio-discussion, a moderator or an introduction. The *Arbeiterfilme* challenged the division between 'information' and 'personal opinion', reinforced by the analogous administrative-departmental divisions. After behind-the-scenes manoeuvres involving the internal WDR hierarchy as well as political pressure and the right-wing national press, such workers' films were no longer commissioned, even though as authors the directors concerned continued to co-produce with television.[66]

The general political situation during the early 1970s, which saw the rise of urban terrorism, and the counter-measures taken by the government including manifest restrictions of civil liberties, made television a particularly sensitive arena. Volker Schlöndorff's contribution to the omnibus film *Germany in Autumn* (*Deutschland im Herbst*, 1978) was a satirical sketch written by Heinrich Böll in which a television programming committee decides to ban the airing of a production of Sophocles' *Antigone*, because members of the committee feel the play takes a pro-terrorist view and shows a brother and sister in open defiance of State authority, under circumstances too reminiscent of the Baader-Meinhof suicides not to appear inflammatory.

Angela Winkler (right) as Antigone in Germany in Autumn *(1978)*

111

The implication was that many projects coming before the programming committees would be vetoed out of political caution, without it appearing as direct editorial pressure on the freedom of expression. Only the best-known victims of such measures (directors whose activity constituted 'events') were able to attract enough attention to make this form of interference public. Fassbinder frequently mobilised the press in order to protest against what he saw as politically motivated censorship. His television series *Soll und Haben*, an adaptation of a ninteenth-century classic by Gustav Freytag intended as the chronologically earliest instalment of his history of Germany, was cancelled even before it went into production after leaks and accusations of anti-semitism.

> The fact that the Director General von Sell vetoed the project, without even reading the existing material or discussing it, is something we had not seen before. He did it to establish a new power potential . . . I realized that a small area of freedom which still existed in television . . . had become impossible.[67]

Fassbinder's skirmishes with cautious committees only strengthened his antipathy to the subsidy system in general and his belief in the virtues of free enterprise. Sheila Johnston quotes an interview where he commented on the difficulties with his backers over *The Third Generation* (*Die Dritte Generation*, 1979):

> In the end, the Westdeutsche Rundfunk withdrew its offer for political reasons. The producer said to me that in the film an opinion is put forward which he is unable to share and did not feel he could defend to the broadcasting house. The representative of the Berlin Senate also backed out . . . When they called if off we were already in the first week of shooting . . . Only by piling up debts without knowing how they are to be repaid can films be made that might one day result in an industry. I can't imagine it any other way because I don't find it such a good idea to try to build up an industry through committees and lobbies – in the end you have to make too many compromises. You just have to do it the capitalist way, on speculation and risk.[68]

Television Co-production

> A particular state's TV operations, its popularity, its appeal to different sectors of the population, its distinctive aesthetic strengths and weaknesses, its openness or hostility to innovatory ideas, all of these factors affect the kind of cinema that is on offer in a country.[69]

West German television, with its regional, largely autonomous networks has had a shaping influence on film production in two major ways. Through its votes on the Film Subsidy Board it can influence the funding of independent projects as a whole, and through the different commissioning editors, notably those of WDR, ZDF, NDR and SDR, it exercises direct power over a crucial sector: that of television co-productions. While during the 1960s and early 1970s a substantial number of projects in the area of television drama were supplied by outside sources, one of the effects of the 1974 Framework Agreement was to bring co-production with independent directors more in-house, and thus turn television administrators into executive film producers. In ways remotely reminiscent of the producer-director alliance prevailing in the commercial film industry during the studio system, West German film-makers developed close and regular working relationships with individual executive editors. Some of the teams at WDR were: Fassbinder and Peter Märthesheimer (who co-wrote some of Fassbinder's scripts), Edgar Reitz and Joachim von Megershausen (also WDR) and von Trotta and Gunther Witte (WDR). Schlöndorff usually works for HR in Frankfurt and Herzog for SDR Baden Baden. The key role at WDR during the 1970s was held by Günter Rohrbach as Head of feature production, and at ZDF by Eckardt Stein. They scouted for talent among newcomers and film school graduates and acted as commissioning editors for the more established directors. Certain networks have preferred house-directors, and film-makers such as Reinhardt Hauff, Volker Vogeler, Peter Lilienthal, Klaus Lemke and Wolfgang Petersen are regularly approached by editors with specific projects, which is the reverse of the author-relationship where film-makers bring their projects to the networks.

On the other hand, there are a number of television directors – Wolfgang Menge, Eberhard Fechner, Peter Beauvais and Ilse Hofmann – with no marked ambition towards cinema and author status, but who none the less have an important role in so far as they specialise in turning topical subjects or 'real life' problems (industrial pollution, divorce, delinquency or truancy, mid-life crisis, drug abuse) into effective television drama.[70]

Their programmes satisfy one of television's social functions, namely to provide journalistic information, or popularise areas of specialised research in a form that maintains a basic consensus between the state and its members. The personalised and dramatised sociological case study has emerged as the most effective and economic way of filling this brief, not only in Germany. The organisation of television in respect of made-for-TV movies, mini-series and drama in West Germany does not differ markedly from that of other European countries. Adaptations of literary bestsellers (*Soweit die Füsse tragen, Tadellöser & Wolf*), long-running family sit-coms, soap operas like the *Black Forest Clinic* and filmed plays form the staple of indigenous product. On the other hand, writers like Heinrich Böll, Peter Weiss, Peter Handke, Max von der Grün and Tankred Dorst have all written or adapted their work for television.

However, in contrast to, say, British television, which because of its traditional links with the theatre tends to make the writer rather than the director the star, German television is notable for the more risk-taking policy of encouraging first-time film-makers. In this respect, socially 'relevant' issues and individual authors can complement each other, rather than stand in opposition. The films of Christian Ziewer, for instance (a director barely known outside Germany), are a good example. Ziewer is considered an *Autor* of the New German Cinema, but he is so much identified with the *Arbeiterfilme*, a typical television venture, that every attempt he has made since to establish an independent identity as a cinema director (*From Afar I See This Country*, 1979, the story of an immigrant worker, and *Death of a White Horse*, 1985, a costume drama set during the sixteenth-century Peasants' War) has been unsuccessful.

Similarly, Peter Lilienthal is considered to be an important *Autor*, known through television. Working mainly for ZDF, Lilienthal has one of the most solid reputations and track-records as a left-liberal director with an excellent knowledge of Latin American issues. Since 1960 he has made over 30 television films, documentaries and feature films, and his forte is effective but unsensationalist dramatisations of the external and internal states of siege in conditions of political repression (*La Victoria*, 1973; *Calm Prevails in the Country*, 1976; *The Uprising*, 1980; *The Autograph*, 1984). Yet when he made a more classically conceived

113

The Third World meets the First: (above) Ziewer's From Afar I See This Country *(1979) and (below) armed insurrection in Vlado Kristl's* The Letter *(1966)*

cinema film, about a small-time Jewish nightclub owner pressurised by the Mafia, with location shooting in New Jersey and an English-language cast starring Joe Pesci (*Dear Mr Wonderful*, 1982), he disappointed the expectations of his politicised, 'contentist' spectators without making the transition to the 'sensibilist' art cinema faction.

The filmography of many West German directors is therefore usefully read not only against the various stages of the Film Subsidy Law and its revisions, but also in the light of the television co-producer, the network and programming slot for which a particular project was commissioned or accepted. This, as we shall see, is especially true of one of the most typical products of television co-production, the women's film, which in many ways encapsulates the achievements of the New German Cinema outside its international auteurs.

If an institutional analysis of German feature film production must focus on the funding structure and the ideological role of the *Autorenfilm*, an investigation of the films' audience-orientation must take account both of the relative anonymity of much of the product broadcast by television, and of the survival and mutation of genre-categories inherited from the cinema. The New German Cinema found, via its funding structure, one part of its domestic audiences on television. Much of the logic of its production comes from commissioning editors filling pre-established programme grids with material that keeps a balance between general relevance of the subject matter and the individualised, recognisably authorial form of the presentation. Kluge has gone so far as to call this the 'Babylonian captivity' of the German cinema: slave to the sub-contract, it has developed neither valid alternatives to the dominant model of the Hollywood feature film nor cinematic forms wholly independent from television.

Within the television programming structure slots such as ZDF's *Das kleine Fernsehspiel*[71] or WDR's 'Third Programme' allowed commissioning editors to accommodate productions whose artistic status needs showcasing, or where the 'personal', 'experimental' or 'politically controversial' element demands a specially designated frame. This meant that even where independent directors had access to the only national audience that still existed, they did so at viewing times and under conditions which marginalised their work or assigned it to a ghetto. Most film-makers, therefore, entertained with the television networks a relationship somewhere between that of a small business, supplying components to a large manufacturer (in this case, individual programmes for the overall schedule) and that of the autonomous entrepreneur who markets, sometimes with the help of a bigger organisation, his own line of products. However, almost without exception, German directors see themselves as film-makers rather than TV directors, and they think of the cinema as the natural home for their work.

From Author to Auteur

The internal contradictions of the authors' cinema, under pressure to prove itself both original and popular, are instructive partly because they indicate to what extent the New German Cinema in Germany itself was as much a matter of keeping alive debates that would validate the films and legitimise the cinema, as it was a struggle for the means of production and the physical making of films.

The potency of *Autorenkino* as a trademark declined at the end of the 1970s, not because the director became less important than the producer or because the international cinema functions anonymously or by genre. On the contrary, during the same period one can observe the increasing importance of the author-producer as brand name in the international film industry, alongside the star. Spielberg, Lucas, Coppola and de Palma are box office draws in their own right almost as much as Clint Eastwood, Burt Reynolds or Robert Redford. What undermined the *Autorenfilm* in Germany as a crucial ideological support of the funding structure were changes in the objective conditions, on both sides of the equation, as it were. With the sheer volume of films increasing, the industrial model re-emerged, now supported by the voracious demands of television.

For most of the 1960s the German cinema's very limited success with the public allowed the *Autorenfilm* to exist intact as a focus and rallying point, however much the individual film-maker's situation might have been at variance with its basic tenets. By the mid-1970s, with the full diversity of cultural and economic funding measures established, the author became a necessary ideological fiction. Split between being, on one side of the funding system, an artist, and on another a self-employed entrepreneur, working under conditions of the craftsman and the bricoleur, in a *metier* dominated by a sophisticated division of labour and capitalist marketing techniques, German film-makers grasped at the concept of the *Autor* as the most authentic and viable self-image. In order to add up to a workable mode of production, in other words, the subsidy system itself, as a multiplication of the sources of financial aid, required the *Autor* as its addressee and counterpart, since he alone could provide a principle of coherence among the maze of conflicting economic and cultural discourses.

In this sense, the author was indeed an institution, in so far as he functioned both as a principle of production coherence and, over time, with the increasing international fame of some of them, also became an 'auteur' of the international art cinema. On the side of the author, self-expression became redefined as self-image, leading to a 'marketing' of the name as itself the seal of quality and a brand name. Caught in the middle were all those film-makers who did not want their work to disappear down television, but did not, or would not, achieve star status either.

4:

In Search of the Spectator 1:
From Oberhausen to Genre Films?

Living Down the Oberhausen Legacy

It seems difficult to establish a stylistic continuity between the Young German Film and the German cinema of the 1970s. Firstly, the political positions supporting the theory of film authorship varied greatly. Secondly, as the previous chapter tried to show, directors represented their situation and self-understanding as *Autoren* in highly specific terms. Reaction to Oberhausen ranged from the political rejection of the very concept of the *Autorenfilm* (and of state funding by the avant-garde) via the commercial exploitation of the new subsidy laws (by

'German tourists in Sardinia': Hans Jürgen Syberberg's Scarabea *(1968)*

'renegades' like Rob Houwer or Hans Jürgen Pohland), to the emergence of young representatives of the *Altbranche* (such as Eckhart Schmidt or Manfred Purzer). But the discontinuity can be traced in and through the films themselves.

By trying to project a new realism and opting for the satirical eye, the Young German Film had, according to critics like Hembus and Patalas, displayed patronising condescension towards its subjects. Syberberg's *Scarabea* was reviewed by Patalas' journal *Filmkritik* in terms which revived such accusations:

> Syberberg shows us a German . . . tourist on Sardinia, who eats like a pig, is loud, chases women, is ignorant about Gottfried Benn, and drinks too much wine . . . Thus prepared, it should come as no surprise that Syberberg has the same arrogant attitude to Sardinia and its people as his protagonist.[1]

By the criteria of *Filmkritik*, *Scarabea* (*Scarabea – Wieviel Erde braucht der Mensch?*, 1968) belongs squarely to the Young German Film, from which the New German Cinema differed less by a change of themes and more by the moral point of view it took of its subjects which, of course, implies an aesthetic choice as well. Syberberg may rightly have felt misunderstood, since the 'classical' realist aesthetic of *Filmkritik* (heavily influenced by Siegfried Kracauer) was not altogether the one which established itself in the New German Cinema either, although the 'morality' of the *mise en scène* in a film by Herzog, Fassbinder or Wenders is, as I shall argue, ultimately closer to that of Kracauer or Bazin than are the – diametrically opposed – realisms of Kluge or Schlöndorff. Syberberg's case is particular, since he seems to have rethought the aesthetic assumptions of his film-making when he moved from the pure fiction film to the mixed forms he first discovered in Werner Schroeter's films.

By the same criteria of the moral point of view, Herzog might be said to have belonged from his very first films to the New German Cinema. Although his documentary *Letzte Worte* (*Last Words*, 1967/68) and his feature *Signs of Life* (1968) have settings rather like *Scarabea* (a remote island in Greece in the case of Herzog) and are both inspired by classic short stories (Syberberg's by Tolstoy, Herzog's by Achim von Arnim) the films differ substantially. For instance, when comparing the treatment of landscape and the human figure in *Signs of Life* with those of *Scarabea*, it becomes clear that a fundamentally new aesthetic is present in Herzog, one that is almost fanatical in its insistence on physicality and presence, and in forcing the spectator to recognise and respect the strange otherness of what s/he sees.

One can discuss the difference starting from two opposed ends. As we have seen in Patalas' critique of Kluge, the objection was to the treatment of the pro-filmic material ('reality by the cart-load') and, therefore, to the director's attitude to the characters ('evidence for a trial'), but also to the treatment of the filmic material (absence of sync-sound, editing) and, therefore, to the discursive relation with the spectator. Herzog (and Straub) are primarily committed to establishing a certain attitude or stance *vis-à-vis* the spectator, which necessarily determines their attitude to the pro-filmic (Straub's form of minimalism, Herzog's insistence on the otherness of a landscape or a people). Syberberg or Kluge attempt to define a strategy (of argument, of persuasion) to which the specifically filmic processes become secondary (hence their preference for mixed film forms, but also the difference between Schroeter's use of opera music or back-projection and Syberberg's). As a consequence, it is only by stressing the differences between the directors in terms of different modes of spectatorial address that one can

118

The human figure in Werner Herzog's (centre) Signs of Life *(1968)*

Shades of Marlene Dietrich: Harry Baer and Ingrid Caven in Fassbinder's Gods of the Plague *(1970)*

Iris Berben, Marquard Bohm, Ulli Lommel in Rudolf Thome's Detectives *(1969)*

Imitation Fassbinder? Ilse Steppat in Kurt Maetzig's Shadows on a Marriage *(1947)*

understand why, for instance, Syberberg felt the need to publish such voluminous commentaries on his own films or why Kluge was at once so central to the film-political development of the New German Cinema and so marginal to its aesthetic programme.

Towards a Genre Cinema?

It has been argued that the influence of *Cahiers du Cinéma* and their enthusiasm for the Hollywood B picture, especially the gangster and film noir genres, signalled towards the late 1960s a new audience-orientation among directors emerging after Oberhausen but who had not formed part of it. In 1967 Klaus Lemke made *48 Hours to Acapulco* and Volker Schlöndorff *A Degree of Murder* (*Mord und Totschlag*), both thrillers that harked back to those of Don Siegel and Sam Fuller in the 1950s. The following years Rudolf Thome made *Detectives* (*Detektive*), and Fassbinder appeared with *Love is Colder Than Death* (*Liebe ist kalter als der Tod*, 1969) and *Gods of the Plague* (*Götter der Pest*, 1970). The films of Lemke and Thome were quite explicitly cinephile exercises in an American genre, somewhere between Howard Hawks' *Rio Bravo* (1958) and Godard's *Bande à part* (1964).[2] German film historians tend to dismiss these films as indicative of an 'overwhelming influence of industrial American culture':

A second generation of young cineastes . . . found their tradition and learnt their

120

Fassbinder imitating: Hanna Schygulla in Lili Marleen *(1980)*

Karlheinz Böhm in Fassbinder's Fox and his Friends *(1975)*

craft in the cinema itself. Socially critical ambitions, the desire to reflect the reality of West Germany or to change it, were articulated if at all, only indirectly. It is significant that quite a few of these directors started as critics; their first films stem from a fascination with the possibilities of the medium itself, which visibly becomes its own subject, and experience of the cinema itself serves as the point of reference . . . In retrospect, these films appear as no more than finger exercises for their directors: Lemke, Thome, and, above all, Fassbinder found their way to new themes and forms. For others – such as Volker Schlöndcrff whose *A Degree of Murder* was the most amusing and masterly attempt in this direction – this game with the stock situations of the genre remained an isolated exercise.[3]

Convincing as this argument may at first appear, such an assessment seems to understate just what importance this brief revival of genres and formula film-making had for the New German Cinema. The idea of finger exercises or exorcism of a cinephile impulse seems shallow, and even the often repeated suggestion that Fassbinder learnt about the use of genre watching Sirk's melodramas, or that a renaissance of the *Heimat* film contributed to the New German Cinema's self-definition as a national cinema, overlooks an important aspect. The re-orientation happened not so much in terms of iconography and even less through formula plots (that is, of the kinds of stories told or the settings used) but in terms of the narrational strategies, of how the spectator was to be involved in the characters. Unlike Godard or Truffaut, who in their first films polemically sought to attach themselves to a particular interpretation of film history (which their characters shared with them), the German independent cinema's experiences with genre – even in the case of Fassbinder and Wenders, the two directors most closely associated with French cinephilia – were not a reaction to the well-made film, the 'tradition of quality', but a reaction to the Oberhausen imitation of that reaction.

It is true that allusionism is part of a complex process whereby film-making assures itself of its own history, and the New German Cinema progressively did just that. This is evident when one considers the case of Fassbinder: the early gangster films, the 1950s Hollywood melodramas, his reworking of the UFA–Stil in *Lili Marleen* (1980) and *Veronika Voss* (1982). It is also evident in his pastiches of so many other historic styles, from quoting specific scenes or shots familiar from German films of the 1950s as in *The Marriage of Maria Braun* and *Lola*, to systematically using well-known German stars from the 1950s in character parts or even in a leading role, as in the case of Karlheinz Böhm for *Fox and his Friends* (1975), *Mother's Küster's Trip to Heaven* (1975), *Effi Briest* (1974) and *Martha* (1973). The career of Niklaus Schilling could serve as an example of a film-maker trying to inscribe himself in a tradition, via allusionism, of the German cinema's own commercial history.[4]

In this context, a glance might be useful at the reaction to Oberhausen on the part of a film-maker like Schlöndorff, who was concerned that the German cinema should not isolate itself in its parochialism. Such a concept is usually associated with a re-evaluation of the strengths of Hollywood genre cinema. But if Wenders and Fassbinder could be said to have explored this path and if Herzog, Schroeter, Syberberg or even Kluge have links with more radical avant-garde traditions, Schlöndorff's films represent quite a different answer to both the Old German Cinema and Oberhausen.

'Tradition of Quality'? The Case of Schlöndorff

Schlöndorff has often chosen formula film-making for the representation of conflict situations, in which the audience could recognise a specific social setting or a moral dilemma, but in a form and through a dramatic development instantly familiar from more classical–conventional American or European models. As such, his target audience is the one which responds to 'big subjects': the middle ground of a national–international film industry on a European scale, but with a potential American market to warrant substantial production values. Having begun in France, as assistant to Alain Resnais and Louis Malle, Schlöndorff's projects and career-moves indicate a careful testing of the modes and formats of the European art cinema and of the liberal tradition of Hollywood.

First of all, he is the director with the closest ties to the German literary establishment. This means that, for the audiences he envisages, the proven literary value of his properties is of significance. But it also implies that, compared to other German *Autoren*, Schlöndorff attaches unusual importance to the professionally well-made script. His first film, *Young Törless* (1965), was taken from Robert Musil's story written in 1906 and shows the literary influence of Joyce and Proust. Schlöndorff and his script writer Herbert Asmodi simplified the complex temporal structure of the story and externalised the stream-of-consciousness narrative into action scenes and set pieces. It was a formula familiar from conventional film adaptations but, in retrospect, it also seems a 'finger exercise' for the more ambitious and even more professional scripts that Jean-Claude Carrière co-wrote for Schlöndorff's other ventures in scaling down modernist fiction, Günter Grass' *The Tin Drum* (*Die Blechtrommel*, 1979) and the Proust adaptation *Swann in Love* (*Eine Liebe von Swann*, 1984).

Between *Young Törless* and *Swann in Love*, Schlöndorff adapted Kleist (*Michael Kohlhaas, The Rebel*, 1969, script by Edward Bond), Brecht (*Baal*, 1969, with Fassbinder in the title role), Henry James (*Georgina's Reasons*; *Georginas Gründe*, 1974), Heinrich Böll (*The Lost Honour of Katharina Blum*), Marguerite Yourcenar (*Coup de grace*; *Der Fangschuss*, 1976), Günter Grass (*The Tin Drum*, 1979), and another German novelist, Nicolas Born (*Circle of Deceit*; *Die Fälschung*, 1981). The apparently unusual project of *Death of a Salesman* (*Tod eines Handlungsreisenden*, 1986), with Dustin Hoffman, is thus a logical continuation for a director working with classical material. *A Degree of Murder* (1967), scripted by the professional screenwriter Gregor von Rezori, was thus an exception only in so far as it belongs to the group of Schlöndorff films (*The Sudden Wealth of the Poor People of Kombach*, 1970, *A Free Woman/Summer Lightning* (*Strohfeuer*, 1972), *The Morals of Ruth Halbfass*, 1971), where he experimented with other forms (the 'New Heimatfilm', the women's film). This was before he identified himself almost completely with the genre of the respectable literary adaptation, enhanced by an international cast (Barbara Steele, David Warner, Charles Aznavour, Jeremy Irons, Alain Delon, Senta Berger, Dustin Hoffman) and the names the New German Cinema itself made famous (Hanna Schygulla, Bruno Ganz, Angela Winkler, Mario Adorf). *The Tin Drum* won Schlöndorff an Oscar, the first ever to be awarded to a film from West Germany.

Schlöndorff has always defended the virtues of calculated commercial productions as the economic support and flagship of a national film industry. But the significance of his work within Germany lay in his ability to 'naturalize' the conventions of both Hollywood film-making and French commercial cinema, in

Schlöndorff's internationalism: Angela Winkler and Charles Aznavour in The Tin Drum *(1979)*

and for German settings and characters (as in *A Free Woman/Summer Lightning*, *The Lost Honour of Katharina Blum* or *The Tin Drum*). His stories and situations are constructed along the lines of Hollywood narrative. That is, the social issues and conflicts are transformed into and dramatised as psychological ones, and the emphasis is on plotting motives, choices, decisions, actions – the very assumptions which for other directors of the New German Cinema such as Herzog or Wenders are anathema and against which they developed their individual styles. The least linear of Schlöndorff's films and also one of his most intriguing, because so much depends on place and atmosphere, on unresolved tensions and unstated motives, is *Coup de grace*, scripted by Margarethe von Trotta and Jutta Brückner, two film-makers quite different from Schlöndorff.

Reviving the Central Hero

Also characteristic of what one might call Schlöndorff's proto-generic cinema modelled on 1970s Hollywood were the films by Reinhardt Hauff, Hans W. Geissendörfer and Wolfgang Petersen. *Knife in the Head, The Brutalization of Franz Blum (Die Verrohung des Franz Blum*, 1973), *The Man on the Wall (Der Mann auf der Mauer*, 1983), *Stammheim* (1986), *The Case of Lena Christ* (1969), *The Consequence* (1977), *Black and White Like Night and Day (Schwarz und weiss wie Tage und Nächte*, 1978) all represent an identifiable formula, in so far

Volker Schlöndorff's Coup de grace *(1976)*

Reinhard Hauff's The Brutalisation of Franz Blum *(1973)*

as they tend to take a social case history or an autobiographical account as the basis for a fictional narrative. They also borrow from the Hollywood investigative or paranoia thriller and construct a scenario around a central character capable of engaging the audience's direct identification.

Hauff in particular has specialised in heroes who generally start off as representatives of normality and ordinariness, but who are caught in an extreme situation and often become fatally drawn into left-wing politics, the lifestyle of sub-cultures, or the criminal world. The topical subjects with respect to contemporary Germany (the urban terrorist scene, the penal system, the early days of the protest movement, the Berlin wall, the trial and triple suicide of the Baader-Meinhoff group) are usually worked into a plot in which the hero finally confronts himself, in a quasi-existential moment. In *Knife in the Head* (*Messer im Kopf*, 1978), for instance, Hauff's best-known film, a young scientist while looking for his girlfriend at a rehabilitation centre for young offenders is accidentally shot by the police raiding the centre for terrorist suspects. The film details his slow recovery from the head wound which leaves him amnesiac and partially paralysed. Outraged by the casual way the police try to cover up their error, he sets out to confront the officer who shot him, and discovers a frightened young man who panicked at the crucial moment. Each man is forced to recognise his own fears and feelings mirrored in the other.

To the extent that such a film works with identification strategies familiar from classical cinema, relies on a strong central character, has a linear narrative and often a political issue as its story pretext, it is a reworking of the mainstream Hollywood problem film. This means that themes and topics associated with the student movement, feminism and terrorism could become film subjects, through a recognisable story format accessible to a general audience. As an attempt to compete with the liberal Hollywood tradition, with a professionally constructed script, suspenseful and tightly organised around the logic of cause and effect, this 'quality cinema' was ideally exploitable both in the cinemas and on television. It was not surprising that some of the films in this category, especially where the central characters were played by established actors such as Bruno Ganz, Angela Winkler, Mario Adorf, Hans Christian Blech or, more recently, by German pop star Marius Müller-Westernhagen, did well in Germany, both critically and financially, although neither Hauff nor Geissendörfer ever achieved authorial status abroad. Theirs is an invisible style at the service of a (self-important) subject.

Reinhard Hauff directing Mathias Kneissl *(1971)*

Representative Figures, Historical Role Models and Literary Heroes

What makes this commercially oriented independent cinema none the less part of the New German Cinema is its penchant for exemplary figures. Bridging the gap between spectators who looked to films for a confirmation of their political views (or their personal experiences) and audiences who went to the cinema in order to be caught up in someone else's life, Hauff's films offer a sort of compromise and a common denominator. This is usually a central character whose behaviour and attitudes makes him or her marginal and a rebel in relation to society, but whose story is sufficiently singular to be representative and affords an opportunity for a classical *mise en scène* to establish an emotive link with audiences.

From *Katharina Blum* to *Christa Klages*, from *Lina Braake* (1975) to *Lena Rais* (1980), from *Maria Braun* to the Maria of *Heimat* (1984), the German 'cinema of quality' presents a portrait gallery of figures whose allegorical status in most cases invites direct identification. A great number of them are women, and theirs is usually a quest for self-discovery, the cautious negotiation of a new identity. In this respect they are intended to lend story and voice, in short, the possibility of a purposeful trajectory to widely shared experiences of social insecurity and turmoil. Given the collectivist aspirations of the 1960s, the turn towards the exemplary individual marked a retreat, a personalisation of social conflict and political struggle, but no doubt a gain in accessibility to audiences expecting to identify in a film with a central, dominant consciousness.

126

Peter Schneider, Tina Engel, Marius Müller-Westernhagen in Margarethe von Trotta's
The Second Awakening of Christa Klages *(1977)*

This search for representative figures was confined neither to contemporary stories and settings nor to women. It is particularly noticeable in the directors' choice of historical material: *Aguirre, Wrath of God* (*Aguirre, der Zorn Gottes*, 1972) is set in the sixteenth century; the Bavarian highwayman and Robin Hood hero of *Mathias Kneissl* (1971) was hanged in 1902; *Michael Kohlhaas* is a figure from the time of the Lutheran Reformation; the famous foundling *Kaspar Hauser* dates from the nineteenth century; *Marie Ward* (1985) was a Catholic nun from the time of Oliver Cromwell and the Counter-Reformation; *Rosa Luxemburg* (1986) was the martyr of the failed German Revolution after the First World War.

During the last two decades the New German Cinema seems to have found more ways than one to satisfy a thirst for biography while celebrating counter-cultural heroes. This may well provide a further clue as to why the prevalence of literary adaptations was in some sense overdetermined. They, too, favoured subjects whose central character, forcefully identified in the title (*Effi Briest*, *Grete Minde*, *Heinrich*, *Lenz*) could act as role models for a generation bereft of historical or national identification figures, especially from what one might call a revolutionary or politically dissident tradition. German history is short on charismatic figures who are not identified with a feudal, patriarchal system. The few there are are mostly found among the protagonists of romantic and post-romantic prose works by Büchner, Kleist, Storm and Fontane, which suggests that the literary adaptation and the historical reconstruction of exemplary lives

Martyrs of the revolution: Barbara Sukowa, Daniel Olbrychski in Margarethe von Trotta's Rosa Luxemburg *(1986)*

tended to aim for a single constituency, reinforcing a predilection for vicariously experienced rebellion and defeat. Both are emotions that, as we saw in Rutschky's hypothetical spectator M, audiences could directly relate to their own situation.

Film Names and Film Titles

The New German Cinema's attempts at targetting audiences through the promise of role models and figures for direct identification can be studied in its titles. Even the most selective list of German films from the past twenty years shows an unusually large proportion of titles not only containing a proper name, but in an almost predictable rhetorical configuration. Straub/Huillet's austere aesthetics in *Chronicle of Anna Magdalena Bach* may not have had many followers, but the title created a trend: *The Lost Honour of Katharina Blum, The Morals of Ruth Halbfass, The Marriage of Maria Braun, The Death of Maria Malibran*. Surnames and Christian names are like a guarantee, to authenticate the fiction. The tendency of joining name to fate gives such titles the pathos of moral value, but it also alludes to the simplicity and crude artistry of a sung ballad or a recited *Moritat*, briefly revived by Bert Brecht in the 1920s and associated with the Left.

128

Some titles connote finality and stoic resignation, others bathos, but most encase the protagonist in a descriptive statement that gives them no escape and rules out suspense. Some are bombastic, some ironic, some sentimental: *The Great Ecstasy of Woodcarver Steiner*, *The Second Awakening of Christa Klages*, [*The Yearning of*] *Veronica Voss*, *The Bitter Tears of Petra von Kant*. Titles underline the symbolic importance attached to the protagonists' fate: *The Brutalisation of Franz Blum*, *The Sudden Wealth of the Poor People of Kombach*, *The Case of Lena Christ*, *The Enigma of Kaspar Hauser*, *The Long Vacations of Lotte Eisner*. A laconic tone stresses the documentary, factual image: *The Willi Busch Report*, *Berlinger – A German Fate*, *Ludwig – Requiem for a Virgin King*, or it speaks with a peremptory authority: *Vera Romeike Cannot be Tolerated*. Some proper names promise history turned myth: *Marie Ward*, *Karl May*, *Hitler*, *Parsifal*, or the mystery of an undisclosed secret life, like *Harlis* (1972), *Heinrich* (1977), *David* (1979), *Celeste* (1981); or are so ordinary that they must have been rescued from the anonymity of the banal case history: *Paule Pauländer* (1975), *Lena Rais* (1980), *Adele Spitzeder* (1972), *Bolwieser* (1976/77), *Anita G* (*Yesterday Girl*, 1966) and *Christiane F* (1981), *Headteacher Hofer* (1974), *Strongman Ferdinand* (*Der Starke Ferdinand*, 1976). Sometimes a name symbolises a culturally divided self: *Johnny West* (1977), *Johnny Glückstadt* (1975), *Whity* (1970), *Gibbi Westgermany* (1980). If foreign distributors have occasionally fought shy of offering their art cinema audiences literal translations of these titles, no doubt anticipating the negative effect of so much straightforward didacticism, it is

Tina Engel and Sylvia Reize in von Trotta's The Second Awakening of Christa Klages *(1977)*

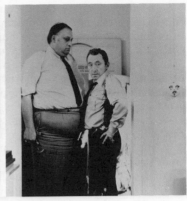

Günther Kaufmann (right) in
Fassbinder's Whity *(1970)*

Heinz Schubert (right) in Kluge's
Strongman Ferdinand (1976)

perhaps no accident that some of the biggest international successes of Herzog
have been films with proper names as titles: *Aguirre, Kaspar Hauser, Stroszek,
Nosferatu, Woyzeck* and *Fitzcarraldo.* Similarly for Fassbinder: *Petra von Kant,
Fox, Martha, Effi Briest, Mother Küster, Maria Braun, Lola, Lili Marleen,
Veronika Voss* – even *Katzelmacher* might be mistaken for a proper name outside
the borders of Upper Bavaria.

'Indulgent to the Point of Irresponsibility': The Outsider

In itself, such a pre-construction of the audience's expectations via a title
emphasising the central protagonist may not be very telling about a film's stance
towards the spectator, except to underline the character-centred, rather than
action-oriented, interest of New German Cinema generally. More important is,
perhaps, how a film presents its protagonists: in a tragic, epic or comic mode –
superior, equal or inferior to the spectator's own moral awareness. Hauff, after
completing *Paule Pauländer* (1975), made a film about the boy who played the
leading role, simply called *The Main Actor* (*Der Hauptdarsteller*, 1977) in which
the responsibility of the director for his character becomes itself the moral issue
and subject.

The emphasis on the outsider, for instance, which is a motif by no means
restricted to the German cinema, none the less offers an especially instructive
example of narrational stances and points of view. The theme functions quite
differently depending on whether s/he is a particular instance of a moral to which
the fable attributes general validity, or whether s/he has the particularity and
irreducibility heightened to the point of appearing radically 'other'.

Werner Herzog, in all his films, makes it difficult if not impossible to entertain
vis-à-vis his characters a stance of condescension and superiority, of derision or
sentimentality. However grotesque, monstrous or apparently pitiful his heroes
are, as spectators we have to take them seriously because the director refuses to
shoot and edit in a way that would permit an ironic distance or an interpreting
context or commentary to interfere with the integrity of the image: 'Truth always

has its hour and its moment, and requires a particular kind of empathy; the problem is to find the right distance, but also to dare to go so close that occasionally one can show things naked and still trust an audience with it.'[5]

Likewise, looking at the characters of Fassbinder's early films, however pathetic and degraded they may appear, what predominates is the straight-faced tone, the 'level' attitude which the camera imposes on the spectator, as Fassbinder himself was the first to point out:

> In contrast to a lot of directors, I do not denounce my characters, on the contrary, I am often indulgent to the point of irresponsibility. When, for instance, in *Jailbait* the father talks about his war experiences, and his views become particularly horrific, then we treated him especially gently, in order to make it plain . . . that a human being is something gentle and tender, and only what he says and thinks is horrible, not what he is.[6]

This tender gaze is not confined to *Jailbait* (*Wildwechsel*, 1972), where the girl, the boy and her father – all equally twisted by their individual histories – are observed with even-handed equanimity. Fassbinder's ridiculous would-be gangsters as well as the heroes and heroines of his melodramas also benefit from a generosity which conveys both a moral attitude and, in the melodramas, acts as a dramaturgical resource.

On the other hand, what makes Schlöndorff a less typical director of the New German Cinema is his invariably manipulative attitude to his characters, as in

Heinz Bennent (right) in Schlöndorff's The Tin Drum *(1979)*

Liebe – kälter als der Tod
Ein Film von Rainer Werner Fassbinder

The would-be gangster and his moll: Ulli Lommel (right) and Hanna Schygulla in Fassbinder's Love Is Colder Than Death *(1969)*

The Lost Honour of Katharina Blum. Schlöndorff had in fact made the outsider his favourite hero. From the sensitive schoolboy Törless (*Young Törless*), via *Michael Kohlhaas, the Rebel* to Oskar Matzerath (in *The Tin Drum*), the director specialised in some of German literature's best-known loners and outcasts. However, by privileging their point of view totally, Schlöndorff gives the spectator the illusion that s/he shares the hero's singular perspective. One only has to imagine how the Herzog of *Even Dwarfs Started Small* (*Auch Zwerge haben klein angefangen*, 1970) might have handled *The Tin Drum*'s central narrative premise and compare it to Schlöndorff's infatuation with recreating a period feel. By making his film seem like a naturalistic homage to Fellini, he may have discovered a truth about Grass that escaped the readers of the novel. But what another film-maker would see as the end-result of a process of which the film is the record – the elaboration of a unique perspective of difference – the *mise en scène* in Schlöndoff's films tends to deliver ready-made, annihilating difference through the conspiratorially shared point of view, often establishing a victim's perspective from the opening scene.

The emphasis on outsiders in the German cinema need thus not only be seen as the sociological phenomenon it undoubtedly also is. Or rather, the sociological significance has in many films the function of a pretext. Outsiders are important for the self-definition of the film-maker engaged in a marginal activity, but they are also ideologically significant stand-ins for the spectator, inviting identification, but one that can entail quite a radical experience of otherness, as in Herzog's documentaries:

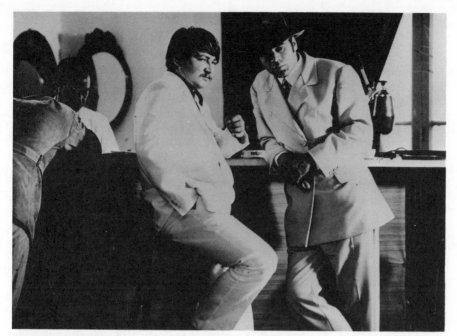

The would-be gangster and his buddy: Karl Scheydt (right) and Rainer Werner Fassbinder in The American Soldier *(1970)*

> There are people (like Fini Straubinger in *Land of Silence and Darkness*) in whom a fire is burning, and which glows even at a distance. One can see the same in Bruno, a strong glow from within. Both have this radical dignity emanating from them, and the radicality comes from them having suffered much and not been broken.[7]

Empathetic but also made uncomfortable, divided but also curious, the spectator watches the mentally handicapped heroes and the deaf-mutes (in *Land of Darkness and Silence*; *Land des Schweigens und der Dunkelheit*, 1971) with a measure of detachment which implies rather than solicits understanding and sympathy. Such films demand from the viewer a different kind of perception, one that is slower, more patient. Yet the outsider in Herzog is never depicted as victim only: as we shall see, an interplay of victimisation and heroism (the privileged figuration in Herzog) of deviancy and excess (as in Fassbinder), flamboyance and perversity (as in Schroeter) characterises many of the most typical films of the New German Cinema. This seems at least in part aimed at preventing the viewer from trying to recognise too readily the same (him or herself) in the different (the other). Such careful articulations of an ambiguous stance are part of the reason why in the German cinema the distinction between documentary and the fiction film is sometimes difficult to draw.

I would therefore argue that none of the distinctions so far suggested for classifying German film production adequately describes the inner logic of the texts or their social significance, unless they include the stance towards the characters, and by extension, identification in general, as one of the criteria.

133

A Matter of *Einstellung*: Wenders versus Kluge

The reasons which made Fassbinder or Wenders approach traditional American genres are several, and quite different from those that brought Schlöndorff, Hauff, or Petersen to literary adaptations or formula film-making. For example, Lemke's *48 Hours to Acapulco* (1967) was an influence on Fassbinder, not so much in its subject (that of a small-time Munich crook caught up in an affair too big for him to handle), but because Lemke's attitude to his characters was to become typical of Fassbinder's. The secret was to take seriously the image the characters have of themselves, because the director is willing to recognise as 'reality' (in *Love is Colder than Death* or *The American Soldier* (*Der amerikanische Soldat*, 1971)) and an inner truth, what are merely the characters' fantasies. Fassbinder wrote: 'The heroes behave like gangsters, but at the same time as they imagine gangsters would behave. The Hollywood stereotype comes through: but Lemke has attempted not to imitate them.'[8]

With this new level of reflection, a different relation of protagonist to spectator was introduced into the films, which was to become part of the audience strategy that typified the New German Cinema in contrast to the Young German Film. It secured it an international public, as well as a national one in the late 1970s: the double inscription of the spectator and of two kinds of reality operating in the films. One might say that via genre films German directors became sensitive towards a new form of realism, which had to do not only with a different attitude to the protagonist, but also with a different approach to time in the cinema.

This applies especially to Wim Wenders, whose relation to genre cinema is rather more nuanced than the phrase about film-makers having 'found their tradition and learnt their craft in the cinema itself' suggests. In fact, Wenders began as an avant-garde director, hostile to both Hollywood and the German cinema. *Same Player Shoots Again* (1967), *Alabama* (1969), *Three American LPs* (1969) and *Silver City* (1968) do not protest verbally against the oppressive dominance of Hollywood. These films dispense with words altogether and let music, the rock music of the 1960s, speak in their place. For the young Wenders, two languages were inadmissible: the German language and post-1950s Hollywood film dramaturgy – his own films and rock music pointing an accusing finger at that to which they referred negatively.[9] Only English or American song lyrics could be trusted to convey authentic states of feeling, and only a cinema of observation, stillness and the long take could reply to the hectic shot-countershot of TV-influenced new Hollywood, where action was always a form of 'pornography – a raping of objects, of people, of feelings, of landscape – of the spectator'.[10]

Wenders, whose stories emphasise *temps morts*, the passage of time when not consumed by action, has always been preoccupied with narrative. But the telling of stories matters only in so far as it is an occasion for creating a specifically filmic sense of time, and allows for characters not driven relentlessly forward by psychological motives and externally imposed causes. One just has to compare *Summer in the City* (1970) to its Hollywood models of the gangster on the run to realise that the *mise en scène* not so much parodies the genre as deprives it of its motivational core. Wenders often cites conventional genre motifs (*Summer in the City* opens with a shot of the hero leaving prison, blinking into the unaccustomed sunlight, and getting into a car that speeds away), but he usually lets them come

Uschi Obermeier (centre) and Marquard Bohm (right) in Rudolf Thome's Red Sun
(1969)

to nothing in order that a temporality other than that of the chase can take over: process not progress. The result is a form of distanciation and foregrounding. Spectator involvement and attention are directed to other aspects of the film, to the empty compositions, for instance, and to the passage of time giving substance to space.

A review of Rudolf Thome's *Red Sun* (1969) – one of the films signalling the turn to American genres – became a way for Wenders to test a new aesthetic position. It was diametrically opposed to that of the Oberhausener or Schlöndorff, but also different from that of Straub or Herzog:

> I used to cut out the comics from the back page of the newspaper and paste them into exercise books. *Red Sun* seemed to me like one of my home-made Phantom and Blondie comics: something very simple, very cheap and very artless has been taken seriously and treated with care. *Red Sun* is one of those extremely rare European films which do not merely set out to copy American films, only to make one wish they had been shot in New York and with Humphrey Bogart in the lead, but which take from the American cinema no more than a certain stance: to display, without buttonholing, for 90 minutes nothing but surface. This frame of mind is evident in each frame: flat compositions, the same lens throughout allows for only a handful of different shot sizes, the banality of the camera movements which never exert themselves beyond what is absolutely necessary, the curious blandness of the colours identical to those in Mickey Mouse cartoons. [The characters] are only

present if they happen to be in shot. They themselves do not know yet how the story ends. The film is prepared to go along with their story, it does not impose itself on them.[11]

Wenders may appear to be aiming at the German film industry's own imitations of Hollywood, trying to rival it on its own ground. But equally significant, the review is also directed (and thereby becomes a programme) against the Young German Film and its moral and ideological buttonholing. With Wenders – via Lemke and Thome as pretext – a realist gestus towards audiences (taken from André Bazin rather than Siegfried Kracauer) dissociates itself from a realist gestus claiming for itself the tradition of Brecht. Wenders' praise for Thome is a condemnation of Kluge and, via Kluge, once more an attack on Oberhausen and its aesthetics. That the theme is a persistent one can be seen from a more recent remark by Thome:

> If a film-maker pokes fun at the people in front of the camera at their expense, that's the worst thing for me. In Alexander Kluge's new film *The Patriot*, there is this scene at the Hamburg SPD Party Congress, I had to leave, I could not bear to watch it, seeing people filmed like that.[12]

The general view of Kluge as a 'Brechtian' director is itself problematic, especially since Kluge's use of montage, voice-over and staged interviews seem to relate as much to the impasse of the non-existent spectator discussed above as to Brecht's theories of realism and anti-illusionism. As has already been pointed out in relation to women film-makers, the most controversial aspect of Kluge's films has often been the attitude the director takes towards his (predominantly female) characters. Kluge's protagonists are invariably the appendages of a discourse that is rarely, if ever, capable of questioning its own authority and, instead, by letting voice-over dominate the image, subjects the characters to the tyranny of the commentary. Although not mentioned by name, Kluge's cinema becomes questionable, in Wenders' terms, for its *Einstellung* – in both senses of that word: its moral stance and the importance it gives to the film frame and duration of the shot.

This argument is made explicit in an article entitled 'Augsburg in August: Desolate' which Peter Handke, collaborator and long-time friend of Wenders, published in *Film* in January 1969, about Kluge's *Artistes at the Top of the Big Top: Disorientated* (1968):

> The reactions of complaisance, discomfort, curiosity, snideness, anger which seeing this film arouse stem from the fact that one constantly recognizes things: names, faces, people, personalities, dramaturgical clichés, phrases, but above all: attitudes [*Einstellungen*]; attitudes of the film towards the things and the people it shows – it is these attitudes alone which create meaning. The cinema has become nothing but a space of meanings . . . the film is full of ready-made significance. Due to the fact that the words are formulated, formulaic, unambiguous and not playfully quoted . . . they make the pictures into picture-puzzles instead of leaving them as images. Instead of looking and then discovering something, the spectator is asked to match words with images.[13]

Fassbinder and the Return to Melodrama

Fassbinder's conception of the audience-oriented film – a Hollywood for Germany – relied primarily on a recourse to genre cinema and, like Wenders',

136

Hanna Schygulla, Fassbinder's archetypal femme fatale (in Gods of the Plague, *1970)*

. . . and mother-substitute (in Katzelmacher, *1969)*

proceeded from a quite radical rethinking of its function in film-making. Even more than Wenders, however, Fassbinder was conscious of the need to establish a double focus for identification as the basis for a subversion or transgressive use of genres. Like Wenders his strategy was to bypass altogether the strong story, the suspense scene drawn from the logic of the action, typical of a genre like the gangster film (or of Hitchcock), and instead focus on the protagonists, as if they were themselves spectators of their own lives.

As in Godard's early films, the interest but also the unease came from characters playing at gangsters or *femmes fatales*, the discrepancy between the role and the person trying to fill it being the most obvious feature. This in turn gave singular prominence to the actor, not so much as the professional performer of a part, but as a kind of impersonator of a role.

The crooks, layabouts, pimps and day-dreaming shop assistants are outsiders aspiring to the prejudices if not the manners of the Bavarian petit bourgeoisie. With this, the outsider ceases to be a victim, nor does he have a privileged perspective: he is a victim only of his self-delusions, for his pretence is to be an insider. Becoming a member of the gang or of a clique makes him subjectively create and reappropriate the world from which he is objectively excluded. The *mise en scène*, on the other hand, seems determined to force the spectator into a quandary. The characters are too foolish, sentimental and pathetic not to give the audience a sense of easy superiority, but too brutalised, emotionally crippled and deformed, and finally also too evil, to become simple figures of fun. Wenders took strong objection to this strategy, especially in *Katzelmacher* (1969):

The most terrible thing about this film is its apathy down to the last detail. The editing is like the listless flicking from channel to channel during Saturday night

137

Barbara Valentin, El Hedi Ben Salem in Fassbinder's Fear Eats the Soul *(1974)*

television, when every new programme makes you only more angry and depressed. And the fact that all the actors look so rigid doesn't come from them having to represent the provinces, but from the rigid schema, which loves to press them into acting as mere puppets, or maybe as in a photo-novel, but with a black bar across the eyes, like people in the newspapers when they don't want to be recognized. 'There isn't a tender bone in her body' one of the women says in the film. Only Hanna Schygulla is so alive among these corpses that one imagines seeing her in colour.[14]

Fassbinder, more than most directors, tested the limits of his 'generosity' towards characters. If the gangster film gave him heroes whose morals and motives should by right make them villains, or at least utterly unappealing types, the melodrama provided a new perspective on the apparently integrated individual. His ability to re-appropriate for a general audience the clichés of a popular genre is usually attributed to his discovery of Douglas Sirk's American melodramas from the 1950s. In Sirk's films the characters are insiders who suddenly discover that they are outsiders, victims, without a privileged insight to redeem their suffering.

In Fassbinder's melodramas, too, the heroes, because they are totally in agreement with the values that victimise them (as in *The Merchant of Four Seasons, Effi Briest* or *Fear Eats the Soul*), are victims without knowing it. But because they are from the very start so ordinary as to be banal, the fact that they are devoid of special insight, but also of grand self-delusions, makes them exemplary figures of victimisation: or rather, of the (social, psycho-sexual) processes that make victims. By representing over and over again within the films

138

Johanna König (centre) in Walter Bockmayer's Jane Is Jane Forever *(1977)*

a masochistic identification with an idealised oppressor, or the tyranny of an idealised self-image, Fassbinder points to the masochistic side in cinematic identification generally. Yet because this masochistic pleasure is not rationalised by a unified and privileged perspective that the spectator is allowed to project on a character – as, say, in the masochistic males usually playing opposite Marlene Dietrich in Josef von Sternberg's films – it is rendered unpalatable, ambiguous, queasy. Often, in Fassbinder's films, the audience experiences an unusually strong sense of spectatorial appellation, without being able to identify with it. It is as if an invisible eye presided over the action, for whose approval it was staged.

However, Fassbinder's approach to genre did not lead to the domestication of an American genre, as, for instance, the French cop thriller in Melville or the Italo-Western. Nor were there obvious imitations of his style by other German film-makers, except perhaps Walter Bockmayer's *Jane is Jane Forever* (*Jane bleibt Jane*, 1977). For Fassbinder himself, although he never abandoned the structural principles of melodrama (its dramatic symmetries and ironic reversals) or the ambiguous pathos that could be derived from treating villains with indulgence, genre seemed ultimately only one way of exploring identification and spectator-orientation on a much broader front. It was a form of intertextuality which gave his film-making a history, but also gave his plea for deviancy and perversion a non-voyeuristic *mise en scène*. Fassbinder, not least because of his prolific output, was able to establish spectatorial expectations which could substitute for genres. Rather than make genres assume the dominant role they have in classical Hollywood film-making, he adapted generic formula primarily to confirm and strengthen his authorial identity. The Sirkean melodrama was perhaps ultimately

139

Frank Ripploh (right) in his Taxi zum Klo *(1981)*

more useful for his critical standing among scholars than for his popularity with audiences.

Fassbinder was a director whose interest in marginal groups is a clear feature of his work. His very concept of film form is inflected by the problem of otherness and the Other, regardless of whether his films deal, for instance, directly with homosexuality (usually not). There are, however, also film-makers (Frank Ripploh and Lothar Lambert) who address themselves not only directly to the representation of homosexuals, but specifically to the *Subkultur*.

Ripploh's *Taxi zum Klo* (1981) was an attempt to treat the homosexual couple as the very image of heterosexual romance, but also as a caricature of 'normal' marital strife. The considerable commercial success of the film was due in large measure to Ripploh's ability to present the dilemmas of his homosexual teacher, torn between love for his steady partner and the need for more furtive thrills, in the form of a situation comedy, to naturalise his trials and tribulations, while at the same time making the milieu seems sufficiently exotic for a certain voyeurism to sustain itself without causing offence. Its depiction of gay life, while not begging for understanding, largely flatters liberal tolerance and ensures that the audience can rely on the central protagonist (played by Ripploh himself) to remain the comic and picaresque hero, and thus a secure point of identification. A competent *mise en scène* ably integrated certain rough edges, such as hand-held camera, improvisation, shaky editing and freewheeling narrative, all typically connoting an 'underground' style.

A number of films by Lambert explored the subject of sexual 'deviancy' in commercially even more acceptable forms, often exploiting the traditional theme of transvestism for its comic potential (*Paso Doble*, 1984). Coming out of the

Berlin of the 1980s, Lambert's film is, with its formulaic plot and slickly calculated appeal, indicative of how little scope for a change in attitude towards the representation of homosexuality actually exists. This is true even when compared with Fleischmann's Bavarian *Jagdszenen* from the late 1960s, despite geographical and class differences. For the fact that Lambert or Ripploh could treat the sexual outsider as a subject for comedy means that they have turned him into an insider which, as we shall see, scarcely reflects the degree to which a militant and articulate group such as the gay movement support a specific film culture.

A New *Heimat* Film?

The first example of the social and sexual outcast treated not only with total sympathy, but more importantly as the zero degree of a moral perspective which, by a stark and deliberate contrast, made normality appear severely pathological, was Peter Fleischmann's *Hunting Scenes from Lower Bavaria* (1969). In this respect the film is a parallel to and invites comparison with Fassbinder's *Katzelmacher* (1969). In *Hunting Scenes* a young mechanic, recently released from jail and suspected of being a homosexual, is hounded by the villagers into leaving. Held back by his pregnant girlfriend he stabs her, flees into the woods and is shot down like a wild animal. Like *Katzelmacher*, the film is less the portrait of an individual than the study of a community. It is comparable to a cruel Chabrolian picture of rural France, or to red-neck films about Appalachian hillbillies and Alabama sheriffs, and it recalls William Faulkner as least as much as it recalls Brecht.

Based on a play by the writer Martin Sperr, it none the less has a distinctly national theatrical tradition to draw on. Playwrights in the 1920s like Marie Luise Fleisser, Odon von Horvath and Ferdinand Bruckner had already radicalised Bavarian folk-drama. They had written plays that used dialect and vernacular forms to dramatise the climate of emotional violence, sexual oppression and alcoholism which went with being geographically cut off from history.

The reappearance of a rural milieu and of Bavarian settings in some of the early films of the New German Cinema was hailed as the 'New' *Heimat* film, reworked from a critical perspective. The chief features of the old *Heimat* film were an Alpine setting, and usually a plot in which a poacher, in love with the daughter of the richest farmer, becomes the defender of the peasantry. The resurrection, around 1971, of Germany's only indigenous and historically most enduring genre attracted much attention, mainly in the context of attempts to win audiences by harking back to populist or at least popular film forms. According to Hans Günther Pflaum, the boom in new *Heimat* films

> was sparked off by the Spaghetti Westerns, the initial successes of Brazil's Cinema Novo, and of course, the young German directors' increasing difficulties in retaining a more extensive public over the long term. The *Heimat* film also seemed to be the only genre that had survived the Nazi era, the post-war years, and the Economic Miracle. Ludwig Ganghofer's novel *Schloss Hubertus* has, for instance, been made into a film no fewer than three times, adapted to the tastes of 1934, 1954, and 1973, and each time it was a success.[15]

These reasons do not add up to a very persuasive argument and, correspondingly, a very disparate list of films appears under the label. Fleischmann's *Hunting Scenes* finds itself side by side with Schlöndorff's *The Sudden Wealth of the Poor People of Kombach* (1970), Reinhard Hauff's *Mathias Kneissl* (1971), Uwe

Margarethe von Trotta and R. W.
Fassbinder in Volker Schlöndorff's The
Sudden Wealth of the Poor People of
Kombach *(1970)*

Angela Winkler in Peter Fleischmann's
Hunting Scenes from Lower Bavaria
(1968)

Brandner's *I Love You, I Kill You* (1971), Volker Vogeler's *Jaider – The Lonely Hunter* (1974), Fassbinder's *Katzelmacher*, Herzog's *Heart of Glass* (*Herz aus Glas*, 1976), Niklaus Schilling's *Night Shade* (*Nachtschatten*, 1972). Some of them, such as Schlöndorff's or Hauff's, were intended as political parables: stories about authoritarian feudal lords, about miscarriages of justice, peasant exploitation, revolts against taxation, outlaws who help the poor and steal from the rich and about farmers who, driven from their land, are pressed into mercenary armies or try to emigrate to America.

Thematically, therefore, there might be a link with Corbucci's Italo-Westerns although, especially in the case of *Kombach*, the influence of Büchner and Brecht is more noticeable than either the Western or the old *Heimat* film: the props, costumes and language point to the 'gestic' use of historic detail of a *Mother Courage*, as does the sardonic irony of the moral. After bungling a robbery of the ducal tax inspector's coach five times, the inhabitants of a small Hessian village finally succeed in becoming rich, although they know they cannot spend the money without arousing suspicion. Grinding poverty and mounting debts finally force them into parting with some of their gold, whereupon they are instantly arrested and eventually hanged. They are even made to confess where the treasure is hidden, in order to receive the last rites, repentant and in a state of grace.

The detailed depiction of the mechanisms of repression, the difficulties of solidarity once circumstances have forced the villagers into the criminal 'underground', and the heroism of failure makes the historical situation of the film (set in 1821) and its storyline directly readable in contemporary terms. A student audience especially could find in it a pedigree for revolutionary action and violence drawn from their own national history. *Kombach* is thus a film which belongs ideologically to the cycle of literary adaptation (in fact, Schlöndorff came across the subject through an amateur historian who had found the account in local records) and the search for counter-cultural heroes.

142

Of the films cited *Jaider* is the only one to use generic codes in plot and setting, combining elements of the Italo-Western with the *Heimat* film. Having become an outlaw because of war and lack of work, Jaider is tracked by a sadistic bounty-hunter in the pay of the local gentry. He escapes several times into the remoter parts of the mountains, but is forced to show himself when his girlfriend is brutally murdered. He takes revenge, trapping the bounty hunter in a barn before setting it alight. The crucial aspect of both the *Heimat* film and the Italo-Western is preserved, that of the outsider or loner at the centre of the narrative. The motif of the poacher in the *Heimat* film betrays the social origin of the genre, since a poacher steals for his own immediate needs what the landed aristocracy has taken from peasants by force. A folk hero, he is the rebel come not from outside, but arising from within the community itself.

Precisely this constellation inspired *Jaider* and is symmetrically inverted in *I Love You, I Kill You*, which shows a closed community both vulnerable to and resisting the outsider. The homosexual love story between a teacher (newly posted to a village entirely controlled by remote landowners) and the gamekeeper (who teaches him to use a rifle, but cannot stop him from using it to poach and is thus forced to hand him over to the authorities) is a bold attempt to bring the existentialism of Kafka's *Castle* to bear on the setting of the *Heimat* film. The very self-conscious and literary use of genre makes the film chiefly interesting for the way it introduces the figure of the Double, and with it a play on identification and otherness which may have influenced Fassbinder in the conception of *Despair* (1978).

Playwright Franz Xaver Kroetz and writer–film-maker Herbert Achternbusch have been much more closely involved in drawing on the generic stereotypes of the *Heimat* film and folk drama than any of the film-makers mentioned so far. Both explore the pseudo-naivety of the village idiot as a catalyst for political (Kroetz) and anarcho-absurdist drama (Achternbusch). Both learnt from Fassbinder the skill of poeticising the wooden inarticulacy of rural or working-class characters, which comes directly from an awareness of the aggressive minimalism inherent in the Bavarian vernacular.

Fassbinder's *Jailbait* (1972) is based on a play by Kroetz, who later alleged that Fassbinder had exploited the characters – a charge which resulted in a legal settlement that imposed cuts on the finished film. The incident may explain why Fassbinder felt moved to defend his sympathetic treatment even of unsympathetic protagonists, for in an open letter he claimed that Kroetz had only protested in order to disguise the debt the play owed to *Katzelmacher* (1969):

> Does it bother you (that through my film), it may be the first time you have really been heard by the people for whom you profess to be writing, and that, this too, has to do with me, like your work with Bavarian dialect?[16]

Heart of Glass was Herzog's attempt to find the strangeness of myth and legend in the heartland of the *Heimat* film. Based on a story by Achternbusch, it shows (between these two at first sight very similar 'folklorists') a radical difference of perception of the genre. Not one of Herzog's successes, the film might have been better had it been written by its director or directed by its writer. *Heart of Glass* never seems to be able to resolve whether it is a *Heimat* film turned inside out, showing the bigotry and rivalries in inbred communities, or whether it celebrates harmony and a oneness-with-nature of the elect. Herzog's tendency to distance his characters at all costs, even if it means fashioning for them a halo of mystical remoteness (apparently achieved by hypnotising the cast) runs counter to

Brunhilde Klöckner   *and Clemens Scheitz in Herzog's* Heart of Glass *(1976)*

Achternbusch's drastic debunking. The problem seems to be that in Herzog's conception, Achternbusch's extraordinary characters remain a gallery of freaks and gargoyles, unable to engage the spectators in the aggressive play of identification and fascination. This Herzog elicits when relying on actors like Kinski and Bruno S, or characters like Fini Straubinger and ski-jumper Steiner. Achternbusch himself, on the other hand, is his own greatest asset in so far as he always brings his mesmerising presence to material even where it is wilfully caricatured.

The *Heimat* as Ice-land: Herbert Achternbusch

The importance of the *Heimat* film and its politically or poetically subversive resurrection towards the early 1970s, then, lay to some extent in the function the outsider had as the figure of an ambivalent play with cinematic identification. The narratives of rebellion and failure, associated with the genre, could represent class antagonisms (as in Hauff, Schlöndorff and Vogeler) and sexual otherness (Fleischmann, Brandner and Fassbinder). However, a second complex seemed to be involved: that of Bavaria, its history, culture and the uses to which the cinema had put them. The latter is crucial to an understanding, for instance, of the films of Achternbusch. His is the most exhaustive attempt to make Bavaria, its language and myths, its politics and geographical position yield both style and subject matter for an entire oeuvre, itself a satirical anthology and radical re-writing of the *Heimat* film. Achternbusch, whose more than a dozen films since 1974 are virtually unknown outside Germany, is the example of a film-maker who has transformed and deformed the codes of a popular genre to such a degree that it has become his unmistakable signature as an author and a performer (he plays the lead in virtually all his films).

Already with his first film *The Andechs Feeling* (*Das Andecher Gëfuhl*, 1974) he set out consciously to subvert and nip in the bud the emergent pieties of the new *Heimat* film. A schoolteacher in his thirties, played by Achternbusch, slowly

144

Harry Baer and Eva Mattes in Fassbinder's Jailbait *(1972)*

drinks himelf to death while flies drown in his beermug. He neglects his wife, fails in his job, beats his children and insults his drinking companions, and all because of a consuming fantasy about a movie star from Munich (Margarethe von Trotta, playing herself but resembling Achternbusch's mother) whom the strength of his spiritual yearning and his alcoholic stupor finally succeed in materialising. Von Trotta's arrival in the village in a roadster, wearing a canary yellow dress and remaining regally aloof, precipitates the events towards a ghoulish and bloody end.

Here the threat of the outsider, so important in the *Heimat* film as the symbol of corruption, sin and sex, is shown to be the figure of desire, whose disavowal alone keeps peace in the idyll. The community itself in Achternbusch's films is nothing but a collection of misfits and outsiders, held together by boredom. Their fantasy is to be the desired object of the townspeoples' fantasy, whose need for an idyll is the villagers' curse and degradation.

Achternbusch's central strategy is to shape his own authorial persona into a mere shell of a personality, to annihilate character and let only bad puns and clichés speak, endowing them, however, with an aura of emotional authenticity and presence. It is a comic technique derived from music hall turns, to which his own exhibitionist performance gives a new twist. Indicative of an avant-garde wing among the Bavarian folk revival, Achternbusch has borrowed from modernist forms of literature and theatre (notably Beckett). He self-consciously works them into the provincial setting and idiom, combining the 'serious' intellectual appeal of *angst* and *Weltschmerz* with popular or debased formal techniques like the

145

Anomie in Austria: Arthur Brauss (right) in Wenders' The Goalie's Fear of the Penalty Kick *(1971)*

cabaret sketch. As a specialist on the *Heimat* film himself, Peter Handke wrote a critical piece on Achternbusch in which he acknowledges the attraction of this form of disguise and warns of what he sees as its dangers:

> Achternbusch ought to know better than any other writer. Why then does he content himself with fantasies taken from the pages of the local paper? The result: slavish – or in Achternbusch's case, simulating slavish – adherence to the cultural cliché that nobody can be represented as an individual anymore, that we have all become damaged, perforated foils for anything and everything already illustrated and pictured: formless beings, ventriloquist existences. Does Achternbusch offer more than merely rhetorical, literally 'sub'-cultural challenge to the world of the newspaper . . . ? Or are his travesties of plastic mythologies a kind of resistance?[17]

Handke, an Austrian writer rather than a Bavarian, tried himself to blend the generic rules of the film noir thriller with the *Heimat* film, in his book *The Goalie's Fear of the Penalty Kick* (*Die Angst des Tormanns beim Elfmeter*). When made into a film by Wenders in 1971, it became a quintessential study of anomie and latent violence in the Hinterland, of the radiant smiles of village idiots, which the outsider, vaguely on the run after a senseless, motiveless crime and feeling himself exposed rather than sheltered by the closed community, can only interpret as threats. But as with Fassbinder, Fleischmann or Achternbusch, there is no magic, mystery or special dignity attributed to village life in Wenders' film. Boredom and the sense of having come to a dead end predominate, while the

146

'plastic myths' are those imported from America: the jukebox, Howard Hawks' *Red Line 2000*, and a handful of dimes and quarters.

A contrary case in this context might serve to illustrate the general point. As we have seen, the commercial cinema of the 1960s and early 1970s actually registered a production boom (mainly due to the indiscriminate nature of the subsidy bonuses) on the strength of several consecutive waves of soft-core porn films. But sex films are actually a good example of the way in which mainstream cinema traditions feed off each other. Sex films in general, but German ones in particular, are parasitic in so far as they are parodies. In Germany the parody is of the *Heimat* film, which the sex films, as it were, strip of its nostalgic and idealist features, thereby not only incidentally pointing to the same ideological function as did Achternbusch. These films show Bavaria as a displaced and degraded utopia, commercialised in the form of the tourist industry, its former rebelliousness 'liberated' as barnyard sex. Thus, the so-called 'yodel wave' – an eloquent example of the kind of vampirism genres are prone to at the bottom end of the commercial market, with titles like *Beim Jodeln juckt die Lederhose* (literally: Yodelling gives me an itch in my leather shorts) – might be said to have 'deconstructed' the genre from within the *Heimat* film industry itself.

One of Syberberg's early documentaries, *Sex Business Made in Pasing* (1969), attempts a sarcastic, deadpan deconstruction of this deconstruction, with an interview–portrait of the German porn film-maker Alois Brummer:

> For the first time [critics] could see the world of cinema in which they lived as it actually was: practical, proletarian art, commercialized, unimaginative, perverted, clean German sex made in Bavaria. The opposite of blue movies and international porn – witlessly funny, an unintentional joke. . . . Alois Brummer, the genial, harmless Lower Bavarian as the most cogent joker symbol of the inhuman wheeler-dealer cinema in its currently lowest stage.[18]

Sex Business Made in Pasing is a film about a doubly false fiction: the exploitation of Bavaria by the *Heimat* film and the exploitation of the *Heimat* film by German soft-core porn. But underneath the crassly naive commercialism of Brummer,

Alois Brummer in Syberberg's Sex Business Made in Pasing *(1969)*   *. . . and one of his films:* How Sweet Is Her Valley? *(1974)*

147

Two ways of parodying the Heimatfilm: (left) Brummer's There's No Sex Like Snow Sex *(1974)*
and (right) Peter Kern, Barbara Valentin in Walter Bockmayer's Flaming Hearts
(1978)

Syberberg discovered a layer of Bavarian blunt thinking, whose realism he could not but admire, even suggesting – especially in the way the motif is later taken up again in the *Ludwig* films, particularly, *Theodor Hierneis/Ludwig's Cook* (1972) – that through its knowing fakery of formulae the pornographic *Heimat* film does achieve a measure of 'materialist' authenticity.

Imagining Bavaria

Handke's misgivings about Achternbusch indicate little sympathy for the absurdist strand of the Munich avant-garde, flirting with popular idioms and 'plastic myths'. But it is precisely the kitsch element which points to the importance of Munich and Bavaria as a context yielding the antinomies, the brutal contrasts so essential for exploring the narrative potential of national stereotypes. As indicated, these are not limited to the *Heimat* film, nor is it merely a matter of a metropolitan artistic bohème going into the provinces. Munich has always been an important film-making city, and since the war has become the main production centre of the German film industry, as well as of its rivals the independents. A Mecca of movie fantasies, Munich was clearly crucial to films like *Gods of the Plague* and *Love is Colder than Death*, but also for Syberberg's *Ludwig – Requiem for a Virgin King* and even Herzog's *Fitzcarraldo*.[19]

Ultimately, the special role Bavaria has in any account of the German cinema resides in the fact that Munich is indeed something of an equivalent of Hollywood. It is the centre of different entertainment industries and of German show-business,

Josef Bierbichler, Annamirl Bierbichler and Herbert Achternbusch in Achternbusch's Bye, Bye Bavaria *(1977)*

with Upper Bavaria, the Alps and Austria as an all-too picturesque backdrop. Thus, the true importance of the *Heimat* film may be that it made Bavaria into an imaginary country. It gave rise to stories and stereotypes that constantly restage the conflicts between an ultra-conservative peasant culture on the one hand, and a cosmopolitan, hedonist, ultra-sophisticated urban culture on the other, but where each side of the divide is itself contradictory and schizophrenic. As in the case of Scotland, Bavaria has become itself a plastic myth, a store of ready-made symbols and part of a semiotically manipulable iconography.[20]

Through the gangster film and melodrama Fassbinder established a one-man studio system, but also a cinema of 'identification with the other'. Through classical *mise en scène* Wenders was able to develop a 'realist' aesthetic of duration over action, of image over narrative. Through the *Heimat* film Achternbusch found a new form of direct address and developed an authentically inauthentic 'persona' out of the very impoverishment and minimalism of this generally despised genre, without heroising it.

The notion, therefore, that the New German Cinema achieved in the 1970s its identity through genres – the *Heimat* film, melodrama, the worker's films, the women's film, youth films, road movies and so on – seems to me to need a very cautious formulation if it is to stand up to scrutiny. By concentrating on the outsider as both a rhetorical and a sociological figure, the significant feature does not seem to have been genre but the search for role models, for representative figures and the strategies of identification.

5:

In Search of the Spectator 2:
Cinema of Experience

Cinema against Television

With television entering the subsidy system, the search for audiences on the domestic front was both accentuated and displaced in emphasis. For the networks the audience was, in one sense, already constituted, ready-made. The programming schedules of television, however, put film directors under quite different constraints. Their films were at the mercy of seemingly arbitrary decisions as to when they were to be shown, while the time slots largely determined whom they would be shown to. On the other hand, television did allow film-makers to address audiences which the traditional cinema had not included at all. For instance, the legitimate demands of minorities to benefit from the principle of 'public interest', as defined in German broadcasting statutes, or the right of special pressure groups to be represented and have their grievances aired, gave rise to an enormous demand for films on the wide range of social issues mentioned earlier.

Titles that in other countries would form part of the vast and amorphous area of docu-drama, often had thrust upon them the status of authorial works and would officially count, rightly no doubt, as part of the New German Cinema: films dealing with racism (*Die Kümmeltürkin geht*), juvenile delinquency (*Nordsee ist Mordsee*), drug abuse (*Christiana F. – Die Kinder vom Bahnhof Zoo*), the yellow press (*Die Verlorene Ehre der Katharina Blum*), the penal sytem (*Die Verrohung des Franz Blum* – no relation), state surveillance (*Der Starke Ferdinand*), prostitution (*Shirins Hochzeit*), urban redevelopment (*Berlin Chamissoplatz*), or unemployment (*Kanackerbraut*).

At the same time, the dominant position of television meant that new audiences, generally younger and more media-conscious, found their way back to the cinema looking for an experience radically different from television. As in other countries, most of these spectators wanted Hollywood blockbusters, sci-fi and special effects extravaganzas, but it also meant that certain German films began to command a cult following among the *Szene* in Berlin or *Subkultur* of Munich. Directors like Lothar Lambert, Rosa von Praunheim, Walter Brockmayer and Uwe Schrader established a reputation with the so-called 'dirty little films' which appealed only to numerically very small audiences. As a result, the market for German films may not have expanded in volume, but it became noticeably more diverse, with the avant-garde/sub-culture/independent cinema sector feeding back into late night television slots.

By the mid-1970s certain broad categories had established themselves for targeting the domestic market: films by and for women (*Das zweite Erwachen*

Natja Brunkhorst (left) in Ulrich Edel's
Christiane F *(1981)*

Frank Ripploh (left) in Taxi zum Klo
(1981)

der Christa Klages, Hungerjahre, Redupers); films with an overtly 'cultural' appeal, dealing with literary works (*Effi Briest, The Tin Drum*), the traditional subjects of the art cinema (*Malou, Tarot*) or maintaining a close association with the legitimate theatre (the Berlin Schaubühne's *Sommergäste, Die Ortliebschen Frauen* or Fassbinder's *Nora Helmer* and *The Bitter Tears of Petra von Kant*); films with a camp sensibility (*The Death of Maria Malibran, Bildnis einer Trinkerin, Madame X*); films aimed at special interest groups which had militant social claims to represent: teachers, homosexuals, trade-unionists (*Vera Romeike Cannot Be Tolerated, Taxi zum Klo, Der aufrechte Gang*); finally, films which, thanks to their cinematic references or stylistic interest, appealed to connoisseurs of the cinema and fostered a nostalgic rediscovery of Hollywood cinema (Wenders' *Kings of the Road* and *The American Friend*).

As we have seen in an earlier chapter, such divisions mostly reflect the fact that under a mixed funding system and outside the commercial market, all films represent a compromise of conflicting expectations and calculations. In most cases audiences responded very much in direct proportion to recognising themselves and their own problems on screen. Paradoxically, the cinephile films at first encountered most resistance. Wenders or Herzog, for instance, did not treat overtly social issues and thus seemed ideologically ambiguous. Without a film culture to place them, films like *Even Dwarfs Started Small* (1970), *Fata Morgana* (1971) or *The Goalie's Fear of the Penalty Kick* (1971) could not relate to personal experience in the way that films made for specific target audiences did. The internationally famous directors thus fared rather badly in Germany itself, until their reputation abroad had filtered back and generated a kind of second order fan interest. Audiences in Germany often knew the names of Fassbinder, Herzog,

Wenders or Syberberg more from the newspapers than from actually having seen their films, and more from seeing their films on television than in the cinemas: 'In cities of less than 80,000 inhabitants people have at most heard the name of the director of *Die Brücke* (*The Bridge*), Bernhard Wicki and, from television, Fassbinder.'[1]

A frequent complaint was that foreign views of the German cinema were based on too small and unrepresentative a sample of films,[2] but also the inverse, namely that the New German Cinema lacked coherence, purpose, unity of style or subject.[3] These contradictory views can only be reconciled if one distinguishes between a concept of the New German Cinema as it constituted itself within the European art cinema, backed by the star directors and functioning largely *outside* Germany, and a New German Cinema as the direct consequence of the subsidy system and with a distinct existence *inside* Germany.

The Spaces of Independent Cinema

Serious cinema-going in Germany had always been a middle-class phenomenon. This is even reflected in the name given to quality cinemas in the 1950s and 1960s. What in France would have been the 'cinémas d'art et essai' were in Germany called *Gildekinos* (from 'Gilde der Filmkunst-Theater', reflecting a distinct burgher mentality). *Gildekinos*, with their subscription schemes and loyalty bonuses, had as their public a self-selected audience mainly for European art films and matinee classics (that is, viewers who shunned Hollywood productions even in auteurist forms).

By the time the mainly student audiences returned to the cinema at the end of the 1960s, not only had the *Gildekinos* all but disappeared, the neighbourhood commercial cinemas had as well. Only the larger cities still boasted first- and second-run houses. Across West Germany no more than a handful of venues, often second-run theatres owned privately, catered for a cine-literate or avant-garde audience. Up to 1970, the best-known of these were in Hamburg, Berlin and Munich, the latter being the traditional city for watching films.[4] By the mid-1970s the number of specialised cinemas, often set up in conjunction with a film-makers' co-op (the Abaton Kino in Hamburg, for example, opened in 1970 and refurbished as a cinema-cum-pub in 1973) or as the breakaway initiative of a film club (the Arsenal, for example, founded in 1970 by the Friends of the German Kinemathek) had increased dramatically. This was partly due – as mentioned earlier – to the publicity generated by a new venture in Frankfurt, where the then Senator for Cultural Affairs had initiated the first 'Kommunale Kino':

> It was an act of self-defence to create a municipal, subsidised cinema, equivalent in status to a theatre. The goal was to further education, entertainment, exploration of film culture through thematically organized programmes, the presentation of new work, the revival of historically important films.[5]

Something akin to a grassroot movement followed, with communal cinemas opening in cities like Cologne, Hanover, Mannheim, Stuttgart, Dortmund, Nürnberg and Göttingen. They were often located in university towns, after reconverting converted supermarkets or taking over boarded-up suburban cinemas.[6] The Arsenal had introduced the idea of programming 'seasons', and it had become the home of the Berlin Film Festival's *Forum des Jungen Films* which showed avant-garde, experimental, New German and Third World films in large numbers, and also ran a nationwide distribution and rental system. In Munich, the city museum cinémathèque had a daily changing programme of film classics. An increasing number of so-called 'Programmkinos' followed suit, breaking with the deeply engrained commercial practice of booking films for a week at a time and instead showing two or three different films a night.

One can distinguish several separate stages in this process of upgrading cinema-going, of which the effort to build up alternative film exhibition not dependent on the first-run houses was perhaps the most crucial. Directors became active as writers, critics and lobbyists, in a way no generation of film-makers had been before them, not even those of the French *nouvelle vague*.[7] Thirdly, directors took the lead by co-founding distribution companies and supporting 'alternative' outlets for independent films. This was the initial idea behind the *Filmverlag der Autoren*, originally a co-operative with Wenders, Fassbinder, Geissendörfer and Uwe Brandner as members.[8]

Kluge, Herzog, Schroeter and others also travelled with their films to film clubs or regional festivals, and participated in discussions with audiences after the screenings. They did this not only for the sake of self-promotion, but from a realisation that the German cinema needed to woo a new public in new spaces. As far as independent films were concerned, directors saw their potential audiences outside both the commercial film industry and outside television, however much financing depended on the latter.

Most of the exhibition initiatives mentioned, therefore, were aimed at identifying the spaces as physically distinct from traditional cinemas. Since portable equipment had brought films into university lecture theatres, community halls and adult education centres, the communal cinemas and cinemathèques tended to keep alive the heroic phase of the student movement in their setting and ambience. As the large picture palaces divided into multiplexes and mini-theatres made watching commercial feature films more and more like squeezing furtively into viewing booths for a pornography show, the idea that alternative films required altogether different venues seemed in fact self-evident. For several years Edgar Reitz and Ula Stöckl ran a cinema pub in Munich, after the example of the Hamburg Abathon. In order to integrate the space with the product, they even made a film specially designed for this venue – *Geschichten vom Kübelkind* – whose individual episodes could be shown in a different order or for performances of varying length.[9]

However isolated an example, such experiments proved that a great number of films were based neither on spectacle nor – as the ideology of the *Autorenfilm* might suggest – were they exercises in self-expression: often the film-makers themselves felt straitjacketed by this concept.[10] If films sought to address spectators with subjects and through protagonists appealing to a relatively small audience segment, they did so from a sense of shared values and assumptions, whereas a commercially oriented cinema has to go for the lowest common denominator. Herein lies a strength and a weakness. The New German Cinema, as I argued earlier, was different from the Young German Film precisely because it was aimed more coherently at an implied spectator. But by aiming at the highest common denominator, as it were, it also courted the risk of being either parochial (the in-group film) or esoteric. The plethora of apparently unclassifiable films was in a sense over-determined: a result not only of the double-headed production context of cinema and television, but of the new distribution situation opening up different possibilities of what was to pass as 'cinema'.

The New Audiences

Although the films shown outside West Germany amounted to merely the proverbial tip of the iceberg, the invisible parts were not just more films: what for an international public represented the New German Cinema often had a different meaning in Germany itself. This was less a matter of misreading than an indication that responses to certain films (such as the literary adaptations or the new *Heimat* films with their counter-cultural heroes) were conditioned by extra-cinematic contexts: the political issues of the day, for instance. The episode in *Germany in Autumn* (1978), showing a television production of *Antigone* being cancelled because of its potential analogies with the trials of the Berlin communes' urban terrorists and the Baader-Meinhof group, has already been mentioned. Kluge's *Occasional Work of a Female Slave* (1973) or Achternbusch's *The Ghost* (*Das Gespenst*, 1982) are in Germany always associated with the respective official attempts to interfere with the projects after pressure from Catholic lobbies.[11]

The most crucial context and reference point for film viewing during the 1970s was, no doubt, the student movement which, in West Germany no less than in France, developed a media consciousness alongside a political consciousness. Between 1968 and 1974 the cinema became a place where one expected not entertainment but information, not distraction but instruction. The Vietnam war had for many people in the West highlighted their general ignorance about world affairs and a lack of understanding about the role of industrial nations in the so-called post-colonial societies. A veritable hunger for information about politics, in the narrow as well as the wider sense of the term, filled the halls, cinemas and meetings where documentaries from Third World countries, testimonies, eye-witness reports, analyses of liberation movements and anti-war protests were shown. In a very specific sense, therefore, independent cinema was able to fill a need that official television only began to service in the later 1970s, when current affairs programmes and special reports increasingly reflected the fact that news as spectacle could be big business.

The sudden politicisation of a whole generation and social group around 1968 meant that audiences returned from the street to the cinema, with different expectations from the ones associated with the Saturday matinees of their childhood. They wanted information that the official media would ignore or suppress. Militant spectators, however, needed no *Programmkino* reviving *Casablanca* or *Stagecoach*, no municipally funded film museums showing restored prints of Murnau's *Faust*. Instead they sought cinemas that could function as a focal point for political opposition and protest – an anti-cinema, anti-television and anti-press medium. They also needed no German *Autorenkino*, if film was to be part of a collective act of self-expression and self-representation. The very media consciousness of the protest movement had helped the cinema, however briefly, to become 'naturalised' as a public arena for symbolic action. The primary audiences for political films were also often the ones most directly involved in the exceptionally virulent and violent protest actions in Berlin and elsewhere. This was a time when not only much of the history of the Federal Republic was opened up for re-examination but when the role of the media, and especially of the popular press, literally came under fire. To quote Michael Rutschky once more:

> The last big demonstration M. had participated in was the Berlin demonstration after the assassination attempt on Rudi Dutschke, which had ended in front of the Springer building, right by the Wall. It was the final straw for M. He found himself

incapable of throwing stones into the glass-fronted building or setting fire to the delivery vans.[12]

Film-makers who wanted to fill these new public spaces had to respond to the new pressure of the political, if only in the sense of being open to discussion and agitation, and having their films appropriated and tested for their use-value rather than consumed as self-sufficient objects. Most directly involved in this process was the Berlin Film School. Here students advocated a role for the cinema modelled on the one it had assumed after the Russian Revolution: that of a totally partisan instrument of agitation, of political education and of a new rationality, as well as a new militancy. In 1968 the Film School was briefly occupied by its students and baptised the 'Dziga-Vertov Academy'. Its most notorious agitprop film was simply called *Manufacturing a Molotov Cocktail*, and it concluded with a shot of the glass-fronted Springer newspaper building. One wonders whether Rutschky's M. discovered the sensibilist cinema of Wenders because he realised, amidst the violence outside the Springer headquarters, that he would never be a revolutionary fire-brand. Or did he know that in the cinema he could, if not learn how to make a Molotov Cocktail, at least watch himself watch the vans burn?

The Audience as Critics

In fact, despite confronting a very splintered audience, directors knew exactly whom their films were reaching. Because of the initial lack of exhibition outlets and the absence of a film culture (outside Hamburg, Berlin or Munich cinephile circles) directors travelling with their films did welcome the unmediated contact. Some, like Rosa von Praunheim, at the time of *Not the Homosexual is Perverse But the Situation in which He Finds Himself* (1970), and to counter largely hostile responses, refused to have the film booked in cinemas unless either he personally or a member of the production team was present to answer questions. Others, like Werner Schroeter, did the same, but felt more ambivalent. Asked about distribution he said in an interview in 1972:

> In recent years, I have been trekking around with my films, in fact I am usually present at the screenings, and it is quite a good method. It does not altogether satisfy me, of course, but right now I see no other concrete possibility (for getting the films to an audience).[13]

Personal appearances with subsequent discussions, bridging the customary separation in time and space between film production and film exhibition, may have entailed a loss of mystique for the cinemas' once paramount aura of glamour and exclusivity. But it was compensated for by the new currency directors gave to film-making as a publicly accountable activity. It became a practical engagement with audiences on the one hand and social reality on the other, thus also conferring a different status on film viewing and cinema-going. A director became comparable to the author reading from his or her work (strengthening the 'authorial' discourse of the New German Cinema), but she/he also met the audience as equals, presenting work intended to contribute, especially in the case of women's films, to the movement's self-definition. This activated the audience, restored to them an identity as social beings, rather than merely as consumers. Many of the discourses surrounding this independent cinema and constituting its justification had to do with creating what was called *Öffentlichkeit* (a 'public sphere') or a *Gegenöffentlichkeit* (an 'alternative public sphere') in which the media would have a radicalising and politicising function:

Compared with the commercially oriented film and its cinemas the alternative cinema has the advantage that it gets closer to the life of people rather than moving away from it, that it takes the spectator with his problems seriously, makes him more responsible than the commercial cinema could ever do. The advantage over television . . . is that our films can be tested in discussions, publications and seminars as to their attitudes to social developments at large . . .[14]

Not all film-makers agreed with this interpretation of a film's function. *Even Dwarfs Started Small*, for instance, was Herzog's way of representing his isolation after the 1968 Oberhausen Festival. The film issued a challenge to the German Left about what Herzog saw as the impossibility of combining political revolution with radical subjectivity. Kluge's *Artistes at the Top of the Big Top: Disorientated* and Reitz' *Cardillac* were also made as a result of direct confrontations with spectators. As mentioned earlier, they were reactions to rows with students at the Berlin Film School. From occasions such as these Kluge concluded that German directors are particularly vulnerable because of their many target audiences:

In the heads of its makers the New German film is subject to accumulated 'programmation'. Precisely because they feel no longer under orders, liberated from the shackles of a producer's directives, they confront a number of partly imaginary, partly contradictory demands, of which they believe that if they fulfil them, their film would derive advantages: the premises of the committees, the national critics, the exhibition sector, hopes of an international festival success, assumptions about spectator-preferences, opinions of colleagues . . . Such a committee in one's head creates a sort of artistic super-ego. Such a super-ego produces scruples. Such scruples lead to vagueness and indeterminacy.[15]

Another way of putting it would be to say that many of the most typical products of this cinema had both a very direct audience response via active and self-selected spectators, and a completely different feedback structure: long-term and mediated. Where the Young German Film had still implicitly, albeit in vain, addressed itself to an imaginary national audience, the New German Cinema went the other way. It tried to escape television by meeting its home audiences among the groups who, with the student movement, had rediscovered the cinema as a new public space, promising very personal experiences, but which through discussions and debates could be verbalised or rationalised in a political discourse. To these audiences film-makers turned with more 'primitive' or tribal forms of publicity than the commercial film industry employed. The directors who toured found that to show their films in the context of specific campaigns, cultural occasions and public events (not necessarily connected with the cinema) gave them better audiences than regular cinemas. Statistically, such audiences were miniscule and in the short term economically insignificant. On the other hand one of Herzog's boasts, that his 'films are made for the next fifty, maybe five hundred years',[16] also seems less of an exaggeration with the possibility that through video, but also via this other film culture, a film might indeed become an object like a novel or a volume of poetry. Spared the perishable shelf life of the best seller, it could (and in some cases has) become a classic without having been a financial success or on general release.

The Idea of *Erfahrung*

During the roundtable discussions in Frankfurt already quoted, Christian Ziewer tried to answer the question:

'What audience do I have'? First of all, a largely bourgeois public interested in self-reflection and culture . . . For parts of this public, 'culture' doesn't just mean getting to know certain forms of expression of social life, but participating in change. I think the decisive factor is that these spectators come to the cinema with certain expectations that differ completely from the ingrained ones of commercial film . . . This is true of bourgeois audiences as well as workers, who realize that film can be a means of life ['Lebensmittel': in German also the word for 'food'].[17]

Between such divergent conceptions as that of Herzog ('films are made for the next fifty years') and Ziewer's ('film can be food'), a film necessarily becomes a very ambiguous object in the rapport between film-maker and audience. As the protest movement lost momentum, the independent cinema, which had to some extent served it, had fallen between two stools. On the one hand it did not occupy the social space nor command the financial resources of a dominant medium (like television) and, on the other, the 'hard' information it could give was more easily and efficiently communicated through other organs of the Left (newspapers, pamphlets, targeted actions). The cinema's claims to social relevance had to be based on another criterion. The touchstone that developed could best be described by the word *Erfahrung*. Indicative of the potentially fertile but also frustrating relations between film, film-maker and spectator, the term invariably turned up in face-to-face encounters between directors and their public. Because it is a word richer in philosophical, emotional and cognitive connotations than the English 'experience', *Erfahrung* had a special topicality during the 1970s. It is in fact closer to the cluster of meanings associated with 'consciousness', as in 'consciousness-raising', than with the relatively pale literal translation.

Thus, while the term *Erfahrung* names experiences of all kinds when related to the cinema, it does suggest also a distance, a self-reflexive dimension, different from group therapy 'consciousness raising'. *Erfahrung* implies a certain form of spectatorship – if only of oneself in the act of introspection, as in the then very fashionable term *Selbsterfahrung*. The notion could preserve a certain ambiguity about going to see a film, appreciating not its entertainment value, but its relevance to personal experiences and problems, which one wanted to have argued out or see confirmed. A passage by Ziewer, explaining the background to *Dear Mother, I'm Fine* (*Liebe Mutter, mir geht es gut*, 1971) is typical in this respect:

The interests, motivation and praxis of the recipients are the starting points. For it is from familiar surroundings that the spectator must derive what is significant. *Liebe Mutter, mir geht es gut*, in its seemingly documentary parts, tries to tie in with the spectator's viewing habits. The language is the language of everyday. The experiences of those directly affected have entered into it.[18]

The result of many of the discussions about audiences and their expectations was a tension between different kinds of realities 'in the spectator's head': that of wanting to experience social emotions (solidarity, empathy, memory) and, conversely, looking to films for a representation of essentially asocial feelings (melancholy, aggression, frustration) or, finally, for a recognition of radical 'otherness'. None of these forms of spectatorship is adequately described by the word 'subjective', and even less by a distinction between 'political' and 'escapist' film-making. Indeed, many of the films of the New German Cinema address the spectator in this triple register of identification, distanciation and otherness. They invite recognition on the basis of consensus, as do many of the women's films, but also recognition as estrangement, as in the case of gay films that invert stereotypes or employ parody. What makes certain films, such as Fassbinder's social melodramas, stand out is that they justify and accommodate both the solipsistic and narcissistic pleasures of going to the movies, without thereby excluding the cinema's role of providing a 'political' experience of otherness.

The issue-oriented films discussed earlier, therefore, have to be seen under the aspect of not only *what* areas of social life or experience they represented, but *how* the spectators' perception of the issue was shaped by a film-maker within the dual horizon of the cinema as simultaneously private experience and social space. The emphasis on *Erfahrung* and *Öffentlichkeit* in the debates surrounding the films allowed the cinema to be seen by its audiences 'horizontally', as it were, as integral to other areas of public life and, equally importantly, integral to the viewers' own experience.

What often seemed to be taken for granted was the extent to which cinema served an audience for confirming or validating individual experience and feelings. Films did not have to ring true to a traditional notion of spectacle or pleasurable involvement. Rather, to a much more specific, differentiated, yet also often diffuse desire, manifested in discussions as a demand, directed at the film-maker, to represent only a 'correct' political or ideologically unambiguous standpoint. The rapidly institutionalised discussions between film-makers and audiences encouraged this need for self-confirmation and self-validation in the guise of criticism and ad hoc political theory on the part of the spectators. But the desire for transparency in the representation and immediacy of contact could also register as disruptive interference. Debates often became very aggressive, confrontational and irrational before ceasing abruptly. When Ulrike Ottinger was asked about audience response to her feminist pirate film *Madame X* (1977), she replied:

Tabea Blumenschein in Ulrike Ottinger's Madame X *(1977)*

Evelyn Künnecke in von Praunheim's I Am an Anti-Star *(1976)*

In general, the discussions (after the screenings) were always very boring for me. Partly of course because it's difficult for people to say anything directly after a film. Only when there is time for a longer discussion does it sometimes get quite interesting. At first it's the same ten questions every time which by now ought to be banned: What did you intend? What does it mean? Who did you make the film for? Is it intended as social criticism? What alternatives do you have to offer? . . . I really get the impression that people feel very helpless (with our films).[19]

Film-makers found it irritating to deal with what seemed to them a very naive appropriation or rejection of the film's 'statement'. Audiences, encouraged not to consume the films as entertainment and judge them accordingly, only had an often awkwardly verbalised personal framework of references and immediate interests to relate the films to. At the 1983 Berlin Film Festival Claudia Alemann made no attempt to conceal her anger and impatience when, after a screening, she was confronted with yet another round of 'who did you make the film for?' and 'what was your intention?'[20]

'Hunger for Experience'

What becomes apparent in the Dichter poll and in Rutschky's symptomatic spectator M. is that the new audiences appeared to expect from the cinema and films something both more and less than what is usually understood by movie entertainment. Instead of forgetting their own lives in the glamour or adventure of another existence, they wanted to become more aware of themselves. Instead of demanding distraction, they wanted concentration, intensity of selfhood rather than self-oblivion. Rutschky coined for this – and other aspects of life for the post-1968 generation – the term *Erfahrungshunger* (hunger for experience):

> The countless restless searching movements, the almost programmatically confusing activities and tendencies which can be observed in the 1970s . . . I see them as the verso and reversal of the utopia which unfolded itself in the 1960s: that of the validity of abstract concepts.[21]

For Rutschky, therefore, the new interest in the cinema during the 1970s was directly related to the loss of faith in the sociological and critical categories of the 1960s. If these had once helped to understand personal reality as part of social reality, they had impoverished the 'realm of the senses' to the point where the external world had become identical with its sociological abstractions. The sensibilist's desire was thus not for a new subjectivity as much as for a new objectivity: 'perception, experience, sensory apperception – not interpretation'. The migration of motifs from film to film, the allusionism and sharing of a common iconography discussed in a subsequent chapter in the context of a reappropriation of a sense of the past, can also be seen as part of this more general translation of analytical insights and political experiences into the forms appropriate to a media reality, as opposed to verbal discourse. The cult of images is thus more than simply the regression to a new irrationalism.

Rutschky himself, of course, operates with abstractions and generalisations. The sort of symptoms he is describing for the generation in their late twenties and early thirties during the last decade not only provides a number of suggestions for seeing the development of the German cinema through the eyes of its audiences. It also confirms the aesthetic stances and programmes of the film-makers as discussed in Chapter 4.

Rutschky's opposition between his primary research object, the sensibilists and

160

Barbara Valentin, Magdalena Montezuma and Irm Hermann in Ulrike Ottinger's
Dorian Gray in the Popular Press *(1983)*

the 'contentists', is thus more apparent than real. It almost seems that one needs more encompassing categories if one is to account not only for the majority of films made in Germany and never seen abroad, but also for the films that do typify the New German Cinema, such as Wenders' or Herzog's. Their origin in a certain conception of and commitment to (non-classical) realism is too obvious to be ignored, but also too awkward to be explained by any reference to either 'documentary' film-making, *cinéma verité*, or to a tradition of neo-realism in the cinema as defined by Bazin.

The reason why 'experience' seems a useful word in this context is that it attenuates the binarism which is usually set up between 'progressive' and 'reactionary' texts, between a cinema of pleasure and a cinema of unpleasure, the 'realist' film and the 'illusionist' film. 'Hunger for experience' as an expectation of spectatorship can thus encompass both the identification and recognition of the spectator's practical interests in the representation, but also the sensations and pleasures associated with going to the cinema. The fact that feeling at home in the cinema, away from home, was sociologically speaking a much more frequent and typical experience for adolescent males than for young women, has left its mark on German film-making, and gives rise to another polarity that needs to be examined. A case will be made that there are specifically male and female notions of experience to be found in the New German Cinema. For it is clear that Rutschky's symptomatic spectator M. is male and that the kind of 'hunger for experience' which characterises his pleasure in the cinema is intimately linked to giving priority to the male spectator position in the cinema. When discussing

161

films made by women for women, the question of the specificity of the experience addressed in the implied spectator will be answered more fully.

I am coining the term 'cinema of experience' to describe a film-making practice aimed not at specific audiences, but at particular spectatorial dispositions, at forms of spectatorship neither identical with the psychoanalytically defined visual pleasure of classical realism, nor different from it in the way the Brechtian term distanciation or the formalist 'defamiliarisation' are used. The argument would be that much of the German cinema solicits distinct forms of spectatorship which need historical as well as textual definitions. So far, I have deliberately concentrated on the social and ideological definition of these domestic audiences. I will later turn to particular instances of the filmic forms which corresponded to such spectator expectations: the documentary, the *Arbeiterfilm*, the women's film and the films that emerged from the gay movement.

The Documentary Bias of the New German Cinema

The more sustained debates about film form in West Germany have always been centred not on spectatorship but on the question of realism. Yet as we have seen in the discussions about the post-Oberhausen fiction films made with documentary methods, it would be too simple to reduce the options to realism versus anti-illusionism, or realism versus fantasy. Likewise, the concepts of realism which directors like Fassbinder and Wenders derived from American genre films to support a *mise en scène* of pathos and perverse identification (Fassbinder) or duration and point of view (Wenders) cannot be phrased in the familiar terms of identification versus distanciation.[22]

It was under the pressure of a more militant engagement with social struggles and target groups that the argument moved from the correct representation of reality as the main criterion of political film-making to focusing instead on the spectator. By asking himself what combination of reportage and fictional transposition of events was more likely to activate the spectators' awareness of a situation, and their ability to perceive it as changeable, Christian Ziewer became typical of this reorientation:

> If a form of perception is to be fostered which helps to understand connections and sharpen an awareness of problems, it is not enough simply to 'sensitise' the spectator. Sensitivity *per se* is merely a blind reflex to the status quo . . . It is the combination of fact and reflection which ignites the spectator's imagination. Contradictions, gaps and the insertion of epic material get the imagination going – an imagination directed towards change.[23]

In Ziewer's remarks, the legacy of Brechtian concepts of realism is most in evidence. They point to a mixed form, where directly observed material and staged recreations are joined. In practice Ziewer's film-making, as exemplified by the workers' films he co-scripted and directed for WDR, largely relied on purely fictional techniques, dramatised situations and the classical realism of the invisible fourth wall (deep-space, scene-dissection and point-of-view structure). As we shall see, Ziewer's position was not the only one, and his films gave rise to fundamental disagreements about the methods and uses of realism in political film-making generally. One implicit critique came from another 'Brechtian' – Alexander Kluge.

In an influential and extensive appendix to the published script of *Gelegenheitsarbeit einer Sklavin* (*Occasional Work of a Female Slave*, 1973), Kluge proposes what he calls an 'antagonistic concept of realism'. Starting from the idea that both documentary and fiction films share an essential deductive mode of representation, Kluge argues that in both cases a set of expectations belonging to the respective genres organises the spectator's observations (and determine the logic of the action). By bracketing off actual connections, both documentary and fiction film exclude other, equally possible correlations between facts:

> The basic elements of film may have become highly specialised (since Méliès and Lumière) but the principle has remained the same: isolated segments of reality, instances of time are formed, and edited together to create a coherence. In the case of the documentary, there are three 'cameras' present, (1) the camera in the technical sense, (2) that in the head of the film-makers, and (3) the genre-'head', formed by the expectations of the spectator who anticipates seeing a documentary . . . What we have to begin to understand is that the camera's much-vaunted documentary authenticity is no different from the total stylization of opera.[24]

For Kluge, the spectator brings to the cinema a mode of perception where facts and desires are never separated – 'desire is the form in which facts are perceived'.[25] The classic realist fiction film accommodates the pressure which desire exerts on the creation of a coherence between events, by the causal nexus of linear sequence and suspense. Against this concept of realism Kluge's antagonistic realism sets a more anthropological model of perception. Its basic assumption is that the spectator's desire is never directed towards confirming reality as it is, but rather takes the form of protest. Whether this protest expresses itself by 'mimicking the oppressor', 'escaping the pressure of the real' (into fantasy) or 'violent redressing of a situation' (through aggression) is less important than the fact that these 'natural' reactions are generally repressed in the interest of 'balanced', rational behaviour. Any 'realist cinema', according to Kluge, therefore has to work with this contradictory state of the spectator's perceptual apparatus. The main objective must be to heighten not the efficacy of the pre-established generic formula or manage aggression and conflict through linear narrative, nor sharpen a specific sense experience (the cardinal sin in Kluge's book of the 'sensibilists'), but

> to produce at all cost the ability to differentiate . . . This assumes an associative method and an organised ability to remember. The result is a restructuring of the spectator's sensuous interest into a sensuous-social interest, a thoroughly analytical 'second instinct'.[26]

Consequently, the cinema's 'means of expression is difference, a basic disharmony between the individual (film-)product and reality, not the easily produced harmony of the individual material with itself'. By this Kluge means any theory of 'pure cinema' or of realism as self-evidence. Thus Kluge is proposing an essentially semiotic theory of filmic signification ('difference'), but he attaches it to a psychological theory of spectatorship. The aim is the 'production of a horizon of experience', as opposed to the 'horizon of expectation' programmed by genre cinema:

> Without such a context for experience (*Erfahrungszusammenhang*) neither motivation nor perception, neither the logic of constellations, nor a judgment about the authenticity of the means of production could shape themselves.[27]

Kluge's stress on differentiation, based on the discontinuity of the filmic process, makes his theory appear similar to Godard's montage theory. But, as his use of the term *Erfahrung* indicates, for him difference is not a way of preserving a radical heterogeneity of signifying materials (as in Godard's systematic confrontation of

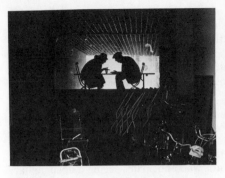

Alexander Kluge's The Power of Feelings *(1983)*

Bruno S before he met Herzog (in Lutz Eisholz's Bruno the Black, *1970)*

sounds and images). Instead it serves to create a new kind of coherence, that of the spectator-subject reconciling facts and desires. Kluge's idea of montage is neither quite the classical filmic one of Eisenstein, nor the agitational one of Vertov. Behaviourist rather than political, more associational than formal-aesthetic, its main function is pragmatic. It provides a rationale for a concept of *Erfahrung* which on the one hand takes account of experience mediated by the filmic apparatus and, secondly, creates a space for the mixture of documentary and fiction film typical of the German cinema. The 'cinema of experience' is thus intimately connected to, but not identical with, documentary.

Kluge, Herzog and Syberberg

It is not often appreciated that virtually every feature film-maker of the first and second generation after Oberhausen started in documentary films. Some, like Kluge, have never felt the need to make a rigid separation between the two modes. Conversely, film-makers such as Klaus Wildenhahn or Peter Nestler who, because their work is classed as documentary, have scarcely ever come to the notice of film critics, have pioneered techniques and espoused styles which were also of consequence to feature film directors. As we have seen in the context of the so-called issue-orientation of the New German Cinema, the filmed essay and the full-length documentary loom large in the volume of annual production. This is mainly because of television's appetite for investigative journalism and docu-drama, but it is equally true that throughout the last 25 years feature film-making in West Germany has renewed itself primarily by its rediscovery of documentary.

Kluge himself is perhaps the most obvious fiction film director relying on documentary methods and material. But where Ziewer would argue for heightening realism by means of dramatised scenes acted by professionals, Kluge's films (such as *The Patriot*, 1979; *The Power of Feelings*, 1983 and *The Blind Director*, 1985) are notorious for the way the documentary gesture is heightened by being made part of the fiction. Kluge invents facts, statistics, historical characters and dates, referring to them as if they were common knowledge. Meanwhile, his fictional characters (in *The Patriot*, for instance) appear at such 'documented' events as the SPD's party political conference, listening to Willy Brandt or the novelist Max Frisch.

164

Physical film-making: Herzog's Signs of Life *(1968)*

Kluge's early short films (*Porträt einer Bewährung, Frau Blackburn wird gefilmt, Feuerlöscher F.A. Winterstein* and *Ein Arzt aus Halberstadt*) are all in some sense portraits of eccentric but also representative individuals (as it happens, often relatives of the film-maker). In retrospect one can see that the shorts are mainly about the problem of how to give the illusion of subjectivity, of having access to a person's inner life, feelings, values, by exploiting the gap between an excess of external objectivity (an accumulation of pseudo-facts), and the pseudo-neutrality of a reticent, but insistently present camera.[28]

In the later feature films, Kluge tries to work the quirkiness of his characters into a larger historical scheme, by means of voice-over commentary and didactic montage techniques. These rationalise erratic behaviour as resistance and protest, in the sense of an 'antagonistic realism' as defined above. The earlier films show rather less editorial and authorial interference. Instead, they restrict themselves to a certain kind of observation, usually of moments and incidents which more story-oriented film-making would consider irrelevant or undramatic, and a documentary film-maker might deem impertinently fictionalised. An example is a scene from *Ein Arzt aus Halberstadt* (*A Doctor from Halberstadt*, 1970), where Kluge's camera lingers on his father trying to rid himself of a fly, shot with the heartless humour of a W.C. Fields comic routine.

Nothing at first glance resembles these films more than the documentaries of Werner Herzog. Herzog, too, is a director who heightens the documentary stance to the point where it becomes itself a powerful fiction. He has often stated that his non-fiction work is essential for an understanding of all his films.[29] From the first features such as *Signs of Life* and *Even Dwarfs Started Small* via *Aguirre* or *Fitzcarraldo* to *Where the Green Ants Dream*, the fiction serves to dramatise a peculiarly physical notion of film-making. Herzog has never ceased shooting documentaries alongside his feature films, recognising no fundamental difference. As in the case of Kluge, Herzog wants to document the fascination that emanates from the fictional or fantastic elements at the very heart of the everyday occurrence. This is eminently the case in his American documentaries *Huie's Sermon* (1980) and *How Much Wood Would A Woodchuck Chuck* (1975/76), as opposed to the 'heightening' of a documentary subject such as the ski-jumper Steiner. Here Herzog focuses on his subject's obsessions: a pet raven and wood-sculptures of exploding universes (*The Great Ecstasy of the Woodcarver Steiner*, 1973/74). Searching for the exemplary within the exotic/ecstatic becomes more of a problem in films as politically explicit (and unfashionable) as his documentary about the Misquito Indians fighting on the side of the Contras against the Sandinista Government in Nicaragua (*The Ballad of the Little Soldier*; *Die Ballade vom kleinen Soldaten*, 1984).[30]

And yet Herzog's approach to documentary differs fundamentally from Kluge's. Coupled with the long passages of *temps morts* and an insistence on place (not only natural landscapes and environments at the edge of civilisation) over social factors determining people's fate, Herzog's inventions of his characters' obsessions (Herr Scheitz's animal magnetism in *Stroszek*, Fitzcarraldo's dream of building an opera house) and collective, fantastic mythologies (e.g. in *Heart of Glass* or *Where The Green Ants Dream*) become part of an almost desperate attempt to fix a reality in its physicality and otherness. By conjuring up the gravity of myth, Herzog makes temporality (often represented in the form of decay) the key to his filmic language. Against Kluge's impatience with filming in real time (especially in his later work), because it inhibits the dialectic of differentiation and interpretation which alone makes reality signify and the eye intelligent, Herzog's main interest is in process. This is true even if the occasions for these processes to become filmable have to be elaborately created first, as in *Aguirre*'s river expedition or in *Fitzcarraldo*'s scheme of winching a steamboat across a mountain.

Both film-makers, compared to more analytical or political documentarists, have an interest in myth and apparently irrational modes of behaviour. It distinguishes them from critical documentarists of the Wildenhahn school as much as from political fiction film-makers like Ziewer. Yet Herzog, especially, brings to his films an attitude of distance which, to mark it off from Brechtian distanciation, might be called ethnographic. Lived intimacy with the film's subjects, a preference for the long take and hand-held camera work, small crews and respectful or reticent narrators who let the subjects speak for themselves are its salient features.[31]

In the case of Herzog it is an ethnography of civilisations, designed to circumvent primarily a sociological and a psychological perspective on his subjects and their lives. Herzog retains (as a technique of *Verfremdung*) a 'stupid' eye, one that is merely curious rather than knowing or demonstrative. In his films *The Flying Doctors of East Africa* (1968/9) or *Fata Morgana* (1971), distance is achieved by the superimposition of (again) pseudo-myths about creation on situations that cry out for a historical or political analysis. The myths provide a frame which is both deliberately inadequate and highly ironic: it implies other models of understanding which are subverted by a commentary at once ludicrous and solemn.

By contrast, Kluge's is not a 'stupid' but a cold eye. His distance comes from a perfect aping of the functionalism become second nature in medical, legal or

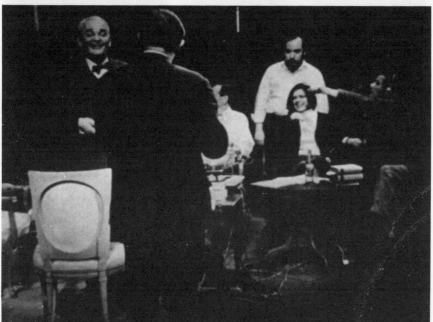

Syberberg as documentarist: Fritz Kortner in Fritz Kortner in rehearsal . . . *(1965)*
and (top right) Winifred Wagner in The Confessions of Winifred Wagner *(1975)*

bureaucratic language.[22] Kluge's protective mimicry is so perfect and of such virtuosity that it is sometimes difficult to see in it the melancholy irony by which he hints at the negative image of a utopia, the gradual disappearance of that *Erfahrungshorizont*. Instead, the mechanical puppets that agitate in his films are often a reminder of the satirical gaze which the critics of Oberhausen found so disagreeable. Others object to the gesture of appropriating reality that seems equally typical. In reviewing *The Patriot* Hartmut Bitomski wrote in *Filmkritik*:

> His film uses up images more than it creates them. Kluge films a situation, but he doesn't seize the moment. When somewhere the police are storming a house to evict squatters, or to remove troublemakers from a supermarket, Kluge is there, his information is obviously reliable. Raw film stock runs past his lens by the yard. Nevertheless, afterwards it always looks as if he had arrived just too late.[33]

In Herzog the danger is an inverse one: that of a fabricated exoticism disguised as immediacy and presence. In his first feature film *Signs of Life*, which deals with a German soldier during the closing stages of World War Two running amok in a garrison on Crete, Herzog suggests that it is not the war, but the landscape, the heat and the valley of the thousand windmills that drive the hero mad, making his revolt an existential and even biblical gesture. Herzog's project, however, must be understood as a reaction to the all-too-knowing, overinterpreting films from *Notabene Mezzogiorno* (1962) to Syberberg's *Scarabea* (1968).

As a fiction film-maker Syberberg might be said to have had a false start with *Scarabea* and *San Domingo* (1970), after which he found himself again as a documentarist. What sets him off from Herzog and Kluge in this respect is that he has always preferred making his documentaries about people with a distinct flair for or professional involvement in show-business and the *mise en scène* of their own lives. His very first film featured Fritz Kortner, the Expressionist actor and theatre-director, rehearsing a scene from a play by Schiller (*Fritz Kortner probt Kabale und Liebe*, 1965). This was followed by *Romy – Anatomie eines Gesichts* (*Romy Schneider – Anatomy of a Face*, 1965), a docu-portrait of the actress Romy Schneider at the time of her relationship with Alain Delon. It is these films, together with *Die Grafen Pocci* (*The Counts of Pocci*, 1967), about an eccentric Bavarian count, that prepared the way for *Ludwig – Requiem for a Virgin King*:

> [*Die Grafen Pocci*] is really the story of a house, Schloss Ammerland near Lake Starnberg. We enter the story via its last owner and his curious life, exceptional for Germany, and look at the psyche, history and everyday philosophy of this beautiful family, whose best-known ancestor invented, a hundred years ago, the Bavarian harlequin for children . . . Undoctrinaire and witty, he was the contemporary of Richard Wagner and Ludwig the Second, and their polar opposite, but, without hostility, a late Romantic.[34]

Equally, Syberberg's five hour interview about and with Winifred Wagner – *Winifred Wagner und die Geschichte des Hauses Wahnfried* (*The Confessions of Winifred Wagner*, 1975) is primarily the documentary of a person's ability to create and live, all external evidence to the contrary, her life as a private, self-created fiction. It is in this respect also similar to *Ludwig*, a film which Syberberg followed up with a fictionalised documentary about Ludwig's cook, Theodor Hierneis, who gives his own version of events, and is shown casually to have benefited handsomely from marketing his former association with the fantastic monarch.

Syberberg has moved from making documentaries about performances, to

Rosa von Praunheim's Our Corpses Are Still Alive *(1981)*

documentaries about show-business people. He has moved from making documentaries about the *mise en scène* of historical figures (*Ludwig, Karl May*) to documentaries about the *mise en scène* of myths and apocalypses (*Our Hitler*, 1977; *Die Nacht*, 1985). Thus he has never ceased to be a documentary filmmaker, except that in his conception of what could be considered document and documentary form, he has borrowed more and more from opera and allegorical modes of spectacle, such as the baroque *teatrum mundi*.

Herzog, Kluge and Syberberg are, in this penchant for documenting the self-enclosing fictions of eccentrics, misfits or naively-evil villains, typical of the Munich School of film-making. Escaping from the sombre or sordid, captured by an idée fixe, the protagonists of their films dramatise themselves, often in an explicitly theatrical or operatic context. As already discussed, Fassbinder made such role play the basis for his gangster films, skilfully exploiting the cinema itself as an inner frame of reference. He also directed for television a personality show celebrating Brigitte Mira, the actress who played the charwoman in *Fear Eats the Soul* (1973). *Like a Bird on a Wire* (*Wie ein Vogel auf dem Draht*, 1974) documents how the once famous and glamorous Mira (a star in the 1950s) rescues her vitality in old age. Another film which comes to mind is Schlöndorff's documentary of the cabaret singer and actress of the German silent cinema, Valeska Gert (*Nur zum Spaß nur zum Spiel*, 1977). Similarly, Rosa von Praunheim's *Evelyn Künnecke – Ich bin ein Anti-Star* (1976) and *Rote Liebe* (*Red Love*, 1981), as well as his fiction films *Berliner Bettwurst* (*The Bedroll*, 1971), and *Unsere Leichen leben noch* (*Our Corpses are Still Alive*, 1981). Films by Walter Bockmayer (*Jane is Jane Forever*, 1977), and by Peter Kern, Kurt Raab and Elfi Mikesch (*Ich denke oft an Hawaii*; *I Often Think of Hawaii*, 1978) spring from a similar attempt to convey emotion

169

Marianne Segerbrecht and Eisi Gulp in Percy Adlon's Sugarbaby *(1985)*

through the popular romantic song, or sentimentally celebrate a consciousness colonised by comic strips, travel agent brochures and romance fiction.

Not all the directors mentioned above can be associated with the Munich School (Praunheim and Mikesch are 'Berlin' film-makers, as we shall see). But slicker, more calculated and internationally successful examples in this vein are the films of Percy Adlon, *Zuckerbaby* (*Sugarbaby*, 1983) and *Bagdad Café* (*Out of Rosenheim*, 1987). *Sugarbaby* is the story of a fat mortician developing a passion for a skinny blond train driver, whom she stalks by stealing and meticulously studying the rota scheme of the Munich underground. The film is a quintessentially Munich product by a director both born and living there. On the other hand, the work of Werner Schroeter and Ulrike Ottinger, which might superficially belong here, constitutes a critique of the 'cinema of experience'. Their films not only try to change the perspective which the traditional cinema has on the outsider, on marginal individuals and 'freaks', but also, how in the absence of a high culture norm, the deformations of popular culture can imply a more radical form of subjectivity which challenges the very concept of experience as confirming self-hood and identity.

6:

In Search of the Spectator 3:
Minority Views

The Sphere of Production and the World of Work

It might well be argued that defining 'experience' as a dichotomy between the drab everyday and the degraded, but also authentic, fantasies of popular culture, is to give in to a typically petit bourgeois romanticism about misfits and déclassés, who have always been the social heroes of intellectuals. However, the Munich indulgence in artifice actually signalled a swing of the pendulum. It marked a veering away from the films, mainly made in Berlin, about the organised working class, its domestic problems and the world of work.

A new interest in working-class experience arose in West Germany at around the same time as the Oberhausen protest, though not at first in relation to the cinema. It was the revival of the kind of documentary literature as practiced in the 1920s and early 1930s that prepared the appearance of the *Arbeiterfilme* and also largely set the terms for the theoretical debate about realism and political film-making. The postwar literary scene in West Germany was dominated by the Group 47, formed in protest against the censorship pressures that the Allied Control Commission had exerted against the liberal-left literary journal *Der Ruf* in 1947.[1] Yet despite these origins, during the 1950s the Group 47 became associated with an apolitical if not conservative concept of literature and commitment. In a comparison between East and West Germany, *The Times* came to the conclusion that:

> In the West, the working class seems to have almost disappeared from the literary map . . . however anti-bourgeois and bohemian West German writers seem to be, however much they reject the inhumanity of modern society, they nonetheless remain within a strikingly bourgeois world and concern themselves with problems carefully separated from the realities of working class existence.[2]

The counter-move came in 1961 from a group of writers, journalists and critics from Dortmund who founded the Group 61, in deliberate and polemical contrast to the Group 47.[3] Their aim was to steer clear of two dangers: that of reviving the worker poet of the early years of socialism, and of imitating the so-called 'Bitterfeld Way', which in the GDR organised workers into writers' collectives and workshops: 'What is important is not the profession or social status of the writer, but only the subject and his ability to represent it artistically.'[4]

The naiveties of this programme did not escape its critics. But the Group 61 encouraged writers like Max von der Grün to write popular fiction about working-class characters, their problems in the workplace and at home and their relation to German history and the new-found prosperity. These were themes which were

171

to be the basis for the fictionalised treatment of labour disputes, social conflict and trade union activity that one finds in the *Arbeiterfilme*. Group 61 was also the first home of Günther Wallraff, whose investigative journalism and unorthodox research methods made him the folk hero of the Left during the 1970s, and the most successful writer ever on the practices of private industry and the actual situation of the working class. His *Industriereportagen* revived the concept of an operational literature in the tradition of Tretiakov and Benjamin, but in the spirit of a Trotskyite Fantomas. He was known to put on a disguise, present himself with borrowed identity papers for labouring jobs in Germany's heavy industries or large manufacturing firms, and record his experiences over several months before writing them up in racy and engrossing prose. Always keeping a step ahead of the fury and legal might of his duped employers, he published devastating reports of safety violations and everyday exploitation of the workforce, of labour camp conditions for Gastarbeiter, housing rackets and other malpractices among virtually all the leading firms and figures whom the economic miracle had made into status symbols of Germany's democratic recovery.[5]

Opponents of the Group 61 had by then founded the *Werkkreis Literatur der Arbeitswelt*, which was particularly active in West Berlin. Its indictment of bourgeois literature was even more radical and contained a case for commercial popular culture:

> For nearly two centuries the bourgeois poet and writer has been preoccupied with the cares and worries of his class, detailing with keen attention the spiritual state of the middle-class and upwards. The social struggle of those he likes to call the broad masses has passed him by virtually without a trace. Economic problems are of interest to this 'conscience of the nation' only under duress, and social themes figure merely as background. The 'broad masses' reward the writer who ignores their problems and interests by not reading his books or only those which at least touch on the unsatisfied desires of the majority: of married bliss without hire purchase payments and rent increases, of Hollywood dreams of glamour and leisure, of a sex life which isn't damaged by assembly line work or the twelve hour shift, of a world where the law is not manipulated and right and wrong are simple options . . . and human beings can be happy.[6]

In contrast to Max von der Grün and even Wallraff, the aim of the *Werkkreis* movement was to get workers to write about themselves, to become through writing partisan and articulate, and to address not a general public but – in the manner of Brecht's learning plays – to generate solidarity and a practical consciousness among members of the organised working class. If their impact was brief and local at best, the *Werkkreis* and the *Gruppe 61*, as well as similar initiatives, raised important issues about the representation of the working class in the press and the media, about shop-floor democracy and the problematic position of trade unions.

Arbeiterfilme

It is against this generally high level of debate, at least among the Left, that the emergence of the *Arbeiterfilme* has to be seen. The films grouped under this category include a documentary, divided into self-contained scenes and episodes, about a factory closure (*Rote Fahnen sieht man besser*; *Red Flags Are More Visible*, 1971); a series of feature films by Christian Ziewer and Klaus Wiese focusing on the internal conflicts between differently politicised workers on the

Hanna Schygulla and Gottfried John in
Fassbinder's Eight Hours Are Not a Day
(1972)

Tilo Prückner and Dagmar Biener in
Marianne Lüdcke/Ingo Kratisch's
Wedded Bliss *(1975)*

shop-floor and how these affect their confrontations with management; a five-part television soap opera (*Familienserie*) *Acht Stunden sind kein Tag* (*Eight Hours Are Not a Day*, 1972), directed by Fassbinder, and depicting the life and work situation of several families; three films made by Marianne Lüdke and Ingo Kratisch, dealing with family life as much as with the work place, and finally Helma Sanders' *Shirins Hochzeit* (*Shirin's Wedding*, 1976), the story of a Turkish girl coming to the Federal Republic to escape an arranged marriage and find her lover, a *Gastarbeiter* in Cologne, whom she eventually meets while working as a prostitute.

The history of the *Arbeiterfilme* and especially the institutional background of their production, is well covered elsewhere.[7] In the context opened up in this chapter, however, the strategies of Ziewer – and the criticism they received in Germany – merit some consideration. *Dear Mother, I'm Fine* (1971), *Snowdrops Bloom in September* (*Schneeglöckchen blühn im September*, 1974) and *Walking Tall* (*Der aufrechte Gang*, 1976) form a kind of trilogy of the conflicts, contradictions and potential for solidarity facing a particular section of the working class, which in the films is assumed to be representative. Ziewer and his co-scenarist Wiese therefore gave particular attention to extensive research on the objective factors shaping the conflicts and, secondly, they analysed for each stage of the confrontations the respective interests involved and the characters' motives (that is, their subjective perception and awareness of these interests). The problem of the scripts, then, was to create figures for identification sufficiently particularised to convey 'some of the naturalism and obsession with detail of other television plays',[8] but also sufficiently generalised to advance the more abstract play of contending forces. The trajectory of the central hero had to be attenuated in favour of a kind of leapfrog progression, whereby:

The working class in Wolfgang Staudte's ... *and in Christian Ziewer's* Snowdrops
The Murderers Are Among Us *(1946)*   Bloom in September *(1974)*

protagonists are lost from view and incidental characters take over the main action. The film is a network of collective relationships. . . . Plots composed of collective activities are not likely to produce figures with whom the viewer can identify throughout the whole film. He can no longer put himself in the place of individual heroes when his attention is being claimed by the relationships between a number of characters . . . The old character dramaturgy that tried to draw generalised conclusions from typical people in typical situations is made obsolete by the laws of reality itself.[9]

A number of problematic assumptions are made in Ziewer's research principles and this passage, notably in the way 'the laws of reality itself' have to vouchsafe for a particular form of dramaturgy and representation. Ziewer justifies fictionalisation and the staged recreation of conflicts partly by objectivist criteria (the drama of false consciousness in the protagonists' heads) and partly by referring to the consciousness of the workers, whose notion of reality is formed by the identification strategies of the fiction film. Yet his dramaturgy is already fixed in advance, even if the precise form and content is the result of specific research. Inadvertently, no doubt, Ziewer becomes a sort of administrator of the workers' own experiences and consciousness. For his dramatisation relies, as in all fiction films, on the premise that the spectator is given access to the characters' inner life, that he sees their point of view. This manipulation of the audiences' position of knowledge which in a conventional film produces suspense or pathos is, in Ziewer's films, a necessary precondition for understanding how the conflict of interests are lived in concrete terms by 'those affected' (*die Betroffenen*).

Yet this access to the inner life is precisely the issue. How can the film-maker with his fictional construction attempt to mediate between the real worker on the shop-floor and the real worker in front of the television screen, and presume to have access to his subjects' subjectivity? As Johannes Beringer put it in a sharp attack on the workers' films in general:

To commit oneself to serving the cause of the working class would have required first of all the realisation that as a director one cannot have a free pass to the reality of the proletariat as easily as to a left-wing film festival. The interests of the working class are by no means automatically identical with those of the film-maker . . . Placed between the emancipatory needs of the workers and the capitalist media's needs to package and sell issues, the film-maker is put in a difficult and dubious position. His role of mediator and go-between cannot arbitrarily change its master:

the subjectivity of his creative effort is the very object of the media . . . The form in which therefore those affected pass on their material, their reports, their experiences, their 'life' is crucial. [Precisely the fact that they have to sell their labour] might dispose them towards keeping their inner life to themselves at least until it is clear in whose interest it is finally administered.[10]

The constant references to verifiable facts and painstaking research are ultimately more a fetish, and the decision to direct attention to 'the world of work' becomes at best a useful exercise in delivering a hitherto unknown slice of life to the attention of a bourgeois public. Beringer's premise is that the work of uncovering social relations is as difficult when one is too close as when one is too far removed: 'The cognitive act resides in finding the right distance to things, as a position which has to be discovered and taken up: the judgement (*Überblick*) over proximity and distance.'[11]

What this might mean in filmic terms is indicated by a review of *Snowdrops Bloom in September*:

We know as much about the work they do at the beginning as we do at the end, the chaps always bang the obligatory hammer three times before they have another round of dialogue. They lower their hammer and start: 'you remember what I told you the other day . . .' not once does somebody bang his finger. Nikolaus Dutsch, an actor by now notorious in Berlin for his roles as the working man, defiantly raises his chin even when someone asks him for the time . . . What [Ziewer] finds he passes off as constructed, what he constructs is supposed to be authentic. He neither possesses a [film] language nor is he without one. As if he had sent

Realism or stereotype? (Christian Ziewer's Dear Mother, I'm Fine, *1971)*

someone off and told him, go and shoot some footage of the work-benches, Ziewer sends himself . . . With the same gesture that [he] allocates meaning to his images and sentences, others allocate housing, or jobs or children to schools. The gesture of bureaucratic terror.[12]

In this cruelly polemical piece Harun Farocki goes on to describe in detail what he perceives as Ziewer's contradictory use of the zoom lens, of actors, of the music, and concludes: 'What a pity that there are so few who understand the politics of cinematic language.'

With hindsight it is perhaps easy to see how the rise of workers' films and literature were themselves historically determined. The major economic recessions of 1966/67 and 1971 cast the spotlight on industrial relations and the working class. Television took the issues on board, aired them, discussed them, fictionalised them and dropped them when it was clear that all the viewers saw was yet another TV genre. This exposure to publicity in print and the visual media may in the long run even have facilitated the structural changes which the moves from a manufacturing base to high technology industries and from national firms to multi-national conglomerates necessitated. Certainly, the very brief flowering of the *Arbeiterfilme* suggests such a conjunctural interpretation, just as Wallraff's promotion to star personality and the half-cynical, half-voyeuristic participation of his readers in his ever more spectacular exploits indicate as much the political vulnerability of his intentions as the limits of his method.

Counter-Cinema and Meta-Television: Klaus Wildenhahn

Ziewer, Wiese, Lüdcke and Kratisch were all identified with the Berlin School. But they were by no means the only tendency at the Film and Television Academy. Farocki, too, was a fellow student of Ziewer's (both film-makers in fact belonged to the rebel generation of 1968, relegated during the days of the Dziga Vertov Academy).

Also affiliated with the Academy and representing a quite different form of political cinema was Klaus Wildenhahn, a documentary film-maker whose films have only ever been shown on television but whose ideas shaped much of the work associated with the Berlin School and documentary generally, even after he ceased teaching there in 1972. Wildenhahn's film-making rejected any attempt at fictionalisation. While he shared Ziewer's commitment to detailed pre-production research, the objective was less agitational and more ethnographic. With his co-director Gisela Tuchtenhagen, he influenced at least initially the films that came out of the women's movement. By the late 1970s Wildenhahn's techniques as adopted by his students had themselves become something of a formula, and the label 'Berlin School' was synonymous with well-meaning but rather stolid documentaries about strike committees and cramped housing conditions, about the educational disadvantages of Turkish children in West Berlin, the difficulties of unionising women or the successes of grass-roots movements in organising anti-nuclear protesters.[13]

Wildenhahn's own films are more difficult to categorise, but his choice of projects indicates two central interests: the interaction of artists (performers, actors, musicians) when creating or rehearsing a work; and communities (farmers, labourers, skilled workers) organising themselves to respond to decisions or events over which they appear to have no control. To the first category belong *Bayreuth Rehearsals* (*Bayreuther Proben*, 1965); *John Cage* (1966); *498 Third*

Avenue (1967, about the Merce Cunningham Ballet in New York), *Harlem Theatre* (1968, with a concluding, unscheduled 'performance' by Bobby Seale); *Bandonion I, II* (1981), and *What are Pina Bausch and her Dancers doing in Wuppertal?* (1983). To the second belong *In der Fremde* (*Far From Home*, 1967), about contract workers building a silo; *Der Hamburg Aufstand* (*Hamburg Insurrection October 1923*, 1971), documenting the surviving traces and memories of one of the rare attempts to establish workers' councils in Germany after the failed Revolution; *Emden Goes to the US I, II* (1976) about the workers' response to the relocation of a VW plant and *Love of the Land* (*Die Liebe zum Land*, 1973/4), investigating the effects of the Common Agricultural Policy on the life and working habits of North German farmers.

The two interests are not unconnected. In one of his earliest films, about an avant-garde music festival in Sicily, Wildenhahn contrasted the urbane life-style of the performers and guests at the festival with the actual life of the local peasants (*A Week of Avant-garde Work for Sicily*; *Eine Woche Avantgarde für Sizilien*, 1965). Similarly, his film about the Pina Bausch dance theatre tries to relate her work to the history of Wuppertal, a former centre of the mining industry and now a town in search of a new role and a sense of identity. What seems more crucial to him than pointing out the social price and privilege of artistic activity or civic sponsorship is to document the dynamics of groups in their relation to a specific place or event. *Bandonion I, II* contrasts the use of the harmonica in German rural communities and its significance in Latin America, where it is both the preferred musical instrument of very conservative German settlers and part of an indigenous tango culture: just the sort of political and historical paradox that appeals to Wildenhahn's low-key sense of irony.

What makes Wildenhahn's work important in the context of this chapter is two-fold: his institutional position, and the wider significance of his documentary style. He seems to have pondered the relation of distance and proximity more than others. Distance in Wildenhahn translates itself into an acknowledged presence of the camera, while proximity comes not from close-ups or reverse-angle, but from observing his subjects and following events often over very long periods of time (from ten weeks to two years).

Wildenhahn is hyper-conscious of the television context in which he works, its possibilities and its constraints. He began by discovering a militant counter-television: as a reporter for WDR in 1964 he covered the Social Democrat Party Congress, and when a member of the executive failed to get re-elected because he had protested against the SPD adopting an unconditional pro-Nato defence policy Wildenhahn had wanted to focus his report on this story. But the footage was re-cut by the editor-in-charge, omitting any mention of the incident. He decided to use the material for a short documentary (*Parteitag 64*): 'One can – or one could – turn an official reporting job around by using the material and follow up a different strand. You can do what Willy Roth has called "counter-reporting" at any official event, if you look carefully.'[14]

But instead of carrying on in a vein that would probably have put an end to his employment, it led him to practice a form of television counter-cinema directed against the *Autorenfilm*. By refusing the independent status of the *Autor* (according to him a 'corner grocer in the industrial landscape' of the media),[15] Wildenhahn none the less supported independent film-making for the quite different kind of public it was able to address, or rather for the different context in which it could address part of the same public as television. The poverty of the *Autorenfilm* was its lack of substantive experience (*Erfahrungsgehalt*), which is an objection similar to Kluge's complaint that sensibilists over-developed one sense at the expense of others. The conclusions Wildenhahn drew from this, however, differed from Kluge's. Where Kluge gives the viewer a disquisition about nerve centres and feet as perceptual organs (*The Patriot*), Wildenhahn, not unlike Straub, wants the spectators to listen with their eyes and see with their ears.

The logical consequence of Wildenhahn's dual career as a television employee and a documentary film-maker was that he preserved in his films this faculty of the attentive eye and ear, while his counter-reporting defined itself more and more across the by now classical principles of *cinéma verité*, as pioneered by Leacock and Pennebaker. Although a good deal more low-key than Wiseman in the choice of his subjects Wildenhahn, like Wiseman, lets his characters represent themselves in their own words without controlling or contextualising them through voice-over commentary.

His editing, however, is less self-consciously rhetorical than Wiseman's and has invested more in representing duration and process, against Wiseman's tough-minded sense of dramatic irony and argumentative structure. Wildenhahn's subjects acknowledge the camera's presence, as if to respond to the film-makers' sympathy and solidarity. Instead of dramatising an event, or waiting for the spectacular moment as Leacock did by building his films around a character's crisis or his or her loss of control, Wildenhahn tries to develop what he calls an 'inner chronology', by focusing on gradual changes in behaviour and attitude:

> You have to trust yourself as a documentarist to find the chronology. But not sensational. Sensational would have been to film the people the day of the dismissals (in *Emden Goes to the US*). Instead, two months later we filmed the effects. That way there's more of the truth of the everyday in it.[16]

If we recall Kluge's remarks about documentary as itself a genre not to be confused with reality, the question arises why Wildenhahn's concept of the 'truth of the everyday' should have had the following it did, in spite of or because of its manifest 'ideology of the real'. What, in other words, is the significance of the genre Wildenhahn helped to create? In the first place his techniques of observation (at a discreet distance, the unobtrusive participation of his camera and team, his insistence on long-term involvement with his subjects – *Lang-zeitbetrachtung* – and the emphasis on process rather than on drama or peripeteia and resolution, however much the situation might invite it) are the expression of an aesthetics of the open-ended and the incomplete: hence the preference for rehearsals or for filming groups in the process of organising defensive actions.

Secondly, Wildenhahn's films are recognisable by their *temps morts* or the moments where apparently nothing happens, but where a crucial 'phatic' rapport between the subjects and the spectators constantly renews itself across the representation, installing a particular rhythm of vision. It naturalises the different ways in which the spectator is vicariously present in the action, deconstructing the voyeurism inherent in the filmic situation and replacing it with the fiction of an interlocutor.

With this in mind, one could isolate two preferred scenarios of the Wildenhahn school. Firstly, the strike or protest action – but where failure or defeat becomes transfigured as a kind of permanent rehearsal (*Emden Goes to the US* and *Love of the Land*, and also films by his disciples like *Flöz Dickebank*, *Kalldorf versus Mannesmann*, both from 1975). Secondly, the interview film 'round the kitchen table' (*Far From Home* (*In der Fremde*), 1975, *Der Hamburger Aufstand*, but also *Sing Iris – Sing*, 1978, *Frauen – Schlußlichter der Gewerkschaft* (*Women – At the Tail-End of Trade Unions*) 1975, and *Flöz Dickebank*) where narratives, made up of patchy reminiscences and pressing problems of the here-and-now, weave a continuity between past and present through the poignant banality of both.

How do such documentaries situate the spectator? Unlike the audience in a fiction film – divided and split through the multiple identification processes that are projected on and contained by the characters (shifting camera positions, shot-reverse or point-of-view shot, along with the divisions or ironies of the dialogue) – the spectators of a Wildenhahn documentary do not experience the pleasures and thrills of fictional division, not even the ones of the candid camera. The morality of Wildenhahn's *mise en scène* demands that the presence of the camera and crew is acknowledged in the diegesis (audible questions coming from off-camera, the look into the lens, the presence of the sound person in the image), thus creating the ambience of the *family visit*.

It is here that the potential discomfort of this viewing position is neutralised by invisible editing and long takes which give the spectator a sense of security in the representation, inscribing into it the temporality of an epic form, whereas the temporality of the visit is actually one of intermittence. Furthermore, the often long focal lenses and a preference for medium shots (rarely are there zooms) maintain a balance of distance and proximity, by redefining the observer's gaze. Rather than the 'cold look' of Kluge, Wildenhahn's ethnographic look promotes solidarity. Yet unlike the 'stupid eye' by which Herzog's documentaries produce shock and distress along with a more ambiguous solidarity, Wildenhahn's reassures because it generates for the audience a secure position of knowledge. This knowledge is enshrined in that intuited chronology, the creation of which is the director's aim in the editing. Its mode of closure, and thus its most powerful subject-effect, is the pleasure that comes from the anticipation of failure and defeat, redeemed by the consolation of time itself. One might call it the elegiac look, falling on objects, places and people alike, because they are all given over to time as the medium and agent of their disappearance, and fetishised in the image.

Such a reading runs counter to the overt ideology of Wildenhahn's work. Politically left-wing and socialist, its message is one of resistance, endurance and, although tied into a love–hate relationship with contemporary Germany, Wildenhahn shows a solid belief in its working class. None the less, I would argue, it is the elegiac look that keeps spectators in their seats, and encourages other film-makers to follow his lead. For it is a look supported by feelings with a wider resonance, and a certain form of pathos which itself relies on a fantasy. The desire is to merge with the object of the look, which in many of the documentaries of the Berlin school is rarely an individual but a collectivity (the working class, women in the factory, immigrant children). Yet in order for this collectivity to become the object of desire, it has to be represented as 'other' and separated from the spectator by a distance. This is precisely the distance which, for example, is collapsed in Ziewer's *mise en scène* of fictional identifications derived from the commercial cinema, in its anxiousness to bring the 'other' close.

In what sense, then, is Wildenhahn's a 'cinema of experience' where Ziewer's is not? Wildenhahn's films tend to engage the spectator in a process ostensibly without goal, a search for moments that can mark the gap (of class, region, age), across which is played out the mini-drama of empathy and solidarity. Yet it is

*Günter Wallraff (far right)
disguised as a Turkish
'Gastarbeiter' in* Ganz Unten
(At the Bottom of the Heap,
1986)

always also a search of the self in the other, supported by the fantasy of merging
with this other through the gaze which, when returned, promises to unite the
viewing subject with him/herself. Wildenhahn's documentaries are thus a kind of
ritual enactment of the sense of separateness and otherness, the merging with the
other and the desire to find in this other the self. It is a transaction accomplished
through the image, where voyeurism gives way to a tender necrophilia – for in
the living (the old, the baffled farmers, the striking workers) the camera already
sees the defeated, even the dead, and it is this which releases the love that allows
the object to be appropriated and incorporated. Wildenhahn's solidarity is
ultimately a solidarity with and of victims.

Such a style and its techniques are not uncontested. Wildenhahn's method has
given rise to arguments with film-makers who saw documentary as providing
counter-information to television, and dealing with situations or people where it
is neither possible nor desirable to be as self-effacingly in love or in sympathy
with one's subject. When Kluge worked on *Der Kandidat* (*The Candidate*, 1980),
a documentary about Franz Josef Strauss at a time when the latter stood for
Federal Chancellor, he successfully dissimulated his sympathies in order to be
able to infiltrate the enemy camp and obtain footage about right-wing circles with
which Strauss had political affiliations. Similarly, when Günter Wallraff extended
his successful raids into the taboo areas of German capitalism by making a film,
Ganz Unten (1986), he and his team, true to his undercover method, chose a
candid camera approach. The objective was to gather material on the criminal
practices of the owner of a labour exchange for Turkish workers. Wallraff dressed
up for the part and had himself hired, accompanied by another worker with a
video camera hidden in his lunchbox. While the technical quality of the pictures
acts as a reminder of the illicit circumstances of their origins and provides the
spectator with a voyeuristic thrill,

> the effort – disguise, hidden camera and microphone – stands in no relation to the
> result, for the images thus recorded are on the whole very banal. The problem of
> the film is that the scandal [it wishes to record] is not as such visible . . . *Ganz
> Unten* depicts the duel between the intrepid investigator and the hard-boiled
> profiteer, both of whom in their own way, stop at nothing. This is a fiction plot,

narrated – in this case – with the monotonous means of the documentary, poorly utilised for illuminating either character or motivation of the avenger, the villain or the victims.[17]

Wildenhahn would have added that such undercover documentations fall outside the province of television, if not outside legality, and perhaps only in certain exceptional political situations should they be considered part of the public interest. By contrast, Wildenhahn's strength is precisely his ability to work within television as an independent film-maker and produce a kind of meta-television. The fact that his films are often, in Wilhelm Roth's memorable phrase, about 'obscure subjects precisely observed'[18] challenges the very assumptions television has of its audiences, not only in so far as television tries to unite viewers around a consensus of values and commonsense views, but because its dominant mode of address is to contextualise images and editorialise them with voice-over sound. Wildenhahn's direct sound and sparing use of verbal commentary demand from the viewer a different form of attention. His films also comment implicitly on another aspect of the television discourse: its preoccupation with preserving on every issue a balance, often forcing into equivalence and an appearance of like and like, realities or arguments that cannot be compared or balanced. Film for Wildenhahn is proof of the incommensurability of the real, and also a reminder of inequalities in society itself, especially in the (very relative) ability of its members to have access to the media, and to secure an equitable representation in sounds and images.

In the disagreements between Wildenhahn and other political film-makers much hinges on the function of the spoken word. Clearly, documentaries with commentary yield different spectator positions and modes of address from those without commentary, and each implies rather different politics of representation. In the wake of 1968, interventionist and agitational film-making saw its role in supplying information that television and the press, especially during civil disturbances, news blackouts or biased reporting, failed to provide. Wildenhahn's method appeared in this context excessively reticent. By contrast, film-makers like Farocki or Bitomski knew they could not trust the image in a political discourse. Sometimes this may be a question of resources, either because of the limited opportunity film-makers had to acquire first-hand footage or its often poor technical quality. More crucial, though, is that images, however documentary by themselves, communicate too much and too little. They have to be decoded since, like the situation they refer to, their meaning is constructed. A non-interfering style of film-making is thus an illusion, and Wildenhahn, by the priority he gives to the image, abandons his discourse to a primacy of vision at the expense of montage and counterpoint, which negates avant-garde political film-making from Eisenstein and Vertov to Godard and Chris Marker. Kluge once referred to the uncommented documentary as suffering from the 'Rumbelstilzkin complex', meaning that its self-effacement and its denial of a place of enunciation invariably backfires, since the author is bound to manifest himself elsewhere.

The political argument inversely mirrors the institutional one. If commissioned by television, film-makers are aware of the ideological constraints inherent in a public institution, but they will also be aware that these restraints are conveyed in terms of formal criteria. Thus films on sensitive subjects will be required either to subscribe to the formal properties of the balanced, neutral and objective documentary, or they will have to be presented from a perspective unambiguously marked as subjective. It is here that Wildenhahn's polemics against the 'Author' status, but also his rejection of the interventionist and analytical documentary, shows itself to be both historically significant and another possible key to an understanding of the logic and development of at least one section of the New German Cinema.

Wildenhahn's work gives both an individual view (that is, partial and not 'balanced') and he enjoys the freedom of not having to appear as the *Autor* within the television institution. His method allows for the norm of television broadcasting to co-exist with the absolute primacy of expression which normally is the prerogative of the authored fiction film. Thus, Wildenhahn would claim, he has the (artistic) advantages of self-expression without the (political) disadvantages of appearing as a ghettoised or lionised author. On the other hand, he might be said to fall into Farocki's second category of television worker: his self-expression coincides miraculously with the views of the apparatus.

Because television is such a crucial factor in providing audiences for Germany's film production generally, the distinction between fiction and documentary film-making became permeable in the other direction, allowing a director like Wildenhahn to make documentaries with fictional methods. The insistence that the subjects present themselves without directorial interference, and his own avoidance of the interview format, reinforce the sense of powerfully imaginary subject positions such as the ones described above. Wildenhahn's preference for groups here has something strategic about it, since they naturally create a level of interaction always short of appearing exhibitionist. Portraying an individual in this way requires a subject both personally reticent and good at talking in front of a camera. One of the more successful films of Wildenhahn disciples was

The mint in Johannes Flütsch and Manfred Stelzer's Monarch *(1979)*

Johannes Flütsch and Manfred Stelzer's *Monarch* (1979), about a man who had perfected a way of 'milking' fruit machines in bars and amusement arcades, and who travelled across Germany in a gold-coloured Mercedes. What in a short film would have remained something of a gag, the story of someone who 'beats the system' becomes, observed over a longer period and treated at near-feature length, a rather moving portrait of the winner as loser. In response to *Monarch's* success, the suppliers of the 'Mint' are rapidly redesigning their machines. At the same time, Monarch's way of making a living turns him as much into a slave to routine as any other working man, even while he talks as if he was enjoying the freedom of the proverbial 'King of the Road'. Stelzer went on to make feature films – mainly comedies.

A crucial point is that Wildenhahn's method is itself one kind of answer to what we saw was the Young German Film's central problem – finding an adequate attitude to its characters and thereby a complex viewing position for the spectator. What at one level holds the New German Cinema together, from Wildenhahn to Wenders, is its similar attitude to characters – even if similar only in relation to the difference that separates their films from those of the Young German Film. From another perspective (the ideological-polemical one) a director such as Wildenhahn feels he has little in common with Wenders, whom he has personally attacked along with the 'sensibilist' tendency in German film-making for what he perceives as the false romanticism of a resigned inwardness. Yet the director diametrically opposed to Wildenhahn is not Herzog or Wenders but Kluge, whose way of interfering with, and manipulation of, sound and image he must heartily detest.

Cinema as Self-Experience: The Woman's Film

The best example of what characterises a cinema of experience is the *Frauenfilm*, which is in some sense the culmination of developments inherent in the New German Cinema from its beginnings. It could combine the ideology of self-expression of the *Autorenfilm* with the social responsiveness of the spectator film; it followed the main tendency of the German documentary, in that its aim was to give a voice to those who 'had been silent too long', and to lend itself to the demands of social minorities. Finally, its aesthetic strategies had to engage with identification, recognition and the question of false consciousness, since they form such a crucial part of women's social existence. What in the present context is of special interest is how the women's film tackled the problem of distance and proximity, how it tried to encourage neither a voyeuristic nor a contemplative stance, but an attitude on the part of the spectator at once concerned and self-reflexive.

Films by and for women in Germany owe their existence to three impulses. Firstly, the history and internal development of the West German women's movement. Secondly, the role of German television in taking up social issues and creating from within the institution spaces for their representation. Thirdly, the initiatives of women who had gained access to the media and who created structures which consolidated and expanded the opportunities for women to become active in all parts of the independent sector.

In a sense the rise of the *Frauenfilm* had to do with a more general change in cultural orientation around 1970, when the impact of the women's movement, along with other radical impulses that came to the fore, had forced the student

Rebecca Pauly in Claudia Alemann's The Trip to Lyon *(1980)*

Left to loosen its rather dogmatic grip on art and intellectual life. In West Germany, more than perhaps elsewhere in the aftermath of 1968, Sartre's ironic dictum that 'materialism is the subjectivity of those who are ashamed of subjectivity' could have been an apt description. Directly exposed to a double oppression and experiencing their social role as marginal, women seemed in a better position than male heterosexual Marxists to keep intact the hopes of social change and the revolutionary ideals of the anti-authoritarian movement.[19]

The West German women's movement shared with the first phase of the student rebellion this anti-authoritarian bias, but it soon also understood itself as 'autonomous'. It was the struggle for women's rights on specific issues, such as abortion, coming from the social base, which created part of the need and also the opportunities for female film-makers. Women became politically visible as never before and when some of them came to make films, either as independent directors or for television, they often had – from direct and practical experience – a very clear sense of the importance and uses of the media in publicising demands and pressing for their recognition. Their films, when dealing with experiences specific to women but also with social problems generally, combined a sense of urgency with strategies that aimed at solidarity through self-representation.

Not only did feminist documentaries and feature films thus provide the clearest example of film-making relying for its primary audiences on the existence of a politically motivated and broadly based social constituency. Since many of the

184

Ida di Benedetto in Ula Stöckl's The Sleep of Reason *(1984)*

women directors came to film only through the women's movement, they never lost sight of the need to address spectators in their specific situation: that of the psychosexual and economic logic of women's oppression and the struggles for a new self-experience.

Yet, at the same time, some of the most remarkable examples of West German film-making in general during the 1970s came from women, and women were also responsible for giving the direction of independent cinema a different shape, notably by their increasing presence in the production and distribution sector, as well as on the technical side. Producers like Regina Ziegler and Renee Gundelach, or Clara Burckner's Basis-Film Verleih, were responsible for providing women directors with logistic and organisational back-up on their films. They were, along with others, also active in lobby groups representing the interests of the film-making community as a whole. By the mid-1970s women had created one of the strongest professional associations, the *Verband der Filmarbeiterinnen* (the Union of Women Film Workers) and, as a consequence, West Germany possesses proportionally more women film-makers than any other film-producing country. If this was partly due to funding sources specifically opened up to women film-makers and women's issues, these opportunities were themselves the result of organised struggles and campaigns.

There had been women film-makers before the 1970s, for instance Ula Stöckl (among the directors of the first Oberhausen generation), Dore O. (known in international avant-garde circles since the late 1960s) and Birgit Hein, film-maker and author of a study of experimental film. Yet even more than with the male directors at Oberhausen, a common forum, or at least the sense of a common project, was necessary in order for their presence to be acknowledged. Since

185

the agenda was at least initially defined by the women's movement, aesthetic or film-theoretical questions took second place (unlike in Britain, where a feminist film theory can almost be said to have preceded feminist film practice).

The leading figure in drawing the media into the women's movement was Helke Sander. She had in 1968 publicly protested at an SDS delegates' congress against the fact that in all the debates about liberation struggles those of women never seemed to be on the agenda. Together with Claudia Alemann, Sander was responsible for organising the first international women's film seminar in Berlin in 1973. In 1974 she founded the first feminist film journal, *frauen und film*, where she initiated the discussion about a feminist film theory and practice with a series of highly polemical essays.[20]

Another factor peculiar to Germany was the institutional base of the *Frauenfilm*. The major source of funding of films on and by women came from television which, with its voracious appetite for issues, discovered the women's question much as it had discovered the working class a few years earlier. Through its current affairs slots, its magazine features and documentary departments, television created the need and the spaces for in-depth reports and analyses. Programmers could go beyond journalism and invite those in the forefront of the women's movement to be involved in long-term projects and series, such as the *Arbeiterfilme*, or films about the Pill, about working women, unionisation, crèches and education. Some of the 'topical' divisions even of the more cinema-oriented feature films of say von Trotta or Jeanine Meerapfel still reflect this origin (see the list mentioned in Chapter 2, from 'Mother–Daughter Relations' to 'Foreign Women in West Germany', p. 53).

A similar influence explains the predominance of documentary or mixed forms, such as the interview–portrait or the semi-fictional day-in-the-life-of film. Women active in the media could not let the chance of television slip by, and had to exploit what Helke Sander once called 'the loopholes left by the financiers in the hope of a feminine treatment of "feminine themes"'.[21] The television background may also be one of the reasons why films that had women as exemplary figures, both in the title and in the narrative, were so frequent – from Lena Rais to Christa Klages, Maria Braun to Rosa Luxemburg. For as Heide Schlüpmann and Carola Gramann noted: 'The New German Cinema, although tendentially a male-oriented cinema, produced at the same time strong female figures of identification and helped to establish actresses'.[22]

Women at Work

The close inter-relation of left-wing politics, feminism and television as it defined the *Frauenfilm* up to the mid-1970s can be studied in three cases: that of Erika Runge, a pioneer in the techniques of participating observation; some of the women directors who graduated from the Berlin Film Academy; and Helma Sanders-Brahms and Helke Sander. Taken together, their work indicates the possibilities but also the limitations under which women began making films.

Erika Runge was a television current affairs producer before she wrote *Bottroper Protokolle* (1968), a study of working-class life that made her famous. She subsequently directed both documentaries (*Why is Mrs B Happy? Women at the Top*) and feature films (*My Name is Erwin and I'm Seventeen, I am a Citizen of the GDR, Michael or the Difficulties with Happiness, Grandad Schulz*). But it was her protocol book and *Why is Mrs B Happy?* that became the archetypes for the interview film and for documentaries of threatened communities, especially as seen through the opinions and reminiscences of women and the older generation. Runge's work came directly out of the documentary and operational literature discussed earlier. *Bottroper Protokolle* records and evokes the vanishing traces of working-class culture through taped and transcribed interviews with a cross-section of people in Bottrop, a small town in the Ruhr affected by pit closures and re-housing schemes. Films like *Flöz Dickebank, Der Kampf um 11% (Fighting for 11%,* 1972), *Kalldorf gegen Mannesmann (Kalldorf versus Mannesmann,* 1975), *Eintracht Borbeck (Borbeck's Team-Spirit,* 1977) and others (mostly made by film students) owe Runge the perspective on their subject matter and Wildenhahn their observational method.

Runge's writing, film-work and investigative journalism made her something of a figurehead among women who had a strong left-wing political commitment, even though few of her other films and none of her features had anything like the success or influence of *Why is Mrs B Happy?* This is the story of one of the women interviewed in *Bottroper Protokolle*, covering 40 years of her life from 1928 to 1968. What was felt to be remarkable about the film was that despite its politically explicit stance, it put its faith in images and its central character:

> The question of this woman's happiness is not a rhetorical one. Runge is seriously concerned with the answer. For according to strict socialist theory, Frau B should not be happy; she should feel herself exploited, or otherwise she would be an example of 'false consciousness'. Runge's images contradict such a simple either-or scheme. There are shots, mostly close-ups, where the face of this woman, in spite of all she has suffered, manifests a kind of happiness . . . which refuses any dogmatic appropriation. Even though the film makes the economic factors explicit, it does not subsume the individual reality under the social conditions.[23]

The final sentence of the preceding extract might well serve as the motto for much of the work produced by the women students at the Berlin Film Academy. Enrolment of women candidates grew from 6 per cent of the annual intake in 1966 to 57 per cent in 1979. Among directors whose work refined Runge's subject and tested the new forms were Valeska Schöttle, Cristina Perincioli, Gisela Tuchtenhagen, Marianne Lüdcke, Ingrid Oppermann, Suzanne Beyeler, Helga Reidemeister and Marlis Kallweit. With the exception of Marianne Lüdcke's films (including the *Arbeiterfilme* she directed with Ingo Kratisch), which have always been fictional dramatisations, most of the Academy's graduates worked on the borderline between documentary, film essay and fiction film, though always on subjects empirically researched and often discussed collectively.

Schöttle's film *Wer braucht wen? (Who Needs Whom?,* 1972), was a fiction film which used the 'putting on the show' plot of the musical in the context of a group of women trying to organise a protest against a lowering of the piece-work rate in their factory. The confrontations which they have with their husbands at home are counter-pointed to their growing sense of solidarity, and unlike documentaries on similar subjects, the perspective is that of comedy. The film comes to a finale with an agit-prop, show-biz pop cabaret show for the assembled workers, a strategy which passes the responsibility for effective change on to the audience.

Perincioli's *Für Frauen 1. Kapitel (For Women, Chapter One,* 1971), about supermarket cashiers organising a protest against their low wages, similarly tries to use humour and comic exaggeration to create a realistic relation between the analysis of the situation and the possibility for change. Oppermann, in her *Women – At the Tail End of Trade Unions,* was more concerned with working out the exact domestic pressures and economic contradictions bearing on factory women's traditional reluctance to join a trade union, and the failure of these unions in representing women members adequately.

Although many of these films were intended as interventions in a particular struggle, the main influence of the work from the Berlin Film Academy in this area was as prototypes for television documentaries. It may have been a crucial weakness of the first phase of the *Frauenfilm* generally that the desire to address not the feminist spectator, but working women in a specific situation, required certain stylistic concessions. For although the documentaries as well as the fiction films were made 'in close collaboration with those affected', the result was often a format undistinguishable from other television features. The radicalism of the political message tended to be absorbed in the film-makers' self-effacement, itself a sign of the fear of not communicating. The question of feminist aesthetics (as opposed to a feminist sensibility with socialist sympathies) may have been posed, but it was not confronted.

Ernst Jacobi (centre) in Helma Sanders-Brahms' The White-Collar Worker *(1972)*

This might explain the career of Helma Sanders-Brahms, another director who also started out making shorts and features about the economic situation of working-class women and men (*Angelika Urban, Salesgirl, Engaged to Marry*, 1969; *Gewalt* (*Violence*, 1971); *Der Angestellte* (*The White-Collar Worker*, 1972); *Die Maschine* (*The Machine*, 1973)) before taking up explicitly feminist positions, as in *Unter dem Pflaster der Strand* (*Beneath the Paving Stones is the Beach*, 1975) and *Shirin's Wedding*, the latter as part of the *Arbeiterfilme*. Helma Sanders-Brahms' background was in television – she worked as a programme announcer – rather than film school, but *Angelika Urban* was a project Sanders-Brahms had to complete with her own money, preferring to withdraw the film from television rather than have it re-cut. Its several festival prizes secured her a basis for further work at both ZDF and WDR, but from 1974 onwards most of her films were produced or co-produced by her own company.

Helma Sanders-Brahms is notable not least for the way her film subjects reflect the changing tendencies and trends within the New German Cinema rather than the issues emerging from the women's movement. After a docu-portrait in the manner of Runge, a number of feature films dealing with working-class issues and one of the most politically didactic film essays ever made (*Die Industrielle Reservearmee*; *The Industrial Reserve Army*, 1971), she tackled a Kleist adaptation (*The Earthquake in Chile*) and an 'actors' film' (the psychodrama of a middle-class couple, *Beneath the Paving Stones is the Beach*), before turning to the much-discussed *Gastarbeiter* problem in *Shirin's Wedding*. When she won the main federal prize for her next project, another Kleist film (*Heinrich*, 1977) planned to coincide with the Kleist bicentenary, she was singled out as the main offender in the general uproar about the *Gremienfilm* and the abuse of literary adaptations.

Germany Pale Mother, her international success, was not only accused of riding the Nazi nostalgia wave but, as the story of a mother–daughter relationship, cashing in on a fashionable subject. This instinct for the *Zeitgeist* on the part of a director who had by then styled herself as an *Autor* was not well received, and Sanders-Brahms became next to Syberberg the least-loved film director in Germany. Like Syberberg she sought compensation in her standing outside Germany and her recent films have often featured stars from the international art cinema (*Flügel und Fesseln* (*The Future of Emily*, 1985), with Brigitte Fossey, Ivan Desny and Hildegard Knef, or *Laputa*, 1986, with Krystyna Janda and Sami Frey). While such choices do not disqualify her films (even the much-reviled *Heinrich* seems to me of considerable interest, and *Die Berührte* (*No Mercy, No Future*, 1981) is in every sense a very radical film) they bring to the surface some of the pressures and determinants at play in the career of a director trying to address the different audiences to which German independent films appealed over the years.

Despite similar beginnings in television documentary and didactic films about controversial issues (*Eine Prämie für Irene* (*A Bonus for Irene*, 1971), *Macht die Pille frei?* (*Does the Pill Liberate Women?*, 1972), *Männerbünde* (*Male Bonding*, 1973)) there could hardly be a greater difference between Helke Sander and her virtual name-sake. While Helma Sanders-Brahms came to see herself as a European auteur, Helke Sander remained a film-maker not only committed to a more clearly defined constituency in Germany itself, but also to a consistently socialist and feminist perspective. One of the very first students of the Berlin Academy, her career can also be read symptomatically in the way that it quite deliberately marks and documents the women's movement and its impact on the private as well as public lives of her characters, at once autobiographical and representative.

While *A Bonus for Irene* was still very much in the tradition of the Berlin Academy films (showing the double pressure on working-class women in factory jobs and with a household to look after), Sander's three semi-autobiographical fiction films (*Redupers*, 1977; *The Subjective Factor*, 1981; *Love is the Beginning of all Terrors*, 1984, in two of which she plays the lead) comprise a sort of trilogy of different stages of a woman's self-realisation, but they are also the history of (someone actively involved in) the German women's movement.

Comparable to Kluge's in at least one respect, Sander's role in the history of

189

the German women's film exceeds the impact of her films. This is partly the result of her writing, especially her articles in *frauen und film*, where in the very first number she delivered a well-researched, lucid and highly polemical attack on 'sexism in the media'.[24] Disadvantaged by ordinary sexism (in the form of the role models imposed on women through schooling and socialisation), disadvantaged within the industry (second-class jobs as assistants, film editors or in the prop or costume departments with less pay and fewer promotion prospects than their male colleagues), women are discriminated against even when they hold positions usually occupied by men, through constantly having to prove themselves, working more and having to perform better just to stay in place. Sander also pointed out that feminists' scope for working with television was curtailed in direct proportion to programme makers' applying certain provisions of the television charter, notably those expressly prohibiting the broadcast of programmes that attack or question the institution of marriage and the family.

Helke Sander (left) in Redupers *(1977)*

But what makes Sander's work exemplary is how these themes of the women's movement are integrated into her films. On one level they are historicised and made concrete in the context of West Berlin and the fate of the German Left; on another, they become quite rigorous questionings of issues of representation and aesthetic form. Instead of the 'personal' being subsumed under the 'political' or directly opposed to it (as tended to happen in the working-class films discussed above and the early feminist documentaries), Sander came to reject any such dualistic conflict model. The 'subjective factor' in her film of that title, for instance, is not some ineffable personal essence, but seems much more the frictions and dissonances that arise from the incoherence of the signs surrounding the heroine, and her resistance to the publicly circulating records of events (such as photographs or materials from the sound archives) which constantly revise, reposition and retouch her own memories. It is the non-convergence, registered painfully as loss or comically as a gag, between these realities which constitute the personal in the political.

In short, Sander radicalised the genre most readily available to women – that of the diary and the autobiographical narrative. For if one were to select one aspect where the *Frauenfilm* has given a new impetus to West German film-making in general, it would be in the rethinking of biography and autobiography. In this respect German women film-makers are perhaps not so different from women film-makers elsewhere, and one might again usefully cite Pam Cook:

> The idea of self-expression suggesting as it does the creation of a private language to convey the personal fantasies and obsessions of a single individual . . . is a concept which, with its emphasis on the personal, the intimate, and the domestic, has always been important to the Women's Movement, and the personal diary form, for instance, has always been a means of self-expression for women to whom other avenues were closed. The suppression of the 'personal', albeit politically correct, brings to the surface specific problems and contradictions for women and for feminist film-makers.[25]

Between the 'suppression of the "personal"' in left politics and its lustful or painful exhibition Sander's films try to chart a different course, in so far as they do not pursue either side of the equation. Instead of compensating the deficit of identity by staging a masquerade, they dramatise the loss of self as a sort of 'bad timing'. In *Love is the Beginning of all Terrors*, the heroine's sharply divided loyalties when trying to live with an unfaithful lover stand for a more fundamental recognition of the impossibility of separating 'self' from 'other'. The love of the title, 'origin of all terrors', is finally nothing but the intensity of which in the film only the jealous woman is capable, of rebelling against but also ridiculing the difference between the sexes. Transposed into another register – the irreconcilability of 'here' and 'now' – it is objectified in the film by snatches of opera sung by a female voice. Sander here at times comes close to conceiving of the problem of female identity and the staging of its impossibility (coded as love) in terms more reminiscent of the music spectacles of Werner Schroeter than of the political–feminist discourses in her earlier films, such as *Redupers* (also known as *Die allseitig reduzierte Persönlichkeit*, 1977). Here Berlin as divided city and the woman as artist-and-mother became the mutually communicating stages for the many divisions of the female self. Yet within her own work the splitting of body from voice, as one of the ways in which difference circulates in *Love is the Beginning of all Terror*, is a logical development from *Redupers* and *The Subjective Factor*, especially in their investigation of the divisions of the female self in the various apparatuses of male power.

However, in the present context, *The Subjective Factor* may be considered almost as the definitive statement of the impasse of the documentary form itself as a women's genre. For in so far as the film traces within its own textual configuration the history of the German women's movement from its socialist beginning to autonomous feminism, it provides a key to the development of a feminist cinema of experience, showing almost as an aside how the question of the body was, even within the woman's movement, bracketed off. Instead, the issues of female representation, both in the political sense and as the separation of voice and image, dominate the film. They, in turn, are central to Sander's

Nikolaus Dutsch and Angelika Rommel in Helke Sander's The Subjective Factor
(1980)

critique of documentary as a film form which places the spectator in too
comfortable a subject position – that of presuming to know through seeing – a
fallacy revealed as soon as the object of the documentary is the film-maker
herself, that is, when the genre becomes autobiographical.

The Subjective Factor takes press photographs and newsreel – the most public
of images – to pose the problem of the subject. Annie a former activist and
leading figure in the breakaway group from the German student movement that
formed the women's caucus (*Weiberrat*, the nucleus of the women's movement),
is visited by her grown-up son who brings her a coffee table book of photographs
documenting the events of 1968. In one of them she spots herself: 'This is me,
here in the car, fronting the protest march, your mother'. The historical document
acts as a trigger for the trauma of the personal since the image, far from reassuring
the subject of her identity, splits her and returns her to the incompatible roles
and irreconcilable temporalities that make up her present life. Its political
correlative is indicated in another crucial scene. In a television studio Annie
comes across newsreel footage of the historic student congress. But when Helke
Sander took the platform and addressed the meeting, the cameras switched off
and only a tape recording survived of her speech. The film confronts the image
of the (fictional) Annie with the voice of the (historical) Helke Sander, precisely
marking the gap where the fact that her integrity as a 'person' is no longer
recoverable (no image to match her voice) becomes a political one. *The Subjective
Factor* records the effort of comprehending the contradictions contained in these

splits, because the search for the biographical in the historical comes face to face with representation and sexual difference.

The Subjective Factor is a settling of scores with documentary film, in that the genre's reticence, its play of distance and proximity is ultimately the displacement of the question of who 'speaks the image'. Throughout Sander's film, the voice-over splits the heroine by addressing her as both Annie (fictional) and as Helke Sander in a constant uncertainty but also as a struggle, about who speaks whom in the space of the film's present, and the time of the film's memory.

In the documentary the elegiac look is itself the veiling of an aggression. This, too, becomes more apparent where it falls on a biographical or autobiographical subject, as in the first film of Jutta Brückner, *Tue Recht und Scheue Niemand* (*Do What is Right, Come What May*, 1975). The film consists of photographs from August Sander's *Menschen des XX. Jahrhunderts* matched on the sound-track with Brückner's own mother's hesitant and muted narrative of her life. At first glance *Tue Recht und Scheue Niemand* fits rather well into the tradition of docu-portraits: the story of an older woman, whose personal reminiscences, anxieties and deeply melancholy disappointment with life merge and are totally congruent with the ideology of her class. It makes her, for the spectator, a representative, indeed a historical document, of the German petit bourgeoisie this century. At the same time, this very realisation annihilates her as an individual, and from the tension between these conflicting positions of knowledge the film derives its pathos, freeing the look to embrace the banal, even to love it under the aspects of its destruction. Yet precisely because the film is so aware of its own process, enacting it before our eyes, Gerda Siepenbrink's story is quite different from the melancholy pathos of a comparable portrait, Eberhard Fechner's *Nachrede auf Klara Heydebreck* (*Obituary for Klara Heydebreck*, 1969).

Fechner had chosen, more or less at random, one of the suicides reported to the West Berlin coroner's office on a given day – a woman in her sixties, living alone and without relatives. By talking to the neighbours, filming her sparse possessions, digging up old photographs and letting the camera look out of her windows, Fechner renders Klara Heydebreck visible in her absence, and although not trying to explain her death, he makes it seem almost inevitable. Her life was blighted by the narrowness of upbringing, the personal tragedies brought by both world wars and the sheer oppressiveness of a home right next to the Berlin wall. Yet from the start the spectators share with the camera not only the knowledge but the meaning of her death. Each sight or object the camera's gaze lingers on becomes a signifier of this life, which it represents as a fetish. By the end we think we know Klara Heydebreck, because we have invested her physical remains with significance. The 'Nachrede' is a necrologue – by a tender necrophiliac.

Here a difference of gender undoubtedly played its part. Fechner's Klara becomes the image of the mother, repossessed after her death through part-objects and their representations, without having to confront, in this passage from image to signification, the fear and scandal of her body and physical death. Characteristically, a film by Elfi Mikesch, *Was soll'n wir denn machen ohne den Tod* (*What Would We Do Without Death?*, 1980), ostensibly about women in a nursing home trying to face their end with fortitude, humour or merely resigning themselves to it, is very much the *mise en scène* of gendered bodies, as well as of their possessions. Gertrud Koch, in a brief review of the film, may have over-stressed the latter when she writes:

The luminous blue glass in the cupboard, the harsh silhouette of a chair on the

Elfi Mikesch's What
Would We Do Without
Death? *(1980)*

balcony are sensuous impressions that transcend the mere reproduction of objects. What these images convey is a sense of fragility, of lost time, of mourning and a holding tight on life and living . . . When she arranges certain images in tableaux, when she illuminates trivial trinkets as if they were precious vessels of memory, then it becomes clear that she expresses her own relationship to death and perhaps also that of a few old women.[26]

The 'and perhaps' is an important qualification, because it seems Mikesch is very careful not to offer the viewer these objects for any metaphoric transfer. Instead, she emphasises their strangeness and their resistance to substituting for the women whose bodies so obstinately refuse to go away. This dual focus makes the film 'irritating' and subverts 'the traditional codes of documentary'. Brückner, too, at the end of *Tue Recht und Scheue Niemand*, shows photos of her mother, jerkily coming to life thanks to optical printing. This is a gesture in which the cinematic apparatus is made to signify the violence of the film-maker's gaze, bringing to the fore something of the ambivalence of the documentary look in general. For the aggression which the film carries is ambiguously coded. Is it directed against the mother, her paralysing and permanent anxiety, her refusal to speak of her sexuality or of her feelings towards her husband? Or is it patriarchal society that stands accused, as it returns, through August Sander's portraits, the spectators' look – narcissistic and self-satisfied, self-righteous even in its submission to duty and the nation? This question arises, not least since these earnest faces seem to be listening to the mother's voice, identifying the audience's (and the film-maker's) ears if not their look, with that of the father, resisting identification with the mother and what her story says.

Self-Representation as Otherness

The redefinition of the 'political' in the wake of autonomous feminism made it inevitable that women film-makers should turn towards that area of experience where they felt most alienated from themselves: 'The women's movement started simply and materialistically with what was nearest, the woman's body, and from there tried to disentangle the violation of women's rights and their subjection.'[27] Yet three of the films most directly concerned with 'what is nearest, the woman's body', Brückner's *Hunger Years* (*Hungerjahre*, 1980), Sanders-Brahms' *No Mercy No Future* (*Die Berührte*, 1981) and Ulrike Ottinger's *Ticket of No Return* (*Bildnis einer Trinkerin*, 1979) devastatingly show that this body is much too near, too real to serve as a perspective for a 'materialist' critique. On the contrary, it is as if, once the body comes into view, all perspectives crumble.

Hunger Years is the story of a young woman growing up in the newly prosperous 1950s, starved of affection and understanding. Without guidance or love to help her cope with sex, she takes out on her body all the bafflement, curiosity and anguish which a stultifyingly prim home unwittingly inflicts on her. The narrative is constructed as a succession and repetition of nodal points around which the trauma forms. By the end it has reduced her to bouts of, alternately, anorexia and bulimia. Beyond the autobiographical case history Brückner's film is conceived as cathartic, a form of auto-analysis in which the director includes the audience:

> What I wanted to describe, and what I failed to create by writing, was a kind of empathy, of identification. I needed pictures to get this sort of identification . . . I made [*Hunger Years*] so as to be able to identify with myself . . . I was trying to create an identity for myself in words – and that's impossible! Eventually I had my identity created step by step through pictures, or rather through the extraction of the forgotten pictures inside me . . . I think that in films for women – and I don't just mean films directed at women as a consumer group – but in films which direct themselves at/to the perception of women (and this perception has been historically conditioned) – well, the [Brechtian] alienation effect is useful but it must only be used at the point where identification threatens to spill over . . .[28]

Making films in order to 'identify with myself': although Brückner here seems to voice a discourse of self-exploration and self-expression which, as we have seen, applies to the feminist author generally, the self with which the heroine of *Hunger Years* tries to identify is the mother. Compared to *Tue Recht und Scheue Niemand*, *Hunger Years* is much less concerned with placing the mother under the eye and ear of patriarchy. Instead it shows how her inaccessibility (as love object, as body to approach and to merge with, as source of the self-confirming gaze) makes the heroine direct the most intense aggression against her own body, subjected to and subjecting it to the terrible régimes and violent rhythms of hysterical bleeding, compulsive eating and self-induced vomiting. Through an Algerian student, himself alien to her culture and discriminated against, she eventually learns to see this body as hers – but only to give to him. The scenes between them take place near water, a turgid, turbid, heavy substance in the film, associated with the maternal. When the man leaves her she tries to commit suicide, no longer sustained by the gaze of this other, whose outsider position had become her own. In the final scene, piling the food from the family fridge in front of her, she celebrates a self-punishing orgy, returning to an oral–anal chaos in which murky indifference seems to blur all boundaries and contours.

In *Hunger Years* the images themselves are marked by a violence, only sometimes represented directly through the characters' actions. Mostly it is the violence of the *mise en scène* itself: a lugubrious half-light, as in the closing scene, shots held for a painfully long time, episodes that make the viewer sense the actors' own discomfort, images difficult to watch in their naked privacy, stripping away the self-protection of a fictional role. None the less, perhaps because the anger that gives the film its elemental brutalism (and also its tenderness) is so desperate, and because Brückner's cinematic space is disorienting without being unintelligible, the spectator can rarely take a distanced view:

(the) mechanism of identification in women as cinema audiences means both greater opportunities for them on the one hand and greater dangers on the other. What I want to discover is how this mechanism can be used . . . so that women identify themselves with their anxieties and fears, with the forgotten areas of their selves, with the repressed areas of their past, with all the things which are neurotically displaced in women . . . That is what I see as the aesthetic and social function of cinema.[29]

Similar observations apply to Brückner's *One Glance and Love Breaks Out* (*Ein Blick – und die Liebe bricht aus*, 1987), a film made up of performance pieces, where different heroines stage over and over again, in a compulsive rhythm reminiscent of Pina Bausch's dance theatre, fantasies of desire, lust, self-humiliation and aggression.

Women with psychic disorders or on the borderline tend to be the subjects of case studies or of snakepit melodramas. Feminist films, on the other hand, have tried to rescue these case histories from the medical–scientific discourses, because mirrored or contained in the clinical symptoms are the very contradictions shaping a 'normal' woman's experience of herself. Helma Sanders-Brahms' *No Mercy No Future*, a history of schizophrenia, records a specifically female breakdown of selfhood, the failure to find a livable identity. It also details the more general horrors of an existence in and out of institutions, at the limits of a society which excludes the ill-adapted and the unassimilated with singular indifference. From an early scene onwards, where the heroine strips naked and lies down in the snow near the barbed wire fence of an army firing range in silent protest over the casualties of Lebanon and El Salvador, the film never lets go of the cold and desolation enveloping its solitary figure.

Sanders-Brahms' story of a daughter from a wealthy bourgeois home who slits her wrists at her parents' linen-covered breakfast table and bleeds into their gold-tap shower bath, is also a metaphor for the more fundamental ambivalence in German feminist films focused on the body. Veronika is 'touched', believing herself inspired by God. She thinks of her body as a vessel of Jesus, thus sanctifying her sexuality which she freely gives to the needy: mostly to old men, a caretaker who clumsily touches her up on a bare iron bedstead, a music hall magician whom she finds weeping on the stairs after his final performance, to cripples or foreigners (Vietnamese, Blacks, Turks, again, figures of the 'other'). Like Brückner's Ursula, Veronika's violence against her own body is the language of a being without image, who opens her veins as she opens her body, physically to obliterate the difference between inside and outside. She lies bleeding in the steaming shower to let her body wash away and merge with the world, or makes love in a pool of her own menstrual blood, because her spiritual eros refuses to recognise the boundaries regulating sexual or racial exclusion and difference, responding to it with an enigmatic, terrifying smile.

The film opens with Veronika's nightmare: in the opaque gloom of an underwater tank divers explore marine life. When one of them has his oxygen mask torn away, the terror of asphyxiation on his face, she wakes up, thrashing and gasping for breath and moaning 'Father, mother, I am so alone'. Both primal scene and birth trauma, it signals the anxiety and desire of total indifferentiation, the loss of self in the maternal element. *No Mercy, No Future* does not resolve this ambivalence even at the end, when a maternal face bends over her,

Daughter and mother in Jutta Brückner's Hunger Years *(1980)*

(above and right) Elisabeth Stepanek in Helma Sanders-Brahms' No Mercy, No Future *(1981)*

'tormenting' her with psychoanalytic questions, to fade out on the word *Anfang* (beginning).

The viewer is always made aware that the setting is Berlin. It is not so much the divided city and symbol of the divisions imposed on women that it is in Helke Sander's *Redupers*, but reminder of a past which gives the heroine's gestures of self-effacing expiation and bodily sacrifice an ironic historical foil. Veronika follows a prostitute on her beat near the Brandenburg Gate, and pimps are busy by the entrance of the restored Reichstag. It is the Berlin of immigrant workers, British and American troops, old people's homes and mental hospitals.

In *Ticket of No Return*, by contrast, Berlin becomes the city of inebriation, a paradise of oblivion. Single, wealthy and beautiful, Ulrike Ottinger's heroine has decided to make it the destination of her final binge, the 'ticket of no return'. However, alcohol is merely a convenient figure signalling an urge towards self-annihilation and the dissolution of an identity similar to *The Hunger Years* and *No Mercy, No Future*. The body has become carapace and prison but infinitely available for disguise and display. Unlike Brückner and Sanders-Brahms, Ottinger makes no concessions to elemental imagery or the rawness of the flesh. Every surface is polished, bathroom mirrors and bar-room metal gleam with a precise

Dressed to kill: Tabea Blumenschein in Ulrike Ottinger's Ticket of No Return *(1979)*

and cold reflection. Even the heroine's attempted suicide/murder becomes a choreographed ballet of open blades against an impeccably coordinated *interieur*.

Ottinger's subject, too, revolves around a process, obsessively repeated but ultimately failing, of discovering a self through the other. Yet in *Ticket of No Return*, as the original title indicates (literally: *Image of a Woman Alcoholic*), it is treated systematically and exclusively through a heroine hyper-conscious of her self-image, and whose quest to lose herself is intertwined with the discovery of her double. This 'other', so unlike her and yet the very image of her own degradation and liberation, is the bag lady Lutze, who joins her on her drinking bouts pushing a supermarket shopping cart and mumbling obscene imprecations. In contrast to the heroine, adorned by fashion, turned into fantastic forms and dressed to kill, the old lady is a shapeless bulk, grotesque and neglected. In tolerating Lutze, the heroine's fascination mingles with aggression, whose object one imagines to be, here too, the body of the mother. The gaze exchanged between the women, often mirrored through glass partitions, is one of recognition, but also of a wary separation in the very acceptance of the identificatory doubling. As in Mikesch' *What Would We Do Without Death?*, the empathy towards the faces of decay and imminent death is almost a nostalgia for the self's own future, and not free of its own form of aggression. Although in the case of Ottinger the real violence is directed against the heroine herself, the very stylisation and beauty of her appearance is displayed as if it meant to hurt the eye.

Against the Cinema of Experience: The *Mise en Scène* of Perversion

The demand for transparency on the part of politicised spectators (and the film-maker's knowledge of his/her target audience) might help to explain why some German films invest so much of their stylistic work into creating complex and ambivalent spectator perspectives, refusing unambiguous strategies of identification and inscribing positions which court the 'helplessness' alluded to by Ottinger in an earlier remark.

For Ottinger especially, the fact that student audiences tended to read films either sociologically or psychologically, associating their own experience and thus minimising the distance (aesthetic or otherwise) between the film and themselves, was one of the reasons to increase the distance within her films through stylisation and narrative deconstruction. This was less in order to counter any 'subjective' appropriation with an objective, distanced presentation of action or characters (as a Brechtian dramaturgy might demand), but on the contrary, to opt for a more radical aestheticism, aimed at exposing the preconstructed nature of the categories of subjectivity and objectivity. Indeed, in *Ticket of No Return*, 'issue-orientation' becomes itself an issue:

> In my new film quasi-documentary scenes alternate with extremely stylised ones. This is so because I noticed especially in films made in Berlin, that a lot of work is documentary – and the films are basically seen by a public already armed with their critical attitude, who go to the cinema in order to see once more on film what they already know from reality. For although they have a critical attitude to reality, or maybe because of it, they don't or don't want to notice what happens around them.[30]

Thus, three female figures, their severity and eccentricity underlined by hounds-

Jutta Brückner's A Thoroughly Neglected Girl *(1976)*

tooth dresses, accompany the heroine like a chorus. Called 'Common Sense', 'The Social Problem' and 'Reliable Statistics' they take the heroine's alcoholism literally, and are thus the ironic stand-ins for all those spectators of the German cinema who expect films, in the words of Farocki, 'to be the agony aunt and show them how to live their lives'. Ottinger, too, in this respect, rejoins the political avant-garde and its opposition to the workers' films. But she is quite different in so far as her films are intended neither as a counter cinema set up in opposition to Hollywood, nor as the practice following on from a theoretical position. She is not a militant film-maker in the usual sense at all, for her films are not even acts of resistance and refusal. Where they implicitly confront other film-making practices, such as documentary, they do so in a dialogue with particular spectator expectations. Ottinger belongs to those film-makers, inspired by the example of Werner Schroeter, who have in fact rejected not only television as a medium and returned to working in film, but who also respond to the 'cinema of experience' with the experience of artifice. Perhaps because Ottinger comes from a fine arts background her search for a specifically feminist aesthetic has taken her not to the literature of feminism or to film theory, but to the visual arts.

The object of this chapter has been to indicate how in the debate about the spectator, 'identification' – in the everyday sense of recognition, and in the filmic sense of a secure position of knowledge – became less and less the touchstone of *Erfahrung* in the cinema. In particular the woman's film broke with pure documentary, moving towards mixed forms and the experimental fiction film. The latter discovered identification in the psychoanalytic sense (the splitting, doubling and dividing of the subject in representation) as its major theme and

Veil of Tears: Tabea Blumenschein in Ulrike Ottinger's Ticket of No Return *(1979)*

the basis of a feminist aesthetics entailing a more complex and unsettling cross-over logic of projections and subject positions. The women film-makers discussed here have all insisted to varying degrees on the otherness of the experiences they depict, refusing to familiarise them as a bridge to spectators, even though they knew – from public discussions – that many in the audience expected films to confirm their views and address the need for a secure and pleasurable position of knowledge. Unlike directors who saw the commercial cinema – the cinema of recognition and repetition – as their antagonists, none of the women film-makers seemed interested in reviving Brechtian techniques of estrangement or endorse either Kluge's or Ziewer's notion of realism.

Brückner's emphasis (in the interview quoted above) on the differing function of the gaze for men and women, and thus of cinematic identification, points in a similar direction. The cutting edge where many of these films tried to situate themselves was not yet another form of realism, as much as it was an attempt to bring into view the mechanisms of self-estrangement attendant upon gender divisions. These divisions and exclusions the film-makers challenged by a *mise en scène* of perversion, paranoia or schizophrenia – modes of perception and consciousness to which film lends itself, precisely because of the mobility of subject positions that an experimental narrative cinema can articulate.

The chapter has also tried to argue that such was also the case in some of the documentaries produced, whereas the feature films which used classical techniques of identification tended not to displace the preconstruction of a stable subject, but merely to reinforce it. By contrast, feminist and gay film-makers are particularly aware of the problems of subjectivity and representation, in so far as they are made to experience their identity not only as transgression of the norm,

201

but as constructed in the image this norm forms of them. Thus it becomes apparent that the notion of a personal cinema, taken to its logical conclusion, actually involves a critique of the 'cinema of experience' if this is based on the concept of the authentic self, or the social and psychological categories that support it. By contrast, the aesthetics of the mirror that one finds in Ottinger, the body politics of Brückner and Sanders-Brahms, or the splits and shifts of the subject-in-history thematised by Helke Sander, all refuse in different ways the fictions of identity.

It is therefore not enough to say that the German 'cinema of experience' is either more subjective or issue-oriented, either more realistic or more unrealistic and stylised than the international commercial cinema and the European art cinema. It is a cinema by and for women and men whose awareness of living an alienated existence includes the knowledge that subjectivity is lived through the images and representations by which this subjectivity is formed. Access to the media, for instance, for a gay culture or subculture must also mean the right to affirm 'perversity' as an aesthetic impulse, especially where society only sees a sexual one, and conversely, to explore sexuality in representations other than those sanctioned by the aesthetics of bourgeois culture.

This was the subject of Rosa von Praunheim's *Not the Homosexual is Perverse but the Situation in which He Finds Himself* (1970), one of the key statements of gay film culture in Germany. Praunheim's (for many gays, controversial) strategy was to block identification on the part of the viewer, by presenting homosexuals as veritable caricatures of homosexual stereotypes.

> 'The film is radical, it doesn't spare homosexuals, it is anti-gay and confirms all the prejudices of heterosexuals.' This is how the liberal press might review the film. [But] we did not want to make a dishonest film about integration, which shows the homosexual as a manly, clean-cut type who has lived with his boy-friend happily and inconspicuously for the last thirty years . . . I am sure that liberals and a lot of gays would have preferred nothing better than a film whose longingly-obsequious gaze beseeches those who are 'normal' for toleration.[31]

What the non-gay spectator is given is an exaggerated but also threatening version not so much of homosexuality but of heterosexuals' fears of homosexuals. Praunheim's intention was to provoke what he called a 'Zwiespalt' (a split, an ambiguity) in the spectator, in order to subvert all available discourses on homosexuality, from the medical discourses about deviancy to the liberal ones about tolerance. In subsequent films Praunheim became less radical, preferring to displace this thorny subject of reverse and perverse identification into comedy, either about uneven couples (as in *The Bedroll*, a more documentary and satirically distanced version of Fassbinder's *Fear Eats the Soul*) or about older women (*Red Love, Our Corpses are Still Alive, Evelyn Künneke – I Am an Anti-Star*) where an ambivalence similar to that shown by women film-makers hovers over the fascination with the maternal body.

Das kleine Fernsehspiel

German independent film-making, as has been said here many times, is unthinkable without television. But even so one needs to make distinctions, because especially in the development of the experimental/experiential feature film not all television was equal. For the woman's film in particular it required a very precise conjunction, since as long as women directors were typecast by being assigned to documentaries on women's issues, they found it virtually impossible to obtain a comparable space for feature projects. The turn to autobiography in the women's movement generally provided for many a point of entry into the fiction film via television, allowing feminists to respond to a demand for self-expression as direct self-representation while not colluding with television's own exhibitionism about topical subjects.

The point of convergence was one of West German television's most remarkable programmes, long recognized as the space where the *Frauenfilm* as fiction film had its breakthrough – *das kleine Fernsehspiel*, the Second Channel (ZDF)'s experimental feature slot. According to Eckart Stein, its programming director, the idea behind *das kleine Fernsehspiel* was to create a 'forum for witnesses to the age'[32] and a showcase for new talent who would be given the opportunity (even if limited in funds and consigned to a late night weekday slot) to express a singular vision, without being bound by either issues or format.

The intention may have initially been to build up a kind of filmic archive of the *Zeitgeist*, and thus to be as transparent as possible towards tendencies and trends as seen through an individual personality and sensibility. As it developed *das kleine Fernsehspiel* not only became a precious source of finance for a first-time film-maker, it also proved the most fertile ground for new narrative forms. The 'small TV play' became a double misnomer, therefore, since the films could be as long as three hours, and they were rarely confined to television. What the Kuratorium had been in the 1960s, *das kleine Fernsehspiel* was in the 1970s. It revived the *Autorenfilm* ostensibly for television, but also for the cinema. Stein knew that the films had to address the two kinds of audiences existing for independent cinema:

> we feel we have a public by now, maybe half of which watches regularly to see what this week's programme is like, the other half has a group interest in what we are doing. A film about homosexual teachers would attract primarily a homosexual public or viewers involved in education; or again for the women's films that we are doing a lot of now we would perhaps have mainly a female audience.[33]

The programme secured an audience by successfully marrying the 'contentists' with the 'sensibilists'. Controversial issues and formal experiment existed side by side, those responsible apparently willing to back both. Over the years the weekly programmes comprised documentaries and feature films, by men and women, first-time film-makers and established ones, German and foreign. Directors known for their avant-garde fiction films such as Raoul Ruiz, Steve Dwoskin, Jean Pierre Gorin and Theodore Angelopoulos made films for ZDF, and by all accounts were virtually given a free hand. Women turning to the ZDF, even with very little experience in film-making, also had *carte blanche*, as Jutta Brückner implies:

> I'm completely self-taught. I've never been to a film school or been an assistant. I got into film through writing screenplays. I wrote the screenplay for Volker Schlöndorff's *Der Fangschuss* together with Margarethe von Trotta . . . So then I decided to make my first film . . . I just wrote a script outline and sent it off to all the TV stations, and ZDF – one of their departments, that is, *das kleine Fernsehspiel* – said they wanted to do it. They are the people who've commissioned most of the recent West German films by women, or have at least co-produced them . . . At that point I really didn't know what to do and I just phoned some friends and said 'I'm making a film' – they all laughed themselves sick. I said, 'No, really, I've already got the money' and they were amazed.[34]

Scenarios of desire: Jutta Brückner's One Glance and Love Breaks Out *(1987) . . .*

The paradox is that whereas in the case of documentaries television determined the forms the films took even where these were not made for television, *das kleine Fernsehspiel*, especially in the area of feminist film-making, seemed to have functioned as a preview theatre for cinema films. The fact that the films originated from within television made it easier to escape the limitations implied by the term *Frauenfilm*, which suggested that women had had their demands met with regards to the media once they had been allocated a special corner and their own genre. To forestall such a conception, women preferred to talk about film-work (*Filmarbeit*) which democratised not only the distinctions between the creative and technical side, but also those between cinema and television.

This applies with equal truth to a male director, Werner Schroeter, who is the German cinema's greatest marginal film-maker. Often unacknowledged, his films (*The Death of Maria Malibran, Willow Springs, The Bomber Pilot, Palermo or Wolfsburg, Kingdom of Naples*) are the prototypes that stand behind almost all forms of the experimental feature film, whether feminist, gay, avant-garde or as in the case of Syberberg, historical. Schroeter, even more than other film-makers, is obliged to work for television and its late-night slots. Yet it is ultimately the cinema, rather than television, that offers him the conceptual space to set up a different relation to an audience. His 'total cinema' is one which, thanks to television taking on the narrative cinema's ideological functions, devotes itself to the areas where painting, music, dance, narrative and performance intersect. Yet it is television alone which has the financial power and the organisational base to support (but also to exploit) someone like Schroeter, who maintains a critical distance both from television's promiscuous pluralism and from the cultural apparatus of the authors' cinema.

. . . and Werner Schroeter's Kingdom of Naples *(1978)*

To what extent the signature of *das kleine Fernsehspiel* is on the work of Jutta Brückner, Helma Sanders-Brahms, Helke Sander, Elfi Mikesch or Ulrike Ottinger is difficult to decide. What is clear is that the programme recognised the potential of a new form of experimental feature film, and by sponsoring it in an international context it allowed women film-makers to find a forum. The role that radical subjectivity has in these worlds of private fantasy and anxiety – radical, in laying bare the non-individual roots of the subject – makes them belong to a recognisable tendency within feminist film generally. Here excess, display, show and spectacle became the political stances of a new aesthetic investment in the female, the maternal and the androgynous body.

However, precisely in this last respect – the politics of the body – German film-makers are very different from each other, a difference that, as I have tried to show, must be located in their approach to identification and the image. Brückner's *Hunger Years*, Sanders-Brahms' *No Mercy No Future*, Schroeter's *Death of Maria Malibran*, Mikesch' *What Would We Do Without Death?* and Ottinger's *Ticket of No Return* can stand for some of the extended possibilities of representing experience as defined in this chapter. The critique film-makers brought to bear on the very concept of *Erfahrung* – the desire of the post-1968 generation for concrete, immediate experience, for appropriating subjectivity as identity and thus reifying it – had to be countered by showing experience to be always a form of loss: more specifically in respect to cinema, the subject's disappearance in the act of representation. And what Helke Sander observes in *The Subjective Factor* is true for many films: 'The effort to acquire [this] information is so great that it is finally the effort itself that becomes the information.'[35]

7:

The New German Cinema's Germany

Experience of Cinema

During the 1970s the cinema in West Germany was seen as a privileged medium of self-representation. It became a vocation to intellectuals who for the most part had not come up through the ranks of a film industry or adopted its formal and technical canons of professionalism. Often self-taught and wanting to make films differently, these directors do not easily fit into the categories that film history has to offer: independent, avant-garde, experimental. It is equally difficult to classify the products generically since, as we have seen, even the most basic distinction between documentary and fiction does not hold, at least not in any way that would account for the many mixed forms that make up the bulk of Germany's so-called independent production.

Instead of invoking an ever-extensible and permeable 'borderline' and thus measuring the films by a norm which they in most cases explicitly repudiate, it has seemed more sensible – though due to the vagueness of the term also quite risky – to propose a different axis of differentiation. It revolves around the term 'experience' which, at least in its German meaning, has been as crucial in the discussions about an alternative cinema as 'realism' was in Britain, and as conceptually spongy. It was the common ground on which film-makers and audiences talked with and past each other. It also marked, if we are to trust Michael Rutschky, the peculiar *Zeitgeist* of the 1970s, to which the New German Cinema so decidedly belonged.

Two kinds of experience, then, are constitutive of this cinema. In line with the observations made in previous chapters, I have called that part of independent production which addressed itself primarily to domestic audiences 'cinema of experience', to distinguish it from the international productions whose horizon of expectation I have called 'experience of cinema'. This distinction is intended to modify and subsume the general/generic opposition realism versus fantasy, as well as those discussed specifically in connection with the New German Cinema: author-oriented versus issue-oriented, contentist versus sensibilist.

In the first case, experience refers to the aspirations of self-selected élites, but also of minorities and disadvantaged groups as recorded through the voices and images of those immediately concerned and affected. Ideally, the form a film of this kind takes is determined by the nature of the experience itself, its most authentic expression and manifestation. To this extent, the medium is treated as (ideally) transparent, which is why neither the pair objective/subjective nor form/content is much help. In the second case, the cinema is recognised as a very specific mode of experience, not to be mistaken for a mere instrument of recording reality. Instead, it creates its own kind of reality, and its own experience of time, memory and duration, of space, place and occasion. The emphasis on the exploration of this form of experience is what distinguishes the 'sensibilism' of Fassbinder, Wenders, Syberberg and Herzog from the cine-literacy of the French *nouvelle vague* on the one hand, and the 'Hawksianisms' of the early Rudolf Thome, Klaus Lemke or Eckart Schmidt on the other. The difference is important because it wants to underline that the work of even the internationally known directors of the German cinema is closer to the 'cinema of experience' than to the films either of other European auteurs or those of genre-based, allusionist, New Hollywood directors.

'Experience of cinema' is akin to but not identical with what is traditionally referred to as cinephilia – love of the cinema as cinema – and thus the opposite of reproducing 'real' experiences. The reason why both belong together none the less is, as I have tried to indicate in the previous chapters, that they valorise, albeit in quite different ways, 'going to the cinema' as a particular kind of event. If, therefore, the cinema of experience becomes more like cinephilia, experience of cinema in the German context is perhaps not quite the fetishism of the cinema that it is usually taken to be. Wim Wenders' cinephilia, for example (representative here of an entire complex of film-making, film criticism and spectatorship, covering a wide political spectrum), defines itself by an experience of intensity, physicality, duration and imaginary plenitude which is well aware of its extra-cinematic historical roots in a particular postwar German childhood and adolescence. Because of this any stark opposition between experience as having to do with real life, and experience as a search for artificial sensations, must

Ivan Desny in Fassbinder's The Marriage of Maria Braun *(1979)* . . .

208

. . . and with Ingrid Caven in Jeanine Meerapfel's Malou *(1981)*

break down. The first is mediated by the technological apparatus of the cinema, while the second is mediated by history, memory and actual lived experience.

Generally, it seems that within the overall divide of film forms – montage versus realism or, in Bazin's phrase, between 'film-makers who believe in the image and film-makers who believe in reality'[1] – the New German Cinema sides with realism, except that it is a realism that believes mainly in the image. Therefore, the distinction between the two forms of experience becomes even less absolute when one considers how much general knowledge of the world and even intimate knowledge of the self is mediated via representations and images. Introspection invariably becomes a form of autoscopia, bringing it ever closer to the narcissistic and nostalgic pleasures derived from the cinema as cinema. These are the aspects of the New German Cinema which the remaining chapters seek to explore further.

'The Dead Souls of Germany'

I would like to speak briefly about loneliness in Germany. It seems to me that it is more hidden and at the same time more painful than elsewhere. Fear is considered a sign either of vanity or it is felt as weakness. And that is why loneliness in Germany is masked, masked by all those treacherous, bright, soulless faces that drift through supermarkets, leisure centres, pedestrian precincts, keep-fit evening classes – the dead souls of Germany.[2]

With these programmatic sentences a rich industrialist from the Rhineland in

209

Wenders' *Wrong Movement* (*Falsche Bewegung*, 1974) takes leave of his guests on the eve of hanging himself from the banister of his rococo staircase. He is played by Ivan Desny, who in Fassbinder's *The Marriage of Maria Braun* (*Die Ehe der Maria Braun*, 1979) is the rich industrialist Oswald. Oswald's relationship with Maria Braun is explicitly based on the proposition that sharing loneliness is the best that two people can achieve. In 1971, after seeing six films by Douglas Sirk and visiting him in Switzerland, Fassbinder wrote:

> People can't live alone, but they cannot live together either. This is why Sirk's movies are so desperate . . . Douglas Sirk looks at these corpses with such tenderness and radiance that we start to think something must be badly wrong if these people are so screwed up and nonetheless, so human. The fault lies with fear and loneliness.[3]

In Jeanine Meerapfel's *Malou* (1981) the heroine, unhappily married to a successful architect, goes on a journey in search of her roots. She visits the grave of her mother and, on the other side of the Rhine, in Alsace, finds the family home of her father, a rich Jewish businessman who had to flee to South America, where her mother became a manic-depressive alcoholic. The father is played by Ivan Desny, and the mother by Ingrid Caven, star of early Fassbinder films and briefly his wife. Caven plays the unattainable but infinitely seductive 'great love' in Fassbinder's first 'Sirkean' film *The Merchant of Four Seasons* (*Der Händler der vier Jahreszeiten*, 1971). In this film Hans Epp, the hero, progressively more isolated in the midst of his family, in-laws and friends, drinks himself to death. Two years later Fassbinder made *Fear Eats the Soul* (*Angst Essen Seele Auf*, 1974), in which fear of social ostracism eats away at the passionate if unorthodox relationship between Emmi, a 60-year-old Munich charwoman, and a Moroccan immigrant worker in his thirties.

It was neither the first nor the last time that the word 'Angst' (fear) would appear in a New German film. From *The Goalie's Fear of the Penalty Kick* (*Die Angst des Tormanns beim Elfmeter*, Wenders, 1972) to *Fear of Fear* (*Angst vor der Angst*, Fassbinder, 1975), *Fear is a Second Shadow* (*Die Angst ist ein zweiter Schatten*, Norbert Kückelmann, 1975) and *Henry Angst* (Ingo Kratisch, 1980) it becomes almost a leitmotif. In *Alice in the Cities* (*Alice in der Städten*, Wenders, 1974) the hero, while taking a bath, confesses to 'Angst vor der Angst', and in *Effi Briest* (Fassbinder, 1974) Effi says of her husband that he keeps her in check by a 'calculated anxiety-machine' ('Angstapparat aus Kalkül'). This is a fair description of what Dennis Hopper in *The American Friend* (*Der amerikanische Freund*, Wenders, 1977) does to Bruno Ganz, when he exploits the frame-maker's fears of suffering from a terminal illness. In the same film Hopper mumbles into his dictaphone that 'the only thing to fear is fear itself' – a double quotation in the context – a line from President Roosevelt's famous address to the Nation, and an ironic acknowledgement that the German cinema had made such sentiments its trademark.

The year before, in *Kaspar Hauser* (Herzog, 1974), over the shot of a ripening wheatfield blown and buffeted by the wind, a voice is heard saying 'do you not hear the awful scream all around us that people call silence?' (a quotation from Georg Büchner's *Lenz*). When Kaspar Hauser is seen head-on for the first time, it is in the central square of a sleepy Biedermeier town at the break of dawn, awkwardly holding a letter to the blank amazement of the townspeople as they open their shutters and windows. Kaspar is a foundling grown to manhood in a cellar, without language, without memory, with no past and, as it turns out, no

Brigitte Mira and El Hedi Ben Salem in Fassbinder's Fear Eats the Soul *(1974)*

Ingrid Caven in Fassbinder's The Merchant of Four Seasons *(1971)*

Bruno S in Herzog's Kaspar Hauser *(1974)*

future. As soon as he reaches the threshold of communication, he is murdered by his erstwhile gaoler and presumed father. The lone figure in the square, the adult child caught in an absurd gesture of pleading supplication, recalls Fassbinder's 'Merchant of Four Seasons', standing by his barrow in a desolate Munich courtyard, surrounded by five-storey tenement buildings. His eyes raised towards the rows of closed windows, he barks with the automatic mourning voice of the rag-and-bone man. This is an image that Herzog in turn, quoting himself and Fassbinder's film, takes up in *Stroszek* (1977) when Bruno S. – the leading actor in both *Kaspar Hauser* and *Stroszek* – finds himself, after a lifetime in and out of prisons, playing the accordion in a Berlin tenement courtyard.

It is no accident that images from these films seem to echo each other in important respects. Loneliness, homelessness, isolation, fear and failure have often been identified as the main preoccupations of the New German Cinema. In what sense, though, are such themes or motifs typically German? Are questions about the Germanness of the films not merely the consequence of the fact that critics, confronted with the work of very different directors from the same country, tend to look for common denominators? Yet many of the films, especially from the mid-1970s onwards, encourage speculations about the national character, referring explicitly to Germany, either in their original titles or their foreign release versions: *Germany in Autumn* (*Deutschland im Herbst*, 1978), *The German*

Theodor Kotulla's Death is My Trade *(1977)*

Sisters (*Die Bleierne Zeit*, in the US: *Marianne and Juliane*, von Trotta, 1981), *Germany Pale Mother* (*Deutschland Bleiche Mutter*, Sanders-Brahms, 1979), *Aus einem deutschen Leben* (Theodor Kotulla, 1977), *Made in Germany and USA* (Thome, 1974) and *Morgen in Alabama* (*A German Lawyer*, Kückelmann, 1984). Edgar Reitz' *Heimat* (1984) is subtitled *Made in Germany*, alluding also to the ambiguous status of many of the films as products-for-export, a status which the New German Cinema acquired during the second half of the 1970s, when it was massively promoted by the German government through its embassies and cultural institutes. As we shall see, such emphasis on Germany and Germanness became part of launching a brand name abroad that could play up to and reinforce a mythology taking shape around postwar German culture and the New German Cinema.

Germany: An Open Wound

At home, therefore, the thematisation of 'Germany' in the late 1970s took quite a different turn from the self-consciousness implied by the revival of formula films and the retooling of the *Heimat* film. The essentially literary orientation of the *Autorenfilm* showed itself also in the primarily 'cultural' definition which the question of national specificity received. In line with the dominant 'romantic-radical' traditions of German intellectuals, film-makers took up the 'German

212

question' in much the same terms in which it had already been raised in the nineteenth century by writers like Hölderlin, Heine and Ludwig Börne. It was seen as 'Die Wunde Deutschland', the wound, caused by the divisions of class, region, religion, political affiliation and nationalist sentiment, that refused to close on the body-politic of the nation-state.

As mentioned earlier, ever since the French Revolution democratic thought and socialist aspirations in Germany found themselves in contradiction with the realities of nationhood. The sense of sharing a common culture or enjoying the pride and identity of the patriot had always been the patrimony of the conservative right. Challenges to the feudal-militarist alliance on the part of radical writers or, later, working-class organisations were met with disparaging references to unpatriotic elements ('vaterlandslose Gesellen') and countered with expulsion or, as in the case of Rosa Luxemburg or Karl Liebknecht, assassination. From Heine and Marx to Fritz Lang and Bert Brecht, self-imposed or forced exile (most often to France) served the German liberal and left intelligentsia as both a confirmation of exclusion and a vantage-point. The constant toying with emigration on the part of Syberberg, Fassbinder, Wenders or Herzog must be understood as a language of symbolic action alluding to historic precedent.[4]

If the New German Cinema eventually turned itself into a myth, it was in terms of antinomies arising out of German history and the culture at large, as interpreted by writers of very different political aspirations. Hölderlin's *Hyperion*, Heine's *Deutschland ein Wintermärchen*, Büchner's *Lenz*, Tucholsky's *Deutschland, Deutschland über Alles*, Rosa Luxemburg's *Letters*, Bloch's *Erbschaft dieser Zeit* and, after the war, the poems of Hans Magnus Enzensberger (*Landessprache*) are some of the reference points for a left-liberal tradition. Novalis, Nietzsche,

Jutta Lampe and Barbara Sukowa in von Trotta's The German Sisters *(1981)*

Wagner, Thomas Mann, Gottfried Benn and Ernst Jünger can stand for the conservative interpretation of the German question.

The language of myth may serve to reconcile individuals, groups or an entire people to an inadequate reality. In Wilhelmine Germany, for instance, the Barbarossa myth had been a way of consoling for historical failure, while the ever-popular Siegfried legend answered to the sense of being the victim of inter- and supra-national conspiracies. Yet myth may also indicate something other than the imaginary resolution to real contradictions. It is a mode of dealing with both positive and negative experiences in a form where fact, desire and memory enter into a single image or coherent narrative, unifying existence for those who live at the margins of history or in opposition to it. The Grail legend or the Parsifal figure have always attracted melancholy rebels.

Myths in this sense can be seen as fables of identity, promises of reconciliation, the assertion of unity in the face of and as protest against fragmentation and division in the fabric of lived continuities. Poised ambiguously between a conservative mystification of social and political realities, and a potential energy for change, literary myth – whether naive as in Karl May's novels, or ironic, as in Thomas Mann – tries to keep alive (in the image of a better past) the promise of a better future. The Faust legend in particular has served historically as a way of investigating the dialectics of unity and division which traverse German history. Yet the very idea of an authentic national experience or a mythic hero point to a culture singularly obsessed with wholeness, unification and identity. These cultural motifs are themselves symptomatic of a history marked by division, particularism, regionalism and decentredness, punctuated by brief and usually disastrous periods of centralised military-bureaucratic rule.

The terms of this debate about a national consciousness – in the 1970s polarised between the fervent self-denying internationalism of the Left and the politically more diffuse regionalism of conservationists – entered the films in typically oblique ways. Thus, Herzog's internationalism is that of a conservative, whereas Achternbusch's regionalism is anarchist. Syberberg's invocation of European culture serves a conservative outlook, while Fassbinder's Germano-centric view is left-wing and anti-capitalist. However, the myths of their cinema have to be reconstructed, rather than simply read off the titles, plots, or personal postures and convictions of the directors. A common stock of motifs, quotations, auto-citations and oppositions suggests that the films together form a kind of synthetic mythology, restating, but also not altogether contained within, the master-narrative of the 'German question'.

Three complexes can be isolated which inform the German cinema's reflections and representations of its Germanness – the question of continuity and discontinuity of German history, especially with respect to Fascism; the family, as a problem of personal identity and patriarchal authority; and finally the issue of legitimacy, which in some sense subsumes the other two. An example might illustrate the point that one is dealing not only with filmic motifs but with a layering of social texts and symbolic actions. When in 1974 Werner Herzog had completed *Kaspar Hauser*, he put the cans of film into a rucksack and set off from Munich by foot in the direction of Paris where, three weeks later, he presented himself and his film at the sickbed of Lotte Eisner.[5] For a director vaunting his spontaneity and unselfconsciousness this was a brilliantly calculated inspiration. In a minor key, it was as redolent of cultural and historic resonances as Willy Brandt's spontaneous genuflection at a memorial to the Warsaw ghetto in 1971 had been an act of political atonement and a gesture of redress for Auschwitz and what it stood for.

Lotte Eisner surrounded by her sons (right Bruno Ganz and, on the ground, Werner Herzog)

That *the* historian of Expressionist cinema, émigre Jew and woman, friend of F.W. Murnau and Fritz Lang, personal assistant to Henri Langlois (founding father of the Cinémathèque and patron saint of the French *nouvelle vague*), should – on what might easily have been her deathbed – give a young German film-maker her blessing, by assuring him that his work was once more 'legitimate German culture', could itself be read as a founding myth of origins and identity. By endorsing continuity, bestowing the right of inheritance, mediating between fathers and sons, enemy nations and two rebel film movements, Lotte Eisner, thanks to Herzog, became the super-mother of the New German Cinema and of a film history conceived as family melodrama, whose key figure is, precisely, the abandoned child.

Looking at some of the most popular films of the 1970s, questions of national, existential or sexual identity are clearly to the fore. In *Aguirre, Kaspar Hauser, Stroszek, Fear Eats the Soul, Despair, The Marriage of Maria Braun, Alice in the Cities, Kings of the Road, The American Friend, Ludwig – Requiem for a Virgin King, Our Hitler, Sisters, or the Balance of Happiness* and *The German Sisters*, these three motifs are rarely treated in isolation. They overlap, are woven into the different strands of the narrative, or are condensed in highly symbolic visual compositions and icons, sacrificing realism and verisimilitude for allegory, fantasy or melodrama. Once again, it rarely is a case of objective or sociological representation, but of a mediated, highly coded depiction of history, society and the family from an emotionally coloured, even partisan perspective. It is a reaction to a reality more than its description, which is why, perhaps too generally and simplistically, the New German Cinema is so often called 'subjective'.

If 'subjective' suggests that the films are impressionistic and therefore unrepresentative, this is misleading. Although they do not share a specific style, they belong together by virtue of this common nexus – the family/legitimacy/identity – explored in different registers. Kaspar Hauser appears in many guises, male and female; the family is generally incomplete or asymmetrical in its power relations, and history in the New German Cinema is almost exclusively seen in the context of Fascism and its delayed aftermath: the radicalisation and polarisation of the 1960s culminating in the wave of urban terrorism in the early 1970s. As in *The German Sisters*, the will to work for renewal and create a utopia (if necessary by force) often justifies itself by a reference to the unexpiated guilt and collective crimes of the Third Reich. The task of a 'past to be mastered', to which the generation who grew up in the 1950s seemed still mortgaged when they made films in the 1970s, demanded that they ask what it meant to be German.

Torn between homesickness, suicide (Wenders' Kings of the Road, *1976)*

Hence German history is present, even where it does not appear as such. In the films that deal with borders and border-crossings (*Alice in the Cities*), with journeys, exiles and exotic adventures (*Aguirre, Madame X*), with America in Europe (*The American Friend*), or with a divided Germany (*Kings of the Road, The Willi Busch Report*) historical traumas are never far away. Especially notable are the many narratives about heroes torn between homesickness and the longing for faraway places (*Signs of Life, Kaspar Hauser* and *Heart of Glass; Alice in the Cities* and *Kings of the Road; Ludwig* and *Karl May; The Trip to Vienna* and *Heimat*). Equally typical is the desire to escape from a narrow milieu, blocked and frustrated by the need for roots and for a sense of belonging (*The Merchant of Four Seasons* and *Fear Eats the Soul*; *The Atlantic Swimmers* and *Servus Bayern*). Many films could carry as their motto Ernst Bloch's dictum that 'utopia is the return to a childhood not yet lived',[6] for they situate history between apocalypse and *tabula rasa*.

Society, as a consequence, is experienced from the vantage point of standing outside, alone and overwhelmed by personal impotence. Desire for change invariably involves rebellion which, as we shall see, is figured primarily as martyrdom or submission, indicating the very problematic but also symptomatic relation of the protagonists to authority. Indeed, it is hardly an exaggeration to argue that the central line of force in these films is the ambivalence between aggression against others and aggression against the self. Put even most starkly, the choice seems to be between murder and suicide, the two often amounting to the same.

The configuration is emblematically present in *Despair* (where the hero kills

. . . *and the longing for faraway places (Edgar Reitz'* Heimat, *1984)*

his double in the mad hope it will be taken as suicide) and also in *Knife in the Head* (the victim of a police raid tries to avenge himself on his assailant, but hesitates when he recognises his own fear in the face of the other). The same is true of *The German Sisters* (the terrorist commits suicide in order to indict the State and punish her parents) and *Sisters, or the Balance of Happiness* (a young woman commits suicide to punish her sister), but equally in *The American Friend* (the terminally ill hero in front of the mirror puts a gun to his mouth before shooting it out with the Mafia). Finally, in *The Lost Honour of Katharina Blum*, where the heroine smashes up her own apartment and then silently waits for the

217

arrival of a newspaper reporter whom she riddles with bullets. It is the prevalence of such configurations that links the films of the cinema of experience to the international prestige productions aimed at an experience of cinema.

Suicide and a disturbed rapport with authority figures point to the family, seen especially in Fassbinder and von Trotta as the key to history and social relations. Crucially in German films, the family is rarely a functioning unit: often the father is weak, absent or unapproachable, the mother bitter, depressive or alcoholic. In *Kaspar Hauser* there is a clear separation between good fathers (like Daumer or the prison warder), bad fathers (the Caligari figure in hat and coat who attacks him in the outdoor privy) and a number of stupid, tyrannical or foppish authority figures (the pastor, the logician, the ring master and Lord Stanhope), indicative of the meshing of authoritarian education, political repression and familial violence. Thus, society is both filtered and interpreted polemically via the family. It allows not only a direct confrontation with the questions of legitimacy (the passing on of power between the generations), and of terrorism (interpreted as a necessary act of violent defence against father figures or aggressively turned inward against the self), but also an often very subtle exploration of the structures of identification and projection governing emotional bonds in postwar Germany. To recognise oneself in the other, who appears alternatively as one's opponent, one's accomplice and one's double, is almost *the* cinematic theme par excellence. Its re-emergence in the New German Cinema as the structure which allows social relations and a view of history to articulate themselves, forms the basic premise of this chapter.

Herzog's Germany

Those directors able to give their successive films the coherence of an oeuvre (notably Fassbinder, Syberberg, Herzog, Wenders, von Trotta and Achternbusch) tend to dramatise the common polarities by a series of variations, often modified from film to film. Werner Herzog's heroes in the major films (*Signs of Life, Even Dwarfs Started Small, Kaspar Hauser, Aguirre, Nosferatu, Heart of Glass, Stroszek, Woyzeck* and *Fitzcarraldo*) can be seen most easily as forming a self-sustaining, internally coherent paradigm. These heroes invariably circle around limit states and try to define what is human – by a dialectic of mankind as destructive and the individual as inwardly destroyed. At a glance, they divide into two symmetrically related groups: the overreachers of *Signs of Life, Aguirre, Nosferatu, Fitzcarraldo* and the underdogs of *Even Dwarfs Started Small, Kaspar Hauser, Stroszek* and *Woyzeck*. Whether supermen or victims, however, Herzog's protagonists are always extreme, marginal and outside, in relation to the centre which is the social world, the world of history, that of ordinary beings. The existential dimension of his characters always seems to take precedence over any social issue against which they might revolt or from which they might suffer. The heroes are either larger or smaller than life, but life for them is precisely the realm of the ordinary, the commonplace, the unremarkable, the bureaucratic, the institutional, the petty and the mediocre. Only *Where the Green Ants Dream* (*Wo die grünen Ameisen träumen*, 1984) is an exception, with a hero who appears to have been chosen for his ordinariness and determination to get involved in a specific, local issue, the fight of a tribe of Australian aborigines to retain their sacred sites. Yet even this hero is a loner: Herzog's characters are unattached and total individualists. Where they are married (Stroszek in *Signs of Life*,

218

Angela Winkler in Schlöndorff/von Trotta's The Lost Honour of Katharina Blum *(1975)*

Dirk Bogarde in Fassbinder's Despair *(1978)*

Bruno Ganz and Angela Winkler in Reinhard Hauff's Knife in the Head *(1978)*

219

Between over-reacher and underdog: the different faces of Klaus Kinski in Herzog's

Nosferatu *(1978)* . . .

. . . Aguirre Wrath of God *(1972)* . . .

. . . *and* Woyzeck *(1978)*

Woyzeck, Aguirre, who has a daughter but no wife) the bond proves to be ineffectual. It merely underscores the character's isolation and solitude rather than promising even the sort of temporary companionship one finds in the more optimistic moments of a Wenders or Fassbinder film. Herzog's heroes do not merely exclude the world of the ordinary, the space where most human beings organise their lives, but exist in a void because of a determination to investigate the limits of what it means to be human at all.

Between man-as-god and man-as-beast, Herzog's films oscillate in a perpetual search for an existential and metaphysical truth which can only be a divided or dialectical quest. For the neat division between super-man and sub-human in his films is only apparent; there is a constant communication between the two poles, as is suggested by external evidence: Stroszek is the name of one of his supermen (in *Signs of Life*), and also the name of Bruno S. in the film of that title. Klaus

Helmut Döhring in Herzog's Even
Dwarfs Started Small *(1970)*

Kinski, who became Herzog's ideal incarnation of the superman (Aguirre and
Fitzcarraldo) also plays one of the sub-humans: Woyzeck, George Büchner's
classic study of the exploitation of man by man. Nosferatu, on the other hand, is
both: superior to human beings by his powers over death, he is less than human
by his exile from the temporal, daytime order of life, desiring the ordinary the
more for being excluded from it. Similarly, the Dwarfs are depicted as physically
sub-human, but in their actions and self-images they see themselves as superior
to the rest of mankind. What unites the super-human and the sub-human in a
single dialectic is that both types of protagonists are failures, and are shown in
stories that exemplify their failure. Jan Dawson was the first to draw attention to
this:

> His preferred heroes, chosen or revealed, are extreme not only in their situation
> (and often in their geographical situation), but also in their isolation . . . an
> impatience, not merely with the more mundane forms of human suffering [runs
> through the films like a seismic fault]. His chosen people are not merely those who
> transcend their limitations, but those who also have hyperbolic limitations to
> overcome. The quality of compassion evident in Herzog's palpable revelations of
> the fate of the afflicted – the blind, the handicapped, the colonized, the oppressed
> (all victims, as much of mankind's segregational practices as of their generic
> afflictions) – is offset not merely by the films' lust for death, but more questionably
> by the fact that he admits no ordinary victims, merely super-victims . . . Even his
> victim figures are supermen – none of them ever appeals to or for pity.[7]

The underlying unity is that Herzog's heroes are solitary rebels, incapable of
solidarity but also incapable of success, and it is this insistence on failure that
redeems their vaulting ambition and their hubris. Or, in another sense, whether
one sees them as supermen or as victims and outcasts depends on where one
places the emphasis, in a fallen world that in Herzog's films aspires to God-like
omnipotence but where a God always mocks men by making them keenly aware

221

Hyperbolic limitations to overcome: Klaus Kinski in Herzog's Nosferatu *(1978)*

of their impotence. Herzog himself qualified Stroszek as someone who had undertaken a 'titanic revolt, but like all of his kind, he had failed and perished' (*Signs of Life*).

The dialectic that propels the characters is therefore not without mythological resonances. Behind his figures stands Hercules, doing other people's dirty work. But even more central is Prometheus – the mythic hero who tried to steal from the Gods, bringing fire down from the heavens for the benefit of mankind, to be eternally exiled and punished for his deed. The role of scapegoats, even the primitive Christ-like suffering of Herzog's heroes, can easily be related to basic Western myths and their derivations. The director himself is quite aware of his mythologising tendency, and able to comment on it ironically. One of his first films, a twelve minute short called, characteristically, *Herakles* (*Hercules*, 1962) sums up this ambivalence succinctly. A body-building contest is intercut with scenes from a scrap metal yard where a huge machine is crushing automobile wrecks into handy parcels. Around this surreal collage Herzog has packed the basic configuration of practically all his subsequent films: heroic effort and endeavour in a mockingly futile situation.

However, more important than confronting the image of the superman with a world dominated by technology is the very possibility or impossibility of revolution. The choice is between degeneration into anarchic revolt, or operatic self-display and exhibitionism. In a very direct sense Herzog's film heroes may thus be construed as having political relevance to the German question in the 1960s and 1970s, two decades that saw intense debates about the possibility of change and revolution in West Germany and industrial societies. Such a direct interpretation of the films as belonging to the arena of the political – with all the attendant misunderstanding this could entail about Herzog and his pessimistic, if not counter-revolutionary outlook – needs to remember how typical the alternative of revolt and self-display, or revolt as self-display, is in the German cinema. It is unique neither to the work nor to the personality of Herzog.

222

Herzog and Syberberg

What informs Herzog's pessimistic insistence on isolation and failure, as worked out in his heroes, is the intertwining opposition of rebellion and submission. One only has to turn to Hans-Jürgen Syberberg, with his much more overtly historical and cultural themes and his direct thematisation of Germany and the German soul, to find the constellation made explicit. In Syberberg's vast panorama – stretching from Ludwig of Bavaria to Hitler – the figure of Wagner occupies a central place as the key to the Germanness of German history since the nineteenth century. This is so because in Wagner the history of the nineteenth century condenses itself into mythology and, as Nietzsche had pointed out, Wagner provided the rising German bourgeoisie with a mythological image of themselves, an image in which the act of revolutionary appropriation of power was only condoned if it was accompanied by an act of submission elsewhere. In Wagner's operas the rebelliousness of a Siegfried finds its symbolic fulfilment in the swooning death wish of Tristan and Isolde, transforming a political act into an erotic gesture, and thus preparing the way for turning politics into depth-psychology. One could even say that in Wagner the rebel-turned-conformist enters German culture as a seductive archetype.

In this respect Syberberg's visionary villains (Ludwig II, Karl May and Himmler/Hitler) have much in common with Herzog's titans. This is especially so with Aguirre and Aguirre's happier brother Fitzcarraldo who, like Ludwig II, devotes his life to building opera houses with fantastic sets and staging baroque spectacles of whom he is the only audience. In a perceptive comment the poet Erich Fried once called Herzog's role in German film culture that of a 'Parsival among the Tuis',[8] brandishing his innocence like a sword. What Siegfried was to the generation of the 1920s – the heroic self-image of a technocratic imagination – Parsifal is for the sensibilists of the 1970s, hoping to find the Holy Grail by concentrating on their inwardness. Syberberg's *Parsifal* (1982) might be interpreted as a comment on this topos when his hero, after refusing either to kill the father-figure or sleep with the mother-figure turns into a girl but retains his male voice.

If one can see in Aguirre and Fitzcarraldo the shape of Ludwig rather than Hitler, then it is even more plausible to see in Syberberg's Karl May not so much the Fenimore Cooper or Kipling of Germany (as the historic Karl May is often described), but the figure of Bruno S., the orphan foundling who compensates for his human disadvantages and afflictions in life with a vision of distant lands, exoticism and heroic deeds worthy of a Siegfried. Seen through Karl May, author of adventure stories, the Herzogian obsession with faraway landscapes, jungles and super-human exploits takes on a distinctly German historical dimension. Despite their seemingly existential emphasis, their apolitical aspects, these films become quite precisely locatable in the social and cultural history of Germany, as a country which lived its politics in the imagination and eventually realised some of its deepest fantasies (of redemption and heroism) in the technocratic nightmares of Nazism and the Final Solution. The myth-logic implicit in both Syberberg's and Herzog's films is one where Siegfried and Parsifal belong together, which means that the Aguirre figures in Herzog are actually characters out of Kaspar Hauser's dreams. This is made more or less explicit in the visions that he narrates on his deathbed: scenes from the Sahara and Iceland stand for the treks, landscapes and pilgrimages that form the backdrop to *Signs of Life*, *Fata Morgana*, and *Aguirre*. In *Stroszek* Bruno S. becomes just such a mythological but also a

Wagner's head between Klingsor and Kundry in Syberberg's Parsifal *(1982)*

grotesque outlaw: ending his life as a cowboy in a Red Indian Amusement Arcade, the dream of the better life and the purity of the vision betrayed to commerce and the cultural cliché.

Herzog, in other words, is committed to a heroic view of life, a heroism that might appear suspect, juvenile or bombastic were it not so clearly marked as a strategy for survival rather than a will to power. The heroic attitude – with its devaluation of the merely ordinary – is first and foremost a perspective, a deliberate stance and vantage point, which allows him to take the measure of the world. As a way of formulating his concern with the quality of life, it points to the emotional and spiritual numbness that in almost all the films of the New German Cinema seems to characterise West German public affairs and private lives. Herzog's heroism is thus an inevitably ironic stance, a form of distance that makes impossible, excessive and extreme demands on the 'self'. It becomes almost a necessary spiritual exercise, a peculiarly German chastisement for the imagination and the senses. What gives the stance its ironic twist is that, as indicated, his heroes are aware of failure from the outset. Where they are Promethean and titanic they none the less persevere in the full knowledge of punishment and of the price there is to pay; where they are saints and holy fools they have no possibility of glory and power in this world, nor is there a next one. Outside society, maimed, handicapped or bearing the mark of Cain, their quest for survival is also a quest for innocence. By stoically courting failure, while challenging everyone and everything, they may well be symptomatic of a flawed and divided self, but they are no fascist versions of the superman. That this vision partakes none the less of a culturally identifiable dualism which is typically German – excluding as it does a secular tradition of democratic humanism – seems undeniable.

No doubt one can also discover at the heart of this dual vision an autobiographical experience, and it is not difficult, though perhaps not very rewarding, to diagnose in the dialectic of hero and victim, rebel and saint, a personal fixation on authority. Herzog's conversion to Catholicism, as mentioned earlier, was a deliberate gesture against his father, whom he blamed for abandoning his family. Preferring the unsteady life of an adventurer and a 'tramp' to being a provider, Herzog's father left his wife to raise her only son. The story Herzog likes to tell about stealing a camera from the very people who refused to help him realise his first film forms part of the same oedipal configuration. Robin Hood becomes Prometheus, and it might not be too fanciful to see in the figures of the adventurer and the tramp who dominate Herzog's films the haunted quest for the paternal image.

But such a masochistic disposition places Herzog, once again, in a particular German historical context – similar to the one discussed by Horkheimer and Adorno in their *Authoritarian Personality*. Yet this does not confine him to a socio-psychological type, either as a personality or as a film-maker. As a Bavarian 'regionalist' Herzog also situates himself within the terms of a specifically German

Cowboy hat and cultural cliché: Clemens Scheitz (left) and Bruno S (centre) in Herzog's Stroszek *(1977)*

The Kaspar Hauser complex in Herzog's Stroszek *(1977)* . . .

debate about anthropology and ecology, which in the 1970s tried to fuse the international concerns of the Left with the German problem of Heimat and 'belonging'. This is why Kaspar Hauser is so central to Herzog and to the New German Cinema. Not only as the subject of one of its best-known films, but as a complex psychoanalytic motif; it is the fantasy of being abandoned, fatherless, with an uncertain relationship to all forms of socialisation, to sexual identity and adulthood, attempting to survive between a good father substitute and a bad father image.

Herzog's work shows a profusion of such polarities and his protagonists embody the two sides of the Kaspar Hauser complex – its active and its passive component. While Kaspar Hauser finds himself abandoned and cast into the world Aguirre, in an act of defiance against God, King, and country, abandons himself, as if to anticipate and preempt the experience of being abandoned by making himself the wilful instrument of his own destruction. The scene where Aguirre leans against the makeshift hut on the raft while Hombrecito, the imbecile Indian, plays for him on a reed pipe is like the tacit recognition of two kinds of Herzog survivors, two complementary figurations of a single idea and identity. In the process, the social world is bracketed off: both Kaspar Hauser and Aguirre seek salvation in a state where society no longer (or not yet) imposes its norms. Perhaps only in *Stroszek*, especially in the scene where the two pimps torment and humiliate Bruno S. (in whose expression pain has given way to a kind of astonished self-abandonment) does the Dostoevskian dialectic of sinner and saint, transposed into the Berlin underworld of destitution and prostitution, frame an overt social critique. Yet even there, the point of view is both more metaphysical

226

. . . and Fassbinder's Fox and his Friends *(1975)*

and less heroic, mainly because of the Kafkesque humour that Bruno S. and Herr Scheitz bring to their roles.

Herzog and Fassbinder

In *Stroszek,* with its stark statement of sadism and masochism, Herzog seems closest to Fassbinder, both in his depiction of a milieu and of a situation of more or less explicit sexual violation and violence among males. However, Fassbinder's heroes are not as easy to typify as those of Herzog, not only because the autobiographical elements are more literal, and therefore enter less into the structure of the films, but also because in so vast an output – over 40 films in barely 15 years – one has to distinguish between different types of heroes, not forgetting that many of them are heroines (as they are not in Herzog).

Fassbinder's early films are less about cultural legitimacy than they are concerned with sexual and class identity. At first these are seen as parallel processes: oppression in the family equals social oppression, a congruence which preoccupied the German Left and the anti-authoritarian movement more than any other subject. The tension in Fassbinder's work comes from the growing realisation that social and sexual crises of identity do not converge, and that to see the father merely as the representative of capitalism in the home is to become a rebel in the image of the oppressor. Fassbinder's 'solution' to the problem of authority and identity and thus the question of the hero was to bring into play two kinds of reversals. Firstly, his female characters were often given strong, rebellious roles. Their failure to achieve a stable identity through revolt was not

227

only motivated by the contradictory 'programming' of needs and desires that women receive in patriarchal society, but pointed to a more general failure of 'oedipal' identity. Fassbinder's second strategy was to replace the oppressor/oppressed model by the sado-masochistic double-bind.

If one takes the films of the middle period (from *The Merchant of Four Seasons* to *Martha*, 1973), it is clear that sado-masochism is the basic structure of interaction between the characters. The discussions of these films as imitations and transpositions of Sirkean melodrama and soap opera have somewhat obscured the significance of the psychological purism and reductionism in Fassbinder's work. Exploitation is still the central motif, regardless of whether the depicted relationship is a heterosexual, male homosexual or a lesbian one. Yet it is *within* exploitation that many of the heroes seek salvation. Submission and service rather than rebellion become the prime motives of his characters' desire, even where the power struggles take on a much more directly social, economic or racial dimension. For it became increasingly evident that the political motifs in *Fox and his Friends* (*Faustrecht der Freiheit*, 1975), *Fear Eats the Soul*, *Mother Küster's Trip to Heaven* (*Mutter Küster's Fahrt zum Himmel*, 1975) and even in *In a Year of Thirteen Moons* (*In einem Jahr mit 13 Monden*, 1978) and *The Third Generation* (*Die dritte Generation*, 1979) were to some extent interchangeable. Whatever the ideological or sexual politics, they did not basically affect the structure of the interaction, nor the mechanisms that Fassbinder wanted to lay bare. These mechanisms, although originating in the family and massively reinforced by the power relations in society at large, can only be lived 'from within' the vicious circles. Masochism to the point of self-abandonment becomes the gesture of freedom that alone restores identity.

Almost all of the films of that period and many of the later ones end in suicide. A persistent will to self-destruction pervades them, which seems to stand in diametrical contrast to the Promethean self-creation so evident in Herzog's films. And yet, as we have seen, it is preserved as its necessary complement in the Kaspar Hauser configuration. For in Fassbinder, too, the family is always incomplete or askew: there are wives and mothers (severe and castrating, notably in *The Merchant of Four Seasons* and many of the roles interpreted by Fassbinder's own mother) but rarely if ever fathers or even father figures. What one sees abundantly are constellations dominated by daughters, by sons and by lovers, as for instance in *The Bitter Tears of Petra von Kant*, *Germany in Autumn*, *The Marriage of Maria Braun* and *Veronika Voss*. Identity in Fassbinder is usually the end-point of a negative trajectory towards accepting the lack, rather than appropriating the fetish-objects of power. Where a character does so, as in *Maria Braun* or *Lola*, the films are structured around those moments where phallic power is shown to be fetishistic, a spectacle which in Fassbinder is always tragic-comic, ironic or grotesque and, in the later films, always tied to the history of West Germany.

Wenders' Germany

To support this brief review of how the family and the question of identity provides the master-narrative in the films of the auteurs of the New German Cinema, it is useful to look at Wenders, since – at least until *Paris, Texas* (1984) – he seems to avoid, even more than Herzog, making the family the emotional or dramatic centre of the story. Generally in Wenders there are only mothers and

Trouble and strife in the home: Karl Scheydt and Irm Hermann in Fassbinder's The Merchant of Four Seasons *(1971)*

Hanna Schygulla and Margit Carstensen in Fassbinder's The Bitter Tears of Petra von Kant *(1972)*

Hollywood maverick and father-figure: Nick Ray in Wenders' The American Friend *(1977)*

Icon of the 1950s: the portable record player, in Wenders' Kings of the Road *(1976)*

Harry Dean Stanton and Hunter Carson looking for Mother . . .

. . . Natasha Kinski in Wenders' Paris, Texas *(1984)*

mother-surrogates (as in *The Goalie's Fear of the Penalty Kick*, *Alice in the Cities* and *Wrong Movement*). The question of rebellion barely arises, since father–son conflicts are almost always displaced, usually to sibling rivalry and an ambiguous homoerotic bond between males (as in *Kings of the Road* and *The American Friend*). An exception is Robert's visit to his father in *Kings of the Road*, where a conflict unresolved since childhood finds its poetically apt expression in the headline article Robert prints on his father's presses while the old man is asleep. The article, true to the paradigm described above, accuses the father of having driven Robert away and his mother to suicide. His companion Bruno, by contrast, visits the house where he once lived alone with his mother, on an island in the middle of the Rhine.

Whereas Herzog went to Lotte Eisner and Fassbinder to Douglas Sirk, Wenders found his substitute fathers in the non-German, Hollywood misfits Sam Fuller and Nicholas Ray. The slow death of Nick Ray on film in *Lightning Over Water* (*Nick's Film*, 1980) or the death of the Hollywood producer and the quasi-suicide of the hero in *The State of Things* (*Der Stand der Dinge*, 1982) are intriguing versions of displaced and yet subtly aggressive oedipal challenges in the work of a director whose films generally avoid any kind of overt violence or even conflict (except in heavily eroticised form, as in *The American Friend*).

The quest of Wenders' exclusively male protagonists in the films for which he is best known (*Alice in the Cities*, *Wrong Movement*, *Kings of the Road*, *The American Friend*, *Paris, Texas*, *Wings of Desire*) is frequently tied to the cultural and national opposition between Germany and the United States. All the films involve hypersensitive men – paradigmatically incarnated in three of them by the actor Rüdiger Vogler – travelling across borders and boundaries, in a different version of the Herzog motif of testing extremities of situation and states of mind. An unpopulated geography or a deserted landscape, even a piece of empty sky, serve as a projective foil for ambiguities and aggressions which can never be expressed directly. America in its dual role as resented but also emulated liberator must stand for the 'other' as opponent, rival and father, in a double bind which in Herzog is mythologised and in Fassbinder sexually charged. The celebrated line from *Kings of the Road*, 'the Yanks have colonized our subconscious', uttered when one of the protagonists cannot get a pop song out of his head, hints at the potentially paranoid or schizoid identity which results from displacing direct conflict. One cannot tell what is inside and what is outside, what is self and what is the Other.

The ambiguity is underscored by another scene from the same film, when the heroes find themselves in an abandoned US patrol post. It marks the moment where the two experience their closest bond, both as physical contact with one another and by discovering a common childhood in the memory of the US occupation of the 1950s. But in this patrol hut they are also at the barbed wire border that separates West Germany from East Germany, the 'free world' from 'communism'. The scene intimates that it might still be preferable to have one's subconscious colonised by rock music, chewing gum and Mickey Mouse than to be an actual colony of the Soviet Union. As Wenders himself has pointed out, without American rock music and American movies as 'life-savers' he would not have survived his childhood without 'going mad'. Here again, a process of

Rüdiger Vogler and Yella Rottländer looking for Mother in Alice in the Cities *(1973)*

231

displacement and substitution ensures that Germany, and the German family, are the implied referent. Compensating for an unsatisfactory family life, American popular culture functions as a surrogate home, which can appease the hunger for experience'.

Exile and travel thus become over-determined: they represent in the very act of revolt against the family, a return to its nurturing functions. This is how one might read the fairy tale told by Philip (Rüdiger Vogler in *Alice in the Cities*) to Alice abandoned by her mother in New York and Amsterdam and vainly searching for her grandmother in the Ruhr. A boy accidentally left in the woods is given rides and guided by all manner of helpers, animal and human, until eventually a highway truck takes him to the sea where, miraculously, his mother is waiting for him. This return to the mother, by a man turned boy again who experiences the destruction of the family as a trauma making him literally schizophrenic, is of course the story of *Paris, Texas*.

Margarethe von Trotta: German Sisters – Divided Daughters

For women directors the family became a film subject largely as the result of two kinds of pressure. With the part played by women in the student protests, the role of the family became of cardinal importance for the movement's self-understanding. Secondly, women like Ulrike Meinhof and Gudrun Ensslin also took a significant lead in the rise of urban terrorism, and film-makers began

Gesine Strempel and Hans Peter Korff in Marianne Rosenbaum's Peppermint-Frieden *(1983)*

looking closely at the social and psychic context of violence and direct action. They did so by exploring to the full the ambiguity in which they found themselves as the daughters of mothers who had both lived through the war and sustained the home front, had borne and brought up children under extraordinarily difficult circumstances, but who – as their daughters remembered only too well – had become rigid, timid and neurotic women in the 1950s, poorly preparing their children to challenge male stereotypes of femininity or to lead independent lives.

As we have seen, quite a number of films made by women directors took up these issues by making questions of parental authority, and especially mother–daughter relationships central to the plot. In the early 1980s Helma Sanders-Brahms' *Germany Pale Mother*, Jeanine Meerapfel's *Malou*, Jutta Brückner's *Hunger Years*, Recha Jungman's *Etwas tut weh* (*Something Hurts*, 1980) and Marianne Rosenbaum's *Peppermint Frieden* (*Peppermint Peace*, 1983) all attempted to establish a link between German history, the postwar period and the particular difficulties confronting a woman in finding a viable identity. Most of them are autobiographical and semi-documentary films, belonging to the 'cinema of experience' discussed in the previous chapter. Among them the films of Margarethe von Trotta stand out, not only as examples of a more classical narrative cinema, but also because, like the author's films of Wenders, Fassbinder or Herzog, the question of identity is treated not at the level of biography or history, but more obliquely as a dramatisation of self and other, of identification and projection.

The paradigm of von Trotta's work is most clearly developed in *Sisters, or the Balance of Happiness*, 1979, a title appropriate for several of her films. In each, the more than fragile balance has to do with the emotional interdependence of two women who are disters either by blood (*Sisters, or the Balance of Happiness*; *The German Sisters*, 1981) or by elective affinity in *The Second Awakening of Christa Klages* (*Das Zweite Erwachen der Christa Klages*, 1977) and *Friends and Husbands* (*Heller Wahn*, 1984). In *Christa Klages*, a nursery teacher robs a bank in order to keep a crèche going. On the run she is pursued not only by the police but, for motives of her own, by the young woman bank teller whom she took hostage during the raid. After a stay in Portugal with a former girlfriend who is recovering from a broken marriage Christa Klages gives herself up. But during the crucial confrontation the bank teller does not identify Christa, and the film ends on this public gesture of disavowal which for both women is a recognition and an awakening.

Most of the themes of von Trotta's later films are present: terrorism as violence for political ends, attempted suicide, isolation and solitary confinement, mothers and daughters. Whereas for Herzog and Wenders negative emotions like anxiety, terror or guilt become cinematically more interesting once they are less steeped in precise political referents, von Trotta 'cannot imagine making a film that does not bear directly on our situation in Germany'.[9] Both *Katharina Blum* (which she co-directed) and *Christa Klages* were based on 'real' incidents with a topicality that was almost journalistic. Yet *The German Sisters*, the fictionalised story of Gudrun Ensslin, told from the point of view of her sister, manages to convey, through symmetries and parallels built into the events, a symbolic dimension that gives mythic status to events that at the time were barely three years old.

In *Sisters . . .* , the story of two daughters of very different temperament sharing an apartment and a family past they cannot disentangle, the drama revolves around a cross-over identification that has fatal consequences for Anna (the younger, more idealist and less assimilated of the two). In order to punish

233

Recognizing the Self in the Other: (left) von Trotta's Sisters, or the Balance of Happiness *(1978)*
and (right) The Second Awakening of Christa Klages *(1977)*

Maria (her older, outwardly successful sister) for making her feel inadequate, Anna commits suicide. Explicitly recalling Bergman's *Persona*, von Trotta's film is none the less very different in so far as the contest between the women is not a Strindbergian power struggle. Rather, it shifts the dependencies and also the violence away from the issue of domination, towards that of fusion and merging with the other – something which Maria, who has accepted the male order through her roles of super-woman and secretary, cannot understand. 'You don't really need me. You only need me needing you', Anna says during an argument. As it turns out, Maria adopts another woman to take Anna's place in her economy of being needed, which suggests that her own identity is balanced around a disguised mother–child situation.

Binary oppositions, plot symmetries, repetitions and visual parallels are structural features very much in evidence in von Trotta's films. In *Christa Klages* the daytime crèche has to close because the landlord wants to open a sex shop; Lena, the bank teller, is both a double of Christa's school friend Ingrid and at one point takes the place of Christa's own young daughter. In *Sisters . . .*, Maria has a double in the severe matron who presides over the typing pool, and the conflict between Maria and Anna is echoed by a blind old woman arguing with her sister. In *The German Sisters* Marianne the terrorist has thrown bombs that have possibly wounded innocent people; her innocent small son becomes the victim of a hideous arson attack when someone finds out the identity of his mother. Juliana works for a feminist magazine, but the editorial meetings are conducted dictatorially.

These parallels and dramatic ironies underscore how far the films are about role reversals, mutually sustaining projections and reflections. Usually, an identification across difference is the driving force of the narrative, with a third woman (or a child) acting as the catalyst or mediator. In *Sisters* Maria finally accepts the Anna within herself, ending the process of repression and projection that killed her sister, but also hinting that she might be in danger of going mad herself. Despite its basis in history, *The German Sisters* follows the same pattern very closely. Here, too, the older one, Juliane (played by the same actress, Jutta

Lampe) replies to Marianne in a moment of exasperation: 'You have succeeded in foisting upon me the life you no longer wanted to lead'. She ends up 'becoming' the dead Marianne, by proxy finding her way back to her own rebellious youth, while also making a more positive commitment to life than her sister by raising Marianne's doubly orphaned child.

In neither film do men have any significant role, and if they help to bring the issues into the open they are dropped as soon as the real conflict gets under way. Von Trotta leaves little doubt that the self-destructive identification patterns derive from a displaced or repressed mother–daughter relationship which, however, forcibly implies the absent father. In *Sisters, or the Balance of Happiness* the mother, having had to bring up her daughters alone, is traumatised by the double role of being father and mother. Under the historical conditions of postwar Germany, the film suggests, a woman could only identify with the male order. From such a point of view she either had to become 'male', or accept for herself the verdict of self-sacrifice and self-annihilation which being female, or rather non-male, entails. *Sisters . . .* is a remarkably acute examination of this dilemma, especially since none of the men – Maria's boss, his son, the song-writer Robert, and Maria's dream-reading friend Fritz – are active representatives of this law, however much they live within it.

Maria, Anna and their mother act out a drama which is not theirs – and yet each one faces it alone. The mother has destroyed herself even before her daughter's suicide; Maria tries to resolve the difficulty of being a sister to Anna by impersonating the father: severe, always right, a model of duty and service. Anna's death-wish, her mother's depressions, and Maria's functional efficiency echo each other in what is finally an empty fortress, a haunted house, cemented through guilt and recrimination, where the mutual interdependence becomes a hall of mirrors in a spiritual and emotional void that no external force – political or emotional – can penetrate or fill. The women all live under the 'old law', so to speak: that of bourgeois morality and Oedipal sin.

The German Sisters depicts the working of this law of the family as the motivational core of urban terrorism. Here the father is not absent, but in his arrogant isolation he is an oppressive presence, unresponsive, denying and remote. What distinguishes Marianne from Anna is that initially she responds by violence against others, rather than herself. It is Marianne's husband who commits suicide out of slighted self-love, while she, by contrast, joins her comrades in a politically motivated protest/suicide. Both films return to the past in the form of flashbacks to the sisters as small girls or through visits to the mother that convey just how much this past impinges psychologically. Yet, where von Trotta's films differ from those of virtually all other German film-makers is in her sense of a specifically German history and sensibility not constructed exclusively around Fascism. Instead, her social ethos has its roots in the German Lutheran Church, over the centuries perhaps the most durable home of bourgeois humanism and liberal thought, with its own tradition of political non-conformism, social work, education, child-care and, more recently, a principled anti-fascism and anti-nuclear militancy.

The conflict is between a sense of impersonal duty towards a common good and the almost inhuman isolation it entails. In *Sisters . . .* Maria's solitude becomes a temptation to use moral righteousness as a weapon in an essentially psychological struggle; and in *The German Sisters* the élitism of unmediated spiritual suffering that makes Protestantism so strong is also what explains emotionally, even if it does not justify, the radicalism with which the terrorists' violence and direct action rupture the social contract. This tissue of moral and historical complications and

Sisters, or the Balance of
Happiness *(1979)*

Sisters, or the Balance of
Happiness *(1979)*

The German Sisters *(1981)*

nuances is what von Trotta catches in her images. Particularly memorable are the brusque or rapid gestures of the women, their energy which can take cold and brutal forms or suddenly suffuses the films with a particular emotional flow; qualities of the *mise en scène* more arresting than the linearity or diagrammatical doubling of the narratives. Through an attention to detail, a density of visual texture and mood, her films locate a certain truth about Germany and her characters, building up an emotional resonance – irresistible and corny at the same time – that makes her a popular film-maker able to move an audience into directly identifying with the characters.

The direction of von Trotta's work has been to make the radically other into the familiar and the extreme into the logical, by a system of formal balances, symmetries and parallels. Yet since such doubling is precisely the thematic centre of many of her films, it is something that remains contradictory and problematic, perhaps not only as an aesthetic strategy but politically as well. One of the catchwords of the 1970s was *Sympathisanten* – sympathizers. From the point of view of the government and the police, it designated all those who overtly – in demonstrations, writings or speeches – expressed sympathy or agreement with 'terrorists' or 'extremists'. Anyone who had a word of explanation or understanding to offer for the reasons behind this type of radical militancy and desperate violence could find himself thus labelled. For instance, because he was the author of *The Lost Honour of Katharina Blum*, novelist Heinrich Böll was branded a terrorist sympathiser by the Springer press.

Such a strategy of isolation and exclusion towards dissenters or those who merely think differently is not only reminiscent of the 'German question' discussed earlier, but imposes on the writer or film-maker a quite distinct task – to create the possibility of reflection through sympathy. Von Trotta's films, 'classical' and even conformist when viewed in terms of an anti-narrative avant-garde, none the less have a political dimension both within and outside feminist positions, in their intense preoccupation with identity, doubling, splitting and the transference between self and other. They can be seen as part of what Andreas Huyssen, discussing postwar German literature and especially the plays of Max Frisch, Rolf Hochhuth and Peter Weiss, has called 'the politics of identification'.[10] He was referring to the strategies each writer adopts in order to link a social or historical situation – in this case the question of the Jews – with a network of identifications and projections based on the primary feelings originating in childhood.

Perhaps the examples cited so far about the New German Cinema rely too much on biography (Herzog and Fassbinder were brought up by mothers abandoned by their husbands; in the case of Wenders or von Trotta one would have to speculate). Yet the fact that, despite different film styles and narratives, their work seems unified by essential motifs, suggests that the permutations represent divergent strategies in response to a common crisis. What in Herzog is revolt against the father, albeit in mythic form, dominates in Fassbinder as castrating submission. Whereas in von Trotta the outcome of oedipal rivalry among sisters spells violence against the self or madness, in Wenders direct oedipal conflict seems to be displaced: it resurfaces in the search – at the level of the narrative – for a soul-mate and a double, and by an emotionally very charged relation of the protagonists to the media of communication and representation. Writing, taking pictures, listening to music on a juke box and watching movies are all seen as activities through which the self is assured of a form of personal identity, the kind of identity typical of the experience of cinema. In the light of the previous chapter, where many of the forms of the cinema of experience were seen to revolve around a desire to identify with the place or body of the mother, both the *Autorenfilme* discussed in this chapter and the cinema of experience share certain fantasy scenarios.

The mysteries of origins manifested in the many Kaspar Hauser stories, the quests of identity and sacrifice undertaken by the seekers of the Holy Grails, the Parsifals and Prometheus figures, the predilection for the literary heroes of Büchner, Kleist and the early Goethe, or the many autobiographies of self-reconstruction and self-destruction suggest that the New German Cinema harbours secrets and nurses wounds, the more intensely felt for not being named or explored directly. When one thinks of the apocalyptic images of Herzog, the self-lacerations of Fassbinder, the pessimistic Jeremiads of Syberberg and the perhaps more urbane, but no less melancholy, films of Wenders, one wonders whether their sense of a lost childhood was the expression of a 'myth of origins' or another form of its repression and displacement. Where children are the main protagonists, as in the films of Hark Bohm, Norbert Kückelmann, Reinhardt Hauff or Ulrich Edel, an all-knowing *mise en scène* and the victim's perspective seem to foreshorten the fable to a case-history or a sentimental chronicle of crime and corruption.

The very topicality and realism of *Nordsee ist Mordsee* (*The North Sea is Murderous*, 1975), *The End of the Rainbow* (*Das Ende des Regenbogens*, 1979), *Die letzten Jahre der Kindheit* (*The Last Years of Childhood*, 1979), *Paule Pauländer* (1975) or *Christiane F.* (1981) deprive such films of anything but a social worker's understanding of their characters. By contrast, the scars of childhood and a personal past as they appear in the adult heroes of early Fassbinder (*The Merchant of Four Seasons*), Herzog (*Kaspar Hauser*) or Wenders (*Kings of the Road*) – often in existential terms, as a general malaise and a depressive sensibility – hint at enigmas and traumas of which the films are tentative and unfocused probings, leaving the spectators as disconsolate as they do the characters. Only when the gaze is directed both backwards and inward, when a delay in time and space doubles perception, does childhood seem to be a cinematically viable subject for the German cinema.

(left) Reinhard Hauff's The Main Actor *(1977)*

(right) Uwe Friessner's The End of the Rainbow *(1979)*

8:

Returning Home to History

The Fatherless Society

The New German Cinema was no longer new when it began to understand its characters' past as history also. Many of the films made in the late 1960s and early 1970s seemed studiously to avoid reference to any precise temporality of events, and in the case of Herzog rarely featured Germany even as geography. Fassbinder and Wenders, as we saw, initially preferred to explore the colonised state of their protagonists' consciousness. But asked why American music, comics and movies had been his 'life savers' in adolescence, Wenders replied: 'Twenty years of political amnesia had left a hole: we covered it with chewing gum and Polaroids.'[1]

Yet barely half a decade later, after Syberberg's *Our Hitler* (1976), Fassbinder's *The Marriage of Maria Braun* (1978), Helma Sanders-Brahms' *Germany Pale Mother* (1979) and Kluge's *The Patriot* (1979) had become international successes, the New German Cinema appeared set to have its identity firmly located in a brooding obsession with Germany's own unredeemed and irredeemable past as a nation. Two questions arise from this. What prepared the ground for film-makers eventually to cut a passage through this 'amnesia' to Nazism and German history as a film subject? Secondly, to what extent did they thematise this amnesia itself, or investigate the conditions of representing German history? The argument that emerges is that the New German Cinema discovered its subjects not only by mythologising the experience of 1968. When turning to German history, directors chose a characteristically oblique and violent route. They found history in the home and Fascism in the family unit, for the fantasies and anxieties which kept so many films enthralled in melancholy introspection begin to become comprehensible if one views them as reactions to a more general problem of identification, thereby sharing in a historical complex: the crisis of authority, the legitimation of power and the Law, the actual and symbolic role of the head of the family. This complex can best be grasped if one looks outside the films to another 'horizon of experience'.

Recent psychological studies have noted that in advanced industrial societies the position of the father as provider and source of parental authority has changed profoundly. In classic Freudian and post-Freudian psychology the individual's sense of personal identity is generally assumed to be the result of successfully repressing incestuous desires that arise out of the male child's identification with the Father and his subsequent rivalry and conflicts with his Father or father image, until the choice of a mother substitute stabilises the situation and assures the legitimacy of the succeeding generation.

Social psychologists like Otto Kernberg and Christopher Lasch have argued

Terminal Angst: Fassbinder's Veronika Voss *(1982)*

that, especially in the consumer-oriented postwar societies of the West, this drama of identification and subject formation is only incompletely accomplished within the bourgeois family. The child's anxieties (that is, the forms in which the repression of incest desires and competition with the male parent manifest themselves) are no longer focused on the feared and loved father, personalised rival and emulated model. Instead of dispersing themselves over the whole field of symbolic and substitutive authority figures (from teachers, government officials, social workers to police, politicians or corporation chairmen), they turn inward, with the consequence that castration anxieties have become more diffuse and irrational, with marked schizoid or paranoid tendencies.

> The decline of institutionalised authority in an ostensibly permissive society does not lead to a 'decline of the superego' in individuals. It encourages instead a harsh, punitive superego that derives most of its psychic energy, in the absence of authoritative social prohibitions, from the destructive, aggressive impulses within the Id. Unconscious, irrational elements in the superego come to dominate its operation. As authority figures in modern society lose their 'credibility', the superego in individuals increasingly derives from the child's primitive fantasies about his parents – fantasies charged with sadistic rage – rather than from internalised ego ideals formed by later experience with loved and respected models of social conduct.[2]

According to Lasch, a different personality type has emerged who depends for his identity entirely on the approval of others. He tries to secure this approval by making others the mirror of his idealised self and by presenting himself to others with a behaviour designed to elicit from them nothing but the image the subject most desires to have of himself. 'Post-industrial man' alternates between states of omnipotence and of worthlessness, sadism and masochism, and in clinical instances ends up a schizophrenic.

Alexander Mitscherlich, as director of the Sigmund Freud Institute in Frankfurt, had investigated the political and historical dimensions of what he called the 'Fatherless Society' some years earlier than Lasch.[3] Taking his cue from the pre-war work of Freud's dissident disciples, such as Wilhelm Reich and Ernst Fromm, as well as the socio-psychological studies which the *Institut für Socialforschung* had devoted to the rise of Hitler and his mass-appeal,[4] Mitscherlich had written several studies on Fascism and its aftermath in West Germany. Nazism, according

. . . *and von Trotta's* Sisters, or the Balance of Happiness *(1979)*

to Mitscherlich, could exert such a firm ideological hold even before the war because it represented the type of belief which, in order to counteract the weakening authority structures within Weimar Germany, had encouraged the original attachment to the mother to transfer itself on to substitute love objects, abstractions such as nation, race, the State: in turn symbolically represented by the Führer.

> [The mass-leader], surprising as it may seem . . . is much more like the image of a primitive mother–goddess. He acts as if he were superior to conscience, and demands a regressive obedience and the begging behaviour that belongs to the behaviour pattern of a child in the pre-Oedipal state . . . The ties to the Führer, in spite of all the protestations of eternal loyalty, never reached the level, so rich in conflict, where the conscience is formed and ties with it are established.[5]

Hitler projected himself not as the ideal father, but as the dutiful son of a beloved mother, and thus as a representative of the primary love-object, prior to and outside Oedipal division. The Nazi sympathiser would thus be a Narcissist who had bypassed repression and failed to acquire the ego-ideal modelled after the Father who was either absent, inaccessible or overshadowed by the mother's authority. Fathers became pure objects of hate and aggression in a psychic world dominated by masochistic and sadistic impulses. Mitscherlich saw in Nazism a regressive solution to the 'fatherless society', a solution which led to latent and disavowed homosexuality and manic-depressive personality structures.

One may wonder whether such a psychoanalytic account does justice to a phenomenon as complex economically and ideologically as German Fascism. What the quotation from Lasch indicates is that the 'Culture of Narcissism' is not confined to Germany, but seems far more a consequence of the capitalist division of labour penetrating the family and extending to the exercise of parental authority. Thus, the peculiarity of the German situation is not explained by such a generalised account. However, Mitscherlich also investigated the psychic situation of the 'sons' of Weimar when they in turn became fathers or, through their wives, left their families the legacy of damaged egos. As far as the postwar German family is concerned, the situation of the fatherless family applies with special historical truth to the sons and daughters who were born during and grew up immediately after the Second World War, whose fathers had either been killed or had spent years as Soviet prisoners of war. Even where they returned alive, their credibility was compromised by active or passive collaboration with a criminal political regime and an indefensible war. It is not surprising, therefore, that the fatherless family recurs with astonishing insistence at a certain point in West German culture and that, in the films, primary relations should be such a contested terrain.

'Mourning Work'

What Mitscherlich tried to explain was why the collapse of the Third Reich had not provoked the kinds of reactions of conscience, guilt and remorse among the German population that world public opinion had expected. Also why, at least in West Germany, evidence of clinical depression had reached, by the early 1960s, epidemic proportions. He accordingly characterised postwar German society as ideologically and emotionally immobilised by its 'inability to mourn',[6] unable to feel either grief for themselves and remorse about the personal share in the disaster, or compassion and understanding for others. The German lower and middle class had experienced Fascism not only as a repressive society, but also as an intensely narcissistic one: parades, public spectacles, even the cult of the Führer were a perpetual form of self-celebration. They could not hate Hitler after the war because of this narcissistic attachment. But neither could they re-establish any kind of continuity with their own past, their experience or their memories.

> The inability to mourn was preceded by a way of loving that was less intent on sharing in the feelings of the other person than on confirming one's own self-esteem. Susceptibility to this form of love is one of the German people's collective character traits. Germans vacillate all too often between arrogance and self-abasement. But their self-abasement bears the mark not so much of humility, as of melancholy.[7]

Instead of confronting this past, Germans preferred to bury it. According to Mitscherlich, the frantic reconstruction and rebuilding effort known as the economic miracle was sustained not only by the Marshall Plan and Nato defences, but by psychological defences as well. These help to explain why the work ethic and the ideologies of effort and self-sacrifice played such an important part in German family life, and why the performance principle took such a ferocious toll on the subsequent generation.

The symptoms of what Mitscherlich terms 'the self-hatred of melancholia' were a 'de-realization' of the very events and experiences of which the parents were the survivors. Psychic disavowal manifested itself in a refusal to see, to notice or to have noticed anything during the Third Reich – the years of 'amnesia' to which Wenders refers.[8]

But without continuity there could be no identity, and without a sense of identity there could be no meaningful relationships either with the outside world or with other people. Diffuse self-pity and guilty resentment fostered sullen resistance or melancholy listlessness: towards not only the victors' attempts to assign responsibility, blame and punishment, but often enough towards an interest in or understanding of history. What Mitscherlich concluded was that the German nation, if it was to have a politically mature and emotionally coherent attitude to its history, would have to undertake collective 'mourning work', making an acknowledgement of loss and of the separation from the love object. It would have to make the passage to independence by reliving and restaging the ambivalences of primary narcissism: the rage and anger of abandonment, and the

242

desire for merging and doubling. If the parent generation was unable to accomplish this task, the problems would return to haunt the children.

This may explain why it took 30 years after the death of Hitler, with another generation grown to adulthood and becoming parents themselves, before one saw in West Germany the first sustained and coherent effort to come to terms with what Fascism meant at the private level – for Germans themselves, for the feelings, ambitions and psyches of the parent generation – and how it affected the children's ability to love or hate, to act responsibly or protest politically.

If in Mitscherlich's account, national socialism and male bonding were the socio-political solutions to the 'fatherless society' after the First World War, one would have to regard the anti-authoritarian student movement, feminism and gay activism as the responses to a similarly constituted crisis in authority and legitimation after the Second World War. The German cinema of the 1970s, both in its auteurist form and as a 'cinema of experience', would thus have its specific historical place and cultural identity as a complex but coherent act of self-representation and self-reflection. In contrast to the regressive-narcissistic solution represented by Nazi ideology and culture, the New German Cinema would have become a 'national' cinema, by helping to undertake the 'mourning work' for Germany. This is certainly the way Syberberg and Kluge have understood their films. But a glance at two distinct yet related examples, not directly connected with the cinema, may illustrate what is at stake. One is found in the literary culture of the 1968 generation, and the other is the tragi-comic history of an anniversary.

Hamlet in Germany

From about 1977 onwards, West German literature saw a veritable wave of autobiographies and fictional auto-analyses by writers in their thirties and at a turning point in their lives. Starting with Bernward Vesper's *Die Reise*,[9] these reports about the self took the form of extended suicide notes, often addressed to, and trying to settle old scores with, a recently deceased parent. Thus, while in the films the narratives revolve around the absent father, the literary testimonies present a reverse but symmetrical picture. *Die Reise* (made into *The Journey* by Markus Imhof, 1986) is the autobiographical account of the son of a well-to-do Nazi writer, trying to resolve the conflict between loving and fearing his father as a father, and hating what he stood for. Unable to confront the fact that his parent's ardent Nazism had turned into an ultra-right, but highly respectable conservatism, and that far from regretting his past, he had become a man disappointed in his son and consumed by sentimental nostalgia for his youth, the hero takes up radical causes and is drawn into militant student circles, together with his girlfriend. She, however, falls under the influence of a trigger-happy, working-class activist, and the two of them, wanted by the police, escape to Sicily, where they are being trained as international terrorists. The hero, too sensitive to commit acts of violence and recognising in his rival the same ruthlessness once shown by his father, kidnaps his own son and brings him home – to his father's abandoned house. Vesper committed suicide before he had completed what is a *roman à clef*, the story of two members of the Baader-Meinhof group: his girlfriend was Gudrun Ensslin and his rival Jan-Carl Raspe.

In an article analysing *Die Reise* Michael Schneider, after reviewing Mitscherlich's theses about the fatherless society and the parent generation's collective amnesia, observes that their conspiracy of silence had 'been bitterly avenged':

> Since the fathers had failed to indict themselves for their monstrous pasts, they were on trial by proxy by the radicalised sons and daughters in 1968 and thereafter. Since the fathers themselves had taken pains to be sure that they would only be seen as fathers, and not as political beings, their offspring chose to do precisely the opposite as a result of their abrupt political emancipation.[10]

Clearly the fathers, as failed world conquerors and politically disenfranchised citizens, felt an obvious need to re-establish their own sense of identity by wielding authority within the home. But the family climate resulting from such flawed authority could only breed radical distrust between fathers and sons or daughters – a distrust which, according to Schneider, influenced the forms the protest movement took in West Germany. In Christoph Meckel's autobiographical essay 'Suchbild', for example, the most traumatic memories are instances where the father projected his own insufficiency on to his children, abusing parental power to confirm himself and strengthen his own battered ego. Yet, as Schneider also points out, the chance discovery of shoeboxes full of old photographs or war diaries locked in desk drawers did not often lead to objective investigations:

> the specific interest which released this literary return to the past was not at all primarily an interest in the fathers and the dark areas of their past, but rather, and to a much greater extent, an interest in [the sons'] own beginnings. The look back . . . is a retrospective look to the roots of their own emotional lives, to the influences at work on them, and to the psychological legacy . . . which seem to surface time and again in the lives of these authors, who are representative of an entire generation.[11]

These sons did not identify with the official optimism of the West German economic miracle but rather with the latent emotions, the ones that the forced optimism and strident efficiency tried to hide. Seeing the fathers' cover-up, seeing through it, but being sons by flesh and blood, they also had to deal with their own internalisation of the father, whose hidden guilt and shame, according to Schneider, returns in the son as self-destructive melancholy:

> By virtue of unconscious identification, they made themselves at home in the resignation, the apathy and depressive moods of their fathers which these had tried to repress and hide behind the facade of frantic reconstruction activity.[12]

In the words of one of these sons, 'the wound had folded inwards'.[13] For the paradox was that only in the wake of disillusioned and disillusioning political activity did these ambivalences find words and expression. The generation of the 1960s began to realise and to accept only in the 1970s that they felt most at home in a melancholy, introverted narcissism. In their politics they had been seduced by utopias that remained abstract, because not informed by the memory of any childhood experiences of happiness. 'To be happy aroused your suspicion' (Schneider quotes one writer, whose posthumous letter to his father might have been written by Kafka) 'because you thought one had successfully eluded your command, that one was happy at your expense'.[14] And Meckel writes: 'In everything and everywhere the frank, honest word was missing. Absent was the living contradiction, because Father would not tolerate argument.'[15] Trying to account not only for the autobiographical literature of the early 1980s but for the political violence of the early 1970s, Schneider concluded that many student rebels had 'found themselves in a "Hamlet" situation':

It was as if the ghosts of their fathers had suddenly appeared before them in Nazi uniforms, and their living fathers with whom they had sat down at the supper table for twenty years had been indicated in the most horrible collective crime committed by any generation this century.[16]

The bombing, the hostage-taking and terrorism that shook the Federal Republic in the aftermath of the student movement seemed to Schneider nothing less than 'murderous and suicidal attempts to tear off the mask from the German bourgeois establishment' behind which they had reason to suspect the faces of their own fathers. The search for the political in the family was thus the most obvious sign that the German student and protest movement was preoccupied with questions of education and socialisation. It was anti-authoritarian rather than egalitarian, despite a Marxist political discourse, and it was fixated on father figures – a feature from which the women's movement had to extricate itself.

Mitscherlich's and Lasch's analyses were criticised by the women's movement not only because they were, like Freud's original formulation of the Oedipus complex, heavily slanted towards giving an account of the male psyche, but because the Freudian analysis of subject formation actually implies a division of gender modelled on a strict division of labour. This makes it difficult to see how reference to such a model can analyse the psychic effects of this division of labour other than by a conservative or nostalgic turn. Instead of looking beyond present society and the psychic structures it engenders, Lasch and Mitscherlich seemed to hanker after a reinstatement of the patriarchial father and the 'rich conflicts' he produced.[17] And as Schneider's analysis of the Hamlet complex of West German writers implies, much the same might be said of the autobiographical literature on the subject of patriarchy in Germany.

May the Eighth: the wound that would not close

In May 1985 Europe commemorated the 40th anniversary of the end of the Second World War. The events surrounding the anniversary gave rise to a good deal of controversy: the President of the United States, honouring a promise he had made to Federal Chancellor Helmut Kohl, visited a German War Cemetery in the small town of Bitburg, where members of the Waffen-SS were buried. In the end, to 'balance' Bitburg, the President also went to Bergen Belsen.

The incident, soon forgotten as so many political media events are, none the less highlighted quite graphically the difficulties that official and unofficial Germany has with its history. Or rather, with the representation – in both senses of that term – of a history that, while for many still part of living memory is also a mediated reality, something created in words and images, which exist, as it were, alongside the events, and whose meanings escape the control of even those who try to manipulate their symbolic significance.[18]

There could be no better example of the way a particular date can return to haunt a people and a generation than this May anniversary. Ten years after the signing of the Surrender, on 5 May 1955 the Allied Forces declared the formal end to the 'Occupied Territory' status of the three Western Zones, and the recognition of the Federal Republic as a Sovereign State. It sealed the fate of Germany as a divided nation, and four days later – on 9 May 1955 – West Germany joined NATO, thereby ensuring the necessary rearmament of Germany but also the fact that subsequent May anniversaries became not only subdued but schizophrenic events.

245

Across the generations: Hildegard Knef in The Murderers Are Among Us *(1946)* . . .

In May 1965 the 20th anniversary was pointedly ignored by the Federal Government. With the Berlin Wall as a massive mortgage on Soviet/West German relations, Bonn politicians boycotted the official Soviet Embassay Reception. Meanwhile, in nearby Hanover, the NPD (the German Neo-Nazi Party) was holding its first Party Congress.

8 May 1970: Chancellor Willy Brandt, in an Extraordinary Session of Parliament, called for the reconciliation of West Germany with its neighbours. The occasion marked the beginning of Brandt's famous 'Ostpolitik', the signing of agreements with the Soviet Union, but also Brandt's public gesture of atonement in Poland, West Germany's friendlier terms towards Czechoslovakia and, above all, the 'normalization' of relations with the German Democratic Republic (the 'other' Germany). Four years later to the day Brandt was forced to resign, after Günter Guillaume, Brandt's personal assistant for many years, was arrested as an East German spy.

May 1975: for over three years the activities of left-wing extremists, but also the signs of a severe economic recession, had been passionately dividing public opinion. The Social Democratic/Liberal alliance of Helmut Schmidt was under pressure to push through Parliament tough anti-terrorist legislation. Only 'citizens with convictions solidly anchored in the Basic Law'[19] could be employed as teachers, or postmen or railway guards. Anyone in local or federal government suspected of belonging to a political party left of the Social Democrats risked losing his/her job. For the official 8 May commemoration speech by the Federal President, many Christian Democrat politicians, among them party leader Kohl, were absent, pleading prior engagements. A year later, on 8 May 1976, Ulrike Meinhof was discovered dead in her cell.

What was there to celebrate or to commemorate for a German government or the German people? The German Democratic Republic never had a problem with 8 May. Having rehearsed in official speeches and reiterated in schools and history books two neat divisions – between Fascists and anti-Fascists (that is, communists) and (more useful for their own population at large) between Fascists and ordinary Germans – they could join the Soviet Union in celebrating the

246

. . . and with Brigitte Fossey (and their earlier selves) in Helma Sanders-Brahms' The Future of Emily *(1985)*

'liberation from Fascism, and the victorious end of the Great Patriotic War', the name the Soviet Union gives to World War Two.

But for West Germans the situation has always been more complex. In 1965 the then Bonn ambassador to Moscow put the dilemma with revealing naivety: how can a German, he asked indignantly, 'drink to his own defeat?'[20] To a political establishment that regarded the end of the war as a personal let-down, the victory celebrations elsewhere in Europe or in the United States were either a frank embarrassment or a reminder of Germany's darkest hour. One could mourn the victims, the sacrifices, the losses: secretly perhaps one's own first, but publicly those of others, the victims of Nazi terror and the War. But how to distinguish among *German* victims between the wholly innocent, the more or less innocent, those guilty by association or acquiescence, and the wholly guilty? And could the Germans be said to be victims of history at all?

Mourning or Celebration

Was 8 May the liberation from a criminal régime, or the collapse of Germany's idealist dreams in ruins and ashes? Which was the real disaster – March 1933, September 1939 or May 1945? Was May 1945 the famous 'Zero Hour' and the chance for a new beginning or, rather, already the return of a period of political restoration, the creeping and scarcely clandestine rehabilitation of former Nazis in positions of power: industry at first, then government, administration, the judiciary, press and education? For May 1985 also saw the publication of a study[21] of the post-1945 careers of prominent Nazis. It makes depressing reading, and even more dispiriting is the long list of names at the very top of the Federal Republic's official representatives in the 1960s and 1970s, whose Nazi record should by rights have barred them from holding any kind of public office. These include Federal Judges, Leaders of State Assemblies, the Head of the Confederation of Industry, Ministers and Secretaries of State, a Federal Chancellor and, not forgetting, three of the six Presidents of the Federal Republic: all in their time active members of the NSDAP or the SS. If they were reinstated, however, it was with the full knowledge and blessing of the United States, who themselves employed the services of Klaus Barbie, the 'Butcher of Lyon', and helped him escape to Latin America, while the CIA, in contravention of US immigration laws, airlifted hundreds of Nazi scientists, rocket-experts and nuclear physicists to New Mexico, Texas or Florida.[22]

The fierce ideological divide between capitalist and communist Germany in the 1950s and 1960s was determined for both sides by the exigencies of the Cold War and superpower rivalry. Germans were mere pawns in the East–West game, a fact which could only increase the sense of political apathy and social amnesia. Since 1945 solutions to the German question, official attitudes to German history and many of the moral and political judgements on the War and Fascism had been, as it were, imposed *from outside*. The defeat of Hitler, the creation of West and East Germany, rearmament and the division of the German nation were seen as external interventions, rather than expressions of a national resolve. Germans were liberated from outside, and they were separated into good Germans and bad Germans from outside; they were declared collectively guilty, and they were given the conditions on which they could collectively redeem themselves. Or so it must have seemed among the multitude of polarisations and splits, divisions and oppositions by which postwar Germans experienced and participated in the recreation and reformulation of themselves as a geographical entity, a nation, a people; but also as individuals with an identity and as families with a history and histories, with private pasts and recollections.

Images of themselves and images of how others saw them competed with each other in a battle of visual representations and semantic identifications which always threatened to shroud once more in partisanship and confusion the historical significance of the events. Not only the period between 1933 to 1945, but the shifts that occurred subsequently, in Germany, in Europe, on a global scale, in the line-up of friend and foe, enemy from within and enemy from without, contributed to insecurity and forced a retrenchment to the private sphere. Mourning or celebration, or neither? A thorn in the side of the Federal Republic's self-representation, 8 May is in this sense the reverse side of Mitscherlich's 'inability to mourn': namely the Germans' inability to celebrate.

Conditions for Representing German History

In the context of Germany's capitulation and the history of its anniversary, the embarrassing *faux pas* and poor judgements of May 1985 seem almost inevitable. They could be called the parapraxes of the political process of democratisation, involuntary manifestations of a historical unconscious, of something obstinately demanding to be heard. Because repressed, rewritten, traded and exchanged over three decades, German history was bound to return. Before, however, examining in more detail how film-makers took account of the 'psychic' and at the same time 'semiotic' dimension of their country's history, some general conditions for representing German history on film in the 1970s have to be mentioned.

The cinema's preoccupation with Fascism during the last two decades is a common and complex European phenomenon, not satisfactorily explained by reference to the German cinema alone. When directors like Syberberg, Fassbinder or Helma Sanders-Brahms turned to Fascism as in some sense the German issue *par excellence*, they were following a lead in so far as an iconography

248

Echoes of Visconti's The Damned *in Wolfgang Petersen's* The Boat *(1981)*

(down to the colour schemes), typical characters and thus a dramaturgy had already established themselves. The ground had been prepared by, among others, Luchino Visconti (*The Damned*), Ingmar Bergman (*The Serpent's Egg*), Liliana Cavani (*The Night Porter*), Lina Wertmuller (*Seven Beauties*), Louis Malle (*Lacombe Lucien*), Joseph Losey (*Mr Klein*) and François Truffaut (*The Last Metro*). The European art cinema, in other words, had already for its part discovered the immense cinematic and photogenic potential of the subject. Hollywood, too, had had its own version of German history fixed for the 1970s in the popular mind by Bob Fosse's *Cabaret*, and by the television series *Holocaust* which proved in Germany to be something of a catalyst.

These film and television spectacles have themselves to be seen in the context of earlier modes of representing Fascism and the World War in the European cinema during the late 1940s and 1950s. To the documentary mode belong Alain Resnais' *Night and Fog* (1956), and a few years later, Michael Romm's *Ordinary Fascism* (1964) and Erwin Leiser's Swedish compilation films (*Mein Kampf*, 1960 and *Deutschland Erwache*, 1965). The neo-realist mode is mainly associated with Roberto Rossellini's films *Rome Open City* (1945), *Paisa* (1946) and *Germany Year Zero* (1948). Given the ambivalent political alliances which in Italy had resisted Fascism, the cautious understatements of neo-realism seemed highly appropriate to a situation that had produced acts of individual courage, rather than organised or collective opposition. By contrast, especially in the immediate postwar years, the heroic–ironic mode offered itself for the depiction of the Resistance in France (from Melville's *Le Silence de la mer* in 1948, to Chabrol's *La Ligne de démarcation* in 1966). In Poland and East European countries a tragic-heroic or allegorical style dramatised the precarious alliance of nationalists

249

and communists in the victory over the Germans (Andrzej Wajda's *Ashes and Diamonds*, 1958, but also Kalatozov's *The Cranes are Flying*, 1957, and Chukhrai's *Ballad of a Soldier*, 1959).

For good reason such 'national' styles were not open to German film-makers directly after the war. Documentaries about Fascism and the war were, to a German audience, necessarily associated with the indoctrination and re-education programme of the Allied Occupation Forces, and thus a version of history imposed from outside. A flashback in *The German Sisters*, for example, shows the two girls sitting through a screening of *Night and Fog* at school, one of them vomiting afterwards in the lavatory, her body rejecting what her mind cannot grasp. Resistance to Hitler, on the other hand, had not only been minimal but came very late and, on the whole, from disaffected members of the class that had helped him to power, such as the military and the grande bourgeoisie.

The very first films to be made in Berlin under Allied Control from 1947 onwards were evidently concerned with the question of how Hitler could have happened, and tried to trace the logic that had led Germans to acquiesce in and to condone a criminal régime. *The Murderers Are Among Us* (*Die Mörder sind unter uns*, 1946), *Somewhere in Berlin* (*Irgendwo in Berlin*, 1946) and *The Blum Affair* (*Affäre Blum*, 1948) all had middle-of-the-road protagonists, ordinary people, caught up and implicated through cowardice and misguidedness. As such, they offered an audience prepared to be contrite the comfort of fatalism and self-pity. Characteristically, the style was close to the dark pessimism of the pre-war films, and showed echoes of the film noir genre as practiced in Hollywood during the 1940s by German émigrés, particularly where a thriller format was employed or a flashback structure. A late and very impressive example of this genre was *Der Verlorene* (*The Lost One*, 1951), directed by and starring Peter Lorre as a former SS doctor whose past inexorably catches up with him.

In retrospect one can see why the thriller element was crucial. Through the mechanisms of suspense it gave the spectator figures of identification whom the narrative could invest with both positive and negative moral attributes, while the investigative structure provided a coherent position of knowledge, with the resolution of the enigma mitigating the politically more sensitive aspects of the subject. It could make for moving cinema, occasionally even reminiscent of French poetic realism, as in *Between Yesterday and Tomorrow* (*Zwischen Gestern und Morgen*, 1947), but it could hardly pass as historical analysis. Only Staudte's *Rotation* (1948) raised the issue of class in the rise of Nazism, while *Shadows on a Marriage* (*Ehe im Schatten*, 1947), the story of a Jewish-Aryan couple who commit suicide rather than leave each other, opted for domestic melodrama to engage the spectator's sympathy for the fate of the Jews.

Other films attempted a more allegorical mode; Helmut Käutner's *In Those Days* (*In jenen Tagen*, 1947) is the story of a car, brand new in 1933 and on the junk yard in 1945 where it is dismantled for spares. In flashbacks one sees it change owner with every significant turning point during the Third Reich. Käutner's style and the episodic structure of the narrative are directly indebted to *Paisa*, while the characters are all victims of the régime: either convinced anti-Nazi, or harassed by the SS, or actively resistant, or soldiers tragically wasted by the Russian winter and invisibly lurking partisans. One wonders how typical the car could have been when the symbolism of its assembly line anonymity stands in such stark contrast to the extraordinary and totally unrepresentative behaviour of its mostly middle-class owners.

Thus the thriller format made it seem as if Nazism had been a conspiracy

Hildegard Knef (left), between fascism and film noir (Harald Braun's Between Yesterday and Tomorrow, *1947)*

German neo-realism:
Renate Mannhardt and Peter
Lorre in The Lost One *(1951)*

Gisela Trowe in Erich Engel's The Blum Affair *(1948)*

251

Ilse Steppat (left) in Kurt Maetzig's Marriage in the Shadows *(1947)*
Hildegard Knef (right) in Wolfgang Staudte's The Murderers Are Among Us *(1946)*

perpetrated by a clique of fanatics, lunatics and underworld criminals. The neo-realist mode, however, was always in danger of becoming frankly apologetic, suggesting that moral decency and individual courage had prevailed throughout and that the war when it came was the universal human tragedy it has always been in the popular mind, like a natural disaster such as a flood or a drought. Or else it incriminated Germans with nothing worse than guilt by association. The Nazi figures that were portrayed had become Nazis, it was suggested, out of greed, spite, lust for power or cowardice and weakness of character: failings located in the protagonists' personality. Yet even such classically generic strategies of identification as these could not hold audiences' attention on the subject. Films dealing with 'the German problem' came to be known disparagingly in the trade

Hans Nielsen, Gisela Tantau . . .
. . . and Alice Treff in Helmut Käutner's In Those Days *(1947)*

Reviving the Trümmerfilm: Eva Mattes in Helma Sanders-Brahms' Germany Pale Mother *(1979)*

and among spectators as *Trümmerfilme* (ruin films), and invariably spelt box office disaster for their producers.

Where the war remained a subject, it was as a backdrop to adventure. The heroic mode surfaced in the 1950s. Religious themes, stoic forbearance, silent resistance, self-sacrifice and devotion to a higher duty became the moral pivots around which war and espionage films turned. Directors – some of them tried and seasoned professionals from the days of Goebbels' film industry in the 1930s and 1940s – were anxious to find stories with good Germans fatally caught up in events and the smaller tragedies of human life, in order to represent the recent past.[23]

Popular Memory or Retro-Scenario?

The revisionism in matters of history practiced by the European art cinema of the 1970s, dubbed 'retro-fashion' but whose emergence in the space of less than a decade was indicative of a profound shift in the understanding of history itself, amounted to a series of displacements of the postwar paradigms. In Italy, from Bertolucci's *The Conformist* to Pasolini's *Salo*, film-makers used the Fascist period as a foil for an exploration of the more ambiguous aspects of sex and death. Most fastened on to the show-values of Fascism and its psychopathology, seeing the apocalyptic, self-destructive and sado-masochistic aspects as prefigurations of the deathwish of contemporary Western civilisation. In France, the tendency was to debunk the myths of the Resistance, those of the Gaullists as much as of the Left, invoking in films like *Lacombe Lucien* a perhaps no less mythical collaborationist France of rural violence and the seductiveness of power. This notion, not of a more accurate history but of the possibility of re-writing history in a form that thanks to the cinema permits the illusion of total credibility because permeated by the paraphernalia of the real, led Jean Baudrillard to talk about history films not as retro-fashion but as 'retro-scenarios'.[24]

According to Baudrillard contemporary societies, locked into political stasis, nostalgically dream and imagine through the cinema – the traditional refuge for myths – a time where history still involved human agents and individual victims, forces and causes that mattered and decisions involving questions of life and death. One attraction of such a history is the excuse it gives for still telling stories with a beginning, middle and an end, and thus for the possibility of conceiving of a personal destiny – the very desire Fascism tried to gratify on a collective scale. The return to history in the cinema is thus for Baudrillard not a move towards coming to terms with the past, but the fetishisation of another trauma altogether: that of the present. What to the Freudian fetishist is the female thigh or laced-up foot, Fascism is to contemporary imagination. It is the last permissible sight that can be possessed as object prior to and in lieu of the traumatic event barred from consciousness. Fascism has become a perversely efficient fetish history, to cover for the absence of history altogether.

Baudrillard's analysis touches on some of the ambiguities which are clearly present in the New German Cinema's turn to history, especially in Syberberg and Fassbinder. For, with his allusion to both fetishism and nostalgia, Baudrillard indicates the psychic dimension – that of projection and identification – undoubtedly at stake for Germans in the cinematic representation of Germany's past. It was not so much Fascism that was traumatic as that which followed. Baudrillard confirms, from a different perspective, what has already been noted in connection with Mitscherlich's 'inability to mourn' and Schneider's analysis of the father–son conflict: the strongly narcissistic component in the return to history and the fact that it is prompted by an autobiographical impulse.

Fassbinder's original title for *The Marriage of Maria Braun* was to have been 'The Marriages of Our Parents'. Both self-representation and the quest for origins crucially inform the German 'cinema of experience' as a whole, even though it was the renewed preoccupation with Fascism which also permitted the film-makers to articulate an internationally recognisable 'experience of cinema' and thus create a generic identity for their films. The German retro-phenomenon ought therefore to be seen both in the European context of 'national cinemas', but also as emerging out of developments more germane to a situation whose pathology and fetishisation involved countering 'amnesia' with a 'working through' and a self-confrontation.

Hitler and Auschwitz, the Second World War and the Final Solution represent events of such enormity that they challenge the very concept of history as a narrative, as a causal nexus of motives and consequences represented in story terms. Nazism could not, on the whole, become for the German cinema a retro-scenario such as *Cabaret* or *Holocaust*, and not only because the very idea behind a 'cinema of experience' militated against making genres out of specific subjects. The reason why the German turn to history has to be seen in a narrower and more local context is that it defined itself across a number of prevailing interpretations of Fascism, the so-called *Faschismus*-Debatte among historians,

'*The marriages of our parents?' Fassbinder's* Effi Briest *(1974)*

for instance, or the arguments behind the *Ostpolitik* of the Social Democrat government. In as much as these issues impinged on the film-makers' conception of history – in Syberberg, von Trotta, Kluge and Sanders-Brahms amongst others – their work can be regarded as contributing to a debate about popular memory. This was, however, more in the form of the introspection which Mitscherlich had called *Trauerarbeit* than along the lines of oral history or reviving working-class traditions. The latter are projects closer to the Wildenhahn school of documentary which, as I tried to show, do their own mourning work.

Trauerarbeit became politically associated with Willy Brandt, particularly after his genuflection at the Warsaw Ghetto memorial. It was a symbolic moment dividing Germans since many of his generation, even from among the Social Democrat Party, were revealingly ambivalent about the gesture. It would have been inconceivable for Brandt's successor, Helmut Schmidt, to perform what seemed such an act of public self-abasement. Schmidt, having served as a soldier in the German Army while Brandt had fought that same Army from exile, consciously presented himself as the average German father and thus as a figure of identification for all those whose own experience of the war – and whose need for legitimation – had been far closer to that of Schmidt than Brandt.

To this extent one can speak of Syberberg's *Our Hitler*, Fassbinder's *The Marriage of Maria Braun*, *Germany in Autumn*, Kluge's *The Patriot* or von Trotta's *The German Sisters* as films loyal to or in the spirit of the Brandt era. Petersen's

255

The Boat, however, by giving a voice to the common man who, trying to do his duty, can admit to fear, weakness and confusion, represents the ethos of a Helmut Schmidt or even a Helmut Kohl. By contrast, Joachim Fest's newsreel compilation film *Hitler – A Career* (*Hitler – eine Karriere*, 1977), based on his own best-selling biography, is a more typical product of the New Right. Fest interprets – in what understands itself to be a critical gesture – Hitler's political success as the consequence of shrewd marketing strategies and techniques in the manipulation of the new mass media. By giving full reign to the fascination inherent in these images and sounds, the film allows the Nazis' own staging and editing of events to be consumed as pure spectacle. What is more, Fest lets the visual pleasure of the subject positions already implied by the propaganda material be mirrored and doubled in a self-confident and smug commentary, giving an illusion of safe distance and secure knowledge about the meaning of the Hitler 'phenomenon'.

> The film was compiled from more than 300,000 ft of film material, including many incomplete and unreleased scenes from domestic and foreign archives; many unusual sequences come from private collections . . . [The film] provides a basis for judgement. [It] cannot change German history: it does not glorify it either. It illuminates it: as much for those who lived through the Hitler period as for those who can no longer imagine what it was like.[25]

Trauerarbeit, as we have seen, implies almost exactly the opposite. It is an acknowledgement of spectatorial divisions in representation, an exploration of the rifts as well as the continuities between past and present, a sensitivity for the intensities and resistances that individual memory opposes to the public images and public discourses about history. More a telling of the stories that go against the grain of the master-narratives of world-political events and charismatic careers, *Trauerarbeit* marks the gaps that occur, and the very obtuseness with which people live their own participation in what posterity comes to regard as significant. In this respect, it is indeed akin to the 'popular memory' and oral history initiatives in France, Italy or Britain which especially after 1968 focused on labour and working-class traditions, but which in Britain and the United States were also associated with the women's movement. Where films in this vein returned to the war period, they tended to demythologise the heroic-dramatic as well as the spectacular modes, as in what is still the best-known example, Marcel Ophuls' *The Sorrow and the Pity*, whose title is itself perhaps the most apposite translation of *Trauerarbeit*.

Michel Foucault has argued that films like Ophuls' are part of the same retro-fashion as Malle's *Lacombe Lucien*, because symptomatic of a typically post-1968 New Right ideological attack on the very concept of history as popular struggle:

> Popular struggles have become for our society, not part of the actual, but of the possible. So they have to be set at a distance. How? Not by providing a direct interpretation, which would be asking to be exposed. But by offering an historical interpretation of those popular struggles which have occurred in France in the past, in order to show that they never really happened.[26]

Foucault speaks from the perspective of 'popular memory', in the sense not of *the* Resistance but of a resistance among the common people against all forms of power and coercion, and an awareness of the materialist core of the historical process that dispenses with political labels and ideological rationalisations. He found this in court records or confessions, such as the detailed account which one

Pierre Rivière gave of his life, as he was being tried and convicted of killing his mother and brothers and sisters.

But Ophuls' film is not, as Foucault seems to assert, an attempt to deprive the French working class of its pride in the Resistance by showing that the vast majority of Frenchmen were implicated in the Nazi Occupation and Vichy as collaborators, fellow-travellers and anti-Semites. Once motives and events are reconstructed from the 'bottom up' and without a preconceived thesis to unify the narrative, even newsreel images no longer assure the viewers of their positions of knowledge. By juxtaposing, in a series of extensive interviews, his subject's attempts to fashion a retrospective coherence out of their actions, and other kinds of evidence – documentary, photographic and analytical – Ophuls does not denounce the interviewees' internal inconsistencies and involuntary contradictions in the name of some other truth as much as he puts before the spectator the very processes by which history is invested with meaning and constructed for a subject.

The same is true of Edgardo Cozarinsky's *One Man's War* (*La Guerre d'un seul homme*, 1981), in which an aristocratic, anti-historical, logistic and at the same time apocalyptic view of war and civilisation by Ernst Jünger is made to comment on German newsreel from the Occupation.[27] The extremity of Jünger's detachment, coupled with the iconographic familiarity of the documentary footage, creates a space of reflection where both newsreel and commentary stand exposed as artifice and leave the spectator with a sense of knowing, in spite of all

Retro-fashion or popular memory? Theodor Kotulla's Death Is My Trade *(1977)*

257

the images one has seen and all the studies one has read, very little about either the meaning or the agents of history.

This is even more apparent in Claude Lanzmann's *Shoah* (1985), where the care over bureaucratic detail, the exact description of place and circumstance, the goading of memory and reminiscence among surviving prisoners, guards of concentration camps and farmers from adjacent communities, suspend all preconceived narratives and explanations. *Shoah* does not invalidate them, but by confronting the sheer enormity of the numbers of victims with their total disappearance, even in the minds of those that helped or were present, the film brings home to the spectator the industrial scale and methods, but also the overwhelmingly particular and physical annihilations involved in the 'Final Solution' – truths not preserved in political, economic or even psychological discourses. In the end, the dead accuse the living, defying any viewer to imagine a history that could contain the palpable reality of their death, and thus spurning even the notion that film or photographs, memorial sites or surviving possessions and objects could in any sense stand for the victims or signify their lives.

Irreconcilable Memories: History as Resistance and *Eigensinn*

Ophuls, Cozarinsky and Lanzmann are all exiles and of Jewish origin, a fact that may indicate why projects such as theirs did not come out of West Germany itself. Only in the most radical films of the avant-garde, such as Straub's *Not Reconciled* (*Nicht Versöhnt*, 1965) or in some of the feminist work discussed in the previous chapter, is there a similar refusal to make the image signify and represent what in fact can only be grasped as bodily loss and absence.

Straub is himself an exile and, viewed from the 1980s, his film, dating from 1963, has become profoundly anticipatory, even though one can above all understand *Not Reconciled* as the deconstruction of the apologetic-allegorical mode noted earlier. In fact, it could be seen as a direct reply to one of the most critically and commercially successful films about West Germany mastering the past, Kurt Hoffmann's pseudo-Brechtian *Aren't We Wonderful* (*Wir Wunderkinder*, 1958). Evidently, at that time, an indulgent identification with well-meaning but timid 'good Germans', engaged in a manichean conflict with the economic profiteers and political opportunists who are the villains, could pass for a serious analysis of the political and ideological continuity between the Third Reich and the Federal Republic. What at first appears as a distancing device (the framing story of a cabaret duo performing irreverent and sarcastic songs) turns out to have the reverse effect: self-irony and satire end up reinforcing the self-pity and sentimental defeatism of the central narrative.

Against the orgies of benevolent understanding, the sympathy for victims and the vague regrets that the guilty never seem to be punished which prevailed in the serious genres of the film industry, Straub's adaptation of Heinrich Böll's novel proved a harsh and unforgiving film, whose diagonals and sharply angled compositions even in the visuals seemed to want to stem the tide of those whose ultimate moral wisdom was that life must go on.[28]

From another perspective *Not Reconciled* was, however, the first film to confront fathers with sons, mothers and sons, brothers and friends, the generations and the sexes, across the political and racial divides opened up by Nazism. By trying to break with the false continuity or community of survivors which the

Angular Obstinacy: Jean-Marie Straub's Not Reconciled *(1963)*

political establishment of the Federal Republic attempted to create in its claim as successor to the German Reich, Straub made a 'terrorist' film.[29] The heroine, the wife, mother and grandmother of two generations of architects and demolition experts, rents a room in a luxury hotel opposite Cologne Cathedral in order to shoot a former Nazi, now Minister for Rearmament, about to step on the hotel balcony to salute a military parade.

In the contrasting and interwoven fates of the Fähmel family Böll had tried to document and satirise the ironies of German history since the 1920s, continuing and thereby rewriting Thomas Mann's *Buddenbrooks*, as it were, from a militant–pacifist position. Straub pared away all of Böll's satire, leaving the spectator with a film that resists the family chronicle, but also narrative and the linear logic of cause and effect. This is done for much the same reason as his male protagonists reject the conciliatory gestures of their former political enemies and persecutors, and the old lady resists German rearmament by violence.

Neither politically nor aesthetically can Straub's film claim to have had many emulators, although its title is echoed in a documentary, *Unversöhnliche Erinnerungen* (*Irreconcilable Memories*, 1979), in which an extended interview with a retired general of the Bundeswehr is intercut with another one man's war, that of a retired bricklayer. What gives these memories and reminiscences exemplary status in their asymmetrical mirroring is that both served in Spain during the Civil War, one as an ace flier in the Condor Legion, the other as a homeless and stateless refugee in the International Brigade. Both profess their love of Germany and yet, as one listens to the stories and arguments, it is clear that in their experiences and outlook they come from different continents, and

259

not only economically or in terms of class and social background. Underneath the apparent peace and prosperity memories are indeed irreconcilable.

However, the film with which the prescience of *Not Reconciled* is most usefully compared is *Germany in Autumn*, a collective venture undertaken in the aftermath of the politically hot autumn of 1977 when West Germany seemed nearer to a civil war than it had been since the 1920s. *Germany in Autumn*, in its overall structure, its montage of documentary material, archive footage and staged scenes, bears the unmistakable stamp of Kluge, the director whose concept of history as *Eigensinn* (obstinacy, a will of its own) has, at least on the face of it, something in common with Straub's notion of resistance.[30]

No film set out more self-consciously than *Germany in Autumn* to undertake collective mourning work, occasioned as it was by two public funerals. During the months September to November, after terrorists had kidnapped Hans Martin Schleyer, the chairman of the West German Confederation of Industry, and hijacked a Lufthansa plane to Mogadishu, the Federal Republic was virtually under a state of siege by its own police and security forces. At home, many children had their first political discussion ever with their parents, and while family members divided against each other more violently than over domestic issues, much of West Germany's history and buried past crystallised as so many paradoxes and ironies were illuminated in one brief flash. The film found such immediate success because it was able to read these events as a double structure, as the hidden configuration of two generations' mythological but also historical coming of age. For the parent generation the deaths at Mogadishu (where youthful German gunmen 'executed' the pilot, but were themselves shot when special units stormed the plane) transgressed too many taboos not to force them, according to Kluge, to confront their own 'lack of memories':

> By themselves, the events did not have all that much to do with war, but the association was '1945' and 'the war'. It is no accident that motion came into people's emotions, asking about Germany and about the past.[31]

For the younger generation the deaths at Stammheim, the maximum security prison where three members of the Baader–Meinhof group committed suicide in solidarity with the Mogadishu hijack, confirmed not only the violence the state was prepared to use against its critics, but the fact that beneath their parents' cautious conservatism lay a militarist mentality and deeply chauvinistic resentments.

Germany in Autumn skilfully weaves together the terrorist present and the Nazi past, by exploiting to the full a series of remarkable, but in the light of what was said about the 'parapraxes' of postwar history, altogether typical parallels and coincidences. From the opening scene it becomes clear that this is a film about fathers and sons, mothers and sons, symbolic fathers and physical fathers, political fathers and rebellious children. For the somewhat over-determined collective family drama that emerged from the events of autumn 1977 was that of Hans Martin Schleyer, himself an eager son under the Nazis (he served in the SS) but by then the father of West German capitalism. His kidnap, carried out by members of a radical terrorist group because of his symbolic political role, was intended to force the government to release a group of political extremists. From captivity, Schleyer wrote a letter to his own son indirectly warning the government not to underestimate the realism and capacity for self-sacrifice of his captors. The Schmidt government refused to be held to ransom by the sons and daughters of its bourgeoisie, and a few days later Schleyer was dead, dumped in the boot of a car.

Edgar Reitz (left) during the shooting of Germany in Autumn *(1978)*

A state funeral was held for him in Stuttgart, home of Daimler Benz and symbol of West Germany's prosperity. It was also the city whose Lord Mayor happened to be the son of Rommel, hero of Hitler's terrorist war, but whom Hitler had condemned to commit suicide, giving him a state funeral at which the son was present, documented by the wartime newsreel of the elaborately staged ceremony. However, there was more to come. After the suicides of Stammheim, a suburb of Stuttgart, local opinion was violently set against allowing the terrorists to be buried there. In a bold gesture, worthy of Willy Brandt, Lord Mayor Rommel, politically a conservative but no doubt historically more sensitive than other members of his city council, decreed that the families of the suicides, and especially Gudrun Ensslin's sister and daughter of a local protestant pastor, should have the right to organise a funeral. Rommel thus became a Creon who didn't stop Antigone from burying her kin.

Intercut into the two funerals, their elaborate preparation and the depiction of the respective mourners – national anthems, the German colours, black coats and tails at one occasion, Joan Baez songs, Palestinian scarves and blue jeans at the other – is an interview with the spiritual father of the Baader–Meinhof group, the lawyer Horst Mahler who was then serving a long prison sentence. From his cell he conducts an authoritative auto-critique of violent extremism, lending the voice of reason to his own recantation. Compared to the narrative echo-effects emanating from the funerals, with a multiplication of moral parallels and visual symmetries, many of the other episodes seem misplaced or anecdotal (apart from Schlöndorff's Antigone sketch and Fassbinder's, which opens the film). *Germany in Autumn* became the transcription of political history into family melodrama.

261

The echo-chamber of analogies around the symbolic father (the parricide/suicide paradigm earlier isolated as typical for the New German Cinema) makes the film, despite its documentary origin,[32] seem closer to a retro-scenario than Kluge might have wished. As in the case of von Trotta's internal rhymes, the dramaturgical strategies of classical narrative give *Germany in Autumn* a powerful illusion of historical depth, in so far as it is through repetition that the cinema's fictions create their own memory.

The character who embodies Kluge's own notion of history as *Eigensinn* is Gabi Teichert, a schoolteacher out with a spade in a snow-covered landscape 'digging for German history'. She reappears as the heroine of *The Patriot*, the film in which Kluge is at his most systematic in working out the conditions of representing German history. The traumatic experience, it emerges, is not Nazism or the Jewish holocaust, but the final years of the war, the time of scattered armies, migrating populations, the refugees and the bombing raids on cities. Emblematically, the complex has in Kluge's work the name 'Stalingrad', the mid-winter battle that brought decisive defeat for Germany and signalled the turning point in the war.

Two major aspects of Kluge's view of the past come together in 'Stalingrad': the non-linear, antagonistic nature of the historic process, as symbolised by war, and the utopian moment of radical change, the possibility of a Zero Hour and a new beginning resulting from the total breakdown of a social system. This second element refers back to German culture's (and the New German Cinema's) fascination with the 'Earthquake in Chile' motif discussed earlier, and the idea that only a cataclysmic event can break up frozen social relations – ice being

A love story and a world war (Alexander Kluge's The Patriot, *1979)*

262

another crucial motif in *The Patriot* but also a cliché of West German cultural pessimism. A nursery rhyme used in the film makes the point:

Was a man not very wise / Built himself a house on ice
Said: O lord, please send me frost / Otherwise my house is lost.
Came the thaw, the house went down / And the little man did drown.[33]

This, according to Kluge, is German history in a nutshell, a symbol of the labour and energy built up over the centuries on tragically unsuitable foundations.

At the same time, Stalingrad in Kluge's system is the retrospectively projected origin of the present, not only in that the Second World War was a rehearsal for the Third, but in the way the historical energies of the twentieth century (Fascism versus Communism, the German working class versus the Russian peasants, mass-destruction of machines and people for the benefit of production) became frozen and preserved like a mammoth in ice. In *The Patriot* the knee joint of a dead soldier – the part standing for the whole but, at the same time, a relation rather than an essence – literally voices this unreclaimed energy. The perspective of the knee joint ('the dead criticise the living') is set in counterpoint to the story of Gabi Teichert. She compulsively 'literalises' metaphors, attacking her books, for instance, with chisels and a saw to extract the facts or playing the alchemist in order to distil the wisdom of the ages. Her private rebellion against the 'official version' of German history suggests that it is not to be found in schoolbooks or at SPD party congresses but, if anywhere, in nursery rhymes, the Brothers Grimm fairy tales and other scraps of popular wisdom. These are usually conservative and

Digging for History (Hannelore Hoger in Kluge's The Patriot, *1979)*

apolitical, irrational and fantastic, but preserve a kind of leverage in the play of uneven forces.

It is here that Kluge's conception touches that of popular memory. The anecdotes, primitive book illustrations, cheap reproductions and riddles that are interspersed in *The Patriot* represent to Kluge what he calls the 'friction-energy' of history, in contrast to illusionist spectacle which to him is always the sign of a 'strategy from above'. The 'strategy from below' is not only one that can see connections between very disparate events, it also resides in malapropisms and unseemly associations, such as thinking of Christmas with goose and cranberry sauce during an air raid because of the smell of burning flesh, or slips of the tongue and generally embarrassing moments in people's lives. The events of *Germany in Autumn* or the Bitburg episode are fascinating to Kluge precisely because an official 'strategy from above' is subverted and made incongruous by the unexpected manifestations of a 'strategy from below'.

Syberberg's German History

Throughout the 1950s history returned triumphantly in the hugely successful *Sissi* films, which involved the nation's millions in the agonising choices facing a young princess destined to become the wife of the future ruler of the Austro-Hungarian Empire. Kluge would no doubt see in these costume spectacles, with their pageantry and melodrama, a flagrant example of postwar amnesia and the repression of history – the least promising tradition to go back to for a recovery of the past. Yet for a project rather similar to Kluge's, this was precisely where Syberberg started when he embarked on his trilogy of films which would bring together Romanticism and Realpolitik, art and politics, by looking at German history not through the eyes of historians but through the rose-tinted vision of mass fantasy: the Hapsburg monarchy and its appeal to the popular imagination.

Syberberg chose three watersheds of German history during the last 100 years. The first is the traditional rivalry between Prussia and Bavaria, which culminated in the defeat of Bavaria and the formation of the German Reich by Bismarck. The second historical pivot is the period of Germany's imperialism, when the aspirations to become a world power ended with the fiasco of the First World War. The third is Hitler, Fascism and the destruction of the Germany founded by Bismarck: the revenge of Munich on Berlin.

Yet Syberberg's films are actually not about these events, but about three marginal, basically pathetic figures. In *Ludwig – Requiem for a Virgin King* it is Ludwig II, the mad King of Bavaria, whose major claim to fame is to have built fairy tale castles in the Alps and put on lavish private performances of Wagner's operas. The second film is about *Karl May*, the pulp writer of boys' adventure fiction, a day-dreamer and recluse, who gave shape to some of the most potent formulas of popular wishful thinking. Finally, *Our Hitler* concentrates more on Hitler's valet, and on the private anxieties of Heinrich Himmler than on Hitler himself, who appears as a mere puppet and mouthpiece of a collective unconscious. Syberberg has chosen apparently apolitical figures and day-dreamers so as to get at the inner lining, as it were, of German history, at the myths and fantasies that sustain a people in its everyday lives, but also capture their superstitions, premonitions and nightmares. As Kluge puts it in *The Patriot*, Grimm's fairy tales are proof that the German people have been working on their wishes for 800 years.

Camping Out and Camping it Up: Kitsch and Death in Syberberg's Ludwig – Requiem for a Virgin King *(1971)*

This is much the same perspective adopted by Syberberg to explore the contradictions of his Ludwig figure. The radicalism with which this decadent aesthete cultivates a homosexual sensibility becomes a political stance where it flamboyantly rejects the aggressive, totalitarian, Prussian side of German Realpolitik. But this protest is equally an escape, the famous German road to

Baroque theatrum mundi in Syberberg's Ludwig – Requiem for a Virgin King *(1971)*

Rainer Werner Fassbinder arguing with his mother (Lilo Pempeit) in Germany in Autumn *(1978)*

inwardness, the flight from reality, practised by failed revolutionaries at least since the Romantic period in the 1820s. The ruthless power politicians, according to Syberberg, have always as their alter ego a sentimental aesthete, and the sadistic realist often hides a masochistic dreamer. By staying close to what he perceives to be the popular residue of history, the sentimental stereotypes, Syberberg wanted to work with the kitsch imagination and what he termed 'cultural refuse'. For him they documented the feelings of common people about events and historical crises, but also contained attitudes that could be called 'realistic' in that cynicism and wishful thinking are present in equal measure.

In the *Hitler* film, however, the question arises whether one could actually treat the emotional and sentimental detritus from this period as if it was now dead. Or did Syberberg succumb to the fascination still contained in the paraphernalia and imagery of Fascism? With regard to the emotions mobilised by the Nazis and their iconography, Syberberg was, after Schroeter's *Bomber Pilot* (1970), the first West German film-maker who presented them directly. In contrast to Joachim Fest he neither reproduced the aesthetic forms by showing original footage as 'documentary', nor accompanied them with a pseudo-objective commentary. Instead, by restaging the emotions through deliberately more primitive technical means (back-projection, puppets, papier mâché sets) Syberberg wanted to mark both the distance and the proximity of this repressed part of Germans' emotional lives. His style might be seen as parody or pastiche, but was more pertinently part of that *Trauerarbeit* which exposes the spectator once more to fascination in order to recognise within oneself what it was one had lost and was secretly disavowing.

That the cinema has an especially ambivalent role in the representation of Nazism derives not least from the fact that German Fascism has left a more complete account, in sight and sound, in visual records and staged celebrations, of itself and its version of history than any previous régime or period. Leni Riefenstahl's *Triumph of the Will* is not so much the record of the 1934 National Socialist Party Congress in Nuremberg as its visual–dramatic–aural or architectural *mise en scène*. What makes the ambivalence and fascination surrounding this film survive all directly political deconstructions of its message is that, through television, one has come to live with its underlying aesthetics: that public events are often staged, that news is made rather than simply happens. In this respect, Syberberg's ironic pastiche is perhaps after all vulnerable to the critique that it belongs to the discourse of the New Right. By producing Fascism's own fascination with 'kitsch and death'[34] it provides a very problematic spectator-position for the nostalgic self. Yet these very terms imply that the question of Fascism in the cinema is part of the wider, no less problematic relationship between history and the cinema generally, and the surplus meaning carried by any history reproduced or represented by film, and more generally, by aural and photographic evidence.[35]

Fassbinder's Germany

The question is particularly relevant in the case of Fassbinder who, from the mid-1970s onwards, set out almost systematically to document German history this century. He took a decision to rewrite it as German film history. But more than anyone else he saw Fascism in relation to the present, and its representation across the dialectics of identification, the splitting and doubling of the self. If *The Marriage of Maria Braun* was to be called 'The Marriages of Our Parents' and be part of an omnibus film, one can get a glimpse of what Fassbinder's contribution might have been like from watching *Germany in Autumn*. In an artlessly casual but carefully scripted interview with his mother he mercilessly interrogates her until she finally confesses that the government she feels happiest with would be a dictatorship – 'but a gentle, benevolent one'. While his mother, in the face of

267

Klaus Löwitsch, Hanna
Schygulla and George Byrd
in The Marriage of Maria
Braun *(1979)*

ever more ubiquitous bureaucratic surveillance systems, wants Hitler back, and most of the intellectuals portrayed in other episodes of the film display a headlong flight into paranoia, Fassbinder toys with another gesture: an act of terrorist exhibitionism which turns the machinery of surveillance, including the cinema, into an occasion for self-display.

Having established via his mother an analogy between the Federal Republic and its own Fascist past, Fassbinder enacts, especially in the scenes with his lover Armin, both the general paranoia following the breakdown of authority, and its narcissistic/exhibitionist obverse, which emerges as the subjective dimension of a Fascist society. Naked, in frontal view, close to the camera, he shows himself mentally falling to pieces under the pressure of police sirens, house searches and the virtual news blackout in the media. The heavy, obese presence of his own body filling the frame, Fassbinder alternates between self-loathing and self-love, an ambiguity projected aggressively on the mother and the lover in turn. The connection between paranoia and narcissistic object choice is made by a double metaphor. Fassbinder cuts from his mother advocating the virtues of conformity and submission to a helpless embrace with his lover as they both roll naked on the floor. Like Hermann Hermann in *Despair*, he tries to escape from paranoia by mirroring himself in his double.[36]

The Marriage of Maria Braun, on the other hand, initiated for the New German Cinema the turn to 'history from below', with its stories and experiences of ordinary people, of families for whom the problem of getting firewood for their stove or cigarettes to use as 'hard currency' on the black market was more acute than Konrad Adenauer's assertion on the radio that Germany would never again rearm. In actual fact, Fassbinder was reinventing the *Trümmerfilme*. By quoting scenes and shots which had become the icons of the postwar period not only through television putting on films from the 1950s, but because they circulated as coffee table books of newsreel photos and other visual memorabilia, the filmmaker could avail himself of – and ironically comment on – the fetish objects of historical truth.

Yet Fassbinder's project was a more ambitious one, especially if one considers his films from the 1970s, not in the order he made them but in the chronology of the periods they depict. They reveal a positively nineteenth century voraciousness for history, and Balzac's *Comédie Humaine* comes to mind, or Trollope, Galsworthy or Thomas Hardy. The wealth of characters and situations, of stories, types and people is astounding in a work that had barely more than a decade, from 1968 to 1982, to develop and fulfil itself. Fassbinder also stretched our notion of German history beyond the decade 1933–45. *Effi Briest*: the Prussian aristocracy in the 1890s; *Berlin Alexanderplatz*: proletarian life in the growing capital of the Reich between 1922 and 1929; *Despair*: the rise of Fascism among the wealthy middle class from 1932 to 1935; *Lili Marleen*: the career of a nightclub singer from 1936 to 1945, among the upper echelons of the Party between Berlin, Munich and Zurich; *The Marriage of Maria Braun*: the economic miracle in the Cologne area from 1945 to 1953; *Lola*: the Adenauer years, and local politics between 1955–1958; *Veronika Voss*: show business, drugs and Munich high-life in the mid 1950s; *The Merchant of Four Seasons*: petty-bourgeois family life in the Munich suburbs around 1960. Other films, such as *The Third Generation* and *In a Year of Thirteen Moons* continued this history up to the mid- and late 1970s.

Kluge had used documentary and newsreel footage, family snapshots and fictional scenes in *The Patriot* for a cut-up representation of the many layers that make up a sense of living in and through history. Syberberg had worked more with an amalgam of camp and kitsch, seen through the mythology of Wagner or Nietzschean philosophy. Fassbinder made a decision to use narrative and to tell stories in his reckoning with German history: to opt, in other words, for the illusion of realism, heightened by stylisation and artifice, and to go for this version of history to the cinema itself. Not only copying the hair-do's, clothes and accessories, the ephemeral aspects of life that constitute what is called a period style, but the gestures. What he had learnt from imitating the American cinema he now much more skilfully extended to the German cinema, producing a sense of disturbing familiarity. It was a controversial move. For Fassbinder it seems that a return to history meant establishing above all a continuity within discontinuity, and thus an acknowledgement of collusion of the present with the past on the basis not so much of a hunger for experience but a hunger for images, so that in the stories he told the repressed of German history did seem to return: the *unheimlich* did become *heimlich* – canny and familiar.

History: The Mother's Story

Fassbinder in this sense might be said to have rediscovered the value of the family. But not as the bastion of strength it had been in the immediate postwar cinema, where mothers and fathers, sons and daughters huddled together to survive the blows of fate, or be reunited in the last reel, but rather as the true battlefield and theatre of war. To this extent the German cinema did find its way back to history by finding German history right in the home. As Alexander Kluge put it: what had to come under scrutiny was how the Nazi régime was able to keep the German family idyll intact right next to the concentration camp.

One film which perhaps more than any other tried to answer this question, while building on the need to tell stories of families and setting out the private consequences of the compromised father, was Helma Sanders-Brahms' *Germany Pale Mother*. The title is taken from a poem by Brecht, spoken in a gravelly voice by Brecht's own daughter Hanne Hiob. A woman's voice-over then informs us that this is the story of her mother, how she met her future husband, their courtship and marriage which coincided with the outbreak of the war. While Hans is at the front, Leni has to cope with his absence. On the few occasions

Elisabeth Trissenaar and Hanna Schygulla
in Fassbinder's The Marriage of Maria
Braun *(1979)*

Eva Mattes in Germany Pale Mother
(1979)

they see each other in the years to follow, it becomes clear that their experience of war is so radically different in emotional and psychic terms as to condemn each to suffer and desire in solitude. For Leni the birth of a child is the beginning of a heroic private war of survival, where mother and daughter exist in and through each other in mutual interdependence and as each other's mirror images. For Hans, the existence of the child confirms his total exclusion from this charmed circle of reinforcing identities.

But it is during the postwar years dedicated to rebuilding and reconstructing the devastated country that the inverse symmetrical destruction of the family becomes evident. Hans' return from captivity and his sullen struggle to impose himself as a father and authority drives a wedge between mother and daughter that makes the mother a physical cripple and a potential suicide, while it turns the daughter into a cheerless, all-too-knowing, inhibited little girl. *Germany Pale Mother* describes the drama of the absent father in the most starkly realistic terms. It derives its pathos from the fact that Hans, an opponent of the Nazi régime, returns from the war an emotionally cold, hard and authoritarian man, hiding his own disappointment and disorientation behind a façade of punishing and self-punishing severity. But it also dramatises, as no other narrative feature film, a woman's resistance to re-entering a reconstituted patriarchy. In Sanders-Brahms' film it is the heroine's body that bears quite literally the physical marks and the mental scars of the German reconstruction effort. *Germany Pale Mother*, in spite of its title, refrains from using the woman as a metaphor and allegorical figure in the way Fassbinder's *Maria Braun*, for instance, can call herself 'the Mata Hari of the Economic Miracle'. Where Maria Braun comes to symbolise the complex relations of substitution and exchange around which Fassbinder has constructed his story, Leni's ravaged face and body remain on the screen well after the film has exhausted its narrative – refusing to release the spectator into meaning.

White telephones and the 'Mata Hari of the Economic Miracle': Klaus Löwitsch and Hanna Schygulla in Fassbinder's The Marriage of Maria Braun *(1979)*

The Impact of *Holocaust*

A sentimental bracketing of the family and the concentration camp characterised the most overtly commercial venture into 'retro-spectacle' – the American NBC television series *Holocaust*. Yet this very conjunction may help to explain why German audiences were so powerfully affected by it as to make *Holocaust* an unprecedented media event.

> More than any documentary or any personal account, this fiction film, although of mediocre quality, provoked a truly emotional outburst: after the first telecast on Monday January 22 1979, the ARD staff received more than 5000 frenzied passionate telephone calls, which constituted a veritable event in the history of the relationship between German television and its public.[37]

The series started a heated public discussion not only about this (in West Germany) least-discussed aspect of the Third Reich, but also about the ethics of turning an occasion of national shame into a family melodrama and thriller. If, however, a soap opera managed what no documentary film, no literary account, no commemorative event had achieved, namely to bring home the horrors of Nazi rule and to open the locked doors of memory, conscience and personal history – as *Holocaust* seemed to do for millions of Germans – then objections on the grounds of aesthetics might be misplaced. *Die Zeit* even went so far as to suggest that a 'wish to forget these events, especially since the impulse to remember them has come from abroad, hides behind a high-minded disapproval of the form'.[38]

Peter Märthesheimer, responsible for acquiring *Holocaust* for German TV and

271

also Fassbinder's scriptwriter on *The Marriage of Maria Braun*, argued that given the very special historical circumstances and 'the mechanism of identification' employed by the programme, its effect was emotionally overwhelming irrespective of its 'artistic' merits.

> [In 1945] individual Germans bore a responsibility alone, without ever having had to bear such responsibility for their own actions . . . these people put their soul on ice . . . [Watching *Holocaust* the viewer was freed] from the horrible, paralysing anxiety that has remained repressed for decades, that we in truth were in league with the murderers. Instead, we are able to experience, as in the psycho-drama of a therapeutic experiment, every phase of the horror which we are supposed to have committed against the other – in ourselves . . . to feel and to suffer it . . . and deal with it as our own trauma.[39]

Is Märthesheimer, to counter objections to German history being 'made in Hollywood', simply spelling out the narrative strategies of every commercial fiction film? And do not the abstract nature and generality of mechanisms of suspense and identification, cut loose from personal memory and its specifics, actually betray the very idea of 'working through' which he seems to advocate?

This might well have been the line taken by Edgar Reitz, who argued that he was glad *Holocaust* had not been made in Germany 'because that would mean its commercial aesthetic which dominates the international market had established itself also in Germany'. With an article entitled 'Let's work on our memories' he participated quite vigorously in the debate sparked off by *Holocaust*:

> If we are to come to terms with the Third Reich and the crimes committed in our country it has to be by the same means we use every day to take stock of the world we live in. We suffer from a hopeless lack of meaningfully communicated experience. One should put an end to thinking in categories in this respect, even where this terrible part of our history is concerned. As far as possible, we must work on our memories. This way, films, literature, images come into being that bring us to our senses and restore our reflexes.[40]

The passage pleads quite explicitly for a 'cinema of experience' in respect of representing history, by contrast to *Holocaust*'s use of an 'experience of cinema' in order to convey the reality of the historical events. Reitz actually provides a very useful definition of both:

> The difference between a scene that rings true and a scene written by commercial scriptwriters, as in *Holocaust*, is similar to that between 'experience' and 'opinion'. Opinions about events can be circulated separately, manipulated, pushed across desks, bought and sold. Experiences, on the other hand, are tied to human beings and their faculty of memory, they become false or falsified when living details are replaced in an effort to eliminate subjectivity and uniqueness. There are thousands of stories among our people that are worth being filmed, that are based on irritatingly detailed experiences which apparently do not contribute to judging or explaining history, but whose sum total would actually fill this gap. Authors all over the world are trying to take possession of their history, but they often find that it is torn out of their hands. The most serious act of expropriation occurs when people are deprived of their history. With *Holocaust*, the Americans have taken away our history.[41]

Heimat

Of the projects trying to counter *Holocaust* on its own terms, the most remarkable was Reitz' sixteen-hour nine-part series *Heimat*, made between 1979 and 1984. Screened on television, after a brief but highly visible release in the cinemas, it served Reitz as a test case of whether, through television, a nation can 'take possession' of its history. The secret of the undoubted impact of *Heimat*, I would argue, lies in Reitz having found a formula which synthesises the autobiographical perspective (of a history from below) with the narrational strategies of identification. A subtle, cinematically highly self-conscious narrative, supported by many parallels and repetitions, ironies and symmetries, gives this story of a rural community and the lives of three generations a complex internal frame of *en-abyme* mirroring effects, comparable to *Germany in Autumn* or *The German Sisters* but on a vastly extended scale – from 1919 to 1982 to be exact.

The title, inadequately translated as 'Homeland', is an intensely emotional concept, always implying both a return to imaginary or real origins and roots, and a totalising, acquisitive gesture. Larger than the nation state, it tries to embrace and unify culture, language, history and geography. Yet *Heimat* also has predominantly rural associations and is therefore closely linked to the land and soil, even to a particular landscape or a region. As such it has been much abused by German nationalists from the Romantics to our day. Every expansionist or annexation policy in German history has been justified by the slogan 'Heimat' or, as with Hitler, 'Heim ins Reich'. To call a New German film *Heimat* was therefore a calculated provocation and was bound to be controversial.

On television the series is a chronicle. First centred on Katharina, the mother-figure who tries to hold the family together, and then on Maria, her daughter-in-law bringing up three sons without a father, the episodes are introduced by Glasisch, a good-natured village idiot, shuffling through a stack of photographs which serve to recapitulate the story and introduce subsequent episodes. For each update Glasisch changes the emphasis, literally able to 'drop' characters and 'pick up' others, depending on the snapshots he chooses. His story-teller stance fosters the sense of scenes which come alive from a family album, but he also balances spectatorial distance and proximity, intimating that he is in love with Maria, but from afar.

Despite the many characters and incidents the main protagonist in *Heimat* is time itself, eating into the characters' features, bearing down on their bodies and hardening their attitudes. Especially revealing is the choice of actors who play Maria's sons at different stages in their lives. Anton becomes stockier and more thickset as his devotion to marketing his optical inventions turns into a mixture of business caution and moral complacency. Ernst, an ace Luftwaffe pilot during the war, becomes ever thinner and more ferret-like after his marriage for money breaks up and he enters the antiques business, scouring the region for peasant furniture and farm implements to sell to Cologne or Düsseldorf nightclubs for their decor. Hermann, the youngest, turns from a vulnerable adolescent troubadour to a coldly elegant composer of electronic *musique concrète*. To all appearances he is a city-bred intellectual, who returns to the village resentfully and in the event too late to make peace with his mother, who once took out her incestuous feelings on the 'dark' woman Hermann was in love with.

It is through the details of the actors' body language, the objects Reitz surrounds the action with, and especially the role these play in both situating the period and the personalities, that the film comes into its own as cinema. Freed from the

273

commentary, the story has a more epic sweep, but unlike other family sagas such as *The Godfather* or *1900*, whose journeys through time take their predominantly male protagonists on quests either into distant parts or towards self-realisation, *Heimat* abandons its males once they abandon the charmed circle of their Schabbach village. The only exception is Eduard, the eldest of the Simon brothers, who figures in the episode set in Berlin during the Nazi seizure of power. He, however, is in many ways the least independent, and his stay in Berlin only highlights his need to return to the Hunsrück region. At one point he voices what is certainly one side of the dialectic on which Reitz has built his film: the feeling that if everything stayed the same as it is now (the year is 1938), he could be happy for ever after. His mother Katharina, though, knows better; the new millennium lives on credit – borrowed money, a borrowed creed and borrowed time.

Heimat's leisurely pace, the emphasis on the changing seasons, the idyllic moments of picnics and outings, are not, as in a Hollywood production, the preludes or counterpoints to dramatic climaxes or scenes of cathartic violence: they *are* the drama. The good things in life – which for Katharina means listening to a Christmas choir, for Pauline going to the movies, for Martina making raisin and potato pancakes and for Maria buying her son a model airplane – are undermined not by the dramatic intrusion of political events or even by the war. Instead it is the scars that the small sins of commission or omission, petty injustices, moments of cowardice, indecision or opportunism leave on life and relationships that destroy the community of Schabbach.

Reitz's plea for a cinema of memory directly communicating individual experience, unprocessed as it were and thus amounting to a collective history, does not translate easily into practice and neither is it altogether his own. It is true that for a German audience there must be literally hundreds of details and scores of incidents that ring absolutely true, because they spark off personal memories and allow an audience to recognise themselves. But *Heimat* is not only a complexly layered film full of implications for the post-1968 political scene in its undercurrent of anti-Americanism, which allows one to see some of the sentiments and resentments that have transformed portions of the New Left into the Green Party. There are echoes of *The Odyssey* and of the Return of the Prodigal Son, but also of Siegfried and Parsifal myths. The women characters, too, allude to biblical as well as mythological figures. *Heimat* also has a more narrowly film–political subtext, for in the opposition between those who stayed behind (or returned), and those who thought they had to seek fame and fortune abroad, one can read the polarities of the New German Cinema itself, between international auteurs (Americanophiles like Herzog and Wenders), and those directors who, like Kluge and Reitz, have remained faithful to their roots.

Reitz had already in earlier films explored the historical and political aspects of that mythical search for origins so typical of postwar German culture. At times it was explicitly related to 1945 as in *Zero Hour* (*Stunde Null*, 1976), which tells of the end of the war in a village near Leipzig as American troops evacuate and cede part of the territorial gains to the Russians. True to the topos fixed by Kleist in *The Earthquake in Chile*, the film details the villagers' depressingly swift accommodation to three different masters in as many months. In another Reitz film, *The Trip to Vienna* (*Die Reise nach Wien*, 1973), the ambiguity of a return to origins and the hope for a fresh start get translated into the dualism of home and abroad, of rootedness in central Europe and emigration to America, thus anticipating many motifs from *Heimat*.

Heimat, Home and Happiness: Marita Breuer and Edgar Reitz

Rüdiger Weigand and Karin Rasenack

and the whole cast for the family album (Reitz' Heimat, 1984)

Fact (Edgar Reitz' Geschichten aus den Hunsrückdörfern, shot while preparing Heimat*)*

. . . and Fiction . . . (Edgar Reitz' Heimat, 1984)

But where *Heimat* is more ambitious than Reitz' previous films, and particularly instructive in relation to *Holocaust*, is in its many references to other films, and to the impact of the mass media, communication and transport. Not only are the first automobiles, the arrival of telephone wires and the building of new roads major events for the village. The film as a whole thematises its conflicts and characterises its protagonists via the instruments of recording, diffusing and consuming experiences in vicarious forms. Paul's interest in radio, Anton's in optics, Eduard's in photography, Ernst's in aviation and Hermann's in electronic music become in the course of the film very complexly handled symbols of (especially) the men's very displaced and mediated relation to experience and their own self-images.

Reitz also includes an extract from a very popular 1938 Zarah Leander film, directed by Carl Froelich, called *Heimat* – another *en-abyme* device, not just because of the title. Zarah Leander is a crucial reference point for several characters in *Heimat*, for the women who stay at home (and dream of Spain, Italy and the south), as well as for the men on the front (who dream of returning

Zero Hour then . . . (Edgar Reitz' Zero Hour, 1976)

. . . and now (Volker Schlöndorff, Jerzy Skolimowski and Bruno Ganz on the 'set' of Circle of Deceit, *1981)*

Dreaming of the South: Marita Breuer and Karin Kienzler in Reitz' Heimat *(1984)*

home). A movie star becomes the convergence of several not quite symmetrically placed fantasies: the very subject of Fassbinder's *Lili Marleen*, based on the life of another Nazi star, Lale Andersen.

In spite of his attack on Hollywood Reitz is thus clearly aware that, in our century, to talk about memory is to talk about images and sounds electronically or optically produced. Audio-visual representations of events, whether newsreel, family snapshots, big screen movies or recorded music, fascinate us with the instant presence they conjure up and their miraculous ability to annihilate time, distance and death. None of us can escape the force of images that always already exist, and to build a counter-memory from scratch would seem as heroic as it is impossible.

Heimat, like *Holocaust*, was a media event. Reitz had argued that whatever happens in future to the cinema as a physical place where films are being shown publicly, what matters is that every country should be able to preserve a space where human beings can 'encounter their own lives, their own world of experience in the constructed and heightened form which is the work of film'.[42] The cinema as a space and event implies, apart from a different relation to the subject, a different relation to the objective world – the environment, the landscape, the cities, the sites of work and production. In order to counter the violence of action narratives which always instrumentalise the real, the most typical films of the New German Cinema did not, finally, invest the exterior world with a 'soul' as critics have claimed. Many of the films, however, offer the spectator a gaze, a way of seeing which, while not denying the violence that comes with rendering everything visible to the eye – even the elegiac look is aware of its inherent

277

aggression – at least does not profit from it. Suspense and action cinema, with its essentially voyeuristic gaze and its 'rape of objects', tends to do just that.

The New German Cinema (of which *Heimat* was perhaps intended as both a summing up and an epitaph), in order to find history, had to turn to the family and the home. Some of the most interesting films tried to get this history into focus by way of what one might call distorting mirrors: the mirrors of terrorism, of family violence and of the clinical disintegration of a personality. Reitz chose a different route. The paradox of his project of 'repossessing our history' is that the cinema, even where it is not a spectacular restaging of the past but a 'working-through' in the sense of filmic *Trauerarbeit*, encounters the fact that photographic memory is especially selective; what it preserves is often a conservative, nostalgic sense of loss. From painful events, too, it can draw the perverse but real pleasures of regret.

A return to history through the subjective, the autobiographical, but even more, a return to history through its images, cannot but be an elegy, a lament, a dwelling on destruction. Thus the trauma of burying and repressing the past – the collective amnesia – which had characterised German society for the first three decades after the war seemed to have been lifted only at the price of nostalgia, of a gratifying identification with victims, and with oneself as victim, if not of history, then of time itself. And since nostalgia is also the emotion typical of the cinema itself *Heimat*, like other films of the German cinema that have returned home to history, works with nostalgia for nostalgia: the memory and recognition of images which have been seen many times before. History has become an old movie, willy-nilly. And that – if the history happens to be that of Germany this century – must give pause for thought.

9:

National or International Cinema?

From Identification to Identity?

By the beginning of the 1980s, then, the New German Cinema had in effect established a thematic and social space where its films could be seen as formally coherent and historically determined. Furthermore, if a film like Ottinger's *Ticket of No Return* (*Bildnis einer Trinkerin*, 1979) satirised not the Hollywood genre film, but its intended alternative, namely the independent New German film, it proved the existence of an identifiable constituency at home as well. For the reason Ottinger could be polemical about audience expectations was the new cinema's own successful presentation of itself as a critical cinema, speaking directly to its audiences and their desire for social relevance and personal commitment. This in turn was an indication that the New German Cinema, despite its heterogeneous output, its cult of individual authorship and marginal appeal when measured against Hollywood genre cinema, had in fact developed identification marks which signalled to its audiences relatively stable spectator expectations.

These, evidently, were recognised more easily in Germany itself. They made cinema in Germany the privileged medium for representing certain images of the nation, but in most cases against the background of social and political history rather than film history. The New German Cinema at home during the 1970s was in some sense a cinema for those who do not go to the cinema. This is what might be meant by the label 'content-oriented': that independent, state-financed cinema actually found itself involved in general political and cultural issues, quite apart from the films' entertainment values. What was at stake was a temporary redefinition and appropriation of the cinema as a kind of public forum in a period of acute polarisation caused by social and economic crises, during which the media had assumed some of the functions and status of civic institutions.

Within Germany, therefore, a sense of coherence for this cinema was rarely associated with the label 'New German Cinema', which was always felt to be a foreign import. Instead one finds the many bi-polar schemes discussed above: contentist/sensibilist, realist/stylised, Berlin school versus Munich school, television versus cinema, progressive versus reactionary, rationalist versus romantic. But as I have tried to argue, not only are these categories insufficient and self-contradictory,[1] they do not convey the actual field of force in which this cinema developed: the redefinition of the media and their general social function. This is why in the German context documentary production seems closer to the fiction films than either of these are to Hollywood. Both documentary and fiction films were united by complementary sets of textual and intertextual references, centred on the question of identification, in its psycho-historical as well as in its specifically filmic sense.

The overall effect was that social issues, self-representation and role models took on some of the functions traditionally assumed in the Hollywood cinema by generic codes, by stars and a stable narrative syntax. The meaning of these stable elements in German film-making in the 1970s, however, derived from debates and assumptions which never took the industrially produced feature films as the norm, not even as a counter-example. Films may have required detailed knowledge and recognition on the part of the spectator (in Ottinger's example, the Berlin documentary school), but this information was present in the film as a stance rather than as its subject matter.

Undeniably, however, it was out of a particular constellation – the absent and at the same time monstrous father in a society still under the sway of patriarchy – that the New German Cinema created some of the main points of reference which gave it emotional appeal and structural coherence, and thus an audience beyond its national boundaries. The themes of isolation, loneliness and despair noted at the beginning of the previous chapter were thus not so much the symptomatic indications of a loss of identity, or a failure of nerve, which is how they struck many left-wing critics, not only in Germany,[2] but elements of a critique. What made this critique original was that it was not formulated in the terms of a critique, but as a playing out, a 'working through': taking the forms of *Trauerarbeit* and melancholy discussed in the previous chapter. It brought into view a stark antithesis around which the first German postwar generation conceived many of its personal narratives: violence against the self or violence against the Other. In many of the realist fiction films the alternative was suicide or terrorism, in 'experimental' and feminist films it found expression in the seemingly endless processes of mirroring and doubling, frequently also only resolved by death. If such were the basic terms of a mythological structure, they also added up to an ideological self-portrait of a generation.

Testing borderlines, limits and extremes, as in the case of Herzog and Wenders, confronting painful memories from their own individual past, like Helma Sanders-Brahms, Jutta Brückner and Helke Sander; living their lives and their sexuality under the public gaze, like Fassbinder or Werner Schroeter, film-makers confronted the law of the father on the side of exhibitionism and narcissism, putting on a spectacle of self-display. Rather than internalise the latent conflicts which German postwar history and the legacy of a particular culture had programmed into them, feminist and gay film-makers in particular tried to restage the traumas in their films, often making the body itself the site of division, transgression and the transformation of sexual identity. The result was a cinema of excess and melancholy, which challenged the norms of cinema almost inadvertently, while seeking the representation of subject positions outside patriarchy and partriarchal definitions of the self. From the potential fate of neurosis and depression that seemed built into the cultural fabric, New German films escaped into 'perversion', the pleasurable side of neurosis.

By focusing so powerfully on negative states and painful experiences, however, they also helped to shape a cultural paradigm that gave to their domestic audiences and to the rest of the world a contemporary myth of Germany in which more and more of their generation – even where they did not share the same historical experiences – could recognise themselves. The film-makers, out of the very absence of a cultural continuity or a national identity in the aftermath of Hitler, fashioned a negative identity whose apparent pessimism was the very condition of its psychological and political truth. This was not only because spectatorial identity and coherence in the cinema is most intensely dramatised in structures of absence and lack. Circulating in almost all the films is an aggression which is also a force of contestation and contradiction. Uncontained within the family, and invested with powerful taboos relating to sexuality and desire, this violence finds its form mainly in the spectacle of gestures and faces both beautiful and pathetic.

The films established, but also changed, horizons of expectations. For the turn to history, the reactions to *Holocaust* and the discussions around a feminist aesthetic contributed to making the notion of 'experience' more complex. With identification no longer based solely on empathy and direct recognition, film forms emerged which allowed the very mechanisms of projection and identification to surface and articulate themselves. In this sense both the identification mechanisms of classical cinema, as well as Brechtian distanciation, were effectively challenged and revised.

The spectrum is a broad one, as we have seen. There were directors interested in validating experience by giving the illusion of presence (Schlöndorff, Hauff and Ziewer), directors who wanted to organise experience as a productive category (Kluge), those who wanted to estrange experience (Herzog) and those who wanted to deconstruct the very nature of cinematic experience (Farocki). Fassbinder, Wenders, Schroeter, Achternbusch, Ottinger, Sanders-Brahms, Sander, but also von Trotta in some of her films, and, more recently, Doris Dörrie, took as their basic theme and material the fact that spectators respond not to content but to images: self-images, mirror-images, spectatorial subject-positions.

It might appear as if film-makers consciously planned their films according to the issues in current film theory. This is of course not the case, since the debates were above all about the politics of film culture. But what I have tried to argue in the previous chapters is that the films addressed distinctive forms of subjectivity and responded – in filmic forms – to such apparently non-filmic issues as 'experience of selfhood', 'identity', 'self-estrangement' (summed up as 'Selbsterfahrung'). This meant that film-makers turned to audiences in forms which – because of the inherently 'cultural' brief – were often very distinct from the identification mechanisms of commercial cinema. The result was films that, far from being either exercises in self-expression or conventionally 'critical', tried to involve the spectator by dramatising and thematising a narcissism ambiguously poised between nostalgia and loss, seducing the spectator via self-oblivion and self-display.

Evidently, some film-makers gave more scope to this process than others, and in more suggestive ways. The question would require a more detailed and more differentiated analysis of individual texts or oeuvres than is possible here. I have discussed elsewhere[3] the imaginary addressee implied in the works of certain film-makers, notably in Fassbinder's films (*The Merchant of Four Seasons, Fear Eats the Soul, Despair, The Marriage of Maria Braun* and *Lili Marleen*), in Syberberg, Wenders, Herzog, Achternbusch, Farocki and Helke Sander. But to what extent there was indeed a 'politics of identification' at work could be seen by the refusal of the film-making community to endorse, for instance, Joachim Fest's *Hitler – eine Karriere* or to adopt the narrative strategies of the *Holocaust* series.

Kluge and the Spectator Film

Looking at the situation in the late-1980s, however, it is clear that there has been a marked shift away from the 'cinema of experience' to a more conventional 'experience of cinema' and to internally generated recognition effects. Such a development was to be expected, not least because a new film culture emerged in Germany itself. It also reflected the successes which an internationally recognisable 'national cinema' achieved without having had recourse to pure formula film-making. Typical of this new thinking was a collection of essays and polemics, edited by Alexander Kluge in 1983, entitled *Bestandsaufnahme: Utopie Film*. One of the most surprising contributions was by Kluge himself, on the 'ingredients' which make a successful German film – in his terms a 'spectator film'. In order to measure the change, one has to recall his arguments for the *Autorenfilm* in the 1960s, and his strictures against the 'film by ingredients'[4] made in the 1970s, sparked off by the poor box office performance of the New German Cinema.

In a detailed gloss on the Dichter poll published in 1972, Kluge had tried to isolate the criteria for a cinema which would be closer to the audience's needs:

Ernest Dichter confronts performance principle and leisure needs. He notes a lack of norms and patterns of behaviour with regard to leisure . . . which also characterise the relations of spectator and cinema. This leads to a resigned attitude on the part of the public and the emergence of a casual audience whose behaviour neither the film producer nor the cinema owner can anticipate reliably. According to this survey, the spectators' needs appear to be unstable . . . Dichter's analysis contains a whole topography of empirical data, which accurately describe the crisis of the cinema in West Germany as well as in its world-wide context. A close application of Dichter's findings in the practice of the German film industry would go a long way.[5]

Yet the conclusions Kluge drew led him to argue for a cinema 'in the spectators' heads', that is, making their own experiences productive. In 1983, in an essay entitled 'What spectators encounter before they see a film', Kluge continues his own research into the factors that come into play when someone decides to go to the cinema. He now isolated four points:

a) title

b) in which cinema and what public sphere does a film appear: the 'direct image' of a film, how many cinemas start it, do the local papers treat it as if one had to have seen it?

c) the links which the direct image of the film has with already well-known films or known extra-cinematic facts or events. Its similarity with films, themes, forms which already enjoy the loyalty of a public. The direct image may also touch the core of an emotion or an interest existing in the spectator but so far not covered by a film. But in this case we have to speak of an indirect image because the rapprochement happens only gradually and over time.

d) word of mouth. This of course can only occur if the film has already had exposure on a sufficiently broad basis.[6]

It will be obvious that these are much more 'market-oriented' criteria, but with features relevant to the German situation, in that they theorise and rationalise the inherent production logic of the New German Cinema over the past decade. As we have seen, German film titles do in fact outline a field of definite associations and convey 'direct images' to the spectator: for instance, the emphasis on cool facticity and understatement, stressing the documentary and exemplary nature of the story, its seriousness and importance. These associations, unusual for an international film, might well influence a non-German audience negatively. Such

titles were, in a commercial context, almost unmarketable, unless their didactic-pathetic tone is taken ironically, as was often the case with Fassbinder's films. On the other hand, they accommodated extremely well the desire, noted in the Dichter poll, of German audiences expecting from the cinema figures to identify with.

If one considers one problem of the New German film, namely not having at its disposal the range of stars that the American cinema could offer its public, one can see that in a sense the titles wanted to compensate for the guarantee of value attached to the stars by shifting this aura of certainty and value from the actor to the character. The very definiteness and peremptory mode of address implicit in the names ensured a certain stability of the referent thus named. Indeed, among the films with the greatest box office success we do find precisely such titles. *The Lost Honour of Katharina Blum, Effi Briest, The Marriage of Maria Braun, Aguirre: Wrath of God, The Enigma of Kaspar Hauser* and *Lina Braake*: the German public is interested in character not action. At the same time, many of the films promise a case history. In this respect, too, the category of the 'issue-oriented' film shows its shortcomings: the case history is not a social issue as such, but rather its subjective, individualised instance. Here the German cinema responded with its own means to the personalisation of social issues as one knows it from Hollywood films, but by inverting the relationship between individual and society. Whereas in the classical genres, such as the Western, the hero becomes the representative of social or cultural values on whose behalf he fights, in German films the individual is always seen as isolated, fighting society as an outsider, in the name of irreducible, often eccentric singularity.

In his 1983 essay Kluge calls the question of the title 'the German cinema's primary challenge'. For him, a good film title is always made up of a combination of indeterminacy and mystery:

> Mystery and indeterminacy can be an excellent point of attraction but not if the enigmatic part is formulated in an indeterminate way. The question of determinacy in a film title is decided by the degree to which a perspective or movement within the title develops, almost invariably based on counterpoint. Generalised openness does not produce an image. The indeterminacy always comes out of a contrast with something determined.[7]

Kluge makes a distinction between titles that associate particular referents (*Anknüpfungstitel*) and unique titles (*Originaltitel*). Taking more or less at random

283

192 film titles, Kluge seems to think that proper name titles gain in direct appeal what they lose in indeterminacy. This would confirm what I have argued earlier: that New German films, having deliberately or by default given up the attempt to address a general audience, were able to home in very precisely on certain target audiences. The titles define therefore quite precisely not so much the content of the film, and even less its style, but the implied spectators and the experience they expect from going to the cinema (Kluge calls this 'anticipatory communication'). To categorise this field of expectations and semi-conscious value judgements, Kluge introduces the terms 'authentic promise' and 'congruence':

> If we imagine the screen to be a skin it is quite clear that audiences intuitively distinguish between an acned skin and a smooth one. I am convinced that the spectator's reaction is in the first instance intuitive, connected with welcome associations, which are rarely if ever fixed as to content. But without content or congruence the first positive skin contact will soon be disavowed, either when the spectator tests for meaning, or at the very latest when he discusses the film with others. Examples of congruence: a film is being shown called 'You Can't Have Everything You Want' starring Christine Kaufmann. First reaction: a good fit. A film is being shown called 'You Can't Have Everything You Want' directed by Margarethe von Trotta: spectator needs more information. The same film with Romy Schneider: sure fire combination. 'You Can't Have What You Want' directed by R.W. Fassbinder starring Karlheinz Böhm: suspicious reaction. . . . The public have a highly developed sense of authentic cinema-fare. Example of authenticity: 'Erwin The Nigger, a Bavarian film by Herbert Achternbusch.' . . . Another example: 50% of interviewees expressed interest, when given the title Aguirre: Wrath of God, 60% knew Klaus Kinski, of which 50% thought it especially exciting to imagine seeing Klaus Kinski as a wrathful god. Although the film was playing at a studio cinema, only 12% had heard of the director Werner Herzog.[8]

In his reliance on the Dichter study and opinion polls such as the ones conducted by the *Filmverlag der Autoren* (even if some of his information is clearly fabricated), Kluge followed a growing tendency among West German filmmakers: the turn towards more 'commercial' criteria. His 'View from the Spectator' coincides rather closely with that of any industry-oriented producer conducting some basic market research and coming to the conclusion that Hollywood must be doing something right:

> The modern [German] film has two competitive disadvantages. Firstly, the orientation factor provided by the stars during the first fifty years of the cinema's history has disappeared. Margaret Mitchell, author of *Gone With the Wind*, wanted Groucho Marx in the lead. The producers were right to insist on Clark Gable. Secondly, in place of the stars we now have more and more subject matter, while at the same time films have lost the simplicity of classical narrative. To tell the story of a film in four sentences has become virtually impossible for most productions during the past twenty years. This prevents a clear orientation of the public, except in special cases, e.g. *The Tin Drum, Christiane F.* and *Maria Braun*, where the subject has collective associations (the first is based on a famous novel, the other two were serialised in the popular press).[9]

The Actor as Intertext

Kluge's apparent change of position can be seen in the context not of the failure of the New German Cinema, but of its successes. For he is quite right to stress the compensatory relationship that exists between actors and subject matter on the one hand, and actors and genre (the four sentence plot) on the other. His, on the whole, rather negative assessment of the situation could be turned positively, by saying that one of the assets the New German Cinema acquired in the 1970s and which crucially distinguished it from the Young German Film, was its actors and actresses. For what has allowed directors to move away from formula plots and make up for the absence of genres have been the 'collective associations' and the cross-referencing made possible by the emergence of a large number of high-visibility character actors alongside the few actors who have succeeded as international stars: Hanna Schygulla, Bruno Ganz, Klaus Kinski. As a counter example, Klaus Maria Brandauer is not associated with the New German Cinema, but with the European art cinema.

(top left) Magdalena Montezuma and Nicola Zarbo in Werner Schroeter's Palermo or Wolfsburg *(1980)*

Wandering Stars: (bottom left) Ingrid Caven in Syberberg's Ludwig – Requiem for a Virgin King *(1971)*

. . . and Eva Mattes in Percy Adlon's Celeste *(1981)*

The importance accorded to the actor from the 1970s onwards in the German Cinema is very striking. Before the 1970s most directors seem deliberately to have chosen either lay actors or players merging with their parts. In keeping with the documentary impulse, the first films of Reitz, Schaaf, Pohland, Spieker, Syberberg and Herzog all seem to have one-off actors in the lead. Schlöndorff experimented with foreign actors: Matthieu Carrière and Barbara Steele for *Young Törless* (1966), David Warner for *Michael Kohlhaas, the Rebel* (1969). With Fassbinder and Schroeter two directors emerged whose *mise en scène* treated their actors as 'stars' well before their talent or reputation legitimated them as such. Schroeter's *Argila* (1969) and *Eika Katappa* (1969) established Magdalena Montezuma as the undisputed star of the German underground, crucial to the films of Schroeter, but also for Ottinger and Elfi Mikesch. Fassbinder's conception of Hanna Schygulla was, as already mentioned, guided by the thought of building up a personal star system.

What gave the use of actors in the German cinema the dimension of a star system was their appearance in the films of different directors, which complemented their roles in the different films by the same director. One might, for instance, construct for the New German Cinema a recognisable identity and an existence as a national cinema entirely on the basis of the different roles and personae that less than a dozen actors and actresses embodied in 40 or 50 films. Without Edith Clever, Angela Winkler, Eva Mattes, Katharina Thalbach, Rüdiger Vogler, Harry Baer, Hanns Zischler, Mario Adorf, Peter Kern, Hark Bohm, Alfred Edel and Gottfried John, among others, backing up Hanna Schygulla, Barbara Sukowa and Bruno Ganz, the New German Cinema would disintegrate into individual films or at best individual directors.

Perennially popular villain: Mario Adorf in Robert Siodmak's The Devil Strikes at Night *(1957) . . .*

. . . and in Schlöndorff/Trotta's The Lost Honour of Katharina Blum *(1975)*

The actors helped establish an intertextuality sufficiently stable to give the impression of a coherent fictional universe, although sufficiently variable to inhibit typecasting. To the persona of Hanna Schygulla belong, besides the roles she played for Fassbinder, also her parts in Wenders, Schlöndorff and von Trotta. Edith Clever is associated with films by Rohmer, Handke and Syberberg. Eva Mattes' role in Sanders-Brahms' *Germany Pale Mother* (1980) implies her role for Herzog (*Stroszek*), which is itself based on the part she played in Fassbinder's *Jailbait* (*Wildwechsel*, 1972). The recognition factor associated with these names was of incalculable benefit when the German Cinema became known abroad. Their 'surplus value' domestically derives in part from the fact that many of the actors are members of extremely well-known and prestigious theatre companies, first and foremost among them Peter Stein's Berlin Schaubühne (Edith Clever, Bruno Ganz, Jutta Lampe and Barbara Sukowa).[10]
It is worth pointing out that the directors who themselves became established as international auteurs have all extensively relied on actors to supply a system of stable references. Werner Herzog's rise to international fame, as the reference to *Aguirre* above reminds one, is intimately connected with Klaus Kinski. But

Rüdiger Vogler:
the Wenders hero
in a Trotta film:
with Jutta Lampe
in The German
Sisters

. . . and with
Hanns Zischler,
Vera Tchechova,
Katharina Böhm
in Rudolf Thome's
Tarot *(1986)*

on his own in
Ingemo Engström's
Escape Route to
Marseille *(1977)*

287

even more it depended on the skill with which Herzog generated a network of cross-references out of Kinski and Bruno S., where one actor complemented the other, across the different films in which they starred. The case of Wenders is equally instructive: he had already made three full-length films before he found, in Rüdiger Vogler, an actor who could develop the Wenders persona and sustain it through the trilogy on which Wenders' reputation rested until *The American Friend*. An intriguing aspect of von Trotta's *The German Sisters* in this context is that Rüdiger Vogler plays a role which is not so much that of a character within the fiction as that of a Wenders persona in a von Trotta film, and thus answering for the spectator the question of what Wenders' attitude might be to left-wing politics, terrorism and the women's movement. Vogler is a particularly interesting actor, in so far as his Wenders persona is a double one, each side having been exploited by other directors perhaps too much in isolation.

The introspective side (*Wrong Movement*) can be found to excess in Ingemo Engstrom's *Last Love* (*Letzte Liebe*, 1979, opposite Angela Winkler), Ingo Kratisch's *The Logic of Feeling* (*Logik des Gefühls*, 1982, playing opposite both Hanns Zischler and Bruno Ganz), whereas the footloose adventurer from *Alice in the Cities* and *Kings of the Road* turns up in Handke's *The Left-Handed Woman* (*Die Linkshändige Frau*, 1978) and Klaus Emmrich's *Kreutzer* (1977). One of the reasons why director Rudolf Thome (ten feature films since 1968) has such a shadowy existence as an *Autor* may well be that between trying to make American genre films in the late 1960s, and Wenders-type actors' films in the 1980s (*Berlin Chamissoplatz*, 1980 stars Hanns Zischler, *Closed Circuit*; *System ohne Schatten*, 1984, features Bruno Ganz and Hanns Zischler, and *Tarot*, 1986, pairs Rüdiger Vogler and Hanns Zischler) he has not fully exploited the narrative images of his leading players. On the other hand, the coherence that exists in Achternbusch's work or that of Helke Sander has much to do with the fact that both directors regularly star in their own films.

Fassbinder was by far the most adventurous and skilful director to exploit the

Hans Christian Blech in Erich Engel's The Blum Affair *(1948)*   *. . . and in Edgar Reitz'* Cardillac *(1969)*

Edith Clever with Peter Handke on the set of The Left-Handed Woman *(1978)*
. . . and as Kundry in Syberberg's Parsifal *(1982)*

advantages of actors as recognition factors. Not only did he appear in his own films and employ his own roster of stars regularly and consistently, especially with respect to minor roles, in order to give each of his films the typical Fassbinder look and feel, he was also instrumental in bringing about a revival of actors from the 1950s and 1960s. Barbara Valentin, Brigitte Mira, Karlheinz Böhm and Adrian Hoven embodied some of Fassbinder's most memorable characters and helped considerably to re-establish a continuity between the cinema of the 1950s and that of the 1970s, something which Fassbinder considered absolutely essential if the New German Cinema was ever to become a 'national' cinema and thus of international importance.

Syberberg actors were often 'borrowed' from other directors (Harry Baer, Peter Kern and Walter Sedlmayr were originally Fassbinder actors) or the stage (André Heller, Edith Clever and Martin Sperr), and he followed suit in the revival of actors from the 'old' German Cinema when for *Karl May* (1974) he cast Helmut Käutner and Christina Söderbaum, a director and an actress associated with the Nazi cinema. By casting Marianne Hoppe (the mother), Hans Christian Blech (Mignon's father) and Ivan Desny (the suicidal industrialist) as the representatives of the parent generation, Wenders engaged for *Wrong Movement* three actors from the 1950s, one of whom had already been 'rediscovered' and another (Desny) was to become the definitive reincarnation of the troubled 'grand bourgeois' in *The Marriage of Maria Braun* (1978), *Malou* (1981) and *Lola* (1981). One wonders, for instance, what might have happened to Kluge as a director, had Alexandra Kluge (Kluge's sister, the 'star' of *Yesterday Girl*, 1966, and in the opinion of many critics what made the film memorable and important) acted consistently in Kluge's subsequent films and been developed as a persona. As it is, Hannelore Hoger, Kluge's female alter ego in *Artistes at the Top of the Big Top: Disorientated* and *The Patriot*, simply is not able to project the kind of presence that Alexandra Kluge has: the latter's brief appearance in *The Power of Feelings* (*Die Macht der Gefühle*, 1983) makes the point forcefully.

'Bonapartism'

Kluge seems to underestimate the contribution that the star directors have made in fostering recognition values at home and abroad through generating forms of cinema other than the one-off film. According to him, they are guilty of 'Bonapartism':

> In the New German Cinema there is, due to varying, individually well definable reasons, a tendency to want to conquer world-power in the cinema with a single film. It is a case of creeping Bonapartism: Syberberg's *Hitler*, Herzog's *Nosferatu*, Wenders' *The American Friend* . . . It is a matter of quietly taking out an option to become the leader, a sort of territorial imperialism which adversely affects the products.[11]

International success, in fact, depended as much on the ability to develop series (in the German cinema these are often trilogies) as on associating a director's or actor's name with a consistent product over several films. In this process, the narrative image projected by actors was a crucial factor, giving not only an identity to the director, but to a New German Cinema film. Thus, within Germany the 'use value' of the commodity 'New German Cinema' or 'independent cinema' was defined by the different groups of spectators appropriating specific films. Often several groups claimed the same film for different use values: *Kings of the Road* was enjoyed by the cinephiles for its echoes of the Hollywood road movie, but also discussed by those more concerned with images of masculinity and the role of women, or the division of Germany and the postwar presence of American culture.[12] Appropriation abroad and perception of the films outside Germany was what finally made the 'New German Cinema'.

The New German Cinema Abroad

If the films often had a difficult passage finding their way to German audiences, few such problems existed for art cinema audiences or for critics and scholars abroad, notably in France, Britain, the United States and Italy. To some extent this has to do with a much better defined film culture in these countries, with criteria and expectations able to absorb or welcome the most diverse manifestations of cinema. Indeed, they need periodically to supply their own market with cultural commodities that can be labelled 'new': new directors, new movements, new national cinemas, renaissances, new alternatives. Whether daily journalists, festival reporters or professional critics, their task is always to create a comprehensible framework, a discourse around the films and the film-makers, which in the case of the New German Cinema meant that writers had several distinct entry points.

In the United States, to choose one example, the films of Fassbinder and Herzog attracted widespread notice at the New York Film Festivals of 1974 and 1975. Two books, James Franklin's *New German Cinema*, and Klaus Phillips' *West German Film-makers*, take this as their starting point. The media coverage put the stress on the personalities of the directors, their eccentric appearance (Fassbinder) or eccentric opinions (Herzog). This gave the New York cultural élite a startling glimpse of West Germany, a country known only in the vaguest terms and without a coherent national image since the Hollywood myth of the jack-booted, heel-clicking German had been allowed to fade during the 1950s in the interest of American foreign policy and good relations with an important ally. Stanley Kauffmann, writing in *The New Republic* in 1977, vividly conveys this new image:

> Accursed Germany. All nations are self-contradictory, but Germany takes it furthest. In the last two centuries, has any other people displayed more self-contradiction – by any measure of intellectual-artistic good or history-shattering evil?
>
> The schism doesn't dwindle. A two-and-a-half hour documentary about Hitler has just been seen in three weeks by 100,000 Germans. And any question about how it's being viewed can be posed against a report in the 'New Statesman' on the booming war nostalgia in Germany – widely popular books and magazines about World War II that emphasise heroism and victories. Yet from this same country comes the New German Cinema. The quick explanation of the contradiction is that abrasion produces art: if the society weren't so enraging, the best people in it would not react against it to the depth of their being. Well, I'm sure there is no art in paradise; still, why don't other enraging countries – no shortage of them – produce comparable films?[13]

Also by 1977, the urban terrorist activities of the Baader–Meinhof group provided renewed topical interest in what had gone wrong with the German economic miracle and the society it had produced ('Hitler's ungrateful grand-children').[14] Eric Rentschler has provided a chronology of the assimilation process of the New German Cinema in the United States,[15] and similar studies have appeared about the way the press welcomed Fassbinder and Wenders in Britain. Sheila Johnston wrote in her Introduction to *Wenders*, 'Coming down from the Mountain':

> 'A totally exciting experience, a film that crystallises a new European consciousness as decisively as those of the New Wave', enthused *Time Out* on the British release of *Alice in the Cities* in 1975. It was a moment when the New German Cinema was in the throes of being discovered and celebrated with indecent haste.[16]

What emerges is that the crystallisation point, where the name 'New German Cinema' acted as both a label of identification and a mark of quality, was reached very quickly. Within the space of eighteen months all major film journals had published either analyses of the 'phenomenon' of the New German Cinema or in-depth studies of its leading figures.[17] It was an instructive example of the powerful amplification effect that the media in the sphere of culture can command, when there is a market ready for it and a certain quantitative presence can translate itself into a qualitative judgement. Secondly, a few years later, Fascism and German history *in* the films helped to project a definition *of* the films in the eyes of the international public, if only as a fascinating enigma, a process which had repercussions at home. The label helped the quite different and distinct films of Fassbinder, Herzog, Wenders and Syberberg to appear as part of a larger totality. It was that of a German renaissance, a German 'invasion', or even as the sign that West Germany had left behind its political backwardness and was ready to assume a world role in culture and the arts again, commensurate to its economic status (West Germany has often been called 'a political dwarf inside an economic giant').

It was not altogether clear whether the individual directors were mere extensions of these metaphoric constructions, each symbolising the dual nature of the German soul, or whether the parts stood for the whole, which was the 'New German Cinema'. In other words, was the New German Cinema simply the combined films of Fassbinder, Wenders and Herzog or were their films examples of the New German Cinema? Yet what for the star directors may have been merely a tautological definition served other, less well known or perhaps less charismatic directors as a useful launch pad. The mere existence of the term, in other words, opened up a new space of definitions and counter-definitions, divisions and sub-divisions, of categories and the unclassifiable, in which any film or group of films from Germany could find its place either within or in opposition to the New German Cinema.

The Scholarly Discourse

The response of film scholars and theorists can be, without too much simplification, divided into two broad categories. Firstly, those who saw the films as part of the European art cinema whose criteria have always been self-expression and personal vision, centred on the director as author. Secondly, those who saw the films as part of an international avant-garde. For the trade press, such as *Variety*, the commercial potential seemed very limited and mainly confined to the campus distribution circuits.[18] For university courses the New German Cinema came as a welcome addition to Foreign Language Programmes[19] and, not surprisingly, stimulated interest especially in the context of postwar German Studies.

Certainly, the films of the star directors lent themselves primarily to an author-based art cinema approach. Fassbinder, Herzog and Wenders not only produced some of their most interesting and challenging work around 1974–1977 (*Kaspar Hauser, Stroszek, Fear Eats the Soul, Despair, Kings of the Road, The American Friend*), but their earlier work could be shown in rapid succession, giving the impression of an even more effervescent and feverish output than was already the case during these first prolific years, after the revised Film Subsidy Bill and the Television Framework Agreement had boosted production both in scale and quantity.

A number of received opinions and clichés soon clustered into serviceable shorthand about these directors-as-authors with an idiosyncratic approach to film. Herzog's mystical romanticism, his Bavarian peasant slyness and unusual visual style, his unconventional narratives, his outsiders, recluses, madmen and outcasts, his love of excess, exhaustion and extremes – all made good copy. The person, his films and heroes could blend into a single personality of quite uncommon magnetism.[20] At the same time, the elements of this myth reminded foreigners of certain typical German attributes and stereotypes sufficiently strongly to make the performance convincing and the impression a lasting one.

In the case of Fassbinder, his counter-cultural lifestyle with a glamorous and flamboyant entourage, his open homosexuality and frankness about drugs and alcohol made him, in the American context, a thoroughly familiar show business figure. All this belonged to the decadent, camp sensibility of the New York demi-monde, the radical chic derided by Tom Wolfe and celebrated by Truman Capote and Andy Warhol.[21] The Warhol reference, often repeated, also served to draw attention to Fassbinder's working environment, his Munich 'factory' which allowed him to turn out film after film with dizzying speed, whilst his life burnt itself out like a Roman candle.

The New German Cinema seemed to have taken up Hitler and Fascism at precisely the point when and where this history had itself acquired a mythical or imaginary dimension, even if the imaginary dimension was that of the unimaginable

Heinz Schubert in Syberberg's
Our Hitler *(1977)*

horrors perpetrated by a legally elected government and supported by an entire people. When Syberberg made his entry on the international scene with *Our Hitler* (1977), it was in part due to having chosen a topic that secured him attention. While his prophetic-oracular, provocatively polemical personal statements made him something of a media personality, it also enabled critics to locate his pronouncements on the state of the western world in general and West Germany in particular within a much more precise geographical and historical landscape than the films of Herzog or even Fassbinder. Their often cramped and claustrophobic family settings evoked sociological rather than historical resonances.

Countries without a strong and continuous tradition of film-making may have to depend on an ability to 'market' the national history as international spectacle for international success. British cinema, for example, enjoyed its most recent 'renaissance' precisely around historical subjects of national glory or defeat (*Gandhi, Chariots of Fire, The Jewel in the Crown, Another Country, The Monocled Mutineer*) and the same seems true of other national cinemas (the New Australian Cinema, with *Gallipoli, Breaker Morant* or *We of the Never Never*). A common historical currency establishes a signifying system of motifs, oppositions, antinomies and structural binarisms: the very stuff of narratives.

Thus, whenever the perspective of critics went outside and beyond the authorial discourse, it found its natural reference point for defining the New German Cinema in Germany's notorious past or its contemporary political troubles. The mystical romanticism seemed as typically German as the despair, anxiety and nihilism. Viewed from the outside, it is easy to form the opinion that German films concentrated on guilt, depression, paranoia, sexual unhappiness, emotional exploitation and social anomie. Many of the films seemed existential parables of nameless terrors and forlorn hopes of bliss. As we saw, the film-makers and the films often seemed only too ready to accommodate such cliché projections. The obsession with isolation and anxiety did make it seem as if all the central protagonists of the New German Cinema were pulled down or held back by guilt as pervasive as it was inevitable. It led from slow decline to suicide (*Effi Briest, Martha, Fox and His Friends, Why Does Mr R Run Amok, The Merchant of Four Seasons, Despair*) to inexplicable death (*Kaspar Hauser*), apocalyptic conflagration

293

The Haunted Screen returns: Klaus Kinski and Isabelle Adjani in Herzog's Nosferatu
(1978)

(*Heart of Glass*), disappearance and suicide (*Aguirre, Stroszek*), to murder disguised as suicide (*Ludwig – Requiem for a Virgin King*), to attempted suicide (*Kings of the Road*), suicide out of *Weltschmerz* (*Wrong Movement*), suicide disguised as illness (*The American Friend*) or violent death as a form of suicide (*The State of Things*).

Such thematic readings posed, however, even within the authorial approach, a certain problem. The temptation was to see these recurrent motifs as expression of the director's autobiography, a view reinforced by the fact that, for instance, Fassbinder often appeared and even sometimes starred in his films (*Katzelmacher, Fox and His Friends, Germany in Autumn*), and that the Herzog legend was built on an almost wilful confusion of the director and his supermen protagonists. Yet, the very prevalence of the various motifs not just within a director's work but across the whole spectrum of films from Germany obliged critics to seek out more embracing categories and, in effect, make Germany itself the collective author of these texts.

This seemed the more plausible since the standard works on the German Expressionist Cinema of the 1920s, Siegfried Kracauer's *From Caligari to Hitler* and Lotte Eisner's *The Haunted Screen* had already, explicitly and implicitly, associated Germany with baring its 'soul' or 'collective mentality' on film. The issue was further compounded by the all-too-ready analogies that writers (and the film-makers themselves to some extent) were prepared to draw between the classic German cinema of the Weimar Republic and its directors – Lang, Murnau, Pabst – and the New German Cinema. Even before Herzog chose to remake Murnau's *Nosferatu*, articles had appeared with such titles as 'Metropolis Now',

and Kurt Raab as Peter Lorre's M in Ulli Lommel's The Tenderness of Wolves *(1973)*

'From Murnau to Munich', or 'From Caligari to *Hitler*'.[22] The metaphor of a tradition and an inheritance was vigorously propagated by Herzog, when he declared that the New German Cinema was 'legitimate German culture', while a film like Wenders' *Kings of the Road* invokes Fritz Lang as almost a totemistic father of the present generation.[23]

The alternative critical approach to the New German Cinema was to see the films in the context of debates around the avant-garde, of modernism, and of a post-narrative, 'deconstructive' cinema. For these views there was, on the face of it, also a good case to be made. The evidence in this instance was the work of Straub and Huillet, of Werner Schroeter, but also certain films by Fassbinder, Syberberg and even Herzog and Wenders. This avant-garde needed to be distinguished from the US underground (Brakhage, Anger) or the Canadian and British structuralist avant-garde (Snow, Gidal, Le Grice) or, finally, the political avant-garde for which Godard may stand as the distinctive European representative. There were, as has already been pointed out, German film-makers much more directly comparable to these avant-garde movements (Klaus Wyborny, Birgit and Wilhelm Hein, Werner Nekes and Dore O., Bastian Clevé and Heinz Emigholz),[24] but these film-makers' work was rarely shown outside very specialised circles. The names generally associated with the New German Cinema could not be fitted into these categories without difficulties.

Yet there was sufficient biographical evidence to make the comparison feasible. Germany had had in the early and mid-1960s quite a strong tradition of avant-garde, experimental, visionary or expanded cinema: the so-called Other Cinema (to distinguish it from the Young German Film), a Co-op movement, performance and video artists, Prokino and various other multi-media artists with a strong interest in film. As we have seen, this avant-garde remained by and large outside the television and state funding systems, since these favoured narrative feature film or at the very least required documentary films. The kind of formal experiment, the theoretical and deconstructive dismantling of the cinema's technological, optical and psychic apparatus which characterises much of the work of the European and North American avant-garde did not fit into the script-based or issue-based allocation of funds practised by the subsidy selection committees. Hellmuth Costard tried to document the exclusionary manoeuvres *vis-à-vis* the avant-garde in his film called *The Little Godard* (meaning himself).[25] Only in the mid-1980s has Werner Nekes been able to get funds for projects, typically involving the history of early film and optical toys (*Film before Film* (*Was geschah wirklich zwischen den Bildern?*), 1985/6) or based, however loosely, on cultural classics (his structural version of Joyce, *Uliisses*, 1982).

While the formal avant-garde thus languished in the late 1960s and played only a minor part in the booming 1970s, it is important to remind oneself that Wim Wenders, for instance, first attracted attention as an avant-garde film-maker with minimalist, anti-narrative films. Along with Thomas Mauch, now better known as the preferred cameraman of Herzog, Kluge, Helma Sanders-Brahms and many others, Wenders formed part of a Munich school of minimalists. Viewed with hindsight Wenders' early shorts (*Same Player Shoots Again, Alabama, Silver City*) now seem quintessentially to belong to the director's later work, but at the time they were just as coherently seen as part of a formalist avant-garde, concerned with the deconstruction of narrative-illusionist cinema and the problem of duration in film.

Werner Herzog's affiliation with the avant-garde is perhaps more tenuous, but none the less real. He has gone on record as being influenced by Brakhage in his conception of film-making, a rare admission of influence from a director almost pathologically committed to affirming the autodidactic, self-created and self-motivated impulse behind his film-making. The fact that the dream visions of the dying Kaspar Hauser are actually super-8 footage shot by Klaus Wyborny and commissioned by Herzog for his film can be seen as the acknowledgement of a debt, rather like that of Fassbinder to Schroeter. Had he not achieved international success with *Aguirre*, Herzog might well have concentrated his career more on making fantastic-surreal documentaries like *Land of Silence and Darkness* (*Land des Schweigens und der Dunkelheit*, 1971), or visionary films like *Fata Morgana* (1974), whose vicinity to the romantic traditions of the American avant-garde is more in evidence.

Fassbinder, for his part, had made the acquaintance of Straub, when his *antiteater* ensemble (the nucleus of what was to become his mini-studio/factory) performed a play by Ferdinand Bruckner, which Straub directed as the central section of his film *The Bridegroom, the Comedienne and the Pimp* (*Der Bräutigam, die Komödiantin und der Zuhälter*, 1968). With some justification, Fassbinder's *Katzelmacher* has been compared to the Straubs' films, especially in its starkly geometrical conception of scenic and dramatic space.[26] The similarity may only be superficial, and Straub has had little sympathy for Fassbinder's subsequent work, but there can be no doubt that Fassbinder was as aware of the materialist-political avant-garde in Germany as he was of Schroeter's films.

Although the influence of the American avant-garde on the New German

Cinema has been slight, and at best intermittent, there is none the less a strongly experimental dimension to much of the work that has come out of the funding structure and the subsidy system, even if its criteria made it necessary for certain formal concerns to displace themselves into less overtly avant-garde modes, as in the case of the feminist films for *Das kleine Fernsehspiel*. What thematic or auteurist analyses of the New German Cinema regularly overlooked was the extent to which German films were also reflections about the cinema itself, not only in its political aspects as they arose from the conditions of production but also formally. Schroeter has been experimenting with music, performance, structuralist repetition and multiple diegesis in a highly original way which, as we saw, influenced Syberberg, Ottinger and Mikesch among others, and was directed towards a conception of representation that owes little to narrative while none the less being totally committed to spectacle.

One of the most fertile contexts in which German film-makers have communicated with an international audience, while sidestepping the label of New German Cinema or avant-garde, has been feminism. The films of Ottinger, Helke Sander and Jutta Brückner have been discussed by American feminists in the light of specific theoretical positions regarding the woman's place in representation, questions of feminine narcissism and visual pleasure or autobiography and enunciation. Films by Sanders-Brahms and von Trotta have contributed to debates on the representation of women by women in commercial and art cinema practices.[27]

In the latter case, work on German women film-makers as well as on the star directors of the New German Cinema has, under the impact of academic film studies and renewed interest in film theory, benefited from critical work focusing on narrative and anti-narrative, representation and subject-position in the contemporary cinema generally, and feminist film-making in particular. Since this theory surfaced particularly strongly in the 1970s, it was chronologically coincidental with the rise of the New German Cinema. In the films of Fassbinder, Wenders, or Herzog, film theory fastened on the fact that their textual systems did not seem to conform to the classical model of Hollywood linear narrative. While theirs were narrative films, they rarely used the models of conflict, enigma and resolution that had become identified with Hollywood narrative. Nor did the films appear to conform to the different kinds of oedipal trajectory which theorists had established for Western fictional narratives. While clearly about these conflicts, they manifestly did not encode them in the same filmic terms. Yet although there was a degree of deviancy from the classical model, this did not seem to make the films 'illegible' within the codes of mainstream cinema.

Consequently a number of studies appeared which investigated the narrative structure of Fassbinder's films, from the vantage point of cinematic modernism,[28] and which analysed the strategies of narrative distanciation, stressing the visible presence of the camera, or pointed to the influence of Brecht.[29] The work of Herzog has been analysed in terms of enunciation, showing to what extent a Lacanian or semiotic reading of *Kaspar Hauser* might be appropriate and illuminating.[30] Equally, the films of Wenders have been examined in the light of recent theories of filmic signification.[31] On the whole, it was clearly important in valorising the New German Cinema as part of film studies and the academic curriculum to be able to use the films positively and as examples of contemporary critical and theoretical problems. The fact that this tended to shift the political implications of the New German Cinema towards more textual politics was in itself not unwelcome, in so far as it balanced and even corrected some of the

297

Irm Hermann in Fassbinder's The Bitter Tears of Petra von Kant *(1972)*

hasty and superficial 'political' readings that film journalists had tried to give of the films.[32]

It is perhaps premature to want to assess the value of the modernist and deconstructive readings given to individual films by New German directors. The fact that there is a polarisation between theoretical readings and culturalist analyses has also to do with the institutional constraint of subjects such as Film Studies and German Studies. However, by far the most common source of interest for a textual analysis, especially with the films of Wenders and Fassbinder, was the possibility of seeing their work connect with the re-working of popular formulas and generic codes that took place in the Hollywood cinema itself; and further, to study the transgressive, parodic or excessive uses German directors made of Hollywood, both as a continuation and a critique of genre-based cinema. From earlier chapters, it will be remembered that there were certain compelling reasons why German directors at a certain point in the history of the New German Cinema wanted to return to a genre cinema, in order both to find a public not mediated by television, and also to free themselves from the odium of making films merely for the members of official subsidy committees. The turn to cinephile forms, especially in the case of Wenders, corresponded to a belief that only by making contact with the emotions and experiences that the cinema had aroused in them as adolescents could Germans of the postwar generation return to their affective roots and childhood memories.

In the Anglo-American context, however, the question of Hollywood and anti-Hollywood had already been part of a much more wide-ranging film cultural debate about progressive or political film-making in relation to classic cinema, initiated by the French (in *Cahiers du Cinéma*'s celebrated article on John Ford's *Young Mr Lincoln*[33]) and in Britain at about the same time by the rediscovery of the films of Douglas Sirk.[34] Film critics and film-makers became interested in the possibilities of describing transgressive practices within the Hollywood mode of production, as well as developing models of textual reading for both industrially and independently produced films. The work of Fassbinder seemed to fit particularly well, with his own explicit and well-documented interest in Sirk and melodrama. The first book to appear in English on the New German Cinema therefore naturally focused on Fassbinder, his relation to the subsidy system on the one hand, and Hollywood genre cinema on the other.[35]

Given the renewed interest in melodrama on the part of feminist film theory, the conjunction of Sirk and Fassbinder proved to be particularly productive in the search for 'deconstructive' practices within the classical cinema as a model for contemporary film-making, although as far as one can tell his style has rarely been imitated. At the same time, Fassbinder's work was very controversial for critics interested in the representation of gay men and homosexuality in the cinema.[36] Even in films like *Fox and His Friends* it seems difficult to speak of a specifically gay sensibility, distinct from Fassbinder's manipulation of generic stereotypes and autocitation, as in the very camp *The Bitter Tears of Petra von Kant* (1972). Another look at *In a Year of Thirteen Moons* (1978), or a comparison with German feminist films, might suggest that there was a distinctly 'sexed'

In a dilemma: Dirk Bogarde between Volker Spengler and Andrea Ferreol in Fassbinder's Despair *(1978)*

aesthetic in Fassbinder after all.[37] Yet taken as a whole, Fassbinder's films are too numerous and explore too systematically different forms of cinema to be amenable to a single reading, be it authorial or textual. The diversity was mainly determined by the possibilities that the mixed economy of German film finance permitted. Yet it also reflected Fassbinder's ambition to be West Germany's first popular and commercially successful director, which meant not only trying to occupy as many sites of production as possible, but also making 'Hollywood films in Germany'. In this respect his work has yet to be analysed in its full significance.

Productive Misreadings

Finally, it can be argued that the reception of German directors in the United States and Britain is an instructive case of productive misreading, in the sense of unifying the diversity and appropriating the films for film history and film theory. The major successes have been in the capitals of Western Europe and on American university campuses; with audiences, in other words, who could afford to ignore the peculiar historical inscription or economic determinants that might have marked the films. Precisely because of a familiarity with models of narrative deconstruction and modernist self-reflexivity, spectators and critics were able to discover a satisfactory meaning in the films, whether of the kind typical for European art cinema or analogous to the critical readings made of classical Hollywood narrative cinema. Such horizons of expectation, as we saw, were not readily available to German audiences, whose response to their own cinema was for political and historical reasons almost too close and visceral to be critical in anything other than a polemical sense.

One of the more puzzling aspects of the history of the New German Cinema is therefore the discrepancy between the directors' reputation abroad, and their status in Germany itself. To over-simplify perhaps, one could say that the New German Cinema was discovered and even invented abroad, and had to be reimported to be recognised as such. Behind this paradox lie a number of inter-related factors. From Oberhausen onwards, film-makers were counting on a foreign audience to secure a position at home, at first economically, since it was always assumed that films could not pay their way on the home market alone. Secondly, in their polemics with German critics, the response from abroad could always be treated as an independent witness for the defence, or even a form of arbitration. Film-makers realised that their standing abroad had a two-fold effect on their reputation at home. It did, for instance, alert the mass circulation press that something extraordinary was indeed happening. *Der Spiegel*, Germany's most widely read news magazine, ran a major article not on the New German Cinema, but on the fact that *Newsweek* had featured the New German Cinema as a cover story in February 1976.[38] Similarly, Syberberg placed an ad in the high-brow weekly *Die Zeit*, alerting readers that if they happened to be in Paris they could see what the Germans couldn't see: a major German film, namely *Our Hitler* (1977). He also presented journalists at the 1977 Berlin Film Festival with a 300-page dossier, which contrasted the German press coverage of the *Hitler* film with that in France and Britain. The foreign press became the leverage to force German critics to take note.

More importantly perhaps, in a situation where the market forces had largely been suspended due to the subsidy system, publicity, journalistic news value and a reputation among foreign critics and film scholars, an invitation by an international festival or even just a fat book of press clippings was the film-maker's capital and currency, the very material basis which might decide how big a slice a director might get of the subsidy cake, and how often. Yet finally, it was also a matter of finance in a more direct sense. As already mentioned earlier, since the vast majority of distribution was handled by American-owned firms, only a solid international reputation would persuade these distributors to release a Herzog or a Wenders film commercially in the European market and in Germany. Their films constituted part of the American export business which Germany had to reimport, like any third world country reimporting its own primary commodities as processed goods.

Marketing a Commodity

Since the State was actively investing in film-making, it was equally aware of the problem of making the product circulate. From the early 1970s onwards the Federal government, through its embassies, its cultural missions and Goethe Institutes, vigorously promoted the New German Cinema abroad.[39] It gave interested audiences access to otherwise unavailable films, conducting seminars, inviting film-makers, supporting lecture tours, retrospectives and special events at colleges, festivals or arts centres. If German film-makers sometimes seemed to hype themselves like pop stars, make oracular announcements like prophets, they were also like athletes selected to represent their countries at Olympic Games.[40] Culture, like sports on an international level, is political. Seeking an international reputation and marketing themselves as brand names, as producers of unique yet recognisable goods of standard quality, was part of the German film-makers' economic condition with which they colluded. The paradox was that at another – textual – level, their work articulated a protest, because as we have seen, it was so often directed against their very circumstances as film-makers.

Some directors protected themselves in other ways. Kluge, while arguing persuasively for the need to break with a 40-year-old 'provincialism in German films',[41] none the less resolutely refused to go on tours abroad or turn himself into an 'author'. Herbert Achternbusch, while subsisting on the cultural circuit like so many other German directors, felt it necessary to document a certain resistance. His account of a sponsored visit to Los Angeles and Berkeley (which he calls 'Birkli' – a Bavarian nonsense word) fairly bristles with inner rage and discomfort:

> At the public discussion we [Achternbusch and Sohrab Shahid Saless] did not say a word, first because the audience wanted to know about [Hark] Bohm and [Reinhard] Hauff, neither of whom were present. As Herzog rightly pointed out, Americans just cannot grasp that there isn't simply one New German Cinema . . . Secondly, the discussion took place before the films were shown, and if I could introduce my films, I would have to be a real windbag, and if someone needs to talk to me after they have seen my films, then they have to be real windbags. Of course, we were supposed to be representatives, against the background of this festival of rejects, we were meant to be the third line, and show that there was lots more territory behind and around the heroes and stars, prove that the German cinema has unlimited potential, we, two nihilists, who every time we make a film barely have the strength to pull away from the slimy embraces of all these forward-looking idiots at home.[42]

Achternbusch is clearly not interested in either the commercial goodwill abroad or the rise in status at home which a successful tour can bring. He once called Herzog 'the best detergent salesman Germany has ever had, because he is the only one who believes in his product', to indicate what he thought of national culture when marketed like a commodity. Yet this was precisely the situation that made the New German Cinema a label and a concept: not whether it could be defined, or given a substance, but that it could be marketed, packaged and circulated ensured that it existed. The mistake of the 'old' German cinema had been to think of films as material goods, similar to machine tools, Mercedes or BMW cars, and to attempt direct and unsuccessful competition with the US and Hollywood. The mistake of the Young German Film had been to try and sell bicycles as if they were Rolls-Royces, or to expect to be congratulated at a motor show for manufacturing bicycles at such a low cost:

> They told us in France – what we don't understand is that you Germans always show off how poor you are in your films. One can tell that you don't have the money, but you are trying to make a virtue out of necessity and advertise the fact that in spite of it, you still make films. But it's bad manners, people here would take it as an insult.[43]

The French, by contrast, have always been highly successful in associating the label 'Made in France' with a variety of material and immaterial products – wine, cheese, Roland Barthes, Chanel No. 5, Exocet missiles, Jacques Derrida – so that Frenchness becomes almost an autonomous signifier of value. This, Herzog and Wenders, Fassbinder and Syberberg appropriated for themselves by making the New German Cinema into just such an autonomous sign.

The strategy of treating artefacts and cultural objects as commodities, in order to make them enter into but also create a market, is much clearer with the New German Cinema than in other cases. It was neither a 'movement' based on personal friendships and loyalties like the *nouvelle vague*, nor united by a common programme or an aesthetic *parti-pris* like neo-realism, nor a political protest like the Cinema Nôvo of Brazil. It was a cinema created around the very contradictions of culture and commodity, of (self-)expression value and (self-)exhibition value, in a modern capitalist economy that depends on export to sustain internal growth, and which in the case of the social-democratic government was prepared to subsidise invisible exports on the assumption that supply would by itself generate demand. The modest commercial successes and the rather more substantial critical successes did in the event sustain an increased volume of production. From barely 60 German films made in 1970, the number shot up to 124 in 1975. The New German Cinema, though it was still produced outside box office returns as these are commonly defined, was intimately connected with the economics of culture.

Films, compared with other artefacts, are cheap and efficient to transport. Unlike a ballet company or a symphony orchestra, a few cans of film can go by diplomatic bag. Unlike literature, films present no insuperable language barriers, and insurance problems pale to insignificance compared with those attendant upon the shipping of paintings or other unique works of art. Yet if the subsidy system tended to reinforce the status of the film-makers as a personality, culture as export detached the individual film from any historical or aesthetically precise context. It came to circulate in as many different forms as there were occasions for exhibition: as media event, 'masterpiece', star vehicle, brand-name product, or as a controversial contribution to sensitive public issues like terrorism or the legacy of Fascism. Films construct themselves in their coherence, meaning and value, not at the points of origin or by a recourse to the makers' intentionality, but in the context and the act of consumption. They remain objects, but they also become texts.

The films of the New German Cinema acquired political meaning in ways not always controlled by their directors, and irrespective of their pragmatic, radical or merely opportunist political opposition to West German society and its institutions. They were, in their function, official representations, sanctioned and sponsored by a country that has had difficulties in profiling itself culturally and politically, except through a relatively recent, though intense, preoccupation with its historical past and its troubled ideological identity as a nation. As we have seen, this is the 'cultural' core around which a certain aesthetic coherence can best be construed, and around which the economic rationale for a very diverse production policy can be explained. These economics of culture make the films political in a general way, but they also tend to depoliticise the individual work and the individual film-maker.

Without Fassbinder, Herzog, Wenders, Syberberg, Schlöndorff or Kluge there would have been no New German Cinema. Each of these directors has had a crucial role to play; they were influential, however, not only through the films they have made, but through their ability to define a stance, a dogma, a theory or myth about the New German Cinema. In other words, they are more than film-makers, they are icons and, in this sense perhaps, they correspond to the idea of a European art cinema 'auteur'. The New German Cinema became a reality at the level of discourse, by the interplay and intertextuality of different media, multiplying and mutually amplifying their effects. Yet as soon as the New German Cinema had been launched as a label, it was part of a range of commodities, a diffuse accumulation of values, not unlike those associated with tourism, through which a country markets its national heritage and past, indeed even its present, if it can be presented as spectacle.

For national cinemas struggling to get into the international market, history (and Nazism in the case of Germany) has become a system of referents to some extent substituting for generic formulas and codes. In films like Schlöndorff's *The Tin Drum*, Petersen's *The Boat* or Fassbinder's *Lili Marleen*, Fascism and its visual paraphernalia function simultaneously within several (generic, psychological, authorial, economic) discourses, so that the filmic status of Fascism, as signifier and referent, becomes quite problematic. This disjunction between sign and referent allows questions of history to become questions of representation in a very precise sense. It allows any number of metaphorical discourses (about outsiders and minorities, about honour and loyalty, family and oedipal rivalry, about showbusiness and warfare) to be supported by the same set of signs.

Between Economics and Semiotics

The extent to which different sites of consumption can generate quite distinct preferred readings, and generate ultimately conflicting constructions of a film, was shown in the case of Herzog's *Fitzcarraldo*. The film tells the story of an Irish rubber planter in South America whose enthusiasm for Caruso makes him want to build an opera house in the jungle, if necessary by hauling a boat across a mountain and opening up a waterway that will generate the cash needed to finance such a scheme. Herzog frequently talked about the project in interviews, ever since completing *Kaspar Hauser*. Clearly the film existed as a recognisably typical Herzog story well before production was underway. The idea of pulling a full-

Alter egos: (above) Werner Herzog directing
Fitzcarraldo *(1981)*
. . . and (right) Klaus Kinski acting
Fitzcarraldo

size river boat across a jungle mountain was entirely in keeping with the absurd and excessive bravado acts associated with Herzog's public persona.

Fitzcarraldo furthermore set expectations that this would be a return for Herzog to the thematic terrain and exotic location of earlier Herzog films, such as *Signs of Life* and *Aguirre*, after more domestic films like *Kaspar Hauser, Nosferatu* and *Woyzeck*. Thus, the film was already situated within two distinct, even if complementary discourses – that of the colourful personality of Herzog himself, and that of his work. *Fitzcarraldo* could inscribe itself into a pattern of continuity and alternation that had already made the Herzog oeuvre into a coherent and unified project.

The actual filming was accompanied by an unusual amount of pre-publicity, although in the context of Herzog's habitual self-promotion this was to be expected. No less than two films were in fact made about Herzog making *Fitzcarraldo*. The circumstances of the production itself provided ample copy for the newspapers. There was Hollywood-type showbusiness gossip about difficulties with the leading actors; Mick Jagger's part being written out of the script, the replacement of Jack Nicholson by Jason Robards, and of Jason Robards by – inevitably – Klaus Kinski. This made the film crystallise around Kinski and Herzog's obviously privileged relationship with his preferred actor, since he had already used him in *Aguirre, Nosferatu* and *Woyzeck* to portray the Herzog persona *par excellence*. However, even more publicity was generated by Herzog's involvement in the tribal and even national politics of Peru, where the shooting took place. It culminated in what at times appeared to be a minor civil war, touching issues about Third World exploitation, the situation of the Amazon Indians, and the European attitude of exoticism *vis-à-vis* the problems of genocide and underdevelopment in Latin America.

When *Fitzcarraldo* was eventually released, much of this publicity did seem to have an adverse effect, making it very difficult to see the film apart from the accretions it had already accumulated. Some critics thought that one of the documentaries made on location about the film, *Burden of Dreams*, 1982, had actually turned out to be the more interesting product of the exercise, while the spectacular scenes of Herzog's film had been anticipated by the pre-publicity. In West Germany, *Fitzcarraldo* was the object of considerable controversy. Herzog himself seemed to think of it as a *Heimat* film transposed to the jungle – a film about Bavaria in other words, with a figure not unlike Mad King Ludwig who had built fantasy castles and had funded lavishly extravagant productions of Wagner's operas. Certainly, Fitzcarraldo can be seen as an anti-hero who, frustrated in his desire for social progress, turns to art and music on a scale symmetrically inverse to his social standing and professional failure. In this sense, *Fitzcarraldo* was indeed a variation on and a reply to Syberberg's *Ludwig – Requiem for a Virgin King*.

A good case can also be made for seeing it as thematically and stylistically close to Werner Schroeter's abiding preoccupation with opera, thus opening up within the conditions of an international super-production space for experimenting with an altogether typical subject and form of the New German Cinema. Indeed, even Kluge had, with *The Power of Feelings* (1983), made a film about opera. The suggestion was therefore not at all implausible, when a German critic pointed out that Herzog could have set his film in Germany itself, and instead of making Fitzcarraldo want to open an opera in the jungle, his hero might have tried to run a cinema in a West German provincial town. For him the film was unambiguously about the plight of West German film-makers, the subsidy system, the love of cinema and the impossibility of the New German Cinema reaching a popular audience in Germany itself.[44]

Finally, for some members of the German left, a film like *Fitzcarraldo* and the reviews it received were nothing less than a sure sign of the victory of the counter-revolution, an aesthetic and ideological defence of irrationalism wilfully betraying the anti-authoritarian work of a whole generation:

> Especially our German intellectuals, tired of politics and theory, flock to and are seduced by Herzog's films. Fed up with enlightenment, to which they used to sacrifice as to a God, they now once more yearn for irrationalism and magic, for cults and occult experiences, for archaic and mystical states, in short, for everything they consider 'dialectical' about 'enlightenment' . . . Let me repeat: the myth of *Fitzcarraldo* is based on the totalitarianism of individual self-realisation, to which corresponds a hero-worship of the victims in the name of absolutes. There may still be a difference between the cult of art as a sacrifice for absolute values, and a politics of sacrifice for an absolute good. But recent German history has shown how little it takes to cross this divide, particularly in times of economic and political crises.[45]

The divergent circuits of international distribution and nationally specific reception make films like *Fitzcarraldo* opaque as texts, but multi-faceted mirrors for any audience seeking confirmation of its own expectations. In one sense, it became a different film depending on whether it was regarded as a product of the international film industry, a work of Werner Herzog's, an example of the New German Cinema or a contribution to an ideological debate between opposing factions in Germany itself, at war over the direction of recent German history and the meaning of the national culture. In another sense, however, it was proof that the New German Cinema and its directors had succeeded. They had established the kind of intertexts and cross-references necessary to make the film circulate as both commodity and text.

International cast: Claudia Cardinale and Klaus Kinski in Herzog's Fitzcarraldo *(1981)*

A National or an International Cinema?

The radical subjectivism in Fassbinder's films, the visionary quality of Herzog's imagination, the anxiously introspective turn of Wenders' heroes and the irrational-ist mythomania of Syberberg have all been noted by critics too many times not to have become commonplaces. But not only do the critical clichés do less than justice to the films themselves, they also disregard the objective conditions which put German directors in the contradictory positions described. Not the least of these contradictions was that the New German Cinema coincided historically and chronologically with the rationalist, anti-bourgeois and anti-'Kultur' phase of 1960s radicalisation. Yet its political function abroad and its semi-official status obliged directors to be at least aware of their cultural mandate. As directors began to address their peculiar dilemma of having an international audience, but finding themselves in several counter-currents domestically (the collection in which the attack on Herzog appeared was actually entitled 'Only Dead Fish Swim With the Current'), they turned first of all to more and more recognisably 'German' issues and subjects in their films. They also treated them from a more and more particularised, limited and extreme angle of vision, knowing that, as Schlöndorff put it, 'only by being aware of its national identity can a film industry be international'.[46]

Quite logically, it led many of them to a rediscovery and revaluation of a specifically Romantic tradition – that of Utopian idealism and radical subjectivity. An Austrian critic duly took the New German Cinema to task for it, seeing mainly a return to the badly skewed relation between art and politics of the days of Caligari:

> The 'new German cinema' . . . sells eccentricity and dreaminess, as one would expect from Germans, mysticism and the sort of individualism that runs away from society. The German brand [of subjective despair] competes with Hollywood disaster movies: social alienation and reification are turned into solid entertainment values. In this form, new-German 'journeys to the soul's interior' hit the international market, and inwardness sits bent over the assembly-line, where Fassbinder puts in a double shift with overtime, and Herzog vows: 'German culture is seriousness and pain'. The Fassbinders, Herzogs and Wenders are certainly no lefties, but they are unthinkable without the backdrop of left-wing student radicalism. They copy the uprising of the 'critique of the critique'. Whether they actually took part in the events hardly matters: their audiences did, and it is their defeat which, in the form of exportable 'Weltschmerz' helps these young cine-talents to worldwide success. However popular such a cinema might be, it doesn't lend itself to an accurate reflection of the state of mind of its public, who consume such films like a drug.[47]

Such ultra-left critiques interpret the 'romantic' tendencies of the New German Cinema as the result of commercial speculation, from a position that rejects the commodity status of culture under capitalism. They are unwilling to concede that this is in fact the very subject of many of the films of Wenders, Herzog or Fassbinder. A case in point might be Fassbinder's use of Fascism in films as

Icy glamour: Hanna Schygulla in Fassbinder's Lili Marleen *(1980)*

. . . and Rosl Zech in Fassbinder's Veronica Voss *(1982)*

different as *Despair*, *The Marriage of Maria Braun* and *Lili Marleen*. The latter project gave rise to accusations of the grossest exploitation on the part of Fassbinder, of trivialising history in order to extract from it a saccharin private melodrama loosely based on the memoirs of a second rate singer, Lale Andersen.

Lili Marleen was not made directly within the subsidy system, except that Fassbinder, for virtually all his films after 1972, was able to collect automatic subsidy. The main source of finance was Luggi Waldleitner, an 'old guard' producer, and his company Roxy-Rialto, with additional Italian interest on account of the male lead, Giancarlo Giannini. Waldleitner, as it happened, owned the rights to the famous song of the title. One way of looking at the film is thus to say that Fassbinder colluded with the process whereby capitalism and the entertainment industry strip history to the skeleton of its use value – that which survives as bankable, which coincides with what is memorable or, in this case, what is hummable.

Was the vulgarity of Nazi nostalgia Fassbinder's price for having had ample production funds in the only currently available valid currency of the international New German Cinema? His film is, however, a film about Fascism only by constructing its narrative around a highly paradoxical but historically authenticated 'montage effect': the fortuitous encounter of a love song and a world war. The wartime popularity of 'Lili Marleen' is what interests Fassbinder, and he is in effect much more concerned with the aggregate states – material and immaterial – of something as ephemeral and apparently trivial as a song, than with either the love story or the paternal melodrama which he and his scriptwriters have built around it.[48] The fact that Waldleitner could acquire a piece of history literally for a song must have seemed to Fassbinder materialism with a vengeance, an ironic rebuttal to Brecht's theory of the 'Messingkauf', which says that an artist's relation to his cultural tradition should be like that of the man who buys a trumpet for its brass value.

Fassbinder's film, where the song is an object to be traded and used, a symbol and a substitute, concentrates on the curious relations that do exist in our culture between show business and power, between entertainment and commerce, between spectacle and warfare. In this sense, and making a very instructive companion piece, *Lili Marleen* is as much about the New German Cinema and the commodity status of culture as *Fitzcarraldo* is about patronage for a despised art in an unsuitable place – the cinema in West Germany.

10:

Conclusion

The Absent Centre

In referring to the 'New German Cinema', the preceding chapters have mostly employed the past tense. But is the patient actually dead? The number of German films at, say, the Berlin Film Festival seems if anything to increase from year to year. Figures from the Film Statistical Yearbook, or those released by the Film Subsidy Board, indicate an annual production of 80 to 100 films, depending on the calculations, and whether, for instance, television films and international co-productions are included. Commercially, too, German films are doing better business nationally and internationally than ever before. Schlöndorff's *Swann in Love* (if counted as a German film), Wolfgang Petersen's *The Boat*, Doris Dörrie's *Men* (*Männer*, 1986), Jean-Jacques Annaud's *The Name of the Rose* (a Franco-German co-production, 1986) and Percy Adlon's *Bagdad Café* (1987) were successes with art cinema audiences and as commercial releases, though most of them hardly exemplify the New German Cinema. Reitz' *Heimat* was a public and a critical triumph for a director who had been making films virtually unnoticed for 25 years. *Heimat* also proved that the German cinema could enter into competition with international television: the series found buyers from several major national television networks. Bernhard Sinkel and Hans Geissendörfer have followed Reitz' lead and directed, respectively, a historical chronicle (*Fathers and Sons*) and a TV soap opera or 'family series' (*Lindenstrasse*).

While Reitz joined the international 'auteurs', Wenders won the Golden Palm at Cannes in 1984 with *Paris, Texas* and the Director's Prize for *Wings of Desire* (1987), while Syberberg's *Parsifal* (1982) did well during the Wagner Centenary Year. Kluge's *The Power of Feeling* (1983) was the director's most successful film since *Strongman Ferdinand* (*Der Starke Ferdinand*, 1976), yet critics were also complaining that he had been 'making the same film for fifteen years'. They found Herzog's *Where the Green Ants Dream* and *Cobra Verde* disappointing, confirming his 'decline' after the lack of box office success for *Fitzcarraldo*. Syberberg's *The Night* (*Die Nacht*, 1985), Sanders-Brahms' *Laputa* (1986) and even von Trotta's *Rosa Luxemburg* (1986) and her *Three Sisters* (1988) aroused much less interest than the directors' previous work, and the feeling became inescapable that the central impulse of a distinctly national cinema had been lost.

What was striking was how many German directors worked abroad on co-productions with other, often non-U.S. film and television industries. Wenders shot *Paris, Texas* in the United States, with French and British co-finance; Herzog made *Green Ants* in Australia, which has seen a revival as a national cinema similar to that in West Germany; Schlöndorff received French film aid for *Swann* in *Love* and did *Death of a Salesman* (*Tod eines Handlungsreisenden*, 1986) for Dustin Hoffman's production company and American Public Broadcast Television; Sanders-Brahms' *The Future of Emily* (*Flügel und Fesseln*, 1985) was mainly shot in France in a co-production with French television; with funds from the Goethe Institute Jutta Brückner made *Ein Blick – und die Liebe bricht aus* (*One Glance and Love Breaks Out*, 1986) in Buenos Aires. Paris was also the unlikely location for parts of *Rita, Ritter* (1984) by Herbert Achternbusch, whose *Blauer Blumen* (1986) was a poetic travel diary of a visit to China. Ulrike Ottinger's most recent film was also shot in China, and Werner Schroeter has made films in the Philippines (*The Smiling Star* or *Der lachende Stern*, 1983), Portugal (*Der Rosenkönig*, 1985) and Argentina (*De l'Argentine*, 1983–85), the latter for French television. The conclusion to be drawn is perhaps that the New German Cinema has dispersed itself to the four corners of the earth and fragmented whatever unity there may have existed during the 1970s.

The image of a centre that can no longer hold inevitably evokes an obvious absence: Fassbinder. His death in 1982 was seen as synonymous with the demise of the New German Cinema. As Wolfram Schütte put it in an obituary:

> The New German Cinema (what remained from Oberhausen and what came after) has many kinds of energy. Alexander Kluge would be its synthesising intelligence, Werner Herzog its athletic will, Wim Wenders its phenomenological power of perception, Werner Schroeter emphatically underscores its emotional side, Herbert Achternbusch is its rebellious stubbornness, and Volker Schlöndorff its craftsman. Rainer Werner Fassbinder, however, would be the heart, the beating, vibrant centre of all these partial impulses, these different aggregate states of its energy . . . He was the pounding heart. Now it has been stopped.[1]

Fassbinder's loss not only for the German Cinema is incalculable, and more historical distance will be needed before the importance of his work can be fully assessed. Within days of his death the inner circle of his collaborators, his entourage and surrogate family sadly fell out with each other.[2] Lawsuits, litigation, court injunctions and libel cases followed in quick succession. A flurry of activity produced a shelf full of biographies, autobiographies, confessions, revelations: mostly from his once close associates and collaborators.[3] *A Man Called Eva* (*Ein Mann wie Eva*, 1984) appeared, starring Eva Mattes as Fassbinder. Among the many bizarre episodes in this marketing of a genius was the attempt by one of his more casual acquaintances to sell copies of a stolen death-mask to visitors at the Venice Festival in 1982.

Decline, dispersal, disintegration: the metaphors abound by which to characterise the death of a movement, the end of a career and the closure of an epoch. But again, such a view would lack all historical perspective, not least because, paradoxically, Fassbinder contributed more to the 'death' of the New German Cinema when he was alive than after his own death. It was his work, the restless exploration of different conditions and possibilities of film-making which, if it did not inaugurate, then at any rate accelerated the changes that have led to the transformations of the New German Cinema into *the* German Cinema, and of the German Cinema into a host of rather heterogeneous forms of film-making, in television and the cinema, at home and abroad.[4]

Fassbinder seems to have been aware of these changes earlier than most of his colleagues, and able to expand his mini-studio to a one-man film industry. His immense productivity helped to build up an infrastructure of technical and artistic skills in several fields very quickly. Working in film and television, but also in the

Fictional biography: Eva Mattes as Fassbinder in Radu Gabrea's A Man Called Eva
(1984)

theatre, his projects were often designed to stretch and extend the technical and organisational possibilities of his team. For WDR he was the first to create a popular television series that seriously engaged with political issues (*Acht Stunden sind kein Tag; Eight Hours are not a Day*, 1972) as well as leading in low budget films with high production values (*The Bitter Tears of Petra von Kant*). He took on subjects which required commercial and international finance, and in his work there is ultimately no opposition between the cultural mode of production and the industrial one: he used the cultural one *as* the industrial one.

Fassbinder had from the start aimed for the fascination that glamour could bring even at a time when the technical means allowed him nothing more than tinsel. This glamour required the existence, if only as a memory, of the international film industry with its typical movie mythology, and the view that the cinema itself is what brings audiences into the cinema. Fassbinder had a make-believe studio system, he had make-believe stars, and he was making make-believe Hollywood films. In his advocacy of a German film industry in the late 1970s, he merely spelled out what he had himself practised since 1968. By the early 1980s he was able to produce wholly uncommercial films such as *In a Year of Thirteen Moons*, politically controversial films such as *The Third Generation* (1979), big budget and fashionable films such as *Lili Marleen*, very private but international art cinema such as *Querelle* (1982), and prestigious national television such as *Berlin Alexanderplatz* (1979/80). Fassbinder's films were often made with 'real money', that is, funds materialising from the dizzyingly complicated profit and loss calculations, the write-off, deferral and refinancing policies, the ceaseless logic of unlimited speculation. When he talked about the fact that films can ultimately only be made by taking risks, he had added 'the capitalist way'.[5] It is in this sense, more than in the genres he revived and imitated, that he finally achieved his ambition to make 'real Hollywood' films.

The End of the *Autorenfilm*?

In January 1983 Günter Rohrbach, Executive Producer at Bavaria Studios, addressed the Federal Association of Film and Television Actors. His title was a calculated provocation: 'The Pernicious Power of Directors'. In it, the former Head of Film Production for the celebrated television channel WDR, and one of the chief promoters of the Television Framework Agreement which put the authors' cinema on its solid financial footing, roundly denounced the tyranny of the film director. Perhaps he did have Fassbinder in mind, with whom he and his director of production, Peter Märthesheimer, had worked many times, both at the WDR and at Bavaria Studios, and last on *Berlin Alexanderplatz*.

The power at the command of directors, once they are established, has practically no equivalent in our society. Although the labour of his team members remains without public recognition, and flows instead wholly towards the director's fame, their loyalty, as a rule, knows no bounds. The director is their leader and a cult figure on whom all eyes rest . . . The team knows of course that their jobs depend on him, that his success can mean work and bread for them in the future. But the emancipatory content of many films today stands in a peculiarly odd relation of tension with the conditions under which they were made.

Directors are also the stars of their films. Insofar as they offer their own person as advertisement and sales point, they oust the actors from a role which traditionally was theirs. Directors give press conferences, appear on television, and let themselves be celebrated at festivals. Many of them have accommodated quite well to this state of affairs. Even Hanna Schygulla in Cannes had to submit to questions about who the woman was at Fassbinder's side.[6]

Rohrbach could not have chosen a more conservative vocabulary to voice his disquiet about the future of the German Cinema. His attack on directors in general, and on cult figures in particular, seemed to revive all the old arguments of the film industry against the *Autorenkino* and selective subsidy. His reasoning, however, attempted to be historical: the *Autorenkino* had fulfilled its mission and purpose, namely to give the German Cinema an artistic reputation. But the star directors could not resolve the dilemma they had themselves helped to bring about: the disappearance of professionals from the industry. Instead of complaining about the lack of competent scriptwriters, and the decline in standards among technicians, editors and art directors, the film-makers, according to Rohrbach, should put their own house in order: they only had themselves to blame. Seeing that real power lay only with directors, and resenting the low status that their craft and skills enjoyed, cameramen and editors were going for directorial assignments themselves.

Rohrbach tried to rewrite the history of the New German Cinema from the film industry's point of view, even though he knew, for instance, that it was only thanks to Fassbinder and one or two other names that the German cinema had been able to break into international markets at all. Furthermore, precisely because the commodity film and the institution cinema have a material as well as an immaterial side, exhibition value will always attach itself to *some* aspect of the cinema – actors, directors, special effects – which will seem excessive when measured by other criteria. But what are the criteria of value? Rohrbach's purpose, however, was less to plead on behalf of technicians or actors than to rehabilitate the producer, the symbol of the commercial film industry. His main arguments were that, given the opportunities for national films on the world market, only experienced producers could successfully exploit the new possibilities of film financing. Secondly, with television itself coming under pressure, its role as patron of the independent sector would have to shrink. Here too, only producers were in a position to protect directors from bureaucratic machinations and the political vagaries of public funding.

What Rohrbach had certainly sensed correctly was a new political toughness about public funding, and also a more widespread discontent:

> We are not against the authors' film, but against the fact that a marginal aspect of the cinema has monopolised the entire spectrum of film-making, and is attempting to immunise this 'new type of cinema' (outside the regulating mechanisms of the market) against all criticism.[7]

This passage is neither from a trade magazine of the old guard, nor a right wing daily paper. It appeared in the three part investigation 'Towards a State Cinema?' already quoted, in *medium*, a scholarly publication on the liberal left. The development seemed to have come full circle, with critics almost taking up the same opposition as after Oberhausen, except that by the 1980s the old right and the young left seemed to have formed an unholy alliance. Two things, however, had changed. Firstly, the author–directors themselves were demanding more overt and transparent power hierarchies. Fassbinder, in an interview given after completing *Despair* with a tax-shelter company and while contemplating making a film in the United States, had the following to say:

> If things get any worse, I'd rather be a streetsweeper in Mexico than a film-maker in Germany. I prefer censorship that is handed to me in black-and-white to the sort of freedom where I'm supplying the censorship myself.[8]

Having produced enough films to acquire, via automatic subsidy, a basic working capital, he could afford a more outspoken rejection of subsidy than most. Secondly, the *Autorenfilm* of 1978 was no longer the *Autorenfilm* of 1963 or even 1968. International success for some directors, the possibilities of American distributors in co-producing German films, and the emergence of many of the *Autoren*'s former production assistants as independent, full-time producers (so-called 'telephone producers', that is, experts of the subsidy system with insider connections to the committees and the television networks and thus basically comparable to American producers setting up the 'package deals') had all prepared the ground once again for a directly commercial approach to film-making.

The Hamburg Declaration, too, only ratified the situation.[9] It marked the end of a development, though not that of state-funding for the cinema, nor that of the involvement of television. Rather, it indicated the point where the New German Cinema began to experience the consequences of its own success and growth, risking the loss of its specifically national development and history, to become a highly diffuse, diversified and fragmented sector of the international television and film industry. The much-vaunted 'pluralism of Hamburg' seemed to signal the dissipation of that moment of self-reflection which had given West Germany a sense of coming to terms not only with its film history, but its history – even if, as we have seen, it was partly rewritten as another film history.

One might conclude from this that, broadly speaking, the surge in film-making in West Germany during the 1970s followed the transfer of power from cinema to television which implied drawing on and absorbing a considerable number of as yet unaffiliated directors, cameramen and related personnel on a freelance basis. With the stabilisation of this labour market by the mid-1980s, the New German Cinema vanished like Cinderella's carriage, leaving, apart from a vast number of individual films hardly ever shown in cinemas either in Germany or abroad, a few internationally known auteurs who might arguably have made a career for themselves even without the film-funding system or elaborate, government-sponsored promotion campaigns. If this is the impression, then it is partly because our account so far has restricted its perspective too narrowly on Germany itself.

The International Situation

The *Autorenfilm* – this was one of the theses of present study – does not name a particular genre of films or range of subjects, but is first of all a political concept. It was intended to create a space for film-making outside that colonised by the international commercial feature film. In the early 1960s the Hollywood product, together with its national variants, seemed to be the enemy. As we saw, while David did not actually slay Goliath at the box office, the New German Cinema was successful in establishing institutional structures – some would say bureaucracies – which substituted for and bypassed the hierarchies of the traditional film industry.

But it seems clear that, apart from the factors discussed in the earlier chapters, the *Autorenfilm* was also aided by a shift in the balance of power between the commercial cinema and its rival, television, which affected not only West Germany but – to look no further – Europe as a whole. If the battlefront that prevailed at the time of Oberhausen had disappeared, it was not the *Autorenkino* that could lay claim to victory, even though its erstwhile enemy, the domestic film industry, seemed to have been swept aside before its very eyes. The forces that finished off the old German cinema were in the process of also swallowing up the *Autorenfilm*, probably without even noticing that they were doing so.

For, over the last decade, the entire picture has changed. None of the old oppositions really holds: not only *Altbranche* and *Jungfilm* have gone, but commerce versus culture, Hollywood versus national cinema, *Autorenkino* versus *Anderes Kino* and even cinema versus television are beginning to be antinomies of the past. In its place we have the so-called 'new media' – video, cable, satellite – which strictly speaking are not new media but, to use the jargon, new delivery systems.[10] Because the club of those who have a stake in owning these systems is possibly even smaller, and by virtue of the enormous investments even more exclusive than the old film industries, their existence and the battles over their control mean that all audio-visual products are affected sooner or later.

So far the signs – in Italy and France for instance – are that the emergence of the media conglomerates clustering around satellite broadcasting and cable television in particular are effectively squeezing out whatever resists or does not fit into the global concept that the old and the new media are building up. They are reducing the diversity of programming on national television and further eroding the admission figures for cinemas. If one takes a longer view of the present situation in Europe one can see that, in the current crisis of the *Autorenfilm*, it is the survival of the cinema itself that is at issue. The *Autorenfilm* is not the only possible or the most precious form of cinema, yet in its German variant it was an extreme, but for its time and on its own terms also very consistent form of film-making, and thus its history can serve as a symptomatic case. This is how it has been discussed here, and not the least of the reasons why the preceding chapters have on the whole refrained from passing value judgements on this or that film or director is the paradigmatic role the New German Cinema occupies within the larger context of cinema history, as distinct from film history.

The Leading Players

What we are witnessing in the 1980s are the takeover battles by which the giants of the print media (newspaper, publishing) are acquiring the audio-visual media on a worldwide scale. The players in this very unevenly matched game are, firstly, international media barons like Robert Maxwell, the Australian Rupert Murdoch, the Canadian Ted Turner and the Italian Silvio Berlusconi, presslords in France, the various backers of Radio Luxemburg, the Bertelsmann Verlag, Axel Springer and Gruner & Jahr in West Germany. They are not only fighting over respective shares in the cable and video business but are busy lobbying governments to amend restrictive legislation and persuading state monopolies like the postal services to grant licences and become themselves suppliers of the necessary informational infrastructure.

Secondly there are the national broadcasting networks and their commercial competitors: in Britain, the BBC and ITV, including Channel Four; in West Germany, the relatively autonomous regional networks, as well as the Second Channel, ZDF. Being producers of feature films either from within their own resources, like the BBC, or by commissioning from independents, as in the case of Channel Four and ZDF, the television networks are in a strong even if precarious position when it comes to supplying the new, deregulated market. WDR, for instance, has built up commercially very extensive relations with Germany's largest studio, the Bavaria Film Atelier in Munich-Geiselgasteig, of which Rohrbach's transfer of post and change of tune were the clearest signs.

Thirdly there are the national and international film distributors. In Britain: Cannon, Rank, and the US Majors; in Germany mostly the US Majors, and small national distributors such as Constantin (Bernd Eichinger), Horst Wendlandt, Filmverlag der Autoren and Laurens Straub's Filmwelt. They compete with one another on two fronts: to supply the cinemas and to get their share of the video market. They may invest in production, because a producer who is not also a distributor loses out on the gross takings of a film. Here, too, the problem is to have a sufficient quantity of product, and to exploit both film and video market skilfully so as not to kill one with the other.

Effective control in the new media is determined by the material supports and access to existing markets, not by the products. Yet access and delivery system together redefine the market for all products including film, for all sites and spaces of consumption, including the cinemas, and in all countries, including those in which *Autorenfilm*, independent, art or avant-garde cinema have a (small) stake in the overall media on offer. The consequences for the cinema are that certain films, usually Hollywood films, are heavily promoted for their start in first-run theatres. But instead of counting on the second-run market, distributors now go straight into the video shops, usually within two or three months of the movie premiere, the haste being partly in order to discourage pirating. Figures suggest that in Germany more than half of the gross income from feature films comes out of video hire.

Finally, in the 1970s United States film and television production became a relatively minor field of diversification for multi-national corporations such as Gulf and Western, the Kinney Corporation or Coca-Cola. Yet however marginal Hollywood might be to the petro-chemical, food, leisure or communication industries, it still dominates the international film industry, and also most of the world's television screens. In film production the 1970s brought another major concentration of capital and resources: fewer films now attract a larger share of the overall investment, and very intensive marketing strategies create no more than a dozen mega-hits annually. These have budgets so vast that they allow the industry to modernise its technology and keep abreast with advanced research (computerisation, sound systems, camera robotics, special effects). The American film industry can thus act in many ways as a production site for developing prototypes, both in terms of manufacturing processes and of types of entertainment spectacles.

Such concentration entails increasing division of labour at the production stage. This is most conspicuous in the preponderance of 'special effects' and in advertising budgets that are, at times, almost as large as net production costs. It has also resulted in a restructuring and reintegration at another level. Not many films are distributed today without a soundtrack available on record or cassette, and a book version in paperback. This fact alone underscores the degree to which the uniqueness of the individual product vanishes in the diversity of its aggregate commodity states, each of which attracts further investment and thus further profit. The record industry, the audio-visual industries of both soft and hardware and the publishing companies form an interdependent system with television, the cinema, advertising and sometimes toy manufacture and fashion design, in which the film and its 'image' are the pretext for productivity, the fuel driving the different subsystems. This myriad of specialised skills and technologies does produce a kind of coherence for the consumer: the commodity film – thanks to its value as entertainment and as a mirror of the spectator's fantasy – glows and scintillates as a total experience of cinema. Such a film retains a ghostly afterimage, as it reverberates and echoes through the media environment in all its incarnations, until it fades or is replaced by a similar, and similarly total, experience.

The economic power and administrative logistics behind the blockbuster's successful synthesis of all the diverse systems which it mobilises and draws upon, are as awesome as they are disturbing. They represent another form of colonisation, of strategic occupation and territorial penetration to which the European film industries and independent film-makers may not be able to respond. For in the reorganisation and redefinition of the market there are a few obvious casualties: the cinemas, for instance, unless they are first-run houses; the so-called non-commercial or 16mm market (affecting students and teachers of film); and, most importantly, the independent feature film, such as the *Autorenfilm*, which has rarely made it into the first-run theatres and thus is unlikely to make it into the video market either. Exceptions are the few films distributed by US Majors (one-offs by Wenders, Fassbinder, Herzog, Schlöndorff, Wolfgang Petersen, Margarethe von Trotta and recently Doris Dörrie).

316

Success of the 1980s: Doris Dörrie's Men *(1986)*

The New German Cinema: An Invention of the Social–Liberal Coalition?

What makes the situation complicated for the film-makers is that the players are often very unevenly matched. Some, like the media empires, always play offensively. Some, like the national broadcasting networks, are usually forced on the defensive, especially at times when they do not have a politically sympathetic government to back them up as in Britain, where the Conservative Party practically declared war on the BBC in the mid 1980s. Italy's coalition governments are too divided, and much too involved in playing political games with and via the media, to implement any kind of restraints. In West Germany the Kohl administration is also busy dismantling the media policy which the Social Democrat/Liberal coalition had built up in the way of defences or at least compensatory mechanisms over the years. Throughout Europe deregulation seems to be the order of the day, partly because the national governments themselves are already in defensive positions *vis-à-vis* their own private enterprise companies.

It is thus possible to see that the kind of protection which the *Autorenfilm* received during the late 1960s and throughout the 1970s was prescient in two ways. It subsidised a 'national' film culture, but it also created media structures that may be able to withstand the onslaught of the new media more effectively, provided they can combine a political response with an economically practicable programming concept. Politically the New German Cinema was the result of

317

lobbyists like Kluge finding sympathetic ears among Social Democrat and Liberal parliamentarians, who in turn exerted pressure on the policies of rewarding national prestige projects including the cinema, along with museums, music festivals, theatre events and sports. Practically, the New German Cinema was financed by television, making films that could also pass as cinema in the specialised markets and at national and international festivals, where a television film could be upgraded to become part of the international art cinema, if critics, journalists, prize-giving juries, distributors or a television buyer from abroad liked it.

The dual strategy corresponded to a division of the *Autorenfilm*, between its creation of a national cinema (which as we saw could range from re-staging national history to the self-representation of special groups such as women or gay sub-cultures) and its support of alternative forms of cinema altogether (non-narrative films, documentary, opera and music drama, dance theatre or film essays). In neither case does 'self-expression' or the notion of the 'artist' in the romantic sense need to play a significant part other than as an ideologically useful bargaining counter. The 'artist' gave the work a cultural cachet within a specific political situation – such as prevailed in West Germany – where film had to bid with (and initially against) the rest of the arts for a share of the overall cultural budget that the State hands out annually. In Britain, by contrast, to describe cinema as 'art' or even 'culture' would give it a bad name, which makes the terms 'independent' or 'freelance' the preferred currency when appealing to State sponsorship or television funding. To that extent the *Autor* was not only a public institution but a strategic fiction, yet one which, although it created its own problems for film-makers, had in the German context a peculiar potency and effectivity.

With this concept if not the term, West Germany was, for most of the 1970s, ahead of the rest of Europe. By the time of the third revision of the Film Subsidy Law in 1974 its subsidy system had been quite finely tuned, combining federal and regional funding, automatic subsidy and project subsidy with Kuratorium money, television co-production agreement and Berlin-Effekt. It gave a boost at all levels, and for a huge variety of film forms and modes, from the medium-to-big budget prestige film like Fassbinder's *The Marriage of Maria Braun* or Schlöndorff's *The Tin Drum*, to avant-garde and experimental films by Schroeter, Achternbusch, Farocki, Sander and Ottinger. This also indicates the historicity of the idea and why, in the 1980s, the term was being dropped and the strategy rethought.

But by the mid-1980s it seemed as if the Germans had to say of themselves 'we blew it'. While France and Britain had learnt from the German experience and began to be more successful in keeping a stake for their product in the national market as well as breaking into the international market, the German cinema, despite its advantages, was apparently unable to build on its real if brief breakthrough during the 1970s. There was no shortage of reasons: had the basis for a full-scale recovery always been too small? Was it the change in government policy? Had the Americans killed some of the geese that laid the golden eggs – Wenders, Herzog and Schlöndorff? Was it Fassbinder's drug overdose? Had distributors not promoted German films, but merely chased international box office hits which do not require a risky outlay when launched on the German market? Was it the telephone producers, who simply milked the subsidy system? Had film critics and journalists been too short-sighted, provincial and masochistic to mount a decent public relations job, not just for this or that film or director,

318

but for a broadly conceived production policy? Was it the film-makers, who had stayed on the defensive, too much concerned with becoming auteurs – with Truffaut, Fellini, Scorsese or Coppola as their models – or hankering after support from the international avant-garde, regardless of the changing conditions, and without fully grasping what was happening in the domestic media situation? Was it the public – in the sense that the generation that had supported the independent *Autorenfilm* during the 1970s had dropped out as an active cinema public, because they had become too old, too busy or too lazy to bother to go to the cinema? Was it the cinemas that had turned into multiplexes showing films in a semi-pornographic environment with bad projection, bad sound and bad service? Or was it the films, not inventive enough, nor exciting enough, nor intelligent enough to interest either a national or an international audience once the novelty had worn off? Whatever the reason, or combination of reasons, instead of celebrating the New German Cinema's twenty-fifth anniversary since Oberhausen, journalists at the 1987 Berlin Film Festival behaved more as if they were attending a wake.[11]

A Missed Opportunity or a Strategic Retreat?

Some of the complaints echoed those made by Rohrbach, namely that in all the years and despite hundreds of films the German cinema still lacked an adequate industrial and technical infrastructure. Others were similar to the ones raised during the years of the Young German Film, such as that funding had created too many first-time film-makers and one-off films, forever making amateurish home movies pass off as authenticity and inspiration.

The criticisms of the industry-oriented faction came down to three: not only did the German cinema lack professionals, the films were, by international standards, often too cheaply made to employ properly trained technicians. Secondly, the German cinema lacked scriptwriters of experience, and therefore neglected narrative; it lacked a feel for dialogue and therefore for character, it had no sense of situation and therefore lacked drama. Consequently, despite a manifest demand on the part of the public for entertainment films with German stars and German settings, the independent cinema was unable to supply them. They had developed no genres of its own, nor credible reworkings of others, and instead taken refuge in exoticisms, camp and kitsch fantasies and lurid evocations of extreme states of mind. Thirdly, German films lacked popular support, not least because they were completely identified with the generation of 1968, currently very much out of favour with those under 30.

A new generation of audiences – and film-makers – now look at these films and find them boring, pretentious and vacuous. Fashion and the generation gap seems to have overtaken the directors faster than they could accumulate expertise and attain maturity in a practice as demanding and specialised as the film business. To these one might add that the subsidy system had made German directors too obsessed with film policy. There was no aesthetic concept, other than a home-made kit of ideas borrowed from *Cahiers du Cinéma* cinephilia of over 30 years ago or from the other arts. Even the political programme of the *Autorenfilm* had collapsed, not just among the doubters but among its most fervent advocates and ideologues.

Bestandsaufnahme: Utopie Film, once the pretty illustrations and amusing anecdotes are discounted, could be seen as Kluge's declaration of defeat. Elegantly and dazzlingly as ever he had accomplished a turnaround, making it seem as if

319

his position had remained the same by calling the *Autorenfilm* now *Zuschauerfilm*. His notion of the associational fit of a title, for instance, could have been borrowed from Paul Schrader, who told an interviewer how he had been fascinated by the associations between 'American' and 'Gigolo', and that once the title had come to him the story wrote itself. And Kluge's idea of the four-line plot is strikingly similar to Steven Spielberg's conviction that a good story is 'something you can weigh in the palm of your hand'.[12]

In defence of the German Cinema of the 1970s one might argue that France, once it had adopted much the same funding system as West Germany, could build on the advantage of a relatively healthy national film culture. It still functions both in Paris and in the provinces to get spectators into the cinemas – that is, outside the very narrow band of 15 to 25-year-olds who, because France has a quota system, are brought up on French films as well as American ones. In Britain, too, even though all governmental aid such as the Eady levy and tax concessions has been removed, Channel Four's commissioning policy and the BFI Production Board, both modelled on the German example, are beginning to maximise the advantages British productions have: better access to the inter-national television market and thus to the new art cinema than many of their European competitors. Thanks to its leading role in the pop music field, Britain is also well placed in the entertainment sector, while for serious drama the prejudice in favour of 'British English' is an additional asset in the United States, where the monarchy, the Empire and stories about the British Establishment seem to possess a perennial appeal.

The German cinema has none of these cultural advantages and no serious hopes of breaking into anything other than the prestige market of the art cinemas, as its domestic 'commercial' successes underline. For the directors of the 1980s are not Werner Herzog or Wim Wenders, but names like Peter F. Bringmann and Carl Schenkel, Dominik Graf and Peter Keglevic, Hartmann Schmige, Stefan Lukschy and Christian Rateuke. The stars are not Hanna Schygulla or Bruno Ganz, but rock singer Marius Müller-Westernhagen, TV comics Didi Hallervorden and Gerhard Polt, stand-up comedian Otto and Jean-Paul Belmondo, ever-popular comic adventurer. His *The Ace of Aces*, a co-production made with Bavarian subsidy funds, was one of the biggest successes of the 1984/85 season. These directors and actors specialise in chase films, in suspense thrillers and humour – their models are William Friedkin, American cop series, the French comedian Louis de Funès and Marty Feldman – precisely the genres and stereotypes the New German Cinema had avoided like the plague. Peter F. Bringmann's *Theo Against the Rest of the World* (*Theo gegen den Rest der Welt*, 1980 – a Belmondo-type chase and adventure comedy with Marius Müller-Westernhagen in the lead) broke all records in 1981, and the two seem set to make more films in the same vein (*The Snowman* (*Der Schneemann*, 1985), for example). Even more popular is Otto, who plays an East Frisian simpleton and whose first film was the most commercially lucrative German production for 30 years.

From Experience to Event

Perhaps the New German Cinema did not 'blow it' after all. If the mass audience preferred German versions of *The French Connection*, or *Kojak*, or Marty Feldman or Louis de Funès, they might be better off with the real thing, and

The new Belmondo: Marius Müller-Westernhagen in Peter F. Bringmann's Theo
Against the Rest of the World *(1980)*

American distributors could be left to run the show, or French directors and co-producers to collect the automatic subsidies for *The Ace of Aces* or *The Name of the Rose*. Many of the complaints against the New German Cinema, even where true, seem misplaced if they implicitly assume the vantage point of an ideal (the home-made mass entertainment film) which is either unattainable or undesirable in practice and as a norm historically about to become obsolete. The developments in the 'new media' as predicted by pundits will rapidly lead to a concentration of the cinemas on highly professional, expensively made (and therefore American) blockbusters and prototypes, with national film industries in Europe supplying medium-to-low-cost broadcast and canned television entertainment.

By 1982 European film-makers were already up in arms over a suggestion that the European Community was thinking of prosecuting member states and forcing them to abandon their respective film subsidy schemes. French, Italian, German and even Greek directors felt that it could not conceivably be in the interest of a united Europe to destroy nationally specific cultural or cinematic traditions by the stroke of a bureaucrat's pen in favour of more harmonisation. 'Every film must declare its nationality and its own cultural identity' pronounced Bertrand Tavernier, who condemned the multi-national cinema of co-productions and poured scorn on the prospect of 'Sophia Loren playing a Berlin housewife, and Catherine Deneuve a Sicilian peasant'. The Eurofilm of the future could join the Golden Delicious Euro-apple: tasteless and bland.[13]

Thus the New German Cinema, behind the times and out of favour with its

321

critics in respect of one kind of product, may actually be ahead in another, perhaps more modest, but crucial area. For as the present study has tried to show, the German cinema, out of its two decades of experiment with film forms and collaboration with television, has acquired expertise in two 'alternative' uses of the cinema, both of which are capable of further developments. Firstly, to combine film *and* television for what one might call, perhaps too pompously, nationally specific but internationally recognisable media events, such as Syberberg's *Hitler* film, Reitz' *Heimat* or Fassbinder's *Berlin Alexanderplatz*. This would be in order to respond in the independent or cultural sector to what in the commercial field is the Hollywood superhit launched in the cinema, but making its money in other aggregate states.

Hence the argument that the *Autorenfilm*, in its typically German form as a 'cinema of experience', is not a certain kind of product as much as it is a certain idea of cinema – and not only an idea of cinema, but of the cinema as both a physical space *and* a discourse. If during the 1970s such films on the whole involved small, politically or socially motivated groups of spectators, the media events mentioned above indicate how these spaces can, thanks to television, become larger occasions. Here the critical reflexivity implied in encountering 'otherness' can combine with that other experience of self – the history/ memory/film history experience – without foregoing what was so crucial about 'going to the movies', the spontaneous creation of a community. Television is finding its own ways of doing this, even though spectators are now sharing the same (blocks of) time rather than a public space with a large number of others.

Secondly, the German cinema has proved itself very inventive in 'minor' formats and hybrid forms. The reason for its eclecticism and its borrowings from so many different cultural models – from pre-cinematic spectacles like the magic lantern to opera, melodrama and the *Gesamtkunstwerk*, from film essay to film tableau, from chronicle to allegorical mystery play, from documentary to requiem, from dramatic monologue to schizo-dialogue – lies in the desire to preserve the cinema as the site of self-alienating experiences, in contrast to television's essentially self-confirming and self-validating function. In this respect, film-makers are inheriting the legacy of a wide cultural field, from literature to protest action, from history to case study. This requires non-narrative as well as narrative forms, a cinema of gestures and faces as much as a cinema of spectacle, and a cinema of the white page and *temps morts* as well as a cinema of *temps forts* and action.

Without constituting a counter-cinema, Fassbinder, Wenders, Schroeter, Herzog, Achternbusch, Ottinger, Sander and Sanders-Brahms, Brückner and von Trotta, Syberberg and Fleischmann, Straub and Farocki and Kluge and Reitz have responded in very different ways to the pressure of (cinema-)history, but they are all aware of the extent to which their works are 'windows' – not on to the world, but on an already programmed screen. Today, films can be made neither just for the cinema nor just for television, but *with* both and *against* both. In a situation where independent film-making's best chance might be to anticipate, test and initiate the types of programming public television will need to compete with and contrast with satellite TV, their films are as much pilots and models of a cinema of the future as the high-tech prototypes out of Hollywood.

Looking back on the 1970s one can perhaps comprehend the extraordinary diversity of the German cinema as the consequence of a vast transcription process. It was an attempt to gather, record and report the images, sounds and stories – including those that the cinema itself produced – which make up the memory of a generation, a nation and a culture, and to translate them, from their many perishable supports in people's minds to the one medium that, after all, promises paradoxically to be the most permanent: the cinema. Literature, popular culture, architecture, fashion, memorabilia and the contents of junk shops have all been enlisted in a vast effort to preserve the traces of lives lived for oblivion. This hastily accumulated visual wealth has not yet been tapped or even properly inspected for its meanings or uses. As a source of understanding the changes from a culture living mainly by the written text to one dominated by the image, the New German Cinema still awaits to be discovered.

Jack Palance in Percy Adlon's Bagdad Café *(1987)*

One can already argue that the period between 1960 and 1985 may well come to signify a quite distinct era in European film history: that of a reprieve, as the cinema handed over to television and was in turn handed over to the 'new media'. In spite of their manifest ideological and formal differences, the various 'Young', 'Other' and 'New' German Cinemas have in common with the *nouvelle vague*, the counter cinemas and independent/avant-garde cinemas of France, Italy and Britain certain historical limit conditions. These are, to some extent, external to the films and the film-makers since the two decades in question saw television take over from the cinema not only its adult mass audiences, but also most of the ideological functions previously shared by cinema, radio and the press: the production and circulation of socially agreed versions of reality. Thus, the cinema has in every case become less and less representative, less and less a 'national cinema' in the sense traditionally conceived. By contrast, few corners of any nation have been allowed to remain hidden from television's own peculiar gaze, which is dramatising, probing, documenting, telling and retelling, and thus constructing spectators and reconstructing their history in its own image, intended as one in which everyone can recognise themselves.

In so far as the beginning of the New German Cinema coincided with the failure of the commercial European film industries to protect their domestic markets from the dominance of Hollywood, and ended with most forms of both commercial and independent film-making agreeing terms with their respective national television networks, the different movements, groups and film forms perhaps only existed while the larger shifts in the technological and ideological environment of the mass media took place, as national cinemas 'lost out' to Hollywood, and the cinema itself 'lost out' to television, and television is 'losing out' to digitalised information. But although many who love the cinema will regret this transformation and transcription, who can say with certainty what is loss and what is gain in a world of signs, images and electronic signals?

Notes and References

Introduction

1. Andrew Sarris, 'The Germans are Coming, the Germans are Coming', *Village Voice*, 27 October 1975.
2. John Sandford, *The New German Cinema* (London: Oswald Wolff, 1980); James Franklin, *New German Cinema: From Oberhausen to Hamburg* (Boston: Twayne, 1983).
3. Klaus Phillips (ed.), *New German Filmmakers: From Oberhausen Through the 1970s* (New York: Ungar, 1984).
4. Eric Rentschler, *West German Film in the Course of Time* (Bedford Hills, New York: Redgrave, 1984).
5. Timothy Corrigan, *New German Film: The Displaced Image* (Austin: University of Texas, 1983).
6. Hans Günther Pflaum and Hans Helmut Prinzler, *Cinema in the Federal Republic of Germany* (Bonn: Inter Nationes, 1983).
7. The terms come from David Riesman's *The Lonely Crowd* (New York: Doubleday/Anchor, 1953) and figure, for instance, in the Hamburg Declaration in 1979: 'We shall not allow ourselves to be other-directed.'

1 Film Industry – Film Subsidy

1. See Charles Eidsvik, 'Behind the Crest of the Wave: An Overview of the New German Cinema', *Literature/Film Quarterly*, vol. 7, no. 3, 1979, pp. 167–181.
2. See Kristin Thompson, *Exporting Entertainment* (London: British Film Institute, 1986).
3. Quoted in Thomas H. Guback, *The International Film Industry* (Bloomington: University of Indiana Press, 1969) p. 125.
4. Guback, p. 134.
5. See Klaus Kreimeier, *Kino und Filmindustrie in der BRD* (Kronberg: Scriptor, 1973) p. 179.
6. Guback, p. 135.
7. Quoted in Kreimeier, p. 31.
8. Quoted in Ute Schmidt and Tilman Fichter, *Der erzwungene Kapitalismus* (Berlin: Klaus Wagenbach, 1971) p. 72.
9. Eberhard Kranz, *Filmkunst in der Agonie* (Berlin, GDR: Henschel Verlag, 1964) p. 84.
10. Guback, p. 134.
11. Henry P. Pilgert, as quoted in Peter Pleyer, *Deutscher-Nachkriegsfilm 1946–1948* (Münster: Verlag C.J. Fahle, 1965) p. 29.
12. Pleyer, p. 30.

13. Wim Wenders, 'Verachten, was verkauft wird', *Süddeutsche Zeitung*, 16 December 1969.
14. 'Directors now try to benefit individually from their international reputation and their success with foreign audiences. The result is surprising: thanks to international distributors, the German public can now – sometimes – get to see German films. To give an example: the four most popular German films of 1979 were distributed by United Artists, Fox, and CIC.' Werner Burzlaff, 'Cinema = Argent × Film', *Cahiers de la Cinémathèque*, no. 32, Spring 1981, p. 140.
15. See Dieter Prokop, *Soziologie des Films* (Luchterhand: Neuwied, 1974) p. 158.
16. For annual figures about the German film industry, see *Filmstatistisches Jahrbuch* and *Filmstatistisches Taschenbuch* (Wiesbaden: Spitzenorganisation der Filmwirtschaft, 1952/53ff and 1963ff). The relative insignificance of the West German film industry within the national economy can also be seen by the following figures: in 1970 only 0.1 per cent of the labour force was active in the film industry, and accounted for less than 0.1 per cent of taxable income. These figures include services in television. Quoted in Burckhard Dreher, *Filmförderung in der Bundesrepublik* (Berlin: Deutsches Institut für Wirtschaftsforschung, Sonderheft III, 1976) pp. 49–50.
17. Barbara Bronnen and Corinna Brocher, *Die Filmemacher* (Munich: C. Bertelsmann, 1973) p. 83.
18. Burzlaff, p. 141.
19. Quoted in Guback, p. 137.
20. 'Periods where the State did not intervene in the area of film do not exist in the Federal Republic. Already at the time of its founding, measures were taken in aid of the film industry. The nearest to a "free market" situation would be the years 1956 to 1964. This period is sandwiched between two massively interventionist phases: from 1950 to 1955 the federal authorities subsidised film production in the form of guaranteed credits, and since 1965 first the Kuratorium Junger Deutscher Film, then from 1967 onwards the Film Subsidy Bill intervened in aid of production. The film industry furthermore gets preferential VAT classification, and since the end of the 1960s has enjoyed further tax concessions . . . The period where state intervention was weakest shows a quite considerable falling off of performance and productivity in the film industry.' Dreher, p. 64.
21. Quoted in Kreimeier, p. 190.
22. For a detailed account of the *Ausfallbürgschaften*, see Dreher, pp. 71–4. Dreher also points out that the situation had changed very little by the 1970s: 'The limited possibilities of spreading the financial risks inherent in film production is due to the fact that German production consists of small enterprise units. In 1972, the annual average output per firm amounted to 1½ feature films.' Dreher, p. 60.
23. Atze Brauner, *Mich gibt's nur einmal, Rückblende eines Lebens* (Berlin: Herbig, 1976) p. 141.
24. See Reinhold E. Thiel, 'Was wurde aus Goebbels' UFA?', in *Film aktuell*, February 1970.
25. Ulrich Kurowski (ed.), . . . *nicht mehr fliehen: Kino in der Ära Adenauer* (Munich: Filmmuseum, 1979) p. 12.
26. See Kreimeier, p. 196.
27. See Pflaum and Prinzler, *Cinema in the Federal Republic of Germany* (Bonn: Inter Nationes, 1983) p. 5 (translation amended).
28. For an assessment of the work of the Kuratorium, see *Kino*, no. 13, 1983–4, pp. 2–36.
29. For a full account of the Film Subsidy Bill, see Pflaum and Prinzler, pp. 98–101.
30. For a list, see Michael Dost, Florian Hopf and Alexander Kluge, *Filmwirtschaft in der BRD und Europa* (Munich: Hanser, 1973) pp. 152–62.

31. Dost *et al.*, p. 168.
32. Bronnen and Brocher, p. 136.
33. Kreimeier, p. 78.
34. See Chris Marker's highly critical but searching article 'Adieu au cinéma allemand?' in *Positif*, no. 12, 1954.
35. Bronnen and Brocher, pp. 136–7.
36. Bronnen and Brocher, p. 152.
37. See Dieter Prokop (ed.), *Materialien zur Theorie des Films* (Munich: Hanser, 1971) pp. 339–82.
38. Dost *et al.*, p. 56.
39. See Helmuth H. Diederichs, 'Filmverlag der Autoren', *epd-Film*, September 1985, pp. 22–6.
40. See Klaus Eder and Alexander Kluge, *Ulmer Dramaturgien: Reibungsverluste* (Munich: Hanser, 1980) p. 31.
41. For an account of the *Kommunale Kinos*, see Hans Helmut Prinzler and Walter Seidler, *Kinobuch 74/75* (Berlin: Deutsche Kinemathek, 1975).
42. *SPD Filmpolitische Leitsätze*, quoted in A. Mayer, 'Auf dem Weg zum Staatsfilm?', *medium*, December 1977, p. 16.
43. Dreher, *Filmförderung in der Bundesrepublick*, p. 45.
44. For a complete reprint of the 1979 version of the Film Subsidy Bill and accounts of the different kinds of funding, see Gisela Hundertmark and Louis Saul (eds.), *Förderung Essen Filme Auf* (Munich: Verlag Ölschläger, 1984).
45. 'It seems to me that, via culturally oriented film subsidy, we are becoming more successful with our top productions in reaching the kind of international level which a nation achieves when it is able to play its part in world culture through its own unique national character. Film thus contributes with its national culture to world culture.' Gerhard Baum, Minister of the Interior, *Kulturelle Filmförderung* (Bonn: Bundesministerium des Inneren, June 1978) p. 11.
46. T.W. Adorno and M. Horkheimer, *Dialectic of Enlightenment* (New York: Herder and Herder, 1972) p. 132.
47. For a striking example of musical terms applied to film-making, see Hans Jürgen Syberberg: 'When I called my Ludwig-film a requiem, it was not to name a mood or an epitaph for a king. I was thinking of a closed, strict system, a stylistic or aesthetic programme analogous to the universal laws of music.' *Syberbergs Filmbuch* (Frankfurt: Fischer, 1979) p. 11.
48. In 1976 the total amount spent by the 11 Federal states on subsidising film culture was in the region of 10 million DM. During the same period they spent 616 million DM on theatres, 253 million DM on historic sites and monuments, 213 million DM on adult education, 163 million DM on museums, 109 million DM on public libraries and 59 million DM on orchestras. See S. Dörrfeldt, 'Das Missverhältnis der Kulturausgaben zum Film' in *Filmförderung in der Bundesrepublik: Ende oder Neubeginn?* (Mannheim: Internationale Filmwoche, 1977) p. 13.
49. Reinhardt Hauff in *Die Filmemacher*, p. 193.
50. Horst von Hartlieb, 'Es muss eine neue Grundentscheidung getroffen werden', in *Filmförderung*, 1977, p. 5.
51. 'Films like *Cross of Iron* [produced by Wolf Hartwig and directed by Sam Peckinpah] are proof that a German film can be a commercial success on the world market.' (Wolf C. Hartwig, 'Handeln- oder es gibt keine deutsche Filmproduktion mehr', *Filmecho/Filmwoche* no. 1, January 1977, p. 13).
52. Hanno Jochimsen, 'Film ins Grundgesetz', *Berlinale Tip*, no. 10/1982, p. 7.
53. Resolution of the 139th session of the Bundestag, 1968. Quoted in Mischa Gallé, 'Zur Frage der Weiterarbeit' in Norbert Kückelmann (ed.), *Kuratorium Junger*

Deutscher Film – Die ersten drei Jahre (Munich: Kuratorium, 1968).

54. 'Subsidy measures, being largely tax concessions for producers as well as distributors, mainly benefitted foreign companies. In 1971 almost one third (20 million DM) went to foreign firms.' Dreher, *Filmförderung in der Bundesrepublik*, p. 178.

55. For an account of film prizes, see Pflaum and Prinzler, *Cinema in the Federal Republic of Germany*, pp. 109–112.

56. 'There is an indirect form of subsidy from the German Foreign Office. In 1977, as an experiment, the Goethe Institute through the services of Inter Nationes, a semi-official agency in Bonn, began to purchase and distribute packages of film from the Filmverlag der Autoren, Cine International and other alternative distributors. The prints would be subtitled free-of-charge and distributed through the Goethe Institute branches, often with the film-maker present for discussion.' Ron Holloway, *Kino*, October 1979, p. 11.

57. Dost *et al.*, p. 56.

58. For a hostile, pro-industry assessment, see Holloway: 'The subsidized film system in West Germany . . . allowed Autoren of every hue to get a strangle-hold on their own productions. Since money-without-risk was there for the asking, a clever (not necessarily competent or talented) director could double his salary by writing, producing, and even (in some cases) acting in his own films. Once the "project" was completed, there was no more cash to be pocketed save to get busy on the next script.' *Kino*, October 1979, p. 8.

59. A fuller account of the various forms of grant aid can be found in my 'German Film Bonanza', *New Statesman*, 8 January 1980.

60. 'Within the EEC, and calculating for the year 1971, Germany is second, after Italy, in terms of the gross volume of its film subsidies.' Dreher, p. 177.

61. Alexander Kluge (ed.), *Bestandsaufnahme: Utopie Film* (Frankfurt: Zweitausendeins, 1983) p. 76.

62. Peter W. Jansen, *The New German Film* (Munich: Goethe Institute, 1982) p. 3.

63. Werner Herzog in *Die Filmemacher*, p. 21.

64. Jansen, p. 3.

65. For a very useful account of German television, see Richard Collins and Vincent Porter, *WDR and the Arbeiterfilm* (London: British Film Institute, 1981).

66. See Sheila Johnston, 'Fassbinder and New German Cinema', *New German Critique*, nos. 24–25, Fall/Winter 1981-2, p. 67.

67. Collins and Porter, pp. 25–39.

68. Sheila Johnston and John Ellis, 'The Radical Film Funding of ZDF', *Screen*, vol. 23, no. 1, May/June 1982, pp. 60–73.

69. See John Fiske and John Hartley, *Reading Television* (London: Methuen, 1978) esp. Chapter 6, and John Ellis, *Visible Fictions* (London: Routledge & Kegan Paul, 1982).

70. 'Die Hamburger Erklärung' in Willi Bär and Hans Jürgen Weber (eds.), *Fischer Film Almanach* (Hamburg: Fischer Taschenbuch, 1980).

2 The Old, the Young and the New: Commerce, Art Cinema and *Autorenfilm*?

1. 'In 1970, West Germany had 40% of the home market, while the United States commanded 30%. In 1976, the German share was reduced to 10%, and the United States had more than 40%.' Ron Holloway, *Kino*, October 1979, p. 8.

2. Michael Gotthelf, 'Dem Deutschen Film auf die Beine helfen', *Frankfurter Allgemeine Zeitung*, 26 September 1981. At the Berlin Film Festival in 1982, Alexander Kluge contested the accuracy of the SPIO figures.

3. 'In Germany, statistics are very exact because the FFA and television are public institutions, and therefore accountable. The biggest German box office success of 1978 was *Moritz Lieber Moritz* by Hark Bohm, with 460,000 spectators. This compares with 4.2 million spectators for *Saturday Night Fever* and 4.45 million for *Star Wars*.' Werner Burzlaff, 'Cinema = Argent × Film', *Cahiers de la Cinémathèque*, no. 32, Spring 1981, p. 141.
4. Pflaum and Prinzler, *Cinema in the Federal Republic of Germany*, p. 87.
5. Gunhild Freese, 'Die Leinwand lebt', *Die Zeit*, 10 October 1975.
6. Eckart Schmidt, in *Deutsche Zeitung*, 2 September 1977.
7. Two 1977 editorials from *Film-Echo*, the official film industry trade journal, convey the general tone and level of the debate:
'The would-be heroes of the new German cinema before and behind the cameras should first of all learn what culture actually means, before they start talking or writing about film-culture . . . The "cultural" side of the Film Subsidy, which has long since become a cover for film-makers to live off the generous salaries they allocate themselves in their budgets, must be sacrificed to the realities of the economic situation in the film industry . . . Imagine, had the funds of the Film Subsidy Board, the Ministry of the Interior and the other regional bodies, instead of pouring into the productions of these inmates of homes for the blind, been paid into a bank, and could now be used by the film industry which identifies with the wishes of the public . . . our cinemas would be out of trouble.' Quoted in Wim Wenders, 'Jetzt fällt die Entscheidung', *Münchner Abendzeitung*, 30 August 1977, p. 12.
8. Olga Grüber, 'Armer Deutscher Film', *Transatlantik*, January 1981, p. 66.
9. Werner Herzog in *Die Filmemacher*, p. 21.
10. See Peter Jansen, *The New German Film* (Munich: Goethe Institute, 1982) p. 3.
11. 'In this field, neither a professional nor a trade union structure nor an organized market is in existence. German films are practically always the result of personal initiative, and the label "authors' cinema" also, in this case, points to the material conditions of film-making.' Burzlaff, p. 139.
12. See Steve Neale, 'Art Cinema as Institution', *Screen*, vol. 22 no. 1, Spring 1981, pp. 11–29.
13. Directors whose films are based on continuity systems other than narrative ones, or who, like Werner Schroeter, use forms of narrativity derived from music and opera, had a much more difficult stand with subsidy commissions and funding authorities. See Wolfram Schütte *et al.*, *Werner Schroeter* (Munich: Hanser, 1983).
14. For the concept of a 'mode of production', see David Bordwell, Janet Staiger and Kristin Thompson, *The Classical Hollywood Cinema – Film Style and Mode of Production* (London: Routledge & Kegan Paul, 1985).
15. Pam Cook, 'The point of self-expression in avant-garde film' in J. Caughie (ed.), *Theories of Authorship* (London: Routledge & Kegan Paul, 1981) p. 272.
16. Werner Herzog in *Die Filmemacher*, pp. 18, 20.
17. Quoted in Sheila Johnston, 'Fassbinder and New German Cinema', unpublished PhD thesis, London University 1979.
18. Quoted in Peter Buchka, 'Wir leben in einem toten Land', *Süddeutsche Zeitung*, 21–22 August 1977.
19. See Alexander Kluge, 'Förderung – die modernste Form der Zensur', *Das Parlament*, 6 October, 1979.
20. When the industry lobby suggested that in order to curb over-production the Subsidy Board should raise both the qualifying threshold and the percentage share that a producer had to invest before becoming eligible for subsidy, and thus make the club of film-makers more exclusive, Kluge wrote: 'More happiness for fewer people by controlling the birth-rate. By analogy, the free-for-all which the

New German Cinema creates by radically opening access to the profession is countered by saying that via the subsidy committees fewer but more highly qualified film-makers should be supported. Clear the woods of the non-talents . . . But the so-called top talents could not arise without the broadly based, overall developments.' Alexander Kluge (ed.), *Bestandsaufnahme: Utopie Film* (Frankfurt: Zweitausendeins, 1983) pp. 171–2.

21. Alfred Andersch, 'Das Kino der Autoren' in *Merkur*, no. 158, 1961.
22. Edgar Reitz in *Die Filmemacher*, p. 110.
23. The term itself was not new in West Germany. In 1950 Wolf-Dietrich Schnurre had recommended 'for the rescue of German cinema' that 'the author . . . must be reporter, poet, photographer, director and cameraman all in one'. Quoted by Leonhard H. Gmür, 'Zur Chronik', *Der Junge Deutsche Film* (Munich: Constantin Verleih, 1967) n.p.
24. See Sheila Johnston, 'The Author as Public Institution', *Screen Education*, nos. 32–33, Autumn/Winter 1979–80, pp. 67–78.
25. Eric Rentschler, *West German Film in the Course of Time* (Bedford Hills, New York: Redgrave, 1984) p. 40.
26. For background to the concept inside and outside Germany, see also Johnston, pp. 70–4.
27. For an application of the term to European art directors, see J. Gelmis, *The Film Director as Superstar* (New York: Doubleday, 1971).
28. Johnston, p. 71.
29. Quoted in Johnston, p. 68.
30. See Wilfried Berghahn, 'Kino der Autoren – Kino der Produzenten', *Die Zeit*, 27 April 1962.
31. Olga Grüber, 'Armer Deutscher Film', *Transatlantik*, January 1981, p. 71.
32. In Germany a tradition of the authors' cinema, in the sense of literary authors 'writing' for the cinema, goes back to 1913 and Hans Heinz Ewers' promotion of the film author, as the cinema began to attract a middle-class audience: 'Today I know that it is as difficult, that it takes as much art to write a good film-script as it does to write a poem, a novel or a play.' Hanns Heinz Ewers, 'Der Film und ich', in Anton Kaes (ed.), *Kino-Debatte* (Tübingen: Max Niemeyer, 1978) pp. 103–4.
33. *Bertolt Brechts Dreigroschenbuch*, vol. I (Frankfurt: Suhrkamp, 1978) pp. 171–2. See also Wolfgang Gersch, *Film bei Brecht* (Berlin, GDR: Henschel Verlag, 1975) pp. 75–100.
34. Quoted in Johnston, p. 69.
35. Johnston, p. 69.
36. See for instance, Arnold Hauser, *The Social History of Art* (London: Routledge, 1962).
37. Quoted in English in Prinzler and Pflaum, *Cinema in the Federal Republic of Germany* (Bonn: Inter Nationes, 1983) p. 5.
38. Reinhard Hauff, in *Die Filmemacher*, p. 193.
39. See J. Hermand, H. Peitsch and K.R. Scherpe (eds), *Nachkriegsliteratur in Westdeutschland 1945–1949*, vol. I (Berlin: Das Argument, 1982).
40. Quoted in Kreimeier, p. 182, but see also Enno Patalas: 'A quarter million DM awaits those films that "raise particularly the esteem of Germany abroad"', in 'Prämien für die Braven', *Filmkritik*, November 1961, p. 465.
41. For the development of the cinema in the GDR, see P.W. Jansen and W. Schütte (eds.), *Film in der DDR* (Munich: Hanser 1977).
42. Werner Schroeter in *Die Filmemacher*, p. 133.
43. This often-quoted statement should perhaps be seen in its full context: 'What I do and others do right now in Germany with film is legitimate German culture:

again we are legitimate. I have to say this because film-making and culture have been abused for the most barbaric purposes in recent history. People often try to link us with the Expressionist films of the 1920s, and it is not true. We do not have any links at all, but what links us is that both Expressionist film in the 1920s and what we do now is legitimate German culture. Lotte Eisner is so important to me because she has declared us legitimate, and she is the only person who has the authority to declare us legitimate.' *New York Times*, Sunday Supplement, 11 September 1977.

44. Werner Schroeter in *Die Filmemacher*, p. 155.
45. Klaus Eder and Alexander Kluge, *Ulmer Dramaturgien: Reibungverluste* (Munich: Hanser Verlag 1980) p. 116.
46. Miriam Hansen makes a similar point, when she writes: 'Nor does it seem appropriate to draw the line between an author-oriented and an issue-oriented New German Cinema', in 'Cooperative Auteur Cinema and Oppositional Public Sphere', *New German Critique*, nos. 24–25, Fall/Winter 1981–2, p. 41. She may have in mind James Franklin, *The New German Cinema: From Oberhausen to Hamburg* (Boston: Twayne, 1983) pp. 44–6.
47. Examples of such issues are: law enforcement and the penal system (*Im Namen des Volkes, Die Verrohung des Franz Blum*), unemployment (*Na Und, Kanackerbraut*), labour disputes and strikes (*Liebe Mutter mir geht es gut*), trade union organisation (*Der aufrechte Gang*), terrorism (*Deutschland im Herbst, Die bleierne Zeit, Die dritte Generation*), the yellow press and sensationalist journalism (*Die verlorene Ehre der Katharina Blum, Dorian Gray im Spiegel der Boule-vardpresse*), the German Communist Party (*Mutter Küsters Fahrt zum Himmel*), right-wing extremism (*Morgen in Alabama*), alcohol and drugs (*Bildnis einer Trinkerin, Veronika Voss*), prostitution (*Shirins Hochzeit*), abortion (*Gelegenheit-sarbeit einer Sklavin*), housing problems (*In Gefahr und größter Not*), urban redevelopment (*Berlin Chamissoplatz*), property speculation (*Schatten der Engel*), the Berlin Wall (*Redupers, Der Mann auf der Mauer*), 'Berufsverbot' and education (*Vera Romeike ist nicht tragbar*), wife-battering (*Der Händler der vier Jahreszeiten*), party-politics (*Die Patriotin*), schizophrenia (*Die Berührte*), bulimia (*Hungerjahre*), police harassment (*Messer im Kopf*), surveillance (*Der starke Ferdinand*), juvenile delinquency (*Wildwechsel, Nordsee ist Mordsee*), racism (*Angst essen Seele auf, Palermo oder Wolfsburg, Die Kümmeltürkin geht*).
48. Gudrun Lakasz-Aden and Christel Strobel, *Der Frauenfilm* (Munich: Heyne, 1985).
49. See H.J. Syberberg, *Syberbergs Filmbuch* (Munich: Hanser, 1979) p. 87.
50. Reprinted in parts in Michael Rutschky, *Erfahrungshunger* (Frankfurt: Fischer, 1982) pp. 167–92.
51. See, for instance, the essays collected in Siegfried Kracauer, *Das Ornament der Masse* (Frankfurt: Suhrkamp, 1963).
52. Rutschky, p. 170.
53. Rutschky, 'Realität träumen', *Merkur*, no. 363, 1978, p. 775.
54. Rutschky, 'Realität träumen', p. 783.
55. See Ernest Dichter International, 'Freizeitbedürfnisse und Präferenzstruktur' in D. Prokop (ed.), *Materialien zur Theorie des Film* (Munich: Hanser, 1971) pp. 339–82.
56. See my 'Murder, Merger, Suicide' in T. Rayns (ed.), *Fassbinder* (London: British Film Institute, 1979) p. 49.
57. Independent production often addresses identifiable spectators as target audiences: women, homosexuals, the old, teenagers, foreign workers, trade unionists, and teachers.
58. Rutschky, *Erfahrungshunger*, p. 171.

59. 'Sie machen uns das Kino tot', *Frankfurter Rundschau*, 2 May 1977; *Frankfurter Allgemeine Zeitung*, 2 May 1977.
60. 'Filmstoffe, ballenweise', *Frankfurter Rundschau*, 30 April 1983.
61. *Filmkritik*, January 1961, pp. 10–15.
62. Reinhold E. Thiel, 'Mutmaßungen über Walter', *Filmkritik*, January 1962, p. 13.
63. Urs Jenny, 'Abschied von Illusionen', in Leonhardt H. Gmühr (ed.), *Der Junge Deutsche Film* (Munich: Constantin, 1967) pp. 102–3.
64. Peter M. Ladiges, *Filmkritik*, December 1968, p. 843.
65. Ladiges, p. 843.
66. Jean-Marie Straub in *Die Filmemacher*, p. 42.
67. Pflaum and Prinzler, pp. 9–10.
68. This may be apocryphal, but it is a story Straub himself is fond of telling (for example, Milwaukee, Wisconsin, March 1982).
69. Joe Hembus, *Der deutsche Film kann garnicht besser sein* (Munich: Rogner & Bernhard, 1981) p. 204.
70. Hembus, p. 200.
71. Jenny, p. 104.
72. Enno Patalas, 'Die toten Augen', *Filmkritik*, December 1968, p. 829.
73. Patalas, p. 828.

3   The Author in the Film: Self-expression as Self-representation

1. Helmut Färber, 'Das Unentdeckte Kino', in A. Kluge (ed.), *Bestandsaufnahme: Utopie Film* (Frankfurt: Zweitausendeins, 1983) pp. 21–2.
2. See Michel Foucault, 'What is an author?' in J. Caughie, *Theories of Authorship* (London: Routledge & Kegan Paul, 1981).
3. Horkheimer and Adorno, *Dialectic of Enlightenment*, p. 133.
4. See Eric Rentschler (ed.), *West German Filmmakers on Film* (New York: Holmes & Meier, 1988).
5. Alexander Kluge, *Die Macht der Gefühle* (Frankfurt: Zweitausendeins, 1984) p. 68. See also Eric Rentschler, 'Kluge, Film History and Eigensinn', *New German Critique*, no. 31, Winter 1984, pp. 115–16.
6. Jean-Marie Straub in *Die Filmemacher*, p. 35.
7. *Die Filmemacher*, p. 35.
8. Vlado Kristl in *Die Filmemacher*, p. 49.
9. Helmut Färber, 'Der Brief', *Filmkritik*, April 1967, p. 204.
10. Vlado Kristl, 'Sekundenfilme', *Filmkritik*, October 1969, p. 610.
11. 'Vlado Kristls *Film oder Macht*', *Filmkritik*, July 1970, p. 371.
12. There is very little in English on *Das Andere Kino*, but a brief introduction can be found in Albie Thoms, 'German Underground', *Afterimage* (London) no. 2, Autumn 1970, pp. 44–5.
13. See Werner Herzog, 'Mit den Wölfen heulen', *Filmkritik*, July 1968, p. 460. Also, 'Gespräch mit Eva M.J. Schmid' in *frauen und film*, no. 35, p. 76.
14. Jürgen Ebert, 'Der Kleine Godard', *Filmkritik*, no. 263, November 1978, p. 607.
15. Informationsblatt no. 12, Internationales Forum des Jungen Films, 1984.
16. See my 'Working on the Margins' in *Monthly Film Bulletin*, October 1983.
17. Harun Farocki, 'Notwendige Abwechslung und Vielfalt', in *Filmkritik*, no. 224, August 1975, pp. 368–9.
18. *Etwas Wird Sichtbar* (typed transcript supplied by director) p. 21.
19. R.W. Fassbinder, 'Klimmzug, Handstand, Salto mortale – sicher gestanden', *Frankfurter Rundschau*, 24 February 1979.
20. Werner Schroeter, 'Nachrede auf Maria Callas', quoted in R. Fischer and J. Hembus (eds.), *Der Neue Deutsche Film* (Munich: Goldmann, 1981) p. 154.

21. Edgar Reitz in *Die Filmemacher*, p. 111.
22. 'Preusse, Dichter, Selbstmörder: ein Interview mit Helma Sanders-Brahms', quoted in Renate Möhrmann, *Die Frau mit der Kamera* (Munich: Hanser, 1980) p. 148.
23. 'Film is not the Art of Scholars but of Illiterates', *New York Times*, Sunday Supplement, 11 September 1977.
24. This is a collage from different interviews with Herzog: from *Filmkritik*, July 1968; *New York Times*, September 1977; *American Film*, May 1980 and one tape-recorded at the Chicago Art Institute, 1978.
25. Hans Jürgen Syberberg, *Hitler – Ein Film aus Deutschland* (Reinbek: Rowohlt, 1978) p. 57.
26. See 'Syberberg, Cinema and Representation' in *New German Critique*, Fall/Winter 1981–2, pp. 108–54.
27. Ernst Bloch, *Erbschaft dieser Zeit* (Frankfurt: Suhrkamp, 1962) p. 19.
28. See 'Fassbinder, Fascism and the Film Industry', *October*, no. 21, p. 118. Waldleitner had his own reasons: 'We had to work with these so-called left-wing directors, because there wasn't a single director in the conservative camp that could be sold outside the Federal Republic.' Quoted in Rainer Werner Fassbinder, *Die Anarchie der Fantasie* (Frankfurt: Fischer, 1986) p. 227.
29. Klaus Eder and Alexander Kluge, *Ulmer Dramaturgien*, p. 105.
30. Oskar Negt and Alexander Kluge, *Öffentlichkeit und Erfahrung* (Frankfurt: Suhrkamp, 1972).
31. See 'Ein Gespräch zwischen Alexander Kluge und Bion Steinborn', *Filmfaust*, no. 26, 1982, pp. 32–64.
32. Peter W. Jansen and Wolfram Schütte (eds.), *Herzog, Kluge, Straub* (Munich: Hanser, 1976) p. 154.
33. See Rainer Lewandowski, *Die Filme von Alexander Kluge* (Hildesheim: Olms, 1980).
34. Renate Möhrmann, *Die Frau mit der Kamera*, p. 9.
35. Möhrmann, p. 16.
36. Pam Cook, 'The point of self-expression in avant-garde film' in J. Caughie (ed.), *Theories of Authorship* (London: Routledge & Kegan Paul, 1979) p. 272–3.
37. Helke Sander, 'Der subjektive Faktor, vertrackt' (Berlin: Basis-Film Verleih, 1981) p. 12.
38. For feminist critiques of Kluge see *frauen und film*, nos 3, 16 and 23, as well as Ruby Rich, 'She Says He Says', *Discourse*, no. 6, Fall 1983, pp. 31–7.
39. Werner Herzog in *Die Filmemacher*, p. 12.
40. Alf Brustellin, quoted in 'Die Verlohrene Ehre des deutschen Films', *lui* (Munich) March 1979.
41. Edgar Reitz, *Liebe zum Kino* (Cologne: Verlag Köln, 1984) p. 167.
42. Werner Herzog in *Die Filmemacher*, p. 12.
43. Hans Jürgen Syberberg, *Hitler ein Film aus Deutschland* (Reinbek: Rowohlt, 1978) p. 7.
44. Werner Herzog in *Die Filmemacher*, p. 13.
45. Rainer Werner Fassbinder in *Die Filmemacher*, p. 177.
46. Quoted in Bill Horrigan, 'Signs of Life', *Chicago Film Center Program*, 1 September 1977.
47. Reitz, *Liebe zum Kino*, p. 166.
48. Johannes Schaaf in *Die Filmemacher*, p. 137.
49. Werner Herzog in *Die Filmemacher*, p. 20.
50. Klaus Eder and Alexander Kluge, *Ulmer Dramaturgien*, pp. 102–3.
51. Quoted in Peter Buchka, 'Dann geht wieder was, dann geht wieder nix', *Süddeutsche Zeitung*, 25 January 1985.

52. See 'Film in Berlin: Der Basis-Film Verleih', *Kinemathek* no. 65, October 1983, p. 105.
53. See Herbert Achternbusch, *Die Atlantikschwimmer* (Frankfurt: Suhrkamp, 1978) p. 148.
54. Quoted in B. Schlicht, 'Nullwachstum', *medium*, November 1978, p. 8.
55. Andreas Meyer, 'Das Gremienkino', *medium*, November 1977, p. 18.
56. Meyer, p. 14.
57. Meyer, p. 18.
58. Meyer, p. 18; see also Sven Hansen, 'Die Inspiration aus dem Bücherschrank', *Die Welt*, 13 January 1979.
59. Volker Schlöndorff in *Die Filmemacher*, p. 76.
60. Examples are Neo-Realism (de Sica and Zavattini), Bertolucci and Moravia, Pasolini in Italy; Resnais and Duras, Robbe-Grillet in France; Losey and Pinter, Richardson and Osborne, David Hare or Alan Bennett in Britain.
61. See Hans C. Blumenberg, 'Bildschirm contra Leinwand', *Die Zeit*, 23 June 1978.
62. Edgar Reitz, 'Das Kino der Autoren lebt', *Liebe zum Kino*, p. 117.
63. Sheila Johnston, 'The Author as Public Institution', *Screen Education*, no. 32–33, Autumn/Winter 1979–80.
64. Rainer Werner Fassbinder, *Filme befreien den Kopf* (Frankfurt: Fischer, 1984) p. 78.
65. Harun Farocki, 'Notwendige Abwechslung und Vielfalt', *Filmkritik*, August 1975, p. 363.
66. See Richard Collins and Vincent Porter, *WDR and the Arbeiterfilm* (London: British Film Institute, 1981).
67. Rainer Werner Fassbinder in *Der Spiegel*, 11 July 1977, p. 141.
68. Quoted in Sheila Johnston, 'Fassbinder and the New German Cinema', *New German Critique*, nos. 24–25, Fall/Winter 1981–2, p. 68.
69. John Ellis, *Visible Fictions* (London: Routledge & Kegan Paul, 1982) p. 225.
70. See *Kino*, no. 22, Spring 1986, an issue devoted to WDR, and especially the interview with Gunther Witte and Martin Wiebel.
71. John Ellis and Sheila Johnston, 'The Radical Film Funding of ZDF', *Screen*, vol. 23, no. 1, May/June 1982, pp. 60–73.

4 In Search of the Spectator 1: From Oberhausen to Genre Films?

1. Klaus Bädekerl, 'Alles kennen – nichts erkennen', *Filmkritik*, April 1969, pp. 226–7.
2. 'I started by going to the movies, with my friend Lemke, and we saw American films, and later those of Godard, and we told each other simple stories . . . I like clichés. With *Supergirl* I wanted to make my dream film, a film that is like American films used to be.' Rudolf Thome, quoted in *Kinemathek*, no. 66, November 1983, pp. 91–3.
3. Pflaum and Prinzler, *Cinema in the Federal Republic of Germany* (Bonn: Inter Nationes, 1983) p. 14 (translation amended).
4. 'At the Berlin film festival of 1977, Niklaus Schilling, asked about the directors that have influenced him, replied with a long list of German names who for him were "father figures", teachers, idols: Leni, Lang, Lubitsch, Murnau, Lamprecht, Hochbaum, Ophuls, von Borsody, Haussler, Fanck, Trenker, Berger, Pewas, Sierck, Bertram, Wisbar, König, Deppe, Staudte, Harlan, Leni Riefenstahl, Stemmle, Steinhoff, Jugert, Hans Müller, Tressler – the reaction: embarrassed silence, incredulous head-shaking, questions which betrayed total ignorance of most of the directors cited.' Andreas Mayer, *medium*, November 1977, p. 15.

5. Peter W. Jansen and Wolfram Schütte (eds.), *Herzog, Kluge, Straub* (Munich: Hanser, 1976) p. 126.
6. Peter W. Jansen and Wolfram Schütte (eds.), *Fassbinder* (Munich: Hanser, 1975) p. 82.
7. *Herzog, Kluge, Straub*, p. 127.
8. Quoted in Joe Hembus, *Der deutsche Film kann garnicht besser sein* (Munich: Rogner and Bernhard, 1981) p. 254.
9. Wenders once described the early years in Munich: 'There was a common content, in the Munich style, for instance, the connection between the car rides and the music. I think the music provides a real link; many of us would have become musicians, if we hadn't made films.' Quoted in Hembus, p. 285.
10. 'Terror der Gesetzlosen', *Süddeutsche Zeitung*, 6/7 September 1969.
11. 'Rote Sonne', *Filmkritik*, January 1970, p. 9.
12. Quoted in *Kinemathek*, no. 66, November 1983, p. 93.
13. Peter Handke, 'Augsburg im August: Trostlos', *Film*, January 1969, p. 31.
14. Wim Wenders, 'Kritischer Kalender', *Filmkritik*, December 1969, pp. 751–2.
15. Pflaum and Prinzler, p. 14 (translation amended).
16. 'Offener Brief and Franz Xaver Kroetz', quoted in Rainer Werner Fassbinder, *Filme befreien den Kopf* (Frankfurt: Fischer, 1984) p. 123.
17. Peter Handke, 'Sätze im Schwarzen oder Ausleiern der Tagträume?', *Die Zeit*, 24 June 1977.
18. Hans Jürgen Syberberg, *Syberbergs Filmbuch* (Frankfurt: Fischer, 1979).
19. One film to feature the strange fauna of Munich's film-making community directly, rather than filtered through historical or generic patina, was Niklaus Schilling's *Expulsion From Paradise* (1976), the story of a German actor who, on the strength of having once starred as a Fellini extra, is trying to break into movies in Munich.
20. A recent example is Manfred Stelzer's *The Chinese Are Coming* (1987), in which a team of workmen from the People's Republic of China visit a Bavarian town and dismantle an industrial plant to ship it back home. In the process, national clichés get their comeuppance.

5 In Search of the Spectator 2: Cinema of Experience

1. Wolf Donner, 'Die Deutschen kommen', *Die Zeit*, 28 December 1975.
2. Eric Rentschler, *West German Film in the Course of Time* (Bedford Hills, New York: Redgrave, 1984) pp. 68–72.
3. On reactions to German films in the US, Wilhelm Roth, 'Nichts für das Durchschnittspublikum', *Stuttgarter Zeitung*, 28 December 1979.
4. Special issue 'Kino in München', *Filmkritik*, December 1975.
5. Quoted in 'Vom Lustspiel bis zur Filmbildung', *Frankfurter Rundschau*, 7 December 1981.
6. For a fuller documentation see H.H. Prinzler and W. Seidler (eds.), *Kinobuch Katalog*, no. 2, 1974–75 (Berlin: Stiftung Deutsche Kinemathek, 1975).
7. See bibliography, and also Eric Rentschler, *West German Filmmakers on Film* (New York: Holmes & Meier, 1988).
8. Jan Dawson, 'The Industry – German Weasels (Filmverlag Follies)', *Film Comment*, May–June 1977.
9. Interview with Ula Stöckl, in Renate Möhrmann, *Die Frau mit der Kamera* (Munich: Hanser, 1980) p. 50.
10. Rosa von Praunheim, 'So schlagen uns die Etablierten tot', *Die Zeit*, 13 May 1977.
11. 'Pro und Contra "Das Gespenst",' *Evangelischer Pressedienst*, June 1983, and report on 'Kunst unter der Knute', *Stuttgarter Zeitung*, 7 September 1988.

12. Michael Rutschky, *Erfahrungshunger* (Frankfurt: Fischer, 1982) p. 172.
13. Werner Schroeter in *Die Filmemacher* (Munich: Berelsmann, 1973) p. 167.
14. Christian Ziewer, quoted in *Kinemathek*, 65, October 1983, p. 5.
15. Alexander Kluge, *Bestandsaufnahme: Utopie Film* (Frankfurt: Zweitausendeins, 1983) p. 151.
16. Interview with Werner Herzog, *Filmkritik*, March 1968, p. 176.
17. Christian Ziewer, *Kinemathek*, 65, pp. 5–6.
18. Christian Ziewer, *Kinemathek*, 65, p. 4.
19. Interview with Ulrike Ottinger in Renate Möhrmann, *Die Frau mit der Kamera* (Munich: Hanser, 1980) p. 191.
20. Harun Farocki is said to have hired a cinema for a press show of *Between Two Wars*, but made admission conditional on the journalists' undertaking to attend his public critique of their reviews. See 'Progress und Prozess', *Filmkritik*, November 1979.
21. Michael Rutschky, *Erfahrungshunger* (Frankfurt: Fischer, 1982) p. 57.
22. The critical literature, especially on Fassbinder, testifies to these difficulties. See for instance Manny Farber and Patricia Patterson, 'Fassbinder', *Film Comment*, November–December 1975.
23. Christian Ziewer, *Kinemathek*, no. 65, October 1983, p. 4.
24. Alexander Kluge, *Gelegenheitsarbeit einer Sklavin, Zur Realistischen Methode*, pp. 202–3.
25. Ibid., p. 204.
26. Ibid., pp. 217–18.
27. Ibid., p. 219.
28. Very little has been written about Kluge's short films, but a description of Kluge's method of observation is made in Erhard Schütz, 'Ein Liebesversuch, oder zeigen, was das Auge nicht sieht', in *Text und Kritik*, nos. 85–86, January 1985.
29. See William von Weert, 'Last Words: Observation on a new language', in T. Corrigan (ed.), *Werner Herzog* (London: Methuen, 1986).
30. For an attack on Herzog's quest for the visionary, see Eric Rentschler, 'The Politics of Vision', in Corrigan (ed.), *Werner Herzog* (London: Methuen, 1986).
31. See my 'An anthropologist's eye' in Corrigan (ed.), *Werner Herzog* (London: Methuen, 1986).
32. See Paul Mog, 'Kälte. Satirische Verhaltensforschung' in Thomas Böhm-Christl, *Alexander Kluge* (Frankfurt: Suhrkamp, 1983).
33. Hartmut Bitomski, 'Aufzeichnungen', *Filmkritik*, November 1979, p. 522.
34. Hans Jürgen Syberberg, *Syberbergs Filmbuch* (Frankfurt: Fischer, 1979) p. 74.

6 In Search of the Spectator 3: Minority Views

1. See Friedhelm Kroll, *Die 'Gruppe 47'* (Stuttgart: J.B. Metzler, 1977).
2. *The Times*, 23 September 1960.
3. See Reinhard Dithmar, *Industrieliteratur* (Munich: Deutsche Taschenbuch Verlag, 1973).
4. Fritz Hüser, 'Arbeiterdichtung heute?', *Volksbühnenspiegel*, vol. 12, no. 6, 1966, p. 11.
5. Günter Wallraff, *Industriereportagen* (Reinbek: Rowohlt, 1970), first published as *Wir brauchen dich* (Reinbek: Rowohlt, 1966).
6. W. Röhner, H. Kammrad and H. Schmid, 'Westberliner Werkstatt im Werkkreis Literatur der Arbeitswelt' (pamphlet, Berlin, 1971).
7. R. Collins and V. Porter, *WDR and the Arbeiterfilm* (London: British Film Institute 1981; but see also C. McArthur, 'Days of Hope', *Screen*, vol. 16, no. 4

and C. MacCabe, 'Days of Hope – A Response to McArthur', *Screen*, nol. 17, no. 1.
8. Christian Ziewer, quoted in Collins and Porter, p. 155.
9. Christian Ziewer in Collins and Porter, p. 157.
10. Johannes Beringer, 'Ranklotzen – Arbeitsweltfilme und Verwandtes', *Filmkritik*, March 1975, pp. 125–7.
11. Ibid., p. 130.
12. Harun Farocki, *Filmkritik*, March 1975, pp. 138–9.
13. See Wilhelm Roth, *Der Dokumentarfilm seit 1960* (Munich: Hanser, 1970).
14. Interview with Klaus Wildenhahn, *Filme*, no. 4, 1980, p. iv.
15. Klaus Wildenhahn, 'Industrielandschaft mit Einzelhändlern', *Filmfaust*, no. 20, 1980.
16. Wildenhahn, quoted in Roth, *Der Dokumentarfilm*, p. 62.
17. 'Ganz Unten', *epd-Film*, March 1986, p. 35.
18. Roth, *Der Dokumentarfilm*, p. 69.
19. See Helke Sander, 'Der subjektive Faktor, vertrackt' (Berlin: Basis Verleih, 1982).
20. See especially *frauen und film*, no. 1, 1974, and no. 6, 1976.
21. Helke Sander, quoted in *Camera Obscura*, no. 4, p. 226.
22. Heide Schlüpmann and Carola Gramann, 'Nachwort', in Gudrun Lukasz-Aden and Christel Strobel, *Der Frauenfilm* (Munich: Heyne, 1985) p. 252.
23. Renate Möhrmann, *Die Frau mit der Kamera* (Munich: Hanser, 1980) pp. 69–70.
24. Helke Sander, 'sexismus in den massenmedien', *frauen und film*, no. 1, 1974.
25. Pam Cook, 'The point of self-expression in avant-garde film', in J. Caughie, *Theories of Authorship* (London: Routledge & Kegan Paul, 1979) p. 272.
26. Gertrude Koch, 'Re-visioning Feminist Film Theory', *New German Critique*, no. 34, Winter 1985, p. 152.
27. Quoted in *Der Frauenfilm*, p. 263.
28. Interview with Jutta Brückner, *Screen Education*, no. 40, Autumn/Winter 1981–2, p. 56.
29. Ibid., pp. 54–7.
30. Interview with Ulrike Ottinger, *Ästhetik und Kommunikation*, no. 37, 1979, pp. 123–4.
31. Rosa von Praunheim, *catalogue Filmschau* (Hamburg, 1972).
32. John Ellis and Sheila Johnston, 'The Radical Film Funding of ZDF', *Screen*, vol. 23, no. 1, 1982, p. 64.
33. Ibid., p. 64.
34. Interview with Jutta Brückner, *Screen Education*, no. 40, p. 48.
35. For further discussion of Helke Sander's films, see Kaja Silverman, 'Helke Sander and the Will to Change', *Discourse*, no. 6, Fall 1983.

7 The New German Cinema's Germany

1. André Bazin, 'The Evolution of Cinematographic Language', *What is Cinema*, vol. I (Berkeley: University of California Press, 1971) p. 24.
2. Peter Handke, *Falsche Bewegung* (Frankfurt: Suhrkamp, 1975) pp. 44–5.
3. Rainer Werner Fassbinder, 'Six Films by Douglas Sirk', in L. Mulvey and J. Halliday (eds.), *Douglas Sirk* (Edinburgh: Edinburgh Film Festival, 1972) p. 104.
4. See Peter Buchka, 'Wir leben in einem toten Land', *Süddeutsche Zeitung*, 20/21 August 1977, and 'Lieber Strassenkehrer in Mexiko', *Der Spiegel*, no. 29, August 1977.
5. See Werner Herzog, *Vom Gehen im Eis* (Munich: Skellig, 1974).

6. Ernst Bloch, *Das Prinzip Hoffnung* (Frankfurt: Suhrkamp, 1973) p. 1628.
7. Jan Dawson, 'Werner Herzog', *Monthly Film Bulletin*, October 1980.
8. Erich Fried, as quoted in *Filmkritik*, June 1977, p. 277.
9. Interview with Margarethe von Trotta, *Filmfaust*, no. 21, 1981.
10. Andreas Huyssen, 'The Politics of Identification', *New German Critique*, no. 19, Winter 1980.

8 Returning Home To History

1. Jan Dawson, *Wim Wenders* (New York: Zoetrope, 1976) p. 7.
2. Christopher Lasch, *The Culture of Narcissism* (New York: Norton, 1979) pp. 40–1.
3. Alexander Mitscherlich, *Society without the Father* (London: Tavistock, 1969) p. 283.
4. T.W. Adorno, E. Frenkel-Brunswik *et al.*, *The Authoritarian Personality* (New York: Harper and Row, 1950).
5. Mitscherlich, p. 284.
6. Alexander and Margarethe Mitscherlich, *The Inability to Mourn* (London: Tavistock, 1975).
7. *The Inability to Mourn*, p. 63.
8. See W.F. Haug, *Der Hilflose Antifaschismus* (Frankfurt: Pahl Rugenstein, 1977).
9. Bernward Vesper, *Die Reise* (Berlin: März Verlag, 1977).
10. Michael Schneider, 'Väter und Söhne, posthum' in *Den Kopf verkehrt aufgesetzt* (Darmstadt und Neuwied: Luchterhand, 1981) p. 18; translated as 'Fathers and Sons Retrospectively', *New German Critique*, no. 31, Winter 1984, pp. 11–12.
11. Schneider, *New German Critique*, p. 23.
12. Schneider, *New German Critique*, p. 37 (translation modified).
13. Paul Kersten, *Der Alltägliche Tod meines Vaters*, quoted by Schneider, *New German Critique*, p. 41 (translation modified).
14. Schneider, *New German Critique*, p. 30 (translation modified).
15. Christoph Meckel, *Suchbild* (Frankfurt: Fischer, 1983) p. 148, quoted by Schneider, *New German Critique*, pp. 26–7 (translation modified).
16. Schneider, *New German Critique*, p. 9.
17. See for instance, Jessica Benjamin, 'The Oedipal Riddle: Authority, Autonomy and the New Narcissism', in John P. Diggins and Mark E. Kahn (eds.), *The Problem of Authority in America* (Philadelphia: Temple University Press, 1981).
18. See Eric Rentschler, 'New German Film and the Discourse of Bitburg', *New German Critique*, no. 36, Fall 1985.
19. See Hans Jochen Brauns and David Kramer, 'Political Repression in West Germany', *New German Critique*, no. 7, Winter 1976.
20. Quoted in Norbert Seitz, 'Die Unfähigkeit zu feiern', *Neue Kritik* (Frankfurt: Verlag Neue Kritik, 1985) p. 10.
21. Ernst Bornemann (ed.), *Das Schwarzbuch* (Munich: Steidl, 1986).
22. See Tom Bower, 'Operation Paperclip', BBC Television, 1987.
23. See Klaus Kreimeier, 'Das Kino als Ideologiefabrik', *Kinemathek*, no. 45, 1971.
24. Jean Baudrillard, *Kool Killer oder der Aufstand der Zeichen* (Berlin: Merve Verlag, 1981).
25. 'Hitler – Eine Karriere', 27th Internationale Film Festspiele Berlin, June/July 1977 (press handout).
26. Michel Foucault, 'Interview: Popular Memory', *Edinburgh Magazine*, no. 2, 1977, p. 24.
27. See my interview with Edgardo Cozarinsky, *Framework*, no. 21, 1983.
28. See Richard Roud, *Straub* (London: Secker & Warburg, 1971).

29. Rosalind Delmar, 'Not Reconciled', *Monthly Film Bulletin*, March 1976.
30. Oskar Negt and Alexander Kluge, *Geschichte und Eigensinn* (Frankfurt: Zweitausendeins, 1981).
31. Quoted in Anton Kaes, 'Über den nomadischen Umgang mit Geschichte', *Text und Kritik*, nos. 85–86, 1985.
32. See Hans Helmut Prinzler, 'Jahresbericht', *Jahrbuch Film 1978/79* (Munich: Hanser, 1979).
33. Quoted in *Filmkritik*, November 1979, p. 5.
34. See Saul Friedländer, *Reflexions of Fascism, An Essay on Kitsch and Death* (New York: Harper & Row, 1984).
35. For a more extended argument, see my 'Myth as the Phantasmagoria of History', *New German Critique*, nos. 24–25, Fall/Winter 1981–2.
36. See also my 'Murder, Merger, Suicide: The Politics of *Despair*', in Tony Rayns (ed.), *Fassbinder* (London: British Film Institute, 1979).
37. Edgar Reitz, 'Statt *Holocaust*: Erinnerungen aufarbeiten', *medium*, May 1979, p. 21.
38. Dieter E. Zimmer, 'Massenmord als Melodrama', *Die Zeit*, 19 January 1979, p. 23.
39. Peter Märthesheimer, Ivo Frenzel (eds), *Der Fernsehfilm 'Holocaust': Eine Nation ist betroffen* (Frankfurt: Fischer, 1979) p. 13.
40. Edgar Reitz, *medium*, pp. 21–2.
41. Ibid.
42. Edgar Reitz, 'Filmgeschichte ist nicht an Lichtspieltheater gebunden', in K. Wetzel (ed.), *Neue Medien contra Filmkultur?* (Berlin: Verlag Volker Spiess, 1987) p. 138.

9   National or International Cinema?

1. The debates in Germany, apart from the 'filmed literature crisis', were dominated by the virtues of the big screen compared to television, and the question of 'amphibious films' (Andreas Meyer, 'Auf dem Weg zum Staatskino?', *medium*, October/November/December 1977 and Hans C. Blumenberg, 'Bildschirm contra Leinwand?', *Die Zeit*, 23 June 1978, p. 28). In the early 1980s it was the split between low-budget films and commercially-oriented productions – 'das kleine' versus 'das große Geld' – which agitated the commentators (Klaus Eder, 'Der Glaube ans große Geld', in H.G. Pflaum (ed.), *Jahrbuch Film 1979/80* (Munich: Hanser, 1979) pp. 100–7 and 'Dreckige kleine Filme', *Die Zeit*, 30 November 1979). Total confusion did arise when critics began to accuse 'author-oriented' film-making, such as Fassbinder's big productions or Herzog's and Wenders' deals with American major companies, as a sell-out to commercial interests, and proclaimed 'issue-orientation' as the true heir of the *Autorenfilm*: 'The noisily propagated work of the "author and producer" is a mystification of the economic and political conditions of production. What the author's film can claim for itself is to have discovered the didactic and target-audience film.' (Bion Steinborn, *filmfaust*, no. 4 (June/July 1977) p. 92.
2. See Raymond Durgnat, 'From Caligari to *Hitler*', *Film Comment*, July/August 1980. Adverse comment also came from Pauline Kael, 'Metaphysical Tarzan', *New Yorker*, 20 October 1975 and John Simon, 'Cinematic Illiterates', *New York*, 20 October 1975.
3. See the entries in the bibliography for references.
4. Klaus Eder and Alexander Kluge, *Ulmer Dramaturgien* (Munich: Hanser, 1980) p. 105.

5. Michael Dost, Florian Hopf and Alexander Kluge, *Filmwirtschaft in der BRD und in Europa* (Munich: Hanser, 1973) pp. 89–90.
6. Alexander Kluge (ed.), *Bestandsaufnahme: Utopie Film* (Frankfurt: Zweitausendeins, 1983) pp. 196–7.
7. Ibid., p. 199.
8. Ibid., pp. 208–9.
9. Kluge's argument is here very close to that of Steven Spielberg or Paul Schrader as discussed, for instance, by David Thomson, *Overexposures* (New York: William Morrow, 1981).
10. About Peter Stein, the Schaubühne and its actors, see Michael Patterson, *Peter Stein* (Cambridge: Cambridge University Press, 1981).
11. *Bestandsaufnahme: Utopie Film*, pp. 227–8.
12. See for instance, Michael Covino, 'Wim Wenders: A Worldwide Homesickness', *Film Quarterly*, Winter 1977–8, pp. 9–19 and Tim Corrigan, 'The Realist Gesture in the Films of Wim Wenders', *Quarterly Review of Film Studies*, Spring 1980, pp. 205–16.
13. Stanley Kauffmann, 'Watching the Rhine', *The Nation*, 20 August 1977.
14. A reference to Jillian Becker's book on the Baader–Meinhof group, *Hitler's Children*, taken up by Diane Jacobs, 'Hitler's Ungrateful Grandchildren', *American Film*, May 1980, pp. 34–40.
15. Eric Rentschler, 'American Friends and the New German Cinema', *New German Critique*, no. 24–25, Fall/Winter 1981–2, pp. 7–35.
16. Sheila Johnston (ed.), *Wenders* (London: British Film Institute Dossier No. 10, 1981) p. 1.
17. See Andrew Sarris, 'The Germans are Coming, The Germans are Coming!', *Village Voice*, 27 October 1975; Penelope Gilliatt, 'Gold', *New Yorker*, 11 April 1977; Stanley Kauffmann, 'Watching the Rhine', *The Nation*, 20 August 1977; Vincent Canby, 'The German Renaissance – No Room for Laughter or Love', *New York Times*, 11 December 1977; Gerald Clarke, 'Seeking Planets That Do Not Exist – The German Cinema is the Liveliest in Europe', *Time Magazine*, 20 March 1978; see the bibliography for the cluster of special issues of periodicals around 1979–80.
18. Ron Holloway, 'German Film Tour 1980', *Kino-German Film* no. 2, Spring 1980.
19. See H. Bernd Moeller, 'Der deutsche Film in amerikanischer Forschung und Lehre', *Film und Fernsehen in Forschung und Lehre*, no. 9, 1986, pp. 97–114.
20. See, for instance, Jonathan Cott, 'Signs of Life', *Rolling Stone*, 18 November 1976, pp. 48–56.
21. See Rob Baker, 'New German Cinema: A Fistful of Myths', *Soho Weekly News*, 23 March 1978, pp. 21–3.
22. 'Classic German cinema died with the Nazis' rise. Has the new generation restored the great tradition?', Diane Jacobs, 'Hitler's Ungrateful Grandchildren', *American Film*, May 1980, p. 34. See also David L. Overbey, 'From Murnau to Munich, New German Cinema', *Sight and Sound*, Spring 1974, pp. 101–3, 115; Ruth McCormick, 'Metropolis Now: The New German Cinema', *In These Times*, 30 July 1979; H.C. Blumenberg, 'Von Caligari bis Coppola: Junge deutsche Filmemacher in Hollywood auf den Spuren von Lubitsch, Murnau und Lang', *Die Zeit*, 22 February 1980.
23. Chris Petit's British independent feature *Radio On* (1979), co-produced by Wim Wenders' company Road Movies, bears the written motto: 'We are the children of Fritz Lang and Werner von Braun'.
24. See Ulrich Gregor, *The German Experimental Film of the 1970s* (Munich: Goethe Institute, 1980).
25. See Jan Dawson, *The Films of Hellmuth Costard* (London: Riverside Studios, 1979).

26. See David Bordwell, *Narration and the Fiction Film* (Madison: Wisconsin University Press, 1985) p. 217 and also David Wilson, 'Anti-Cinema Rainer Werner Fassbinder', *Sight and Sound*, Spring 1972, pp. 99–100, 113.
27. See, for instance, E. Ann Kaplan, 'The Search for the Mother/Land in Sanders-Brahms' *Germany Pale Mother*' in Eric Rentschler (ed.), *German Film and Literature* (London: Methuen, 1986) pp. 289–304.
28. John Hughes, 'Fassbinder and Modernism', *Film Content*, November–December 1975, pp. 11–13.
29. See Hans Bernd Moeller, 'Brecht and Epic Film Medium', *Wide Angle*, vol. 3, no. 4, 1980, pp. 4–11 and Roswitha Mueller, 'Brecht the Realist and New German Cinema', *Framework*, no. 25, 1984, pp. 42–51.
30. See Kaja Silverman, 'Kaspar Hauser's "Terrible Fall" into narrative' and Timothy Corrigan, 'Wenders' *Kings of the Road*: The Voyage from Desire to Language', *New German Critique*, no. 24–25, Winter/Fall 1981/2, pp. 73–107.
31. Timothy Corrigan, *New German Film: The Displaced Image* (Austin: University of Texas Press, 1983).
32. New York journalism is especially enamoured of the metaphoric political hyperbole.
33. *Cahiers du Cinéma* collective, 'Young Mr Lincoln', *Screen*, vol. 13, no. 3, Autumn 1972.
34. Laura Mulvey and Jon Halliday (eds.), *Douglas Sirk* (Edinburgh: Edinburgh Film Festival, 1972).
35. Tony Rayns (ed.), *Fassbinder* (London: British Film Institute, 1976).
36. See Richard Dyer, 'Reading Fassbinder's Sexual Politics', in T. Rayns (ed.), *Fassbinder*, pp. 54–64 and Andrew Britton, 'Fox and His Friends, Foxed', *Jump Cut*, no. 19, November 1977, pp. 22–3.
37. See Robert Burgoyne, 'Narrative and Sexual Excess', *October*, no. 21, Summer 1982, pp. 51–62.
38. *Der Spiegel*, 11 February 1976.
39. See the bibliography for a list of English-language pamphlets published by the Goethe Institute.
40. 'The Federal Government must restrict itself in the area of cultural politics – to use the terminology of sports – to supporting the top talents, rather than give funds on a broad basis.' Siegbert von Köcknitz, for the Ministry of the Interior, quoted in *filmfaust* no. 4, June/July 1977, p. 67.
41. Dost/Hopf/Kluge, p. 73.
42. Herbert Achternbusch, *Es ist ein Leichtes beim Gehen den Boden zu berühren* (Frankfurt: Suhrkamp, 1980) p. 145.
43. Reitz in Bronnen and Brocher, *Die Filmemacher* (Munich: C. Bertelsmann, 1973) p. 103.
44. Hans Günther Pflaum, 'Midlife Crisis 1981–1982', *Jahrbuch Film 1981/82* (Munich: Hanser, 1982). On *Fitzcarraldo* as a political media event see Michael Goodwin, 'Herzog the God of Wrath', *American Film*, June 1982 and Elizabeth and Leon Mercadet, 'Paranoia in Eldorado', *Time Out*, London, 12 February 1982.
45. Michael Schneider, *Nur tote Fische schwimmen mit dem Strom* (Cologne: Kiepenheuer & Witsch, 1984) pp. 298–9.
46. Quoted in B. Jeremias, 'Wer schlägt uns denn das Kino tot?', *Frankfurter Allgemeine Zeitung*, 2 May 1977.
47. Jörg Friedrich Krabbe, 'Die Neuen Caligaris', *Neues Forum*, July/August 1976, p. 59.
48. For a more detailed analysis of *Lili Marleen* see my 'Fassbinder, Fascism and the Film Industry', *October* 21, Summer 1982, pp. 115–40.

10   Conclusion

1. Wolfram Schütte, 'Das Herz', in W. Schütte and P.W. Jansen (eds.), *Fassbinder* (Munich: Hanser, revised edition 1982).
2. See Fritz Müller-Scherz, 'Fassbinders Erben', *Transatlantik*, December 1982.
3. Harry Baer, *Schlafen kann ich, wenn ich tot bin* (Cologne: Kiepenheuer & Witsch, 1982); Kurt Raab and Karsten Peters, *Die Sehnsucht des Rainer Werner Fassbinder* (Munich: C. Bertelsmann, 1982); Gerhard Zwerenz, *Der langsame Tod des Rainer Werner Fassbinder* (Munich: Münchner Edition Schneekluth, 1982).
4. See interview in *Der Spiegel*, 'Wir sind nicht mehr der Jungfilm', 18 June 1979.
5. Interview in *Frankfurter Rundschau*, reprinted in Rainer Werner Fassbinder, *Die Anarchie der Phantasie* (Frankfurt: Fischer, 1986) p. 136.
6. Günter Rohrbach, 'Die verhängnisvolle Macht der Regisseure', *medium*, April 1983, pp. 40–1.
7. Andreas Mayer, 'Auf dem Wege zum Staatskino III', *medium*, December 1977.
8. Interview in *Der Spiegel*, reprinted in *Die Anarchie*, p. 97.
9. 'Hamburger Erklärung', reprinted in *medium*, November 1979, p. 27.
10. See Kraft Wetzel (ed.), *Neue Medien contra Filmkultur?* (Berlin: Verlag Volker Spiess, 1987).
11. Berlin Festival, 'Der deutsche Film ist tot', *Berlinale Journal*, 27 February 1987.
12. Both examples are quoted in David Thomson, *Overexposures* (New York: William Morrow, 1981) p. 79.
13. See Ian Christie and Thomas Elsaesser, 'Bring on the Clones', *Guardian*, 4 March 1982.

Bibliography

The bibliography is necessarily selective, and concentrates on 1) book-length studies in English, 2) pamplets in English produced in conjunction with the Goethe Institute, 3) published scripts and 4) material, mainly in English and German, which has either been referred to, or has seemed sufficiently substantial to warrant inclusion. Bibliographical entries on individual directors can also be found in the books listed below, and in the studies edited by Peter W. Jansen and Wolfram Schütte.

1 Books on New German Cinema (in English)

Timothy Corrigan, *New German Film: The Displaced Image* (Austin, Texas: University of Texas Press, 1983).
James Franklin, *New German Cinema: From Oberhausen to Hamburg* (Boston: Twayne, 1983).
Hans Günther Pflaum and Hans Helmut Prinzler, *Cinema in the Federal Republic of Germany* (Bonn: Inter Nationes, 1983).
Klaus Phillips (ed.) *New West German Filmmakers: From Oberhausen Through the 1970s* (New York: Frederick Ungar, 1984).
Eric Rentschler, *West German Film in the Course of Time* (Bedford Hills, New York: Redgrave, 1984).
—— (ed.) *German Film and Literature: Adaptations and Transformations* (London and New York: Methuen, 1986).
—— (ed.) *West German Filmmakers on Film* (New York: Holmes & Meier, 1988).
John Sandford, *The New German Cinema* (London: Oswald Wolff, 1980).

2 Pamphlets and Special Issues of Journals (in English)

Thomas Elsaesser, *Seven Films for Seven Decades* (London: Goethe Institute, 1985).
Bruno Fischli, *The Third Reich in Films of the Federal Republic of Germany* (Munich: Goethe Institute, 1982–4).
Ulrich Gregor, *The German Experimental Film of the Seventies* (Munich: Goethe Institute, 1980).
Peter W. Jansen, *The New German Film* (Munich: Goethe Institute, 1982).
Claudia Lenssen, *Women's Cinema in Germany* (Munich: Goethe Institute, 1980).
Wolfgang Limmer, *Fassbinder* (Munich: Goethe Institute, 1973).
Ingo Petzke, *German Experimental Films* (Munich: Goethe Institute, 1981).
Hans Helmut Prinzler, *Satire, Irony, Humour in Federal German Films* (Munich: Goethe Institute, 1980).
Wilhelm Roth, *The Federal Republic of Germany as Reflected in its Documentary Films* (Munich: Goethe Institute, 1980).
Karl Saurer and Gabriele Voss, *Location Germany* (Munich: Goethe Institute, 1982).

Horst Schäfer and Elke Ried, *Youth Film from the Federal Republic of Germany* (Munich: Goethe Institute, 1982).
Ernst Schürmann (ed.) *A Tribute to Das Kleine Fernsehspiel/ZDF* (Berkeley/San Francisco: Pacific Film Archive/Goethe Institute San Francisco, 1979).
Discourse, no. 6, Fall 1983, (ed.) Roswitha Mueller.
Kino-German Film, appearing 2–3 times a year since October 1979, (eds.) Ron and Dorothea Holloway.
Literature/Film Quarterly, vol. 7 no. 3, 1979, (ed.) James Welsh.
New German Critique, no. 24–25, Winter/Fall 1981–2, (eds.) David Bathrick and Miriam Hansen.
Persistence of Vision, no. 2, Fall 1985, (ed.) Tony Pipolo.
Quarterly Review of Film Studies, Spring 1980, (ed.) Eric Rentschler.
Wide Angle, vol. 3 no. 4, 1980, (ed.) Peter Lehman.

3   Books and Screenplays by German Directors

Herbert Achternbusch, *Schriften*, vols 3–8 (Frankfurt: Suhrkamp, 1978ff).
Ingemo Engstrom and Gerhard Theurig, 'Dossier: *Escape Route to Marseille*', *Framework*, no. 18 (1982) pp. 22–9.
Harun Farocki, *Zwischen zwei Kriegen* (ed.) Peter Nau (Munich: Verlag Filmkritik, 1978).
Rainer Werner Fassbinder, *Antiteater I, II* (Frankfurt: Suhrkamp, 1973–4).
——, *Filme Befreien den Kopf*, (ed.) Michael Töteberg (Frankfurt: Fischer, 1984).
——, *Die Anarchie der Phantasie*, (ed.) Michael Töteberg (Frankfurt: Fischer, 1986).
——, *The Marriage of Maria Braun* (ed.) Joyce Rheuban (New Brunswick: Rutgers University Press, 1986).
——, *Berlin Alexanderplatz* (ed.) Harry Baer (Frankfurt: Zweitausendeins, 1980).
——, *Querelle: the Film Book* (eds.) Dieter Schidor and Michael McLernon (Munich: Schirmer/Mosel, 1982).
——, *Schatten der Engel* (Frankfurt: Zweitausendeins, 1976).
Werner Herzog, *Drehbücher I–II* (Munich: Skellig, 1977).
——, *Vom Gehen im Eis* (Munich: Skellig, 1978).
——, *Of Walking on Ice* (New York: Tanam, 1980).
——, *Drehbücher III* (Munich: Hanser, 1979).
——, *Screenplays* (New York: Tanam Press, 1980).
Alexander Kluge, *Lebensläufe. Anwesenheitsliste für eine Beerdigung* (Frankfurt: Suhrkamp, 1974).
——, *Attendance List for a Funeral*, translated by Leila Vennewitz (New York: McGraw-Hill, 1966).
——, *Schlachtbeschreibung* (Olten: Walter Verlag, 1964).
——, *The Battle*, translated by Leila Vennewitz (New York: McGraw-Hill, 1967).
——, *Lernprozesse mit tödlichem Ausgang* (Frankfurt: Suhrkamp, 1973).
——, *Neue Geschichten. Heft 1–18 'Unheimlichkeit der Zeit'* (Frankfurt: Suhrkamp, 1977).
——, *Gelegenheitsarbeit einer Sklavin: Zur realistischen Methode* (Frankfurt: Suhrkamp, 1975).
——, *Die Patriotin* (Frankfurt: Zweitausendeins, 1979).
——, *Die Macht der Gefühle* (Frankfurt: Zweitausendeins, 1984).
——, *Der Angriff der Gegenwart auf die übrige Zeit* (Frankfurt: Syndikat, 1985).
——, (ed.) *Bestandsaufnahme: Utopie Film* (Frankfurt: Zweitausendeins, 1983).
—— and Oskar Negt, *Öffentlichkeit und Erfahrung* (Frankfurt: Suhrkamp, 1972).
——, *Geschichte und Eigensinn* (Frankfurt: Zweitausendeins, 1981).
Ulrike Ottinger, *Madame X – eine absolute Herrscherin* (Frankfurt: Roter Stern, 1979).

343

——, *Freak Orlando, Kleines Welttheater in fünf Episoden* (Berlin: Medusa, 1981).
Rosa von Praunheim, *Sex und Karriere* (Munich: Rogner & Bernhard, 1976).
——, *Army of Lovers* (London: Gay Men's Press, 1980).
——, *Rote Liebe. Ein Gespräch mit Helga Goetz* (Cologne: Prometh, 1982).
Edgar Reitz, *Liebe zum Kino* (Cologne: Verlag Köln 78, 1984).
Edgar Reitz and Peter Steinbach, *Heimat. Eine deutsche Chronik* (Nördlingen: Greno, 1985).
Helma Sanders-Brahms, *Deutschland Bleiche Mutter* (Reinbek: Rowohlt, 1980).
Volker Schlöndorff and Günter Grass, *Die Blechtrommel als Film* (Frankfurt: Zweitausendeins, 1979).
Volker Schlöndorff, *Die Blechtrommel, Tagebuch einer Verfilmung* (Neuwied: Luchterhand, 1979).
Volker Schlöndorff, Nicolas Born and Bernd Lepel, *Die Fälschung als Film und der Krieg im Libanon* (Frankfurt: Zweitausendeins, 1981).
Werner Schroeter, Oskar Panizza, Antonio Salines, *Liebeskonzil* (Munich: Schirmer/Mosel, 1982).
Jean-Marie Straub and Danièle Huillet, 'Scenarios of *History Lessons* and *Introduction to Arnold Schönberg's "Accompaniment to a Cinematographic Scene"'*, Screen*, vol. 17 no. 1, (Spring 1976) pp. 54–83.
——, *Klassenverhältnisse* (ed.) Wolfram Schütte (Frankfurt: Fischer, 1984).
Hans Jürgen Syberberg, *Syberbergs Filmbuch* (Frankfurt: Fischer, 1979).
——, *Hitler. Ein Film aus Deutschland* (Reinbek: Rowohlt, 1978).
——, *Die Freudlose Gesellschaft* (Munich: Hanser, 1981).
——, *Parsifal* (Munich: Heyne, 1982).
——, *Der Wald steht schwarz und schweiget* (Zurich: Diogenes, 1984).
Margarethe von Trotta, Willi Bär and Hans Jürgen Weber, *Schwestern oder die Balance des Glücks* (Frankfurt: Fischer, 1979).
—— and Luisa Franca, *Das Zweite Erwachen der Christa Klages* (Frankfurt: Fischer, 1980).
—— and Hans Jürgen Weber, *Die Bleierne Zeit* (Frankfurt: Fischer, 1981).
——, *Heller Wahn* (Frankfurt: Fischer, 1983).
——, *Rosa Luxemburg* (Nördlingen: Greno, 1986).
Wim Wenders, *Emotion Pictures* (Frankfurt: Verlag der Autoren, 1986).
Wim Wenders and Peter Handke, *Falsche Bewegung. Essays und Filmkritiken* (Frankfurt: Suhrkamp, 1975).
Wim Wenders and Fritz Müller-Scherz, *The Film by Wim Wenders: Kings of the Road*, transl. by Christopher Doherty (Munich: Filmverlag der Autoren, 1976).
—— and Chris Sievernich, *Nick's Film/Lightning over Water* (Frankfurt: Zweitausendeins, 1981).
—— and Sam Shepard, *Paris, Texas* (ed.) Chris Sievernich (Nördlingen: Greno, 1984).
Klaus Wildenhahn, *Über synthetischen und dokumentarischen Film* (Frankfurt: Kommunales Kino, 1975).

4 General Bibliography

Wilfried Adam, *Das Risiko in der deutschen Filmwirtschaft* (Berlin: 1959).
Theodor W. Adorno and Max Horkheimer, *Dialectic of Enlightenment* (New York: Herder and Herder, 1972).
Alfred Andersch, 'Das Kino der Autoren', *Merkur*, no. 158 (1961) pp. 332–48.
Nigel Andrews, 'Hitler as Entertainment', *American Film*, vol. 3 no. 6 (April 1978) pp. 50–3.
Gideon Bachmann, 'The Man on the Volcano: A Portrait of Werner Herzog', *Film Quarterly*, vol. 31 no. 3 (Fall 1977) pp. 2–10.

Klaus Bädekerl, 'Alles kennen nichts erkennen', *Filmkritik* no. 148 (April 1969) pp. 225–7.

Rob Baker, 'New German Cinema – A Fistful of Myths', *Soho Weekly News*, 23 March 1978, pp. 21–3.

Angelika Bammer, 'Through a Daughter's Eyes', *New German Critique*, no. 36 (Fall 1985) pp. 91–110.

Sigrid Bauschinger *et al.* (eds.) *Film und Literatur. Literarische Texte und der neue deutsche Film* (Berne: Francke, 1984).

Wilfried Berghahn, 'Kino der Autoren – Kino der Produzenten', *Die Zeit*, 27 April 1962.

Ernst Bloch, *Erbschaft dieser Zeit* (Frankfurt: Suhrkamp, 1962).

——, *Das Prinzip Hoffnung* (Frankfurt: Suhrkamp, 1973).

Hans C. Blumenberg, 'Glanz und Elend des neuen deutschen Films', *Die Zeit*, pt I–II, 2–9 September 1977.

——, 'Von Caligari bis Coppola: Junge deutsche Filmemacher in Hollywood auf den Spuren von Lubitsch, Murnau und Lang', *Die Zeit*, 22 February 1980.

——, 'Bildschirm contra Leinwand', *Die Zeit*, 23 June 1978.

——, 'Der Aufstand der Trittbrettfahrer', *Tip Magazin*, 12 August 1983, pp. 6–7.

Hans-Michael Bock (ed.) *Cinegraph. Lexikon zum deutschsprachigen Film* (Munich: Edition Text & Kritik, 1984 ff).

Hark Bohm, 'Lauter Erfolge ohne Publikum', *Der Spiegel*, 7 August 1978, pp. 132–5.

Thomas Böhm-Christel, *Alexander Kluge* (Frankfurt: Suhrkamp, 1983).

Atze Brauner, *Mich gibt's nur einmal, Rückblende eines Lebens* (Berlin: Herbig, 1976).

Bert Brecht, 'Der Dreigroschenprozess: Ein Soziologisches Experiment' in *Bertolt Brechts Dreigroschenbuch*, vol. I (Frankfurt: Suhrkamp, 1978).

Andrew Britton, 'Fox and his Friends: Foxed', *Jump Cut*, no. 16 (November 1977) pp. 22–3.

Barbara Bronnen and Corinna Brocher, *Die Filmemacher. Zur neuen deutschen Produktion nach Oberhausen* (Munich: C. Bertelsmann, 1973).

Wolfgang Bruckner *et al.*, 'Die Verlohrene Ehre des deutschen Films', *lui* (Munich), no. 3 (March 1979) pp. 96–103.

Peter Buchka, 'Wir leben in einem toten Land', *Süddeutsche Zeitung*, 21–22 August 1977.

——, 'Dann geht wieder was, dann geht wieder nix', *Süddeutsche Zeitung*, 25 January 1985.

——, *Augen kann man nicht kaufen. Wim Wenders und seine Filme* (Munich: Carl Hanser, 1983).

——, 'Schwanengesang: Abschied vom neuen deutschen Film', in H. G. Pflaum, *Jahrbuch Film 83/84* (Munich: Carl Hanser, 1983).

Robert Burgoyne, 'Narrative and Sexual Excess', *October*, no. 21, Summer 1982, pp. 51–62.

Werner Burzlaff, 'Cinéma = Argent × Film', *Les Cahiers de la Cinémathèque*, no. 32 (Spring 1981) pp. 138–45.

Erica Carter, 'Interview with Ulrike Ottinger', *Screen Education*, no. 41 (Winter/Spring 1982) pp. 34–42.

Vincent Canby, 'The German Renaissance – No Room for Laughter or Love', *New York Times*, 11 December 1977, Section D, p. 15.

Gerald Clarke, 'Seeking Planets That Do Not Exist – The German Cinema is the Liveliest in Europe', *Time Magazine*, 20 March 1978, pp. 51–3.

Ian Christie (ed.) 'The Syberberg Statement', *Framework*, no. 6 (Autumn 1977) pp. 12–18.

Françoise Colin (ed.) *Jutta Brückner, Cinéma Regard Violence* (Brussels: Les Cahiers du Grif, 1982).
Michael Covino, 'Wim Wenders: A Worldwide Homesickness', *Film Quarterly*, vol. 31 no. 2 (Winter 1977/78) pp. 9–19.
Jonathan Cott, 'Signs of Life', *Rolling Stone*, 18 November 1976, pp. 49–56.
Pam Cook, 'The point of self-expression in avant-garde film' in J. Caughie (ed.) *Theories of Authorship* (London: Routledge & Kegan Paul, 1981).
Richard Collins and Vincent Porter, *WDR and the Arbeiterfilm* (London: British Film Institute, 1981).
Timothy Corrigan (ed.) *Werner Herzog* (London and New York: Methuen, 1986).
——, 'On the edge of history: the radiant spectacle of Werner Schroeter', *Film Quarterly* vol. 37 no. 4 (Summer 1984) pp. 6–18.
——, 'Werner Schroeter's operatic cinema', *Discourse*, no. 3 (Spring 1981) pp. 46–59.
Francis Courtade, *Jeune Cinéma Allemand* (Lyon: Serdoc, 1969).
David Curtis, *Experimental Cinema* (New York: Dell Publishing, 1971).
Jan Dawson, 'Filming Highsmith', *Sight and Sound*, vol. 47 no. 1 (Winter 1977/78) pp. 30–6.
——, 'The Sacred Terror: shadows of terrorism in the New German Cinema', *Sight and Sound*, vol. 48 no. 4 (Autumn 1979) pp. 242–5.
——, 'The Industry – German Weasels (Filmverlag Follies)' *Film Comment*, vol. 13 no. 3 (May–June 1977) pp. 33–4.
——, 'A Labyrinth of Subsidies', *Sight and Sound* (Winter 1980/81) pp. 14–20.
—— (ed.) *The Films of Hellmuth Costard* (London: Riverside Studios, 1979).
——, *Wim Wenders* (New York: New York Zoetrope, 1976).
——, *Alexander Kluge and 'The Occasional Work of a Female Slave'* (New York: New York Zoetrope, 1977).
——, 'Germany in Autumn and Eine Kleine Godard', *Take One*, vol. 6 no. 12 (November 1978) pp. 14–15, 44–5.
——, 'In Memoriam: Jan Dawson', *Monthly Film Bulletin*, October 1980.
David Denby, 'The Germans are Coming! The Germans are Coming!', *Horizon*, vol. 20 no. 1 (1977) pp. 89–90.
Helmut H. Diederichs, 'Märkte, Wüsten, Oasen – Zur bundesdeutschen Kinosituation', *medium*, 4/78 (April 1978) pp. 18–23.
——, 'Filmverlag der Autoren', *epd-Film* (September 1985), pp. 22–6.
Ernest Dichter International, 'Freizeitbedürfnisse und Präferenzstruktur' in D. Prokop (ed.) *Materialien zur Theorie des Films* (Munich: Hanser, 1971) pp. 339–82.
Wolf Donner, 'Die Deutschen kommen', *Die Zeit*, 21 November 1975.
Siegfried Dörrfeldt, 'Das Missverhältnis der Kulturausgaben zum Film' in *Filmförderung in der Bundesrepublik: Ende oder Neubeginn* (Mannheim: Internationale Filmwoche, 1977) pp. 13–15.
Michael Dost, Florian Hopf and Alexander Kluge, *Filmwirtschaft in der BRD und Europa, Gotterdämmerung auf Raten* (Munich: Hanser, 1973).
Raymond Durgnat, 'From Caligari to Hitler', *Film Comment*, vol. 16 no. 4 (July–August 1980) pp. 59–70.
Burkhardt Dreher, *Filmförderung in der Bundesrepublik* (Berlin: Deutsches Institut für Wirtschaftsforschung, Sonderheft III, 1976).
Jürgen Ebert and Harun Farocki, 'Der Kleine Godard', *Filmkritik* no. 263 (November 1978) pp. 607–16.
Klaus Eder, 'Der Glaube ans große Geld', in H. G. Pflaum (ed.) *Jahrbuch Film 79/80* (Munich: Carl Hanser, 1979) pp. 100–7.
—— and Alexander Kluge, *Ulmer Dramaturgien. Reibungsverluste* (Munich: Hanser, 1980).

Charles Eidsvik, 'Behind the Crest of the Wave: An Overview of the New German Cinema', *Literature/Film Quarterly*, vol. 7 no. 3 (1979) pp. 167–81.

John Ellis, 'Art, Culture and Quality', *Screen*, vol. 19 no. 3 (Autumn 1978) pp. 9–49.

——, *Visible Fictions* (London: Routledge & Kegan Paul, 1982).

—— and Sheila Johnston, 'The Radical Film Funding of ZDF', *Screen*, vol. 23 no. 1 (May/June 1982) pp. 60–73.

Thomas Elsaesser, 'The Post-War German Cinema' in T. Rayns (ed.) *Fassbinder* (London: British Film Institute, 1976) pp. 1–16.

——, 'A Cinema of Vicious Circles', in T. Rayns (ed.) *Fassbinder* (London: British Film Institute, 1976) pp. 24–36.

——, 'German Film Bonanza', *New Statesman*, 8 January 1980.

——, 'Mother Courage and Divided Daughters', *Monthly Film Bulletin*, July 1983.

——, 'Memory, Home and Hollywood', *Monthly Film Bulletin*, Februray 1985.

——, 'Heimat', *American Film*, May 1985.

——, 'Syberberg's Parsifal', *Monthly Film Bulletin*, May 1983.

——, 'Primary Identification and the Historical Subject: Fassbinder's Germany', *Cinetracts*, no. 11 (Fall 1980) pp. 43–52.

——, 'Murder, Merger, Suicide' in T. Rayns (ed.) *Fassbinder* (London: British Film Institute, 2nd edn, 1979) pp. 37–53.

——, 'Working on the Margins', *Monthly Film Bulletin*, October 1983.

——, 'Syberberg, Cinema and Representation', *New German Critique*, nos. 24–25 (Fall/Winter 1981–2) pp. 108–54.

——, 'Fassbinder, Fascism and the Film Industry', *October*, no. 21 (1982) pp. 115–40.

——, 'Herbert Achternbusch and the German Avantgarde', *Discourse*, no. 6 (Fall 1983) pp. 92–112.

——, 'It Started with these Images: Filmmaking after Brecht in West Germany', *Discourse* no. 7 (Fall 1985) pp. 95–120.

——, 'Between Bitburg and Bergen Belsen', *On Film*, no. 14 (Spring 1985) pp. 38–40.

——, 'Germany's America: Wim Wenders and Peter Handke' in Susan Hayward (ed.) *European Cinema* (Birmingham: Aston University, 1985).

——, 'American Graffiti – Neuer Deutscher Film zwischen Avant-garde und Postmoderne' in A. Huyssen and K. Scherpe (eds.) *Postmoderne: Zeichen eines kulturellen Wandels* (Reinbek: Rowohlt, 1986) pp. 302–28.

——, 'Public Bodies and Divided Selves: German Women Film-makers in the 80s', *Monthly Film Bulletin*, December 1987.

——, 'A retrospect on the New German Cinema', *German Life and Letters*, vol. 41 no. 3, April 1988.

Hanns Heinz Ewers, 'Der Film und ich', in Anton Kaes (ed.) *Kino-Debatte* (Tübingen: Max Niemeyer, 1978) pp. 103–4.

Manny Farber and Patricia Patterson, 'Fassbinder', *Film Comment*, November–December 1975, pp. 5–7.

Harun Farocki, 'Notwendige Abwechslung und Vielfalt', *Filmkritik*, no. 223 (August 1975) pp. 363–9.

Helmut Färber, *Baukunst und Film* (Munich: Helmut Färber, 1977).

——, 'Der Brief', *Filmkritik* 4/67 (April 1967) pp. 203–4.

——, 'Das Unentdeckte Kino', in A. Kluge (ed.) *Bestandsaufnahme: Utopie Film* (Frankfurt: Zweitausendeins, 1983) pp. 15–29.

Rainer Werner Fassbinder, 'Seven Films by Douglas Sirk' in Jon Halliday and Laura Mulvey (eds.) *Douglas Sirk* (Edinburgh: Edinburgh Film Festival, 1971).

——, 'Insects in a Glass Case: Random Thoughts on Claude Chabrol', *Sight and Sound*, vol. 45 no. 4 (Autumn 1976) pp. 205–6, 252.

——, 'Klimmzug, Handstand, Salto mortale – sicher gestanden', *Frankfurter Rundschau*, 24 February 1979.

'Film in Berlin: Der Basis-Film Verleih', *Kinemathek*, no. 65, October 1983.

'Film in Berlin: Regina Ziegler Produktion', *Kinemathek*, no. 64, October 1983.

Filmstatistisches Jahrbuch (Wiesbaden: Spitzenorganisation der Filmwirtschaft, 1952–53ff).

Filmstatistisches Taschenbuch (Wiesbaden: Spitzenorganisation der Filmwirtschaft, 1963ff).

John Fiske and John Hartley, *Reading Television* (London: Methuen, 1978).

Robert Fischer and Joe Hembus (eds.) *Der Neue Deutsche Film 1960–1980* (Munich: Goldman, 1981).

Michel Foucault, 'What is an author?' in J. Caughie (ed.) *Theories of Authorship* (London: Routledge & Kegan Paul, 1981).

——, 'Interview: Film and Popular Memory', *Edinburgh Magazine*, no. 2 (1977) pp. 20–5.

Jim Franklin, 'Forms of Communication in Fassbinder's *Angst Essen Seele Auf*', *Literature/Film Quarterly*, no. 7 (Summer 1979) pp. 182–200.

Gunhild Freese, 'Die Leinwand lebt', *Die Zeit*, 10 October 1975.

Saul Friedländer, *Reflexions of Nazism – An Essay on Kitsch and Death* (New York: Harper and Row, 1984).

Theo Fürstenau, *Wandlungen im Film* (Pullach, Berlin: Verlag Dokumentation, 1970).

Michael Geisler, 'Heimat and the German Left', *New German Critique*, no. 36 (Fall 1985) pp. 25–66.

Jo Gelmis, *The Film Director as Superstar* (New York: Doubleday, 1970).

Wolfgang Gersch, *Film bei Brecht* (Berlin, GDR: Henschel Verlag, 1975).

Penelope Gilliatt, 'Gold', *New Yorker*, 11 April 1977.

Leonhard H. Gmühr, 'Zur Chronik', *Der Junge Deutsche Film* (Munich: Constantin Verleih, 1967).

Olga Grüber, 'Armer Deutscher Film', *Transatlantik*, January 1981, pp. 66–74.

Michael Goodwin, 'Herzog The God of Wrath', *American Film*, June 1982, pp. 36–51, 72–3.

Michael Gotthelf, 'Dem Deutschen Film auf die Beine helfen', *Frankfurter Allgemeine Zeitung*, 26 September 1981.

Alan Greenberg, *Heart of Glass* (Munich: Skellig, 1976).

Ulrich Gregor, 'The German Film in 1964: Stuck at Zero,' *Film Quarterly*, vol. 18 no. 2 (Winter 1964) pp. 7–21.

——, *Geschichte des Film ab 1960* (Munich: C. Bertelsmann, 1978).

Thomas H. Guback, *The International Film Industry* (Bloomington, Indiana: Indiana University Press, 1969).

'Hamburger Erklärung', *medium*, November 1979, pp. 27–8.

Peter Handke, 'Augsburg im August: Trostlos', *Film*, January 1969.

——, 'Vorläufige Bemerkungen zu Landkinos und Heimatfilmen', in *Ich bin ein Bewohner des Elfenbeinturms* (Frankfurt: Suhrkamp, 1972).

Miriam Hansen, 'Cooperative Auteur Cinema and Oppositional Public Sphere', *New German Critique*, nos. 24–25 (Fall/Winter 1981–2) pp. 36–56.

——, 'Alexander Kluge, Cinema and the Public Sphere: The Construction Site of Counter-History', *Discourse*, no. 6 (Fall 1983) pp. 53–74.

——, 'Visual Pleasure, Fetishism and the Problem of the Feminine/Feminist Discourse', *New German Critique*, no. 31 (Winter 1984) pp. 95–108.

—— (ed.), 'Dossier on Heimat', *New German Critique*, no. 36 (Fall 1985) pp. 3–24.

Sven Hansen, 'Die Inspiration aus dem Bücherschrank', *Die Welt*, 13 January 1979.

Patricia Harbord, 'Interview with Jutta Brückner', *Screen Education*, no. 40 (Autumn/Winter 1981–2).

Horst von Hartlieb, 'Es muß eine neue Grundentscheidung getroffen werden', *Filmförderung in der Bundesrepublik: Ende oder Neubeginn?* (Mannheim: Internationale Filmwoche, 1977) pp. 2–8.

Arnold Hauser, 'The Film Age', *The Social History of Art*, vol. 4 (London: Routledge, 1962).

Ronald Hayman, *Fassbinder Filmmaker* (London: Weidenfeld and Nicolson, 1984).

David Head, 'Der Autor muß respektiert werden' – Schlöndorff/Trotta's *Die verlorene Ehre der Katharina Blum* and Brecht's Critique of Film Adaptation', *German Life and Letters*, vol. 32 no. 3 (April 1979) pp. 248–64.

Joe Hembus, *Der deutsche Film kann garnicht besser sein. Ein Pamphlet von gestern, eine Abrechnung von heute* (Munich: Rogner & Bernhard, 1981).

J. Hermand, H. Peitsch and K. R. Scherpe (eds) *Nachkriegsliteratur in Westdeutschland 1945–1949*, vol. I (Berlin: Das Argument, 1982).

Werner Herzog, 'Mit den Wölfen heulen', *Filmkritik*, July 1968 pp. 460–1.

——, 'Why is There "Being" at All, Rather than Nothing?', *Framework*, no. 3 (Spring 1976) pp. 24–7.

——, 'Interview', *Filmkritik*, March 1968 pp. 176–9.

——, 'Interview', *American Film*, May 1980.

——, 'Interview' at the Chicago Art Institute, 11 February 1978.

——, Hark Bohm and Uwe Brandner, 'Wir sind nicht mehr der Jungfilm', *Der Spiegel*, 18 June 1979.

——, 'Laudatio auf Lotte Eisner', *Film-Korrespondenz*, 30 March 1982, pp. I–II.

Manfred Hohnstock and Alfons Bettermann (eds.) *Der Deutsche Filmpreis, 1951–1980* (Cologne: Bundesministerium des Inneren, 1980).

Ron Holloway, 'A German Breakthrough?', *Kino-German Film* (October 1979) pp. 4–17.

——, 'Who's Who in West German Film Industry: A Directory of Directors and Filmmakers over the Period 1957–1977', *Variety*, 22 June 1977, pp. 51, 54, 58, 70.

John Hughes, 'Fassbinder and Modernism', *Film Comment*, November–December 1975, pp. 11–13.

Gisela Hundertmark and Louis Saul (eds.) *Förderung Essen Filme Auf* (Munich: Ölschläger, 1984).

Andreas Huyssen, 'The Politics of Identification', *New German Critique*, no. 19 (Winter 1980) pp. 117–36.

Diane Jacobs, 'Hitler's Ungrateful Grandchildren', *American Film*, May 1980, pp. 34–40.

Peter W. Jansen and Wolfram Schütte (eds.) *Werner Schroeter* (Munich: Hanser, 1980).

—— (eds.) *Herzog, Kluge, Straub* (Munich: Hanser, 1976).

—— (eds.) *Fassbinder* (Munich: Hanser, 1975, 3rd edn 1982).

—— (eds.) *Film in der DDR* (Munich: Hanser, 1977).

—— (eds.) *Werner Herzog* (Munich: Hanser, 1979).

—— (eds.) *Rosa von Praunheim* (Munich: Hanser, 1983).

—— (eds.) *Herbert Achternbusch* (Munich: Hanser, 1982).

Karen Jaehne, 'The American Fiend', *Sight and Sound*, vol. 47 no. 2 (Spring 1978) pp. 101–3.

——, 'Old Nazis in New Films: The German Cinema Today', *Cineaste*, vol. 9 no. 1 (1978) pp. 32–5.

Frederic Jameson, 'In the Destructive Element Immerse', *October*, no. 17 (Summer 1981) pp. 99–118.

Urs Jenny, 'Abschied von Illusionen', in Leonhardt H. Gmühr, *Der Junge Deutsche Film* (Munich: Constantin Verleih, 1967) pp. 96–111.

Dierk Joachim and Peter Nowotny, *Kommunale Kinos in der BRD* (Münster: Selbstverlag der Herausgeber, 1978).

Hanno Jochimsen, 'Film ins Grundgesetz', *Berlinale Tip*, no. 10, February 1982.

Sheila Johnston, 'The Author as Public Institution', *Screen Education*, nos. 32–33 (Autumn/Winter 1979–80) pp. 67–78.

——, 'A Star is Born: Fassbinder and the New German Cinema', *New German Critique*, nos. 24–25 (Fall/Winter 1981–2) pp. 57–72.

—— (ed.) *Wim Wenders* (London: British Film Institute Dossier No. 10, 1981).

Oskar Kalbus, *Die Situation des deutschen Films* (Wiesbaden: 1956).

Stanley Kauffman, 'Watching the Rhine', *The Nation*, 20 August 1977.

Pauline Kael, 'Metaphysical Tarzan', *New Yorker*, 20 October 1975.

Anton Kaes, 'Distanced Observers: Perspectives on the New German Cinema', *Quarterly Review of Film Studies* (Summer 1985) pp. 238–45.

Liticia Kent, 'Werner Herzog: Film is not the Art of Scholars but of Illiterates', *New York Times*, Sunday Supplement, 11 September 1977.

Alexander Kluge, 'Förderung – Die modernste Form der Zensur', *Das Parlament*, no. 40 (6 October 1979) p. 11.

Gertrud Koch, 'Ex-Changing the Gaze: Re-visioning Feminist Film Theory', *New German Critique*, no. 34 (Winter 1985) pp. 139–53.

Jörg Friedrich Krabbe, 'Die neuen Caligaris', *Neues Forum*, July/August 1976, pp. 59–64.

Eberhard Kranz, *Filmkunst in der Agonie* (Berlin, GDR: Henschel Verlag, 1964).

Vlado Kristl, 'Sekundenfilme', *Filmkritik*, October 1969 pp. 610–11.

——, 'Tod dem Zuschauer', *Informationsblatt*, no. 12 (Berlin: Internationales Forum des Jungen Films, 1984).

Klaus Kreimeier, *Kino und Filmindustrie in der BRD. Ideologieproduktion und Klassenwirklichkeit nach 1945* (Kronberg: Scriptor Verlag, 1973).

——, 'Das Kino als Ideologiefabrik', *Kinemathek*, no. 45, November 1971.

Marion Kroner, *Film – Spiegel der Gesellschaft? Inhaltsanalyse des jungen deutschen Films von 1962 bis 1969* (Heidelberg: Quelle und Meyer, 1973).

Norbert Kückelmann (ed.) *Kuratorium Junger Deutscher Film – Die ersten drei Jahre* (Wiesbaden: 1968).

Ulrich Kurowski (ed.) . . . *nicht mehr fliehen: Kino in der Ära Adenauer* (Munich: Filmmuseum, 1979).

——, '1945–1960: Eine kleine (west)deutsche Filmgeschichte', *epd-Film* July 1985 pp. 22–6.

'Kuratorium Junger deutscher Film', *Kino-German Film*, no. 13, 1983–4, pp. 3–33.

Claudia Lenssen, 'Filmstoffe, ballenweise', *Frankfurter Rundschau*, 30 April 1983.

Rainer Lewandowski, *Die Filme von Alexander Kluge* (Hildesheim: Olms, 1980).

——, *Die Oberhausner. Rekonstruktion einer Gruppe, 1962–1982* (Diekholzen: Regie Verlag, 1982).

Arthur Lubow, 'Cinema's New Wunderkinder', *New Times*, 14 November 1975, p. 55.

Gudrun Lukasz-Aden and Christel Strobel, *Der Frauenfilm* (Munich: Heyne, 1985).

Peter Märtesheimer and Ivo Frenzel (eds.) *Der Fernsehfilm Holocaust. Eine Nation ist betroffen* (Frankfurt: Fischer, 1979).

Judith Mayne, 'Female Narration, Women's Cinema: Helke Sander's *Redupers*', *New German Critique*, nos. 24–25 (Winter/Fall 1981–2) pp. 155–71.

Chris Marker, 'Adieu au cinéma allemand?', *Positif*, no. 12, 1954.

Colin MacCabe, 'Memory, Phantasy, Identity', *Edinburgh Magazine* no. 2 (1977) pp. 13–17.

Ruth McCormick, 'Metropolis Now: The New German Cinema', *In These Times*, 30 July 1979.

—— (ed.) *Fassbinder* (New York: Tanam Press, 1981).

Andreas Meyer, 'Auf dem Weg zum Staatsfilm?', pts I–III, *medium*, October/November/December 1977.

Alexander Mitscherlich, *Society without the Father* (London: Tavistock, 1969).

—— and Margarethe Mitscherlich, *The Inability to Mourn* (London: Tavistock, 1975).

Renate Möhrmann, *Die Frau mit der Kamera: Filmemacherinnen in der Bundesrepublik* (Munich: Carl Hanser, 1980).

Hans-Bernhard Moeller and Carl Springer, 'Directed Change in the Young German Film: Alexander Kluge and *Artists Under the Big Top: Perplexed*', *Wide Angle*, vol. 2 no. 1 (1977) pp. 14–21.

——, 'New German Film and its Precarious Subsidy and Finance System', *Quarterly Review of Film Studies*, Spring 1980.

——, 'Brecht and "Epic" Film Medium', *Wide Angle*, vol. 3 no. 4 (1980) pp. 4–11.

Peter Nau, 'Römerberg Stenogramme', *Filmkritik*, June 1977 pp. 274–5.

Steve Neale, 'Art Cinema as Institution', *Screen*, vol. 22 no. 1 (Spring 1981) pp. 11–39.

Alfred Nemeczek, 'Ganz schön heruntergekommen', in H. G. Pflaum (ed.) *Jahrbuch Film 1978/79* (Munich: Carl Hanser, 1978) pp. 167–78.

Neuer Deutscher Film – Eine Dokumentation (Mannheim: Verband der Filmclubs e.V., 1967).

Hans-Joachim Neumann, *Der deutsche Film heute* (Frankfurt/Berlin: Ullstein Verlag, 1986).

Jürgen Noltenius, *Die FSK der Filmwirtschaft und das Zensurverbot* (Göttingen: 1958).

David L. Overbey, 'From Murnau to Munich. New German Cinema', *Sight and Sound*, vol. 43 no. 2 (Spring 1974) pp. 101–3, 115.

Enno Patalas, 'Autorität und Revolte im deutschen Film: Nationale Leitbilder von Caligari bis Canaris', *Frankfurter Hefte*, January 1956.

——, 'Prämien für die Braven', *Filmkritik*, January 1961 p. 465.

——, 'Die toten Augen', *Filmkritik*, December 1968 pp. 825–33.

——, 'German Cinema since 1945' in R. Roud (ed.) *Cinema: A Critical Dictionary* (London: Secker and Warburg, 1980).

Ruth Perlmutter, 'Visible Narrative, Visible Woman', *Millenium Film Journal*, no. 6 (Spring 1980) pp. 18–30.

Peter Pleyer, *Deutscher Nachkriegsfilm 1945–1948* (Münster: C. J. Fahle, 1965).

——, *Nationale und soziale Stereotypen im gegenwärtigen deutschen Spielfilm* (Munich: Institut für Publizistik/Verlag Regensberg, 1968).

Vincent Porter (ed.) *Film and Television Policy: West Germany and Great Britain* (London: Polytechnic of Central London, 1976).

Hans Helmut Prinzler and Walter Seidler, *Das Kinobuch 74/75* (Berlin: Stiftung Deutsche Kinemathek, 1975).

Dieter Prokop, *Soziologie des Films* (Neuwied: Luchterhand, 1974).

—— (ed.) *Materialien zur Theorie des Films* (Munich: Hanser, 1971).

John Pym, 'Syberberg and the Tempter of Democracy', *Sight and Sound*, vol. 46 no. 4 (Autumn 1977) pp. 227–30.

Tony Rayns, 'Forms of Address: Three German Filmmakers', *Sight and Sound*, vol. 44 no. 1 (Winter 1974/75) pp. 2–7.

—— (ed.) *Fassbinder* (London: British Film Institute, 1976, 1979).

Robert and Carol Reimer, 'Nazi-retro Filmography', *Journal of Popular Film and Television*, Summer 1986, pp. 81–92.

Eric Rentschler, 'The Use and Abuse of Memory: New German Film and the Discourse of Bitburg', *New German Critique*, no. 36 (Fall 1985) pp. 67–90.

——, 'Kluge, Film History and Eigensinn', *New German Critique*, no. 31 (Winter 1984) pp. 1109–24.

Ruby Rich, 'She Says He Says', *Discourse*, no. 6 (Fall 1983) pp. 31–46.

Georg Roeber and Gerhard Jacoby, *Handbuch der Medienbereiche: Film* (Pullach: 1973).

Günter Rohrbach, 'Die verhängnisvolle Macht der Regisseure', *medium*, April 1983, pp. 40–1.

Alvin Rosenfeld, *Imagining Hitler* (Bloomington, Indiana: Indiana University Press, 1985).

Richard Roud, *Straub* (London: Secker & Warburg, 1971).
Wilhelm Roth, *Der Dokumentarfilm seit 1960* (Munich: C. J. Bucher, 1982).
Michael Rutschky, *Erfahrungshunger* (Frankfurt: Fischer, 1982).
——, 'Realität träumen', *Merkur*, no. 363 (July 1978) pp. 773–85.
Helke Sander, *Der subjektive Faktor, vertrackt* (Berlin: Basis-Film Verleih, 1981).
——, 'sexismus in den massenmedien', *frauen und film*, no. 1, 1974.
Helma Sanders-Brahms, 'Preusse, Dichter, Selbstmörder', *Berliner Hefte*, January 1976 pp. 79–84.
——, 'Meine Kritiker, meine Filme und ich', *Kirche und Film* (September 1980) pp. 9–13.
——, 'A Desert for Dreamers', in Vincent Porter (ed.) *Film and Television Policy: West Germany and Great Britain* (London: Polytechnic of Central London, 1976).
John Sandford, 'The New German Cinema', *German Life and Letters*, vol. 32 no. 3 (April 1979) pp. 206–28.
Andrew Sarris, 'The Germans are Coming, The Germans are Coming!', *Village Voice*, 27 October 1975, pp. 137–8.
Ellen Seiter, 'Women's History, Women's Melodrama', *German Quarterly* (Fall 1986) pp. 569–81.
Johannes Semler, *Vorschläge zur Ordnung der deutschen Filmwirtschaft* (Wiesbaden: 1954).
Marc Silberman, 'Cine-Feminists in West Berlin', *Quarterly Review of Film Studies* (Spring 1980) pp. 217–32.
——, 'Women Filmmakers Working in West Germany', *Camera Obscura*, no. 6 (1980) pp. 122–52.
Kaja Silverman, 'Helke Sander and the will to change', *Discourse*, no. 6 (Fall 1983) pp. 10–30.
——, 'Kaspar Hauser's "Terrible Fall" into narrative', *New German Critique*, nos. 24–25 (Winter/Fall 1981–2) pp. 73–93.
Burghard Schlicht, 'Nullwachstum', *medium*, November 1978.
Walter Schmieding, *Kunst oder Kasse – Der Ärger mit dem deutschen Film* (Hamburg: Rütten & Loening, 1961).
Michael Schneider, *Den Kopf verkehrt aufgesetzt* (Neuwied: Luchterhand, 1981).
——, *Nur tote Fische schwimmen mit dem Strom* (Cologne: Kiepenheuer & Witsch, 1984).
——, 'Fathers and Sons Retrospectively', *New German Critique*, no. 31 (Winter 1984) pp. 3–51.
Roland Schneider (ed.) *Cinéma Allemand* (Paris: CinemAction, 1984).
Ute Schmidt and Tilman Fichter, *Der erzwungene Kapitalismus* (Berlin: Klaus Wagenbach Verlag, 1971).
Bion Steinborn, 'Die Idee des Zuschauerfilms ist so alt wie das Kino selbst', *filmfaust*, no. 4 (June/July 1977) pp. 75–96.
——, 'Ein Gespräch zwischen Alexander Kluge und Bion Steinborn', *filmfaust*, no. 26 (1982) pp. 32–64.
Helmut Schödel, 'Die Riesen des Wahnsinns: Über Alexeij Sagerer, Vlado Kristl und Herbert Achternbusch', *Die Zeit*, 7 September 1979.
Wolfram Schütte, 'Herrscht Ruhe im Land?', *Frankfurter Rundschau*, 6 August 1977.
John Simon, 'Cinematic Illiterates', *New York*, 20 October 1975.
Susan Sontag, 'Eye of the Storm', *New York Review of Books*, 21 February 1980, pp. 36–43.
Giovanni Spagnoletti (ed.), *Nuovo Cinema Tedesco negli anni Sessanter 1960–1970* (Milan: Ubulibri, 1985).
Hans Jürgen Syberberg, 'Form is Morality', *Framework*, no. 12 (1980) pp. 11–15.
Reinhold E. Thiel, 'Was wurde aus Goebbels' UFA?', *Film aktuell*, February 1970.

Paul Thomas, 'Fassbinder: The Poetry of the Inarticulate', *Film Quarterly*, Winter 1976–77, pp. 2–17.

'Rudolf Thome', *Kinemathek*, no. 66, November 1983.

Albie Thoms, 'German Underground', *Afterimage* (London) no. 2 (Autumn 1970) pp. 44–55.

Kristin Thompson, *Exporting Entertainment* (London: British Film Institute, 1986).

Amos Vogel, 'A Nation Comes Out of Shell-Shock', *Village Voice*, 4 May 1972, pp. 87–8.

Gene Walsh (ed.) *Images at the Horizon. A Workshop with Werner Herzog, conducted by Roger Ebert* (Chicago: Facets Multi-media, 1979).

'WDR', *Kino-German Film*, no. 22 (Spring 1986).

Wim Wenders, 'Verachten, was verkauft wird', *Süddeutsche Zeitung*, 16 December 1969.

——, 'Jetzt fällt die Entscheidung', *Abendzeitung* (Munich), 30 August 1977, p. 12.

——, 'Kritischer Kalender', *Filmkritik*, December 1969 pp. 751–2.

Ernst Wendt, 'Wir sind wieder wer', *Film 1967*, pp. 43–50.

Kraft Wetzel, 'Vom Jungen Film zum Deutschen Kino', *Frankfurter Allgemeine Zeitung*, 4 March 1982.

——, 'Die Krise des Neuen deutschen Films', *Media Perspektiven*, no. 2 (1987) pp. 90–9.

—— (ed.) *Neue Medien kontra Filmkultur?* (Berlin: Verlag Volker Spiess, 1987).

Klaus Wildenhahn, 'Industrielandschaft mit Einzelhändlern', *Filmfaust*, no. 20 (1980).

David Wilson, 'Anti-Cinema: Rainer Werner Fassbinder', *Sight and Sound*, Spring 1972, pp. 99–100, 113.

Karsten Witte, *Im Kino. Hören und Sehen* (Frankfurt: Fischer, 1985).

——, 'Film ist ein Persönlichkeitsgeschäft', *medium*, 3/78 (March 1978) pp. 10–15.

'Young German Film', *Film Comment*, Spring 1970, pp. 32–45.

Siegfried Zielinski, 'History as Entertainment and Provocation', *New German Critique*, no. 19 (Winter 1980) pp. 81–96.

Friedrich Zimmermann, 'Das Publikum muß immer mitbestimmen', *Die Welt*, 12 January 1985.

Jack Zipes, 'The Political Dimensions of The Lost Honor of Katharina Blum', *New German Critique*, no. 12 (Fall 1977) pp. 75–84.

Gerhard Zwerenz, 'Die falschen Stoffe', in H. G. Pflaum (ed.) *Jahrbuch Film 1977/78* (Munich: Carl Hanser, 1978).

Filmography

Abbreviations

d: director   *c*: camera   *m*: music   *r*: running time
sc: script   *ed*: editor   *l.p.*: leading players   *p*: production

Die Abfahrer (*On the Move*)
d: Adolf Winkelmann – *sc*: Adolf Winkelmann and Gerd Weiss – *c*: David Slama –
ed: Helga Schnurre – *m*: Schmetterlinge – *l.p.*: Detlev Quant, Ludger Schneider,
Beate Brockstedt – *r*: 97 min, col – *p*: Adolf Winkelmann/WDR Cologne 1978

Abschied von Gestern (*Yesterday Girl*)
d/sc: Alexander Kluge, based on his story *Anita G.* – *c*: Edgar Reitz, Thomas Mauch –
ed: Beate Mainka – *l.p.*: Alexandra Kluge, Hans Korte, Alfred Edel, Günther Mack –
r: 88 min, b/w – *p*: Kairos Film Munich/Independent Film Berlin 1966

Acht Stunden sind kein Tag (*Eight Hours are not a Day*)
5 part TV series – *d/sc*: Rainer Werner Fassbinder – *c*: Dietrich Lohmann – *ed*: Marie
Anne Gerhardt – *m*: Jean Geponint (=Jens Wilhelm Petersen) – *l.p.*: Gottfried John,
Hanna Schygulla, Luise Ullrich, Werner Finck, Kurt Raab, Renate Roland, Irm
Hermann, Herb Andres – *r*: 101 min (pt. 1), 100 min (pt. 2), 92 min (pt. 3), 88 min
(pt. 4), 89 min (pt. 5), col – *p*: Westdeutscher Rundfunk (Peter Märthesheimer)
Cologne 1972

Achtundvierzig Stunden bis Acapulco (*48 Hours to Acapulco*)
d: Klaus Lemke – *sc*: Max Zihlmann – *c*: Hubs Hagen, Niklaus Schilling – *m*: Roland
Kovac – *l.p.*: Christiane Krüger, Dieter Geissler, Monika Zinnenberg, Rod Carter –
r: 81 min, col – *p*: Seven Star (Joseph Kommer) Munich 1967

Adele Spitzeder
d: Peer Raben – *sc*: Martin Sperr, Peer Raben – *c*: Michael Ballhaus – *m*: Peer
Raben – *l.p.*: Ruth Drexel, Ursula Strätz, Peter Kern, Rosemarie Fendel – *r*: 92 min,
col – *p*: Filmverlag der Autoren Munich/WDR Cologne 1972

Adolf und Marlene (*Adolf and Marlene*)
d/sc: Ulli Lommel – *c*: Michael Ballhaus – *m*: Liszt, Wagner – *l.p.*: Kurt Raab; Margit
Carstensen, Harry Baer – *r*: 88 min, col – *p*: Albatros Film Munich/Trio Film Duisburg
1977

Affäre Blum (*The Blum Affair*)
d: Erich Engel – *sc*: R.A. Stemmle – *c*: Friedl Behn Grund, Karl Plintzner – *ed*:

Lilian Seng – *m*: Herbert Trantow – *l.p.*: Hans Christian Blech, Gisela Trowe, Arno Paulsen, Gerhard Bienert, Maly Delschaft – *r*: 110 min, b/w – *p*: Defa (Herbert Uhlich) Berlin 1948

Aguirre, der Zorn Gottes (*Aguirre, Wrath of God*)
d/sc: Werner Herzog – *c*: Thomas Mauch, Francisco Joan, Orlando Macchiavello – *ed*: Beate Mainka-Jellinghaus – *m*: Popol Vuh – *l.p.*: Klaus Kinski, Helena Rojo, Rui Guerra, Peter Berling – *r*: 93 min, col – *p*: Werner Herzog Filmproduktion Munich/Hessischer Rundfunk Frankfurt 1972

Alabama
d/sc/ed: Wim Wenders – *c*: Robby Müller, Wim Wenders – *m*: The Rolling Stones, Jimi Hendrix, Bob Dylan – *l.p.*: Paul Lys, Werner Schroeter, Muriel Schrat – *r*: 22 min, b/w – *p*: Hochschule für Fernsehen und Film Munich 1969

Albert Warum? (*Albert – Why?*)
d/sc/ed: Josef Rödl – *c*: Karlheinz Gschwindl – *l.p.*: Fritz Binner, Michael Eichenseer, Georg Schiessl, Elfriede Bleisteiner – *r*: 105 min, b/w – *p*: Hochschule für Fernsehen und Film (HFF) Munich 1978

Alice in den Städten (*Alice in the Cities*)
d: Wim Wenders – *sc*: Wim Wenders, Veith von Füstenberg – *c*: Robby Müller, Martin Schäfer – *ed*: Peter Przygodda – *m*: Irmin Schmid, 'Can' – *l.p.*: Rüdiger Vogler, Yella Rottländer, Lisa Kreuzer, Edda Köchel – *r*: 110 min, b/w – *p*: Produktion 1 im Filmverlag der Autoren (Peter Genée) Munich/WDR Cologne 1973

Die allseitig reduzierte Persönlichkeit-Redupers (*Redupers/The All-round Reduced Personality*)
d/sc: Helke Sander – *c*: Katia Forbert – *ed*: Ursula Höf – *l.p.*: Helke Sander, Frank Burckner, Ronny Tanner, Gesine Strempel, Gislind Nabakowski – *r*: 98 min, b/w – *p*: Basis Film Berlin/ZDF Mainz 1977

. . . als Diesel geboren (*Born for Diesel*)
d/sc: Peter Przygodda and Braulio Tavares Neto – *c*: Martin Schäfer – *ed*: Peter Przygodda – *m*: Raimondo Sodre, Irmin Schmidt – *r*: 117 min, col – *p*: Road Movies Berlin/Wim Wenders Filmproduktion Munich 1979

Der amerikanische Freund (*The American Friend*)
d: Wim Wenders – *sc*: Wim Wenders, Fritz Müller-Scherz after the novel *Ripley's Game* by Patricia Highsmith – *c*: Robby Müller – *m*: Jürgen Knieper – *l.p.*: Bruno Ganz, Dennis Hopper, Gerard Blain, Lisa Kreuzer, Sam Fuller, Nicholas Ray – *r*: 110 min, col – *p*: Road Movies Berlin/Wim Wenders Filmproduktion Munich/WDR Cologne 1977

Der amerikanische Soldat (*The American Soldier*)
d/sc: Rainer Werner Fassbinder – *c*: Dietrich Lohmann – *ed*: Thea Eymèsz – *m*: Peer Raben – *l.p.*: Karl Scheydt, Elga Sorbas, Margarethe von Trotta, Hark Bohm, Ingrid Caven, Rainer Werner Fassbinder, Ulli Lommel, Irm Hermann – *r*: 80 min, b/w – *p*: antiteater Munich 1970

Das Andechser Gefühl (*The Andechs Feeling*)
d/sc: Herbert Achternbusch – *c*: Jörg Schmidt-Reitwein – *ed*: Karin Fischer – *l.p.*: Herbert Achternbusch, Margarethe von Trotta, Barbara Gass, Walter Sedlmayr, Reinhard Hauff – *r*: 68 min, col – *p*: Herbert Achternbusch/Bioskop Munich 1974

Angelika Urban, Verkäuferin, Verlobt (*Angelika Urban, Salesgirl, Engaged to Marry*)
d/sc: Helma Sanders-Brahms – *c*: Horst Bever – *r*: 38 min, b/w – *p*: (Helma Sanders) 1969

355

Der Angestellte (*The White-Collar Worker*)
d/sc: Helma Sanders – *c*: André Dubreuil – *l.p.*: Ernst Jacobi, Gieselheid Hönsch, Peter Arens, Wolfgang Kieling – *r*: 99 min, col – *p*: WDR Cologne 1971–2

Der Angriff der Gegenwart auf die übrige Zeit (*The Blind Director*)
d/sc: Alexander Kluge – *c*: Thomas Mauch, Werner Lüring, Hermann Fahr, Judith Kaufmann – *ed*: Jane Seitz – *l.p.*: Jutta Hoffmann, Armin Müller-Stahl, Michael Rehberg, Rosel Zech – *r*: 113 min, col – *p*: Kairos Film Munich/ZDF Mainz 1986

Die Angst des Tormanns beim Elfmeter (*The Goalie's Fear of the Penalty Kick*)
d: Wim Wenders – *sc*: Wim Wenders, based on the novel by Peter Handke – *c*: Robby Müller – *ed*: Peter Przygodda – *m*: Jürgen Knieper – *l.p.*: Arthur Brauss, Kai Fischer, Erika Pluhar, Libgart Schwarz, Rüdiger Vogler – *r*: 101 min, col – *p*: Produktion 1 im Filmverlag der Autoren (Thomas Schamoni, Peter Genée) Munich 1971

Angst essen Seele auf (*Ali/Fear Eats the Soul*)
d/sc: Rainer Werner Fassbinder – *c*: Jürgen Jürges – *ed*: Thea Eymèsz – *m*: archive – *l.p.*: Brigitte Mira, El Hedi Ben Salem, Barbara Valentin, Irm Hermann, R.W. Fassbinder, Marquard Bohm, Walter Sedlmayr – *r*: 93 min, col – *p*: Tango (Rainer Werner Fassbinder, Michael Fengler) Munich 1974

Die Angst ist ein zweiter Schatten (*Fear is a Second Shadow*)
d/sc: Norbert Kückelmann – *c*: Jürgen Jürges – *ed*: Gerd Berner – *l.p.*: Astrid Fournell, Gunther Maria Halmer, Dieter Hasselblatt, Anita Mally – *r*: 101 min, col – *p*: FFAT (Norbert Kückelmann)/SWF Baden-Baden 1975

Angst vor der Angst (*Fear of Fear*)
d: Rainer Werner Fassbinder – *sc*: Rainer Werner Fassbinder, based on an idea by Asta Scheib – *c*: Jürgen Jürges, Ulrich Prinz – *ed*: Liesgret Schmitt-Klink, Beate Fischer-Weiskirch – *m*: Peer Raben – *l.p.*: Margit Carstensen, Ulrich Faulhaber, Brigitte Mira, Irm Hermann, Kurt Raab, Ingrid Caven, Lilo Pempeit – *r*: 88 min, col – *p*: WDR (Peter Märthesheimer) Cologne 1975

Argila
d/sc/c/ed: Werner Schroeter – *m*: Donizetti, Meyerbeer, Bruch, Beethoven, Verdi, Liszt, Vivaldi, Caterina Valente – *l.p.*: Gisela Trowe, Magdalena Montezuma, Carla Aulaulu – *r*: 36 min, col b/w – *p*: Werner Schroeter 1969

Armee der Liebenden oder Aufstand der Perversen (*Army of Lovers*)
d/sc/ed: Rosa von Praunheim in cooperation with Mike Shepard – *c*: Rosa von Praunheim, Ben van Meter, Michael Oblovitz, John Rome, Werner Schroeter, Bob Schub, Nikolai Ursin, Juliane Wang, Lloyd Williams – *r*: 107 min, col – *p*: Rosa von Praunheim Berlin 1979

Die Artisten in der Zirkuskuppel: ratlos (*Artistes at the Top of the Big Top: Disorientated*)
d/sc: Alexander Kluge – *c*: Günter Hörmann, Thomas Mauch – *ed*: Beate Mainka-Jellinghaus – *l.p.*: Hannelore Hoger, Alfred Edel, Sigi Graue, Bernd Hoeltz – *r*: 103 min, b/w – *p*: Kairos (Alexander Kluge) Munich 1968

Ein Arzt aus Halberstadt (*A Doctor from Halberstadt*)
d/sc: Alexander Kluge – *c*: Alfred Tichawsky, Günter Hörmann – *ed*: Maximiliane Mainka – *l.p.*: Dr.med. Ernst Kluge – *r*: 29 min, b/w – *p*: Kairos (Alexander Kluge) 1970

Das As der Asse (*Ace of Aces*)
d: Gérard Oury – *sc*: Danièle Thompson – *c*: Xaver Schwarzenberger – *m*: Victor Cosma – *l.p.*: Jean Paul Belmondo, Marie-France Pisier, Rachid Ferrache – *r*: 103 min, col – *p*: Gaumont Paris/Cerito/Rialto Munich 1982

Die Atlantikschwimmer (*The Atlantic Swimmers*)
d/sc: Herbert Achternbusch – *c*: Jörg Schmidt-Reitwein – *ed*: Karin Fischer – *l.p.*: Herbert Achternbusch, Heinz Braun, Alois Hitzenbichler, Sepp Bierbichler, Barbara Gass, Margarethe von Trotta – *r*: 81 min, col – *p*: Herbert Achternbusch Buchdorf 1975

Auch Zwerge haben klein angefangen (*Even Dwarfs Started Small*)
d/sc: Werner Herzog – *c*: Thomas Mauch, Jörg Schmidt-Reitwein – *ed*: Beate Mainka-Jellinghaus – *m*: Florian Fricke – *l.p.*: Helmut Döhring, Paul Glauer, Gisela Hertwig – *r*: 96 min, b/w – *p*: Werner Herzog Filmproduktion Munich 1970

Auf Biegen und Brechen (*By Hook or by Crook*)
d: Hartmut Bitomsky – *sc*: Hartmut Bitomsky and Harun Farocki – *c*: Bernd Fiedler – *ed*: Sybille Windt – *m*: Jürgen Knieper – *l.p.*: Jo Bolling, Christine Kaufmann, Lisa Kreuzer, Harry Baer – *r*: 94 min, col – *p*: City/Maran/Big Sky Berlin/SDR Munich 1976

Der aufrechte Gang (*Walking Tall*)
d/sc: Christian Ziewer – *c*: Ulli Heiser – *ed*: Stefanie Wilke – *m*: Erhard Grosskopf – *l.p.*: Claus Eberth, Antje Hagen, Wolfgang Liere, Walter Prüssing – *r*: 115 min, col – *p*: Basis Film Berlin/WDR Cologne 1976

Aus der Ferne sehe ich dieses Land (*From Afar I See this Country*)
d: Christian Ziewer – *sc*: Antonio Skarmetta and Christian Ziewer – *c*: Gerard Vandenberg – *ed*: Stefanie Wilke – *m*: Andariegos, Omero Caro – *l.p.*: Pablo Lira, Annibal Rayna, Valeria Villaroel, Peter Lilienthal, Alf Bold – *r*: 98 min, col – *p*: Basis Film GmbH Berlin/WDR Cologne 1979

Aus einem deutschen Leben (*Death is my Trade*)
d: Theodor Kotulla – *sc*: Theodor Kotulla, based on the novel *La Mort est mon metier* by Robert Merle – *c*: Dieter Naujeck – *ed*: Wolfgang Richter – *m*: Eberhard Weber – *l.p.*: Götz George, Elisabeth Schwarz, Hans Korte, Kai Taschner, Elisabeth Stepanek – *r*: 145 min, col – *p*: Iduna/WDR Cologne 1977

Baal
d: Volker Schlöndorff – *sc*: Volker Schlöndorff, from the play by Bertolt Brecht – *c*: Dietrich Lohmann – *l.p.*: Rainer Werner Fassbinder, Margarethe von Trotta, Sigi Graue, Hanna Schygulla – *r*: 87 min, col – *p*: HR Frankfurt/BR Munich/Hallelujah-Film 1969

Baby
d/sc: Uwe Friessner – *c*: Wolfgang Dickmann – *ed*: Tanja Schmidbauer – *m*: 'Spliff' – *l.p.*: Udo Seidler, Reinhard Seeger, Volkmar Richter – *r*: 114 min, col – *p*: Basis Film Verleih Berlin/WDR Cologne 1985

Die Ballade vom kleinen Soldaten (*The Ballad of the Little Soldier*)
d: Werner Herzog, Denis Reichle – *c*: Jorge Vignao, Michael Edols – *ed*: Maximiliane Mainka – *r*: 44 min, col – *p*: Werner Herzog Filmproduktion Munich/SDR Stuttgart 1985

Bandonion-Deutsche Tangos/Tango im Exil (*German Tangos/Tangos in Exile*)
d: Klaus Wildenhahn, Rainer Komers, Günter Westerhoff – *r*: 55 min (pt. 1), 46 min (pt. 2), col – *p*: Norddeutscher Rundfunk Hamburg 1981

Bayreuther Proben (*Bayreuth Rehearsals*)
d: Klaus Wildenhahn, Rudolf Körösi, Jürgen Keller, Herbert Selk – *r*: 69 min (also a 31 min version), b/w – *p*: NDR Hamburg 1965

Der Beginn aller Schrecken ist Liebe (*Love is the Beginning of all Terrors*)
d: Helke Sander – *sc*: Helke Sander, Dörte Haak – *c*: Martin Schäfer – *ed*: Barbara von Weitershausen – *m*: Heiner Goebbels – *l.p.*: Helke Sander, Lou Castel, Rebecca Pauly, Katrin Seybold – *r*: 117 min, col – *p*: Provobis Film Hamburg 1986

Beim jodeln juckt die Lederhose (*There's No Sex Like Snow Sex*)
d: Alois Brummer – *sc*: Alois Brummer – *c*: Hubertus Hagen – *ed*: not stated – *m*: Fred Strittmater – *l.p.*: Judith Fritsch, Franz Muxeneder, Rosl Mayr – *r*: 85 min, col – *p*: AB Filmproduktion Munich 1974

Bengelchen liebt kreuz und quer (*Bengelchen Loves Back to Front*)
d/sc: Marran Gosov – *c*: Hubs Hagen, Niklaus Schilling – *m*: Martin Böttcher – *l.p.*: Harald Leipnitz, Sybille Maar, Renate Roland – *r*: 88 min, col – *p*: Rob Houwer 1968

Berlin Alexanderplatz
d: Rainer Werner Fassbinder – *sc*: Rainer Werner Fassbinder, based on the novel by Alfred Döblin – *c*: Xaver Schwarzenberger – *ed*: Juliane Lorenz – *m*: Peer Raben – *l.p.*: Gerhard Lamprecht, Barbara Sukowa, Hanna Schygulla, Ivan Desny, Gottfried John, Ingrid Caven, Brigitte Mira – *r*: TV film, 81 min (pt. 1), 59 min (each part from pt. 2–pt. 13), 111 min (epilogue), col – *p*: Bavaria/RAI for WDR (Peter Märthesheimer) 1979–80

Berlin Chamissoplatz
d: Rudolf Thome – *sc*: Jochen Brunow, Rudolf Thome – *c*: Martin Schäfer – *ed*: Ursula West – *m*: 'Ohpsst', Evi und die Evidrins – *l.p.*: Sabine Bach, Hanns Zischler, Wolfgang Kinder – *r*: 112 min, col – *p*: Anthea/Moana/Rudolf Thome/Polytel 1980

Berliner Bettwurst (*The Bedroll*)
d/sc/c/m/ed: Rosa von Praunheim – *l.p.*: Luzi Kryn, Dietmar Kracht, Steven Adamschewski – *r*: 81 min, col – *p*: Rosa von Praunheim 1971

Berliner Stadtbahnbilder (*Berlin S-Bahn Pictures*)
d: Alfred Behrens – *c*: Jürgen Jürges, Fritz Poppenberg, Michael Kuball – *ed*: Ursula Höf – *r*: 60 min, col – *p*: Basis Film Berlin/ZDF Mainz 1982

Berlinger – Ein deutsches Abenteuer (*Berlinger – A German Fate*)
d/sc: Bernhard Sinkel and Alf Brustellin – *c*: Dietrich Lohmann – *ed*: Heidi Genée – *m*: Joe Haider – *l.p.*: Martin Benrath, Hannelore Elsner, Tilo Prückner, Lina Carstens, Walter Ladengast, Evelyn Künnecke – *r*: 115 min, col – *p*: ABS (Brustellin-Sinkel)/Independent Munich (Heinz Angermeyer) 1975

Die Berührte (*No Mercy No Future*)
d: Helma Sanders-Brahms – *sc*: Helma Sanders-Brahms after texts by Rita G. – *c*: Thomas Mauch – *ed*: Ursula West – *m*: Manfred Opitz, Harald Grosskopf – *l.p.*: Elisabeth Stepanek – *r*: 100 min, col – *p*: Helma Sanders-Brahms Filmproduktion Berlin 1981

Besonders Wertvoll (*Quality Rating: Excellent*)
d/sc: Hellmuth Costard – *l.p.*: (voice of) Dr H.C. Toussaint – *r*: 11 min, col – *p*: Hellmuth Costard Hamburg 1968

Bierkampf (*Beer Battle*)
d/sc: Herbert Achternbusch – *c*: Jörg Schmidt-Reitwein – *ed*: Christl Leyrer – *l.p.*: Herbert Achternbusch, Annamirl Bierbichler, Sepp Bierbichler, Gerda Achternbusch, Barbara Gass – *r*: 85 min, col – *p*: Herbert Achternbusch/ZDF Mainz 1977

Bildnis einer Trinkerin (*Ticket of No Return*)
d/sc/c: Ulrike Ottinger – *ed*: Ila von Hasperg – *m*: Peer Raben – *l.p.*: Tabea Blumenschein, Magdalena Montezuma, Lutze, Monkia von Cube, Nina Hagen, Kurt Raab, Eddie Constantine, Volker Spengler – *r*: 108 min, col – *p*: Autorenfilm 1979

Bis zum Happy End (*To the Happy End*)
d: Theodor Kotulla – *sc*: Hans Stempel – *c*: Peter Sickert – *m*: Beethoven, Mozart – *l.p.*: Klaus Löwitsch, Beatrix Ost, Christof Hege – *r*: 94 min, b/w – *p*: Iduna 1968

Ein bisschen Liebe (*A Little Love*)
d: Veith von Fürstenberg – *sc*: Veith von Fürstenberg, Max Zihlmann – *c*: Robby Müller – *l.p.*: Burkhard Schlicht, Brigitte Berger, Eva Maria Herzig – *r*: 81 min, b/w – *p*: Wim Wenders/Veith von Fürstenberg 1974

Die bitteren Tränen der Petra von Kant (*The Bitter Tears of Petra von Kant*)
d: Rainer Werner Fassbinder – *sc*: Rainer Werner Fassbinder, based on his play – *c*: Michael Ballhaus – *ed*: Thea Eymèsz – *m*: The Platters, The Walker Brothers, Giuseppe Verdi – *l.p.*: Margit Carstensen, Hanna Schygulla, Irm Hermann, Eva Mattes, Katrin Schaake, Gisela Fackeldey – *r*: 124 min, col – *p*: Tango (Rainer Werner Fassbinder, Michael Fengler) Munich 1972

Blaue Blumen (*Blue Flowers*)
d/sc/c: Herbert Achternbusch – *c*: Adam Olech, Herbert Schild (=Herbert Achternbusch) – *ed*: Micki Joanni – *r*: 72 min, col – *p*: Herbert Achternbusch Filmproduktion Buchendorf 1984

Die Blechtrommel (*The Tin Drum*)
d: Volker Schlöndorff – *sc*: Jean-Claude Carrière, Franz Seitz, Volker Schlöndorff based on the novel by Günter Grass – *c*: Igor Luther – *ed*: Suzanne Baron – *m*: Maurice Jarre, Friedrich Mayer – *l.p.*: Angela Winkler, Mario Adorf, Heinz Bennent, Charles Aznavour, Daniel Olbrychski, Katharina Thalbach, David Bennent – *r*: 144 min, col – *p*: Franz Seitz Film/Bioskop (Eberhard Junkersdorf)/Hallelujah/Artemis/Argos (Anatole Dauman) Paris/HR Frankfurt in cooperation with Jadran-Film Zagreb and Film Polski Warsaw 1979

Die Bleierne Zeit (*The German Sisters/Marianne and Juliane*)
d/sc: Margarethe von Trotta – *c*: Franz Rath – *ed*: Dagmar Hirtz – *m*: Nicolas Economou – *l.p.*: Jutta Lampe, Barbara Sukowa, Rüdiger Vogler, Doris Schade – *r*: 106 min, col – *p*: Bioskop Filmproduktion (Eberhard Junkersdorf) Munich 1981

Ein Blick und die Liebe bricht aus (*One Glance and Love Breaks Out*)
d/sc: Jutta Brückner – *c*: Marcello Camorino – *ed*: Jutta Brückner, Ursula Höf – *m*: Brynmor Llewelyn Jones – *l.p.*: Elida Araoz, Rosario Blefari, Regina Lamm, Margarita Munoz – *r*: 86 min, col – *p*: Joachim von Vietinghoff Filmproduktion Berlin 1986

359

Blue Velvet
d/sc: Matthias Weiss – *c*: Frank Fiedler – *m*: Soft Machine – *r*: 57 min, col – *p*: Hochschule für Fernsehen und Film Munich 1970

Bolwieser
d: Rainer Werner Fassbinder – *sc*: Rainer Werner Fassbinder, based on the novel by Oskar Maria Graf – *c*: Michael Ballhaus – *ed*: Ila von Hasperg, Juliane Lorenz – *m*: Peer Raben – *l.p.*: Kurt Raab, Elisabeth Trissenaar, Bernhard Helfrich, Udo Kier, Volker Spengler, Armin Meier – *r*: 201 min (TV version in 2 pts), col – *p*: Bavaria Atelier GmbH Munich for ZDF Mainz 1976–7

Der Bomberpilot (*The Bomber Pilot*)
d/sc/c: Werner Schroeter – *m*: F. Liszt, J. Strauss, Zarah Leander, G. Verdi, J. Sibelius, Peter Alexander, W.A. Mozart, L. Bernstein, Caterina Valente, G. Bizet, F. Lehar – *l.p.*: Carla Aulaulu, Mascha Elm, Magdalena Montezuma – *r*: 65 min, col – *p*: Werner Schroeter for ZDF Mainz 1970

Das Boot (*The Boat*)
d: Wolfgang Petersen – *sc*: Wolfgang Petersen based on the book by Lothar Günther Buchheim – *c*: Jost Vacano – *ed*: Hannes Nikel – *m*: Klaus Doldinger – *l.p.*: Jürgen Prochnow, Herbert Grönemeyer, Klaus Wenneman – *r*: 130 min, col – *p*: Bavaria/Radiant/WDR Cologne 1981

Der Bräutigam, die Komödiantin und der Zuhälter (*The Bridegroom, the Comedienne and the Pimp*)
d: Jean Marie Straub and Danièle Huillet – *sc*: Jean Marie Straub, incorporating the play *Krankheit der Jugend* by Ferdinand Bruckner, abridged and produced by Jean Marie Straub; and extracts from the poetry of San Juan de la Cruz – *c*: Klaus Schilling, Hubs Hagen – *ed*: Danièle Huillet, Jean Marie Straub – *m*: J.S. Bach – *l.p.*: James Powell, Lilith Ungerer, Rainer Werner Fassbinder, Peer Raben, Irm Hermann, Hanna Schygulla – *r*: 23 min, b/w – *p*: Janus Film und Fernsehen (Klaus Hellwig) Munich 1968

Der Brief (*The Letter*)
d/sc: Vlado Kristl – *c*: Wolf Wirth – *ed*: Eva Zeyn – *m*: Gerhard Bommersheim – *l.p.*: Vlado Kristl, Mechtild Engel, Eva Hofmeister, Horst Manfred Adloff, Peter Berling – *r*: 82 min, b/w – *p*: Peter Genée/Kuratorium Junger Deutscher Film 1966

Das Brot des Bäckers (*The Baker's Bread*)
d: Erwin Keusch – *sc*: Erwin Keusch, Karl Saurer – *c*: Dietrich Lohmann – *ed*: Lilo Krüger – *m*: Axel Linstädt ('Improved Sound Ltd') – *l.p.*: Gerhard Lamprecht, Bernd Tauber, Maria Lucca, Sylvia Reize – *r*: 116 min, col – *p*: Artus Film Munich/ZDF Mainz 1976

Die Brücke (*The Bridge*)
d: Bernhard Wicki – *sc*: Michael Mansfeld, Karl-Wilhelm Vivier, Bernhard Wicki based on the novel by Manfred Gregor – *c*: Gerd von Bonin, Horst Fehlhaber – *ed*: C.O. Bartnig – *m*: Hans Martin Majewski – *l.p.*: Volker Bohnet, Fritz Wepper, Michael Hinz, Volker Lechtenbrink, Cordula Trantow, Günter Pfitzmann – *r*: 105 min, b/w – *p*: Fono-Film (Hermann Schwerin, Jochen Severin) 1959

Bruno – der Schwarze, es blies ein Jäger wohl in sein Horn (*Black Bruno*)
d/sc: Lutz Eisholz – *c*: Joseph Dayan – *l.p.*: Bruno S., Roland Neumann, Lotte Pause, Elisabeth Sauer – *r*: 81 min, col – *p*: Deutsche Film und Fernsehakademie Berlin 1970

Burden of Dreams
d: Les Blank – *sc*: not credited – *c*: Les Blank – *ed*: Maureen Gosling – *m*: extract from Vivaldi – *l.p.*: Werner Herzog, Klaus Kinski, Claudia Cardinale – *r*: 95 min, col – *p*: Flower Films San Francisco, in association with José Koechlin von Stein 1982

Cardillac
d: Edgar Reitz – *sc*: Edgar Reitz, based on the story *Das Fräulein von Scuderi* by E.T.A. Hoffmann – *c*: Dietrich Lohmann – *ed*: Maximiliane Mainka – *l.p.*: Hans Christian Blech, Catana Cayetano, Gunter Sachs, Heidi Stroh, Urs Jenny – *r*: 97 min, col b/w – *p*: Edgar Reitz Produktion Munich 1969

Celeste
d/sc: Percy Adlon – *c*: Renato Fortunato – *ed*: Clara Fabry – *m*: Cesar Franck (Bartholdy Quartet) – *l.p.*: Eva Mattes, Jürgen Arndt, Norbert Wartha, Wolf Euba – *r*: 107 min, col – *p*: pelemele Film GmbH (Eleonore Adlon)/BR Munich 1981

Chapeau Claque (*Top Hat*)
d/sc: Ulrich Schamoni – *c*: Igor Luther – *ed*: Regina Heuser – *l.p.*: Ulrich Schamoni, Anna Henkel, Jürgen Barz, Karl Dall, Ingo Insterburg, Rolf Zacher, Wolfgang Neuss – *r*: 94 min, col – *p*: Bärenfilm (Regina Ziegler) 1974

Chinesisches Roulette (*Chinese Roulette*)
d/sc: Rainer Werner Fassbinder – *c*: Michael Ballhaus – *ed*: Ila von Hasperg, Juliane Lorenz – *m*: Peer Raben – *l.p.*: Anna Karina, Macha Méril, Ulli Lommel, Brigitte Mira, Alex Allerson, Margit Carstensen, Andrea Schober, Armin Meier – *r*: 86 min, col – *p*: Albatros Film Munich (Michael Fengler)/Les Films du Losange Paris 1976

Christiane F. – Wir Kinder vom Bahnhof Zoo (*Christiane F.*)
d: Ulrich Edel – *sc*: Herman Weigel, based on the book by Kai Hermann and Horst Rieck (taken from taped interviews) – *c*: Justus Pankau, Jürgen Jürges – *ed*: Jane Seitz – *m*: Jürgen Knieper, David Bowie – *l.p.*: Natja Brunkhorst, Thomas Haustein, Jens Kuphal, David Bowie – *r*: 128 min, col – *p*: Solaris Berlin/Maran-Film/Popular-Film Stuttgart/CLV-Filmproduktions GmbH 1981

Chronik der Anna Magdalena Bach (*Chronicle of Anna Magdalena Bach*)
d: Jean-Marie Straub – *sc*: Jean-Marie Straub and Danièle Huillet – *c*: Ugo Piccone, Saverio Diamanti, Giovanni Canfarelli, Hans Kracht, Uwe Radon, Thomas Hartwig – *ed*: Danièle Huillet – *m*: J.S. Bach, Leo Leonius – *l.p.*: Gustav Leonhardt, Christiane Lang, Paolo Carlini – *r*: 94 min, b/w – *p*: Franz Seitz Munich/RAI Rome/ IDI Cinematografica Rome/Straub-Huillet Munich/Filmfond eV Munich/HR Frankfurt/Telepool Munich 1968

Der Damm (*The Dam*)
d/sc: Vlado Kristl – *c*: Gerard Vandenberg – *l.p.*: Petra Krause, Vlado Kristl, Felix Potisk, Erich Glöckler – *r*: 80 min, b/w – *p*: Detten Schleiermacher 1964

Dark Spring
d/sc: Ingemo Engström – *c*: Bernd Fiedler – *l.p.*: Edda Köchl, Ilona Schult, Irene Wittek, Klara Zet, Ingemo Engström, Gerhard Theuring – *r*: 92 min, col – *p*: Hochschule für Fernsehen und Film, Munich 1971

David
d: Peter Lilienthal – *sc*: Peter Lilienthal, Jurek Becker, Ulla Ziemann, based on the novel *Den Netzen entronnen* by Joel König – *c*: Al Ruban – *ed*: Siegrun Jäger – *m*:

Wojciek Kilar – *l.p.*: Mario Fischel, Valter Taub, Irena Vrkljan, Eva Mattes, Hanns Zischler, Erika Runge – *r*: 125 min, col – *p*: Joachim von Vietinghoff/Pro-Jekt/FFAT (Peter Lilienthal)/Zweites Deutsches Fernsehen Mainz 1979

Deadlock
d/sc: Roland Klick – *c*: Robert van Ackeren – *ed*: Jane Sperr – *m*: 'The Can' – *l.p.*: Mario Adorf, Anthony Dawson, Marquard Bohm, Mascha Elm Rabben – *r*: 94 min, col – *p*: Roland Klick 1970

De l'Argentine (*About Argentina*)
d/sc: Werner Schroeter – *c*: Werner Schroeter, Carlos Bernardo Wajsman – *ed*: Catherine Brasier, Claudio Martinez – *m*: excerpt from Mahler's 'Kindertotenlieder' – *l.p.*: Enrique Pinti, Libertad Leblanc, Cipe Lincovsky – *r*: 90 min, col – *p*: FR3/Out One Prods Paris 1983–5

Detektive (*Detectives*)
d: Rudolf Thome – *sc*: Max Zihlmann – *c*: Hubs Hagen, Niklaus Schilling – *m*: Kristian Schultze – *l.p.*: Iris Berben, Marquard Bohm, Ulli Lommel, Walter Rilla – *r*: 91 min, b/w – *p*: Eichberg (Carol Hellman) Munich 1969

Desperado City
d/sc: Vadim Glowna – *c*: Thomas Mauch – *ed*: Helga Borsche – *m*: Stanley Walden – *l.p.*: Siemen Rühaak, Beate Finckh, Vera Tschechowa, Karin Baal, Vadim Glowna, Witta Pohl, Stanley Walden – *r*: 97 min, col – *p*: Atossa-Film Munich 1980

Deutschland bleiche Mutter (*Germany Pale Mother*)
d/sc: Helma Sanders-Brahms – *c*: Jürgen Jürges – *ed*: Elfi Tillack, Uta Periginelli – *m*: Jürgen Knieper – *l.p.*: Eva Mattes, Ernst Jacobi, Elisabeth Stepanek, Rainer Friedrichsen, Fritz Lichtenhahn – *r*: 145 (120) min, col – *p*: Helma Sanders-Brahms/Literarisches Colloquium Berlin/Westdeutscher Rundfunk Cologne 1979

Deutschland im Herbst (*Germany in Autumn*)
d: Alf Brustellin, Rainer Werner Fassbinder, Alexander Kluge, Maximiliane Mainka, Edgar Reitz, Katja Ruppé, Hans Peter Cloos, Bernhard Sinkel, Volker Schlöndorff – *sc*: Rainer Werner Fassbinder, Heinrich Böll, Peter Steinbach – *c*: Michael Ballhaus, Jürgen Jürges, Bodo Kessler, Dietrich Lohmann, Jörg Schmidt-Reitwein – *ed*: Beate Mainka-Jellinghaus – *l.p.*: Rainer Werner Fassbinder, Hannelore Hoger, Katja Ruppé, Angela Winkler, Heinz Bennent, Helmut Griem, Vadim Glowna, Enno Patalas, Horst Mahler, Mario Adorf, Wolf Biermann – *r*: 116 mins, col/bw – *p*: Pro-Ject Filmproduktion/Filmverlag der Autoren/Hallelujah Film/Kairos Film Munich 1978

Dorian Gray im Spiegel der Boulevardpresse (*Dorian Gray in the Popular Press*)
d/sc/c: Ulrike Ottinger – *ed*: Eva Schlensag – *m*: Peer Raben – *l.p.*: Veruschka von Lehndorff, Delphine Seyrig, Tabea Blumenschein, Irm Hermann, Magdalena Montezuma, Barbara Valentin – *r*: 150 min, col – *p*: Ulrike Ottinger Filmproduktion 1983–4

Drei amerikanische LPs (*Three American LPs*)
d/c/ed: Wim Wenders – *sc*: Peter Handke – *m*: Van Morrison, Harvey Mandel, Creedence Clearwater Revival – *r*: 12 min, col – *p*: Wim Wenders/HR Frankfurt 1969

Die dritte Generation (*The Third Generation*)
d/sc/c: Rainer Werner Fassbinder – *ed*: Juiliane Lorenz – *m*: Peer Raben – *l.p.*: Harry

Baer, Hark Bohm, Margit Carstensen, Eddie Constantine, Günther Kaufmann, Udo Kier, Bulle Ogier, Lilo Pempeit, Hanna Schygulla, Volker Spengler, Y Sa Lo, Vitus Zeplichal – *r*: 111 min, col – *p*: Tango Film/Pro-Ject (Harry Baer) 1979

Eine Ehe (*A Marriage*)
d/sc: Rolf Strobel, Heinrich Tichawsky – *c*: Heinrich Tichawsky – *l.p.*: Heidi Stroh, Peter Graaf, Mischa Gallé – *r*: 120 min, b/w – *p*: Strobel-Tichawsky 1969

Die Ehe der Maria Braun (*The Marriage of Maria Braun*)
d: Rainer Werner Fassbinder – *sc*: Peter Märthesheimer, Pea Fröhlich, Rainer Werner Fassbinder based on an idea by Rainer Werner Fassbinder – *c*: Michael Ballhaus – *ed*: Juliane Lorenz, Franz Walsch (=Rainer Werner Fassbinder) – *m*: Peer Raben – *l.p.*: Hanna Schygulla, Klaus Löwitsch, Ivan Desny, Gottfried John, Günter Lamprecht, Gisela Uhlen, Elisabeth Trissenaar – *r*: 120 min, col – *p*: Albatros (Michael Fengler)/Trio (Hans Eckelkamp)/WDR Cologne 1979

Ehe im Schatten (*Shadows on a Marriage*)
d: Kurt Maetzig – *sc*: Kurt Maetzig, based on the novella *Es wird schon nicht so schlimm* by Hans Schweikart – *c*: Friedl Behn Grund – *m*: Wolfgang Zeller – *l.p.*: Paul Klinger, Ilse Steppart, Klaus Holm – *r*: 105 min, b/w – *p*: Defa Berlin 1947

Eika Katappa
d/sc/ed: Werner Schroeter – *c*: Werner Schroeter, Robert van Ackeren – *m*: Verdi, Beethoven, Mozart, Puccini, Richard Strauss, Johann Strauss, Krystof Penderecki, Gaspare Spontini, Vincenzo Bellini, Ambroise Thomas, Conchita Supervia a.o. – *l.p.*: Magdalena Montezuma, Rosa von Praunheim, Giesela Trowe, Carla Aulaulu, Alix von Buchen – *r*: 144 min, col, b/w – *p*: Werner Schroeter 1969

Eins + Eins = Drei (*One Plus One is Three*)
d/sc: Heidi Genée – *c*: Gernot Roll – *ed*: Helga Beyer – *m*: Andreas Koebner – *l.p.*: Adelheid Arndt, Dominik Graf, Christoph Quest, Hark Bohm – *r*: 85 min, col – *p*: Genée & Von Fürstenberg Munich 1979

Eintracht Borbeck (*Borbeck's Team-Spirit*)
d/sc/ed: Susanne Beyeler, Rainer März and Manfred Stelzer – *r*: 51 min, b/w – *p*: Deutsche Film und Fernsehakademie Berlin 1977

Emden geht nach USA (*Emden Goes to the US*)
d/sc/ed: Klaus Wildenhahn and Gisela Tuchtenhagen – *r*: 61 min (pt. 1), 62 min (pt. 2), 59 min (pt. 3), 59 min (pt. 4), b/w – *p*: NDR Hamburg/WDR Cologne 1976

Das Ende des Regenbogens (*The End of the Rainbow*)
d/sc: Uwe Frießner – *c*: Frank Brühne – *ed*: Stefanie Wilke – *m*: Alexander Kraut, Klaus Krüger, Michael Nuschke, Matthias Kaebs – *l.p.*: Thomas Kufahl, Slavica Rankovic, Udo Samel, Henry Lutze – *r*: 107 min, col – *p*: Basis Film Berlin (Clara Burckner)/WDR 1979

Endstation Freiheit (*Last Stop Freedom*)
d: Reinhard Hauff – *sc*: Burkhard Driest – *c*: Frank Brühne – *ed*: Peter Przygodda – *m*: Irmin Schmidt – *l.p.*: Burkhard Driest, Rolf Zacher, Katja Ruppé, Kurt Raab, Hans Noever, Hark Bohm, Irm Hermann, Marquard Bohm – *r*: 112 min, col – *p*: Bioskop (Eberhard Junkersdorf)/Planet/ZDF 1980

Engelchen oder Die Jungfrau von Bamberg (*Little Angel, The Virgin from Bamberg*)
d: Marran Gosov – *sc*: Marran Gosov, Franz Geiger – *c*: Werner Kurz – *ed*: Monica

Wilde – *m*: Jacques Loussier – *l.p.*: Gila von Weitershausen, Ulrich Koch, Dieter Augustin, Hans Clarin, Christof Wackernagel – *r*: 81 min, col – *p*: Rob Houwer 1968

Erdbeben in Chili (*The Earthquake in Chile*)
d: Helma Sanders-Brahms – *sc*: Helma Sanders-Brahms, based on the novella by Heinrich von Kleist – *c*: Dietrich Lohmann – *l.p.*: Julia Pena, Victor Alcazar, Juan Amigo, Maria Jesus Hoyos – *r*: 87 min, b/w – *p*: Filmverlag der Autoren/ZDF Mainz 1974

Es (*It*)
d/sc: Ulrich Schamoni – *c*: Gerard Vandenberg – *ed*: Heidi Rente (=Heidi Genée) – *l.p.*: Sabine Sinjen, Bruno Dietrich, Ulrike Ullrich, Rolf Zacher, Tilla Durieux, Marcel Marceau, Berhard Minetti – *r*: 86 min, b/w – *p*: Horst Manfred Adloff 1965

Es herrscht Ruhe im Land (*Calm Prevails in the Country*)
d: Peter Lilienthal – *sc*: Antonio Skarmeta, Peter Lilienthal – *c*: Robby Müller – *ed*: Susi Jäger – *m*: Angel Parra – *l.p.*: Charles Vanel, Mario Pardo, Eduardo Duran, Zita Duarte – *r*: 104 min, col – *p*: FFAT-Film (Peter Lilienthal)/ZDF/ORTF 1975

Etwas tut weh (*Something Hurts*)
d/sc: Recha Jungmann – *c*: Rüdiger Laske, Merian Szura – *ed*: Ilona Grundmann, Esther Dayan – *m*: Frank Wolff – *l.p.*: Simone Maul, Anja Burak, Hermann Schäfer, Recha Jungmann – *r*: 72 min, col – *p*: Spree-Jungmann Frankfurt 1980

Etwas wird sichtbar (*Before Your Eyes: Vietnam*)
d/sc: Harun Farocki – *c*: Ingo Kratisch, Wolf-Dieter Fallert, Ebba Jahn – *ed*: Johannes Beringer – *m*: Markus Spies – *l.p.*: Hanns Zischler, Inga Humpe, Bruno Ganz, Hartmut Bitomsky, Olaf Scheuring, Ingrid Oppermann, Klaus Wohlfahrt – *r*: 114 min, b/w – *p*: Harun Farocki Filmproduktion 1981

Evelyn Künnecke – Ich bin ein Anti-Star (*Evelyn Künnecke – I am an Anti-Star*)
d/sc/ed: Rosa von Praunheim – *c*: Ed Lieber – *l.p.*: Evelyn Künnecke, Angele Durand, Christina and Dietmar Kracht – *r*: 81 min, col – *p*: Rosa von Praunheim for WDR Cologne 1976

Der Fall Lena Christ (*The Case of Lena Christ*)
d: Hans W. Geissendörfer – *sc*: Hans W. Geissendörfer, from the autobiography *Erinnerungen einer Überflüssigen* by Lena Christ, and Peter Bendix's *Der Weg der Lena Christ* – *c*: Robby Müller – *ed*: Wolfgang Hedinger – *m*: Franz Meyer – *l.p.*: Heidi Stroh, Edith Volkmann, Sophie Strelow, Paul Stieber-Walter – *r*: 90 min, b/w – *p*: Bayrischer Rundfunk Munich 1969

Falsche Bewegung (*Wrong Movement*)
d: Wim Wenders – *sc*: Peter Handke, based on motifs from the novel *Wilhelm Meister* by J.W. Goethe – *c*: Robby Müller – *ed*: Peter Przygodda, Barbara von Weitershausen – *m*: Jürgen Knieper – *l.p.*: Rüdiger Vogler, Hanna Schygulla, Hans Christian Blech, Peter Kern, Ivan Desny, Nastassja Nakszynski, Marianne Hoppe – *r*: 103 min, col – *p*: Solaris (Peter Genée, Bernd Eichinger)/WDR 1974

Die Fälschung (*Circle of Deceit*)
d: Volker Schlöndorff – *sc*: Jean Claude Carrière, Volker Schlöndorff, Margarethe von Trotta, Kai Hermann based on the novel by Nicolas Born – *c*: Igor Luther – *l.p.*: Bruno Ganz, Hanna Schygulla, Jerzy Skolimowski, Gila von Weitershausen – *r*: 110 min, col – *p*: Bioskop Munich/Artemis Paris/Argos Paris/HR Frankfurt 1981

Familienglück (*Wedded Bliss*)
d/sc: Marianne Lüdcke and Ingo Kratisch – c: Ingo Kratisch, Wolfgang Kniffe – ed: Siegrun Jäger, Ursula Höf – m: Peter Fischer – l.p.: Tilo Prückner, Dagmar Biener, Ursula Diestel – r: 107 min, col – p: Regina Ziegler/WDR Cologne 1975

Der Fangschuss (*Coup de Grace*)
d: Volker Schlöndorff – sc: Geneviève Dormann, Margarethe von Trotta, Jutta Brückner based on the novel by Marguerite Yourcenar – c: Igor Luther – ed: Jane Sperr, Henri Colpi – m: Stanley Myers – l.p.: Matthias Habich, Rüdiger Kirschstein, Margarethe von Trotta, Mathieu Carrière, Valeska Gert, Axel von Eschwege – r: 95 min, b/w – p: Bioskop Film Munich (Eberhard Junkersdorf)/Argos Film Neuilly (Anatole Dauman)/HR Frankfurt 1976

Fata Morgana
d/sc: Werner Herzog – c: Jörg Schmidt-Reitwein – ed: Beate Mainka-Jellinghaus – m: Händel, Mozart, Couperin, Blind Faith, Leonard Cohen – l.p.: Wolfgang von Ungern-Sternberg, James William Gledhill, Eugene des Montagnes; Lotte H. Eisner (narrator) – r: 79 min, col – p: Werner Herzog Filmproduktion Munich 1971

Faustrecht der Freiheit (*Fox and his Friends*)
d/sc: Rainer Werner Fassbinder – c: Michael Ballhaus – ed: Thea Eymèsz – m: Peer Raben – l.p.: Rainer Werner Fassbinder, Peter Chatel, Karlheinz Böhm, Rudolf Lenz, Karl Scheydt, Kurt Raab, Harry Baer – r: 123 min, col – p: Tango/City Munich 1975

Film oder Macht (*Film or Power*)
d/sc/c: Vlado Kristl – l.p.: Christine Meier, Marlene Zargos, Heinz Badewitz, Wolf Wondratschek, Denyse Noever, Jelena, Madeleine, Pepe Stephan and Vlado Kristl – r: 100 min, b/w – p: Vlado Kristl, Karl Schedereit, Pitt Brockner 1970

Der Findling (*The Foundling*)
d: George Moorse – sc: George Moorse, based on the novella by Heinrich von Kleist – c: Gerard Vandenberg – m: Wilfried Schröpfer – l.p.: Rudolf Fernau, Julie Felix, Titus Gerhardt – r: 74 min, b/w – p: Bayerischer Rundfunk (Hellmut Haffner) Munich/Literarisches Colloquium (Walter Höllerer) Berlin 1967

Fitzcarraldo
d/sc: Werner Herzog – c: Thomas Mauch – ed: Beate Mainka-Jellinghaus – m: 'Popol Vuh' – l.p.: Klaus Kinski, Claudia Cardinale, José Lewgoy, Paul Hittscher – r: 158 min, col – p: Werner Herzog Filmproduktion Munich/Pro-Ject Filmproduktion at Filmverlag der Autoren Munich/ZDF Mainz 1981

Die flambierte Frau (*The Woman in Flames*)
d: Robert van Ackeren – sc: Robert van Ackeren, Catharina Zwerenz – c: Jürgen Jürges – ed: Tanja Schmidbauer – l.p.: Gudrun Landgrebe, Mathieu Carrière, Hanns Zischler, Gabriele LaFari – r: 106 min, col – p: Robert van Ackeren, Dieter Geissler Munich 1983

Flammende Herzen (*Flaming Hearts*)
d/sc: Walter Bockmayer, Rolf Bührmann – c: Horst Knechtel, Peter Mertin – m: Michael Rother (Karl Valentin, Evelyn Künnecke, Peter Kern, Peter Kraus) – l.p.: Peter Kern, Barbara Valentin, Katja Ruppé – r: 95 min, col – p: Enten-Produktion Cologne (Bockmayer and Bührmann) ZDF Mainz 1978

Die Fliegenden Ärzte von Ostafrika (*The Flying Doctors of East Africa*)
d/sc: Werner Herzog – c: Thomas Mauch – ed: Beate Mainka-Jellinghaus – r: 45 min, col – p: Werner Herzog Filmproduktion, Munich 1968–9

Flöz Dickebank (*We've Woken Up in the Meantime*)
d/sc: Johannes Flütsch, Klaus Helle, Marlies Kallweit – *r*: 67 min, b/w – *p*: Deutsche Film und Fernsehakademie Berlin 1975

Fluchtweg nach Marseille (*Escape Route to Marseille*)
d/sc: Gerhard Theuring, Ingemo Engström – *c*: Axel Block – *ed*: Heidi Murero, Elke Hager – *m*: Pablo Casals – *l.p.*: Katharina Thalbach, Rüdiger Vogler, François Mouren-Provensal – *r*: 92 min (pt. 1), 115 min (pt. 2), col – *p*: Ingemo Engström, Gerhard Theuring/WDR Cologne 1977

Flügel und Fesseln (*The Future of Emily*)
d/sc: Helma Sanders-Brahms – *c*: Sacha Vierny, Lars Barthel, Hans-Günther Bücking – *ed*: Ursula West – *m*: Jürgen Knieper – *l.p.*: Hildegard Knef, Brigitte Fossey, Ivan Desny, Hermann Treusch – *r*: 107 min, col – *p*: Helma Sanders Filmproduktion/Literarisches Colloquium Berlin/ZDF Mainz/Les Films du Losange Paris 1985

Fontane Effi Briest (*Effi Briest*)
d: Rainer Werner Fassbinder – *sc*: Rainer Werner Fassbinder, based on the novel by Theodor Fontane – *c*: Dietrich Lohmann, Jürgen Jürges – *ed*: Thea Eymèsz – *m*: Camille Saint-Saëns and others – *l.p.*: Hanna Schygulla, Wolfgang Schenck, Karlheinz Böhm, Ulli Lommel, Ursula Strätz, Hark Bohm, Irm Hermann – *r*: 141 min, b/w – *p*: Tango 1974

498, Third Avenue
d/sc: Klaus Wildenhahn, Rudolf Körösi, Herbert Selk – *r*: 83 min, b/w – *p*: NDR 1967

Die Frau gegenüber (*The Woman Across the Street*)
d/sc: Hans Noever – *c*: Walter Lassally – *ed*: Christa Wernicke – *m*: Robert Eliscu, Munich Factory – *l.p.*: Franciszek Pieczka, Petra Maria Grühn, Jody Buchmann, Brigitte Mira, Jiri Menzel – *r*: 103 min, b/w – *p*: DNS (Kerstin Dobbertin, Denyse Noever, Elvira Senft)/BR Munich 1978

Frauen an der Spitze (*Women at the Top*)
d/sc: Erika Runge – *c*: Klaus Jähnig – *r*: 44 min, col – *p*: 1969

Frauen – Schlusslichter der Gewerkschaft (*Women – At the Tail-End of Trade Unions*)
d/sc: Ingrid Oppermann, Johanna Kootz, Gisela Steppke – *r*: 59 min, col – *p*: Deutsche Film und Fernsehakademie Berlin 1975

Freak Orlando
d/sc/c: Ulrike Ottinger – *ed*: Dörte Völz – *m*: Wilhelm D. Siebert – *l.p.*: Magdalena Montezuma, Delphine Seyrig, Albert Heins, Eddie Constantine, Franca Magnani – *r*: 126 min, col – *p*: Ulrike Ottinger Filmproduktion Berlin/Pia Frankenberg Musik- und Filmproduktion/ZDF Mainz 1981

Fremde Stadt (*Foreign City*)
d: Rudolf Thome – *sc*: Max Zihlmann – *c*: Martin Schäfer – *m*: John Andrews – *l.p.*: Roger Fritz, Karin Thome, Peter Moland, Martin Sperr, Hans Noever, Stefan Abendroth, Werner Umberg – *r*: 106 min, b/w – *p*: Carina 1972

Das Freudenhaus (*Bordello*)
d: Alfred Weidenmann – *sc*: Alfred Weidenmann, based on the novel by Henry Jaeger – *c*: Ernst W. Kalinke – *ed*: Suzanne Paschen – *m*: Otto Schuett – *l.p.*: Herbert

Fleischmann, Karin Jacobsen, Paul Edwin Roth – *r*: 92 min, col – *p*: Studio-Film 1970

Fritz Kortner probt Kabale und Liebe (*Fritz Kortner rehearses Schiller's* Intrigue and Love)
d: Hans Jürgen Syberberg – *c*: Kurt Lorenz, Konrad Wickler – *r*: 110 min, b/w – *p*: Bayrischer Rundfunk Munich 1965

Für Frauen 1. Kapitel (*For Women, Chapter One*)
d: Christina Perincioli – *r*: 36 min, col – *p*: Deutsche Film und Fernsehakademie Berlin 1971

Ein ganz und gar verwahrlostes Mädchen (*A Thoroughly Neglected Girl*)
d/sc: Jutta Brückner – *c*: Eduard Windhager – *ed*: Eva Schlensag – *l.p.*: Rita Rischak, Erika Prahl, Manfred Fischer – *r*: 80 min, col, b/w – *p*: Jutta Brückner/ZDF Mainz 1976

Der gekaufte Traum (*The Bought Dream*)
d: Helga Reidemeister, Eduard Gernart – *sc*: Helga Reidemeister, Eduard Gernart in cooperation with the Bruder family – *c*: Sophokles Adamidis, Gerhardt Braun, Klaus Helle, Helga Reidemeister – *ed*: Eduard Gernart – *r*: 79 min, col – *p*: Deutsche Film und Fernsehakademie Berlin 1977

Gelegenheitsarbeit einer Sklavin (*Occasional Work of a Female Slave*)
d: Alexander Kluge – *sc*: Alexander Kluge, Hans Drawe, Alexandra Kluge – *c*: Thomas Mauch – *ed*: Beate Mainka-Jellinghaus – *l.p.*: Alexandra Kluge, Franz Bronski, Sylvia Gartmann, Traugott Buhre, Alfred Edel, Ursula Dirichs, Ortrud Teichart – *r*: 91 min, b/w – *p*: Kairos-Film Munich 1973

Die Generalprobe (*Dress Rehearsal*)
d: Werner Schroeter – *c*: Franz Weich – *r*: 90 min, col – *p*: ZDF Mainz 1980

Georginas Gründe (*Georgina's Reasons*)
d: Volker Schlöndorff – *sc*: Peter Adler, based on the story by Henry James – *c*: Sven Nykvist – *l.p.*: Edith Clever, Joachim Bissmeier, Margarethe von Trotta – *r*: 65 min, col – *p*: Bavaria for WDR Cologne/ORTF Paris 1974

Geschichten aus den Hunsrückdörfern (*Stories from the Hunsrück Villages*)
d/sc/c: Edgar Reitz – *ed*: Heidi Handorf – *m*: Nikos Mamangakis – *r*: 117 min, col – *p*: Edgar Reitz Munich 1981

Geschichten vom Kübelkind (*Stories of the Bucket Baby*)
d/sc: Edgar Reitz and Ula Stöckl – *c*: Edgar Reitz – *l.p.*: Kristine de Loup, Werner Herzog – *r*: 23 episodes, total length 260 min – *p*: Edgar Reitz Munich 1970

Das Gespenst (*The Ghost*)
d/sc: Herbert Achternbusch – *c*: Jörg Schmidt-Reitwein – *ed*: Ulrike Joanni – *l.p.*: Herbert Achternbusch, Annamirl Bierbichler – *r*: 88 min, b/w – *p*: Herbert Achternbusch Filmproduktion Buchendorf 1982

Gewalt (*Violence*)
d/sc: Helma Sanders-Brahms – *c*: Alain Derobé – *l.p.*: Werner Umberg, Angelika Bender – *r*: 91 min, col – *p*: Helma Sanders Filmproduktion/ZDF Mainz 1971

Gibbi Westgermany
d/sc: Christel Buschmann – *c*: Frank Brühne – *ed*: Jane Sperr – *l.p.*: Jörg Pfennigwerth,

Eva-Maria Hagen, Kiev Stingel, Eric Burdon, Hans Noever – *r*: 90 min, col – *p*: Bioskop (Eberhard Junkersforf) 1980

Die Gläserne Zelle (*The Glass Cell*)
d: Hans W. Geissendörfer – *sc*: Hans W. Geissendörfer and Klaus Bädekerl, after the novel by Patricia Highsmith – *c*: Robby Müller – *m*: Niels Walen – *l.p.*: Helmut Griem, Brigitte Fossey, Bernhard Wicki – *r*: 95 min, col – *p*: Roxy Film (Luggi Waldleitner)/Solaris (Bernd Eichinger)/Bayrischer Rundfunk Munich 1978

Das goldene Ding (*The Thing of Gold*)
d/sc: Ula Stöckl, Edgar Reitz, Alf Brustellin, Nicos Perakis – *c*: Edgar Reitz – *ed*: Hannelore von Sternberg – *m*: Nikos Mamangakis – *l.p.*: Christian Reitz, Oliver Jovine, Konstantin Sautier, Alf Brustellin, Reinhard Hauff, Katrin Seybold – *r*: 118 min, col – *p*: Edgar Reitz/WDR Cologne 1971

Götter der Pest (*Gods of the Plague*)
d: Rainer Werner Fassbinder, Michael Fengler – *sc*: Rainer Werner Fassbinder – *c*: Dietrich Lohmann – *ed*: Franz Walsch(=Rainer Werner Fassbinder) – *m*: Peer Raben – *l.p.*: Harry Baer, Hanna Schygulla, Margarethe von Trotta, Günther Kaufmann, Carla Aulaulu, Ingrid Caven, Yaak Karsunke – *r*: 91 min, b/w – *p*: antiteater Munich 1970

Die Grafen Pocci – einige Kapitel zur Geschichte einer Familie (*The Counts of Pocci – Some Chapters towards the History of a Family*)
d/sc: Hans Jürgen Syberberg – *c*: Kurt Lorenz, M. Lippl – *r*: 92 min, col – *p*: Hans Jürgen Syberberg 1966–7

Grete Minde
d: Heidi Genée – *sc*: Heidi Genée, based on the novel by Theodor Storm – *c*: Jürgen Jürges – *ed*: Heidi Genée, Helga Beyer – *m*: Niels Janette Walen – *l.p.*: Katerina Jacob, Siemen Rühaak, Hannelore Elsner, Tilo Prückner, Hans Christian Blech, Käte Haack – *r*: 102 min, col – *p*: Solaris (Peter Genée, Bernd Eichinger)/Sascha/ZDF 1976

Die grosse Ekstase des Bildschnitzers Steiner (*The Great Ecstasy of the Woodcarver Steiner*)
d/sc: Werner Herzog – *c*: Jörg Schmidt-Reitwein, Francisco Joan, Frederik Hettich – *ed*: Beate Mainka-Jellinghaus – *m*: Popol Vuh – *l.p.*: Walter Steiner – *r*: 45 min, col – *p*: Werner Herzog Filmproduktion for SDR Stuttgart 1973–4

La guerre d'un seul homme (*One Man's War*)
d: Edgardo Cozarinsky – *sc*: Edgardo Cozarinsky, based on the Paris Diaries of Ernst Jünger – *c*: archive material – *ed*: Christine Aya, Véronique Auricoste – *m*: Hans Pfitzner, Richard Strauss, Arnold Schönberg, Franz Schreker – *r*: 105 min, b/w – *p*: Marion's Films Paris/INA Paris/ZDF Mainz 1981

Günter Wallraff – Ganz unten (*At the Bottom of the Heap*)
d: Jörg Gfrörer – *sc*: Günter Wallraff – *c*: Jörg Gfrörer, Dieter Oeckl – *ed*: Peter Kleinert, Tom Meffert – *m*: Heinrich Uber, Mehmet Ipek – *l.p.*: Günter Wallraff – *r*: 106 min, col, b/w – *p*: KAOS Film & Video Team Cologne/Pirat Film/Radio Bremen 1986

halbe – halbe (*Half and Half*)
d/sc: Uwe Brandner – *c*: Jürgens Jürges – *m*: Peer Raben, Munich Factory, J.J. Cale –

l.p.: Peter Hallwachs, Bernd Tauber, Ivan Desny – *r*: 106 min, b/w – *p*: DNS Film Munich (Kerstin Dobbertin, Denyse Noever, Elvira Senft)/NDR 1978

Der Hamburger Aufstand Oktober 1923 (*Hamburg Insurrection, October 1923*)
d/*sc*/*c*/*ed*: Klaus Wildenhahn, Reiner Etz, Gisela Tuchtenhagen – *r*: 41 min (pt. 1), 46 min (pt. 2), 40 min (pt. 3), b/w – *p*: Deutsche Film und Fernsehakademie Berlin 1971

Hammett
d: Wim Wenders – *sc*: Dennis O'Flaherty, Ross Thomas, based on the novel by Joe Gores – *c*: Joe Biroc – *ed*: Peter Przygodda – *m*: John Barry – *l.p.*: Frederic Forrest, Peter Boyle, Marilu Henner, Roy Kinnear – *r*: 96 min, col – *p*: Zoetrope (Francis Ford Coppola) 1980–1

Der Händler der vier Jahreszeiten (*The Merchant of Four Seasons*)
d/*sc*: Rainer Werner Fassbinder – *c*: Dietrich Lohmann – *ed*: Thea Eymèsz – *m*: 'Buona Notte' (Rocco Granata) – *l.p.*: Hans Hirschmüller, Irm Hermann, Hanna Schygulla, Andrea Schober, Kurt Raab, Klaus Löwitsch, Karl Scheydt, Ingrid Caven – *r*: 89 min, col – *p*: Tango (Rainer Werner Fassbinder, Michael Fengler) 1972

Harlem Theater
d: Klaus Wildenhahn, Christian Schwarzwald – *r*: 110 min (also in a 59 min version), b/w – *p*: NDR Hamburg 1968

Harlis
d: Robert van Ackeren – *sc*: Robert van Ackeren, Joy Markert, Iris Wagner – *c*: Dietrich Lohmann, Lothar E. Stickelbrucks – *ed*: Gibbie Shaw, Doerte Voelz – *m*: Mahler, C.A.M. – *l.p.*: Mascha Rabben, Gabi Larifari, Ulli Lommel, Rolf Zacher – *r*: 86 min, col – *p*: Inter West (Wenzel Lüdecke)/Robert van Ackeren Filmproduktion Munich 1972

Der Hauptdarsteller (*The Main Actor*)
d: Reinhard Hauff – *sc*: Reinhard Hauff, Christel Buschmann – *c*: Frank Brühne – *ed*: Stefanie Wilke – *m*: Klaus Doldinger – *l.p.*: Mario Adorf, Michael Schweiger, Vadim Glowna, Hans Brenner, Rolf Zacher, Doris Dörrie – *r*: 88 min, col – *p*: Bioskop Film Munich (Eberhard Junkersdorf)/WDR Cologne 1977

Hauptlehrer Hofer (*Schoolmaster Hofer*)
d: Peter Lilienthal – *sc*: Peter Lilienthal, Herbert Brödl, Günter Herburger, based on the story by Günter Herburger – *c*: Kurt Weber, Ulrich Heises – *ed*: Heidi Genée – *m*: Robert Eliscu – *l.p.*: André Watt, Sebastian Bleisch, Kim Parnass, Tilo Prückner – *r*: 105 min, col – *p*: FFAT (Peter Lilienthal)/WDR Cologne 1974

Heimat
d: Edgar Reitz – *sc*: Edgar Reitz, Peter Steinbach – *c*: Gernot Roll – *ed*: Heidi Handorf – *m*: Nikos Mamangakis – *l.p.*: Marita Breuer, Michael Lesch, Dieter Schaad, Gudrun Landgrebe, Willi Burger, Gertrud Bredel, Rüdiger Weingang, Karin Rasenack, Jörg Hube, Michael Kausch – *r*: 924 min (11 parts) – *p*: Edgar Reitz Filmproduktion GmbH Munich/WDR Cologne/SFB Berlin 1984

Heinrich
d: Helma Sanders-Brahms – *sc*: Helma Sanders-Brahms, based on letters, documents and writings of Heinrich von Kleist – *c*: Thomas Mauch – *ed*: Margot Löhlein – *m*: Mozart, Bach, Beethoven – *l.p.*: Heinrich Giskes, Grischa Huber, Hannelore Hoger,

Heinz Hönig, Lina Carstens, Fritz Lichtenhahn, Le Théatre du Soleil – *r*: 124 min, col – *p*: Regina Ziegler/WDR 1977

Heinrich Penthesilea von Kleist
d: Hans Neuenfels – *sc*: Hans Neuenfels, based on the play 'Penthesilea' by Heinrich von Kleist – *c*: Thomas Mauch – *ed*: Evelyn Schmidt – *m*: Heiner Goebbels – *l.p.*: Elisabeth Trisenaar, Hermann Treusch, Verena Peter – *r*: 144 min, col – *p*: Regina Ziegler Filmproduktion Berlin 1982

Heller Wahn (*Friends and Husbands/A Labour of Love*)
d/sc: Margarethe von Trotta – *c*: Michael Ballhaus – *ed*: Dagmar Hirtz – *m*: Nicolas Economou – *l.p.*: Hanna Schygulla, Angela Winkler, Peter Striebeck – *r*: 105 min, col – *p*: Bioskop Munich/Les Films du Losange, Paris/WDR Cologne 1982

Henry Angst
d: Ingo Kratisch – *sc/ed*: Ingo Kratisch, Jutta Sartory – *c*: Martin Streit, Mike Fallert – *m*: Chuck Berry, John Cage, Mozart – *l.p.*: Klaus Hoffmann, Daphne Moore, Heidrun Polack, Rüdiger Vogler, Hanns Zischler, Harun Farocki – *r*: 100 min, col – *p*: Regina Ziegler/Ingo Kratisch 1980

Herakles (*Hercules*)
d/sc/ed: Werner Herzog – *c*: Jaime Pacheco – *m*: Uwe Brandner – *l.p.*: Mr Germany 1962 – *r*: 12 min, b/w – *p*: Werner Herzog 1962 (revised 1965)

Herz aus Glas (*Heart of Glass*)
d: Werner Herzog – *sc*: Herbert Achternbusch and Werner Herzog – *c*: Jörg Schmidt-Reitwein and Michael Gast – *ed*: Beate Mainka-Jellinghaus – *m*: Popol Vuh and the Studio Frühe Musik – *l.p.*: Josef Bierbichler, Stefan Güttler, Clemens Scheitz, Sonja Skiba, Brunhilde Klöckner – *r*: 94 min, col – *p*: Werner Herzog Filmproduktion Munich 1976

Highway 40 West – Reise in Amerika (*US Highway 40 West*)
d/sc: Hartmut Bitomsky – *c*: Axel Block – *ed*: Mathias von Gunten – *r*: 170 min, col – *p*: Big Sky Berlin 1981

Hitler – ein Film aus Deutschland (*Our Hitler*)
d/sc: Hans Jürgen Syberberg – *c*: Dietrich Lohmann – *ed*: Jutta Brandstaetter – *m*: Wagner, Mozart, Beethoven – *l.p.*: André Heller, Harry Baer, Heinz Schubert, Peter Kern, Hellmut Lange, Martin Sperr, Alfred Edel – *r*: 420 min, col – *p*: TMS (Hans Jürgen Syberberg)/Solaris (Bernd Eichinger)/WDR Cologne/INA Paris/BBC London 1977

Hitler – eine Karriere (*Hitler – A Career*)
d: Christian Herrendoerfer and Joachim C. Fest – *sc*: Joachim C. Fest – *ed*: Fritz Schwaiger, Elisabeth Imholte, Karin Haban – *m*: Hans Posegga – *r*: 155 min – *p*: Interart (Werner Rieb) 1977

How Much Wood Would a Woodchuck Chuck
d/sc: Werner Herzog – *c*: Thomas Mauch, Francisco Joan, Ed Lachmann – *ed*: Beate Mainka-Jellinghaus – *m*: Shorty Eager and the Eager Beavers – *r*: 44 min, col – *p*: Werner Herzog Filmproduktion Munich 1975–6

Huie's Sermon
d/sc: Werner Herzog – *c*: Thomas Mauch – *ed*: Beate Mainka-Jellinghaus – *l.p.*:

Bishop Huie L. Rogers – *r*: 42 min, b/w – *p*: Werner Herzog Filmproduktion Munich 1980

Hungerjahre (*Hunger Years*)
d/sc: Jutta Brückner – *c*: Jörg Jeshel – *ed*: Anneliese Krigar – *m*: Johannes Schmölling – *l.p.*: Britta Pohland, Sylvia Ulrich, Claus Jurichs – *r*: 114 min, b/w – *p*: Jutta Brückner/ZDF 1980

Ich bin Bürger der DDR (*I am a Citizen of the GDR*)
d/sc: Erika Runge – *c*: Michael Ballhaus – *l.p.*: Peter Wappler and family, members of the 'Georgi Dimitroff' Brigade – *r*: 88 min – *p*: 1972

Ich dachte, ich wäre tot (*I Thought I Was Dead*)
d/sc: Wolf Gremm – *c*: David Slama – *ed*: Dorothee Gerlach – *m*: Peter Schirrmann – *l.p.*: Y Sa Lo, Alexander Bzik, Reinhard Bock, Ingrid Bzik – *r*: 80 min, col – *p*: Regina Ziegler Berlin 1973

Ich denke oft an Hawaii (*I Often Think of Hawaii*)
d/sc/c: Elfi Mikesch – *l.p.*: Carmen, Ruth and Tito Rossol – *r*: 85 min, col – *p*: Laurens Straub/Oh Muvie/ZDF Mainz 1978

Ich heiße Erwin und bin 17 Jahre (*My Name is Erwin and I'm Seventeen*)
d/sc: Erika Runge – *c*: Rudolf Körösi – *ed*: E. Gochwilm – *l.p.*: Erwin Walther, Heinz Günther Penckmann, Irmgard Penckmann – *r*: 74 min, b/w – *p*: Bavaria Atelier for WDR Cologne 1970

Ich liebe dich, ich töte dich (*I Love You, I Kill You*)
d/sc: Uwe Brandner – *c*: André Dubreuil – *ed*: Heidi Genée – *m*: Uwe Brandner, Mozart, Hötter, Olanf, 'Spieldose' – *l.p.*: Rolf Becker, Hannes Fuchs, Helmut Brasch, Rudolf Thome – *r*: 95 min, col – *p*: Uwe Brandner 1971

Im Land meiner Eltern (*In the Country of my Parents*)
d/sc: Jeanine Meerapfel – *l.p.*: Anna Levine, Luc Bondy, Sarah Haffner – *r*: 86 min, col – *p*: Jeanine Meerapfel Berlin 1981

Im Lauf der Zeit (*Kings of the Road*)
d/sc: Wim Wenders – *c*: Robby Müller, Martin Schäfer – *ed*: Peter Pryzgodda – *m*: Axel Linstädt (Improved Sound Ltd) – *l.p.*: Rüdiger Vogler, Hanns Zischler, Lisa Kreuzer, Marquard Bohm – *r*: 176 min, b/w – *p*: Wim Wenders Filmproduktion/WDR Cologne 1976

Im Namen des Volkes (*In the Name of the People*)
d/concept: Ottokar Runze – *c*: Michael Epp, Paul Ellmerer – *l.p.*: prisoners of Strafanstalt Hamburg-Fuhlsbüttel – *r*: 128 min, col – *p*: Ottokar Runze 1974

In der Fremde (*Far From Home*)
d: Klaus Wildenhahn – *sc*: Egon Monk, Klaus Wildenhahn – *c*: Rudolf Körösi – *ed*: Karin Baumhöfer – *r*: 81 min (also in a 63 min version), b/w – *p*: NDR Hamburg 1967

In der Fremde (*Far from Home*)
d: Sohrab Shahid Saless – *sc*: Sohrab Shahid Saless, Helga Houzer – *c*: Ramin Reza Molai – *m*: 'Super Top' – *l.p.*: Parviz Sayyad, Gihan Anasal, Muhammet Temizkan – *r*: 91 min, col – *p*: Provobis Hamburg/Neue Filmgruppe Teheran 1975

In einem Jahr mit 13 Monden (*In a Year of Thirteen Moons*)
d/sc/c: Rainer Werner Fassbinder – *m*: Peer Raben – *l.p.*: Volker Spengler, Ingrid Caven, Elisabeth Trissenaar, Gottfried John, Eva Mattes – *r*: 124 min, col – *p*: Tango Film/Pro-Ject Film Munich 1978

In Gefahr und Grösster Not brint der Mittelweg den Tod (*In Danger and in Deep Distress, the Middle Way Spells Certain Death*)
d/sc: Alexander Kluge and Edgar Reitz – *c*: Edgar Reitz, Alfred Hürmer, Günter Hörmann – *ed*: Beate Mainka-Jellinghaus – *m*: Wagner, Verdi and others – *l.p.*: Dagmar Bödderich, Jutta Winkelmann, Norbert Kentrup, Alfred Edel, Kurt Jürgens – *r*: 90 min, b/w – *p*: RK (Edgar Reitz, Alexander Kluge) 1974

In jenen Tagen (*In Those Days*)
d: Helmut Käutner – *sc*: Helmut Käutner, Ernst Schnabel – *c*: Igor Oberberg – *m*: Bernd Eichhorn – *l.p.*: Erich Schellow, Gert Schäfer, Helmut Käutner, Werner Hinz – *r*: 111 min, b/w – *p*: Camera (Helmut Käutner) Hamburg 1947

Die industrielle Reservearmee (*The Industrial Reserve Army*)
d/sc: Helma Sanders-Brahms – *c*: Wolfgang Hageney, Marco Brkic – *r*: 45 min, b/w – *p*: Helma Sanders Filmproduktion 1971

Irgendwo in Berlin (*Somewhere in Berlin*)
d/sc: Gerhard Lamprecht – *c*: Werner Krien – *m*: Erich Einegg – *l.p.*: Harry Hindemith, Hedda Sarow, Charles Kentschke, Fritz Rasp – *r*: 86 min, b/w – *p*: Defa Berlin 1946

Jagdszenen aus Niederbayern (*Hunting Scenes from Lower Bavaria*)
d: Peter Fleischmann – *sc*: Peter Fleischmann based on the play by Martin Sperr – *c*: Alain Derobe – *ed*: Barbara Mondry, Jane Seitz – *l.p.*: Martin Sperr, Angela Winkler, Hanna Schygulla, Else Quecke – *r*: 88 min, b/w – *p*: Rob Houwer Film Munich 1968

Der Jäger vom Fall (*The Hunter of the Falls*)
d: Harald Reinl – *sc*: Werner P. Zibaso, after the novel by Ludwig Ganghofer – *c*: Ernst W. Kalinke – *m*: Ernst Brandner – *l.p.*: Gerlinde Döberl, Alexander Stephan, Siegfried Rauch, Klaus Löwitsch – *r*: 90 min, col – *p*: CTV 72 Munich 1974

Jaider – der einsame Jäger (*Jaider, the Lonely Hunter*)
d: Volker Vogeler – *sc*: Volker Vogeler, Ulf Miehe – *c*: Gerard Vandenberg – *ed*: Henri Sokal – *m*: Eugen Illin – *l.p.*: Gottfried John, Rolf Zacher, Sigi Graue, Johannes Schaaf, Arthur Brauss, Louis Waldon – *r*: 94 min, col – *p*: Bavaria (Helmut Krapp)/Triglav 1971

Jane bleibt Jane (*Jane is Jane Forever*)
d: Walter Bockmayer and Rolf Bührmann – *sc*: Walter Bockmayer – *c*: Peter Mertin – *ed*: Inge Gielow – *l.p.*: Johanna König, Karl Blömer, Peter Chatel – *r*: 88 min, col – *p*: Enten-Produktion Cologne (Bockmayer and Bührmann)/ZDF Mainz 1977

Jeder für sich Gott gegen alle (*The Enigma of Kaspar Hauser*)
d/sc: Werner Herzog – *c*: Jörg Schmidt-Reitwein and Michael Gast, Klaus Wyborny – *ed*: Beate Mainka-Jellinghaus – *m*: Pachelbel, Orlando di Lasso, Albinoni, Mozart – *l.p.*: Bruno S., Walter Ladengast, Brigitte Mira, Hans Musäus, Enno Patalas, Willy Semmelrogge, Elis Pilgrim, Alfred Edel, Herbert Achternbusch – *r*: 109 min, col – *p*: Werner Herzog Filmproduktion Munich/ZDF Mainz 1974

Jet Generation
d: Eckhart Schmidt – *sc*: Eckhart Schmidt, Roger Fritz – *c*: Gernot Roll – *m*: David

Llywellyn – *l.p.*: Dginn Moeller, Roger Fritz, Isi Ter Jung, Jürgen Draeger – *r*: 94 min, col – *p*: Roger Fritz 1968

John Cage
d: Klaus Wildenhahn, Rudolf Körösi, Herbert Selk – *r*: 58 min, b/w – *p*: NDR Hamburg 1966

Johnny Glückstadt
d: Ulf Miehe – *sc*: Ulf Miehe, Walter Fritzsche, based on the novella *Ein Doppelgänger* by Theodor Storm – *c*: Jürgen Jürges – *ed*: Heidi Genée – *m*: Eberhard Schoener – *l.p.*: Dieter Laser, Marie-Christine Barrault, Johannes Schaaf, Tilo Prückner, Uwe Dallmeier – *r*: 94 min, b/w – *p*: Independent (Heinz Angermeyer)/Maran/SDR Stuttgart 1975

Johnny West
d/sc: Roald Koller – *c*: Bahram Manocherie – *ed*: Gertie Kühle – *m*: Winfred Lovett, 'The Manhattans', 'The Platters', 'Missus Beastly' – *l.p.*: Rio Reiser, Kristina van Eyck – *r*: 103 min, col – *p*: Multimedia/Sunny Point/Faust/Terra/HR Frankfurt 1977

Der junge Törless (*Young Torless*)
d: Volker Schlöndorff – *sc*: Volker Schlöndorff, Herbert Asmodi based on the novel *Die Verwirrungen des Zöglings Törless* by Robert Musil (1906) – *c*: Franz Rath – *ed*: Claus von Boro – *m*: Hans Werner Henze – *l.p.*: Matthieu Carrière, Marian Seidowsky, Bernd Tischer, Herbert Asmodi – *r*: 87 min, b/w – *p*: Franz Seitz Filmproduktion Munich/Nouvelles Editions de Films (Louis Malle) Paris 1966

Kalldorf gegen Mannesmann (*Kalldorf versus Mannesmann*)
d/sc/c: Suzanne Beyeler, Rainer März, Manfred Stelzer – *r*: 75 min, b/w – *p*: Deutsche Film und Fernsehakademie Berlin 1975

Kampf um ein Kind (*Fight for a Child*)
d/sc: Ingemo Engström – *c*: Axel Block – *ed*: Gerhard Theuring – *m*: J.S. Bach – *l.p.*: Lisa Kreuzer, Hartmut Bitomsky, Muriel Theuring, Monique Armand, Harun Farocki, Veith von Fürstenberg – *r*: 135 min, col – *p*: Ingemo Engström for WDR Cologne 1974–5

Der Kampf um 11% (*Fighting for 11%*)
d: Michael Busse, Thomas Mitscherlich, Jü Peters – *r*: 98 min, b/w – *p*: Deutsche Film und Fernsehakademie Berlin 1972

Kanakerbraut (*White Trash*)
d: Uwe Schrader – *sc*: Uwe Schrader, Daniel Dubbe – *c*: Klaus Müller-Laue – *l.p.*: Peter Franke, Brigitte Janner, Gerhard Olschweski – *r*: 62 min, col – *p*: Deutsche Film und Fernsehakademie Berlin Uwe Schrader 1984

Der Kandidat (*The Candidate*)
d/sc: Alexander Kluge, Stefan Aust, Volker Schlöndorff, Alexander von Eschwege – *c*: Igor Luther, Werner Lüring, Jörg Schmidt-Reitwein, Thomas Mauch, Bodo Kessler – *ed*: Inge Behrens, Beate Mainka-Jellinghaus, Jane Sperr, Mulle Goetz Dickopp – *r*: 129 min, col, b/w – *p*: Pro-Ject/Bioskop/Kairos (Theo Hinz, Volker Schlöndorff, Alexander Kluge) 1980

Karl May
d/sc: Hans Jürgen Syberberg – *c*: Dietrich Lohmann – *ed*: Ingrid Broszat – *m*: Chopin,

Liszt, Mahler and others – *l.p.*: Helmut Käutner, Kristina Söderbaum, Käthe Gold, Willy Trenk-Trebitsch, Attilla Hörbiger, Lil Dagover, André Heller – *r*: 187 min, col – *p*: TMS (Hans Jürgen Syberberg)/ZDF Mainz 1974

Katz und Maus (*Cat and Mouse*)
d: Hansjürgen Pohland – *sc*: Hansjürgen Pohland based on the novella by Günter Grass – *c*: Wolf Wirth – *ed*: Christa Pohland – *m*: Attila Zoller – *l.p.*: Lars Brandt, Peter Brandt, Wolfgang Neuss, Claudia Bremer, Herbert Weissbach, Ingrid van Bergen – *r*: 88 min, b/w – *p*: modern art film, Berlin/Zespol Rytm Warsaw 1967

Katzelmacher
d: Rainer Werner Fassbinder – *sc*: Rainer Werner Fassbinder based on his play – *c*: Dietrich Lohmann – *ed*: Franz Walsch (=Rainer Werner Fassbinder) – *m*: Franz Schubert – *l.p.*: Hanna Schygulla, Rudolf Waldemar Brem, Lilith Ungerer, Elga Sorbas, Irm Hermann, Harry Baer, Hans Hirschmüller, Rainer Werner Fassbinder – *r*: 88 min, b/w – *p*: antiteater-X-Film (Peer Raben) 1969

Kelek
d/sc/c/ed: Werner Nekes – *r*: 60 min, b/w – *p*: Werner Nekes Hamburg 1968

Klassen Feind (*Class Enemy*)
d: Peter Stein – *sc*: based on the play by Nigel Williams – *c*: Robby Müller – *ed*: Inge Behrens – *l.p.*: Greger Hansen, Stefan Reck, Jean Paul Raths, Udo Samel – *r*: 125 min, col – *p*: Regina Ziegler Filmproduktion Berlin/Pro-Ject Filmproduktion/Filmverlag der Autoren Munich 1983

Der kleine Godard an das Kuratorium junger deutscher Film (*The Little Godard*)
d: Hellmuth Costard – *c*: Bernd Upnmoor, Hans-Otto Walter, Hanno Hart, Hellmuth Costard – *ed*: Susanne Paschen – *m*: Thomas Wachweger – *l.p.*: Hellmuth Costard, Bernhard Kiesel, Werner Grassmann, Ivan Nagel, Hark Bohm, Rainer Werner Fassbinder, Michael Ballhaus, Harry Baer, Uwe Nettelbeck, Dieter Meichsner, Jean Luc Godard – *r*: 81 min, col – *p*: Toulouse-Lautrec-Institute (Hellmuth Costard)/ZDF 1978

Kolossale Liebe (*Mighty Love*)
d: Jutta Brückner – *sc*: Jutta Brückner, based on the correspondence of Rahel Varnhagen – *c*: Horst Heisler, Franz Müllegger, Jürgen Rotter, Jürgen von Wins – *ed*: Barbara Block – *l.p.*: Kirsten Dene, Ulrich Gebauer, Lutz Weidlich, Richard Münch – *r*: 132 min, col – *p*: ZDF Mainz 1984

Der Komantsche (*The Comanche*)
d/sc: Herbert Achternbusch – *c*: Jörg Schmidt-Reitwein – *ed*: Heidi Handorf – *l.p.*: Herbert Achternbusch, Alois Hitzenbichler, Barbara Gass, Annamirl Bierbichler, Sepp Bierbichler, Judith Achternbusch – *r*: 80 min, col – *p*: Herbert Achternbusch/ZDF Mainz 1979

Die Konsequenz (*The Consequence*)
d: Wolfgang Petersen – *sc*: Alexander Ziegler, Wolfgang Petersen, based on the novel by Alexander Ziegler – *c*: Jörg-Michael Baldenius – *ed*: Johannes Nikel – *m*: Nils Sustrate – *l.p.*: Jürgen Prochnow, Ernst Hannawald, Walo Lüönd, Edith Volkmann – *r*: 95 min, b/w – *p*: Solaris (Bernd Eichinger)/WDR Cologne 1977

Kopfstand Madam! (*Stand on Your Head, Lady*)
d: Christian Rischert – *sc*: Christian Geissler, Alfred Neven DuMont, Christian

Rischert – *c*: Fritz Schwennicke – *ed*: Christian Rischert – *m*: Carlos Diernhammer, Manfred Niehaus, Otto Weiss – *l.p.*: Miriam Spoerri, Herbert Fleischmann, Heinz Bennent – *r*: 82 min, b/w – *p*: Arcis (Christian Rischert)/Dumont 1967

Krawatten für Olympia (*Ties for the Olympic Games*)
d/sc: Stefan Lukschy and Hartmann Schmiege – *c*: Norbert Bunge – *ed*: Stefan Lukschy – *m*: Wilhelm Dieter Siebert – *l.p.*: Michael Beermann, Sylvia Dudek, Erika Fuhrmann – *r*: 80 min, b/w – *p*: Deutsche Film und Fernsehakademie Berlin 1976

Kreutzer
d: Klaus Emmerich – *şc*: Klaus Emmerich, Klaus Voswinkel – *c*: Frank Brühne – *ed*: Thea Eymèsz – *m*: Franz Hummel – *l.p.*: Rüdiger Vogler, Axel Wagner, Jörg Hube, Vitus Zeplichal, Edith Volkmann, Kurt Weinzierl – *r*: 91 min, col – *p*: Multimedia/Sunny Point/BR Munich 1977

Krieg und Frieden (*War and Peace*)
d: Alexander Kluge, Volker Schlöndorff, Stefan Aust, Axel Engstfeld – *sc*: Heinrich Böll, Alexander Kluge – *c*: Werner Lüring – *ed*: Beate Mainka-Jellinghaus, Carola Mai – *l.p.*: Jürgen Prochnow, Gunther Kaufman, Manfred Zapatka – *r*: 120 min, col and b/w *p*: Pro-Ject Film Produktion/Bioskop-Film/Kairos Film 1982

Die Kümmeltürkin geht (*Melek Leaves*)
d: Jeanine Meerapfel – *sc*: Jeanine Meerapfel – *c*: Johann Feindt – *ed*: Klaus Volkenborn – *m*: Jakob Lichtmann – *l.p.*: Melek Tez, the Kantemir family, Niyazi Türgay – *r*: 88 min, col – *p*: Journal Film KG/Klaus Volkenborn 1984

Der kurze Brief zum langen Abschied (*Short Letter Long Goodbye*)
d: Herbert Vesely – *sc*: Herbert Vesely, after the novel by Peter Handke – *c*: Petrus Schloemp – *m*: Brian Eno – *l.p.*: Thomas Astau, Geraldine Chaplin, Alexander Hey – *r*: 97 min, col – *p*: Intertel Munich/ZDF Mainz 1976–7

Der lachende Stern (*The Smiling Star*)
d: Werner Schroeter – *sc/c*: Werner Schroeter – *ed*: Christel Orthmann, Werner Schroeter – *r*: 110 min, col – *p*: Luxor Film Peter Kern/ZDF Mainz 1983

Land des Schweigens und der Dunkelheit (*Land of Silence and Darkness*)
d/sc: Werner Herzog – *c*: Jörg Schmidt-Reitwein – *ed*: Beate Mainka-Jellinghaus – *m*: J.S. Bach, A. Vivaldi – *l.p.*: Fini Straubinger, Heinrich Fleischmann, Resi Mittermeier – *r*: 85 min, col – *p*: Werner Herzog Filmproduktion Munich 1971

Die langen Ferien der Lotte H. Eisner (*The Long Vacation of Lotte H. Eisner*)
d/sc: Sohrab Shahid-Saless – *ed*: Heidi Handorf – *r*: 60 min, b/w – *p*: Westdeutscher Rundfunk 1979

Der lange Jammer (*The Wailing Wall*)
d: Max Willutzki – *sc*: Max Willutzki, Horst Lange, Aribert Weis – *c*: Rolf Deppe, René Perraudin – *ed*: Regina Heuser – *m*: Dieter Siebert, 'Lokomotive Kreuzberg' – *l.p.*: Günter Kieslich, Heinz Giese, Heinz Meurer, Walter Clasen – *r*: 86 min, col – *p*: Basis Film Berlin OHG (Max Willutzki) 1973

Laputa
d/sc: Helma Sanders-Brahms – *c*: Eberhard Heick – *ed*: Eva Schlensag – *m*: Matthias Meyer – *l.p.*: Sami Frey, Krystyna Janda – *r*: 92 min – *p*: Joachim von Vietinghoff Berlin 1986

Laokoon und Söhne (*Laocoon and his Sons*)
d: Ulrike Ottinger, Tabea Blumenschein – sc: Ulrike Ottinger – c: Ulrike Ottinger – r: 49 min, b/w – p: Ulrike Ottinger 1972–4

Lebenszeichen (*Signs of Life*)
d: Werner Herzog – sc: Werner Herzog based on the story *Der tolle Invalide auf dem Fort Ratonneau* by Achim von Arnim – c: Thomas Mauch – ed: Beate Mainka-Jellinghaus, Maximiliane Mainka – m: Stavros Xarchakos – l.p.: Peter Broglé, Wolfgang Reichmann, Athina Zacharopoulou, Wolfgang von Ungern-Sternberg, Werner Herzog – r: 90 min, b/w – p: Werner Herzog Filmproduktion Munich 1968

Lena Rais
d: Christian Rischert – sc: Manfred Grunert – c: Gerard Vandenberg – ed: Annette Dorn – m: Eberhard Schoener – l.p.: Krista Stadler, Tilo Prückner, Nikolaus Paryla, Kai Fischer – r: 116 min, col – p: Multimedia/Christian Rischert/ZDF 1980

Lenz
d: George Moorse – sc: George Moorse based on the novella by Georg Büchner – c: Gerard Vandenberg – ed: Christa Wernicke – m: David Llywellyn – l.p.: Michael König, Louis Waldon, Sigurd Bischof, Grischa Huber, Rolf Zacher, Klaus Lea – r: 130 min, col – p: Literarisches Colloquium Berlin/Barbara Moorse Workshop 1960–71

Letzte Liebe (*Last Love*)
d/sc: Ingemo Engström – c: Ingo Kratisch – ed: Gerhard Theuring – m: J.S. Bach – l.p.: Rüdiger Vogler, Angela Winkler, Therese Affolter, Rüdiger Hacker, Hildegard Schmahl – r: 125 min, col – p: Ingemo Engström and Gerhard Theuring/ZDF 1979

Das letzte Loch (*The Last Hole*)
d/sc: Herbert Achternbusch – c: Jörg Schmidt-Reitwein – ed: Ulrike Joanni – l.p.: Herbert Achternbusch, Annamirl Bierbichler, Franz Baumgartner, Alois Hitzenbichler – r: 92 min, b/w – p: Herbert Achternbusch Filmproduktion Buchdorf 1981

Der letzte Schrei (*The Latest Fad*)
d: Robert van Ackeren – sc: Robert van Ackeren, Joy Markert, Iris Wagner – c: Dietrich Lohmann – ed: Clarissa Ambach – m: C.A.M. – l.p.: Delphine Seyrig, Barry Foster, Peter Hall, Udo Kier, Rolf Zacher, Jean-Pierre Bonnin – r: 96 min, col – p: Inter West (Wenzel Lüdecke)/Robert van Ackeren 1975

Letzte Worte (*Last Words*)
d/sc: Werner Herzog – c: Thomas Mauch – ed: Beate Mainka-Jellinghaus – m: Cretan folk music – r: 13 min, b/w – p: Werner Herzog Filmproduktion Munich 1967–8

Die letzten Jahre der Kindheit (*The Last Years of Childhood*)
d: Norbert Kückelmann – sc: Norbert Kückelmann, Thomas Petz and others – c: Jürgen Jürges – ed: Jane Seitz-Sperr – m: Markus Urchs – l.p.: Gerhard Gundel, Norbert Bauhuber, Dieter Mustafoff, Jörg Hube, Ernst Hannawald – r: 104 min, col – p: FFAT (Norbert Kückelmann)/ZDF Mainz 1979

Die letzten Tage von Gomorrha (*The Last Days of Gomorrha*)
d/sc: Helma Sanders-Brahms – c: Dietrich Lohmann – m: 'The Can' – l.p.: Mascha Rabben, Matthias Fuchs, Ernst Jacobi, Alfred Edel, Magdalena Montezuma, Consuela Neal, Rainer Langhans – r: 102 min, col – p: Bavaria/WDR Cologne 1974

Liebe ist kälter als der Tod (*Love is Colder Than Death*)
d/sc: Rainer Werner Fassbinder – *c*: Dietrich Lohmann – *ed*: Franz Walsch (=Rainer Werner Fassbinder) – *m*: Peer Raben, Holger Münzer – *l.p.*: Hanna Schygulla, Rainer Werner Fassbinder, Hans Hirschmüller, Katrin Schaake, Ingrid Caven, Ursula Strätz, Irm Hermann, Wil Rabenbauer (=Peer Raben), Kurt Raab, Rudolf Waldemar Brem, Yaak Karsunke – *r*: 88 min, b/w – *p*: antiteater-X-Film (Peer Raben, Thomas Schamoni) 1969

Liebe Mutter, mir geht es gut (*Dear Mother, I'm Fine*)
d/sc: Christian Ziewer – *c*: Jörg Michael Baldenius – *ed*: Stefanie Wilke – *l.p.*: Clause Eberth, Niklaus Dutsch, Heinz Herrmann – *r*: 87 min – *p*: WDR Cologne/Basis-Film Berlin 1971

Liebesnächte in der Taiga (*Code Name Kill*)
d: Harald Philipp – *sc*: Werner P. Zibaso, Harald Philipp, based on the novel by Heinz G. Konsalik – *c*: Helmut Meewes – *ed*: Inge Taschner – *m*: Manfred Hübler – *l.p.*: Thomas Hunter, Marie Versini, Rolf Boysen – *r*: 105 min, col – *p*: Franz Seitz Filmproduktion 1967

Eine Liebe von Swann (*Swann in Love*)
d: Volker Schlöndorff – *sc*: Peter Brook, Jean-Claude Carrière, Volker Schlöndorff after Marcel Proust's *Un Amour de Swann* – *c*: Sven Nykvist – *ed*: Francoise Bonnot – *m*: Hans Werner Henze – *l.p.*: Jeremy Irons, Ornella Muti, Alain Delon, Marie-Christine Barrault, Fanny Ardant – *r*: 110 min, col – *p*: Gaumont Paris/Bioskop Munich/WDR Cologne 1984

Die Liebe zum Land (*Love of the Land*)
d: Klaus Wildenhahn – *sc*: Klaus Wildenhahn, Gisela Tuchtenhagen – *c*: Thomas Hartwig – *ed*: Gisela Tuchtenhagen – *r*: 77 min (pt. 1), 73 min (pt. 2), b/w – *p*: NDR Hamburg 1973–4

Lightning over Water (*Nick's Movie*)
d: Nicholas Ray, Wim Wenders – *sc*: Wim Wenders – *c*: Edward Lachman, Martin Schäfer – *ed*: Peter Przygodda, Wim Wenders – *m*: Ronee Blakley – *l.p.*: Nicholas Ray, Wim Wenders, Susan Ray, Tom Farrell, Ronee Blakley – *r*: 91 min, col – *p*: Road Movies Filmproduktions GmbH, Berlin (Renée Gundelach)/Wim Wenders Filmproduktion Berlin/Viking Film Stockholm 1980

Lili Marleen
d: Rainer Werner Fassbinder – *sc*: Manfred Purzer, Rainer Werner Fassbinder – *c*: Xaver Schwarzenberger – *ed*: Juliane Lorenz, Franz Walsch (=Rainer Werner Fassbinder) – *m*: Peer Raben – *l.p.*: Hanna Schygulla, Giancarlo Giannini, Mel Ferrer, Christine Kaufmann, Hark Bohm, Karin Baal, Udo Kier, Gottfried John – *r*: 121 min, col – *p*: Roxy-Film Munich (Luggi Waldleitner)/Rialto-Film Berlin (Horst Wendlandt)/BR Munich/CIP 1980

Lina Braake
d/sc: Bernhard Sinkel – *c*: Alf Brustellin – *ed*: Heidi Genée – *m*: Joe Haider – *l.p.*: Lina Carstens, Fritz Rasp, Herbert Bötticher, Erica Schramm, Benno Hoffmann – *r*: 85 min, col – *p*: Bernhard Sinkel Filmproduktion/WDR 1975

Die linkshändige Frau (*The Left-Handed Woman*)
d/sc: Peter Handke – *c*: Robby Müller – *ed*: Peter Przygodda – *m*: J.S. Bach – *l.p.*: Edith Clever, Markus Mühleisen, Bruno Ganz, Michel Lonsdale, Angela Winkler,

Bernhard Wicki, Bernhard Minetti, Rüdiger Vogler, Hanns Zischler, Gérard Depardieu – *r*: 119 min, col – *p*: Road Movies Berlin (Renée Gundelach)/Wim Wenders Produktion Munich 1978

Logik des Gefühls (*The Logic of Feeling*)
d: Ingo Kratisch – *sc*: Jutta Sartory – *c*: David Slama, Martin Streit – *m*: Hanns Zischler – *l.p.*: Rüdiger Vogler, Daphne Moore, Grischa Huber, Hanns Zischler – *r*: 95 min, b/w – *p*: Ingo Kratisch Filmproduktion/Literarisches Colloquium Berlin 1981–2

Lohn und Liebe (*Love and Wages*)
d/sc/c: Marianne Lüdcke and Ingo Kratisch – *ed*: Susanne Lahaye – *m*: Peter Fischer – *l.p.*: Erika Skrotzki, Evelyn Meyka, Nicolas Brieger, Hans Peter Hallwachs – *r*: 98 min, col – *p*: Filmverlag der Autoren/WDR Cologne 1974

Lola
d: Rainer Werner Fassbinder – *sc*: Peter Märthesheimer, Pea Fröhlich dialogues by Rainer Werner Fassbinder – *c*: Xaver Schwarzenberger – *ed*: Juliane Lorenz, Franz Walsch (=Rainer Werner Fassbinder) – *m*: Peer Raben – *l.p.*: Barbara Sukowa, Armin Mueller-Stahl, Mario Adorf, Matthias Fuchs, Helga Feddersen, Karin Baal, Ivan Desny, Hark Bohm – *r*: 113 min, col – *p*: Rialto-Film Berlin (Horst Wendlandt)/Trio-Film Duisburg/WDR Cologne 1981

Ludwig – Requiem für einen jungfräulichen König (*Ludwig – Requiem for a Virgin King*)
d/sc: Hans Jürgen Syberberg – *c*: Dietrich Lohmann – *ed*: Peter Przygodda – *m*: Richard Wagner – *l.p.*: Harry Baer, Balthasar Thomas, Peter Kern, Peter Moland, Günther Kaufmann, Rudolf Waldemar Brem, Siggi Graue, Ursula Strätz, Daniel Schmid, Peter Przygodda – *r*: 139 min, col – *p*: TMS (Hans Jürgen Syberberg)/ZDF 1972

Machorka Muff
d/ed: Jean Marie Straub and Danièle Huillet – *sc*: Jean Marie Straub and Danièle Huillet, based on the story *Hauptstädtisches Journal* by Heinrich Böll – *c*: Wendelin Sachtler – *m*: J.S. Bach, François Louis – *l.p.*: Erich Kuby, Renate Langsdorff, Rolf Thiede – *r*: 17 min, b/w – *p*: Straub-Huillet Munich/Atlas Film Duisberg/Cineropa-Film 1963

Die Macht der Gefühle (*The Power of Feelings*)
d/sc: Alexander Kluge – *c*: Thomas Mauch, Werner Lüring – *ed*: Beate Mainka-Jellinghaus – *l.p.*: Hannelore Hoger, Alexandra Kluge, Edgar M. Boehlke, Klaus Wennemann – *r*: 115 min, col – *p*: Kairos Film (Alexander Kluge) Munich 1983

Macht die Pille frei? (*Does the Pill Liberate Women?*)
d/sc: Helke Sander, Sarah Schumann – *c*: Gisela Tuchtenhagen – *r*: 40 min – *p*: Helke Sander Filmproduktion Berlin 1972

Madame X – eine absolute Herrscherin (*Madame X*)
d/sc/c: Ulrike Ottinger – *ed*: Dörte Völz – *m*: Eric Satie, Reynaldo Hahn, Francis Poulenc, Rossini – *l.p.*: Tabea Blumenschein, Yvonne Rainer, Roswitha Janz, Ulrike Ottinger – *r*: 141 min, col – *p*: Autorenfilm Ulrike Ottinger/Tabea Blumenschein 1977

Made in Germany and USA
d/sc: Rudolf Thome – *c*: Martin Schäfer, Michael Ballhaus – *ed*: Gisela Dombek – *m*:

378

Christoph Buchwald – *l.p.*: Karin Thome, Eberhard Klasse, Alf Bold, Victoria Evans – *r*: 145 min, b/w – *p*: Rudolf Thome Berlin 1975

Mädchen, Mädchen (*Girls, Girls*)
d: Roger Fritz – *sc*: Roger Fritz, Eckhart Schmidt – *c*: Klaus König – *ed*: Heidi Genée – *m*: 'The Safebreakers', Fatty George, Wilson Pickett and David Llywellyn – *l.p.*: Helga Anders, Jürgen Jung, Hellmut Lange, Renate Grosser, Klaus Löwitsch, Monika Zinnenberg – *r*: 104 min, b/w – *p*: Roger Fritz Munich 1966

Madeleine, Madeleine
d/sc: Vlado Kristl – *sc*: Vlado Kristl – *c*: Wolf Wirth – *m*: Erich Ferstl – *l.p.*: Madeleine Sommer, Rolf Huber – *r*: 10 min, col – *p*: Houwer Film Munich 1963

Mahlzeiten (*Mealtimes*)
d: Edgar Reitz – *sc*: Edgar Reitz, in cooperation with Alexander Kluge and Hans Dieter Müller – *c*: Thomas Mauch – *ed*: Beate Mainka-Jellinghaus – *m*: Maurice Ravel – *l.p.*: Heidi Stroh, Georg Hauke, Nina Frank, Ruth von Zerboni – *r*: 95 min, b/w – *p*: Edgar Reitz Munich 1966

Malatesta
d: Peter Lilienthal – *sc*: Peter Lilienthal, Heathcote Williams, Michael Koser – *c*: Willy Pankau – *ed*: Annemarie Weigand – *m*: George Gruntz – *l.p.*: Eddie Constantine, Christine Noonan, Vladimir Pucholt – *r*: 80 min, col, b/w – *p*: Manfred Durniok/SFB 1970

Malou
d/sc: Jeanine Meerapfel – *c*: Michael Ballhaus – *ed*: Dagmar Hirtz – *m*: Peer Raben – *l.p.*: Grischa Huber, Ingrid Caven, Helmut Griem, Ivan Desny, Marie Colbin, Peter Chatel – *r*: 93 min, col – *p*: Regina Ziegler Berlin 1981

Der Mann auf der Mauer (*The Man on the Wall*)
d: Reinhard Hauff – *sc*: Peter Schneider – *c*: Frank Brühne – *ed*: Peter Przygodda – *m*: Irmin Schmidt – *l.p.*: Marius Müller-Westernhagen, Julie Carmen, Towje Kleiner, Karin Baal – *r*: 105 min, col – *p*: Bioskop Film Munich/Paramount 1983

Ein Mann wie Eva (*A Man Like Eva*)
d/sc: Radu Gabrea – *c*: Horst Schier – *ed*: Dragos-Emanuel Wittkowski – *m*: Guiseppe Verdi – *l.p.*: Eva Mattes, Lisa Kreuzer, Werner Stocker, Charles Regnier – *r*: 86 min, col – *p*: Horst Schier, Laurens Straub/Atlas Trio Film/Impuls Film/Maran Film 1984

Männer (*Men*)
d/sc: Doris Dörrie – *c*: Helge Weindler – *ed*: Raimund Bartelmes – *m*: Claus Bantzer – *l.p.*: Heiner Lauterbach, Uwe Ochsenknecht, Ulrike Kriener – *r*: 98 min, col – *p*: Olga Film Munich/ZDF Mainz 1986

Männerbünde (*Male Bonding*)
d/sc: Helke Sander and Sarah Schumann – *c*: WDR camera team – *r*: 45 min, col – *p*: WDR Cologne 1973

Marie Ward
d/sc: Angelika Weber – *c*: René Perraudin – *ed*: Juliane Lorenz – *m*: Elmer Bernstein – *l.p.*: Hannelore Elsner, Irm Hermann, Julia Lindig, Matthieu Carrière, Mario Adorf – *r*: 111 min, col – *p*: Hermes Film Munich/Bayrische Rundfunk Munich 1985

Die Marquise von O. (*The Marquise of O.*)
d: Eric Rohmer – *sc*: Eric Rohmer, Peter Iden, after the novella by Heinrich von

Kleist – *c*: Nestor Almendros – *ed*: Cécile Decugis – *l.p.*: Peter Lühr, Edda Seipel, Edith Clever, Bruno Ganz, Otto Sander, Ruth Drexel, Bernhard Frey – *r*: 102 min, col – *p*: Janus Film (Klaus Hellwig)/Artemis/Les Films du Losange Paris/HR 1976

Martha
d: Rainer Werner Fassbinder – *sc*: Rainer Werner Fassbinder, inspired by the short story *For the Rest of Their Lives* by Cornell Woolrich – *c*: Michael Ballhaus – *ed*: Liesgret Schmitt-Klink – *m*: G. Donizetti – *l.p.*: Margit Carstensen, Karlheinz Böhm, Barbara Valentin, Ingrid Caven, Günter Lamprecht, Peter Chatel, Gisela Fackeldey – *r*: 112 min, col – *p*: WDR Cologne 1973

Die Maschine (*The Machine*)
d/sc: Helma Sanders-Brahms – *c*: Carlos Bustamente, Hubert Neuerburg – *l.p.*: workers of Bauer-Druck AG, Cologne – *r*: 54 min, b/w – *p*: Helma Sanders Filmproduktion 1973

Mathias Kneissl
d: Reinhard Hauff – *sc*: Martin Sperr, Reinhard Hauff – *c*: W.P. Hassenstein – *ed*: Jean-Claude Piroué – *m*: Peer Raben – *l.p.*: Hans Brenner, Evan Mattes, Alfons Scharf, Ruth Drexel, Hanna Schygulla, Volker Schlöndorff, Kurt Raab, Irm Hermann, Gustl Bayrhammer, Franz Peter Wirth, Rainer Werner Fassbinder, Martin Sperr – *r*: 94 min, col – *p*: Bavaria (Philippe Pilliod)/WDR Cologne 1971

Messer im Kopf (*Knife in the Head*)
d: Reinhard Hauff – *sc*: Peter Schneider – *c*: Frank Brühne – *ed*: Peter Przygodda – *m*: Irmin Schmidt – *l.p.*: Bruno Ganz, Angela Winkler, Hans Christian Blech, Hans Brenner, Udo Samel, Hans Noever – *r*: 108 min, col – *p*: Bioskop Film (Eberhard Junkersdorf)/Hallelujah Film Munich/WDR Cologne 1978

Michael Kohlhaas – der Rebell (*Michael Kohlhaas, the Rebel*)
d: Volker Schlöndorff – *sc*: Volker Schlöndorff, Edward Bond, Clement Biddle Wood based on the novella by Heinrich von Kleist – *c*: Willy Kurant – *ed*: Claus von Boro – *m*: Stanley Myers – *l.p.*: David Warner, Anna Karina, Relja Basic, Anita Pallenberg, Gregor von Rezzori, Peter Weiss – *r*: 99 min, col – *p*: Oceanic/Rob Houwer/Columbia 1969

Michael oder die Schwierigkeiten mit dem Glück (*Michael, or the Difficulties with Happiness*)
d/sc: Erika Runge – *c*: Petrus Schloemp – *l.p.*: Patrick Kreutzer, Ingrid Zeuner, Ernst Späth – *r*: 83 min – *p*: 1975

Mitten ins Herz (*Straight Through the Heart*)
d/sc: Doris Dörrie – *c*: Michael Göbel – *ed*: Thomas Weigand – *l.p.*: Beate Jensen, Josef Bierbichler, Gabriele Litty – *r*: 91 min, col – *p*: OLGA Film, Munich/WDR Cologne 1983

Monarch
d/sc/c: Johannes Flütsch and Manfred Stelzer – *ed*: Elisabeth Förster – *l.p.*: Diethard Wendlandt – *r*: 85 min, col – *p*: Regina Ziegler Berlin 1979

Die Moral Der Ruth Halbfass (*The Morals of Ruth Halbfass*)
d: Volker Schlöndorff – *sc*: Volker Schlöndorff, Peter Hamm – *c*: Klaus Müller-Laue, Konrad Kotowski – *ed*: Claus von Boro – *m*: Friedrich Meyer – *l.p.*: Senta Berger, Helmut Griem, Peter Ehrlich, Margarethe von Trotta, Walter Sedlmayr – *r*: 89 min,

col – *p*: Hallelujah Film (Volker Schlöndorff)/HR Frankfurt 1971

Mord und Totschlag (*A Degree of Murder*)
d: Volker Schlöndorff – *sc*: Volker Schlöndorff, Gregor von Rezzori, Niklas Frank, Arne Boyer – *c*: Franz Rath – *ed*: Claus von Boro – *m*: Brian Jones – *l.p.*: Anita Pellenberg, Hans Peter Hallwachs, Manfred Fischbeck, Werner Enke – *r*: 86 min, col – *p*: Rob Houwer Munich 1967

Die Mörder sind unter uns (*The Murderers are Among Us*))
d/sc: Wolfgang Staudte – *c*: Friedl Behn-Grund, Eugen Klagemann – *ed*: Hans Heinrich – *m*: Ernst Roters – *l.p.*: Ernst Wilhelm Borchert, Hildegard Knef, Erna Sellmer, Arno Paulsen – *r*: 90 min, b/w – *p*: Defa (Herbert Uhlig) Berlin 1946

Morgen in Alabama (*A German Lawyer*)
d: Norbert Kückelmann – *sc*: Norbert Kückelmann, Thomas Petz, Dagmar Kekulé – *c*: Jürgen Jürges – *ed*: Susi Jäger – *m*: Markus Urcks – *l.p.*: Maximilian Schell, Lena Stolze, Wolfgang Kieling – *r*: 126 min, col – *p*: FFAT Munich/Pro-Jekt Film Munich 1984

Moritz Lieber Moritz (*Moritz Dear Moritz*)
d/sc: Hark Bohm – *c*: Wolfgang Treu – *ed*: Jane Sperr – *m*: Klaus Doldinger – *l.p.*: Michael Kebschull, Kerstin Wehlmann, Uwe Enkelmann, Dschingis Bowakow, Marquard Bohm, Uwe Dallmeier – *r*: 96 min, col – *p*: Hamburger Kino-Kompanie (Hark Bohm) Hamburg 1978

Mutter Küsters Fahrt zum Himmel (*Mother Küster's Trip to Heaven*)
d: Rainer Werner Fassbinder – *sc*: Rainer Werner Fassbinder, Kurt Raab – *c*: Michael Ballhaus – *ed*: Thea Eymèsz – *m*: Peer Raben – *l.p.*: Brigitte Mira, Ingrid Caven, Karlheinz Böhm, Margit Carstensen, Irm Hermann, Gottfried John, Armin Meier, Kurt Raab – *r*: 120 min, col – *p*: Tango Film Munich 1975

Na und . . . ! (*So What . . . !*)
d: Marquard Bohm, Helmut Herbst – *sc*: Marquard Bohm – *c*: Niels Peter Mahlau – *ed*: Marlis Detjens – *l.p.*: Marquard Bohm, Petra Krüger – *r*: 22 min, b/w – *p*: Cinegrafik Hamburg 1967

Nachrede auf Klara Heydebreck (*Obituary for Klara Heydebreck*)
d: Eberhard Fechner – *c*: Rudolf Körös – *ed*: Brigitte Kirsche – *r*: 60 min, b/w – *p*: Norddeutscher Rundfunk 1969

Die Nacht (*The Night*)
d/sc: Hans Jürgen Syberberg – *c*: Xaver Schwarzenberger – *ed*: Jutta Brandstätter – *m*: J.S. Bach, R. Wagner – *l.p.*: Edith Clever – *r*: 180 min (pt. 1), 180 min (pt. 2), col – *p*: TMS Film Munich 1985

Die Nacht mit Chandler (*The Night with Chandler*)
d/sc: Hans Noever – *c*: Kurt Lorenz, Martin Schäfer – *ed*: Helga Beyer – *m*: 'Ton Steine Scherben' – *l.p.*: Agnes Dünneisen, Rio Reiser, Thomas Stücke, Vania Vilers – *r*: 87 min, col – *p*: Olga (Elvira Senft)/BR Munich 1978

Nachtschatten (*Night Shade*)
d/sc/ed: Niklaus Schilling – *c*: Ingo Hamer – *m*: Grieg – *l.p.*: Elke Hart, John van Dreelen, Max Krügel – *r*: 96 min, col – *p*: Visual (Elke Haltaufderheide) 1972

Der Name der Rose (*The Name of the Rose*)
d: Jean-Jacques Annaud – *sc*: Andrew Birkin, Gérard Brach, Howard Franklin, Alain

Godard based on the novel by Umberto Eco – *c*: Toniono Dellicolli – *ed*: Jane Seitz – *m*: James Horner – *l.p.*: Sean Connery, F. Murray Abraham, Christian Slater, Elya Baskin, Helmut Qualtinger – *r*: 100 min, col – *p*: Neue Constantin Film Munich (Bernd Eichinger)/Christaldifilm/Films Ariane Paris 1986

Neapolitanische Geschwister (*Kingdom of Naples*)
d: Werner Schroeter – *sc*: Werner Schroeter, Wolf Wondratschek – *c*: Thomas Mauch – *ed*: Werner Schroeter, Ursula West – *m*: Robert Pregadio – *l.p.*: Romeo Giro, Antonio Orlando, Tiziana Ambretti, Maria Antoniella Riegel, Cristina Donadio – *r*: 136 min, col – *p*: Dieter Geissler Munich/P.B.C. Rome/ZDF Mainz 1978

Nebelland (*Fog Country*)
d/sc: Claudia von Alemann – *c*: Dieter Vervuurt – *ed*: Monique Dartonne – *m*: Dietrich Stern – *l.p.*: Brigitte Röttgers, Grant Johnson, Eos Schophol, Jean Badin – *r*: 94 min, col – *p*: Alemann Filmproduktion Frankfurt for ZDF Mainz 1981–2

Der Neger Erwin (*Erwin the Nigger*)
d/sc: Herbert Achternbusch – *c*: Jörg Schmidt-Reitwein – *ed*: Heidi Handorf – *l.p.*: Herbert Achternbusch, Annamirl Bierbichler, Helga Loder, Alois Hitzenbichler, Sepp Bierbichler, Helmut Neumayer – *p*: Herbert Achternbusch 1980

Neun Leben hat die Katze (*The Cat has Nine Lives*)
d/sc: Ula Stöckl – *c*: Dietrich Lohmann – *m*: Manfred Eicher – *l.p.*: Liane Hielscher, Christine de Loup, Jürgen Arndt – *r*: 91 min, col – *p*: Ula Stöckl, Thomas Mauch 1968

Neurasia
d/sc/c/ed: Werner Schroeter – *m*: Percy Sledge, Jazz and 'Hawaii-music' – *l.p.*: Carla Aulaulu, Magdalena Montezuma, Rita Bauer – *r*: 41 min, b/w – *p*: Werner Schroeter 1969

Nicht der Homosexuelle ist pervers, sondern die Situation, in der er lebt (*Not the Homosexual is Perverse, but the Situation in which He Finds Himself*)
d: Rosa von Praunheim – *sc*: Rosa von Praunheim, Martin Dannecker, Sigurd Wurl – *c*: Robert van Ackeren – *ed*: Jean-Claude Peroué – *l.p.*: Bernd Feuerhelm, Berryt Bohlen, Ernst Kuchling – *r*: 67 min, col – *p*: Bavaria (Werner Kliess)/WDR Cologne 1970

Nicht fummeln, Liebling (*Don't Fumble, Darling*)
d: May Spils – *sc*: May Spils, Werner Enke, Peter Schlieper, based on an idea by C. Karich – *c*: Hubs Hagen, Niklaus Schilling – *ed*: May Spils, Ulrike Froehner – *m*: Kristian Schulze – *l.p.*: Werner Enke, Gila von Weitershausen, Henry van Lyck, Benno Hoffmann, Elke Hart, Otto Sander – *r*: 87 min, b/w – *p*: Cinemova (Hans Fries) 1970

Nicht Versöhnt (*Not Reconciled*)
d/ed: Jean-Marie Straub and Danièle Huillet – *sc*: Jean-Marie Straub, Danièle Huillet, based on the novel *Billiard at Half-past Nine* by Heinrich Böll – *c*: Wendelin Sachtler, Gerhard Ries, Christian Schwarzwald – *m*: Béla Bartok, J.S. Bach – *l.p.*: Henning Harmsen, Karlheinz Hargersheim, Heinrich Hargersheim, Martha Ständer – *r*: 55 min, b/w – *p*: Straub/Huillet Munich 1965

Nordsee ist Mordsee (*The North Sea is Murderous*)
d/sc: Hark Bohm – *c*: Wolfgang Treu – *ed*: Heidi Genée – *m*: Udo Lindenberg – *l.p.*:

Uwe Enkelmann, Dschingis Bowakow, Marquard Bohm – *r*: 86 min, col – *p*: Hamburger Kino Kompanie (Hark Bohm)/SDR Stuttgart 1975

Nosferatu – Phantom der Nacht (*Nosferatu*)
d: Werner Herzog – *sc*: Werner Herzog, based on the novel *Dracula* by Bram Stoker and the film *Nosferatu – Eine Symphonie des Grauens* by F.W. Murnau – *c*: Jörg Schmidt-Reitwein and Michael Gast – *m*: Florian Fricke/'Popol Vuh', Richard Wagner, Charles Gounod – *l.p.*: Klaus Kinski, Isabelle Adjani, Bruno Ganz, Roland Topor, Walter Ladengast – *r*: 107 min, col – *p*: Werner Herzog Filmproduktion Munich/Gaumont Paris/ZDF Mainz 1978

Notabene Mezzogiorno
d/sc: Hans Rolf Strobel and Heinz Tichawsky – *c*: Heinz Tichawsky – *r*: 55 min, b/w – *p*: Strobel-Tichawsky Munich 1962

Novembermond (*November Moon*)
d/sc: Alexandra von Grote – *c*: Bernard Zitzermann – *ed*: Susanne Lahayse – *m*: Egisto Macchi – *l.p.*: Gaby Osburg, Christiane Millet, Danièle Delorme – *r*: 106 min, col – *p*: Ottokar Runze Filmproduktion Berlin/Sun 7 Productions Paris 1985

Nur zum Spass – nur zum Spiel (Kaleidoskop Valeska Gert)
d/sc: Volker Schlöndorff – *c*: Michael Ballhaus – *ed*: Gisela Haller – *m*: Friedrich Mayer – *l.p.*: Valeska Gert, Pola Kinski – *r*: 60 min, col – *p*: Bioskop (Eberhard Junkersdorf)/ZDF Mainz 1977

Ob's stürmt oder schneit (*Come Rain or Shine*)
d/sc: Doris Dörrie, Wolfang Berndt – *c*: Jörg Schmidt-Reitwein – *ed*: Norbert Herzner – *m*: Rico Moreno – *l.p.*: Maria Stadler – *r*: 83 min, col – *p*: Hochschule für Fernsehen und Film (HFF) Munich 1977

Opa Schulz (*Grandad Schulz*)
d/sc: Erika Runge – *c*: Ulrich Burtin – *l.p.*: Erhard Dhein – *r*: 86 min – *p*: 1975

Otto – der Film (*Otto – the Movie*)
d: Xaver Schwarzenberger, Otto Waalkes – *sc*: Bernd Eilers, Robert Gerhardt, Peter Knorr, Otto Waalkes – *c*: Xaver Schwarzenberger – *m*: Herb Geller – *l.p.*: Otto Waalkes, Jessika Cardinahl, Elisabeth Wiedemann – *r*: 86 min, col – *p*: Rialto Film Berlin/Rüssel Video Hamburg 1985

Palermo oder Wolfsburg (*Palermo or Wolfsburg*)
d: Werner Schroeter – *sc*: Werner Schroeter, Giuseppe Fava – *c*: Thomas Mauch – *ed*: Werner Schroeter, Ursula West – *m*: Alban Berg, Sicilian folk music – *l.p.*: Nicola Zarbo, Calogero Arancio, Padra Pace, Magdalena Montezuma, Brigitte Tilg, Otto Sander, Ula Stöckl – *r*: 175 min, col – *p*: Thomas Mauch and Eric Franck Berlin/Artco Geneva/ZDF Mainz 1980

Panische Zeiten (*Panic Times*)
d: Udo Lindenberg, Peter Fratzscher – *sc*: Udo Lindenberg, Kalle Freynik – *c*: Bernd Heinl – *ed*: Helga Borsche, Barbara von Weitershausen – *m*: Udo Lindenberg – *l.p.*: Udo Lindenberg, Leata Galloway, Walter Kohut, Vera Tschechowa, Hark Bohm, Eddie Constantine – *r*: 101 min, col – *p*: Udo Lindenberg/Amazonas/Roba Musik/Regina Ziegler Berlin 1980

Paris, Texas
d: Wim Wenders – *sc*: Wim Wenders, Sam Shepard – *c*: Robby Müller – *ed*: Peter

Przygodda – *m*: Ry Cooder – *l.p.*: Harry Dean Stanton, Nastassja Kinski, Bernhard Wicki, Dean Stockwell, Aurore Clement, Hunter M. Carson – *r*: 148 min, col – *p*: Gray City New York/Road Movies Berlin/Pro-Ject Film Munich/Argos Paris 1984

Parsifal
d: Hans Jürgen Syberberg – *c*: Igor Luther – *ed*: Jutta Brandstaedter, Marianne Fehrenberg – *m*: Richard Wagner – *l.p.*: Armin Jordan, Martin Sperr, Robert Lloyd, Michael Kutter, Edith Clever – *r*: 250 min, col – *p*: TMS Film Munich/BR Munich/Gaumont Paris 1982

Parteitag 64 (*Party Congress 64*)
d/sc: Klaus Wildenhahn, Rudolf Körösi – *r*: 18 min, b/w – *p*: NDR Hamburg 1964

Paso Doble
d: Lothar Lambert – *sc*: Lothar Lambert, Dagmar Beiersdorf, based on an idea by Albert Heins – *c*: Helmut Röttgen – *ed*: Lothar Lambert, Berena Neumann, Doreen Heins – *m*: Albert Kittler – *l.p.*: Albert Heins, Ulrike S., Mustafa Iskandarani, Morteza Ghazanfari – *r*: 90 min, col – *p*: Igelfilm Produktion Hamburg 1984

Die Patriotin (*The Patriot*)
d/sc: Alexander Kluge – *c*: Jörg Schmidt-Reitwein, Petra Hiller, Thomas Mauch, Charlie Scheydt, Werner Lüring, Reinhard Oefle, Günter Hörmann – *ed*: Beate Mainka-Jellinghaus – *l.p.*: Hannelore Hoger, Alfred Edel, Dieter Mainka, Kurt Jürgens – *r*: 121 min, col and b/w – *p*: Kairos Film Munich (Alexander Kluge)/ZDF Mainz 1979

Paule Pauländer
d: Reinhard Hauff – *sc*: Burkhard Driest – *c*: Jürgen Jürges – *ed*: Inez Regnier – *m*: Richard Palmer-James – *l.p.*: Manfred Reiß, Angelika Kulessa, Manfred Gnoth, Tilo Prückner – *r*: 94 min, col – *p*: Bioskop/WDR 1975

Peppermint Frieden (*Peppermint Peace*)
d/sc: Marianne S.W. Rosenbaum – *c*: Alfred Tichawsky – *ed*: Gérard Samaan – *m*: Konstantin Wecker – *l.p.*: Peter Fonda, Saskia Tyroller, Gesine Stremple, Cleo Kretschmer, Konstantin Wecker, Hans Brenner, Gérard Samaan – *r*: 112 min, col and b/w – *p*: Nourfilm Munich 1983

Der Pfingstausflug (*The Whitsun Outing*)
d/sc: Michael Günther – *c*: Michael Epp – *ed*: Inge P. Drestler – *m*: Hans Martin Majewski – *l.p.*: Elisabeth Bergner, Martin Held, Edda Seipel – *r*: 90 min, col – *p*: Ottokar Runze/ZDF Mainz/SRG 1979

Pioniere in Ingolstadt (*Pioneers in Ingolstadt*)
d: Rainer Werner Fassbinder – *sc*: Rainer Werner Fassbinder based on the play by Marieluise Fleisser – *c*: Dietrich Lohmann – *ed*: Thea Eymèsz – *m*: Peer Raben – *l.p.*: Hanna Schygulla, Harry Baer, Irm Hermann, Rudolf Waldemar Brem, Walter Sedlmayr, Klaus Löwitsch – *r*: 83 min, col – *p*: Janus-antiteater 1971

Playgirl
d/sc: Will Tremper – *c*: Wolfgang Lührse, Benno Bellenbaum – *ed*: Ursula Möhrle – *m*: Peter Thomas – *l.p.*: Eva Renzi, Harald Leipnitz, Paul Hubschmid – *r*: 91 min, b/w – *p*: Will Tremper Berlin 1966

Der Plötzliche Reichtum der armen Leute von Kombach (*The Sudden Wealth of the Poor People of Kombach*)
d: Volker Schlöndorff – *sc*: Volker Schlöndorff, Margarethe von Trotta based on the

1825 chronicle of the Subach stage-coach robbery – *c*: Franz Rath – *ed*: Claus von Boro – *m*: Klaus Doldinger – *l.p.*: Reinhard Hauff, Georg Lehn, Karl-Josef Cramer, Margarethe von Trotta, Rainer Werner Fassbinder, Joe Hembus – *r*: 102 min, b/w – *p*: Hallelujah (Eberhard Junkersford)/HR Frankfurt 1970

Eine Prämie für Irene (*A Bonus for Irene*)
d/sc: Helke Sander – *c*: Christoph Roth – *l.p.*: Gundula Schroeder, Sarah Schuhmann – *r*: 50 min – *p*: Helke Sander Filmproduktion 1971

Der Preis fürs Überleben (*The Price of Survival*)
d/sc: Hans Noever – *c*: Walter Lassally – *ed*: Christa Wernicke – *m*: Joe Haider – *l.p.*: Michel Piccoli, Martin West, Marilyn Clark, Kurt Weinzierl – *r*: 107 min, col – *p*: DNS (Deyse Noever, Elvira Senft, Kerstin Dobbertin)/Popular (Hans H. Kaden)/Les Films 66 Paris/BR Munich 1980

Der Prozess (*The Trial*)
d: Eberhard Fechner – *c*: Frank Arnold, Nils-Peter Mahlau, Bernd Schofeld – *ed*: Brigitte Kirsche – *r*: 3 parts, 90 min each, col, b/w – *p*: NDR Hamburg 1976–84

Quartett im Bett (*Quartet in Bed*)
d/sc: Ulrich Schamoni – *c*: Josef Kaufmann – *m*: Ingo Insterburg, Peter Ehlebracht – *l.p.*: Jacob Sisters, Rainer Basedow, Dieter Kursawe – *r*: 95 min, col – *p*: Peter Schamoni Film Produktion 1968

Querelle
d: Rainer Werner Fassbinder – *sc*: Burkhard Driest, Rainer Werner Fassbinder based on the story *Querelle de Brest* by Jean Genet – *c*: Xaver Schwarzenberger – *ed*: Juliane Lorenz – *m*: Peer Raben – *l.p.*: Brad Davis, Franco Nero, Jeanne Moreau, Laurent Malet, Hanno Pöschl, Günther Kaufmann – *r*: 107 min, col, CinemaScope – *p*: Planet-Film Munich (Dieter Schidor) 1982

Die Reinheit des Herzens (*Pure of Heart*)
d/sc: Robert van Ackeren – *c*: Dietrich Lohmann – *ed*: Johannes Nikel – *m*: Peer Raben – *l.p.*: Elisabeth Trissenaar, Mathias Habich, Heinrich Giskes, Marie Colbin, Herb Andress – *r*: 104 min, col – *p*: Bavaria (Peter Märthesheimer)/Pro-Ject 1980

Die Reise (*The Journey*)
d: Markus Imhof – *sc*: Markus Imhof, Martin Wiebel – *c*: Hans Liechti – *ed*: Ursula West – *m*: Franco Ambrosetti – *l.p.*: Markus Boysen, Corinna Kirchhoff, Claude Oliver Rudolph, Will Quadflieg, Alexander Mehner – *r*: 110 min, col – *p*: Regina Ziegler Filmproduktion Berlin/Limbo Film AG Zürich/WDR Cologne/Schweizerische Radio- und Fernsehgesellschaft Berne 1986

Eine Reise ins Licht (*Despair*)
d: Rainer Werner Fassbinder – *sc*: Tom Stoppard after the novel by Vladimir Nabokov – *c*: Michael Ballhaus – *ed*: Reginald Beck, Juliane Lorenz – *m*: Peer Raben – *l.p.*: Dirk Bogarde, Andréa Ferréol, Bernhard Wicki, Volker Spengler, Klaus Löwitsch, Peter Kern, Roger Fritz – *r*: 114 min, col – *p*: NF Geria II/Bavaria Munich/SFP Paris (Peter Märthesheimer, Dieter Minx) 1978

Die Reise nach Lyon (*The Trip to Lyon*)
d/sc: Claudia von Alemann – *c*: Hille Sagel – *ed*: Monique Dartonne – *m*: Frank Wolff – *l.p.*: Rebecca Pauly, Denise Peron, Jean Badin, Sarah Stern – *r*: 106 min, col – *p*: Alemann Filmproduktion Frankfurt 1980

Die Reise nach Wien (*The Trip to Vienna*)
d: Edgar Reitz – *sc*: Edgar Reitz, Alexander Kluge – *c*: Robby Müller – *m*: Hans Hammerschmidt – *l.p.*: Elke Sommer, Hannelore Elsner, Mario Adorf, Nicolas Brieger – *r*: 102 min, col – *p*: Edgar Reitz/WDR Cologne 1973

Rheingold (*Rhinegold*)
d/sc: Niklaus Schilling – *c*: Ernst Wild – *ed*: Thomas Nikel – *m*: Eberhard Schoener – *l.p.*: Rüdiger Kirschstein, Gunter Malzacher, Elke Haltaufderheide – *r*: 91 min, col – *p*: Visual Filmproduktion Elke Haltaufderheide Munich 1978

Rita, Ritter
d/sc: Herbert Achternbusch – *c*: Jörg Schmidt-Reitwein – *ed*: Ulrike Joanni – *m*: Tom Waits – *l.p.*: Annamirl Bierbichler, Christiane Cohendi, Armin Müller-Stahl, Barbara Valentin, Eva Mattes – *r*: 90 min, col – *p*: Herbert Achternbusch Buchendorf 1984

Romy. Anatomie eines Gesichts (*Romy Schneider: Anatomy of a Face*)
d: Hans Jürgen Syberberg – *c*: Kurt Lorenz – *r*: 90 min, later cut by Syberberg to 60 min, b/w – *p*: Rob Houwer 1965

Rosa Luxemburg
d/sc: Margarethe von Trotta – *c*: Franz Rath – *ed*: Dagmar Hirtz – *m*: Nicolas Economou – *l.p.*: Barbara Sukowa, Daniel Olbrychski, Otto Sander, Adelheid Arndt – *r*: 112 min, col – *p*: Bioskop Film Munich/Pro-Jekt Film Munich/Regina Ziegler Filmproduktion Berlin 1986

Der Rosenkönig (*The Rose King*)
d: Werner Schroeter – *sc*: Werner Schroeter, Magdalena Montezuma – *c*: Elfi Mikesch – *ed*: Juliane Lorenz – *l.p.*: Magdalena Montezuma, Mostéla Djadjam, Antonio Orlando – *r*: 103 min, col – *p*: Werner Schroeter Filmproduktion/Juliane Lorenz Filmproduktion/Futura Film Munich 1984–6

Rotation
d: Wolfgang Staudte – *sc*: Wolfgang Staudte, Erwin Klein – *c*: Bruno Mondi – *ed*: Lilian Seng – *m*: H.W. Wiemann – *l.p.*: Paul Esser, Irene Korb, Karl-Heinz Deickert, Brigitte Krause – *r*: 84 min, b/w – *p*: Defa (Herbert Uhlig) 1948

Rote Fahnen sieht man besser (*Red Flags are More Visible*)
d/sc: Theo Gallehr and Rolf Schübel – *c*: Karsten H. Müller – *ed*: Christel Suckow – *m*: Dieter Süverkrüp – *r*: 99 min, col – *p*: Radio Bremen/WDR Cologne/Cinecollectif Hamburg 1971

Rote Liebe (*Red Love*)
d: Rosa von Praunheim – *sc*: Rosa von Praunheim based on the novel *Wassilissa Malegyna* by Alexandra Kollantai – *c*: Mike Kuchar – *m*: 'Ideal', Jakob Lichtmann, 'Din-A-testpicture' – *l.p.*: Helga Goetze, Sascha Hammer, Mark Eins, Eddie Constantine – *r*: 80 min, col – *p*: Rosa von Praunheim Berlin 1981

Rote Sonne (*Red Sun*)
d: Rudolf Thome – *sc*: Max Zihlmann – *c*: Bernd Fiedler – *ed*: Jutta Brandstaedter – *m*: Tommaso Albinoni, 'The Nice', 'The Small Faces' – *l.p.*: Marquard Bohm, Uschi Obermeier, Diana Körner, Sylvia Kekulé – *r*: 89 min, col – *p*: Independent (Heinz Angermeyer) 1970

Salome
d: Werner Schroeter – *sc*: Werner Schroeter based on the play by Oscar Wilde – *c*:

Robert van Ackeren – *ed*: Ila von Hasperg – *m*: G. Donizetti, W.A. Mozart, Rosita Serano, R. Strauss, R. Wagner, H. Meyerbeer, G. Verdi, H. Berlioz, Marie Ceboteri – *l.p.*: Mascha Elm-Rabben, Magdalena Montezuma, Ellen Umlauf, Thomas von Keyserling – *r*: 81 min, col – *p*: Ifage for ZDF 1971

Same Player Shoots Again
d/sc/c: Wim Wenders – *m*: 'Mood Music' – *l.p.*: Hanns Zischler – *r*: 12 min, b/w tinted – *p*: Wim Wenders 1967

San Domingo
d: Hans Jürgen Syberberg – *sc*: Hans Jürgen Syberberg based on the novella *Die Verlobung von San Domingo* by Heinrich von Kleist – *c*: Christian Blackwood – *ed*: Ingrid Fischer – *m*: 'Amon Düül' – *l.p.*: Alice Ottawa, Michael König, Hans Georg Behr, Carla Aulaulu – *r*: 128 min, b/w – *p*: TMS (Hans Jürgen Syberberg) 1970

Der sanfte Lauf (*The Gentle Course*)
d: Haro Senft – *sc*: Haro Senft, Hans Noever – *c*: Jan Curik – *ed*: Thurid Söhnlein – *m*: Erich Ferstl – *l.p.*: Bruno Ganz, Verena Buss, Wolfgang Büttner, Hans-Dieter Asner – *r*: 88 min, b/w – *p*: Haro Senft 1967

Satansbraten (*Satan's Brew*)
d/sc: Rainer Werner Fassbinder – *c*: Jürgen Jürges – *ed*: Thea Eymèsz, Gabi Eichel – *m*: Peer Raben – *l.p.*: Kurt Raab, Margit Carstensen, Helen Vita, Volker Spengler, Ingrid Caven, Marquard Bohm, Ulli Lommel, Y Sa Lo – *r*: 112 min, col – *p*: Albatros/Trio 1976

Scarabea-Wieviel Erde braucht der Mensch? (*Scarabea*)
d: Hans Jürgen Syberberg – *sc*: Hans Jürgen Syberberg based on the novella *Wieviel Erde braucht der Mensch* by Leo Tolstoi – *c*: Petrus Schloemp – *ed*: Barbara Mondry – *m*: Eugen Thomass – *l.p.*: Walter Buschoff, Nicoletta Machiavelli, Franz Graf Treuberg – *r*: 130 min, col – *p*: TMS (Hans Jürgen Syberberg) Munich 1968

Der scharlachrote Buchstabe (*The Scarlet Letter*)
d: Wim Wenders – *sc*: Wim Wenders, Bernardo Fernandez, Tankred Dorst based on the novel by Nathaniel Hawthorne and the scenario *Der Herr klagt über sein Volk in der Wildnis Amerika* by Tankred Dorst and Ursula Ehler – *c*: Robby Müller – *ed*: Peter Przygodda – *m*: Jürgen Knieper – *l.p.*: Senta Berger, Hans Christian Blech, Lou Castel, Yella Rottländer, Rüdiger Vogler – *r*: 90 min, col – *p*: Filmverlag der Autoren/Elias Querejeta Madrid/WDR Cologne 1973

Schatten der Engel (*Shadow of Angels*)
d: Daniel Schmid – *sc*: Rainer Werner Fassbinder, Daniel Schmid based on the play *Der Müll, die Stadt und der Tod* by Rainer Werner Fassbinder – *c*: Renato Berta – *ed*: Ila von Hasperg – *m*: Peer Raben – *l.p.*: Klaus Löwitsch, Ingrid Caven, Rainer Werner Fassbinder, Boy Gobert, Ulli Lommel, Irm Hermann, Harry Baer – *r*: 101 min, col – *p*: Albatros (Michael Fengler) 1975

Der Schatz im Silbersee (*The Treasure of the Silver Lake*)
d: Harald Reinl – *sc*: after the novel by Karl May – *c*: Ernst W. Kalinke – *ed*: Hermann Haller – *m*: Martin Böttcher – *l.p.*: Lex Barker, Pierre Brice, Herbert Lom, Götz George – *r*: 111 min, col – *p*: Rialto Film Hamburg/Jadran Film Zagreb 1962

Der Schlaf der Vernunft (*The Sleep of Reason*)
d/sc: Ula Stöckl – *c*: Axel Block – *ed*: Christel Orthmann – *m*: Helmut Timpelan,

Hugo Wolf – *l.p.*: Ida di Benedetto, Pina Esposito, Christina Scholz, Ingrid Oppermann, Manfred Salzgeber – *r*: 82 min, b/w – *p*: Ula Stöckl Filmproduktion/Common Film Produktion/ZDF Mainz 1983–4

Schloß Hubertus (*Hubertus Castle*)
d: Hans Deppe – *sc*: Willy Rath, Peter Ostermayr, after the novel by Ludwig Ganghofer – *c*: Karl Attenberger, Peter Haller – *m*: Franz R. Friedl – *l.p.*: Hansi Knoteck, Paul Richter, Friedrich Ulmer – *r*: 85 min, b/w – *p*: Dialog Film (Peter Ostermayr) Munich 1934

Schluchtenflitzer (*Ravine Racer*)
d/sc: Rüdiger Nüchtern – *c*: Jürgen Jürges – *ed*: Manja Rock – *m*: Jörg Evers – *l.p.*: Hans Kollmannsberger, Hans Brenner, Ruth Drexel, Eva Mattes – *r*: 121 min, col – *p*: Monika Nüchtern/Bayrische Rundfunk Munich 1979

Schneeglöckchen blühn im September (*Snowdrops Bloom in September*)
d: Christian Ziewer – *sc*: Christian Ziewer, Klaus Wiese – *c*: Kurt Weber – *ed*: Stefanie Wilke – *m*: 'Lokomotive Kreuzberg' – *l.p.*: Claus Eberth, Wolfgang Liere, Horst Pinnow, Claus Jurichs – *r*: 108 min, col – *p*: Basis/WDR Cologne 1974

Der Schneemann (*The Snowman*)
d: Peter F. Bringmann – *sc*: Matthias Selig, after the novel by Jörg Fanser – *c*: Helge Weindler – *ed*: Annette Dorn – *m*: Paul Vincent Gunia – *l.p.*: Marius Müller-Westernhagen, Polly Eltes, Towje Kleiner, Manuela Riva – *r*: 106 min, col – *p*: Bavaria-Atelier Munich/NF Geria II Filmgesellschaft Munich/ZDF Mainz 1985

Der Schneider von Ulm (*The Tailor from Ulm*)
d: Edgar Reitz – *sc*: Edgar Reitz, Petra Kiener – *c*: Dietrich Lohmann, Martin Schäfer – *m*: Nikos Mamangakis – *l.p.*: Hannelore Elsner, Tilo Prückner, Vadim Glowna, Dieter Schidor, Marie Colbin, Rudolf Wessely – *r*: 115 min, col – *p*: 'Schneider von Ulm' Produktionsgemeinschaft Edgar Reitz/Peter Genée Filmproduktion & Co/Veith von Fürstenberg Filmproduktion GmbH Munich/ZDF 1978

Schonzeit für Füchse (*Closed Season for Foxes*)
d: Peter Schamoni – *sc*: Günter Seuren based on his novel – *c*: Jost Vacano – *ed*: Heidi Rente (=Heidi Genée) – *m*: Hans Posegga – *l.p.*: Helmut Förtnbacher, Christian Doermer, Andrea Jonasson, Monika Peitsch, Willy Birgel, Hans Posegga – *r*: 92 min, b/w – *p*: Peter Schamoni 1966

Schwarz und weiss wie Tage und Nächte (*Black and White like Day and Night*)
d: Wolfgang Petersen – *sc*: Karl-Heinz Willschrei, Jochen Wedegärtner, Wolfgang Petersen – *c*: Jörg-Michael Baldenius – *ed*: Johannes Nikel – *m*: Klaus Doldinger – *l.p.*: Bruno Ganz, Gila von Weitershausen, René Deltgen, Ljubo Tadic, Joachim Wichmann – *r*: 103 min, col – *p*: Monaco/Radiant/ORF/WDR Cologne 1978

Schwestern – oder Die Balance des Glücks (*Sisters, or the Balance of Happiness*)
d: Margarethe von Trotta – *sc*: Margarethe von Trotta in cooperation with Luisa Francia and Martje Grohmann – *c*: Franz Rath – *ed*: Annette Dorn – *m*: Konstantin Wecker – *l.p.*: Jutta Lampe, Gudrun Gabriel, Jessica Früh, Konstantin Wecker – *r*: 95 min, col – *p*: Bioskop (Eberhard Junkersdorf)/WDR Cologne 1979

Die Sehnsucht der Veronika Voss (*Veronika Voss*)
d: Rainer Werner Fassbinder – *sc*: Peter Märthesheimer, Pea Fröhlich – *c*: Xaver Schwarzenberger – *ed*: Juliane Lorenz – *m*: Peer Raben – *l.p.*: Rosel Zech, Hilmar

Thate, Cornelia Froboess, Armin Mueller-Stahl, Elisabeth Volkmann, Rudolf Platte, Doris Schade – *r*: 105 min, col – *p*: Laura Film GmbH/Tango Film in cooperation with Rialto-Film/Trio-Film and Maran-Film 1982

Sekundenfilme
d/sc: Vlado Kristl – *l.p.*: Rolf Schesswandter – *r*: 17 short films varying in length between 10 seconds and 3 minutes = 22 min, col – *p*: Bayrische Rundfunk Munich 1968

Septemberweizen (*September Wheat*)
d/sc/c/ed: Peter Krieg – *m*: Rolf Riehm – *r*: 96 min, col – *p*: Teldok Freiburg/ZDF Mainz 1980

Servus Bayern (*Bye Bye Bavaria*)
d/sc: Herbert Achternbusch – *c*: Jörg Schmidt-Reitwein – *ed*: Christl Leyrer – *l.p.*: Annamirl Bierbichler, Herbert Achternbusch, Heinz Braun, Sepp Bierbichler – *r*: 84 min, col – *p*: Herbert Achternbusch Produktion Buchendorf/SDR Stuttgart 1977

Sex Business Made in Pasing
d/sc: Hans Jürgen Syberberg – *c*: Christian Blackwood – *l.p.*: Alois Brummer – *r*: 96 min, b/w – *p*: TMS (Hans Jürgen Syberberg) Munich 1969

Shirins Hochzeit (*Shirin's Wedding*)
d/sc: Helma Sanders-Brahms – *c*: Thomas Mauch – *ed*: Margot Löhlein – *m*: Ö.S. Livaneli – *l.p.*: Ayten Erten, Jürgen Prochnow, Aras Ören, Hans Peter Hallwachs – *r*: 120 min, b/w – *p*: Westdeutscher Rundfunk (Volker Canaris) Cologne 1976

Silver City
d/sc/c: Wim Wenders – *m*: 'Mood Music' – *r*: 25 min, col – *p*: Wim Wenders Munich 1968

Sing, Iris – Sing
d/sc: Gisela Tuchtenhagen, Monika Held – *c*: Gisela Tuchtenhagen – *ed*: Helga Brandt – *r*: 90 min, b/w – *p*: NDR Hamburg 1977–8

Sommergäste (*Summer Visitors*)
d: Peter Stein – *sc*: Botho Strauß after the play by Maxim Gorki – *c*: Michael Ballhaus – *ed*: Siegrun Jäger – *m*: Peter Fischer – *l.p.*: Wolf Redl, Edith Clever, Ilse Ritter, Michael König, Jutta Lampe, Bruno Ganz, Otto Sander – *r*: 115 min, col – *p*: Regina Ziegler Film/SFB Berlin 1975

La Soufrière
d/sc: Werner Herzog – *c*: Jörg Schmidt-Reitwein, Ed Lachman – *ed*: Beate Mainka-Jellinghaus – *m*: Rachmaninov, Brahms, Mendelssohn, Wagner – *r*: 31 min, col – *p*: Werner Herzog Filmproduktion Munich 1976

So weit das Auge reicht (*As Far as the Eye Can See*)
d/sc: Erwin Keusch – *c*: Dietrich Lohmann – *ed*: Bettina Lewertoff – *m*: Axel Linstädt (Improved Sound Ltd), Bernd Tauber – *l.p.*: Bernd Tauber, Aurore Clément, Jürgen Prochnow – *r*: 137 min, col – *p*: prokino (Stephan Hutter, Erwin Keusch)/Les Films du Losange Paris (Margaret Menegoz)/Cactus Zurich (Toni Stricker)/DRS 1980

Stammheim
d: Reinhard Hauff – *sc*: Stefan Aust – *c*: Frank Brühne, Günther Wulf – *ed*: Heidi

Handorf – *m*: Marcel Wengler – *l.p.*: Ulrich Pleitgen, Ulrich Tukur, Therese Affolter, Sabine Wegner – *r*: 107 min, col – *p*: Bioskop Munich/Thalia Theater Hamburg 1986

Der Stand der Dinge (*The State of Things*)
d: Wim Wenders – *sc*: Wim Wenders, Robert Kramer – *c*: Henri Alekan, Martin Schäfer, Fred Murphy – *ed*: Barbara von Weitershausen, Peter Przygodda – *m*: Jürgen Knieper – *l.p.*: Isabelle Weingarten, Rebecca Pauly, Patrick Bauchau, Paul Getty III, Samuel Fuller, Roger Corman, Allen Goorwitz – *r*: 120 min, b/w – *p*: Road Movies GmbH Berlin/Wim Wenders Produktion Berlin/Pro-Ject Filmproduktion Munich/ZDF Mainz in cooperation with Pari Film Paris/Musidora Madrid/Film International Rotterdam/Artificial Eye London 1982

Der Starke Ferdinand (*Strongman Ferdinand*)
d/sc: Alexander Kluge, based on his story *A Bolshevik of Capital* – *c*: Thomas Mauch and Martin Schäfer – *ed*: Heidi Genée, Agape von Dorstewitz – *l.p.*: Heinz Schubert, Verena Rudolph, Heinz Schimmelpfennig, Siegfried Wischnewski, Hark Bohm – *r*: 97 min, col – *p*: Kairos Film (Alexander Kluge)/Reitz Film Munich 1976

Mit starrem Blick aufs Geld (*With Her Eyes Fixed on the Money*)
d/sc: Helga Reidemeister – *l.p.*: Hilde Kuhlbach, Heinz Hönig – *r*: 108 min, col – *p*: Basis Film Berlin 1982

Strohfeuer (*A Free Woman*)
d: Volker Schlöndorff – *sc*: Volker Schlöndorff, Margarethe von Trotta – *c*: Sven Nykvist – *ed*: Suzanne Baron – *m*: Stanley Myers – *l.p.*: Margarethe von Trotta, Friedhelm Ptok, Martin Lüttge, Walter Sedlmayr, Eli Pilgrim – *r*: 101 min, col – *p*: Hallelujah (Eberhard Junkersdorf)/Hessischer Rundfunk Frankfurt 1972

Stroszek
d/sc: Werner Herzog – *c*: Thomas Mauch, Ed Lachmann, Wolfgang Knigge and Stefano Guidi – *ed*: Beate Mainka-Jellinghaus – *m*: Chet Atkins, Sonny Terry – *l.p.*: Bruno S., Eva Mattes, Clemens Scheitz, Burkhard Driest, Alfred Edel, Norbert Grupe – *r*: 108 min, col – *p*: Werner Herzog Filmproduktion Munich/ZDF Mainz 1977

Stunde Null (*Zero Hour*)
d: Edgar Reitz – *sc*: Edgar Reitz, Peter Steinbach – *c*: Gernot Roll – *ed*: Ingrid Broszat, Annette Dorn – *m*: Nicos Mamangakis – *l.p.*: Kai Taschner, Annette Jünger, Herbert Weissbach – *r*: 108 min, b/w – *p*: Edgar Reitz/Solaris (Bernd Eichinger) Munich/WDR Cologne 1976

Der subjektive Faktor (*The Subjective Factor*)
d/sc: Helke Sander – *c*: Martin Schäfer – *ed*: Ursula Höf, Dörte Völz – *m*: Heiner Goebbels, Alfred Harth – *l.p.*: Angelika Rommel, Nikolaus Dutsch, Lutz Weidlich, Dominik Bender, Johanna Sophia – *r*: 138 min, col – *p*: Helke Sander Berlin/ZDF Mainz 1980

Summer in the City
d/sc: Wim Wenders – *c*: Robby Müller – *ed*: Peter Przygodda – *m*: The Kinks, Lovin' Spoonful, Chuck Berry – *l.p.*: Hanns Zischler, Edda Köchl, Libgart Schwarz, Wim Wenders – *r*: 125 min, b/w (145 min) – *p*: Hochschule für Fernsehen und Film Munich 1970

Supermarkt (*Supermarket*)
d: Roland Klick – *sc*: Roland Klick, Georg Althammer, Jane Sperr – *c*: Jost Vacano –

ed: Jane Sperr – *m*: Peter Hesslein, Udo Lindenberg – *l.p.*: Charly Wierzejewski, Eva Mattes, Michael Degen, Hans Michael Rehberg, Alfred Edel – *r*: 84 min, col – *p*: Roland Klick Film/Independent (Heinz Angermeyer) 1973

System ohne Schatten (*Closed Circuit*)
d: Rudolf Thome – *sc*: Jochen Brunow – *c*: Martin Schäfer – *ed*: Ursula West – *l.p.*: Bruno Ganz, Dominique Laffin, Hanns Zischler – *r*: 119 min, col – *p*: Anthea Film Munich/Moana-Film Berlin 1984

Tagebuch (*Diary*)
d: Rudolf Thome – *sc*: Rudolf Thome, based on the novel *Die Wahlverwandtschaften* by J.W. Goethe – *c*: Martin Schäfer – *l.p.*: Angelika Kettelhack, Cynthia Beatt, Rudolf Thome, Holger Henze – *r*: 146 min, b/w – *p*: Rudolf Thome Berlin 1975

Tagebuch eines Liebenden (*Diary of a Lover*)
d: Sohrab Shahid Saless – *sc*: Sohrab Shahid Saless, Helga Houzer – *c*: Mansur Yazdi – *ed*: Christel Orthmann – *m*: Rolf Bauer – *l.p.*: Klaus Salge, Eva Manhardt, Edith Hildebrandt – *r*: 92 min, col – *p*: Provobis 1977

Tarot
d: Rudolf Thome – *sc*: Max Zihlmann, based on the novel *Die Wahlverwandtschaften* by J.W. Goethe – *c*: Martin Schäfer – *ed*: Dörte Volz – *m*: Oliver Zenz – *l.p.*: Hanns Zischler, Vera Tschechova, Rüdiger Vogler, Katharina Böhm – *r*: 110 min, col – *p*: Moana Film Berlin/Anthea Film Munich/ZDF Mainz 1986

Tätowierung (*Tattooing*)
d: Johannes Schaaf – *sc*: Johannes Schaaf, Günter Herburger – *c*: Wolf Wirth – *ed*: Dagmar Hirtz – *m*: George Gruntz – *l.p.*: Helga Anders, Christof Wackernagel, Rosemarie Fendel, Alexander May, Heinz Schubert – *r*: 88 min, col – *p*: Rob Houwer 1967

Die 1000 Augen des Dr Mabuse (*The 1000 Eyes of Dr Mabuse*)
d: Fritz Lang – *sc*: Fritz Lang and Oskar Wutting, after an idea by Jan Fethke – *c*: Kay Loeb – *ed*: Walter and Waltraute Wischniewsky – *m*: Bert Grund – *l.p.*: Peter van Eyck, Dawn Addams, Wolfgang Preiss, Gert Froebe – *r*: 103 min, b/w – *p*: CCC (Atze Brauner), Berlin 1960

Taxi zum Klo
d/sc: Frank Ripploh – *c*: Horst Schier – *ed*: Gela-Marina Runne – *m*: Hans Wittstadt – *l.p.*: Frank Ripploh, Bernd Broaderup, Tabea Blumenschein, Magdalena Montezuma – *r*: 92 min, col – *p*: Laurens Straub, Frank Ripploh, Horst Schier, Berlin 1981

Theo gegen den Rest der Welt (*Theo against the Rest of the World*)
d: Peter F. Bringmann – *sc*: Matthias Seelig – *c*: Helge Weindler – *ed*: Annette Dorn – *m*: Lothar Meid – *l.p.*: Marius Müller-Westernhagen, Guido Gagliardi, Claudia Demarmels, Ursula Strätz, Marquard Bohm – *r*: 109 min, col – *p*: tura film (Michael Weidemann)/Popular-Film (Hans H. Kaden)/Trio-Film (Hans Eckelkamp)/WDR 1980

Theodor Hierneis oder: wie man ehem. Hofkoch wird (*Theodor Hierneis/Ludwig's Cook*)
d: Hans Jürgen Syberberg – *sc*: Hans Jürgen Syberberg, Walter Sedlmayr – *c*: Herman Reichmann – *l.p.*: Walter Sedlmayr – *r*: 84 min, col – *p*: TMS (Hans Jürgen Syberberg) Munich 1972

Der Tiger von Eschnapur/Das Indische Grabmal (*The Indian Tomb*)
d: Fritz Lang – *sc*: Fritz Lang, Werner Lüdecke, after an original script by Thea von Harbou and Fritz Lang – *c*: Richard Angst – *ed*: Walter Wischniewsky – *m*: Michel Michlet, Gerhard Becker – *l.p.*: Debra Paget, Paul Hubschmid, Walter Reyer, Claus Holm – *r*: 97 min (pt. 1), 101 min (pt. 2), col – *p*: CCC (Atze Brauner), Berlin 1959

Tobby
d/sc: Jürgen Pohland – *c*: Wolf Wirth – *m*: Manfred Burzlaff – *l.p.*: Tobias Fichelcher, Eva Häussler, Manfred Burzlaff – *r*: 83 min, b/w – *p*: modern art film (Hansjürgen Pohland) 1961

Tod dem Zuschauer (*Death to the Spectator*)
d/sc/c/ed: Vlado Kristl – *l.p.*: Milan Horacek, Dietrich Kuhlbrodt, Hans Jürgen Masch, Kiev Stingl – *r*: 110 min, col – *p*: Vlado Kristl Filmproduktion 1983

Der Tod des Empedokles (*The Death of Empedocles*)
d: Jean-Marie Straub and Danièle Huillet – *sc*: Jean-Marie Straub and Danièle Huillet, after the dramatic poem by Friedrich Hölderlin – *ed*: Danièle Huillet – *l.p.*: Andreas von Rauch, Howard Vernon – *r*: 132 min, col – *p*: Germany/France 1986

Der Tod der Maria Malibran (*The Death of Maria Malibran*)
d/sc/c: Werner Schroeter – *ed*: Werner Schroeter, Ila von Hasperg – *m*: Johannes Brahms, Ludwig van Beethoven, Ambroise Thomas, Candy Darling, Catarina Valente, Igor Stravinsky, J. Rogers, W.A. Mozart, Marlene Dietrich, Luigi Cherubini, G.F. Handel, Giacomo Puccini, Giacchino Rossini – *l.p.*: Magdalena Montezuma, Christine Kaufmann, Candy Darling, Ingrid Caven – *r*: 104 min, col – *p*: Schroeter for ZDF 1971

Der Tod des weissen Pferdes (*Death of a White Horse*)
d/sc: Christian Ziewer – *c*: Gerard Vandenberg – *m*: Erhard Grosskopf – *l.p.*: Thomas Anzenhofer, Angela Schanelec, Udo Samel, Peter Franke – *r*: 92 min, col – *p*: Basis-Film Verleih Berlin/WDR Cologne 1985

Tod eines Handlungsreisenden (*Death of a Salesman*)
d: Volker Schlöndorff – *sc*: Arthur Miller – *c*: Michael Ballhaus – *ed*: David Ray, Mark Burns – *m*: Alex North – *l.p.*: Dustin Hoffman, Kate Reid, John Malkovich – *r*: 140 min, col – *p*: Roxbury/Punch Productions/HM TV Company 1985

Traumstadt (*Dream City*)
d: Johannes Schaaf – *sc*: Johannes Schaaf, Rosemarie Fendel, Russel Parker, based on the novel *Die andere Seite* by Alfred Kubin – *c*: Gerard Vandenberg, Klaus König – *ed*: Russel Parker, Petra von Oelffen – *m*: Eberhard Schoener – *l.p.*: Per Oscarsson, Rosemarie Fendel, Eva-Maria Meineke – *r*: 124 min, col – *p*: Independent (Heinz Angermeyer)/Maran 1973

Tue recht und scheue niemand (*Do What Is Right, Come What May*)
d/sc: Jutta Brückner – *c*: Francisco Alcala-Toca – *r*: 60 min, b/w – *p*: Jutta Brückner for ZDF 1975

Uliisses
d: Werner Nekes – *sc*: Werner Nekes based on *The Odyssey* by Homer, *Ulysses* by James Joyce and *The Warp* by Niel Oram – *c*: Bernd Upnmoor – *m*: Anthony Moore, Helga Schneid – *l.p.*: Armin Wölfl, Tabea Bloomenschein, Ken Campbell, Werner Nekes, Dore O., Bernd Upnmoor, Neil Cunningham – *r*: 94 min, col – *p*: Werner Nekes Produktion Mühlheim 1982

Die unendliche Geschichte (*The Neverending Story*)
d: Wolfgang Petersen – *sc*: Wolfgang Petersen, Herman Weigel, based on the novel by Michael Ende – *c*: Jost Vacano – *ed*: Jane Seitz – *m*: Klaus Doldinger – *l.p.*: Noah. Hathaway, Barret Oliver, Toni Stronach – *r*: 101 min, col – *p*: Neue Constantin (Bernd Eichinger) Munich/Bavaria Atelier Munich 1984

Unsere Leichen leben noch (*Our Corpses are Still Alive*)
d/sc/ed: Rosa von Praunheim – *c*: Stephen Köster – *m*: Hans Wittstadt – *l.p.*: Lotti Huber, Luzi Kryn, Inka Köhler, Madlen Lorei – *r*: 90 min, col – *p*: Rosa von Praunheim Film/HR Frankfurt 1981

Unter dem Pflaster ist der Strand (*Beneath the Paving Stones is the Beach*)
d: Helma Sanders-Brahms – *sc*: Helma Sanders, Grischa Huber, Heinrich Giskes – *c*: Thomas Mauch – *l.p.*: Grischa Huber, Heinrich Giskes, Gesine Strempel, Heinz Hönig – *r*: 103 min, b/w – *p*: Helma Sanders/ZDF Mainz 1975

Die Unterdrückung der Frau ist vor allem an dem Verhalten der Frauen selber zu erkennen (*The oppression of women shows itself first of all in the behaviour of women themselves*)
d/sc/c: Hellmuth Costard – *l.p.*: Christoph Hemmerling – *r*: 65 min, col – *p*: Hellmuth Costard 1969

Unterm dirndl wird Gejodelt (*How Sweet is Her Valley*)
d: Alois Brummer – *sc*: Peter Genzer – *c*: Hubertus Hagen – *ed*: Jürgen Wolter – *m*: Fred Turnow – *l.p.*: Gisela Schwartz, Annemarie Wiese, Annemarie Wendel – *r*: 90 min, col – *p*: Brummer Filmproduktion 1974

Unversöhnliche Erinnerungen (*Irreconcilable Memories*)
d/sc/c/ed: Klaus Volkenborn, Johann Feindt, Karl Siebig – *m*: Andi Brauer – *l.p.*: Ludwig Stillger, Henning Strümpell – *r*: 92 min, col – *p*: Journal-Film Berlin (Klaus Volkenborn)/ZDF Mainz 1979

Vamos a matar, Compañeros (*Compañeros*)
d: Sergio Corbucci – *sc*: Dino Maiuri, Massimo de Rita, Fritz Ebert, Sergio Corbucci, based on an idea by Sergio Corbucci – *c*: Alejandro Ulloa – *ed*: Eugenio Alabiso – *m*: Ennio Morricone – *l.p.*: Franco Nero, Tomas Milian, Jack Palance – *r*: 118 min, col – *p*: Tritone Filmindustria Rome/Atlantida Film Madrid/Terra Filmkunst Berlin 1970

Vera Romeike ist nicht tragbar (*Vera Romeike Cannot Be Tolerated*)
d: Max Willutzki – *sc*: Renke Korn, Max Willutski – *c*: Dietrich Lohmann – *m*: Dieter Siebert – *l.p.*: Rita Engelmann, Dieter Eppler, Manfred Günther – *r*: 102 min, col – *p*: Basis-Film (Max Willutzki) Berlin 1976

Der Verlorene (*The Lost One*)
d: Peter Lorre – *sc*: Peter Lorre, Benno Vigny, Axel Eggebrecht – *c*: Vaclav Vich – *m*: Willy Schmidt-Gentner – *l.p.*: Peter Lorre, Karl John, Helmut Rudolf, Renate Mannhardt – *r*: 98 min, b/w – *p*: Arnold Pressburger 1951

Die verlorene Ehre der Katharina Blum (*The Lost Honour of Katharina Blum*)
d: Volker Schlöndorff and Margarethe von Trotta – *sc*: Volker Schlöndorff, Margarethe von Trotta based on the story by Heinrich Böll – *c*: Jost Vacano – *ed*: Peter Przygodda – *m*: Hans Werner Henze – *l.p.*: Angela Winkler, Mario Adorf, Dieter Lase, Heinz Bennent, Hannelore Hoger, Jürgen Prochnow – *r*: 106 min, col – *p*: Paramount-Orion

(Willi Benninger)/Bioskop Munich (Eberhard Junkersforf)/WDR 1975

Vermischte Nachrichten (*Odds and Ends*)
d/sc: Alexander Kluge – *c*: Werner Lüring, Thomas Mauch – *ed*: Jane Seitz – *l.p.*:
Marita Breuer, Rosel Zech, Sabine Wegner, André Jung, Sabine Trooger, Beate
Holle – *r*: 103 min, col – *p*: Kairos Film Munich 1987

Die Verrohung des Franz Blum (*The Brutalisation of Franz Blum*)
d: Reinhard Hauff – *sc*: Burkhard Driest based on his novel – *c*: W.P. Hassenstein –
ed: Jane Sperr – *m*: Mike Lewis – *l.p.*: Jürgen Prochnow, Burkhard Driest, Tilo
Prückner, Eike Gallwitz, Kurt Raab, Karlheinz Merz – *r*: 104 min, col – *p*: Bioskop
Film Munich (Eberhard Junkersdorf)/WDR Cologne 1973

Die Vertriebung aus dem Paradies (*The Expulsion from Paradise*)
d/sc/ed: Niklaus Schilling – *c*: Ingo Hamer – *m*: Gaetano Donizetti, Verdi, 'Drupi',
Suzan Avilés – *l.p.*: Herb Andress, Elke Haltaufderheide, Ksenija Protic, Jochen
Busse, Andrea Rau, Herbert Fux, Wolfgang Lukschy – *r*: 119 min, col – *p*: Visual
(Elke Haltaufderheide) 1977

Von wegen 'Schicksal' (*Who says 'Destiny'?*)
d: Helga Reidemeister – *sc*: Helga Reidemeister, Irene Rakowitz – *c*: Axel Brandt –
ed: Elisabeth Förster – *l.p.*: Irene Rakowitz and her family – *r*: 117 min, b/w – *p*:
Literarisches Colloquium Berlin/Deutsche Film und Fernsehakademie Berlin/ZDF
Mainz 1979

Warnung vor einer heiligen Nutte (*Beware of a Holy Whore*)
d/sc: Rainer Werner Fassbinder – *c*: Michael Ballhaus – *ed*: Franz Walsch (=R.W.
Fassbinder), Thea Eymèsz – *m*: Peer Raben, Gaetano Donizetti, Elvis Presley, Ray
Charles, Leonard Cohen, Spooky Tooth – *l.p.*: Lou Castell, Eddie Constantine, Hanna
Schygulla, Marquard Bohm, Rainer Werner Fassbinder, Ulli Lommel, Margarethe von
Trotta, Herb Andress, Werner Schroeter – *r*: 103 min, col – *p*: antiteater-X-Film
Munich/Nova International (Peer Raben) Rome 1971

Warum hast Du mich wachgeküßt? (*Why Did You Wake Me with Your Kisses?*)
d/sc/c: Hellmuth Costard – *r*: 3 min, col – *p*: Hellmuth Costard Hamburg 1967

Warum ist Frau B. glücklich? (*Why is Mrs B Happy?*)
d/sc: Erika Runge – *r*: 43 min, b/w – *p*: Erika Runge 1968

Warum läuft Herr R Amok (*Why Does Mr R Run Amok?*)
d/sc: Rainer Werner Fassbinder, Michael Fengler – *c*: Dietrich Lohmann – *ed*: Franz
Walsch (=R.W. Fassbinder), Michael Fengler – *m*: Christian Anders – *l.p.*: Kurt
Raab, Lilith Ungerer, Amadeus Fengler, Harry Baer, Hanna Schygulla, Peer Raben,
Irm Hermann, Ingrid Caven – *r*: 88 min, col – *p*: antiteater/Maran Munich 1970

Was geschah wirklich zwischen den Bildern? (*Film Before Film*)
d/sc: Werner Nekes – *c*: Bernd Upnmoor, Christoph Schlingensief, Serge Roman –
ed: Astrid Nicklaus – *r*: 83 min, col – *p*: Werner Nekes Filmproduktion Mühlheim
1985–6

Was ich bin, sind meine Filme (*What I Am Are My Films*)
d/sc: Christian Weisenborn, Erwin Keusch – *c*: Martin Schäfer, René Perraudin –
l.p.: Werner Herzog, Laurens E. Straub – *r*: 95 min, col – *p*: Nanuk (Christian
Weisenborn, Erwin Keusch)/WDR Cologne 1978

Was soll'n wir denn machen ohne den Tod (*What Would We Do without Death?*)
d/sc/c: Elfi Mikesch – *ed*: Elfi Mikesch, Renate Merck, Anke-Rixa Hansen – *m*: Gysel, Traute Hagelstein – *l.p.*: Barbara Gold, Edith London, Steve Adamschewski – *r*: 105 min, col and b/w – *p*: Oh Muvie Film Berlin in cooperation with ZDF Mainz 1980

Was tun Pina Bausch und ihre Tänzer in Wuppertal? (*What are Pina Bausch and her Dancers doing in Wuppertal?*)
d: Klaus Wildenhahn, Wolfgang Jost – *r*: 120 min, col – *p*: NDR/WDR 1982–3

Wer braucht wen? (*Who Needs Whom?*)
d/sc: Valeska Schöttle – *r*: 70 min, col – *p*: Deutsche Film und Fernsehakademie Berlin 1972

Der Westen leuchtet (*Light Trap*)
d/sc: Niklaus Schilling – *c*: Wolfgang Dickmann – *ed*: Niklaus Schilling, Moune Barius – *m*: Michael Rueggeberg, Gianna Nanini, Patchwork, C.M. von Weber – *l.p.*: Armin Müller-Stahl, Beatrice Kessler, Melanie Tressler, Harry Baer, Gunther Malzacher – *r*: 107 min, col – *p*: Visual Filmproduktion Munich (Elke Haltaufderheide) 1986

Whity
d/sc: Rainer Werner Fassbinder – *c*: Michael Ballhaus – *ed*: Franz Walsch (=R.W. Fassbinder), Thea Eymèsz – *m*: Peer Raben – *l.p.*: Günther Kaufmann, Hanna Schygulla, Ulli Lommel, Harry Baer – *r*: 95 min, col, CinemaScope – *p*: Atlantis Film/antiteater-X-Film 1970

Wie ein Vogel auf dem Draht (*Like a Bird On the Wire*)
d: Rainer Werner Fassbinder – *sc*: Rainer Werner Fassbinder, Christian Hohoff – *c*: Erhard Spandel – *m*: Ingfried Hoffmann, Kurt Edelhagen Orchestra – *l.p.*: Brigitte Mira, Evelyn Künnecke – *r*: 44 min, col – *p*: WDR Cologne 1974

Wie man einen Molotov Cocktail herstellt (*Manufacturing a Molotov Cocktail*)
d/sc/c/ed: anonymous – *r*: 4 min, b/w – *p*: Deutsche Film und Fernsehakademie Berlin 1968

Die Wildente (*The Wild Duck*)
d: Hans W. Geissendörfer – *sc*: Hans W. Geissendörfer based on the play by Henrik Ibsen – *c*: Robby Müller – *ed*: Jutta Brandstätter – *m*: Niels Janette Walen – *l.p.*: Jean Seberg, Bruno Ganz, Peter Kern, Anne Bennent, Heinz Bennent – *r*: 105 min, col – *p*: Solaris Film (Bernd Eichinger)/Sascha Film Munich/WDR Cologne 1976

Wilder Reiter GmbH (*Wild Rider Ltd*)
d/sc: Franz Josef Spieker – *c*: Wolfgang Fischer – *ed*: Barbara Mondry – *m*: Erich Ferstl – *l.p.*: Herbert Fux, Bernd Herzsprung, Chantal Cachin, Rainer Basedow, Laurens Straub, Ekkehard Aschauer (=Philipp Sonntag), Tilo Prückner, Monika Zinnenberg – *r*: 104 min, b/w – *p*: Horst Manfred Adloff 1966

Wildwechsel (*Jailbait*)
d: Rainer Werner Fassbinder – *sc*: Rainer Werner Fassbinder, based on the play by Franz Xaver Kroetz – *c*: Dietrich Lohmann – *ed*: Thea Eymèsz – *m*: Beethoven – *l.p.*: Jörg von Liebenfels, Ruth Drexel, Eva Mattes, Harry Baer, Hanna Schygulla, Kurt Raab, Karl Scheydt, Klaus Löwitsch – *r*: 102 min, col – *p*: Intertel 1972

Der Willi Busch Report (*The Willi Busch Report*)
d/sc/ed: Niklaus Schilling – *c*: Wolfgang Dickmann – *m*: Patchwork – *l.p.*: Tilo

Prückner, Dorothea Moritz, Kornelia Boje, Eike Gallwitz – *r*: 120 min, col – *p*: Visual (Elke Haltaufderheide) 1979

Willow Springs
d/sc/c: Werner Schroeter – *m*: Saint-Saëns, The Andrews Sisters – *l.p.*: Magdalena Montezuma, Christine Kaufmann, Ila von Hasperg – *r*: 78 min, col – *p*: Schroeter for ZDF Mainz 1972–3

Winifred Wagner und die Geschichte des Hauses Wahnfried von 1914–1975 (*The Confessions of Winifred Wagner*)
d/sc: Hans Jürgen Syberberg – *c*: Dietrich Lohmann – *ed*: Agape Dorstewitz – *m*: Wagner – *l.p.*: Winifred Wagner – *r*: 300 min, b/w – *p*: Hans Jürgen Syberberg 1975

Wir Wunderkinder (*Aren't We Wonderful*)
d: Kurt Hoffmann – *sc*: Heinz Pauck, Günter Neumann, based on the novel by Hugo Hartung – *c*: Richard Angst – *ed*: Hilwa von Boro – *l.p.*: Hansjörg Felmy, Robert Graf, Johanna von Koczian, Elisabeth Flickenschildt, Ingrid van Bergen, Liesl Karstadt, Lina Carstens – *r*: 108 min, b/w – *p*: Filmaufbau (Hans Abich) 1958

Wo die grünen Ameisen träumen (*Where the Green Ants Dream*)
d/sc: Werner Herzog – *c*: Jörg Schmidt-Reitwein – *ed*: Beate Mainka-Jellinghaus – *m*: Gabriel Faure, Richard Wagner, Klaus Jochen Wiese, Ernst Bloch, Wandjuk Marika – *l.p.*: Bruce Spence, Wandjuk Marika, Ray Marika, Ray Barrett, Norman Kaye, Nicolas Lathouris – *r*: 100 min, col – *p*: Werner Herzog Filmproduktion Munich 1984

Eine Woche Avantgarde für Sizilien (*An Avant-garde Week for Sicily*)
d: Klaus Wildenhahn, Rudolf Körösi, Herbert Selk – *r*: 43 min, b/w – *p*: NDR Hamburg 1965

Die Wollands (*The Wolland Family*)
d: Marianne Lüdcke and Ingo Kratisch – *sc*: Marianne Lüdcke, Ingo Kratisch, Johannes Mayer – *c*: Ingo Kratisch, Martin Streit – *ed*: Esther Dayan – *l.p.*: Nicolas Brieger, Peter Fitz, Jörg Friedrich, Heinz Hermann – *r*: 92 min, col – *p*: Deutsche Film und Fensehakademie Berlin 1972

Woyzeck
d: Werner Herzog – *sc*: Werner Herzog, based on the play by Georg Büchner – *c*: Jörg Schmidt-Reitwein, Michael Gast – *m*: String Quartet Telc, Vivaldi, Benedetto Marcello – *l.p.*: Klaus Kinski, Eva Mattes, Wolfgang Reichmann, Josef Bierbichler, Willy Semmelrogge, Herbert Fux – *r*: 81 min, col – *p*: Werner Herzog Filmproduktion Munich 1978

Wundkanal
d/sc: Thomas Harlan – *c*: Henri Alékan – *ed*: Patricia Mazny – *l.p.*: Alfred 'F', Robert Kramer – *r*: 112 min, col – *p*: Quasar Film Berlin/Wieland Schulz-Keil Paris 1984

Die Zärtlickeit der Wölfe (*The Tenderness of Wolves*)
d: Ulli Lomnmel – *sc*: Kurt Raab – *c*: Jürgen Jürges – *ed*: Thea Eymèsz, Franz Walsch (=Rainer Werner Fassbinder) – *m*: Peer Raben, based on motifs by Bach and pop-songs – *l.p.*: Kurt Raab, Jeff Roden, Margit Carstensen, Rainer Werner Fassbinder, Heinrich Giskes, Rosl Zech, Ingrid Caven – *r*: 95 min, col – *p*: Tango (Rainer Werner Fassbinder, Michael Fengler) 1973

Zuckerbaby (*Sugar Baby*)
d/sc: Percy Adlon – *c*: Johanna Heer – *ed*: Jean Claude Pironé – *m*: 'Dreieier' – *l.p.*:

Marianne Segebrecht, Eisi Gulp – *r*: 86 min, col – *p*: Pelemele Munich 1985

Zur Sache, Schätzchen (*Let's Get Down to Business, Darling*)
d/ed: May Spils – *sc*: May Spils, Werner Enke – *c*: Klaus König – *m*: Kristian Schultze –
l.p.: Werner Enke, Uschi Glas, Henry van Lyck, Inge Marschall – *r*: 80 min, b/w – *p*:
Peter Schamoni 1967

Das zweite Erwachen der Christa Klages (*The Second Awakening of Christa Klages*)
d: Margarethe von Trotta – *sc*: Margarethe von Trotta and Luisa Franca – *c*: Franz
Rath – *m*: Klaus Doldinger – *l.p.*: Tina Engel, Katharina Thalbach, Marius Müller-
Westernhagen, Peter Schneider, Sylvia Reize, Sepp Bierbichler – *r*: 93 min, col – *p*:
Bioskop-Film Munich (Eberhard Junkersdorf)/WDR 1977

Zwischen Gestern und Morgen (*Between Yesterday and Tomorrow*)
d: Harald Braun – *sc*: Harald Braun, Herbert Witt – *c*: Günther Anders – *m*: Werner
Eisbrenner – *l.p.*: Viktor de Kowa, Winnie Markus, Viktor Staal, Willy Birgel, Sybille
Schmitz, Hildegard Knef – *r*: 107 min, b/w – *p*: Neue Deutsche Filmgesellschaft
Munich 1947

Zwischen Zwei Kriegen (*Between the Wars*)
d/ed: Harun Farocki – *sc*: Harun Farocki based on his radio play *Das große
Verbindungsrohr* – *c*: Axel Block, Melanie Walz, Ingo Kratisch – *l.p.*: Ingemo
Engström, Jürgen Ebert, Michael Klier, Hartmut Bitomsky – *r*: 83 min, b/w – *p*:
Harun Farocki Berlin 1978

Directory of New German Cinema Directors

The following list comprises biographical data and filmographies of 58 West German directors associated with the Young German Film and the New German Cinema. Two sources have been particularly useful in compiling it – Giovanni Spagnoletti, *Il Nuovo Cinema Tedesco negli anni Sessanta* (Milan: Ubulibri, 1985) and Hans Günther Pflaum and Hans Helmut Prinzler, *Cinema in the Federal Republic of Germany* (Bonn: Inter Nationes, 1983).

Herbert Achternbusch

Born in Munich 23/11/1938. Attended Art School in Nuremberg. A painter for ten years, while earning a living on building sites. Writes prose, poetry, plays and filmscripts as well as making films. His work includes a radio play (1971) and the screenplay for Werner Herzog's *Herz aus Glas* (*Heart of Glass*, 1976). Federal Film Prize in 1982 for *Das letzte Loch*. Plays the lead in most of his films. Lives in Buchendorf near Munich.

Films as director: *Das Kind ist tot* (*The Child is Dead*, 8mm short, 1970), *6. Dezember 1971* (8mm short, 1971), *Das Andechser Gefühl* (*The Andechs Feeling*, 1974), *Die Atlantikschwimmer* (*The Atlantic Swimmers*, 1975), *Bierkampf* (*Beer Battle*, 1976–7), *Servus Bayern* (*Bye Bye, Bavaria*, 1977), *Der junge Mönch* (*The Young Monk*, 1978), *Der Komantsche* (*The Comanche*, 1979), *Der neger Erwin* (*Erwin the Nigger*, 1980), *Das letzte Loch* (*The Last Hole*, 1981), *Der Depp* (*The Village Idiot*, 1982), *Das Gespenst* (*The Ghost*, 1982), *Rita, Ritter* (1983), *Die Olympiasiegerin* (*The Woman Who Won at the Olympics*, 1983), *Der Wanderkrebs* (*Cancer at Large*, 1984), *Blaue Blumen* (*Blue Flowers*, 1985), *Heilt Hitler* (1986), *Wohin* (*Whither*, 1987).

Robert van Ackeren

Born in Berlin 22/12/1946 of Dutch parents. Studied at the Berlin College of Optics and Photography, and also contributed to the Literary Colloquium. Started film-making in 1964, making his first feature film in 1970. Professor in the Art and Design Department at the Cologne Polytechnic. Winner of the 1973 Federal Film Prize for *Harlis*. Lives in Berlin. Has also worked as cameraman, among others on: *Dieser Mann und Deutschland* (dir. Heinz von Cramer, 1966), *Tamara* (dir. Hansjürgen Pohland, 1967), *Bübchen* (dir. Roland Klick, 1967–8), *Hans im Glück* (dir. Thomas Struck, 1968), *Brandstifter* (dir. Klaus Lemke, 1969), *Der Kerl liebt mich – und das soll ich glauben?* (dir. Marran Gosov, 1969), *Eika Katappa* (dir. Werner Schroeter, 1969), *Deadlock* (dir. Roland Klick, 1970), *Der Drücker* (dir. Franz Josef Spieker, 1970), *Nicht der Homosexuelle ist pervers, sondern die Situation in der er lebt* (dir. Rosa Von Praunheim, 1970), *Salome* (dir. Werner Schroeter, 1971).

Films as director: *Einer weiss mehr* (*Someone Knows More*, short, 1964), *19. September* (short documentary, 1965), *Wham* (short, 1965), *Sticky Fingers* (1966), *Der magische Moment* (*The Magic Moment*, 1966), *Nou Nou* (short, 1967), *Eva* (short, 1967), *Ja* *und Nein (Yes and No*, short, 1968), *Die endlose Reise (The Endless Journey*, 1968), *Für immer und ewig (For Ever and a Day*, short, 1969), *Blondie's Number One* (1970), *Küss mich, Fremder (Kiss Me, Stranger*, film in several episodes, 1971), *Harlis* (1972–3), *Der letzte Schrei (The Latest Fad*, 1974–5), *Belcanto* (1977), *Das andere Lächeln (The Other Smile*, 1977), *Die Reinheit des Herzens (Pure of Heart*, 1979–80), *Deutschland privat (Germany at Home*, anthology of super-8 home movies, 1980), *Die flambierte Frau (The Woman in Flames*, 1982–3), *Die Venusfalle (The Venus Trap*, 1987)

Percy Adlon
Born in Munich 1/6/1935. Studied history of art, drama and German. Acting roles until 1961, then worked as a radio broadcaster and editor of a literary radio series with the Bayrischer Rundfunk. First documentary short in 1970, first of several long documentaries in 1973 (*Tomi Ungerers Landleben*). Founded his own production company (pelemele FILM) with Elenore Adlon in 1978. Lives in Munich.
Films as director: *Der Vormund und sein Dichter, Unterhaltung am Koffer, Wir sind Babylon* (all 1979), *Herr Kischott* (TV feature, 1979), *Im Haus des Affenmalers Gabriel Max* (1979), *Celeste* (1981), *Fünf letzte Tage (Five Last Days*, 1982), *Fluchtwege eines friedliebenden Mannes (Escape Routes of a Peace-Loving Man*, 1982), *Die Schaukel (The Swing*, 1983), *Zuckerbaby (Sugar Baby*, 1986), *Out of Rosenheim (Bagdad Cafe*, 1987)

Claudia Alemann
Born in Seebach (Thuringia) 23/3/1943. Studied sociology in Berlin and film at the Institut für Filmgestaltung (Ulm) from 1964 to 1968. Together with Helke Sander organised the first International Seminar of Women Film-makers in West-Berlin (1973). Has written radio plays, books and essays. In 1967 and 1969 did two television documentaries on the Festivals in Knokke and Oberhausen. Has lived in Frankfurt since 1969, where she also founded her own production company (Alemann Filmproduktion).
Films as director: *Einfach* (short, 1966), *Lustgewinn* (short, 1967), *Fundevogel* (short feature film, 1967), *Das ist nur der Anfang – der Kampf geht weiter (This is only the beginning – the fight continues*, documentary, 1968–9), *Brigitte* (semi-documentary short, 1970), *Algier* (documentary short, 1970), *Kathleen und Eldridge Cleaver* (documentary short, 1970), *Germaine Greer* (TV, semi-documentary short, 1971), *FLQ Montreal* (documentary short, 1971), *Anti-imperialistischer Frauenkongress in Toronto* (documentary short, 1971), *Tu luc van doan – aus eigener Kraft* (short documentary compilation, 1971), *Arbeitsunfall* (TV documentary short, 1972), *Zeitarbeit* (TV documentary short, 1972), *Es kommt darauf an, sie zu verändern* (documentary, 1972–3), *Namibia* (documentary, 1973), *Filme der Sonne und der Nacht: Ariane Mnouchkine* (documentary, 1977), *Die Reise nach Lyon (The Trip to Lyon*, 1980), *Flora Tristan* (1980), *Nebelland* (TV feature, 1981–2), *Frauenzimmer* (TV feature, 1984)

Walter Bockmayer
Born in Fehrbach near Pirmasens in 1948. Commercial training, male nurse, theatre cloakroom attendant, publican in Cologne. Collaborated on all his films with Rolf Bührmann (born 1942). Since 1970 several short and long films in super-8.
Films as director: *Nymphomanie* (super-8, 1970), *Jane bleibt Jane (Jane is Jane Forever*, 1977), *Flammende Herzen (Flaming Hearts*, 1978), *Looping* (1981), *Kiez – Aufstieg und Fall eines Luden (Kiez*, 1983)

Hark Bohm
Born in Hamburg 18/5/1939. Raised on the island of Amrum, military service in the

Navy. From 1960 to 1966 studied law and took bar exams. At first a dealer's assistant in a gallery in Munich, then junior defence lawyer, for a time under Dr Norbert Kückelmann. In 1969 gave up judicial practice. Worked with Alexander Kluge and Rolf Thome. Founder member of the Filmverlag der Autoren. Worked as an actor (Fassbinder). Founded his own production company (Hamburger Kino Kompanie Hark Bohm) in 1974.

Films as director: *Wie starb Roland S.?* (*How did Roland S. Die?*, short, 1970), *Einer wird verletzt, träumt, stirbt und wird vergessen* (*Someone is Injured, Dreams, Dies and Is Forgotten*, short, 1971), *Tschetan, der Indianerjunge* (*Tschetan, the Indian Boy*, 1972), *Ich kann auch 'ne Arche bauen* (*I Can also Build an Ark*, TV feature, 1973), *Wir pfeifen auf den Gurkenkönig* (*We Can Do Without the Cucumber King*, two-part TV feature, 1974), *Nordsee ist Mordsee* (*The North Sea is Murderous*, 1975), *Wölfe* (*Wolves*, documentary, 1976), *Moritz, lieber Moritz* (*Moritz, Dear Moritz*, 1977), *Nicht mit uns* (*Count Us Out*, 1979), *Beobachtung an Wölfen* (*Observation on Wolves*, documentary, 1980), *Der Fall Bachmeier – Keine Zeit für Tränen* (*No Time for Tears – The Bachmeier Case*, 1983), *Yasemin* (1987)

Peter F. Bringmann

Born in Hanover 1946. Studied at the Hochschule für Fernsehen und Film in Munich from 1968 to 1971. Lives in Munich.

Films as director: *Kein Grund zur Unruhe* (1974), *Ein Haus für uns Bürger* (TV feature, 1975), *Aufforderung zum Tanz* (TV feature, 1976), *Paul kommt zurück* (TV feature, 1977), *Der Tag, an dem Elvis nach Bremerhaven kam* (*The Day Elvis Came to Bremerhaven*, TV feature, 1978), *Theo gegen den Rest der Welt* (*Theo against the Rest of the World*, 1980), *Die Heartbreakers* (*The Heartbreakers*, 1982), *Der Schneemann* (*The Snowman*, 1985)

Jutta Brückner

Born in Düsseldorf 25/6/1941. Studied politics, philosophy and history in Berlin, Paris and Munich, PhD in 1973. Has written film scripts (*Der Fangschuß* together with Margarethe von Trotta, dir. Volker Schlöndorff, 1974, and *Eine Frau mit Verantwortung*, dir. Ula Stöckl, 1977), radio plays, essays in film theory and film reviews since 1973. Since 1985 professor at the Hochschule der Künste, Berlin. Lives in Berlin.

Films as director: *Tue recht und scheue niemand* (1975), *Ein ganz und gar verwahrlostes Mädchen* (1977), *Hungerjahre* (1979), *Laufen Lernen* (1980), *Die Erbtöchter* (six-part omnibus film with Ula Stöckl and Helma Sanders-Brahms, episode *Luftwurzeln*, 1983), *Kolossale Liebe* (1984), *Ein Blick – und die Liebe bricht aus* (*One Glance – and Love Breaks Out*, 1986)

Alf Brustellin

Born in Vienna 27/7/1940. Studied German and worked as a film critic. Cameraman on Bernhard Sinkel's *Lina Braake*, scripted Sinkel's *Taugenichts* (1977), *Kaltgestellt* (1980) and *Bekenntnisse des Hochstaplers Felix Krull* (1981). Died 11/11/1981 in Munich after an automobile accident.

Films as director: *Kluge, Leni und der Löwe* (*Kluge, Leni and the Lion*, TV short, 1968), *Geschichten aus meinem Alter* (*Stories from my Age*, TV short, 1970), *Das goldene Ding* (*The Golden Thing*, 1971, together with Ula Stöckl, Edgar Reitz and Nicos Perakis), *Die Stadt der Hunde* (*City of Dogs*, TV short, 1972), *Berlinger – Ein deutsches Abenteuer* (1975), co-directed by Bernhard Sinkel, *Der Mädchenkrieg* (*The War of Girls*, 1976–7), co-directed by Bernhard Sinkel), *Deutschland im Herbst* (*Germany in Autumn*, omnibus film, one episode, 1977–8), *Der Sturz* (*The Fall*, 1978)

Hellmuth Costard

Born in Holzhausen near Leipzig 1/11/1940. Studied psychology at Hamburg where he was a member of the university's film and TV group, gaining initial practical experience of film work. Attempted to make a film in 1964 (together with friends in Persia) about the Kurdish liberation struggle. Abandoned his studies in 1966. Caused a scandal at the 1968 Oberhausen Short Film Festival with *Besonders Wertvoll*. Experiments with super-8 and Timecoder, as well as technical inventions. Lives in West Berlin.

Films as director: *Asta-Spot* (short, 1964), *Tom ist doof* (*Tom Is Dumb*, short, 1965), *Klammer auf, Klammer zu* (*Open Brackets, Close Brackets*, short, 1966), *After Action* (short, 1967), *Warum hast Du mich wachgeküsst?* (*Why did you wake me with your kisses?*, short, 1967), *Besonders Wertvoll* (*Quality Rating: Excellent*, 1968), *Die Unterdrückung der Frau ist vor allem an dem Verhalten der Frauen selber zu erkennen* (*The Oppression of women shows itself first of all in the behaviour of women themselves*, 1969), *Die Postkarte* (*The Postcard*, super-8 short, 1969), *Und niemand in Hollywood der versteht, daß schon viel zu viele Gehirne umgedreht wurden* (*And no one in Hollywood understands that far too many brains have been turned already*, TV feature, 1970), *Fußball wie noch nie* (*Football as never before*, TV documentary, 1970), *Der Elefantenfilm* (*The Elephant Film*, short, 1971), *Teilweise von mir – Ein Volksstück* (*Partly Mine – a Folk Play*, 1972), *Ein Nachmittag mit Onkel Robert* (*An Afternoon with Uncle Robert*, TV short, 1975), *Der kleine Godard an das Kuratorium junger deutscher Film* (*The Little Godard*, 1977–9), *Witzleben* (co-directed by Jürgen Ebert, 1980–1), *Echtzeit* (*Realtime*, co-directed by Jürgen Ebert, 1980–2), *Documentary on the production of microchips* for ZDF (c. 1985)

Doris Dörrie

Born in Hanover 1955. Abitur in 1973, studied drama, acting and film at the University of the Pacific, Stockton, and the New School for Social Research, New York until 1975. From 1975–8 at the Hochschule für Fernsehen und Film, Munich.

Films as director: *Ob's stürmt oder schneit* (*Come Rain or Shine*, documentary, 1976), *Ene, Mene, Mink* (short, 1977), *Der erste Walzer* (*The First Waltz*, 1978), *Hättest was gescheites gelernt* (TV documentary, 1978), *Paula aus Portugal* (*Paula from Portugal*, 1979), *Katharina Eiselt, 85, Arbeiterin* (*Katharina Eiselt, 85, Working Woman*, TV documentary, 1980), *Von Romantik keine Spur* (*Not a Trace of Romance*, TV documentary, 1980), *Dazwischen* (*In between*, TV feature, 1981), *Unter lauter Schafen* (*Among Sheep*, TV documentary, 1981), *Mitten ins Herz* (*Straight through the Heart*, 1983), *Im Innern des Wals* (*Inside the Whale*, 1984), *Männer* (*Men*, 1985), *Paradies* (*Paradise*, 1986)

Ingemo Engström

Born in Jakobstad, Finland 15/10/1941. Studied psychology, medicine and literature in Helsinki, Hamburg and Munich. Studied at the Hochschule für Fernsehen und Film Munich from 1967 to 1970. Worked for the magazine *Filmkritik*, for Swedish journals and Finnish radio. Lives in Munich.

Films as director: *Candy Man* (1968), *Dark Spring* (1970), *Zwei Liebende und die Mächtigsten dieser Erde* (*Two Lovers and the Mighty on Earth*, documentary fiction, 1973), *Kampf um ein Kind* (*Fight for a Child*, 1974–5), *Erzählen* (*Narrating*, documentary with Harun Farocki, 1975), *Fluchtweg nach Marseille* (TV documentary fiction in two parts, with Gerhard Theuring, 1977), *Letzte Liebe* (*Last Love*, 1979), *Flucht nach Norden* (*Flight North*, 1986)

Harun Farocki

Born 1943. Studied at the Deutsche Film und Fernsehakademie. Short films in collaboration with Hartmut Bitomski. Regular contributor to *Filmkritik*. His feature-length films are self-financed. Earns his living with magazine features and children's programmes for television.

Films as director: *Die Worte des Vorsitzenden* (*Words of the Chairman*, 1968), *Nicht löschbares Feuer* (*Unextinguishable Fire*, 1969), *Die Teilung aller Tage* (*The Division of the Days*, with Hartmut Bitomski, 1970), *Eine Sache, die sich versteht* (*Something that Goes without Saying*, with Hartmut Bitomski, 1971), *Der Ärger mit den Bildern* (*The Trouble with Images*, 1973), *Erzählen* (*Narrating*, with Ingemo Engström, 1975), *Zwischen zwei Kriegen* (*Between the Wars*, 1977), *Der Geschmack des Lebens* (*The Taste of Life*, 1979), *Etwas wird sichtbar* (*Before your Eyes: Vietnam*, 1981–2), *Wie Man Sieht* (*As You See*, 1986–7)

Rainer Werner Fassbinder

Born in Bad Wörishofen 31/5/1945. Grew up in Augsburg and Munich. Took acting classes and joined the 'action-theater' in 1967. In 1968 co-founded 'antiteater', the core of his later collaborators. From 1969 to 1977 two parallel careers as theatre director and film-maker, in Munich, Bremen, Berlin, Frankfurt, Bochum and Hamburg. Co-founder of the Filmverlag der Autoren. Since 1971 with his own production company, Tango Films. Federal Film Prizes in 1970, 1971, 1972, 1978, 1979, 1982. Golden Bear in Berlin for *Veronika Voss*. Acted in his own films. Died in Munich 10/6/82.

Films as director: *Der Stadtstreicher* (*The City Tramp*, 1965 short); *Das kleine Chaos* (*The Little Chaos*, 1966 short); *Liebe ist kälter als der Tod* (*Love Is Colder Than Death*, 1969), *Katzelmacher* (1969), *Götter der Pest* (*Gods of the Plague*, co-directed by Michael Fengler, 1969), *Warum läuft Herr R. Amok?* (*Why Does Herr R. Run Amok?*, 1969); *Rio das Mortes* (1970), *Das Kaffeehaus* (*The Coffee House*, television version of stage production, 1970), *Whity* (1970); *Die Niklashauser Fart* (*The Nicklehausen Journey*, TV film, 1970); *Der Amerikanische Soldat* (*The American Soldier*, 1970); *Warnung vor einer Heiligen Nutte* (*Beware of a Holy Whore*, 1970); *Pioniere in Ingolstadt* (*Pioneers in Ingolstadt*, TV film, 1970); *Der Händler der vier Jahreszeiten* (*The Merchant of Four Seasons*, 1971); *Bremer Freiheit* (*Bremen Coffee*, television version of stage production, 1972); *Die bitteren Tränen der Petra von Kant* (*The Bitter Tears of Petra von Kant*, 1972); *Wildwechsel* (*Jailbait*, 1972); *Acht Stunden sind kein Tag* (*Eight Hours Are Not a Day*, five part television series, 1972); *Welt am Draht* (*World on a Wire*, two part television series, 1973); *Angst Essen Seele Auf* (*Fear Eats the Soul*, 1973); *Nora Helmer* (television version of stage production, 1973); *Martha* (television film, 1973); *Fontane Effi Briest* (*Effi Briest*, 1974); *Faustrecht der Freiheit* (*Fox and His Friends*, 1974); *Wie ein Vogel auf dem Draht* (*Like A Bird On A Wire*, TV show with Brigitte Mira, 1974); *Mutter Küsters Fahrt zum Himmel* (*Mother Kuster's Trip to Heaven*, 1975); *Angst vor der Angst* (*Fear of Fear*, television film, 1975); *Satansbraten* (*Satan's Brew*, 1976); *Ich will doch nur dass ihr mich liebt* (*I Only Want You to Love Me*, television film, 1976); *Chinesisches Roulette* (*Chinese Roulette*, 1976); *Bolwieser* (*The Station Master's Wife*, two part television film, 1977); *Eine Reise ins Licht* (*Despair*, 1977); *Frauen in New York* (*Women in New York*, television version of stage production, 1977); *Deutschland im Herbst* (*Germany in Autumn*, one episode, 1978); *In einem Jahr mit dreizehn Monden* (*In a Year of Thirteen Moons*, 1978); *Die Ehe der Maria Braun* (*The Marriage of Maria Braun*, 1978); *Die dritte Generation* (*The Third Generation*, 1979); *Berlin Alexanderplatz* (thirteen part television series, 1980); *Lili Marleen* (1980); *Lola* (1981); *Theater in Transe* (*Theater in a Trance*; video-production of international theatre festival, 1981); *Die Sehnsucht der Veronika Voss* (*Veronika Voss*, 1981); *Querelle* (1982)

Eberhard Fechner

Born in Liegnitz (Silesia), 21/10/1926. Grew up in Berlin. Worked in the Accounts Department of UFA. Soldier during the last year of the war. Acting School at the Deutsche Theater, Berlin-East from 1946–8, then actor in Berlin, Bremen, Hanover and Hamburg. 1961–3 assistant director at Giorgio Strehler's Piccolo Teatro in Milan.

Theatre director and actor in Konstanz and Bremen. Since 1966 director of television drama and documentaries. Works mainly for NDR and lives in Hamburg. **Films as director:** *Selbstbedienung* (*Self Service*, 1966), *Vier Stunden von Elbe 1* (*Four Hours of Elbe One*, 1967), *Damenquartett* (*Ladies' Quartet*, 1968), *Der Versager* (*The Failure*, 1969), *Nachrede auf Klara Heydebreck* (*Obituary for Klara Heydebreck*, 1969), *Gezeiten* (*Tides*, 1969), *Klassenphoto* (*Class Photograph*, 1969–70), *Frankfurter Gold* (*Frankfurt Gold*, 1970–1), *Geheimagenten* (*Secret Agents*, 1971), *Aus nichtigem Anlass* (*For No Good Reason*, 1973), *Unter Denkmalschutz* (*Listed Building*, 1974), *Tadellöser & Wolff* (TV film in two parts, 1974–5), *Lebensdaten* (*Chronologies*, 1975), *Die Comedian Harmonists* (two-part documentary 1975–6), *Winterspelt 1944* (feature film, 1977), *Ein Kapitel für sich* (*A Chapter by Itself*, TV film in three parts, 1978–9), *Im Damenstift* (*Religious Orders*, documentary, 1983), *Der Prozess* (three-part TV documentary, 1976–84)

Peter Fleischmann
Born in Zweibrücken 26/7/1937. Studied at the Deutsches Institut für Film und Fernsehen in Munich. Worked as lighting engineer, production manager and assistant director. Scholarship at the Institut des Hautes Etudes Cinématographique in Paris. Worked as assistant for the directors Jacques Rozier and Robert Menegoz, Jean Chapot, Jacques Dewever. Founded his own production firm (Hallelujah Film) with Volker Schlöndorff in 1971. Lives in Munich.
Films as director: *Die Eintagsfliege* (short, 1957), *Un noir pour madame* (*One Night for Madame*, short, 1962), *Brot der Wüste* (*Bread of the Desert*, short, 1962), *Die Sandrose* (short, 1962), *Interview mit Fritz Lang* (*Interview with Fritz Lang*, short, 1963), *Der Test* (*The Test*, short, 1964), *Alexander und das Auto ohne linken Scheinwerfer* (*Alexander and the Car Without the Left Headlight*, short, 1965), *Herbst der Gammler* (documentary, 1967), *Jagdszenen aus Niederbayern* (*Hunting Scenes from Lower Bavaria*, 1968–9), *Das Unheil* (*The Bane*, 1970), *Dorotheas Rache* (*Dorothea's Revenge*, 1973), *Der dritte Grad* (*The Third Degree*, 1974–5), *Rückkehr nach Unholzing/Unholzing – Acht Jahre danach* (TV documentary, 1976), *Die Hamburger Krankheit* (*The Hamburg Disease*, 1978–9), *Der Frevel* (*Mischief*, 1983)

Hans W. Geissendörfer
Born in Augsburg 6/4/1941. Studied German, drama, psychology and African languages at the Universities of Marburg, Erlangen, Vienna and Zurich (1962–7). Made super-8 and Underground films. After breaking off his studies travelled in Europe, Asia and Africa. Worked as assistant director to Gerorge Moorse on *Liebe und so weiter*. Federal Film Prizes: 1970 as the best young director for *Jonathan*, 1976 for *Sternsteinhof*, 1978 for *Die gläserne Zelle*, 1982 for *Der Zauberberg*. A member of the Filmverlag der Autoren. Lives in Munich.
Films as director: *Befriedigung* (*Satisfaction*, 8mm documentary, 1966), *Dynamitfischerei* (*Dynamite Fishing*, 8mm documentary, 1967) *Fastentage in Griechenland* (*Days of Fasting in Greece*, 8mm documentary, 1967), *Netzfischfang im Ägäischen Meer* (*Net Fishing in the Aegean Sea*, 8mm documentary, 1967), *Eins & Eins* (*One & One*, 8mm short, 1968), *Manfred Schoof Quintett* (8mm documentary, 1968), *Anna Kahn* (8mm short, 1968), *Der Fall Lena Christ* (*The Case of Lena Christ*, TV feature, 1968), *Jonathan* (1969), *Eine Rose für Jane* (*A Rose for Jane*, TV feature, 1970), *Carlos* (TV feature, 1971), *Marie* (TV feature, 1972), *Die Eltern* (*The Parents*, TV feature, 1973), *Perahim – Die zweite Chance* (*Perahim – The Second Chance*, TV feature, 1974), *Lobster* (TV series, 1975), *Sternsteinhof* (*Sternstein Manor*, 1975–6), *Die Wildente* (*The Wild Duck*, 1976), *Die Gläserne Zelle* (*The Glass Cell*, 1977), *Theodor Chindler* (TV series, 1978–9), *Der Zauberberg* (*The Magic Mountain*, 1980–1), *Edith's Tagebuch* (*Edith's Diary*, 1982–3)

Wolf Gremm
Born in Freiburg 26/2/1942. Attended music college. Studied literature, psychology and theatre in Heidelberg, Vienna and Berlin. Studied Film at the Deutsche Film und Fernsehakademie Berlin.

Films as director: *Jeden Tag* (*Every Day*, short, 1967), *Anfänge* (*Beginnings*, short, 1967), *Vier Gesten* (*Four Gestures*, 1968), *14 Tage* (*Fortnight*, documentary, 1969), *Berliner Bilderbogen: 20. Berliner Festwochen* (TV documentary, 1971), *Der Große Verschleiß* (1971), *Oh, Donna Clara* (TV Feature, 1972), *Lohnt das ganze Theater?* (TV documentary, 1972), *Die vom Leben Erschöpften* (1973), *Hört, hört!* (*Hear, Hear*, TV documentary, 1973), *Ich dachte ich wäre tot* (*I Thought I Was Dead*, 1973), *Meine Sorgen möcht' ich haben* (1974), *The Moodies* (TV show, 1974), *Tod im U-Bahnschacht* (TV feature for the 'Tatort' series, 1975), *Die Brüder* (*The Brothers*, 1976), *Tod oder Freiheit* (*Death or Liberty*, 1977), *Die Schattengrenze* (TV feature, 1978), *Fabian* (1979), *Kein Reihenhaus für Robin Hood* (1980), *Nach Mitternacht* (*After Midnight*, 1981), *Kamikaze 1989* (1981), *Das letzte Jahr* (*The Last Year*, documentary, 1982)

Reinhard Hauff
Born in Marburg (Lahn) 23/5/1939. Studied literature and sociology. Assistant director on shows, documentaries, TV plays and feature films. Worked on some 20 TV shows between 1966–8. Transferred from light entertainment to documentaries and feature films in 1969. Since 1973 in charge of his own production company 'Bioskop Film' (in conjunction with Volker Schlöndorff). Chief organiser of the 1979 Film-Makers' Film Festival in Hamburg. Federal Film Prize in 1979 for *Messer im Kopf*, Grand Prix (Golden Bear) of the Berlin Film Festival 1986 for *Stammhein*. Married to writer/director Christel Buschmann. Lives in Munich.

Films as director: *Untermann – Obermann* (TV documentary, 1969), *Die Revolte* (*The Revolt*, 1969), *Ausweglos* (*No Way Out*, TV documentary, 1969), *Offener Haß gegen Unbekannt* (*Open Hatred against a Person or Persons Unknown*, TV feature, 1970), *Mathias Kneissl* (TV feature, 1970–1), *Haus am Meer* (*House by the Sea*, TV feature, 1972), *Desaster* (*Disaster*, TV feature, 1972–3), *Die Verrohung des Franz Blum* (*The Brutalisation of Franz Blum*, 1973–4), *Zündschnüre* (*Fuses*, TV feature, 1974), *Paule Pauländer* (1975), *Der Hauptdarsteller* (*The Main Actor*, 1977), *Messer im Kopf* (*Knife in the Head*, 1978), *Endstation Freiheit* (*Last Stop Freedom*, 1980), *Der Mann auf der Mauer* (*The Man on the Wall*, 1982), *Zehn Tage in Calcutta* (*Ten Days in Calcutta*, TV documentary, 1984), *Stammheim* (*Stammheim – The Trial*, 1985) *Linie 1* (1988)

Werner Herzog
Born Werner Stipetic in Munich 5/9/42. Studied history, literature and drama in Munich and Pittsburg. Broke off studies and taught himself film-making. Silver Bear at the 1968 Berlin Film Festival for *Lebenszeichen*. Awarded Prix Spécial at the 1975 Cannes Film Festival for *Jeder für sich und Gott gegen alle*. Director's Prize at Cannes in 1982 for *Fitzcarraldo*. All three films won Federal Film Prizes. His own production company (Werner Herzog Filmproduktion) since 1963 in Munich. Has published several books. Lives in Munich.

Films as director: *Herakles* (*Hercules*, short, 1962), *Spiel im Sand* (*Playing in the Sand*, short, 1964), *Die beispiellose Verteidigung der Festung Deutschkreutz* (*The Unparalleled Defence of the Fortress Deutschkreutz*, short, 1966), *Lebenszeichen* (*Signs of Life*, 1967), *Letzte Worte* (*Last Words*, short, 1967–8), *Maßnahmen gegen Fanatiker* (*Measures against Fanatics*, short, 1968), *Die fliegenden Ärzte von Ostafrika* (*The Flying Doctors of East Africa*, documentary, 1968–9), *Fata Morgana* (experimental, 1968–70), *Auch Zwerge haben klein angefangen* (*Even Dwarfs Started Small*, 1969–70), *Behinderte Zukunft* (*Handicapped Future*, documentary, 1970), *Land des Schweigens und der Dunkelheit* (*Land of Silence and Darkness*, documentary, 1970–1),

Aguirre, der Zorn Gottes (*Aguirre, Wrath of God*, 1972), *Die große Ekstase des Bildschnitzers Steiner* (*The Great Ecstasy of the Woodcarver Steiner*, documentary, 1973–4), *Jeder für sich und Gott gegen alle* (*Every Man For Himself and God Against All, or The Enigma of Kaspar Hauser*, 1974), *How Much Wood Would a Woodchuck Chuck?* (documentary, 1975–6), *Mit mir will keiner spielen* (*No-one Will Play With Me*, short, 1976), *Herz aus Glas* (*Heart of Glass*, 1976), *La Soufrière* (documentary, 1976), *Stroszek* (1976–7), *Nosferatu – Phantom der Nacht* (*Nosferatu*, 1978), *Woyzeck* (1978), *Huie's Sermon* (documentary, 1980), *Glaube und Währung* (documentary, 1980), *Fitzcarraldo* (1980–1), *Wo die grünen Ameisen träumen* (*Where the Green Ants Dream*, 1983), *Ballade vom kleinen Soldaten* (documentary, 1984), *Gasherbrumm, der leuchtende Berg* (documentary, 1984–5), *Cobra Verde* (1987)

Erwin Keusch
Born in Zurich 22/7/1946. Studied German, psychology, history and theatre at Zurich University (1965–8) and in Munich (from 1968 onwards). Became a self-taught film-maker, first experimental films, later films for television. Founded his own production company (Nanuk Film) together with Christian Weisenborn in 1974.
Films as director: *Geni* (*Eugen*, 1968), *Pietro* (short, 1968–9), *Carina nett, lieb* (short, 1969), *Das kleine Riesenrad* (short, 1970), *Das kleine Welttheater* (documentary short, 1970), *Lehrlinge* (1971–2), *Aseptische Operation* (short, 1972), *Es drängen sich keine Maßnahmen auf* (short, 1973), *La Salle blanche* (short, 1973), *Der zweite Bildungsweg* (TV short, 1973), *Die Prinzengarde – Wer wird Fußballstar?* (short TV documentary, 1974–5), *Manfred Weckwerth* (short TV documentary, 1975–6), *Werner Herzog dreht Stroszek* (short TV documentary, 1976), *Das Brot des Bäckers* (*The Baker's Bread*, 1976), *Der Rasen ihrer Träume* (TV documentary, together with Christian Weisenborn, 1974–7), *Was ich bin sind meine Filme* (documentary together with Christian Weisenborn, 1977–8), *Telearena* (1978), *So weit das Auge reicht* (*As Far as the Eye Can See*, 1980), *Ein Mann fürs Leben* (TV feature, 1980), *Der Hunger, der Koch und das Paradies* (together with Karl Saurer, 1981), *Wunder und Narben* (documentary together with Norbert Wieder, 1981), *Unter deutschen Dächern – Konsumkathedralen* (TV documentary together with Norbert Wieder, 1981), *Kerbels Flucht* (TV feature, 1983), *Der Fahnder* (TV feature, 1984), *Gerichtliches Nachspiel* (TV feature, 1984), *Das leise Gift* (TV feature, 1984), *Ein Mann fürs Leben, Teil 2* (TV feature, 1984), *In der Bärengrube* (1985), *Der Flieger* (*The Flyer*, 1986)

Roland Klick
Born in Hof 4/7/1939. Jazz musician and painter, studied theatre history and attended the Deutsches Institut für Film und Fernsehen in Munich.
Films as director: *Weihnacht* (*Christmas*, short, 1963), *Ludwig* (short, 1964), *Zwei* (*Two*, short, 1965), *Jimmy Orpheus* (1966), *Bübchen* (*Little Boy*, also *The Little Vampire*, 1967–8), *Deadlock* (1970), *Supermarkt* (1973), *Lieb Vaterland magst ruhig sein* (1975–6), *Derby-Fieber* (TV documentary, 1979), *White Star* (1983)

Alexander Kluge
Born in Halberstadt 14/2/1932. Studied law, history and church music. PhD thesis on University Administration. Lawyer, chief initiator of the Oberhausen Manifesto in 1962 and active in film politics throughout the 1960s and 1970s. From 1962 onwards director of the Film Institute at the Hochschule für Gestaltung (Ulm). In 1963 founded his own production company, Kairos-Film. Special Prize at the 1966 Venice Film Festival for *Abschied von Gestern*. Venice Grand Prix for *Artistes at the Top of the Big Top: Disorientated* in 1968. Federal Film Prizes in 1967, 1969 and 1979. Since 1973 Professor of Sociology at the University of Frankfurt. Has published numerous volumes of sociological and historical studies, among them *Geschichte und Eigensinn* (with Oskar Negt, 1981) and edited *Bestandsaufnahme Utopie Film* (1983). Awarded the Fontane Prize in 1984. Lives in Munich and Frankfurt.

Films as director: *Brutalität in Stein* (short, with Peter Schamoni, 1960), *Rennen* (short, 1961), *Lehrer im Wandel* (short, 1962–3), *Porträt einer Bewährung* (short, 1964), *Abschied von Gestern* (*Yesterday Girl*, 1965–6), *Frau Blackburn, geb. 5.Jan 1872 wird gefilmt* (short, 1967), *Die Artisten in der Zirkuskuppel: Ratlos* (*Artistes at the Top of the Big Top: Disorientated*, 1967), *Feuerlöscher E.A. Winterstein* (short, 1968), *Die unbezähmbare Leni Peikert* (TV film, 1969), *Der große Verhau* (*The Big Mess*, 1969–70), *Ein Arzt aus Halberstadt* (short, 1970), *Wir verbauen 3 × 27 Milliarden Dollar in einen Angriffsschlachter* (short, 1971), *Willi Tobler und der Untergang der 6.Flotte* (*Willi Tobler and the Sinking of the Sixth Fleet*, 1971), *Besitzbürgerin, Jahrgang 1908* (short, 1973), *Gelegenheitsarbeit einer Sklavin* (*Occasional Work of a Female Slave*, 1973), *In Gefahr und größter Not bringt der Mittelweg den Tod* (*In Danger and in Deep Distress, the Middle Way Spells Certain Death*, co-director Edgar Reitz, 1974), *Der starke Ferdinand* (*Strongman Ferdinand*, 1975), *Die Menschen die das Staufer-Jahr vorbereiten* (short with Maximiliane Mainka, 1977), *Nachrichten von den Staufern* (two shorts with Maximiliane Mainka, 1977), *'Zu böser Nacht schleich ich heut nacht so bang'* (revised version of Willi Tobler, 1977), *Deutschland im Herbst* (*Germany in Autumn*, omnibus film, 1977–8), *Die Patriotin* (*The Patriot*, 1977–9), *Der Kandidat* (*The Candidate*, 1980), *Biermann-Film* (short, with Edgar Reitz, 1982), *Krieg und Frieden* (*War and Peace*, omnibus film, 1982–3), *Auf der Suche nach einer praktisch-realistischen Haltung* (short, 1983), *Die Macht der Gefühle* (*The Power of Feelings*, 1983), *Der Angriff der Gegenwart auf die übrige Zeit* (*The Blind Director*, 1985), *Vermischte Nachrichten* (*Odds and Ends*, 1987)

Theodor Kotulla
Born in Chorzow (Königshütte) 20/8/1928, studied journalism, German literature, philosophy. Film critic (*filmforum, Frankfurter Hefte, film 56, Filmkritik*). Published several books.
Films as director: *Camus und Algier* (TV documentary, 1964); *Zum Beispiel Bresson* (short, 1966), *Panek* (short, 1968), *Vor dem Feind* (short, 1968), *Bis zum Happy End* (1968), *Ohne Nachsicht* (1971), *See the Music* (documentary 1971), *Aus einem deutschen Leben* (1977), *Der Fall Maurizius* (TV film, 1981), *Der Angriff* (*Aggression*, 1987)

Vlado Kristl
Born in Zagreb 24/1/1923, studied at the Academy of Arts in Zagreb. Poet, painter, made his first short in 1962 in Yugoslavia. 1963 moved to West Germany.
Films as director: *Arme Leute* (short co-directed with P. Schamoni, 1963), *Madeleine-Madeleine* (short, 1963), *Der Damm* (1964), *Autorennen* (short, 1964), *Maulwürfe* (short, destroyed, 1965), *Prometheus* (short animated cartoon, 1966), *Der Brief* (1966), *Die Utopen* (short animated cartoon, 1967), *Sekundenfilme* (short TV film, 1967–8), *100 Blatt Schreibblock* (short, 1968), *Italienisches Capriccio* (short, 1969), *Film oder Macht* (1970), *Obrichkeitsfilm* (1971), *Berlinale* (short, super-8, 1971), *Dächer der Ruinen* (super-8, 1971), *Tigerkäfig* (short, super-8, 1971), *Akademismus* (super-8, 1972), *Literaturfilmung* (short, 1973), *Horizonte* (short, 1973), *Diese Gedichte* (1975), *Am Abend kommt die Nacht* (short super-8, 1975), *Die Verräter des jungen deutschen Films schlafen nicht* (short, 1982), *Tod dem Zuschauer* (1983)

Norbert Kückelmann
Born in Munich, 1/5/1930. Studied law and took bar exams. Has practised as a solicitor in Munich since 1958. Co-founder, with Alexander Kluge and Hans Rolf Strobel, of the Kuratorium Junger Deutscher Film. Feature film-maker since 1972, Federal Film Prizes in 1973, 1980 and 1984. Co-owns the production company FFAT with Peter Lilienthal. Lives in Munich.
Films as director: *Die Sachverständigen* (*The Experts*, 1972), *Die Schießübung*

(*Shooting Practice*, 1974), *Die Angst ist ein zweiter Schatten* (*Fear is a Second Shadow*, 1975), *Die letzten Jahre der Kindheit* (*The Last Years of Childhood*, 1979), *Morgen in Alabama* (*A German Lawyer*, 1983)

Klaus Lemke
Born in Landsberg 13/10/1940. Studied history of art and philosophy. Film critic for *Film*. After lack of success with *Negresco*** he began a second career in television.
Films as director: *Kleine Front* (short co-directed with Werner Enke, 1965), *Drei* (short, 1965), *Flipper* (short, 1966), *Duell* (short, 1966), *Henker Tom* (short, 1966), *Ein Haus am Meer* (short, 1966), *48 Stunde bis Acapulco* (1967), *Negresco*** – *Eine Tödliche Affäre* (1968), *Brandstifter* (TV film, 1969), *Mein schönes kurzes Leben* (TV, 1970), *Rocker* (TV film, 1972), *Liebe so schön wie Liebe* (1972), *Sylvie* (TV film, 1973), *Paul* (TV film, 1974), *Teenager-Liebe* (TV film, 1975), *Idole* (TV film, 1976), *Die Sweethearts* (TV film, 1976), *Moto-Cross* (TV film, 1977), *Amore* (TV film, 1978), *Ein komischer Heiliger* (1979), *Der Allerlezte* (TV film, 1979), *Flitterwochen* (1980), *Wie die Weltmeister* (1981), *Der Kleine* (1983)

Peter Lilienthal
Born Berlin, 27/11/1929. Emigration to Uruguay in 1939. Worked in a bank. Studied at the Hochschule für Bildende Kunst in Berlin. Long career in television before making feature films. Has his own production company (with Norbert Kückelmann) FFAT. Lives in Munich.
Films as director: *El Joven del trapecio volante* (*Uruguay*, 1965), *Studie 23* (short animated cartoon, 1958), *In Handumdrehen verdient* (short TV film, 1959), *Die Nachbarskinder* (short TV film, 1960), *Biographie eines Schokoladentages* (TV film, 1961), *Der 18. Geburtstag* (TV film, 1962), *Stück für Stück* (TV film, 1962), *Picknick im Felde* (short TV film, 1962), *Schule der Geläufigkeit* (TV film, 1963), *Striptease* (short, TV film, 1963), *Guernica – Jede Stunde verletzt und die letzte tötet* (short, TV film, 1963), *Das Martyrium des Peter O'Hey* (TV film, 1964), *Marl – Porträt einer Stadt* (TV documentary, 1964), *Seraphine – oder die wundersame Geschichte der Tante Flora* (TV film, 1965), *Unbeschriebenes Blatt* (TV film, 1965), *Der Beginn* (TV film, 1966), *Abgründe* (TV film, 1966), *Verbrechen mit Vorbedacht* (TV film, 1967), *Tramp – oder der einzige und unvergleichliche Lenny Jakobsen* (TV film, 1968), *Horror* (TV film, 1969), *Malatesta* (1970), *Ich, Montag/Ich, Dienstag/Ich, Mittwoch/Ich Donnerstag* (*Porträt Gombrowitz*, TV documentary, 1970), *Die Sonne Angreifen* (TV film, 1971), *Jakob von Gunten* (TV film, 1971), *Noon in Tunisia* (TV documentary, 1971), *Start Nr 9* (TV documentary, 1972), *Shirley Chisholm for President* (TV documentary, 1972), *La Victoria* (1973), *Ikarus* (TV film, 1973), *Hauptlehrer Hofer* (*Headteacher Hofer*, 1975), *Es herrscht Ruhe im Land* (*Calm Prevails in the Country*, 1976), *Kadir* (TV documentary, 1977), *David* (1979), *Kindheit in Amacueda* (TV film, 1979), *Der Aufstand* (*The Uprising*, 1980), *Dear Mr Wonderful* (1982), *Das Autogramm* (*The Autograph*, 1984), *Das Schweigen des Dichters* (*The Poet's Silence*, 1986)

Marianne Lüdcke
Born in Berlin 22/7/1943. Trained in fashion and design, then took acting lessons. Through Ingo Kratisch came to work at the Deutsche Film und Fernsehakademie Berlin in 1971. Together they made a series of very successful 'workers' films', until, after five years' of collaboration with Kratisch, she decided to direct on her own.
Films as director: *Akkord* (*Piece Work*, documentary, co-directed by Ingo Kratisch, 1971), *Die Wollands* (*The Wolland Family*, co-directed by Ingo Kratisch, 1972), *Lohn und Liebe* (*Love and Wages*, co-directed by Ingo Kratisch, 1973), *Familienglück* (*Wedded Bliss*, co-directed Ingo Kratisch, 1975), *Die Tannerhütte* (*The Tanner Hut*, co-directed by Ingo Kratisch, 1976), *Die große Flatter* (*Homeless*, 1978–9)

Elfi Mikesch
Born in Judenburg (Austria), 31/5/1940. Trained as a photographer. Moved to Berlin in 1966 and worked under the name of 'Oh Muvie' as assistant to Rosa von Praunheim. Published photo-books and cover-designs, notably for *Frauen und Film*. Federal Film Prize in 1978. Has her own production company Oh Muvie. Lives in Berlin.
Films as director: *Charisma* (short, 1970), *Family Sketch* (short, 1975), *Ich denke oft an Hawaii* (*I Often Think of Hawaii*, 1977–8), *Execution – A Study of Mary* (experimental short, 1979), *Was soll'n wir denn machen ohne den Tod* (*What Would We Do Without Death*, 1979–80), *Macumba* (1981), *Die blaue Distanz* (*The Blue Distance*, short, 1982), *Das Frühstück der Hyäne* (*The Hyena's Breakfast*, short, 1982), *Verführung: die grausame Frau* (*Seduction: The Cruel Woman*, co-directed by Monika Treut, 1984–5)

Werner Nekes
Born in Erfurt 29/4/1944, studied linguistics and psychology. Co-founder of the Hamburg Filmcooperative and (1970–2) Professor at the Hamburg Hochschule für Bildende Kunst.
Films as director: *Tom Doyle and Eva Hesse* (short super-8, 1965), *Fehlstart* (short, 1966), *Start* (short, 1966), *Artikel* (short, 1966), *Bogen* (short, 1967), *Schnitte für Ababa* (short, 1967), *schwarzhuhnbraunhuhnschwarzhuhnweisshuhnrothuhnweiss oder putt-putt* (short, 1967), *Kratz-, Beiss-, Licht-, Loch- und Flicker-filme* (1967), *jüm-jüm* (co-directed with Dore O, 1967), *Das Seminar* (co-director Bazon Brock, 1967), *Gurtrug Nr.1* (short, 1967), *Gurtrug Nr.2* (short, 1967), *Ach, wie gut dass niemand weiss* (short, 1967), *Körper* (short, 1967), *Operation* (short, 1967), *vis-à-vis* (short, 1968), *Gruppenfilm* (Film collective, 1968), *zipzibbelip* (short, 1968), *Mama, da steht ein Mann* (short, 1968), *Tarzans Kampf mit dem Gorilla* (short, 1968), *Muhkuh* (short, 1968), *Kelek* (1968), *Nebula* (1969), *Palimpsest* (1965–9), *Abbandono* (1970), *Space-cut* (1971), *Aus Altona* (short, 1972), *T-WO-MEN -I-IV* (1972), *Arbatax* (short, 1973), *Diwan* (series of 5 films, 1973), *Makimono* (1974), *Photophtalmia* (short, 1975), *Amalgam I–IV* (1975/76), *Falun* (1976), *Lagado* (1976–7), *Mirador* (1978), *Bei der Lichtbildnerin* (short, 1978), *Horly* (short, 1978), *Hurrycan* (1978–9), *Little Night* (short, 1979), *Peggy und die anderen* (TV documentary, co-director Bazin Brock, 1981), *Beuys* (short, co-director Dore O, 1981), *Uliisses* (co-director Dore O, 1980–2), *Nekes* (co-director Dore O, 1982), *Blick aus dem harmonischen Gefängnis* (short, 1982), *Was geschah wirklich zwischen den Bildern* (*Film Before Film*, 1983)

Ulrike Ottinger
Born in Konstanz, 6/6/1942. Studied art in Munich 1959–61. Lived in Paris as painter and photographer 1961–8. Founded and ran gallery 'Galerie-Press' and film-club 'Visuell' in Konstanz. Moved to Berlin in 1973, started film-making with Tabea Blumenschein. In 1983 directed theatre play in Stuttgart.
Films as director: *Berlinfieber-Wolf Vostell* (short, 1973), *Laokoon & Söhne* (short feature, co-directed by Tabea Blumenschein, 1972–4), *Die Betörung der Blauen Matrosen* (short feature, co-directed by Tabea Blumenschein, 1975) *Madame X – eine absolute Herrscherin* (*Madame X*, 1977), *Bildnis einer Trinkerin* (*Ticket of No Return*, 1979), *Freak Orlando* (1981), *Dorian Gray im Spiegel der Boulevardpresse* (*Dorian Gray in the Popular Press*, 1983), *China – Die Künste, der Alltag* (*China, the arts and daily life*, 1987)

Wolfgang Petersen
Born Emden 14/3/1941, attended the Hamburg School of Drama and became an assistant director. Studied history of drama before going on to the Deutsche Film und Fernsehakademie in Berlin.
Films as director: *Der Eine – der Andere* (short, 1967), *Ich nicht* (short, 1968), *Ich*

werde dich töten, Wolf (1970), *Blechschaden* (TV film, 1971), *Anna und Toto* (TV film, 1971), *Strandgut* (TV film, 1971), *Nachtfrost* (TV film, 1972), *Jagdrevier* (TV film, 1972), *Smog* (TV film, 1972), *Van der Valk und die Reichen* (TV film, 1973), *Einer von uns beiden* (1973), *Aufs Kreuz gelegt* (TV film, 1974), *Die Stadt im Tal* (TV film in 2 parts, 1974), *Stellenweise Glatteis* (TV film, 1974), *Kurzschluss* (TV film, 1975), *Hans im Glück* (TV film, 1976), *Vier gegen die Bank* (TV film, 1976), *Reifezeugnis* (TV film, 1976), *Planübung* (TV film, 1976–7), *Die Konsequenz* (*The Consequence*, TV film, 1977), *Schwarz und weiss wie Tage und Nächte* (*Black and White like Night and Day*, TV film, 1978), *Das Boot* (*The Boat*, 1981), *Die unendliche Geschichte* (*The Neverending Story*, 1983–4), *Enemy Mine* (1985)

Rosa von Praunheim
Pseudonym of Holger Mischwitzki. Born Riga 25/11/1942, studied at the School of Applied Arts in Offenbach and at the Hochschule für Bildende Künste, Berlin. Collaborated with Werner Schroeter, assistant director to Gregory Markopoulos in 1968. Published articles in film journals and various books. Lives in Berlin and Frankfurt.

Films as director: *Von Rosa von Praunheim* (short, 1967), *Grotesk – burlesque – pittoresk* (co-directed by Werner Schroeter, 1968), *Rosa Arbeiter auf Goldener Strasse* (short, 1968), *Schwestern der Revolution* (short, 1969), *Samuel Beckett* (short, 1969), *Was die Rechte nicht sieht. . . . kommt erst recht aus dem Ohr hinaus* (short, 1970), *Macbeth – Oper von Rosa von Praunheim* (TV film, 1970) *Die Bettwurst* (*The Bedroll*, 1970), *Nicht der Homosexuelle ist pervers sondern die Situation, in der er lebt* (*Not the Homosexual is Perverse, but the Situation in which He Finds Himself*, 1970), *Sylvester 70/71* (short, incomplete, 1971), *Homosexuelle in New York* (short, 1971), *Leidenschaften* (1971–2), *Berliner Bettwurst* (*Berlin Bedroll*, 1973), *Axel von Auersperg* (TV film, 1973), *Rosa von Praunheim zeigt* (short, 1973), *Monolog eines Stars* (TV film, 1974), *Underground and Emigrants* (TV film, 1975–6), *Porträt Marianne Rosenberg* (short, TV, 1976), *Ich bin ein Antistar* (TV, 1976), *Frühling für Frankfurt* (short, TV, 1977), *Der 24. Stock* (TV documentary in 2 parts, 1977), *Porträt George und Mike Kuchar* (short, 1977), *Tally Brown, New York* (TV film, 1977–8), *Armee der Liebenden oder Aufstand der Perversen* (*Army of Lovers*, TV, film, 1972–9), *Todesmagazin oder: wie werde ich ein Blumentopf?* (*Death Magazine, or to Become a Flower Pot*, TV film, 1979), *Gräfin von Richthofen* (short, 1979), *Rote Liebe* (*Red Love*, 1980–2), *Unsere Leichen leben noch* (*Our Corpses are Still Alive*, TV film, 1981), *Mein New York* (short, TV film, 1982), *Stadt der verlorenen Seelen – Berlin Blues* (1982–3), *Horror Vacui* (1983–4), *Anita, Tänzerin des Lasters* (1987)

Edgar Reitz
Born in Morbach (Hunsrück) 1/11/1932. Studied journalism, literature and theatre history. Production assistant, cameraman and film editor with various film companies. Since 1957 director of short films and industrial documentaries. Co-signatory of the Oberhausen Manifesto. With Alexander Kluge and Detten Schleiermacher founded the Institute of Film Composition at the Hochschule für Gestaltung in Ulm where he taught art direction, photography and editing. Cameraman on Kluge's *Yesterday Girl*. Since 1966 feature films. Federal Film Prize in 1975 and 1977. Lives in Munich.

Films as director: *Schicksal einer Oper* (co-director Bernhard Dorries, 1957–8), *Baumwolle* (documentary, 1959), *Krebsforschung I und II* (documentary short, 1960), *Yucatan* (short, 1961), *Kommunikation* (short, 1961), *Post und Technik* (documentary short, 1961), *Weltärztekongress* (short, 1961), *Geschwindigkeit* (short, 1962–3), *Varia-Vision* (short, 1964–5), *Binnenschiffahrt* (short, 1965), *Die Kinder* (short, 1966), *Mahlzeiten* (*Mealtimes*, 1966–7), *Fussnoten* (1967), *Uxmal* (incomplete, 1968), *Filmstunde* (documentary, 1968), *Cardillac* (1968–9), *Geschichten von Kübelkind* (*Stories of the Bucket Baby*, co-directed by Ula Stöckl, 1969–70), *Kino Zwei* (TV film, 1971), *Das goldene Ding* (*The Golden Thing*, co-directed by Alf Brustellin, Ula Stöckl and Nicos Perakis, 1971–2), *Die Reise nach Wien* (1973), *In Gefahr und grösster Not bringt der Mittelweg den Tod* (*In Danger and in Deep Distress, the Middle Way spells Certain Death*, co-directed by Alexander Kluge, 1974), *Altstadt – Lebensstadt* (documentary short, 1975), *Picknick* (documentary short, 1975), *Wir gehen wohnen* (documentary short, 1975), *7 Jahre – 70 Jahre* (short, 1975), *Stunde Null* (*Zero Hour*, 1976), *Deutschland im Herbst* (*Germany in Autumn*, episode 'Grenzstation', 1977– 8), *Der Schneider von Ulm* (*The Tailor from Ulm*, 1978), *Susanne tanzt* (short, 1979), *Geschichten aus den Hunstrückdörfern* (documentary, 1981), *Biermann – Film* (short, co-directed by Alexander Kluge, 1983), *Heimat* (1980–4)

Christian Rischert
Born in Munich 9/12/1936. Studied accountancy, then graphic design. Took over animation studio and in 1959 founded the production company Arcis, making advertising and industrial shorts. Specialised in documentaries about gastronomy. Since 1971 Christian Rischert Filmproduktion. Federal Film Prize in 1980. Lives in Munich.
Films as director: *Kopfstand Madam!* (*Stand on Your Head, Lady*, 1966), *Die Anpassung* (*Adapting*, TV film, 1969), *Berührungen* (*Touching*, TV film, 1971), *Der Tod des Fischers Marc Leblanc* (*Death of the Fisherman Marc Leblanc*, 1976), *Venedig – die Insel der Glückseligen am Rande des Untergangs* (*Venice – On the Brink of Going Down*, 1977), *Lena Rais* (1979), *Ein Orchester* (*An Orchestra*, 1981), *Wenn ich mich fürchte* (*When I'm Afraid*, 1983–4)

Erika Runge
Born in Halle 22/11/1939, studied history of literature and theatre. PhD, television journalist and writer, author of numerous books. At first documentarist, then feature films since 1970. Lives in Berlin.
Films as director: *Soll eine Frau soviel verdienen wie ein Mann?* (*Should a Woman Earn as much as a Man?*, TV, 1966), *Warum ist Frau B. glücklich* (*Why is Mrs B Happy?*, TV documentary, 1968), *Frauen an der Spitze – auf dem Weg zur Emanzipation?* (*Women at the Top – on their Way to Emancipation?*, TV documentary, 1969), *Ich heisse Erwin und bin 17 Jahre* (*My Name is Erwin and I'm Seventeen*, 1970), *Ich bin Bürger der DDR* (*I am a Citizen of the GDR*, TV film, 1972), *Michael oder Die Schwierigkeit mit dem Glück* (*Michael, or the Difficulties with Happiness*, TV film, 1975), *Opa Schulz* (*Grandad Schulz*, TV film, 1975), *Wenn eine Betriebsratvorsitzende ein Kind bekommt* (*When a Member of the Executive has a Baby*, TV documentary, 1978), *Porträts von Berlinern* (*Berlin Portraits*, TV documentary in three parts, 1980–2), *Lisa und Tschepo – eine Liebesgeschichte* (*Lisa and Tschepo*, TV film, 1981), *Ein Chilene in Berlin* (*A Chilean in Berlin*, TV documentary, 1983).

Ottokar Runze
Born in Berlin 19/8/1925, fought in the war and was taken prisoner. Acted for the Deutsche Theater in East Berlin, then director at West Berlin theatres. Theatre director in Munich, Hamburg and Berlin. For a time, head of a television company.
Films as director: *Das Echo* (TV film, 1963), *Das ozeanische Fest* (TV film, 1963), *Ein gutes Gewissen* (short TV film, 1966), *Duell um Aimee* (TV film, 1967), *Des Broadways liebstes Kind* (TV documentary in 3 parts, 1969), *Scheidung auf Englisch* (TV film, 1970), *Leiche gesucht* (TV film, 1970), *Viola und Sebastian* (1971), *Pinkville* (co-directed by Georg Tabori, 1972), *Scheinwelt* (short, 1973), *Der Lord von Barmbeck* (1973), *Im Namen des Volkes* (*In the Name of the People*, 1974), *Gerettetes Venedig* (short, 1974), *Das Messer im Rücken* (*Knife in the Back*, 1975), *Verlorenes Leben* (*A Lost Life*, 1975), *Die Standarte* (*Battle Flag*, 1976–7), *Der Mörder* (*The Murderer*, 1979), *Peter Frankenfeld* (TV documentary, 1980), *Stern ohne Himmel* (*Star without*

Sky, 1981), *Feine Gesellschaft – beschränkte Haftung* (*Nice Company – Limited Liability*, 1982), *Der Schnüffler* (*The Snoop*, 1983), *Das Ende vom Anfang* (*The End of the Beginning*, 1983).

Helke Sander
Born in Berlin 31/1/1937. Studied drama, psychology and German. Theatre and television director in Finland. Attended the Deutsche Film und Fernsehakademie in Berlin. Founder and director of *Frauen und Film* in 1966, author of documentaries and film critic on the daily press. Since 1980 Professor of Film at the Hochschule für Bildende Künste in Hamburg. Has published a collection of short stories. Lives in Berlin.

Films as director: *Subjektitude* (short, 1966), *Silvo* (short, 1967), *Brecht die Macht der Manipulateure* (documentary, 1967), *Kindergärtnerin, was nun?* (short, 1969), *Kinder sind keine Rinder* (short, 1969/70), *Eine Prämie für Irene* (*A Bonus for Irene*, 1971), *Macht die Pille frei?* (*Does the Pill Liberate Women?* documentary, 1972), *Männerbünde* (*Male Bonding*, 1973), *Die allseitig reduzierte Persönlichkeit – Redupers* (*Redupers*, 1977), *Der subjektive Faktor* (*The Subjective Factor*, 1980–1), *Der Beginn aller Schrecken ist Liebe* (*Love is the Beginning of all Terrors*, 1984), *Nr.1 Aus Berichten der Wach – und Patrouillendienste* (*Report from the Surveillance Services*, short, 1984)

Helma Sanders-Brahms
Born in Emden, 20/11/1940. Studied drama, German literature and English. Acting classes, then television presenter at WDR. Assistant director with Pasolini. Since 1970 own production company. Federal Film Prize in 1977. Lives in Berlin.
Films as director: *Angelika Urban, Verkäuferin, verlobt* (documentary, 1969), *Gewalt* (TV film, 1971), *Die industrielle Reservearmee* (1971), *Der Angestellte* (*The White-Collar Worker*, TV film, 1972), *Die Maschine* (documentary, 1973), *Die letzten Tage von Gomorrha* (*The Last Days of Gomorrha*, TV film, 1974), *Erdbeben in Chile* (*The Earthquake in Chile*, TV film, 1975), *Unter dem Pflaster ist der Strand* (*Beneath the Paving Stones Is the Beach*, 1975), *Shirins Hochzeit* (*Shirin's Wedding*, 1976), *Heinrich* (1977), *Vringsvedeeler Triptycon 1. Im Reiche des Schokoladenkönigs. 2. Rierkooche – Madonna. 3. Joseph und die Gerechtigkeit* (TV documentary in 3 parts, 1980), *Deutschland, bleiche Mutter* (*Germany Pale Mother*, 1980), *Die Berührte* (*No Mercy No Future*, 1981), *Erbtöchter/Les Fille hereditaires* (omnibus film, one episode, 1983), *Flügel und Fesseln* (*The Future of Emily*, 1984), *Alte Liebe* (*Old Love*, documentary, 1985), *Laputa* (1986)

Johannes Schaaf
Born in Stuttgart 7/4/1933. Studied medicine before becoming assistant director in the theatre. Produced plays in Ulm, Bremen, Munich, Salzburg and Vienna. Also works as actor. As film-maker mainly active in television.
Films as director: *Ein ungebetener Gast* (*An Uninvited Guest*, TV film, 1963), *Hotel Iphigenie* (TV, 1964), *Im Schatten einer Großstadt* (*In the Shadow of a Metropolis*, TV film, 1965), *Die Gegenprobe* (*Proof to the Contrary*, TV, 1965), *Große Liebe* (*Big Love*, TV, 1966), *Der Mann aus dem Bootshaus* (*The Man from the Boathouse*, TV, 1966–7), *Tätowierung* (*Tattooing*, 1967), *Trotta* (1971), *Traumstadt* (*Dream City*, 1973), *Die Dienstreise* (*The Business Trip*, TV, 1976–7)

Ulrich Schamoni
Born in Berlin, 9/11/1939. Took acting classes and worked as an assistant director in the theatre. Published a novel in 1961. Since 1965 author of documentaries and short films. Brother of Peter Schamoni and Thomas Schamoni, both also film-makers.
Films as director: *Hollywood in Debatschka Pescara* (short, 1965), *Geist und ein wenig*

Glück (documentary short, 1965), *Es* (*It*, 1965), *Lockenköpfchen* (short, longer version: *Der kahle Sänger*, TV film, 1966), *Alle Jahre wieder* (*Year In Year Out*, 1966–7), *Quartett im Bett* (*Quartet in Bed*, 1968), *Für meine Kinder – von Vati* (short, 1969), *Wir – Zwei* (*The Two of Us*, 1969), *Eins* (*One*, 1971), *Mein Bruder Willi* (short, 1972), *Chapeau Claque* (*Top Hat*, 1973), *Was wären wir ohne uns?* (TV series in 4 parts, 1978), *Das Traumhaus* (*The Dream House*, 1980), *So lebten sie alle Tage – Geschichten und Berichte aus dem alten Preussen* (*That's How They Lived – Stories and Reports from Old Prussia*, TV film, 1984)

Niklaus Schilling
Born in Basel (Switzerland), 23/4/1944. 1960–3 apprenticeship as decorator and designer. 1963, assistant cameraman for various Swiss television productions. Moved to Munich in 1965, and worked as cameraman for Klaus Lemke, Rudolf Thome, May Spils, Jean-Marie Straub. Since 1968 collaboration with the actress and producer Elke Haltaufderheide. 1971 founded production company. Federal Film Prize in 1978 for *Rheingold*. Since 1983 works with video-transfer techniques. Lives in Munich.
Films as director: *Cosmos Action Painting* (8mm short, 1961), *Verlorene Stunden* (short, 1965), *Flug 601* (short, 1966), *Auftrag ohne Nummer* (short, 1967), *Einsamer Morgen* (short, 1968), *Nachtschatten* (*Night Shade*, 1971), *Die Vertreibung aus dem Paradies* (*Expulsion from Paradise*, 1976), *Rheingold* (*Rhinegold*, 1977–8), *Der Willi Busch Report* (*The Willi Busch Report*, 1979), *Zeichen und Wunder* (*Signs and Miracles*, 1981), *Der Westen leuchtet* (*The Light Trap*, 1982), *Die Frau ohne Körper und der Projektionist* (*The Woman without Body and the Projectionist*, 1983), *Dormire* (1984–5)

Volker Schlöndorff
Born in Wiesbaden, 31/3/1939. Studied economics and political science in Paris and attended the Institut des Hautes Etudes Cinématographiques. Worked as assistant director on productions by Louis Malle, Jean-Pierre Melville and Alain Resnais. Between 1974 and 1976 directed operas in Berlin and Frankfurt. Married to Margarethe von Trotta. Has two production companies: Hallelujah-Film (with Peter Fleischmann) and Bioskop (with Reinhard Hauff). Federal Film Prizes in 1966, 1967, 1971, 1977 and 1979. Golden Palm at Cannes for *The Tin Drum*, which also won an Oscar. Since 1985 directs plays for American television. Lives in Munich.
Films as director: *Wen kümmerts . . .* (short, 1960), *Der junge Törless* (*Young Törless*, 1965–6), *Mord und Totschlag* (*A Degree of Murder*, 1966–7), *Ein unheimlicher Moment* (short, 1967), *Michael Kohlhass – Der Rebell* (*Michael Kohlhaas, the Rebel*, 1968–9), *Baal* (TV film, 1969), *Der plötzliche Reichtum der armen Leute von Kombach* (*The Sudden Wealth of the Poor People of Kombach*, 1970), *Die Moral der Ruth Halbfass* (*The Morals of Ruth Halbfass*, 1971), *Strohfeuer* (*Summer Lightning*, 1972), *Übernachtung in Tirol* (*Overnight Stay in Tyrol*, TV film, 1973), *Georginas Gründe* (*Georgina's Reasons*, TV film, 1974), *Der verlorene Ehre der Katharina Blum* (*The Lost Honour of Katharina Blum*, co-directed by Margarethe von Trotta, 1975), *Der Fangschuß* (*Coup de grace*, 1976), *Nur zum Spass – nur zum Spiel. Kaleidoskop Valeska Gert* (documentary, 1977), *Deutschland im Herbst* (*Germany in Autumn*, co-directors Alf Brustellin, Rainer Werner Fassbinder, Alexander Kluge, Maximiliane Mainka, Edgar Reitz, Katja Ruppe, Hans Peter Cloos and Bernhard Sinkel, 1977–8), *Die Blechtrommel* (*The Tin Drum*, 1978–9), *Der Kandidat* (*The Candidate*, co-directed by Alexander Kluge, Stefan Aust and Alexander von Eschwege, 1979–80), *Die Fälschung* (*Circle of Deceit*, 1980–1), *Krieg und Frieden* (*War and Peace*, co-directed by Alexander Kluge, Stefan Aust and Axel Engstfeld, 1982–3), *Un amour de Swann/Eine Liebe von Swann* (*Swann in Love*, 1983), *Death of a Salesman* (1985)

Daniel Schmid
Born in Flims (Switzerland) 26/12/1941. Studied history, history of art, political science

and journalism. In 1966 moved to West Germany and attended the Deutsche Film and Fernsehakadmie in Berlin. Assistant on productions by Lilienthal, Fassbinder and collaborated with Werner Schroeter. Between 1966 and 1968 worked on several 'film feuilletons' for SFB. Returned to make films in Switzerland in 1980.

Films as director: *Exhibition Alan Jones* (short, 1969), *Miriam* (short, 1969), *Hänsel und Gretel* (incomplete, 1970), *Thut alles im Finstern, Eurem Herrn das Licht zu ersparen* (short, 1970), *Heute Nacht oder nie* (*Tonight or Never*, 1972), *La paloma* (1973–4), *Schatten der Engel* (*Shadow of Angels*, 1976), *Violanta* (1977), *Notre Dame de la Croisette* (1980), *Hecate* (1981–2), *Mirage de la vie* (Swiss TV documentary, 1983), *Il bacio di Tosca* (1983–4)

Eckhart Schmidt
Born Sternberg, 31/10/1938. Studied English, German literature and history of drama. 1962 became film critic for the *Bayerischer Rundfunk*, the *Süddeutsche Zeitung* and the review *Film*. After a long interruption he returned to the cinema in 1981 with mostly commercial productions.

Films as director: *Nachmittags* (short, 1964), *Die Flucht* (short, 1966), *Jet Generation* (1968), *Erotik auf der Schulbank* (*Sex at School*, 1968), *Männer sind zum Lieben da!* (*Men are Made for Love*, 1970), *Der Fan* (*The Fan*, 1982), *Das Gold der Liebe* (*The Gold of Love*, 1983), *Die Story* (1984), *Loft* (1985)

Werner Schroeter
Born in Georgenthal (Thuringia) 7/4/1945. Studied psychology. Worked as a journalist until his first tentative work with 8mm film. Theatrical director at the Hamburg, Kassel and Bochum opera. Since 1967 has produced mostly TV and experimental films.

Films as director: *Verona* (8mm short, probably identical to *Zwei Katzen*, 1967), *Callas Walking Lucia* (8mm short, 1968), *Callas Text mit Doppelbeleuchtung* (8mm short, 1968), *Maria Callas Porträt* (8mm short, 1968), *Mona Lisa* (8mm short, 1968), *Maria Callas singt 1957 Rezitativ und Arie der Elvira aus Ernani 1844 von Guiseppe Verdi* (8mm short, 1968), *Übungen mit Darstellern* (9 rolls 8mm, not edited, 1968), *La morte d'Isotta* (8mm, 1968), *Himmel Hoch* (8mm, short, 1968), *Paula – 'je reviens'* (1968), *Grotesk – Burlesk – Pittoresk* (8mm, co-director Rosa von Praunheim, 1968), *Faces* (8mm short, 1968), *Aggressionen* (short, 1968), *Neurasia* (1968), *Argila* (1968), *Virginia's Death* (short, 1968), *Eika Katappa* (1969), *Nicaragua* (1969), *Der Bomberpilot* (*The Bomber Pilot*, TV film, 1970), *Anglia* (1970), *Salome* (TV film, 1971), *Macbeth* (TV film 1971), *Funkausstellung 1971 – Hitparade* (TV video, 1971), *Der Tod der Maria Malibran* (*The Death of Maria Malibran*, TV film, 1972), *Willow Springs* (TV film, 1973), *Der Schwarze Engel* (*The Black Angel*, TV film, 1974), *Johannas Traum* (short, 1971–5), *Flocons d'or/Goldflocken* (*Goldflakes*, 1976), *Regno di Napoli/Neapolitanische Geschwister* (*Kingdom of Naples*, 1978), *Palermo oder Wolfsburg* (*Palermo or Wolfsburg*, 1980), *Weisse Reisse* (*White Journey*, 1980), *Die Generalprobe/La répétition générale* (*Dress Rehearsal*, 1980), *Der Tag der Idioten* (*Day of Idiots*, 1982), *Das Liebeskonzil* (*Lovers' Council*, 1982), *Der lachende Stern* (*The Smiling Star*, 1983), *De l'Argentine* (*About Argentina*, 1983–5), *Der Rosenkönig* (*Rose King*, 1985)

Bernhard Sinkel
Born in Frankfurt 1940. Studied law. Worked for two years as head of the documentation section for the magazine *Der Spiegel*.

Films as director: *Clinch* (TV feature, 1973), *Lina Braake* (1974), *Berlinger – Ein deutsches Abenteuer* (co-directed by Alf Brustellin, 1975), *Taugenichts* (*Good-for-Nothing*, 1977), *Der Mädchenkrieg* (*The War of the Girls*, co-directed by Alf Brustellin, 1976–7), *Deutschland im Herbst* (*Germany in Autumn*, one episode, 1977), *Kaltgestellt*

(*Neutralised*, 1981), *Die Bekenntnisse des Hochstaplers Felix Krull* (*The Confessions of Felix Krull, Confidence Man*, 1982), *Väter und Söhne* (*Fathers and Sons*, TV series, 1985)

May Spils
Born in Twistringen (near Bremen) 29/7/1941. Trained as a foreign language secretary. Took acting classes, moved to Munich and worked as a fashion model. Met Peter Schamoni, Klaus Lemke and Werner Enke, who helped her set up her first short film. Collaboration with Werner Enke on her subsequent films.
Films as director: *Das Porträt* (*The Portrait*, short, 1966), *Manöver* (*Maneuver*, 1966), *Zur Sache, Schätzchen* (*Let's Get Down to Business, Darling*, 1968), *Nicht fummeln, Liebling* (*Don't Fumble, Darling*, 1970), *Hau drauf, Kleiner* (*Give It to Them, Shorty*, 1974), *Wehe, wenn Schwarzenbeck kommt* (*Beware of Schwarzenbeck*, 1979), *Mit mir nicht, du Knallkopf* (*Not with Me, You Idiot*, 1983)

Manfred Stelzer
Born in Augsburg 22/9/1944. A toolmaker by trade, studied at the Deutsche Film und Fensehakademie in Berlin 1971–7. Began making documentaries for television in 1972. Switched to making feature films in 1981.
Films as director: *Allein machen sie dich ein* (TV documentary, co-directed by Suzanne Beyeler, Rainer März, 1972), *Kalldorf gegen Mannesmann* (documentary, co-directed Suzanne Beyeler, Rainer März, 1974), *Wir haben nie gespürt, was Freiheit ist* (documentary, co-directed Johannes Flütsch, 1975), *Eintracht Borbeck* (documentary, co-directed Suzanne Beyeler, Rainer März, 1976), *Weiter Weg* (documentary, co-directed Johannes Flütsch, Marlies Kallweit, 1977), *Monarch* (co-directed Johannes Flütsch), *Die Perle der Karibik* (*Pearl of the Carribbean*, 1981), *Schwarzfahrer* (*Midnight Blues*, 1983), *Geschichten aus 12 und einem Jahr* (documentary, 1985), *Die Chinesen kommen* (*The Chinese are Coming*, 1987)

Ula Stöckl
Born in Ulm, 5/2/1938. Studied languages in Paris and London, before working as a secretary. Attended the Hochschule für Gestaltung in Ulm.
Films as director: *Antigone* (short, 1964), *Haben Sie Arbitur?* (short, 1965), *Sonnabend 17 Uhr* (short, 1966), *Neun Leben hat die Katze* (*The Cat has Nine Lives*, 1968), *Geschichten von Kübelkind* (*Stories of the Bucket Baby*, co-director Edgar Reitz, 1969–70), *Sonntagsmalerei* (*Sunday Painting*, TV film, 1971), *Das goldene Ding* (*The Golden Thing*, TV film, co-directors Edgar Reitz, Alf Brustellin and Nicos Perakis, 1971), *Hirnhexen* (TV film, 1972), *Der kleine Löwe und die Grossen* (TV film, 1973), *Ein ganz perfektes Ehepaar* (*A Perfect Couple*, TV film, 1974), *Hase und Igel* (TV film, 1974), *Popp und Mingel* (TV film, 1975), *Erikas Leidenschaften* (*Erica's Passion*, TV film, 1976), *Eine Frau mit Verantwortung* (*A Woman with Responsibility*, TV film, 1978), *Die Erbtöchter/Les filles héréditaires* (episode, 'Den Vätern vertrauen gegen alle Erfahrung', 1983), *Der Schlaf der Vernunft* (*The Sleep of Reason*, 1984), *Peter und die Taube* (*Peter and the Pigeon*, TV film, 1984)

Jean-Marie Straub
Born in Metz, 8/1/1933. Studied literature at Strasbourg and Nancy then in Paris. Assisted on productions by Jacques Rivette. 1958 emigrated to West Germany and 1969 to Italy. All his films are co-directed by his wife Danièle Huillet.
Films as director: *Machorka-Muff* (short, 1962), *Nicht versöhnt oder Es hilft nur Gewalt, wo Gewalt herrscht* (*Not Reconciled*, 1964–5), *Chronik der Anna Magdalena Bach* (*Chronicle of Anna Magdalena Bach*, 1967), *Der Bräutigam, die Komödiantin und der Zuhälter* (*The Bridegroom, the Comedienne and the Pimp*, short, 1968), *Les yeux ne veulent pas en tout temps se fermer ou Peut-être qu'un jour Rome se permettra*

de choisir à son tour (*Othon*, 1969), *Geschichtsunterricht* (*History Lessons*, 1972), *Einleitung zu Arnold Schönbergs 'Begleitmusik zu einer Lichtspiel-scene'* (short, 1972), *Moses und Aron* (*Moses and Aaron*, 1974), *Fortini/Cani* (1976), *Toute Révolution est un coup de dés* (short, 1977), *Dalla nube alla resistenza* (*From the Cloud to the Resistance*, 1978–9), *Zu früh/zu spät* (*Too Early, Too Late*, 1980–1), *En rachachant* (short, 1982), *Klassenverhältnisse* (*Class Relations*, 1983), *Der Tod des Empedokles* (*The Death of Empedocles*, 1987)

Hans Jürgen Syberberg
Born in Nossendorf (Pommerania) 8/12/1935. Moved to West Germany in 1953. Studied history of art and literature in Munich. Doctoral dissertation on Friedrich Dürrenmatt. 1962 Assistant director at the Munich Kammerspiele. Since 1963 freelance for Bavarian Radio and Television. Feature films and documentaries since 1965. Federal film prizes in 1966, 1970, 1972, 1973. Founded his own production company (TMS) in 1976. Published several polemical books and articles. Lives in Munich.
Films as director: *Fünfter Akt, Siebte Szene. Fritz Kortner probt Kabale und Liebe* (documentary, 1965), *Romy. Anatomie eines Gesichts* (documentary, 1965), *Fritz Kortner spricht Monologue für eine Schallplatte* (documentary, 1966), *Wilhelm von Kobell* (short, 1966), *Die Grafen Pocci* (documentary 1966/67), *Scarabea – Wieviel Erde braucht der Mensch* (*Scarabea*, 1968), *Sex Business – Made in Pasing* (documentary, 1969), *San Domingo* (1970), *Nach meinem letzten Umzug* (documentary, 1970), *Ludwig – Requiem für einen jungfräulichen König* (*Ludwig – Requiem for a Virgin King*, 1972), *Theodor Hierneis oder: Wie man ehem. Hofkoch wird* (*Theodor Hierneis/ Ludwig's Cook*, 1972), *Karl May* (1974), *Winifred Wagner und die Geschichte des Hauses Wahnfried von 1914–1975* (*The Confessions of Winifred Wagner*, 1975), *Hitler – Ein Film aus Deutschland* (*Our Hitler*, 1976–7), *Parsifal* (1981–2), *Die Nacht* (*The Night*, 1984–5)

Rudolf Thome
Born in Wallau (Lahn) 14/11/1939. Abitur. Studied German literature and history in Munich. 1962–8 film critic of the *Süddeutsche Zeitung*, *Film* and *Filmkritik*. 1966–7 worked for a Building Society. Moved to Berlin in 1973. Since 1974 worked for the Arsenal and the Internationale Forum des jungen Films. Film critic for the Berlin daily, *Der Tagesspiegel*. Since 1967 runs his own production company Rudolf Thome Filmproduktion. Also managing director of Moana Film GmbH. Lives in West Berlin.
Films as director: *Die Versöhnung* (short 1964–5), *Stella* (short 1966), *Galaxis* (short feature 1967), *Jane erschießt John, weil er sie mit Ann betrügt* (short feature 1967–8), *Detektive* (*Detectives*, 1968), *Rote Sonne* (*Red Sun*, 1969), *Supergirl* (1970), *Fremde Stadt* (*Alien City*, 1972), *Made in Germany and USA* (1974), *Tagebuch* (*Diary*, 1975), *Beschriebung einer Insel* (*Description of an Island*, ethnographic feature 1977–9), *Hast du Lust, mit mir einen Kaffe zu trinken?* (short feature 1980), *Berlin Chamissoplatz* (1980), *System ohne Schatten* (*System without Shadow*, 1982–3), *Tarot* (1986–7), *Das Mikroscop* (*The Microscope*, 1988)

Margarethe von Trotta
Born in Berlin, 21/2/1942. Studied German literature and French in Munich and Paris. Acting School in Munich. Theatre work in Stuttgart and Frankfurt. Since 1968 actress in television productions and feature films, directed by Lemke, Schlöndorff, Fassbinder, Hauff, Chabrol, Achternbusch. Began writing screenplays in 1970. Federal Film Prizes in 1978 and 1982. Golden Lion at Venice in 1981 for *The German Sisters*. Married to Volker Schlöndorff. Lives in Munich.
Films as director: *Die verlorene Ehe der Katharina Blum* (*The Lost Honour of Katharina Blum*, co-directed Volker Schlöndorff, 1975), *Das zweite Erwachen der Christa Klages* (*The Second Awakening of Christa Klages*, 1977), *Schwestern oder die*

Balance des Glücks (*Sisters, or the Balance of Happiness*, 1979), *Die Bleierne Zeit* (*The German Sisters*, 1981), *Heller Wahn* (*Friends and Husbands*, 1982), *Rosa Luxemburg* (1986), *Drei Schwestern* (*Three Sisters*, 1988)

Wim Wenders

Born in Düsseldorf, 14/8/1945. Briefly studied medicine and philosophy, before being admitted to the Hochschule für Film und Fernsehen in Munich in 1967. Wrote reviews and articles for *Filmkritik, Süddeutsche Zeitung, Twen*. Founder-member of the Filmverlag der Autoren. Has his own production company Wim Wenders Filmproduktion, and co-owns Road Movies and Gray City Inc. Federal Film Prizes in 1975, 1978, 1981. In 1982 directed a play by his friend Peter Handke in Salzburg. Collected writings published under the title *Emotion Pictures*. Lives in Berlin.

Films as director: *Schauplätze* (short, 1967), *Same Player Shoots Again* (short, 1967), *Klappenfilm* (short, 1968), *Silver City* (short, 1968), *Alabama: 2000 Light Years* (short 1968–9), *Drei Amerikanische LPs* (short, 1969), *Polizeifilm* (short, 1969–70), *Summer in the City* (1969–70), *Die Angst des Tormanns beim Elfmeter* (*The Goalie's Fear of the Penalty Kick*, 1971), *Der scharlachrote Buchstabe* (*The Scarlet Letter*, 1972), *Alice in den Städten* (*Alice in the Cities*, 1973), *Aus der Familie der Panzerechsen/Die Insel* (two short television features for children's series, 1974), *Falsche Bewegung* (*Wrong Movement*, 1974–5), *Im Lauf der Zeit* (*Kings of the Road*, 1975–6), *Der amerikanische Freund* (*The American Friend*, 1976–7), *Nick's Film* (*Lightning over Water*, 1979–80), *Hammett* (1980–2), *Der Stand der Dinge* (*The State of Things*, 1982), *Reverse Angle – New York City, March 1982* (short, 1982), *Chambre 666* (short, 1982), *Paris, Texas* (1983–4), *Tokyo-Ga* (documentary, 1984–5), *Himmel über Berlin* (*Wings of Desire*, 1987)

Klaus Wildenhahn

Born in Bonn 19/6/1930. Raised in Berlin, where he studied sociology, journalism and political science. Lived in London until 1958, working as a hospital nurse. Since 1959 with NDR, from 1960–4 in the current affairs department, then the TV drama department, and since 1981 in the Educational Programme. 1968–72 lecturer at the Deutsche Film und Fernsehakademie Berlin. Published book on the theory of documentary film-making. Lives in Hamburg and Cologne. All his films are documentaries.

Films as director: *Der merkwürdige Tod des Herrn Hammersköld* (*The Strange Death of Mr Hammersköld*, 1961), *Der Tod kam wie bestellt* (*Death Came On Order*, 1962), *Parteitag 1964* (*Party Congress*, 1964), *Bayreuther Proben* (*Bayreuth Rehearsals*, 1965), *Eine Woche Avantgarde für Sizilien* (*An Avant-garde Week for Sicily*, 1965), *Smith, James O. – Organist, USA* (1965), *John Cage* (1966), *498 Third Avenue* (1967), *In der Fremde* (*Far from Home*, 1967), *Heiligabend auf St Pauli* (*Christmas Eve in St Pauli*, 1967–8), *Harlem Theater* (1968), *Der Reifenschneider und seine Frau* (*The Wheelwright and his Wife*, 1968–9), *Institutssommer* (*Summer at the Institute*, 1969), *Der Hamburger Aufstand Oktober 1923* (*The Hamburg Uprising, October 1923*, 1971), *Harburg bis Ostern* (*Harburg till Easter*, 1972), *Die Liebe zum Land* (*Love of the Land*, 1974), *Fünf Bemerkungen zum Dokumentarfilm* (*Five Observations about Documentary Film*, 1974), *Der Mann mit der roten Nelke* (*The Man with the Red Carnation*, 1974–5), *Emden geht nach USA* (*Emden Goes to the US*, 1975–6), *Im Norden das Meer, im Westen der Fluß, im Süden das Moor, in Osten Vorurteile* (*To the North the Sea, to the West the River, to the South the Moors, and to the East Prejudices*, 1975–6), *Der Nachwelt eine Botschaft – Ein Arbeiterdichter* (*A Message for Posterity – A Working Class Poet*, 1979–80), *Bandonion 1: Deutsche Tangos/Bandonion 2: Tangos im Exil* (*German Tangos/Tangos in Exile*, 1981), *Was tun Pina Bausch und ihre Tänzer in Wuppertal?* (*What are Pina Bausch and her Dancers doing in Wuppertal?*, 1982–3), *Ein Film für Bossak und Leacock* (*A Film for*

Bossak and Leacock, 1983–4), *Yorkshire: 10 Tage Juli, November, Dezember 84* (*Ten Days in Yorkshire*, 1984–5)

Christian Ziewer
Born in Danzig (Gdansk) 1/4/1941. Grew up in Berlin. Studied electrical engineering for three years, before changing to social history and philosophy. Assistant director at various theatres. Assistant producer on feature film, traineeship at Bavaria studios. 1966–8 student at the Deutschen Film und Fernsehakademie in Berlin. Co-founded of Basis-Film Verleih GmbH. Lives in Berlin.

Films as director: *Karl Moll, Jahrgang 30* (short, 1967), *Einsamkeit in der Großstadt* (documentary short, co-directed by Klaus Wiese, 1968), *Kinogramm I und II* (short, co-directed by Max Willutzki), *Kinogramm III* (short, co-directed by Klaus Wiese and Max Willutzki), *Liebe Mutter, mir geht es gut* (*Der Mother, I'm Fine*, 1971–2), *Schneeglöckchen blühn im September* (*Snowdrops Bloom in September*, 1973–4), *Der aufrechte Gang* (*Walking Tall*, 1975–6), *Aus der Ferne sehe ich dieses Land* (*From Afar I See This Country*, 1977–8), *Der Tod des Weißen Pferdes* (*Death of a White Horse*, 1984)

417

Index

419

428

61 0 29